THE PAPERS OF ULYSSES S. GRANT

THE PAPERS OF

ULYSSES S. GRANT

Volume 14: February 21–April 30, 1865

Edited by John Y. Simon

ASSOCIATE EDITOR

David L. Wilson

EDITORIAL ASSISTANT

Sue E. Dotson

═══

SOUTHERN ILLINOIS UNIVERSITY PRESS

CARBONDALE AND EDWARDSVILLE

Library of Congress Cataloging in Publication Data (Revised)

Grant, Ulysses Simpson, Pres. U.S., 1822–1885.
  The papers of Ulysses S. Grant.

  Prepared under the auspices of the Ulysses S. Grant Association.
  Bibliographical footnotes.
  CONTENTS: v. 1. 1837–1861—v. 2. April–September 1861.
—v. 3. October 1, 1861–January 7, 1862.—v. 4. January 8–March 31,
1862.—v. 5. April 1–August 31, 1862.—v. 6. September 1–December 8, 1862.—v. 7. December 9, 1862–March 31, 1863.—v. 8.
April 1–July 6, 1863.—v. 9. July 7–December 31, 1863.—v. 10.
January 1–May 31, 1864.—v. 11. June 1–August 15, 1864.—v. 12.
August 16–November 15, 1864.—v. 13. November 16, 1864–February 20, 1865.—v. 14. February 21–April 30, 1865.

  1. Grant, Ulysses Simpson, Pres. U.S., 1822–1885. 2. United
States—History—Civil War, 1861–1865—Campaigns and battles
—Sources. 3. United States—Politics and government—1869–1877
—Sources. 4. Presidents—United States—Biography. 5. Generals—
United States—Biography. I. Simon, John Y., ed. II. Wilson, David
L. 1943–. III. Ulysses S. Grant Association.
E660.G756 1967   973.8'2'0924   67–10725
ISBN–0–8093–1198–4 (v. 14)

To Carl Haverlin

Contents

Maps and Illustrations

===

Introduction

——

By late February, 1865, the Confederate States of America neared military collapse. Lieutenant General Ulysses S. Grant had steadily extended his lines around Petersburg, moving ever closer to cutting the last supply lines to Richmond, while Major General William T. Sherman advanced his army through South Carolina northward toward an eventual union with Grant. General Robert E. Lee still maintained a virtual stalemate near Richmond, but Confederates could not assemble an effective army to stop Sherman, nor the strength necessary to counter massive U.S. cavalry expeditions throughout the South. Grant's only source of anxiety was the possibility that Lee might successfully evacuate his army southward, enabling him to prolong the war another year. If Lee remained trapped at Petersburg, Grant expected to end the war with a spring campaign.

On March 25, Lee launched a last desperate effort to break Grant's lines at Fort Stedman. Lee surprised the garrison and captured nearby entrenchments as well, but his depleted forces could not withstand the inevitable counterattack and fell back with heavy losses. Major General Philip H. Sheridan arrived at City Point on March 26 with the army that had crushed Confederate Lieutenant General Jubal A. Early's forces in the Shenandoah Valley. Grant thought that after a few days of rest and new shoes for the horses this added force would enable him to push Lee to eventual defeat. On March 27, Grant and Sherman met with President Abraham Lincoln on the *River Queen* at City Point to discuss the termination of the conflict.

Despite all warning signs, the collapse of Lee's army still seemed dazzlingly swift. Conscious of previous missed opportunities to break Lee's lines, Grant took personal command and gave a leading role to Sheridan, who had proved an aggressive and relentless commander. Grant abandoned his earlier policy of issuing orders through Major General George G. Meade and conciliating the officers of the Army of the Potomac; in the final battles he paid scant attention to Meade's nominal command of the Army of the Potomac and upheld Sheridan's removal of Major General Gouverneur K. Warren from command of the 5th Army Corps. Grant opened his Appomattox campaign on March 29, pushing westward, and on April 2, the Confederates abandoned their Petersburg line and evacuated Richmond. On April 7, Grant wrote to Lee about "the hopelessness of further resistance" and asked for the surrender of his army. Lee inquired about terms and fended off the inevitable for two days while his hard-pressed forces dwindled.

When Lee surrendered, Grant turned toward the achievement of peace with the same determination with which he waged war. Within the latitude allowed him by Lincoln, Grant gave Lee the most generous terms possible, ordered his troops to refrain from triumphal cheering, and himself spurned a conqueror's entrance into Richmond in favor of a quick trip to Washington to end the war. Even the assassination of Lincoln, part of a plot Grant believed to include himself, did not lessen this resolve. On April 22, President Andrew Johnson rejected the general armistice that Sherman had negotiated with General Joseph E. Johnston and ordered Grant to North Carolina to oversee resumption of hostilities. Johnston surrendered to Sherman on April 26 on the same terms Grant gave Lee. From North Carolina, Grant wrote to his wife: "The suffering that must exist in the South next year, even with the war ending now, will be beyond conception. People who talk of further retalliation and punishment, except of political leaders, either do not conceive of the suffering endured already or they are heartless and unfeeling and wish to stay at home, out of danger, whilst the punishment is being inflicted."

Grant at Appomattox was at the height of his career, and his correspondence reflects his self-confidence, mastery of himself and his armies, and his balance of view. The letter written in the parlor of the McLean house while Lee and others looked on exhibits the same directness and spontaneity as his other military correspondence. "When I put my pen to the paper," Grant recalled, "I did not know the first word that I should make use of in writing the terms. I only knew what was in my mind, and I wished to express it clearly, so that there could be no mistaking it." Afterthoughts flowed gracefully and logically into the letter. "As I wrote on, the thought occurred to me that the officers had their own private horses and effects, which were important to them, but of no value to us; also that it would be an unnecessary humiliation to call upon them to deliver their side arms." A few minor alterations and corrections enabled Grant's concise letter to serve as the basis of Lee's surrender. Grant the writer explains Grant the soldier.

We are indebted to W. Neil Franklin and Karl L. Trever, both recently deceased, for searching the National Archives; to Mary Giunta, Anne Harris Henry, Sara Dunlap Jackson, and Daniel Preston for further assistance in the National Archives; to Harriet Simon for proofreading; and to William J. Smith, a graduate student at Southern Illinois University, for research assistance.

Financial support for the period during which this volume was prepared came from Southern Illinois University, the National Endowment for the Humanities, and the National Historical Publications and Records Commission.

JOHN Y. SIMON

February 20, 1984

Editorial Procedure

---

1. Editorial Insertions

A. Words or letters in roman type within brackets represent editorial reconstruction of parts of manuscripts torn, mutilated, or illegible.

B. [. . .] or [— — —] within brackets represent lost material which cannot be reconstructed. The number of dots represents the approximate number of lost letters; dashes represent lost words.

C. Words in *italic* type within brackets represent material such as dates which were not part of the original manuscript.

D. Other material crossed out is indicated by ~~cancelled type~~.

E. Material raised in manuscript, as "4th," has been brought in line, as "4th."

2. Symbols Used to Describe Manuscripts

AD	Autograph Document
ADS	Autograph Document Signed
ADf	Autograph Draft
ADfS	Autograph Draft Signed
AES	Autograph Endorsement Signed
AL	Autograph Letter
ALS	Autograph Letter Signed
ANS	Autograph Note Signed

D	Document
DS	Document Signed
Df	Draft
DfS	Draft Signed
ES	Endorsement Signed
LS	Letter Signed

3. Military Terms and Abbreviations

Act.	Acting
Adjt.	Adjutant
AG	Adjutant General
AGO	Adjutant General's Office
Art.	Artillery
Asst.	Assistant
Bvt.	Brevet
Brig.	Brigadier
Capt.	Captain
Cav.	Cavalry
Col.	Colonel
Co.	Company
C.S.A.	Confederate States of America
Dept.	Department
Div.	Division
Gen.	General
Hd. Qrs.	Headquarters
Inf.	Infantry
Lt.	Lieutenant
Maj.	Major
Q. M.	Quartermaster
Regt.	Regiment or regimental
Sgt.	Sergeant
USMA	United States Military Academy, West Point, N. Y.
Vols.	Volunteers

4. Short Titles and Abbreviations

ABPC	*American Book-Prices Current* (New York, 1895–)

CG	*Congressional Globe* Numbers following represent the Congress, session, and page.
J. G. Cramer	Jesse Grant Cramer, ed., *Letters of Ulysses S. Grant to his Father and his Youngest Sister, 1857–78* (New York and London, 1912)
DAB	*Dictionary of American Biography* (New York, 1928–36)
Garland	Hamlin Garland, *Ulysses S. Grant: His Life and Character* (New York, 1898)
HED	*House Executive Documents*
HMD	*House Miscellaneous Documents*
HRC	*House Reports of Committees* Numbers following *HED, HMD,* or *HRC* represent the number of the Congress, the session, and the document.
Ill. AG Report	J. N. Reece, ed., *Report of the Adjutant General of the State of Illinois* (Springfield, 1900)
Johnson, Papers	LeRoy P. Graf and Ralph W. Haskins, eds., *The Papers of Andrew Johnson* (Knoxville, 1967–)
Lewis	Lloyd Lewis, *Captain Sam Grant* (Boston, 1950)
Lincoln, Works	Roy P. Basler, Marion Dolores Pratt, and Lloyd A. Dunlap, eds., *The Collected Works of Abraham Lincoln* (New Brunswick, 1953–55)
Memoirs	*Personal Memoirs of U. S. Grant* (New York, 1885–86)
O.R.	*The War of the Rebellion: A Compilation of the Official Records of the Union and Confederate Armies* (Washington, 1880–1901)
O.R. (Navy)	*Official Records of the Union and Confederate Navies in the War of the Rebellion* (Washington, 1894–1927) Roman numerals following *O.R.* or *O.R.* (Navy) represent the series and the volume.
PUSG	John Y. Simon, ed., *The Papers of Ulysses S. Grant* (Carbondale and Edwardsville, 1967–)
Richardson	Albert D. Richardson, *A Personal History of Ulysses S. Grant* (Hartford, Conn., 1868)
SED	*Senate Executive Documents*
SMD	*Senate Miscellaneous Documents*

SRC   *Senate Reports of Committees* Numbers following *SED, SMD,* or *SRC* represent the number of the Congress, the session, and the document.

USGA Newsletter   *Ulysses S. Grant Association Newsletter*

Young   John Russell Young, *Around the World with General Grant* (New York, 1879)

5. *Location Symbols*

CLU	University of California at Los Angeles, Los Angeles, Calif.
CoHi	Colorado State Historical Society, Denver, Colo.
CSmH	Henry E. Huntington Library, San Marino, Calif.
CSt	Stanford University, Stanford, Calif.
CtY	Yale University, New Haven, Conn.
CU-B	Bancroft Library, University of California, Berkeley, Calif.
DLC	Library of Congress, Washington, D.C. Numbers following DLC-USG represent the series and volume of military records in the USG papers.
DNA	National Archives, Washington, D.C. Additional numbers identify record groups.
IaHA	Iowa State Department of History and Archives, Des Moines, Iowa.
I-ar	Illinois State Archives, Springfield, Ill.
IC	Chicago Public Library, Chicago, Ill.
ICarbS	Southern Illinois University, Carbondale, Ill.
ICHi	Chicago Historical Society, Chicago, Ill.
ICN	Newberry Library, Chicago, Ill.
ICU	University of Chicago, Chicago, Ill.
IHi	Illinois State Historical Library, Springfield, Ill.
In	Indiana State Library, Indianapolis, Ind.
InFtwL	Lincoln National Life Foundation, Fort Wayne, Ind.
InHi	Indiana Historical Society, Indianapolis, Ind.
InNd	University of Notre Dame, Notre Dame, Ind.
InU	Indiana University, Bloomington, Ind.
KHi	Kansas State Historical Society, Topeka, Kan.

MdAN	United States Naval Academy Museum, Annapolis, Md.
MeB	Bowdoin College, Brunswick, Me.
MH	Harvard University, Cambridge, Mass.
MHi	Massachusetts Historical Society, Boston, Mass.
MiD	Detroit Public Library, Detroit, Mich.
MiU-C	William L. Clements Library, University of Michigan, Ann Arbor, Mich.
MoSHi	Missouri Historical Society, St. Louis, Mo.
NHi	New-York Historical Society, New York, N.Y.
NIC	Cornell University, Ithaca, N.Y.
NjP	Princeton University, Princeton, N.J.
NjR	Rutgers University, New Brunswick, N.J.
NN	New York Public Library, New York, N.Y.
NNP	Pierpont Morgan Library, New York, N.Y.
NRU	University of Rochester, Rochester, N.Y.
OClWHi	Western Reserve Historical Society, Cleveland, Ohio.
OFH	Rutherford B. Hayes Library, Fremont, Ohio.
OHi	Ohio Historical Society, Columbus, Ohio.
OrHi	Oregon Historical Society, Portland, Ore.
PCarlA	U.S. Army Military History Institute, Carlisle Barracks, Pa.
PHi	Historical Society of Pennsylvania, Philadelphia, Pa.
PPRF	Rosenbach Foundation, Philadelphia, Pa.
RPB	Brown University, Providence, R.I.
TxHR	Rice University, Houston, Tex.
USG 3	Maj. Gen. Ulysses S. Grant 3rd, Clinton, N.Y.
USMA	United States Military Academy Library, West Point, N.Y.
ViHi	Virginia Historical Society, Richmond, Va.
ViU	University of Virginia, Charlottesville, Va.
WHi	State Historical Society of Wisconsin, Madison, Wis.
Wy-Ar	Wyoming State Archives and Historical Department, Cheyenne, Wyo.
WyU	University of Wyoming, Laramie, Wyo.

Chronology

====

FEB. 21. The siege at Petersburg continued. USG refused to allow the French consul at Richmond to pass through U.S. lines to Washington, and he planned a cav. expedition for Maj. Gen. Philip H. Sheridan.

FEB. 21. Maj. Gen. William T. Sherman continued to march his army northward through the Carolinas with a goal of uniting with USG at Petersburg.

FEB. 21. Robert Todd Lincoln, President Abraham Lincoln's son, arrived at City Point to assume duties on USG's staff.

FEB. 22. USG arranged transportation to Philadelphia for Maj. Gen. George G. Meade upon learning of the death of Meade's son. Maj. Gen. John G. Parke temporarily commanded the Army of the Potomac and USG instructed him to be ready at all times for a C.S.A. attack.

FEB. 22. U.S. forces commanded by Maj. Gen. John M. Schofield occupied Wilmington, N.C., closing the last major Southern port.

FEB. 23. USG protested to Secretary of War Edwin M. Stanton against giving a new command to Maj. Gen. Benjamin F. Butler.

FEB. 24. USG informed Stanton about the growing number of C.S.A. deserters entering U.S. lines.

FEB. 25. Maj. Gen. Edward O. C. Ord started informal discussions with C.S.A. Lt. Gen. James Longstreet. These continued on Feb. 27.

FEB. 26. USG assured a nervous Lincoln that the Shenandoah Valley would not be left unprotected during Sheridan's absence on a cav. expedition.

FEB. 27. USG sent Bvt. Brig. Gen. Cyrus B. Comstock to observe Maj. Gen. Edward R. S. Canby's operations against Mobile.

FEB. 28. USG provided evidence that the British government had manufactured fuses for use by C.S.A. forces.

MAR. 1. USG instructed Meade to prepare to attack if Gen. Robert E. Lee detached forces to oppose Sherman's campaign in the Carolinas.

MAR. 2. USG reported to Stanton that Lee was too weak to send a force against Washington, and Sheridan underscored this point by defeating C.S.A. forces in an engagement at Waynesboro, Va.

MAR. 2. Lee requested a meeting with USG to discuss peace terms, a result of the conversations between Ord and Longstreet.

MAR. 3. Lincoln directed USG not to hold a conference with Lee except for the capitulation of the Army of Northern Va., and USG informed Lee the following day that he had no authority to discuss peace terms.

MAR. 4. USG sent an expedition to break up illicit trade on the Rappahannock River.

MAR. 4. Lincoln inaugurated for a second term.

MAR. 6. Clara Rachel Grant, USG's sister, died.

MAR. 8. Vexed by trade permits given to unscrupulous parties, USG issued orders the following day suspending trade with areas in rebellion.

MAR. 9. USG urged Canby to expedite the campaign against Mobile.

MAR. 10. USG learned that C.S.A. naval personnel may have been sent to disrupt traffic on the Mississippi and Ohio rivers.

MAR. 11. U.S. Representative Elihu B. Washburne presented to USG a gold medal authorized by a Joint Resolution of Congress to honor the victory at Chattanooga in 1863.

MAR. 12. USG sent supplies to White House, Va., anticipating the arrival of Sheridan's expedition.

MAR. 13. USG noted Canby's slowness in moving against Mobile, and informed Stanton the next day that Sheridan would be sent to the Gulf Coast when he could be spared.

MAR. 14. USG protested to Lee about the murder of white officers of Negro troops after their capture by C.S.A. forces. He also instructed Meade to have the Army of the Potomac ready to pursue Lee on short notice, and decided to bring Sheridan and his cav. to Petersburg.

MAR. 16. USG learned that Sherman had occupied Fayetteville, N.C., on March 11. Stanton arrived at City Point to confer with USG, returning to Washington on March 18.

MAR. 18. Sheridan arrived at White House, Va., after breaking the James River Canal and Virginia Central Railroad.

MAR. 19. USG instructed Sheridan to prepare for offensive operations west of Petersburg.

MAR. 19–21. C.S.A. forces defeated by Sherman in the battle of Bentonville, N.C., and Schofield occupied Goldsboro, N.C., on March 21.

MAR. 20. USG instructed Maj. Gen. John Pope to prepare to move into Tex.

MAR. 21. USG called attention to the fact that Negro troops had gone unpaid for over six months.

MAR. 24. USG ordered Meade and Ord to prepare for offensive operations west of Petersburg to begin on March 29.

MAR. 24. Lincoln arrived at City Point, having been invited by USG.

MAR. 25. C.S.A. forces attacked Fort Stedman at Petersburg. After Lee made initial gains, U.S. forces repulsed the attack and inflicted heavy losses.

MAR. 27.   Sherman arrived at City Point to consult with USG about final strategy, meeting with Lincoln, Sheridan, Ord, and Meade. Sherman returned to N.C. the following day.

MAR. 27.   Ord began crossing to the south side of the James River with three divs. to reach his position for the assault.

MAR. 28.   U.S. forces under Meade, Sheridan, and Ord in place for offensive operations. USG had decided to accompany this movement and to direct operations personally.

MAR. 29.   USG at Gravelly Run as the Appomattox campaign began, determined to make this offensive the final campaign against Lee.

MAR. 30.   USG at Gravelly Run reported to Lincoln that the campaign progressed well. Although urged to cancel the offensive because of heavy rain, USG decided to press on after conferring with Sheridan.

MAR. 31.   USG switched his hd. qrs. to Dabney's Mill in the afternoon as operations continued. He directed Meade to reinforce Sheridan at Five Forks.

APRIL 1.   USG at Dabney's Mill learned of Sheridan's victory at the battle of Five Forks and ordered an assault all along the lines for the following morning.

APRIL 2.   U.S. forces captured the lines at Petersburg and the C.S.A. government evacuated Richmond. USG moved his hd. qrs. to the Banks House near the Boydton Plank Road, and invited Lincoln to visit the captured works.

APRIL 3.   USG met with Lincoln at a private home inside Petersburg, leaving during the early afternoon to accompany U.S. forces pursuing Lee's army, spending the night at Sutherland's Station on the South Side Railroad.

APRIL 3.   U.S. forces commanded by Maj. Gen. Godfrey Weitzel entered Richmond at 8:15 A.M.

APRIL 4.   USG at Wilson's Station on the South Side Railroad as the pursuit of Lee's army continued.

APRIL 5.   USG started from Wilson's Station early in the morning, arrived at Nottoway Court House in the late afternoon, passed through Burkeville, arriving at Jetersville on the Richmond and Danville Railroad in the late evening near Sayler's Creek.

APRIL 6. USG at Jetersville as Sheridan defeated C.S.A. forces at the battle of Sayler's Creek, the last major engagement between the Army of the Potomac and the Army of Northern Va. USG returned to Burkeville in the evening to spend the night.

APRIL 7. USG at Farmville wrote to Lee asking for his surrender.

APRIL 8. USG at Farmville continued correspondence with Lee.

APRIL 9. Lee surrendered the Army of Northern Va. to USG in the house of Wilmer McLean at Appomattox Court House.

APRIL 10. USG talked privately with Lee at Appomattox Court House. He arrived at Prospect Station on the South Side Railroad in the evening.

APRIL 11. USG at Burke's Station.

APRIL 12. USG at City Point, then left for Washington during the afternoon.

APRIL 12. C.S.A. forces surrendered Mobile to Canby.

APRIL 13. USG established hd. qrs. at Washington.

APRIL 14. USG left Washington to visit his children at Burlington, N.J., declining an invitation to attend Ford's Theatre that evening with the Lincolns.

APRIL 14. Lincoln assassinated, dying the following morning.

APRIL 14. U.S. forces officially raised the flag at Fort Sumter, S.C.

APRIL 15. USG learned of Lincoln's assassination and left Burlington at 6:00 A.M. to return to Washington, arriving at 1:00 P.M. Late in the afternoon he directed Ord to arrest certain C.S.A. officials in Richmond, suspending the order during the evening.

APRIL 15. Andrew Johnson sworn in as President.

APRIL 16. USG decided to send Maj. Gen. Henry W. Halleck to command at Richmond.

APRIL 17.   USG ordered Canby to prepare for a campaign in Tex. and directed Maj. Gen. George H. Thomas to withdraw the bulk of U.S. forces from east Tenn.

APRIL 18.   Sherman signed a general surrender agreement with C.S.A. Gen. Joseph E. Johnston subject to the approval of Johnson.

APRIL 19.   USG instructed Ord about the treatment of paroled C.S.A. prisoners at Richmond.

APRIL 21.   USG learned of the extent of Sherman's accord and recommended to Stanton that a cabinet meeting be called. Johnson disapproved the agreement and directed USG to go to N.C. to oversee resumption of hostilities. USG left Washington at midnight.

APRIL 22.   USG stopped briefly at Fort Monroe to instruct Halleck to send Sheridan's cav. toward N.C.

APRIL 23.   USG at Beaufort, N.C.

APRIL 24.   USG reached Raleigh, N.C., and conferred with Sherman.

APRIL 26.   USG approved Sherman's second surrender agreement with Johnston containing the same terms granted to Lee.

APRIL 29.   USG at Washington returning from his trip to N.C. He informed Julia Dent Grant that their home in Philadelphia was ready for occupancy.

APRIL 30.   USG directed that special precautions be taken along the Mississippi River to prevent C.S.A. President Jefferson Davis from escaping into the West.

The Papers of Ulysses S. Grant
February 21–April 30, 1865

To Robert Ould

In field Virginia, February 21, *18645*.

JUDGE RO. OULD,
AGENT OF EXCHANGE, C. S. A.
SIR:

Enclosed please find communication of Major General E. O. C. Ord, U. S. Vols. in relation to the Insane Asylum at Williamsburg, Virginia, with endorsement of the Secretary of War thereon, and enclosures. If the proposition contained in said endorsement for the supply of this Asylum is accepted, please communicate such acceptance to me, together with any other matter touching the manner of its supply, &c., you may desire in order that immediate measures may be taken to carry the same into effect.

Very Respectfully
Your Obedient Servant
U. S. GRANT
Lieutenant General

LS, Virginia State Library, Richmond, Va.

On Feb. 9, 1865, Maj. Gen. Edward O. C. Ord wrote to Secretary of War Edwin M. Stanton. "There is an insane asylum at Williamsburg—within our lines—under care of our appointees—and whose bills I am called on to pay—as there is no appropriation for such places—the bills are paid from a civil fund that has accrued from fines penalties—taxes—&c under Genl. Butlers administration —as I presume I shall have no authority to collect such fund—Some other mode must be taken to meet the bills—or the Insane people should be sent some where else—I recommend they be sent to the Asylum at or near Washington for it will not do to let them starve, and they can be supported much easier at the north than where they now are" Copy, DNA, RG 108, Letters Received. *O.R.*, I, xlvi, part 2, 503. On Feb. 15, Asst. Secretary of War Charles A. Dana endorsed this letter. "Refferred to Lieutenant Genera[l] Grant to cause the rebel authorities to be informed that these insane people will not be supported by the United States, but must be provided for by them; and to propose that a part of the fund lately raised for the relief of rebel prisoners by the Sale of cotton in New York be appropriated to this purpose" Copy, DNA, RG 108, Letters Received. *O.R.*, I, xlvi, part 2, 503.

On March 2, Governor William Smith of Va. wrote to C.S.A. Agent of Exchange Robert Ould. "I had the honor to receive, under your cover of the 25th Feby, 1865, a letter from Lt. Gen'l Grant, enclosing a communication from Maj. Gen'l Ord, endorsed by the Asst. Secy of War of the U. S., and likewise one from Col. Webster, Chf Quartermaster—all in relation to the lunatics now at Williamsburg, under the authority and control of the Federal Government, the authorities of which communicate the determination of that Gov't to support said lunatics no longer. These papers also contain the proposition to apply a part of the proceeds of cotton recently shipped by the Confederate Govt for the benefit of her prisoners, to the support of the lunatics in question. These lunatics were a charge upon the State of Virginia so long as they were in the Confederate lines, and such charge will be cheerfully resumed when they and their asylum are restored to her possession. But, of course, Virginia cannot ask that resources designed for one humane and benevolent object, and which belong to the Confederate Government, should be appropriated as suggested. She is ready and anxious, however, to resume the care of these unhappy persons, when allowed to do so under circumstances which will ensure their comfort and protection. I see no way of accomplishing this humane and benevolent result, except by restoring possession of the Asylum, with its inmates, &c, to Virginia, making neutral ground of the Corporation of Williamsburg, with the right to trade for the necessary supplies within the lines of the United States and the Confederate States; exchanging such articles as we may have for such supplies as these unfortunates may require; the Superintendent and other necessary employees being bound; whenever they enter the lines of the United States, to make no revelations, upon their return, to the prejudice of that country. If such an arrangement as this could be made, I should be much gratified, and you will oblige me by using your best efforts to promote it." LS, DNA, RG 108, Letters Received. On March 6, Ould endorsed this letter to USG. AES, *ibid.*

To Edwin M. Stanton

(Cipher)   City Point, Va. Feb.y 21st 1865 [*11:30* A.M.]
HON. E. M. STANTON, SEC. OF WAR, WASHINGTON.
Mr. Paul, French Consul at Richmond, has just presented himself at our lines and requests permission to go to Washington. As it has been but a short time since he went to Richmond I have declined to permit him to pass. I ~~will be guided however by~~ would like your directions in this matter.

U. S. GRANT
Lt. Gn

ALS (telegram sent), OCIWHi; copies, DLC-USG, V, 46, 73, 108; (marked as received at noon) DNA, RG 107, Telegrams Received in Cipher; *ibid.*, RG 108, Letters Sent. *O.R.*, I, xlvi, part 2, 608. On Feb. 25, 1865, Secretary of War Edwin M. Stanton telegraphed to USG. "You were right in refusing a pass to the French Consul through your lines   In the present condition of things, the Department recognizes the right of no one to pass through our lines, unless in the service and by your direction." LS (telegram sent), DNA, RG 107, Telegrams Collected (Bound); telegram received (at 12:30 P.M.), *ibid.*, RG 108, Letters Received. *O.R.*, I, xlvi, part 2, 685.

On Feb. 21, Lt. Col. John E. Mulford had telegraphed to USG. "Monsieur Paul French Consul at Richmond is here & desires to go to Washington   Shall I receive him   Answer." ALS (telegram sent), DNA, RG 107, Telegrams Collected (Unbound); telegram received, *ibid.*, RG 108, Letters Received. On the same day, USG telegraphed to Mulford. "Mr. Paul went to Richmond but a few ~~days~~ months since and can not be allowed to return North now. If he has any communications for the French Government they can be ~~sent~~ received by you to be forwarded. I have Submitted the application to the Sec'y of War." ALS (telegram sent), OClWHi; copies, DLC-USG, V, 46, 73, 108; DNA, RG 108, Letters Sent; USG 3. The last sentence is not in USG's hand.

On March 3, Alfred Paul, Richmond, wrote to USG. "On the 21st of the last month I left Richmond to cross the lines at Bulware's Landing, where, at my great surprise, Lieut. Col. Mulford, of the U. S. Army, informed me that the permanent order issued some time ago from the War Department, to allow my crossing the lines freely and at any time, had been suspended, and therefore it was necessary that he should make an application for a special permit for me to go to Washington. Having received yet no communication about this matter, I have, General, the honor of requesting of you to be kind enough to let me know whether you have any objection to my going through the lines for the service of my Government. Expecting a favorable answer, . . ." LS, DNA, RG 108, Letters Received.

To Edwin M. Stanton

(Cipher)   City Point Va. Feb.y 21st 1865 [2:00 P.M.]
HON. E. M. STANTON, SEC. OF WAR, WASHINGTON.

Warren or Humphreys either would be good men to put in command of the Dept. of West Va. Warren I would suggest. Brig. Gen. Carroll is a very active officer and I think would do well to take the place of Kelley. I will telegraph to Gen. Sheridan to hold commanders on the B & O. road responsible for every disaster.

U. S. GRANT
Lt. Gn.

ALS (telegram sent), OClWHi; copies, DLC-USG, V, 46, 73, 108; (marked as received at 2:25 P.M.) DNA, RG 107, Telegrams Received in Cipher; *ibid.*, RG 108, Letters Sent. *O.R.*, I, xlvi, part 2, 608. On Feb. 21, 1865, 11:30 A.M. and 8:00 P.M., Secretary of War Edwin M. Stanton telegraphed to USG. "The fre-

Grant's Area of Operations, 1865

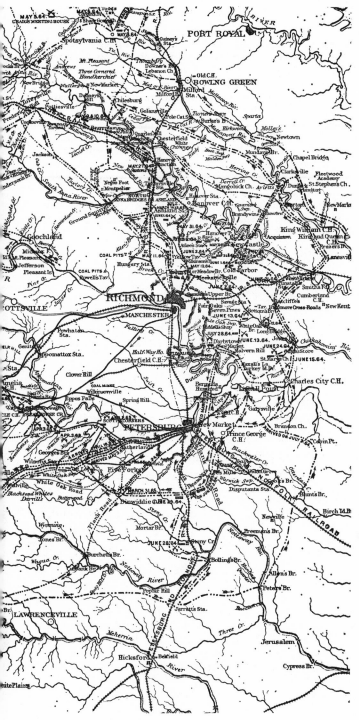

O.R. Atlas, *plate LXXIV, no. 1*

quent surprises in Sheridans command has ~~ex attracted~~ excited a good deal of observation recently. Friday ~~or Sat~~ an entire detachment of one hundred and ten men were captured ~~whi~~ of which [I] have seen no report from him. It was my design yesterday to reccommend ~~him~~ that Crook be ordered out of Cumberland to his front but in the press of business it was not done. There has been ~~gross~~ negligence I am afraid along that whole line for months, and I have been in daily apprehension of disaster, so that Crooks misfortune is not unexpected. can you ~~not~~ excite more vigilance." "Gen Warren has a young wife in Baltimore and of course family connections. I do not think he will suit for ~~the~~ Crooks Department. Humphreys will do better but he would not be the right man. Can you not think of some one else. ~~I think~~ Ought not Crooks & Kelly ~~should~~ both be mustered out of ~~serv~~ service for gross negligence? and as an example even if they should be afterward restored." ALS (telegrams sent), DNA, RG 107, Telegrams Collected (Bound); telegrams received (the second on Feb. 22), *ibid.*, RG 108, Letters Received. *O.R.*, I, xlvi, part 2, 608. See telegram to Edwin M. Stanton, Feb. 22, 1865.

To Maj. Gen. George G. Meade

(Cipher)   City Point, Va, Feb.y 21st *1864*5. [*2:30* P.M.]
MAJ. GEN. MEADE,

At the same time I telegraphed you on the subject of the proposed raid I telegraphed to Sheridan as to the practicability of him starting from where he is, in person, to reach Sherman, going by way of Lynchburg. I do not want to send both. Sherman has but little over 4000 Cavalry and Schofield none. The main object is to reinforce Sherman in that arm of service. I may yet send the proposed reinforcement to Wilmington. Going by Lynchburg would give us great advantages in cutting the Central road, Va. & Tenn, road the Danville road south of Danville and the Canal. If a Division is sent from here it would have to be Greggs to save time.

U. S. GRANT
Lt. Gn

ALS (telegram sent), Mrs. Arthur Loeb, Philadelphia, Pa.; telegram received, DNA, RG 94, War Records Office, Army of the Potomac. *O.R.*, I, xlvi, part 2, 609. On Feb. 21, 1865, 1:30 P.M., Maj. Gen. George G. Meade had telegraphed to USG. "Genl. Getty does not seem inclined to command the Cavalry—I will see Crawford & Ayres probably the latter is the best man—One difficulty is the evident separation from this army with which those who have been identified desire to remain—How would it do to bring another division here & send it?—Would this require too much time?" ALS (telegram sent), DNA, RG 94, War Records

Office, Army of the Potomac; telegram received, *ibid.*, RG 108, Letters Received. *O.R.*, I, xlvi, part 2, 609. On Feb. 22, 11:00 A.M., Meade telegraphed to USG. "Neither Ayres or Crawford feel like taking the cavalry under existing circumstances—How would it do to transfer Kautz to this command It seems to me this is the best & only arrangement we can make for immediate action—I will see you as soon as my train arrives—" ALS (telegram sent), DNA, RG 94, War Records Office, Army of the Potomac; telegram received, *ibid.*, RG 108, Letters Received. *O.R.*, I, xlvi, part 2, 630.

To Maj. Gen. George G. Meade

By Telegraph from City Point
Dated Feby 21 *1864*5.

To MAJ GENL MEADE

There is a regiment of Infy garrisoning Fort McHenry Baltimore Would it interfere with your army to send a heavy artillery regt to take its place and bring it to the army of the Potomac If not you may send the regt to releive the one at Fort McHenry without further orders. Please answer

U S GRANT
Lt Genl

Telegram received (at 4:40 P.M.), DNA, RG 94, War Records Office, Army of the Potomac; copies (2), Meade Papers, PHi. *O.R.*, I, xlvi, part 2, 609. Misdated Feb. 20, 1865, in USG letterbooks.

On Feb. 21, 4:18 P.M., Maj. Gen. Henry W. Halleck had telegraphed to USG. "The 91st New-York regt was changed by Genl Banks, without authority, into an artillery regt. The order was disapproved. The regt is now in Fort-Mc-Henry Baltimore, & the Adjt Genl recommends that it be sent to Army of Potomac as an Infantry regt, & that a regiment of artillery serving there as Infantry take its place in Baltimore. As such a change might interfere with operations in the field, the matter is referred for your action." ALS (telegram sent), DNA, RG 107, Telegrams Collected (Bound); telegram received, *ibid.*; (at 4:20 P.M.) *ibid.*, RG 108, Letters Received. *O.R.*, I, xlvi, part 2, 609.

At 5:00 P.M. and 11:30 P.M., Maj. Gen. George G. Meade telegraphed to USG. "Do you know the strength of the Regiment of Infantry at Baltimore—We think a good deal of our Heavy's they are about as good fighters as we have—I ~~can~~ will however send one of them as you desire—I have telegraphed for returns to see which is the weakest of them." "I have ordered to Baltimore the 7th N. Y. Heavy Artillery 37 officers & 571 enlisted men present —Total present & absent 44. officers 1115 men directing the C. O to report to the C. O. of Fort McHenry or to the C. O Middle Dept—Please have the regiment it is to relieve notified. Deserters just in report that Heths division on our left is under orders to move at a moments notice—No issue of rations for an extended movement and this may be either in anticipation of a movement from us, or to attempt an attack—We are all ready, for the latter contingency—" ALS (telegrams sent), DNA, RG 94, War Records Office, Army of the Potomac; copies, *ibid.*, RG 393, Army of the Potomac, Letters Sent; Meade Papers, PHi. *O.R.*, I, xlvi, part 2, 610. On Feb. 22, 10:00 A.M., USG telegraphed to Halleck. "The 7th N. Y. Heavy Artillery, 37 Officers & 571 men is ordered to relieve the Infantry Regt. at Fort McHenry. Please order the latter to the Army of the Potomac." ALS (telegram sent), OClWHi; telegram received (at 10:15 A.M.), DNA, RG 94, Letters Received, 215A 1865.

On Feb. 27, 2:00 P.M., Halleck telegraphed to USG. "The 91st New York regt leaves Baltimore to-day for Army of the Potomac. The artillery regt [to] replace it should be on [th]e way. Genl Morris says he will not have sufficient guards till it arrives" ALS (telegram sent), *ibid.*, RG 107, Telegrams Collected (Bound); telegram received, *ibid.*; *ibid.*, RG 108, Letters Received. *O.R.*, I, xlvi, part 2, 717. On the same day, USG telegraphed to Halleck. "The Seventh New York Heavy Artillery were shipped from here for Baltimore on the 22d, and should have reached there several days ago." Printed as received at 5:20 P.M. *ibid.*

On March 3, 2:30 P.M., Halleck telegraphed to USG. "The regiment sent to Baltimore is not half as strong as the one taken away & Genl Morris thinks his Dept has not a sufficient force. He has represented the matter to Genl Hancock, but the latter thinks he can spare no troops for Baltimore." ALS (telegram sent), DNA, RG 107, Telegrams Collected (Bound); telegram received, *ibid.*; *ibid.*, RG 108, Letters Received. *O.R.*, I, xlvi, part 2, 803. At 4:00 P.M., USG telegraphed to Halleck. "If Gen. Morris requires more troops he can have the 3d Regular Infantry which was sent here but a short time since. If there are any new regiments raised in the states East of the state of Ohio let them all report to Gen. Hancock." ALS (telegram sent), Free Library of Philadelphia, Philadelphia, Pa.; copies, DLC-USG, V, 46, 74, 108; DNA, RG 108, Letters Sent. *O.R.*, I, xlvi, part 2, 803.

A telegram of Feb. 21 from USG to Maj. Gen. Edward O. C. Ord exists only in incomplete form, containing the last words: "with the efficency of the army." Telegram received, Ord Papers, CU-B. The docket summarizes the contents: "Deserters report that Heaths Devission on our left is under marching orders" *Ibid.*

To Maj. Gen. George G. Meade

(Cipher)   City Point, Va, Feb.y 21st *1865*

Maj. Gen. Halleck, Washington

As we are

Maj. Gen. Meade,

My order does not contemplate payment for Arms brought in by deserters. I do not know however but it would be good policy to amende the order so as to make it an inducement for them to bring their Arms with them. Until the order is changed all Arms brought in will have to be turned over to the ordnance officer without payment being made.

U. S. GRANT
Lt. Gn

ALS (telegram sent), OClWHi; telegram received (at 9:10 P.M.), DNA, RG 94, War Records Office, Army of the Potomac. *O.R.*, I, xlvi, part 2, 610. On Feb. 21, 1865, 8:45 P.M., Maj. Gen. George G. Meade had telegraphed to USG. "Fifty four deserters received today at Prov. Marshalls—including one capt 59. Ala one sergeant & 3 corporals. They report no changes or movements—The capt states that Hood's army is being transported by rail into Georgia—He says the soldiers will not stand the enlistment of colored troops.—Some 12 of these men brought in their arms—Can they be compensated for them & does your order intend payment for arms & accoutrements." ALS (telegram sent), DNA, RG 94, War Records Office, Army of the Potomac; telegram received (at 8:45 P.M.), *ibid.*, RG 108, Letters Received. *O.R.*, I, xlvi, part 2, 610.

To Maj. Gen. Philip H. Sheridan

(Cipher)   City Point, Va, Feb.y 21st *18645.* [2:00 P.M.]
MAJ. GEN. SHERIDAN, WINCHESTER VA.

The number of surprises in West Va. indicates negligence on the part of officers and troops in that Dept. Hereafter when these disasters occur cause an investigation to be made by one of your Staff Officers of the circumstances and when there has been neglect punish it. I have recommended Warren or Humphreys U. S. as Crooks successor and Carroll to take the place of Kelley. If you want any change from this telegraph me at once before assignments are made.

U. S. GRANT
Lt. Gn

ALS (telegram sent), OClWHi; telegram received (at 5:00 P.M.), DNA, RG 107, Telegrams Collected (Bound); *ibid.*, Telegrams Collected (Unbound). *O.R.*, I, xlvi, part 2, 619. See telegram to Edwin M. Stanton, Feb. 21, 1865, 2:00 P.M. On Feb. 21, 1865, Maj. Gen. Philip H. Sheridan telegraphed to USG. "A party of from fifty to sixty rebel Cavalry surprised Genl Crooks pickets at Cumberland at three o'clock this morning, entered the City and captured Generals

Crook and Kelly and carried them off. I ordered the cavalry at New Creek to Moorefield and sent from here to same place via Wardensville but have but little hopes of re-capture as the party is going very rapidly. I think the party belongs to McNeils band" Telegram received (at 6:00 A.M.), DNA, RG 108, Letters Received; copies (2), DLC-Philip H. Sheridan. Printed as addressed to Maj. Gen. Henry W. Halleck in *O.R.*, I, xlvi, part 2, 620. On Feb. 21, Sheridan telegraphed to USG. "I would prefer Genl: Gibbon to either Genl: Humphreys, or Warren, if you can let me have him—if not I prefer Humphreys to Warren— There is, and has been, an inexcusable carlessness on the part of the Officers and Troops in the Dept: of West Va: I have dismissed subject to the appl of the President in all cases. There is on the B. & O. R. R. (or crossing it) from Martinsburg to Parkersburg (14000) fourteen thousand effective Troops—and there was at Cumberland of this force between (3500) & (4000) thirty five hundred & four thousand men, still they have been asking for more—I hope to get off from here about saturday, if possible—I have a canvass pontoon train en route from Washington which I would like to take—" Telegram sent, DNA, RG 107, Telegrams Collected (Unbound); telegram received, *ibid.*, Telegrams Collected (Bound); (on Feb. 22) *ibid.*, RG 108, Letters Received. *O.R.*, I, xlvi, part 2, 619–20.

To Gen. Robert E. Lee

City Point Va, Feby 22nd 1865

GENERAL R. E. LEE
COM'DG ARMIES CONFED- STATES
GENERAL!

Your communication of this date,[1] relating to the refusal of Maj, Gen, Schofield to receive Federal prisoners sent to Wilmington for exchange, is received and in answer thereto I have to state that Gen, Schofield was on the 20th inst informed and directed as follows "That the Confederate Authorities would deliver a large number of our prisoners to us near Wilmington during the present and ensuing weeks," and that if our Agent of Exchange was not there, to receive them and send them to Annapolis,[2] At the date of his refusal to receive them, concerning which you write, it is not probable these instructions had reached him, but unless something unusual happened to the Vessel that carried them, they have reached him by this time. These instruction[s] will be repeated, I have therefore to request that the prisoners be kept in the vicinity of

Wilmington, for nothing on our side shall prevent their being received in accordance with my agreement with Judge Ould,

> Very Respectfully
> Your obt svt
> U. S. GRANT
> Lieut, General

Copies, DLC-USG, V, 46, 73, 108; DNA, RG 108, Letters Sent. *O.R.*, II, viii, 290. See telegram to Maj. Gen. John M. Schofield, Feb. 22, 1865.

　　1. On Feb. 21, 1865, Gen. Robert E. Lee wrote to USG. "I am informed by the Secretary of War of the Confederate States that Genl: Schofield refuses to receive the prisoners sent to Wilmington for exchange according to the agreement entered into with Commissioner Ould by yourself. This will cause great hardships to these prisoners as they will have to be marched across the Country without adequate provision for their subsistence or comfort. On the score of humanity I would ask that Gen: Schofield be instructed to receive them in accordance with the agreement on the faith of which they were sent to Wilmington" LS, PHi. *O.R.*, II, viii, 285–86.
　　2. See telegram to Maj. Gen. John M. Schofield, Feb. 20, 1865.

To Edwin M. Stanton

(Cipher)　　　　　　　　　　City Point, Va, Feb.y 22d *1865*. [*noon*]
HON. E. M. STANTON, SEC. OF WAR, WASHINGTON,

　　I do not think Crook & Kelly should be mustered out of service before there is an investigation of the circumstances of their capture. It may prove they had taken proper precautions and the neglect has been the fault of some one else.[1] ~~Humphries is one of our best Corps commanders and hence~~ I think Humphries will prove one of our best Corps Commanders hence I would not care to have him leave here. I asked Gen. Halleck some time since to order Crocker from New Mexico.[2] If he is within reach I scarsely know his equal to take Crooks place. If he can not be reached I will name some one else probably Terry who from the number of Division commanders with Schofields army ranking him is occupying an unimportant position.

　　　　　　　　　　　　　　　U. S. GRANT Lt. Gn

ALS (telegram sent), OClWHi; copies, DLC-USG, V, 46, 73, 108; (marked as received at 1:35 P.M.) DNA, RG 107, Telegrams Received in Cipher; *ibid.*, RG 108, Letters Sent. *O.R.*, I, xlvi, part 2, 627–28.

    1. On March 5, 1865, USG telegraphed to Lt. Col. John E. Mulford. "Have you understood whether Gens Crooke and Kelly are to be delivered up? If so I will send for two Generals in their place." ALS (telegram sent), Kohns Collection, NN; telegram received (at 4:45 P.M.), Ord Papers, CU-B. See telegram to Edwin M. Stanton, March 21, 1865.

    2. On Dec. 28, 1864, 11:00 A.M., USG telegraphed to Maj. Gen. Henry W. Halleck. "Genl M. M Crocker writes to me that his health is so far ~~recovered~~ improved that he can take the field and desires to do so. I have never seen but three or four Division commanders his equal and we want his services. Please order him to report to Gen Thomas" Telegram received (at 11:45 A.M.), DNA, RG 107, Telegrams Collected (Bound); copies, *ibid.*, RG 94, ACP, C733 CB 1863; *ibid.*, RG 107, Telegrams Received in Cipher; *ibid.*, RG 108, Letters Sent; DLC-USG, V, 45, 71, 107. *O.R.*, I, xlv, part 2, 388. See *ibid.*, p. 443; telegram to Maj. Gen. Henry W. Halleck, March 2, 1865.

To Edwin M. Stanton

(Cipher)   City Point, Va, Feb.y 22d/65 [*11:00* P.M.]
HON. E. M. STANTON, SEC. OF WAR WASHINGTON
All points on the coast now being taken from the rebels except Mobile (if Wilmington is not now in our possession it will be within forty-eight hours I think) makes me believe that the French Rebel Rams will go to Mobile Bay to cut off our troops there from supplies. I have good reason to believe orders have gone from Richmond to hold Mobile at all hazards. This strengthens ~~my~~ this theory. ~~They~~ These Rams may have started for a different destination but as they will likely stop at some port near our coast to fill up with coal & supplies they ~~will prob~~ can get final orders. I think it ~~will be~~ advisable to notify the Navy Dept. and Canby of this theory so they can prepare for it.

                        U. S. GRANT
                        Lt. Gen.

ALS (telegram sent), OClWHi; copies, DLC-USG, V, 46, 73, 108; (marked as received at 11:50 P.M.) DNA, RG 107, Telegrams Received in Cipher; *ibid.*, RG 108, Letters Sent. *O.R.*, I, xlvi, part 2, 628; *ibid.*, I, xlix, part 1, 754.

    On Feb. 18, 1865, Secretary of State William H. Seward wrote to Secretary of War Edwin M. Stanton. "Telegrams and despatches from United States diplomatic agents and Consuls in Europe, indicate that one or more iron clad rams are about to be despatched from France and Spain, and may already have started to attack a port or ports of this country. The information is not definitive enough to enable me to designate the precise point of attack, but it is inferred that it may be either Wilmington or Charleston. I have imparted this intelligence to the Secretary of the Navy, but it is also deemed advisable to apprize you of it in order that, all practicable precautions may be adopted towards meeting any such attack" LS, DNA, RG 108, Letters Received. On Feb. 20, Asst. Secretary of War Charles A. Dana endorsed this letter to USG. ES, *ibid.* On Feb. 23, Seward wrote to USG. "We have this day received reliable information to the effect that the insurgent ram, intelligence respecting which at first excited some apprehension, is likely to be indefinetely detained either at Ferrol in Spain, or Lisbon, in Portugal. It is consequently beleived that you will have no occasion to take into account the probability of her appearance in Hampton Roads, as an element of your military combinations" LS, *ibid.* *O.R.,* I, xlvi, part 2, 653.

To Edwin M. Stanton

City Point, Va, Feb.y 22d *18645.*

HON. E. M. STANTON
SEC. OF WAR,
SIR:

Since so many Brevet Commissions have been given, I would respectfully recommend the following Staff Officers serving with me who have at least fully performed their respective duties in the Campaign of 1864 and so far in 1865, towit:

Brig. Gen. Jno. A. Rawlins to be Maj. Gen. by Brevet. Lt. Col. Horace Porter, A D C. ~~Lt Col~~ Col. F. T. Dent, and Lt. Col. O. E. Babcock,[1] A D C Aides de Camp; Lt. Col. T. S. Bowers, A. A. G., Lt. Col. E. S. Parker, A. A. G and Lt. Col. Adam Badeau, Military Secretaries, to be Colonels by brevet, and Capt. Peter T. Hudson Act. Aid-de-Camp to be Maj. by brevet.

Very respectfully
your obt. svt.
U. S. GRANT
Lt. Gn.

ALS, Mrs. Walter Love, Flint, Mich. Dated Feb. 20, 1865, in DLC-USG, V, 46, 73, 108; DNA, RG 108, Letters Sent. *O.R.,* I, xlvi, part 2, 596. On Feb. 22, Lt. Col. Theodore S. Bowers telegraphed to Capt. George K. Leet. "General Grant forwarded a letter in the mail this morning addressed to the Secretary of War recommending staff officers for brevet He desires you to return it" ALS (telegram sent), DNA, RG 107, Telegrams Collected (Unbound). On Feb. 23, Leet telegraphed to Bowers. "Letter referred to in your dispatch of yesterday will be returned by todays mail." ALS (telegram sent), *ibid.*, Telegrams Collected (Bound).

1. On Feb. 9, Bowers issued Special Orders No. 30. "Lieut Col. O E Babcock, A d C, will proceed without delay to and report to Maj. Gen. J. M. Schofield, at Fort Fisher or vicinity, for temporary duty, as per verbal instructions given him by the Lieut General Comdg. Upon the completion of his instructions he will rejoin these Headquarters." Copies, DLC-USG, V, 57, 63, 64, 65. *O.R.*, I, xlvii, part 2, 358.

To Bvt. Brig. Gen. William Hoffman

City Point, Va, Feb.y 22d 1865 [*7:30* P.M.]
BRIG. GN. HOFFMAN, WASHINGTON.

Please send here for exchange all Naval Prisoners at Fort Lafayette and Fort Delaware. If Campbell and Mars [*Marr*] have not been sent from Johnson's Island have them sent forward at once. Some 15.000 of our prisoners will be received within the next six days, taking all in Va & N. C. and those that were in S. C.

U. S. GRANT
Lt. Gn

ALS (telegram sent), OClWHi; telegram received (at 8:00 P.M.), DNA, RG 107, Telegrams Collected (Bound); *ibid.*, RG 249, Letters Received. *O.R.*, II, viii, 289.

On Feb. 22, 1865, Brig. Gen. John W. Turner telegraphed to Brig. Gen. John A. Rawlins. "A relative of my mothers Charles. A. Peabody is a rebel prisoner of war confined at Camp Douglass. He was conscripted into the rebel service and captured at Nashville. He is only too glad to get out of the rebel service and wishes to take the oath and remain north till the close of the war—my Father has applied to the Commissary General for his release, but I suppose it has been overlooked in the crowd of business at that office—in the mean time being in delicate health he is gradually failing and will probably die if kept in confinement much longer—Does Gen Grant like to act in such cases. I dont ask do not wish to ask it, if he prefers it to take the usual routine, only it being a case for clemency and if not speedily acted upon I fear the boy will die" ALS (telegram sent), DNA, RG 107, Telegrams Collected (Unbound); telegram received, *ibid.*, RG 108, Letters Received. At 10:00 P.M., USG telegraphed to Bvt. Brig. Gen. William Hoffman. "Please direct the discharge of Charles A. Peabody, rebel prisoner confined at Camp Douglas, on his taking the oath of allegiance." ALS (telegram sent), OClWHi; telegram received (at 10:40 P.M.), DNA, RG 107, Telegrams Collected (Bound); (at 11:00 P.M.) *ibid.*, RG 249, Letters Received.

To Maj. Gen. George G. Meade

City Point, Va, Feb.y 22d *1865*

MAJ. GEN. MEADE,

If you will come immediately in I will arrange to have you sent down the river so as to take the Baltimore boat this evening. I have spoken to Gn. Ingalls who will have a boat ready for you here on arrival and will have the train bring you in at once. I sincerely condole with you for your berievement.

U. S. GRANT
Lt. Gn.

ALS (telegram sent), OClWHi; copies, DLC-USG, V, 46, 73, 108; DNA, RG 108, Letters Sent. *O.R.*, I, xlvi, part 2, 629. On Feb. 22, 1865, 10:00 A.M., Maj. Gen. George G. Meade telegraphed to USG. "A telegram announces the death of my son yesterday—With your permission I should like to go home for a day or two.—" ALS (telegram sent), CtY; telegram received (at 10:00 A.M.), DNA, RG 108, Letters Received. *O.R.*, I, xlvi, part 2, 629. At 11:00 A.M., Meade telegraphed to USG. "My thanks are due for your dispatch and kindness. I will leave here at once, and hope to connect with the Baltimore boat this evening, so that a special train will not be required." *Ibid.* John Sergeant Meade died on Feb. 21. See George Meade, *The Life and Letters of George Gordon Meade* (New York, 1913), II, 263–64, where the footnote concerning Gen. Meade's whereabouts is incorrect.

At 1:30 P.M., USG prepared a telegram to Secretary of War Edwin M. Stanton, then changed the addressee to Maj. Gen. Henry W. Halleck. "Please direct Gen. Humphries who is now in Washington to return immediately to his command. He has yet four or five days leave which he will have to take another time when he can be better spared." ALS (telegram sent), OClWHi; copies, DLC-USG, V, 46, 73, 108; DNA, RG 94, Letters Received, 212A 1865; (marked as received at 1:30 P.M.) *ibid.*, RG 107, Telegrams Received in Cipher; *ibid.*, RG 108, Letters Sent. Printed as received at 1:40 P.M. in *O.R.*, I, xlvi, part 2, 629.

On Feb. 13, Brig. Gen. John A. Rawlins telegraphed to Meade and to Maj. Gen. Edward O. C. Ord. "The Lt Genl has returned to his Hd Qrs at City Point" Telegram received (at 12:35 P.M.), DNA, RG 94, War Records Office, Army of the Potomac; (at 12:45 P.M.) Ord Papers, CU-B. Printed as addressed to Meade in *O.R.*, I, xlvi, part 2, 548. On the same day, Lt. Col. Theodore S. Bowers telegraphed to Meade. "Gen Grant has returned and will be pleased to see you any time today" Telegram received (at 12:45 P.M.), DNA, RG 94, War Records Office, Army of the Potomac. *O.R.*, I, xlvi, part 2, 548. At 10:00 P.M., Meade telegraphed to USG. "Maj. Genl. Humphreys was promised a leave of absence on the return of Genl. Warren some weeks since—Just as he was about leaving your order was received forbidding leaves to General officers—Since then military operations have interposed. He now desires to go—Have you any objections to my permitting him to leave, His line is all established." ALS (telegram sent), DNA, RG 94, War Records Office, Army of the Potomac; telegram received (at 10:15 P.M.), *ibid.*, RG 108, Letters Received. *O.R.*, I, xlvi, part 2, 548. On the same day, USG telegraphed to Meade. "Gen. Humphries may be allowed to take his leave now subject to being recalled at any time by telegraphic orders." ALS (telegram sent), Kohns Collection, NN; telegram received (at 10:25 P.M.), DNA, RG 94, War Records Office, Army of the Potomac. *O.R.*, I, xlvi, part 2, 549.

On Feb. 22, noon, Meade twice telegraphed to USG. "Three negro women have just come in to our lines—report the R. Rd. finished to Stoney Creek, and the Cavalry hitherto at Bellefield have been ordered to move up to Stoney Creek & transfer the depot from Bellefield to Stoney Creek—The cavalry at Bellefield was understood to be W. H. F Lee's division & part of Butlers division.—These women were at a house last night just outside of our lines where they saw the cavalry men on their way to join their regiments these women came from the vicinity of Bellefield—& gave the above news." "The salute ordered by the Sec. of War is now being fired. I have just learned un-officialy that Genl. Miles comd. 2d corps yesterday advanced & straightened his picket line, driving away for this purpose—part of the enemies pickets—This may account for the report of deserters last evening that Heths division was ordered to be ready to move at a moments notice—Miles movement has been construed into a threatened advance—" ALS (telegrams sent), DNA, RG 94, War Records Office, Army of the Potomac; telegrams received (the first at noon), *ibid.*, RG 108, Letters Received. Both printed, the second as received at 12:15 P.M., in *O.R.*, I, xlvi, part 2, 630–31.

On Feb. 21, Bvt. Brig. Gen. Edward D. Townsend issued General Orders No. 24 directing a "national salute" in honor of the recapture of Fort Sumter. *Ibid.*, p. 611. A copy was sent by telegraph to USG. Memorandum, DNA, RG 107, Telegrams Collected (Bound). See *O.R.*, I, xlvi, part 2, 630. On Feb. 22, USG telegraphed to Stanton. "I had a salute of 100 guns fired at 12. M. yesterday in honor of the occupation of Charleston and Columbia, Your order is sent out to have the salute repeated" Copies, DLC-USG, V, 46, 73, 108; (marked as received at 10:20 A.M.) DNA, RG 107, Telegrams Received in Cipher; *ibid.*, RG 108, Letters Sent.

To Maj. Gen. Edward O. C. Ord

City Point, Va, Feb.y 22d 1865. [*11:00* A.M.]
MAJ. GEN. ORD, FT. MONROE,

I have no objection to a truce to ascertain the cause of the accident to the Steamer Shultz but I object to valuable machinery being gathered where we can prevent it to be used against us. It can never be used again to facilitate exchanges of prisoners, ~~hence~~

~~there is~~ and unless it is shown that the accident occured from a torpedo put in the water by us there is no claim upon us for its recovery.

U. S. GRANT

Lt. Gen.

ALS (telegram sent), OClWHi; telegrams received (2—at 11:00 A.M.), Ord Papers, CU-B. *O.R.*, I, xlvi, part 2, 646. On Feb. 22, 1865, 10:00 A.M., Maj. Gen. Edward O. C. Ord, Fort Monroe, telegraphed to USG. "Have just recd. an application of Col Ould recommended by Col Mulford that a truce be had on that part of the river where the flag of truce boat Shuttz was sunk, that the boat may be overhauled and that which is valuable about her appropreated and to find out the cause of the accident. On account of facilities it will offer to rebels to come back to the flag I approve the application" Telegram received, DNA, RG 108, Letters Received. *O.R.*, I, xlvi, part 2, 646. On Feb. 23, 8:45 A.M., Ord telegraphed to USG. "Will a truce from 9 till four to morrow—be too long to offer—to discover source of accident—the rebels occupy the river bank on one side—and we ~~do not~~ only occupy by night the other where the accident occured" ALS (telegram sent), Ord Papers, CU-B; telegram received (at 9:45 A.M.), DNA, RG 108, Letters Received.

On Feb. 22, 1:07 P.M., USG telegraphed to Ord. "Return to your command on receipt of this, or as soon after as you can. Your presence may be required." ALS (telegram sent), OClWHi; telegram received, Ord Papers, CU-B; (press) DNA, RG 107, Telegrams Collected (Bound). *O.R.*, I, xlvi, part 2, 647.

At 4:30 P.M., Ord, Norfolk, telegraphed to Brig. Gen. John A. Rawlins. "About twelve deserters (rebels) arrive in these lines daily. Shall they be sent to City Point or to Old Point, take oath, and then go North?" *Ibid.*, p. 646. On the same day, USG telegraphed to Ord. "Direct Provost Marshals. at all points in your Dept. East of this place to report to the Provost Marshal General at City Point for instructions as to disposition to be made of deserters coming in to them." ALS (telegram sent), OClWHi; telegram received, Ord Papers, CU-B; (press) DNA, RG 107, Telegrams Collected (Bound). *O.R.*, I, xlvi, part 2, 647.

To Maj. Gen. John G. Parke

City Point, Va, Feb.y 22d 1865

MAJ. GEN. PARKE, COMD.G A. P.

As there is a possibility of an attack from the enemy at any time, and especially an attempt to break your center, extra viggilence should be kept up both by pickets and the troops on the line. Let commanders understand that no time is to be lost awaiting orders if an attack is made in bringing all their reserves to the point of danger. With proper activity in this respect I would have no objection to seeing the enemy get through.

U. S. GRANT
Lt. Gn.

ALS (telegram sent), OClWHi; telegram received (at 2:20 P.M.), DNA, RG 94, War Records Office, Army of the Potomac. *O.R.*, I, xlvi, part 2, 631–32.

On Feb. 22, 1865, Lt. Col. Theodore S. Bowers telegraphed to Maj. Gen. John G. Parke. "General Grant desires that you please report the number of deserters from the enemy that came in on your front yesterday and to-day, and each day hereafter." Printed as received at 7:30 P.M. *ibid.*, p. 632. On the same day, Parke telegraphed to Bowers. "The Pro Mar reported this a m that fifty four deserters from the enemy had arrived at these Head. qurs—There have been reported thus far today forty three—" Telegram received, DNA, RG 108, Letters Received. Printed as sent at 8:25 P.M. in *O.R.*, I, xlvi, part 2, 632.

Also on Feb. 22, Parke telegraphed to USG and to Brig. Gen. John A. Rawlins. "I have as yet rec'd no report. It is confined entirely to the right of my line. Fort McGilvery and Battery No 5. No. musketry is heard. The national salute has just opened" "The firing was commenced by our people opening from No 5 upon a train of Cars on Richmond & Petersburg R R. The Enemy replied from Chesterfield Goose Neck & their General Mortar Batteries in front of the Line from Steadman to our right" Telegrams received, DNA, RG 108, Letters Received; copies, *ibid.*, RG 393, 9th Army Corps, Telegrams Sent. *O.R.*, I, xlvi, part 2, 642.

To Maj. Gen. John G. Parke

City Point, Va, Feb.y 22d *1865* [*midnight*]

MAJ. GN. ₱PARKE, A. P.

We will see what the morning brings forth now befor ordering the reconnoisance. I did not care about them going farther than just to ascertain if any movment was going on around our flank or if any troops were moving off towards the Weldon road. We may be able to learn this from deserters arriving during the night.

U. S. GRANT
Lt. Gn

ALS (telegram sent), OClWHi; telegram received (at midnight), DNA, RG 94, War Records Office, Army of the Potomac. *O.R.*, I, xlvi, part 2, 633. On Feb. 23, 1865, 12:20 A.M., Maj. Gen. John G. Parke telegraphed to USG. "I am now trying to ascertain whether or not I shall push out my pickets in front of Heth & wilcox or after daylight. If they leave for weldon some of my pickets will be put in position to determine the time of the movement if it be possible 7 deserters confirm the first report made in regard to Hills Corps" Telegram received (at 12:33 P.M. [A.M.?]), DNA, RG 108, Letters Received; copies, *ibid.*, RG 393, Army of the Potomac, Letters Sent; Meade Papers, PHi. *O.R.*, I, xlvi, part 2, 653.

On Feb. 22, Parke telegraphed to USG transmitting a telegram from Maj. Gen. Horatio G. Wright to Bvt. Maj. Gen. Alexander S. Webb. "Your dispatch directing Strengthening trench guards &c is received. A deserter from Mahones Div. states that Hills Entire Corps has been under orders to move at a moments notice since an hour before daylight this morning and says the rumor is that they are to move toward Weldon. He thinks the above orders were given to Hills Corps only." Telegram received (at 7:45 P.M.), DNA, RG 108, Letters Received. *O.R.*, I, xlvi, part 2, 639. On the same day, USG telegraphed to Parke. "Great vigilance will be necessary to prepare to receive an attack or to advance if it should prove that one Corps is ordered away. I think it advisable to push a Cavalry reconnoisance out early in the morning to see if any movement of the enemy can be discovered." ALS (telegram sent), OClWHi; telegram received (at 8:20 P.M.), DNA, RG 94, War Records Office, Army of the Potomac. *O.R.*, I, xlvi, part 2, 632. At 10:10 P.M., Parke telegraphed to USG. "The number of deserters reported to day should have been 45, not 43. The deserter reported by Gen Wright as conveying information concerning Hill's corps, is not sustained by the report of others. The 2nd Corps picket line was advanced last night, & in so doing startled the enemy & caused Heth to put 3 brigades under arms. I do not think that I am warranted to conclude that Hill is prepared to move. Since Lee's ~~army~~ cavalry has moved up to Stony Creek I will require some of my infantry to support a cavalry reconnoissance. To meet the anticipated attack of Lee on my centre all now available will be called upon in case of alarm. Still the reconnoissance can be made, and if you desire it I will issue the necessary orders tonight." Copies, DNA, RG 393, Army of the Potomac, Letters Sent; Meade Papers, PHi. *O.R.*, I, xlvi, part 2, 632–33.

To Maj. Gen. John M. Schofield

City Point Va.
Feb. 22d [*186*]5

MAJ GEN. J. M. SCHOFIELD
FT FISHER.

Gen. Lee reports to me today that you refused to receive our prisoners sent by him to Wilmington for exchange—I informed him in reply that you had not probably received my directions at that date—You will please receive all—prisoners that the rebels may have to deliver to you and forward them to Annapolis—They were sent to Wilmington by special agreement and should they fall into

your hands by the fortunes of [wa]r, we would still be in honor
bound to regard them as delivered to us by the enemy

U. S. GRANT
Lieut. Gen'l.

Telegram received (at 3:00 P.M.—press), DNA, RG 107, Telegrams Collected
(Bound); copies, *ibid.*, RG 108, Letters Sent; *ibid.*, RG 393, Dept. of N. C.,
Telegrams Received; DLC-USG, V, 46, 73, 108; USG 3. *O.R.*, II, viii, 289. On
Feb. 22, 1865, USG telegraphed to the operator, Fort Monroe. "Please put up
to Gen. Schofield and deliver to Capt. James a. q. m. and request that he send it
by first vessel." Telegram received (press), DNA, RG 107, Telegrams Collected
(Bound). On Feb. 28, Maj. Gen. John M. Schofield wrote to USG. "I have just
received your despatch of the 22d, containing Genl Lees statement that I had
refused to receive our prisoners. Genl Lee is mistaken as to the fact. I did not
refuse to receive them, but replied to Genl Hoke that I had received no official
information of any arrangement by which prisoners were to be delivered to me,
and asked on what terms they were to be delivered. I intended to receive them,
if his answer should be satisfactory, without waiting for your instructions. It
would have been impossible to have received the prisoners at the time and place
named by Genl Hoke without suspending operations against Wilmington. Therefore no unnecessary delay was occasioned by my waiting for further information
before receiving the prisoners. I have also agreed to a proposition from Lt. Genl
Hardee to receive about one thousand sick and convalescent prisoners from the
Department of South Carolina. They are to be sent in on the Manchester road
tomorrow. I enclose herewith copies of all correspondence with Genl Hardee,
Genl. Hoke and Col. Hatch, Assist Agent of Exchange." ALS, *ibid.*, RG 108,
Letters Received. *O.R.*, II, viii, 317. The enclosures are *ibid.*, pp. 238, 268, 286,
290, 296–97.

On Feb. 24, 6:00 P.M., USG telegraphed to Lt. Col. John E. Mulford. "I
answered Gen. Lee's note on the subject of Schofields ~~receiving~~ refusing to receive
prisoners at Wilmington by saying that orders were sent to Schofield on the 20th
to receive them. and that the order would be repeated. It was repeated." ALS
(telegram sent), OClWHi; copies, DLC-USG, V, 46, 73, 74, 108; DNA, RG
108, Letters Sent; USG 3.

To Maj. Gen. Philip H. Sheridan

City Point, Va, Feb.y 22d 1865 [*1:30* P.M.]
MAJ. GEN. SHERIDAN, WINCHESTER VA.

Paynes[1] Brig. of Cavalry has arrived here from the Valley.
Wickham's Brigade arrived some time since. Two passenger trains
and two freight trains are now run daily over the Central road.
There is also great activity on the Fredericksburg road. Many sup-

plies have been collected on the Northern Neck and many more are smuggled in from Phila and other places and taken to Richmond over this road. 70.000 pounds of bacon alone have gone to Richmond the last week over that road. Can not Augur send a force to break that trade up? It is reported that all troops from the Valley except those brought here have gone to Lynchburg.

U. S. GRANT
Lt. Gn.

ALS (telegram sent), OClWHi; telegram received (at 3:05 P.M.), DNA, RG 107, Telegrams Collected (Bound); *ibid.*, Telegrams Collected (Unbound). *O.R.*, I, xlvi, part 2, 649–50. On Feb. 23, 1865, Maj. Gen. Philip H. Sheridan telegraphed to USG. "I have telegraphed to Genl Auger in reference to the northern neck. There is ~~there~~—also in Essex, & King and Queen Counties, and in ~~the~~ fact in the section of Country from Bowling Green down to Urbanna— between the Rappahannock and Mattapony Rivers, a large amount of Provisions and Forage—Last Summer when I was in this section, I found the finest crops of Corn, I ever saw—and every acre was planted—I think some supplies are being gathered west of the Shenandoah Valley in the little Mountain Valley—from Warm Springs to Parisburg [*Pearisburg*] on ~~new~~ New River—Rosser's brigade of Cavly: also Imboden, Jackson, and McCausland are in the above named section—It has been raining here for the last 12 hours, the snow is going fast" Telegram sent, DNA, RG 107, Telegrams Collected (Unbound); telegram received (at 5:00 P.M.), *ibid.*, Telegrams Collected (Bound); (at 6:00 P.M.) *ibid.*, RG 108, Letters Received. *O.R.*, I, xlvi, part 2, 665. See *ibid.*, p. 666.

1. William H. Payne, born in 1830 in Va., commonwealth attorney, Fauquier County, Va., before the Civil War, entered the war as capt., Black Horse Cav., in Sept., 1861, and was appointed brig. gen. as of Nov. 1, 1864. His cav. brigade served in the div. of Maj. Gen. Fitzhugh Lee. See "Brilliant Eulogy on Gen. W. H. Payne From Good Old Rebels Who Don't Care," *Southern Historical Society Papers*, XXXV (1908), 285–353.

To Edwin M. Stanton

City Point, Va, Feb.y 23d 1865

HON. E. M. STANTON,
SEC. OF WAR,
SIR:

I see by the papers that an effort is being made to induce the President to appoint Gen. Butler "Provost Marshal" of Charleston and South Carolina. I can not believe this will be done but write to respectfully enter my protest.—There are many reasons which I might give why General Butler should not be placed on duty again, but I think two of them are sufficient: his order to his troops on being relieved from duty, and his Lowell speach.[1]

> Very respectfully
> your obt. svt.
> U. S. GRANT
> Lt. Gn.

ALS, DNA, RG 94, Letters Received, 1077G 1865. *O.R.*, I, xlvii, part 2, 537. On Feb. 25, 1865, 12:40 P.M., Secretary of War Edwin M. Stanton telegraphed to USG. "Your letter of the 23d received. There is no occasion ~~for any~~ to expect the President will make any order against your wishes. ~~while I am here.~~ The reasons mentioned by you have already been presented and, are conclusive." ALS (telegram sent), DNA, RG 107, Telegrams Collected (Bound); telegram received (at 12:16 P.M.), *ibid.*, RG 108, Letters Received. *O.R.*, I, xlvii, part 2, 562.

1. See *ibid.*, I, xlvi, part 2, 70–71; *New York Times*, Jan. 30, 1865.

To Edwin M. Stanton

City Point Va, Feby 23d 1865

HON, E. M. STANTON
SECY OF WAR
SIR

Under the law, and existing orders, we are now losing Colonel's by reason of the experation of their term of service, who as Brigade Commanders are indispensible   In most of these cases the Colonels are willing to be remustered for the un expired term of their regiments; but do not feel willing to muster-in for three years, more,   I would respectfully and earnestly recommend that authority be given to retain such officers as are necessary for the service,   With such authority only such officers as it is really desirable to retain in service, would be retained, It would be a great help if this authority was given for retaining only such Colonels, as are Commanding Brigades, I would however prefer seeing it extended to all Colonel's whose time expires before that of the regiment they Command, or where regiments are reduced below the number entitling them to a Colonel.

I would respectfully ask for an early answer to this, because in a few days, some of our best Best. Brigade Commanders, will go out of service if the authority here asked is not granted in time to save them,

Very Respectfully,
Your obt svt
U. S. GRANT
Lieut, General

Copies, DLC-USG, V, 46, 73, 108; DNA, RG 108, Letters Sent. *O.R.*, I, xlvi, part 2, 651–52. On Feb. 27, 1865, 9:30 P.M., Bvt. Brig. Gen. Edward D. Townsend telegraphed to USG. "Referring to your letter of the twenty third (23) instant, relative to the remuster and retention of Colonels of regiments, under certain circumstances, the Secretary of War, hereby grants authority to remuster, under their existing commissions, and for the unexpired terms of their regiments, all Colonels willing to remain and whose retention in service may be approved by you. This authority may be excercised even if regiments are below the minimum; provided they have not lost, or will not lose, their regimental organization, by companies thereof being mustered out. The remusters will be made on expiration of existing terms of service and by the proper commissaries of musters each case first receiving approval from your HeadQuarters the same to be filed with the remuster in rolls and to refer to this authority, The authority herein contained will cease after the coming spring campaign shall have ended unless renewed by the Secretary of War—" Telegram sent (incomplete), DNA, RG 107, Telegrams Collected (Unbound); telegram received (at 9:30 P.M.) and incomplete copy, *ibid.*, RG 108, Letters Received. At 11:20 P.M., Lt. Col. Theodore S. Bowers transmitted this telegram to Maj. Gen. John G. Parke. *O.R.*, I, xlvi, part 2, 719.

On Feb. 23, Maj. Gen. Edward O. C. Ord wrote to Brig. Gen. John A. Rawlins. "I enclose a case Br Genl (by brevet) T. M. Harris—according to the ruling in this case our most valuable officers are being *ordered* out of service—Br Genl Bell was ordered out of service before he was killed in *it* Br Genl Harris —and Jourdan—are also *ordered* out of service—Col Cullen is *ordered* out of service, and I beg leave to state that if these orders are to go into effect I be relieved from command of this army—for with the best officers ~~going~~ being ordered out—I do not feel myself competent to command the new Troops—and new Officers—" ALS, DNA, RG 108, Letters Received. *O.R.*, I, xlvi, part 2, 663–64.

To Charles A. Dana

———

City Point, Va, Feb.y 23d/65 [*7:30* P.M.]

HON. C. A. DANA, ASST. SEC. OF ~~THE~~ WAR WASHINGTON,

I have here the same information of the intentions and movements of the enemy contained in your dispatch of this evening. We are watching closely and I do not entertain the slightest fear for the result. I know of no false information which could benefit us by having it communicated to the enemy just now.

U. S. GRANT
Lt. Gn

ALS (telegram sent), OClWHi; copies, DLC-USG, V, 46, 73, 108; (marked as received at 7:40 P.M.) DNA, RG 107, Telegrams Received in Cipher; *ibid.*, RG 108, Letters Sent. *O.R.*, I, xlvi, part 2, 652. On Feb. 23, 1865, 3:30 P.M., Asst. Secretary of War Charles A. Dana telegraphed to USG. "I have positive and official ~~news~~ information from Richmond to the effect that Lee is calling in all outlying detachments, bridge guards, and small posts, in order to strength his army for a grand effort. This effort is expected to be made within the next ten days, and is spoken of with confidence in intimate governm[*ent*] circles. No ~~peop~~ persons have been allowed to visit Richmond from the country around since about the tenth instant. ~~C. A. DAN~~ If you wish any false information to be given to the Rebel authorities, I have the means of conveying it so that it will be believed. It will take seven to ten days to reach them." ALS (telegram sent), DNA, RG 107, Telegrams Collected (Bound); telegram received (marked as sent at 3:00 P.M.), *ibid.*, RG 108, Letters Received. *O.R.*, I, xlvi, part 2, 652.

To Bvt. Brig. Gen. William Hoffman

———

City Point, Va, Feb.y 23d *18645*.

BRIG. GN. WM HOFFMAN, WASHINGTON.

You may send forward all citizen prisoners whose homes are within the rebel lines and who are not awaiting trial on grave charges, or who are not undergoing sentence. After this is done send me a list of citizen prisoners still held and the charges upon which they are retained.

U. S. GRANT
Lt. Gn.

ALS (telegram sent), OClWHi; telegram received (at 3:00 P.M.), DNA, RG 107, Telegrams Collected (Bound); *ibid.*, RG 249, Letters Received. *O.R.*, II, viii, 294. On Feb. 23, 1865, Bvt. Brig. Gen. William Hoffman telegraphed to USG. "Naval prisoners have been ordered from Forts-Lafayette and Delaware for exchange. All prisoners who are or have been in irons or close confinement have been ordered forward for exchange Shall I forward citizens for exchange." ALS (telegram sent), DNA, RG 107, Telegrams Collected (Unbound); telegram received (at 2:40 P.M.), *ibid.*, RG 108, Letters Received. *O.R.*, II, viii, 294. USG endorsed the telegram received to Lt. Col. John E. Mulford. "Communicate the above dispatch to Col. Ould, I have directed that all Citizen prisoners whose homes are within the Southern lines except those on trial or under sentence for grave offences be sent here for exchange. Also that a list of all others, and the charges upon which they are detained be sent to me." AES (incomplete), DNA, RG 108, Letters Received; copies, DLC-USG, V, 46, 73, 108. On Feb. 23, Mulford telegraphed to USG. "There are confined in the South a class of prisoners not included in the arrangemt for exchg of Mercht Service men made last week, being persons who have been taken on rivers & bays; engaged in marine pursuits on private account, such as freighters, oystermen, & sutler Vessels including officers crews & in some cases passengers, the reason why these were not included was on account of my being unauthorized, to agree to give army equivalents for any excess the enemy might hold, Mr Ould now proposes ~~to~~ that we release mutually all persons captured on the High Seas & inland waters without regard to numbers, or upon the same basis of equivalents agreed upon for Governmt transport service men seamen rating as privates & the Officers, a grade or two above This proposition involves the release of all blockade runners, and would also include the captors of the Chesapeak &c unless exceptions in cases of that class were made, I can see no objection with my limited knowledge of this class of persons held by us—to an arrangement for the relief of those held by the enemy Our authorities have from time to time discharged unconditionally numbers of prisoners captured on board blockade running Vessels. I think however there are quite a number of this class of prisoners held by us at Fts Delaware Lafayette & Warren—As these are now the only prisoners who have not been arranged for I respectfully call your attention to the subject and await instructions," ALS (telegram sent), DNA, RG 107, Telegrams Collected (Unbound); telegram received, *ibid.*, RG 108, Letters Received. *O.R.*, II, viii, 294–95.

On Feb. 25, 12:32 P.M., Hoffman telegraphed to USG. "Under Gen. Orders No. 6 Jany 18, and your telegram of the 17th inst, all rebel prisoners in close confinement or in irons have been ordered to be forwarded for exchange. This embraces soldiers and citizens, spies, murderers, guerrills &c. A history of each case is sent with them so that exceptions can be made if deemed advisable. From your telegram of the 23 I judge that you did not intend your order to have such a general bearing. If so they may be stopped at City-Point." ALS (telegram sent), DNA, RG 107, Telegrams Collected (Unbound); telegram received (at 12:20 P.M.), *ibid.*, RG 108, Letters Received. *O.R.*, II, viii, 306. On Feb. 26, 11:00 P.M., USG telegraphed to Hoffman. "Send no more Rebel prisoners for exchange, except those who have been in close confinement, until further orders. I do not want to get ahead in the deliveri[es]." ALS (telegram sent), Kohns Collection, NN; telegram received (at 11:15 P.M.), DNA, RG 107, Telegrams Collected (Bound); *ibid.*, RG 249, Letters Received. *O.R.*, II, viii, 309. On Feb. 27, Hoffman telegraphed to USG. "Your telegram of yesterday is received and will be observed. Maj. Genl. Sheridan has sent Guerrillas to Fort-McHenry, not to be exchanged during the war   Shall they be held after the exchange of other prisons" ALS (telegram sent), DNA, RG 107, Telegrams Collected (Unbound); telegram received (at 3:50 P.M.), *ibid.*, RG 108, Letters Received. *O.R.*, II, viii, 313.

On March 3, Hoffman wrote to USG. "Some months since twenty six citizen prisoners were, by order of the Secretary of War, sent from the Old Capitol to Fort Delaware to be held as hostages for Union citizens held at Salisbury, N. C. In the meantime some of them have been discharged on taking the Oath of allegiance and others are applying to do so. Pursuant to your telegram of the 23rd ult, and with the approbation of the War Department, I have directed that such of these men as still remain at Fort Delaware who desire to be exchanged, be forwarded to City Point for exchange, or to be disposed of as you may think proper. They will be on a list by themselves. All citizen prisoners of the class designated in your telegram of the 23rd have been ordered to be forwarded for exchange and I will furnish you a list of those who remain, with the charges against them, as soon as reports are received from the camps where they are held." LS, DNA, RG 108, Letters Received. *O.R.*, II, viii, 335.

To Maj. Gen. John G. Parke

City Point, Va, Feb.y 23d 1865

MAJ. GEN. PARKE, COMD.G A. P.

The regiment of Cavalry ordered from the front can be mounted by taking public horses in the hands of employees of the Q. M. Dept. at City Point. I will have it attended to. A large number of horses can be got in the same way out of the A. P. to fill up what is required by the balance of the Cavalry.

U. S. GRANT
Lt. Gn.

ALS (telegram sent), OClWHi; telegram received, DNA, RG 94, War Records Office, Army of the Potomac. *O.R.*, I, xlvi, part 2, 654. Earlier on Feb. 23, 1865, USG had telegraphed to Maj. Gen. John G. Parke. "Please send to this place as soon as praciticable one good regiment of Cavalry to be transferred to Genl Schofields Command and advise me of the time it will reach City Point & the probable strength of the regt" Telegram received (at 4:50 P.M.—misdated Feb. 21), DNA, RG 393, Army of the Potomac, Miscellaneous Letters Received; copies, *ibid.*, RG 108, Letters Sent; DLC-USG, V, 46, 73, 108; Meade Papers, PHi. *O.R.*, I, xlvi, part 2, 654. On the same day, Parke telegraphed to Lt. Col. Theodore S. Bowers. "The thirteenth Penna Cavalry will report at City Point Va by twelve noon tomorrow in obedience to telegram of this date from Genl Grant. Strength present with this Army five hundred & twenty men. Serviceable horses four hundred and thirty six (436) unserviceable horses forty one, aggregate present and absent eight hundred eleven (811) men   The regiment will report with all the men present in this army. Is the Regt strong enough—" Telegram received, DNA, RG 108, Letters Received; copy, *ibid.*, RG 393, Army of the Potomac, Letters Sent. *O.R.*, I, xlvi, part 2, 654.

At 9:45 A.M., Parke telegraphed to USG. "From deserters I am now informed that no corps of the enemy has been ordered off—From the movement of Miles pickets the enemy concluded that an attack from was to be expected & on their right. Heths Div was moved to the right of their line to meet this. Gen Wright Telegraphs 9:05 a m—A deseter from Heths Div just brought in says that the Div has not moved but confirms the general statement that the troops are under marching orders" Telegram received (at 9:40 A.M.), DNA, RG 108, Letters Received; copies, *ibid.*, RG 393, Army of the Potomac, Letters Sent; Meade Papers, PHi. *O.R.*, I, xlvi, part 2, 653. At 10:40 A.M., Bvt. Maj. Gen. Alexander S. Webb, chief of staff for Parke, telegraphed to Bowers. "Fifty-seven deserters reported this morning. General Wright reports forty-seven came in on his front during the night. This leaves only ten for the rest of the line. I think this number will be increased by later reports." *Ibid.* On the same day, Parke telegraphed to USG. "The above contains the second repot about the Hospitals being about to be moved. One man says the details left his Division 'Mahons' to go North of the Appomattox tom remove Hospitals" Telegram received, DNA, RG 108, Letters Received. *O.R.*, I, xlvi, part 2, 661. Parke transmitted a telegram from Maj. Gen. Horatio G. Wright to Webb, which had been received at 5:45 P.M. "A deserter just in who represents himself as having been on guard at the Bridge over the Appomattox at Petersburg yesterday—says that nine piece of artillery passed the bridge going in direction of Richmond and that an officer told him that 59 piece were to be moved. He also says that a Hospital steward told him that orders had been issued to pack up their supplies and be ready to move. He further says that orders had been issued by Gen Lee to the citizens of Petersburg to remove all Cotton and Tobacco within 7 days. He thinks that order was issued yesterday—" Copy, DNA, RG 108, Letters Received. *O.R.*, I, xlvi, part 2, 661. At 10:15 P.M., Parke telegraphed to USG. "The deserter from Mahones who guarded the Bridge in Petersburg between the two Cotton Factories has been twice examined at these Head Qurs. Gen Webb has just examined him. His story is straightforward and concise—I have no doubt the nine Brass Guns were taken from the front of 9th Corps last night and I am prepared to credit his statement that many have been taken away. I have directed Wright to move out his picket line in the morning. We are watching close" Telegram received (at 10:15 P.M.), DNA, RG 108, Letters Received; copies, *ibid.*, RG 393, Army of the Potomac, Letters Sent; Meade Papers, PHi. *O.R.*, I, xlvi, part 2, 654–55.

On Feb. 24, 11:00 A.M., USG telegraphed to Secretary of War Edwin M. Stanton. "The number of deserters in twenty four hours up to 12 last night was 87 to the Army of the Potomac and about 40 to the Army of the James, There is an average of about 12 per day in addition received at Norfolk. Forty five have come into the A. P since 12 last night" Copies, DLC-USG, V, 46, 74, 108; DNA, RG 108, Letters Sent. *O.R.*, I, xlvi, part 2, 668. Listed as dated Feb. 23 in Stan. V. Henkels, Catalogue No. 1194, June 8, 1917, p. 53.

To Maj. Gen. John G. Parke

By Telegraph from City Pt
Dated Feby 23 *1864*5.

To MAJ GEN PARKE

The Richmond Examineg today says: We learned officially at a late hour last night that Gen J. E. Johnston Was yesterday ordered by the Government to report to Gen Lee for duty.

It is believed that Gen Johnston will be immediately appointed to command the army in front of sherman. Judging from the tone of the papers there seems to be a growing determination to put the negroes into the service.

U S. GRANT.
Lt Genl.

Telegrams received (3), DNA, RG 94, War Records Office, Army of the Potomac; *ibid.*, RG 393, Army of the Potomac, Cav. Corps, Letters and Telegrams Received; copies, Meade Papers, PHi; William C. Banning, Silver Spring, Md. Addressed to Secretary of War Edwin M. Stanton in *O.R.*, I, xlvi, part 2, 652. Copies were sent to all corps commanders. The information had been sent to USG by Maj. Gen. Edward O. C. Ord. *Ibid.*, I, xlvii, part 2, 536.

On Feb. 23, 1865, 4:30 P.M., USG telegraphed to Stanton. "Deserters to-day report Sherman in Charlottesville. The Richmond papers of to-day, true to their word of yesterday, give give no news." ALS (telegram sent), OClWHi; copies (marked as sent at 3:00 P.M.), DLC-USG, V, 46, 73, 108; (marked as received at 5:00 P.M.) DNA, RG 107, Telegrams Received in Cipher; *ibid.*, RG 108, Letters Sent. *O.R.*, I, xlvii, part 2, 536. At 4:00 P.M., Maj. Gen. John G. Parke had telegraphed to USG. "Deserters report a rumor in enemy's camp to the effect that Sherman is in Charlotte." Copy, DNA, RG 393, Army of the Potomac, Letters Sent. *O.R.*, I, xlvi, part 2, 654; (misdated Feb. 15) *ibid.*, p. 565.

To Elihu B. Washburne

City Point Va. Feb.y 23d *1864*5.

DEAR WASHBURN,

Enclosed I send you a letter just received from Col. Duff late of my Staff. I should be delighted if an Act should pass Congress giving the commander of the Army a "Chief of Staff" with the rank of Brig. Gn. in the Regular Army. It is necessary to have such an officer and I see no reason why the law should not give it. It would also reward an officer who has won more deserved reputation in this war than any other who has acted throughout purely as a Staff Officer.

I write to you instead of to Duff knowing your personal friendship for Rawlins as well as myself, and because you are in a place to help the thing along if you think well of it.

I sent you yesterday copy of an order sent from here to Gen. W.[1]

Yours Truly

U. S. GRANT

P. S. Mrs. Grant will not be in Washington to attend the inaugeration but will be returning North soon after. She would like Mrs. W. to make her a long visit if she can before she returns West. Can you not make a run down here and bring Mrs. Washburn with you?

Everything looks like dissolution in the South. A few days more of success with Sherman will put us where we can crow loud.

U. S. G.

ALS, IHi. On Feb. 21, 1865, William L. Duff, Washington, wrote to USG. "A Bill was introduced to day in the House 'To provide for the appointment of a Chief of Staff to the Lt Genl Commanding the Armies of the U S with the rank and pay of a Brigadier General in the United States Army—' The bill was referred to the Military Committee—The bill was framed by friends of yours & Rawlings who believed that nothing would gratify you more than to have the opportunity (as the bill provides for the office to be filled on your nomination or recommendation) of complimenting & rewarding one of ~~whose~~ whose services had been so valuable. I was sent for to see if I knew what view you would take of the matter—I stated of course that I was not now on your staff nor authorized in any way to speak for you but at the same time I stated that I was well aware of the high appreciation in which you held Rawlings and believed it would be very gratifying to you that the bill should be favorably reported on and passed— I was then requested & undertook to communicate with you and ascertain your views—The bill will be kept before the Committee until I receive your answer. A Bill ~~was als~~ is to be introduced to day for the appointment of another Lieut Genl indicating Genl Sherman as the officer to be honored—I am assured that on an expression of opinion from you that the bill for the appointment of a chief of Staff would be agreeable to you and conduce to the good of the service it would go through" ALS, DLC-Elihu B. Washburne. On Feb. 24, Capt. George K. Leet telegraphed to Lt. Col. Theodore S. Bowers. "Hillyer wishes to know whether Gen. Grant has written a letter approving the Chief of Staff bill. If he has, when was the letter sent and to whom addressed. Please answer immy." ALS (telegram sent), DNA, RG 107, Telegrams Collected (Bound). On the same day, USG telegraphed to Leet. "Colonel Hilyer will find answer to Colonel Duffs letter with mr. Washburne It was mailed this morning" Telegram received (press), *ibid.*

On March 3, 3:00 P.M., USG telegraphed to Secretary of War Edwin M. Stanton. "I would respectfully recommend John A. Rawlins for the appointment of Brig. Gen. & Chief of Staff under the Bill which has just passed the two ~h~Houses of Congress. Will you please do me the favor to endorse this recommendation favorably?" ALS (telegram sent), Ford Collection, Minnesota Historical Society, St. Paul, Minn.; copies, DLC-USG, V, 46, 74, 108; DNA, RG 94, ACP, R29 CB 1869; *ibid.*, RG 108, Letters Sent. *O.R.*, I, xlvi, part 2, 801. At 6:00 P.M., Stanton telegraphed to USG. "The nomination of General Rawlins will be sent in immediately and with great pleasure." ALS (telegram sent), DNA, RG 107, Telegrams Collected (Bound). *O.R.*, I, xlvi, part 2, 801.

1. See telegram to Edwin M. Stanton, Feb. 3, 1865.

To Abraham Lincoln

(Cipher)   City Point, Va, Feb.y 24th 1865 [*1:00* P.M.]
A. LINCOLN, PRESIDENT.

Send Prior on here and we will exchange him. He can do us no harm now. Capt. Lincoln reported on the ~22d~1st and was assigned to duty at my Hd Qrs.

                         U. S. GRANT
                         Lt. Gn.

ALS (telegram sent), OClWHi; telegram received (at 1:15 P.M.), DNA, RG 107, Telegrams Collected (Bound); DLC-Robert T. Lincoln. *O.R.*, I, xlvi, part 2, 668. On Feb. 24, 1865, 9:30 A.M., President Abraham Lincoln telegraphed to USG. "I am in a little perplexity. I was induced to authorize a gentleman to bring R. A. Pryor here with a view of effecting an exchange of him. But since then I ~have~ have seen a despatch of yours showing that you specially object to his exchange—Meantime he has reached here & reported to me. It is an ungracious thing for me to send him back to prison, and yet inadmissable for him to remain here long—Can not you help me out with it? I can conceive that there may be difference to you in days; and I can keep him a few days to accommodate on that point. I have not heard of my son's reaching you." ALS (telegram sent), DNA, RG 107, Telegrams Collected (Bound); telegram received (marked as sent at 9:00 A.M.), *ibid.*, RG 108, Letters Sent. *O.R.*, I, xlvi, part 2, 668. Lincoln, *Works*, VIII, 314. See telegram to Bvt. Brig. Gen. William Hoffman, Feb. 7, 1865. On Feb. 24, USG wrote to Lt. Col. John E. Mulford. "Roger A, Prior is on his way here for Exchange I do not want him permitted to pass our lines until John C, Dent is within them" Copies, DLC-USG, V, 46, 74, 108; DNA, RG 108, Letters Sent.

To Edwin M. Stanton

(Cipher)   City Point, Va, Feb.y 234d *1865* [*11:00* A.M.]
HON. E. M. STANTON, SEC. OF WAR, WASHINGTON
I would respectfully recommend the appointment of Schofield as
Brig. Gen. in the Regular Army. He ought to have had it from the
battle of Franklin.

U. S. GRANT
Lt. Gn.

ALS (telegram sent), OClWHi; copies, DLC-USG, V, 46, 73, 74, 108; (marked
as received at 11:00 A.M.) DNA, RG 107, Telegrams Received in Cipher; *ibid.*,
RG 108, Letters Sent. *O.R.*, I, xlvii, part 2, 545.

On Feb. 24, 1865, 5:00 P.M., USG telegraphed to Secretary of War Edwin
M. Stanton. "Has any assignment been made to the Command of the Dept. of
West Va.? Is not Hartsuff a suitable man to take Kelly's place? I do not know
him myself." ALS (telegram sent), OClWHi; copies, DLC-USG, V, 46, 73, 74,
108; (marked as received at 6:00 P.M.) DNA, RG 107, Telegrams Received in
Cipher; *ibid.*, RG 108, Letters Sent. *O.R.*, I, xlvi, part 2, 669. On Feb. 25,
Stanton telegraphed to USG. "No commander for the Department of West-
Virginia has yet been appointed. Hartsuff, in my opinion, is not fit for any-thing.
I will suggest to you a commander some time to-day or to-morrow. Schofield's
nomination will be made, as requested, subject, however, to his obedience to
orders. I am not satisfied with his conduct in seizing the hospital boat Spalding
to make it his own quarters. I have directed him to give it up. If he obeys the
order promptly, I will send in his nomination; otherwise I will not. I wish you
would instruct him as to the impropriety of an officer using hospital boats for
their own personal accommodation, or using or employing transports for their
quarters, at a vast expense to the Government. There has been too much of such
practice already, and he takes rather an early start in such irregularities." LS
(telegram sent), DNA, RG 107, Telegrams Collected (Bound); telegram received (at 12:30 P.M.), *ibid.*, RG 108, Letters Received. *O.R.*, I, xlvi, part 2,
686; *ibid.*, I, xlvii, part 2, 561–62. See telegram to Edwin M. Stanton, Feb.
25, 1865.

To Maj. Gen. Edward O. C. Ord

(Cipher)   City Point Va. Feb.y 24th *18645*. [*4:30* P.M.]
MAJ. GN. ORD.

Is it not possible now to find a place between the Appomattox
and James where, by concentrating all your reserves, a hole might

be made through the lines of the enemy? It will be well to have this matter looked into.

U. S. GRANT

Lt. Gn

ALS (telegram sent), OClWHi; telegram received, Ord Papers, CU-B; DNA, RG 107, Telegrams Collected (Unbound). *O.R.*, I, xlvi, part 2, 679. On Feb. 24, 1865, 5:15 P.M., Maj. Gen. Edward O. C. Ord telegraphed to USG. "was just examining the subject of Bermuda front—have ordered a careful inspection by Turner and an engineer officer to morrow early—will report result" ALS (telegram sent), Ord Papers, CU-B; telegram received (marked as sent at 5:30 P.M.), DNA, RG 108, Letters Received. Printed as sent at 5:30 P.M. in *O.R.*, I, xlvi, part 2, 679. At 3:30 P.M., Ord had telegraphed to Brig. Gen. John A. Rawlins. "Deserters from Bermuda H̶u̶n̶d̶r̶e̶d̶ Front—report that the three brigades near Swift Creek—Grimes Division left yesterday morning Some thought for Charlotte others thought for thier right—Coxes Brigade Same division was left on Piquet—" ALS (telegram sent—addressed to USG, readdressed to Rawlins), DNA, RG 108, Letters Received; telegram received (at 3:40 P.M.), *ibid.* *O.R.*, I, xlvi, part 2, 678. See *ibid.*, p. 682.

On the same day, 4:10 P.M. and 4:40 P.M., Ord telegraphed to Rawlins. "I am in urgent need of a Chief Quartermaster. It is believed tha[t] Bvt Brig Genl Dodge is needed by Gen Schofield Please have Lt Col J. B. Howard Chief Q. M 24th Army Corps ordered here at once" ALS (telegram sent), DNA, RG 107, Telegrams Collected (Unbound); telegram received, *ibid.*, RG 108, Letters Received. *O.R.*, I, xlvi, part 2, 678. "I want a good Brigadier Genl in place of Wild —who has charges against him—and does not Satisfy Genl Weitzell—can not Genl Curtis be ordered to report to me for that Division" ALS (telegram sent), Ord Papers, CU-B; telegram received (marked as sent at 4:30 P.M.), DNA, RG 108, Letters Received. Printed as sent at 4:30 P.M. in *O.R.*, I, xlvi, part 2, 679. On the same day, Rawlins telegraphed to Ord. "Gen Curtis is away wounded when he returns you can have him if the place is still vacant. How would Graham or Marston do? Request has been made to have LtCol Howard a. q. m ordered to report to you" Telegram received, Ord Papers, CU-B; copies, DLC-USG, V, 46, 74, 108; DNA, RG 108, Letters Sent. *O.R.*, I, xlvi, part 2, 679. On the same day, USG telegraphed to Maj. Gen. Henry W. Halleck. "Please order Lieut Col J. B Howard Chf Q̶r̶ M̶r̶ Master twenty fourth (24) Army Corps to report at once to Maj Gen Ord for duty in the field He is now on an Examining board His services are much needed" Telegram received (at 8:30 P.M.), DNA, RG 94, Letters Received, 221A 1865; copies, *ibid.*, RG 108, Letters Sent; DLC-USG, V, 46, 74, 108. *O.R.*, I, xlvi, part 2, 669. See *ibid.*, p. 689.

To Maj. Gen. Edward O. C. Ord

———

City Point, Va, Feb. 24th *1865*

MAJ. GN. ORD.

If Longstreet wishes to send his family North, to stay, they will be received at my Hd Qrs. and sent where he wishes. I do not think he would concent to send them here to return again. If however he will let them come, even to go back again you may let them come.

yours &c.

U. S. GRANT

Lt. Gn.

ALS, Dr. S. P. Katsivelos, New York, N. Y. According to C.S.A. Lt. Gen. James Longstreet, the first of his meetings with Maj. Gen. Edward O. C. Ord took place on Feb. 21, 1865, although the first meeting with contemporary documentation occurred on Feb. 25. Longstreet, *From Manassas to Appomattox* (Dallas, 1896), p. 583; *O.R.*, II, viii, 315; *ibid.*, I, xlvi, part 2, 1259. See letter to Maj. Gen. Edward O. C. Ord, [*Feb. 27, 1865*].

To Maj. Gen. John M. Schofield

City Point Va Feb. 24 1865

MAJ GEN J. M SCHOFIELD
COMDG DEPT OF N C.
GENERAL.

Richmond papers have ceased to give information of Sherman's movements. I presume however he is now past Charlotte with his advance, and moving towards Goldsboro, by the most practicable route. He may follow the railroad north for some distance past Charlotte, but this will depend on the movements and apparent strength of the enemy. I learn of nothing leaving here recently except three Brigades of Battles Division[1] numbering possibly 3500 men   They left their position between the James and Appomattox yesterday morning. I hope, and know you will, push out and form a connection with Sherman at the earliest practicable moment. If you reach Goldsboro and have a fair prospect of getting your road finished soon, it may be unnecessary for Sherman to come down to the coast. Make every effort to communicate with Sherman at once. You probably will find some citizen, who can be trusted to carry a note in cipher to Sherman. He has, I think a cipher operator with him.

Every effort has been made to get your troops, and all else

called for by you, through. But the ice has kept every thing back very much. Teams will be forwarded rapidly. I have also ordered one regiment of cavalry to you numbering about 600 effective.[2] I would send an entire Division from Sheridans Army, but I have ordered him to move on the Va. Central road and James river Canal. He will probably go to Lynchburg, and if information there received justifies it, he will go on and join you and Sherman. If you and Sherman are once united you can keep as far in the interior of North Carolina as you may be able to supply your selves. ~~With the large force you will have united you can keep as far in the interior of North Carolina as you may be able to supply yourselves.~~ With the large force you will have united, Raleigh may not be found too far off.

I congratulate you and the Army under you for the brilliant success of which I have as yet received but the meagre report sent by Admiral Porter.[3] On receipt of the news I immediately telegraphed asking to have your name sent into the Senate for the appointment of Brig Gen in the Regular Army, stating that I thought you should have the appointment for the battle of Franklin. I hope within a day or two to be able to congratulate you on your confirmation.—

Desertions from the Rebel Army are growing very numerous. Many are now bringing their arms with them. This morning 45 came in in a single squad and from a single regiment, a South Carolina regiment at that.

> Very respectfully
> Your obedt Servt
> U S. GRANT
> Lieut General.

Copies, DLC-USG, V, 46, 73, 108; DNA, RG 108, Letters Sent. *O.R.*, I, xlvii, part 2, 558. On Feb. 28, 1865, Maj. Gen. John M. Schofield, Wilmington, N. C., wrote to USG. "I have just received your letter of the 24th. Please accept my thanks for your generous appreciation of our success in the capture of Wilmington. My latest information of Genl Sherman is that on the 24th one of his main columns was about midway between Columbia and Charlotte and the other seventeen miles from Camden on the road to Fayettville. This comes from the mail carrier from Fayettville and is thought by those who know him to be reliable. I had supposed Genl Sherman further advanced, but the roads are bad and he probably has to move quite slowly. Very heavy rains have fallen lately.

The roads in this region are very bad, but they will dry very quickly after the rain ceases. In the region Genl Sherman is marching through the mud will last much longer. I have men out to get information of his movements, but I find it extremely difficult to obtain any one at all trustworthy who is willing to carry a despatch to him. But I hope to get one tomorrow. Genl Sherman can send to me much more easily and no doubt has already done so. Hardee was ordered to this place from Charleston, but we came in just in time to cut him off. He then turned toward Fayetteville. I think Hoke will go in the same direction, and both try to unite with Beauregard about Greensboro. This I derive from a telegraph operator's report of the correspondence between Bragg and Hardee the day before we got Wilmington. My wagons and animals are coming very slowly. Storm and fog have made it impossible to cross Cape Fear bar nearly all the time for several days. It must be four or five days yet before we can fairly begin work on the railroad. I had hoped much more from Palmers movement, but he has done nothing. Instead of pushing out as ordered he came here to see me about it, and was detained by the fog. He probably did not get back until today. I sent Cox back with him, with orders to take command and move forward at once, so that the railroad could be repaired. I intend to move from here by the fifth or sixth with whatever transportation I can get by that time. If the railroad here is not ready for me I will push through and unite with Cox, unless I learn that Sherman is coming this way to get supplies here. His instructions to Col. Wright were to have the road to Goldsboro ready for him *by the 13th of March*. That I think we can make, and will do more if possible. I hope, when Genl Sherman hears I have Wilmington, he will come in as far as Fayettville. Then we will be all right, and can unite wherever we please. The cavalry has begun to arrive. A regiment will do very well for the present." ALS, DNA, RG 108, Letters Received. *O.R.*, I, xlvii, part 2, 619–20.

On Feb. 19, Schofield, Fort Anderson, telegraphed to USG. "I have the honor to report the success of our operations against Ft Anderson & the adjacent works on both sides of the Cape Fear river. Yesterday while the gunboats maintained a heavy fire upon Fort Anderson I pressed the enemy on both sides of the river and sent a force under Gen Cox about 16 miles around a swamp to turn the enemys right. This force made its way along a narrow defile between two swamps and completely turned the enemys position. As soon as the movement became known to the enemy he abandoned his works and retreated towards Wilmington. We captured ten (10) guns uninjured and a considerable amount of ammunition. We have about fifty (50) prisoners. The loss in killed or wounded is small on either side. The troops are pursuing the enemy and the gunboats are moving up the river. Fort Anderson & its collateral works are very strong & rendered almost inaccessable by swamps; a small force could have held them until their supplies were exhausted. My information is that the rebels have a line of defence behind Town Creek where they propose to make a stand; If so, it can probably be only a short one. Only four (4) brigades of my troops have arrived from Washington and no transportation but I will keep at work with what I have" Telegram received (on Feb. 23, 11:00 A.M.), DNA, RG 107, Telegrams Collected (Bound); (on Feb. 23, 10:55 A.M.) *ibid.*, RG 108, Letters Received; copies, *ibid.*, RG 107, Telegrams Received in Cipher; *ibid.*, RG 393, Dept. of N. C., Letters Sent; DLC-John M. Schofield. *O.R.*, I, xlvii, part 2, 492–93. On the same day, Bvt. Brig. Gen. Cyrus B. Comstock telegraphed to USG. "Day before yesterday Coxes Div. moved to Smithville and then toward Ft. Anderson. Yesterday it closed up on Ft Anderson and entrenched a line under navy fire close to the enemys to be held by two brigades, With the balance of his comd. and Ames Div. which had been sent to Smithville Cox then was started on the flank movement for the rear of Ft. Anderson making about ten (10) miles by dark. The enemy evacuated Ft Anderson during the night and the lines in front of Terry this morning. They will at once be followed towards Wilmington" Telegram received (on Feb. 23, 11:00 A.M.), DNA, RG 107, Telegrams Collected (Bound); (on Feb. 23, 10:55 A.M.) *ibid.*, RG 108, Letters Received; copy, *ibid.*, RG 107, Telegrams Received in Cipher. *O.R.*, I, xlvii, part 2, 493. On the same day, Schofield wrote to USG. "I now begin to feel the need of cavalry; and will probably feel it much more soon. I therefore respectfully request that a regiment, at least, be sent me as soon as practicable." ALS, PHi. *O.R.*, I, xlvii, part 2, 493.

On Feb. 22, Schofield wrote to USG. "I have the satisfaction of announcing the capture of Wilmington. On the 19th, after the capture of Fort Anderson, we found the enemy in position behind Town Creek and opposite to its mouth on the East side of the river. During the night I transferred Genl Ames Division, which had been operating with Genl Cox against Fort Anderson, to the East bank to rejoin Genl Terry. On the 20th Genl Terry pushed the enemy back to a point about four miles from Wilmington, where he appeared in force behind strong entrenchments. Genl Terrys loss was about fifty men killed and wounded. Genl Cox crossed Town Creek by the use of a single flatboat, attacked and drove the enemy in confusion from the field, capturing three hundred and seventy five prisoners and two pieces of artillery. Yesterday the enemy concentrated nearly his entire force against Genl Terry and prevented any further advance. Genl Cox pushed forward to the crossing of Brunswick river and secured possession of the main portion of a ponton bridge which the enemy fired on his approach. By the use of the boats Genl Cox put some men on Eagles Island and threatened to cross the river above Wilmington. The enemy at once set fire to his military and naval stores, steamers, boats, cotton ~an~ &c, and commenced his retreat at dark. Our troops entered the city soon after daylight this morning. The enemy has gone toward Goldsboro and Genl Terry is in pursuit. Our loss in killed and wounded since we left Fort fFisher is probably only about two hundred men. That of the enemy is not much larger in killed and wounded but we have taken about eight hundred prisoners beside a large number of stragglers and deserters. A large amount of heavy artillery and a few field pieces have fallen into our hands. The Admiral is now clearing away the obstructions in the river, and we hope to get the transports up today." ALS, DNA, RG 108, Letters Received. *O.R.*, I, xlvii, part 2, 535.

On Feb. 24, Schofield twice wrote to USG. "After the capture of Wilmington, Genl Terry pursued the enemy as far as the North East River, where he found the railroad and ponton bridges destroyed. The bridge over Smith's creek is also destroyed. I have not learned whether any damage has been done to the railroad beyond the river. I shall push forward as soon as I can get any means of transportation. Wagons are beginning to arrive, and I hope the delay will not be long. The rebel Agent of Exchange has informed me that he will deliver ten thousand of our prisoners at the point where the railroad crosses the North East River, and I have agreed to receive them at that point. I presume he will commence to deliver them today. I am making all possible provision for the care of the sick, which will no doubt be a large proportion of the whole number. I have sent Genl Rugers Division of the 23d Corps to Newburn, and shall send either Genl Terry or Genl Cox there to command the troops operating from that point.

I will go there or remain with the troops operating from this place as may seem advisable. I will also keep transports enough for a short time to carry a division from one point to the other if it become necessary. I have heard nothing yet of the troops you have ordered Genl Gilmore to send me, but presume they must be along in a very few days. I can land them here or at Beaufort according to circumstances. I have asked for the assignment of Genl Cox and Genl Terry to corps commands, both because the strength of my command renders it desirable and because it will enable me to leave either the one or the other in command of the column which I may not be with at any time. Moreover it will make the organization of my Army correspond with that of Genl Shermans other grand divisions. I hope, for these reasons, my request may be complied with. I presume Genl Sherman, upon hearing of the fall of Wilmington, will send his cavalry this way to communicate with me and inform me of his progress. I shall also make constant efforts to communicate with him by means of scouts. I propose to repair both railroads toward Goldsboro as rapidly as possible. I shall also make such preparation as I can to send supplies to Genl Sherman by the river toward Fayettville in case he should call for them." "I respectfully request that the troops in this Department which do not belong to the 23d A. C. may be organized into an Army Corps, and that Maj Genl Alfred H. Terry be assigned to its command. Also that Maj Genl J. D. Cox may be assigned to the command of the 23d Army Corps." ALS, DNA, RG 108, Letters Received. *O.R.*, I, xlvii, part 2, 558–59. On the same day, 10:00 P.M., Comstock, Fort Monroe, telegraphed to USG. "Our troops entered Wilmington on the morning of the 22d inst. After the evacuation of Fort Anderson Schofield directed Cox to follow its garrison towards Wilmington while Terry followed Hoke on the East side of the river   The latter took up a new line four miles from Wilmington but was so closely pressed by Terry that he could send no troops to the west side   On that side the rebels made a stand behind Town Creek but on the 20th Cox crossed his troops below them on a flat boat attacked them in rear & routed them taking 2 guns & three hundred prisoners   On the 21st Cox pushed to the Brunswick River opposite Wilmington where the [*bridges*] were on fire & on his arrival the rebels began burning cotton and rosin in the city & left it that night   Our captures including ~~Fort Fisher~~ Ft Anderson amount to about 700 prisoners & 30 guns. Citizens state that the rebels burned 1000 bales of cotton and 15000 barrels of rosin   The union feeling showed itself quite strongly in the city   Terry followed Hoke northward" Telegram received (at 10:45 P.M.), DNA, RG 107, Telegrams Collected (Bound); (at 11:30 P.M.) *ibid.*, RG 108, Letters Received; copy, *ibid.*, RG 107, Telegrams Received in Cipher. *O.R.*, I, xlvii, part 2, 559–60.

On Feb. 25, Schofield telegraphed to USG. "Please have two engines and some flat cars sent here at once, so that Col Wright can commence work. None have arrived at this place or Newburn." ALS (telegram sent—transmitted from Fort Monroe, March 5, 2:30 P.M.), DNA, RG 107, Telegrams Collected (Unbound); telegram received (on March 5), *ibid.*, RG 108, Letters Received.

1. The div. formerly commanded by Brig. Gen. Cullen A. Battle, who was seriously wounded in 1864, was then commanded by Brig. Gen. Bryan Grimes, whose movements had been reported that day. See telegram to Maj. Gen. Edward O. C. Ord, Feb. 24, 1865.

2. See *O.R.*, I, xlvii, part 2, 560.

3. On Feb. 22, Asst. Secretary of War Charles A. Dana telegraphed to USG. "Lieut. Cushing has just arrived bearing a despatch from Admiral Porter

to the Secretary of the Navy announcing the occupation of Fort Anderson by Schofield's troops on ~~the~~ Sunday morning. ~~A~~ I subjoin a copy of the Admirals dispatch for your information." ALS (telegram sent), DNA, RG 107, Telegrams Collected (Bound); telegram received (at 3:30 P.M.), *ibid.*, RG 108, Letters Received. The enclosure is printed in *O.R.* (Navy), I, xii, 33–34. The message to which USG referred in his letter to Schofield is *ibid.*, p. 45. Also on Feb. 22, Lt. Col. Theodore S. Bowers telegraphed to Maj. Gen. George G. Meade and Maj. Gen. Edward O. C. Ord. "Intelligence just recd. from Ft Fisher announces the occupation of Ft Anderson by Gen. Schofields troops on Sunday morning" Telegram received, Ord Papers, CU-B; copies, DLC-USG, V, 46, 73, 108; DNA, RG 107, Telegrams Collected (Unbound); *ibid.*, RG 108, Letters Sent; *ibid.*, RG 393, 25th Army Corps, Telegrams Received; Meade Papers, PHi. Printed as addressed to Maj. Gen. John G. Parke in *O.R.*, I, xlvi, part 2, 631; (as transmitted by Brig. Gen. John W. Turner to Ord) *ibid.*, p. 647.

On Feb. 24, USG telegraphed to Ord and Parke. "Announce to your troops the Capture of Wilmington on the 22d inst. by the troops under Schofield & Terry. Fire a shotted salute in honor of the event at 4 p. m this afternoon." ALS (facsimile telegram sent), Stan. V. Henkels, Catalogue No. 1194, June 8, 1917, p. [52]; telegram received (at 10:52 A.M.), DNA, RG 94, War Records Office, Army of the Potomac; *ibid.*, Miscellaneous War Records. *O.R.*, I, xlvi, part 2, 670.

To Lt. Col. John E. Mulford

City Point Va, Feby 24th [*1865*]

LIEUT, COL, MULFORD
AG'T OF EX- JONES LANDING

You may say to Col, Ould that by despatches from Col, Hoffman I learn that all prisoners who have been in close confinement, or irons, whether under charges or sentence, or not, have been ordered here for exchange. This includes spies, murderers, and persons guilty of whatever offences[1] I have also sent requesting orders to be made to allow prisoners of War to purchase freely both provisions of all kinds and Clothing[2]

U, S, GRANT
Lieut, Gen'l

Telegram, copies, DLC-USG, V, 46, 74, 108; DNA, RG 108, Letters Sent; USG 3. *O.R.*, II, viii, 301. Listed as dated Feb. 25, 1865, in Stan. V. Henkels, Catalogue No. 1194, June 8, 1917, p. 54. On Feb. 25, 4:30 P.M., Lt. Col. John E. Mulford, Varina, Va., telegraphed to USG. "Your despatch in regard to prisoners in close confinemt & priviledges of purchase for prisons, received I will communicate the information to Mr Ould" ALS (telegram sent), DNA, RG 107,

Telegrams Collected (Unbound); telegram received (at 4:45 P.M.), *ibid.*, RG 108, Letters Received. *O.R.*, II, viii, 306.

On Feb. 24, USG telegraphed to Mulford. "If Capt, Richard N, Hewett Miles Louisiana Legion, is among the Rebel Officers now ready for Exchange, please send him to my Head Quarters" Copies, DLC-USG, V, 46, 74, 108; DNA, RG 108, Letters Sent; USG 3. On the same day, Col. Charles W. Hill, 128th Ohio, Sandusky, Ohio, who commanded the Johnson's Island prison, telegraphed to USG. "Captain Richard N Hewitt Miles Legion Louisiana left here for Point Lookout last monday in a party of One hundred 100 Officers for exchange." Telegram received (at 9:00 P.M.), DNA, RG 107, Telegrams Collected (Unbound).

1. On Feb. 1, C.S.A. Agent of Exchange Robert Ould wrote a letter requesting that John E. Boyd, "imprisoned for life at hard labor at Fort McHenry be treated as a prisoner of war[.]" DLC-USG, V, 49. On Feb. 20, USG endorsed this letter. "Respy. referred to Brig Gen W. Hoffman, Comy. Gen of Prisoners who will please forward the within named prisoner for release" Copy, *ibid.*, V, 58. On Feb. 25, Bvt. Brig. Gen. William Hoffman telegraphed to USG. "I have ordered Sergt. Boyd, prisoner at Fort-McHenry, whose delivery is ordered at the request of Mr. Ould, to be forwarded though he is under sentence to be confined during the war." ALS (telegram sent), DNA, RG 107, Telegrams Collected (Unbound); telegram received (at 3:00 P.M.), *ibid.*, RG 108, Letters Received. *O.R.*, II, viii, 306. See *ibid.*, I, xlvi, part 2, 109, 130.

2. On Feb. 6, Ould wrote to Mulford. "The Confederate officers who were delivered yesterday and who left Johnsons Island on the 27th of January, state that the Order of Aug 10, 1864 is still rigidly enforced. They also complain of the amount of food given to them, alleging that it is barely sufficient to keep them from starvation. In view of the recent agreement made with Gen. Grant for the purpose of reliev[in]g prisoners, I again make the request that all restrictions on both sides which prevent prisoners from receiving contributions public or private or from making purchases of proper articles, be immediately removed." LS, DNA, RG 108, Letters Received. *O.R.*, II, viii, 187. On Feb. 24, Mulford endorsed this letter. "Respectfully forwarded to Hd. Qrs. Armies of U. S. with the statement that Mr. Ould has again complained that no abatement in former orders has been made further than to allow prisoners to 'purchase vegetables.' He has requested me to call the attention of the Lieut. Gen'l. to the fact that under the agreement our Prisoners were permitted to purchase in market whatever they could pay for; and receive such contributions as might be offered them. He claims a reciprocal arrangement, and I think the welfare, comfort and almost existence of prisoners whom they do, or may hereafter hold depends upon a continuance of the privilege to receive the benefit of outside supplies." ES, DNA, RG 108, Letters Received. *O.R.*, II, viii, 187–88. On Feb. 25, USG endorsed this letter. "Respectfully forwarded to the Sec. of War with the recommendation that Prisoners of War be allowed to purchase food and clothing freely where they have the means of paying for them. We are the ga[i]ners by this agreement." AES, DNA, RG 108, Letters Received. *O.R.*, II, viii, 188. On Feb. 27, 4:00 P.M., Maj. Gen. Henry W. Halleck telegraphed to USG. "Your endorsement of the 25th on letter of Judge Ould has been approved by the Secty of War & Genl Hoffman ordered to carry it into effect." ALS (telegram sent), DNA, RG 107, Telegrams Collected (Bound); telegram received, *ibid.*; *ibid.*, RG 108, Letters Received.

To Dr. Henry S. Hewit

———

City Point. Va, Feb.y 24th 1865—

DEAR DR.

Your two letters in relation to securing the appointment of your son to West Point were duly received. Neither of them give the name of your son, and without that I cannot make the application. I did have his name and age I believe, and have it yet, but cannot find it. If you will send these I will take great pleasure in writing a letter to the President on the subject, and in speaking to him besides, if I should visit Washington ~~again~~ again in time.

Mrs Grant and Jesse are with me and desire to be remembered to you—

Yours Truly

U. S. GRANT

Copy, ViU. On March 14, 1865, USG wrote to Secretary of War Edwin M. Stanton. "I would respectfully recommend Nathaniel Hewit Jr. for the appointment of Cadet, at large, to West Point. He was Sixteen years of age last November, and a native of Fairfield Connecticut. He is a son of Surg. H. S. Hewit at present of the volunteer service but for many years an Asst. Surg. in the Regular Army." ALS, DNA, RG 94, Cadet Applications.

To Dr. Edward D. Kittoe

———

City Point, Va, Feb. 24th *1865*

DEAR DR.

Your letter asking my aid in securing duty "in the field" for Capt. Smith was duly received. I wrote to Gov. Oglesby at once asking him to give Smith a Colonelcy in an Illinois regiment and hope he will do it. I have not been quite so prompt in answering you and have no very good excuse to offer for this neglect.

Every thing now seems to be working well for the final overthrow of the rebellion. In three weeks more I do not believe there will be a Rebel Army in the field capable of resisting the advance of 10,000 Cavalry. This is my candid judgement only I may, in view of the bad roads that may be expected during next month, fix the time for this final triumph a little to short.

Remember me to the Galenans generally. Mrs. Grant joins me in regards to yourself and family—Rawlins is pretty well. The balance of the Staff are all well.

Yours Truly

U. S. GRANT

ALS, IHi. The name of the addressee is inserted in an unknown hand in the salutation. See letter to Richard J. Oglesby, Feb. 18, 1865.

To Edwin M. Stanton

City Point Va, Feby 25th 1865 [*1:30* P.M.]

HON, E. M. STANTON
SECY OF WAR
WASHINGTON D. C.

Gen, Comstock has just returned from Wilmington, He say's that Gen, Schofield arrived at the Cape Fear River without his transportation and as he had to move about on the water, asked the Quartermaster if there was a boat ~~there~~ he could use temporarily as well as not He was told the Spaulding was doing nothing When Gen, Comstock left the Spaulding was to be loaded with wounded and some escaped prisoners, I will have an order made prohibiting the use of Boats for Head Quarters

U, S, GRANT
Lieut, Gen

Telegram, copies, DLC-USG, V, 46, 74, 108; DLC-John M. Schofield; DNA, RG 108, Letters Sent. *O.R.*, I, xlvii, part 2, 562. See telegram to Edwin M. Stanton, Feb. 24, 1865.

On Feb. 25, 1865, Lt. Col. Theodore S. Bowers issued Special Orders No. 39. "I The using of water transportation of any kind for officers quarters, or for head quarters of commanding officers of whatever grade is positively prohibited throughout the Armies of the United States, except when their commands are afloat or in transit by water. Any officer violating this order will be liable to summary dismissal from the service. It is made the special duty of officers of the Inspector Generals Department to report to these Head Quarters any and all violations of this order, and a failure to do so will subject them to summary dismissal from the service. II Brevet Brig Gen. C. B. Comstock, A d C., will proceed to Washington D C., on public business. Upon the execution of the same he will rejoin these Headquarters" Copies, DLC-USG, V, 57, 63, 64, 65. *O.R.*, I, xlvi, part 2, 688–89.

To Edwin M. Stanton

(Cipher)   City Point, Va, Feb.y 25th 1865 [2:30 P.M.]
~~MAJ. GEN. HALLECK, WASHINGTON.~~ HON. E. M. STANTON,
SEC. OF WAR, WASHINGTON

One of my staff officers who has just returned from Wilmington says nothing has been done to save the large amount of Ordnance and Ordnance stores captured on Cape Fear River. ~~Please direct the Chief of Ordnance to take immediate steps~~

I think the Chief of Ordnance should be required to take immediate steps to secure all Ordnance stores captured on the coast.

U. S. GRANT
Lt. Gn.

ALS (telegram sent), Morristown National Historical Park, Morristown, N. J.; copies, DLC-USG, V, 46, 74, 108; DNA, RG 108, Letters Sent. Printed as received at 7:30 P.M. in *O.R.*, I, xlvii, part 2, 562. On Feb. 26, 1865, 12:25 P.M., Secretary of War Edwin M. Stanton telegraphed to USG. "The Chief of Ordnance sent yesterday an ordnance officer to Cape Fear river to ~~attend to~~ secure the ~~orda~~ captured ordnance & ordnance stores. I have made the appointment of Schofield Brigadier General in regular army" ALS (telegram sent), DNA, RG 107, Telegrams Collected (Bound); telegram received, *ibid.*, Telegrams Collected (Unbound); (at 6:00 P.M.) *ibid.*, RG 108, Letters Received. *O.R.*, I, xlvii, part 2, 582; (misdated Feb. 24) *ibid.*, p. 546. See telegram to Edwin M. Stanton, Feb. 24, 1865.

On Feb. 26, Maj. Gen. Quincy A. Gillmore telegraphed to Maj. Gen. Henry W. Halleck and USG reporting, among other things, the amount of captured ordnance at Charleston. Telegrams received (2—on March 1, 5:00 P.M.), DNA, RG 107, Telegrams Collected (Bound). *O.R.*, I, xlvii, part 1, 1008.

To Edwin M. Stanton

(Cipher)   City Point, Va, Feb.y 25th 1865 [3:30 P.M.]
HON. E. M. STANTON, SEC. OF WAR, WASHINGTON.

I am very much pleased with the interest Commodore Radford seems to take in his duties and the way he talks. Adm.l Farragut can tell better than I can how he will do when danger comes. The probabilities of an attack from the Rebel Navy on the first rise in the river is anticipated and every preparation made to receive it. I have not the slightedst apprehension about the result and rather desire it. We are far differently prepared now, both on land and water, from what we were the last time the Rebel Iron clads come down.

I think we must very soon use either Adm.l Farragut or Porter in capturing Galveston. It will be but a very short time I hope before we will be able to spare the troops for this purpose from here or from Cape Fear River.

U. S. Grant
Lt. Gn.

ALS (telegram sent), PPRF; copies, DLC-USG, V, 46, 74, 108; DNA, RG 108, Letters Sent. *O.R.*, I, xlvi, part 2, 686. On Feb. 25, 1865, 2:00 P.M., Secretary of War Edwin M. Stanton telegraphed to USG. "Do you feel that entirely secure against the rebel rams at Richmond and satisfied with the Naval Commander there or would you prefer to have Farragut. There appears to be nothing else of importance for him." ALS (telegram sent), DNA, RG 107, Telegrams Collected (Bound); telegram received, *ibid.*, RG 108, Letters Received. *O.R.*, I, xlvi, part 2, 686.

On Feb. 22, Lt. Col. Theodore S. Bowers issued Special Orders No. 36. "Brig Gen R. Ingalls, Chief Q. M., Armies operating against Richmond, will cause two barges loaded with stone or sand bags to be sunk in the channel of the James river under the direction of Commodore Radford, U S. Navy." Copies, DLC-USG, V, 57, 63, 64, 65. *O.R.*, I, xlvi, part 2, 633. On Feb. 28, Commodore William Radford, U.S.S. *Dumbarton*, wrote to USG. "The barges were sunk as soon as they arrived—at the place designated" ALS, DNA, RG 94, War Records Office, Army of the Potomac. *O.R.*, I, xlvi, part 2, 733; *O.R.* (Navy), I, xii, 57.

On March 2, 9:00 P.M., Bvt. Maj. Peter S. Michie telegraphed to USG. "Genl Barnard by telegraph d directs me to report to you the following extract from my letter to him on James River obstructions. 'I made an inspection to day (Feby 28th) and find that the obstructions are as is represented in the accompanying chart except that schooner No 4 is reported to have drifted away, leaving an opening in the north channel sufficient to pass an iron clad, and in the south channel there is also space enough to pass a vessel. The naval officer, Lt Hays who has had charge of these obstructions says that it will require 5 more schooners sunk in the north channel or two (2) more in the south channel to make them impassable at ordinary high tide. At present there is a considerable freshet running in the river, and the water is some three to four feet higher than ordinary so that the nav[y] reports that the rebel iron clads can come down over the middle ground or bar between the two channels but think they will not attempt it because the tide current is too strong to steer the vessels—" ALS (telegram sent), DNA, RG 107, Telegrams Collected (Unbound); telegram received (marked as sent at 8:50 P.M., received at 9:15 P.M.), *ibid.*, RG 108, Letters Received. *O.R.*, I, xlvi, part 2, 790.

To Maj. Gen. Henry W. Halleck

City Point Va, Feby 25th [*1865, 1:00* P.M.]

MAJ. GEN, HALLECK
WASHINGTON

Gen, Gilmore's dispatch of the 21st received.[1] I scarcely see a contingency under which it will be necessary at present to open Rail Road communication in South Carolina   It is well enough to occupy Georgetown until Sherman is in communication from the Sea coast,   It is barely possible though not probable, that he may require supplies from Georgetown

I expect nothing of the kind, however

U. S. GRANT
Lieut, Gen,

Telegram, copies, DLC-USG, V, 46, 74, 108; DNA, RG 108, Letters Sent. Printed as received at 2:00 P.M. in *O.R.*, I, xlvii, part 2, 563. On Feb. 25, 1865, 10:30 A.M., Maj. Gen. Henry W. Halleck telegraphed to USG. "On the 19th orders were sent to Genl Gillmore to send all white troops not required to hold most important sea-ports, to Cape Fear River. He had not recieved it when he wrote his despatch of the 21st. I do not see the policy of opening any rail roads from charleston, but will await your orders on Gillmore's requisition." ALS (telegram sent), DNA, RG 107, Telegrams Collected (Bound); telegram received, *ibid.*; *ibid.*, RG 108, Letters Received. *O.R.*, I, xlvii, part 2, 562–63. See *ibid.*, p. 574.

On Feb. 17, Maj. Gen. Quincy A. Gillmore, Hilton Head, S. C., wrote to Halleck asking permission to send troops to Ga. to encourage Unionism. *Ibid.*, p. 464. On Feb. 22, Halleck endorsed this letter. "Respectfully referred to Lt Genl Grant, with the remark that Genl Gillmore has been ordered, as directed, to send all white troops not required to hold the sea ports, to Cape Fear River." AES, PPRF. *O.R.*, I, xlvii, part 2, 464. On Feb. 25, USG endorsed this letter. "Please inform Gen. Gilmore that he will comply with orders sent to him to send his surplus troops to Cape Fear River. We want to use our troops in putting down those in Arms against us and not in what has always proven a useless attempt to get up Union sentiment by a show of strength and diplomacy where there is no resistance. Mounted men at Savannah may be necessary but to get them they must be mounted in the country." AES, PPRF. *O.R.*, I, xlvii, part 2, 464.

On Feb. 25, USG endorsed a letter from Gillmore recommending that the troops in his dept. be organized into the 10th Army Corps. "Disapproved. If the 10th Corps is revived it should be composed of the men, serving here under Gen Terry. There are but few white troops now in the Dept of the South, that have given the 10th Corps its reputation"   Copy, DLC-USG, V, 58. See *O.R.*, I, xlvii, part 2, 604.

1. On Feb. 21, Gillmore telegraphed (and wrote the same message) to Halleck. "Arrived here from Charleston this morning and shall return there tomorrow after the arrival of the Arago with northern mails There are eight locomotives and other rolling stock in Charleston but I want some engineers to run them. I also want a good R. R. Supt. and some workmen I am already advancing on the Wilmington R R & hope to be able to aid Sherman by reaching the Santee River with supplies for him. I have no news from Sherman later than his reported capture of Columbia. I hope to capture Georgetown in a few days, either by an attack from the sea or by moving down ~~the~~ with a force north of the Santee river" Telegram received (on Feb. 25), DNA, RG 108, Letters Received; copy, *ibid.* Printed as received on Feb. 25, 1:25 A.M., in *O.R.*, I, xlvii, part 2, 525.

To Maj. Gen. Edward O. C. Ord

By Telegraph from City Pt.
Dated Febry 25th *18645.*

To MAJ GEN ORD.

Early is said to have moved down the nine mile road yesterday & to be occupuying now a large field, or race course between the York river & Fredericksburg roads. This may indicate an advance of the rebel rams & an attack on you. Great vigilance ought to be observed on your right, & in case of firing on the river every man should be got under arms & in his place.

U. S. GRANT.
Lt Genl

Telegram received (at 10:30 P.M.), Ord Papers, CU-B; copies, DLC-USG, V, 46, 73, 108; DNA, RG 108, Letters Sent. *O.R.*, I, xlvi, part 2, 697.

On Feb. 25, 1865, USG twice telegraphed to Maj. Gen. Edward O. C. Ord. "Troops on the Bermuda front as well as the those on your extreme right should be notified to be extra watchful during the continuance of present high water." Telegram received, Ord Papers, CU-B; copies, DLC-USG, V, 46, 73, 108; DNA, RG 108, Letters Sent. *O.R.*, I, xlvi, part 2, 697. "Charge officers commanding Pickets on the river to keep a close lookout for the enemy's Rams to-night. They may take advantage of present high water to pay us another visit." ALS (telegram sent), Kohns Collection, NN; copies, DLC-USG, V, 46, 74, 108; DNA, RG 108, Letters Sent. *O.R.*, I, xlvi, part 2, 697. On the same day, Ord telegraphed to USG. "Deserters corroborate report as to the evacuation going on of Petersburg. One says that Col. Elliott 25th Va told the men they could see the advantage of it soon—The rumor prevails in rebel camp that Hills Corps has gone or is ~~going~~ leaving for Beauregard—I will be down to see you this evening—Gen Turners report not favorable" Telegram received, DNA, RG 108, Letters Received. *O.R.*, I, xlvi, part 2, 697–98. On the same day, USG telegraphed to Ord. "Do not come down tonight." Telegram received (at 5:45 P.M.), DNA, RG 94, War Records Office, Miscellaneous War Records. *O.R.*, I, xlvi, part 2, 698.

Also on Feb. 25, Lt. Col. Edward W. Smith, adjt. for Ord, twice telegraphed to Lt. Col. Theodore S. Bowers, first at 10:35 A.M. "The following despatch recieved from the lookout at Cobbs Hill dated 9.50 a. m. 'Another column of the enemy numbering about one thousand men moving towards Swift Creek by same route as the Column I reported in my 9.20 A m despatch SERGT BAIRD' The 9.20 despatch has not been recieved and he is ordered to repeat it—Gen Ord is at the front" ALS (telegram sent), DNA, RG 107, Telegrams Collected (Unbound); telegram received (at 10:40 A.M.), *ibid.*, RG 108, Letters Received. *O.R.*, I, xlvi, part 2, 698. "The 9.20 despatch from Cobbs Hill referred to in previous telegram reads as follows 'Two regiments of Rebel Infantry about 800 men in all and fully equipped for march are moving inside and parallel with enemy's line towards Swift Creek SERGT BAIRD'" ALS (telegram sent), DNA, RG 107, Telegrams Collected (Unbound). *O.R.*, I, xlvi, part 2, 699. On the same day, Bowers telegraphed to Smith. "Signal dispatches received—Please ascertain in what direction these troops are moving to or from Richmond" Telegram received, DNA, RG 108, Letters Received. *O.R.*, I, xlvi, part 2, 699. Capt. Lemuel B. Norton drafted a reply at the foot of the telegram received. "The rebel troops ~~reported~~ mentioned were moving from north to south inside of their intrenchments and towards Swift Creek" ADfS, DNA, RG 108, Letters Received. On the same day, Smith telegraphed to Bowers. "The troops mentioned were moving from North to South inside their intrenchments" ALS (telegram sent), *ibid.*, RG 107, Telegrams Collected (Unbound); telegram received (at 12:25 P.M.), *ibid.*, RG 108, Letters Received. *O.R.*, I, xlvi, part 2, 699. Also on Feb. 25, Smith telegraphed to USG transmitting a telegram of the same day from Brig. Gen. Charles K. Graham, Bermuda Hundred. "At 9 this morning three columns of th enemy were moved towards Petersburg—I think they came by Rail Road from Richmond to the Depot in front of our lines Teams accompained the columns—The enemys pickets were relieved at 9 a m today" Telegram received, DNA, RG 108, Letters Received. *O.R.*, I, xlvi, part 2, 700.

Also on Feb. 25, USG telegraphed to Commodore William Radford. "I think it not impossible that the enemy may send the rams down tonight or during present high water I have directed vigilence on the part of pickets to notice and report any such movement" Telegram received, DNA, RG 45, Area 7; *ibid.*, RG 94, War Records Office, Army of the Potomac; copies, *ibid.*, RG 108, Letters Sent; DLC-USG, V, 46, 74, 108. *O.R.*, I, xlvi, part 2, 686; *O.R.* (Navy), I, xii, 51.

To Maj. Gen. John G. Parke

City Point, Va, Feb.y 25th *1865* [5:50 P.M.]

MAJ. GEN. PARKE,

Deserters in from the rebel lines North of the James this afternoon still say that it is reported among them that Hill's Corps has left, or is leaving, to join Beaurigard. Have you received deserters to-day from that Corps? If such a movement is discovered we must endeavor to break a hole through some place in front of the 9th Corps. Reserves from the 2d 5th & 6th can be used to reinforce the 9th in such a move.

U. S. GRANT
Lt. Gen.

ALS (telegram sent), PHi; telegram received (at 7:20 P.M.), DNA, RG 94, War Records Office, Army of the Potomac. *O.R.*, I, xlvi, part 2, 687. Both the telegram sent and telegram received carried notations stating that the message had been delayed because the wires were down. On Feb. 25, 1865, 8:30 P.M., Maj. Gen. John G. Parke telegraphed to USG. "Your dispatch of 5.50 P. M. was delayed 2 hours the wire was down. The last deserter from Hill came from Mahones Div & reported at 10 a. m. & reports 'no movement' From 9th Corps front as result of Artillery fire I hear from Tidball. The enemys reply to our fire indicated no change whatever in their Artillery They fired from mortars and guns as usual. I cannot yet find out that any of Hill's Corps has moved." ALS (telegram sent), DNA, RG 107, Telegrams Collected (Unbound); telegram received, *ibid.*, RG 108, Letters Received. *O.R.*, I, xlvi, part 2, 688. On the same day, USG telegraphed to Parke and all corps commanders transmitting information from the *Richmond Examiner*. Telegram received (at 8:55 P.M.), DNA, RG 94, War Records Office, Army of the Potomac; copy, Meade Papers, PHi. *O.R.*, I, xlvi, part 2, 688; (printed as addressed to Secretary of War Edwin M. Stanton) *ibid.*, I, xlix, part 1, 766. At 11:00 P.M., Parke telegraphed to USG. "We have now received ten deserters from Johnsons Division in front of 9th A. C. and five deserters from 9th Fla. Mahones Division in front of 6th Corps. They repeat the report concerning cotton & Tobacco. No extra rations issued, picket no stronger, have heard that heavy Guns had been removed. Johnsons Div. still strengthening their works and doubling abattis" Telegram received, DNA, RG 108, Letters Received; copies, *ibid.*, RG 393, Army of the Potomac, Letters Sent; Meade Papers, PHi. *O.R.*, I, xlvi, part 2, 688.

On Feb. 24, Parke had telegraphed to USG at 11:45 A.M., and twice to Brig. Gen. John A. Rawlins, at 3:05 P.M. and midnight. "The present firing is by Genl Potter & by my order to determine what guns are still left in his front." ALS (telegram sent), DNA, RG 94, War Records Office, Army of the Potomac; copy, *ibid.*, RG 393, Army of the Potomac, Letters Sent. *O.R.*, I, xlvi, part 2, 670. "A deserter from the 5th. Ala. doing Provost Guard duty north of South-Side R. R. & near the city states—that Early's corps crossed the upper or western bridge on the appamattox yesterday morning, & through the day—After crossing, marched West along the South-side R. R.—This cannot be either Gordon or Pegram. Our artillery this morning ~~draw~~ drew a response from the usual Batteries on our right—On the left, or rather from the Signal tower at Fort Fisher, the Signal Officers report ~~th~~ no apparent change in the position of the enemy's guns or batteries.—this morning" ALS (telegram sent), DNA, RG 94, War Records Office, Army of the Potomac; telegram received, *ibid.*, RG 108, Letters Received. *O.R.*, I, xlvi, part 2, 670. "One hundred & fourteen (114) deserters have been received today—represinting every Division in our front. They State no troops

had moved from their camps & confirm the previous report about marching
Orders &c—about orders to remove Stores to the north of the Appomattox—
From those who have Come in Since dark 35 in number we learn that there has
been no Change in the ordinary issue of rations"   Telegram received, DNA, RG
108, Letters Received. *O.R.*, I, xlvi, part 2, 670.

On Feb. 25, 10:50 A.M., Bvt. Maj. Gen. Alexander S. Webb telegraphed to
Lt. Col. Theodore S. Bowers. "The above is sent for your information. Up to 12
o'clock last night 134 deserters in twenty-four hours." *Ibid.*, p. 693. The enclosure is *ibid.* On the same day, USG telegraphed to Parke. "Deserters from
Genl Ords front today say that it is reported in their lines that Petersburg is
being Evacuated. Make every effort to ascertain if this report is true. The great
number of deserters Coming in on your front enables you however to know all
movements of the enemy I suppose." Telegram received (at 2:10 P.M.), DNA,
RG 94, War Records Office, Army of the Potomac; copies, *ibid.*, RG 108, Letters
Sent; DLC-USG, V, 46, 74, 108; Meade Papers, PHi. *O.R.*, I, xlvi, part 2, 687.
At 3:30 P.M. and 3:55 P.M., Parke telegraphed to USG. "From deserters I
learn that Rhodes Divn moved west on S. S. R. R. on Wednesday without Artillery—that 28 pieces of artillery left Petersburg for Chesterfield depot—that
10 carloads of cheveaux-de-frise arrived in Petersburg over S. S. R. R. last night.
I have ordered Genl Potter to open on enemy's line in his front with his batteries."
"The two following despatches just rec'd.—Owing to the fog & haze, the signal
officers have a very limited view—I have directed Gen: Potter to open with the
guns on the 9th corps front, and report whether or not any response is elicited."
Telegrams sent, DNA, RG 94, War Records Office, Army of the Potomac; telegrams received (at 3:30 P.M. and 4:00 P.M.), *ibid.*, RG 108, Letters Received.
O.R., I, xlvi, part 2, 687. The enclosures are *ibid.*, pp. 693–94, 695–96.

On Feb. 27, 10:30 A.M., Parke telegraphed to USG. "No change has been
observed in the position, nor movement of the enemy reported in our front—The
Pro: Mar. reports this A. M. 90 (ninety) deserters. ~~from~~ One of these ~~reports~~
states that Rodes' Division camped near Sutherland Station S. S. R. R. on Friday
Ev'g." ALS (telegram sent), DNA, RG 94, War Records Office, Army of the
Potomac; telegram received, *ibid.*, RG 108, Letters Received. *O.R.*, I, xlvi, part
2, 718.

On Feb. 28, 11:20 A.M., Parke telegraphed to USG. "The Pro. Mar: reports
22 deserters this A. M.—No movement or changes reported within enemy's
lines." ALS (telegram sent), DNA, RG 393, Army of the Potomac, Miscellaneous Letters Received; copy, *ibid.*, Letters Sent.

To Maj. Gen. John M. Schofield

City Point, Va, Feb.y 25th 18645.

MAJ. GEN. SCHOFIELD, ~~CARE~~ ~~CAPT.~~ ~~JAMES~~
FORTRESS MONROE,

Do not hesitate about making any changes in commanders you
may think necessary. I supposed Palmer had Kinston before this.

I think by all means you should get Goldsboro' and hold and supply it as soon as possible. If you have information of Sherman coming in at any other point you will of course want to meet him with supplies. ~~I take it that whilst you are moving on Goldsboro' a small force will protect supplies sent to Fayetteville or elswhere~~. If he should come to Fayetteville you could send supplies after his arrival there. Prepare to send ~~them~~ supplies forward to Fayetteville the moment you know Sherman is coming in there.

U. S. GRANT

Lt. Gen.

Operator at Fort Monroe will plase put this up to Gen. Schofield and deliver ~~them~~ to Capt James with request to send by first boat

U S GRANT

Lt G

ALS (telegram sent), PPRF; telegram received (press), DNA, RG 107, Telegrams Collected (Bound). *O.R.*, I, xlvii, part 2, 578–79. The postscript is not in USG's hand. On Feb. 25, 1865, USG telegraphed to Capt. William L. James, Fort Monroe. "stop the boat bound for Fort Fisher until I send you a despatch for Gen Schofield" Telegram received (dated only "25"), DNA, RG 107, Telegrams Collected (Unbound).

To Maj. Gen. Philip H. Sheridan

(Cipher)   City Point, Va, Feb. 25 *1865* [*7:30* P.M.]
MAJ. GEN. SHERIDAN, WINCHESTER VA,

Gen. Sherman's movements will depend on the amount of opposition he meets from the enemy. If strongly opposed he may possibly have to fall back to Georgetown S. C. and fit out for a new start. I think however all danger of the necessity for going to that point has passed. I believe he has passed Charlotte. He will now aim to connect with Schofield about Goldsboro'. He may ~~have to make~~ take Fayetteville ~~and first~~ on his way to Goldsboro. If you reach Lynchburg you will have to be guided in your after movements by the information you obtain. Before you could possibly reach Sherman I think you would find him moving from Goldsboro towards Raleigh or engaging the enemy strongly posted at one or

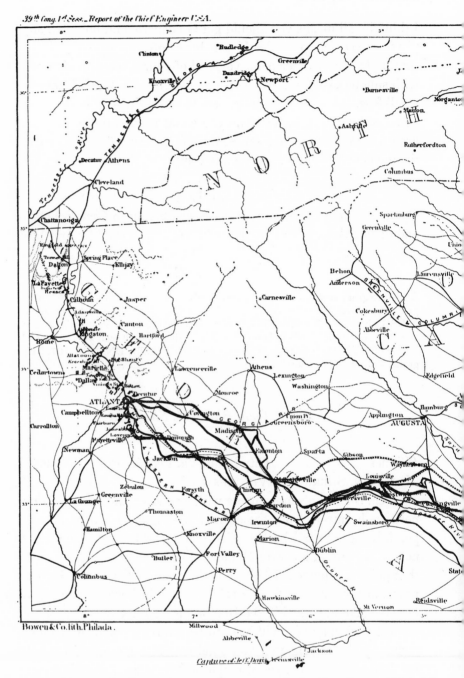

Sherman's Campaigns in Georgia and the Carolinas, 1864–65

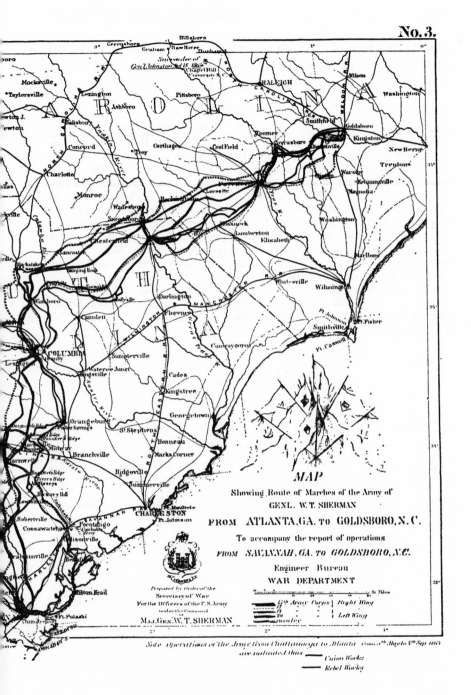

MAP

Showing Route of Marches of the Army of

GENL. W. T. SHERMAN

FROM ATLANTA, GA. TO GOLDSBORO, N. C.

To accompany the report of operations

FROM SAVANNAH, GA. TO GOLDSBORO, N.C.

Engineer Bureau

WAR DEPARTMENT

Prepared by Order of the
Secretary of War
For the Officers of the U.S. Army
under the Command
of
MAJ.GEN.W.T. SHERMAN

the other of these places with rail-road communications opend from his Army to Wilmington or New Berne.

U. S. GRANT

Lt. Gen.

ALS (telegram sent), Abraham Lincoln Book Shop, Chicago, Ill.; (incomplete facsimile) Sotheby Parke-Bernet, Sale No. 3655, June 11, 1974, No. 223; telegram received (at 9:00 P.M.), DNA, RG 107, Telegrams Collected (Bound); *ibid.*, Telegrams Collected (Unbound). *O.R.*, I, xxxiv, part 1, 46–47; *ibid.*, I, xxxvi, part 1, 50; *ibid.*, I, xxxviii, part 1, 39; *ibid.*, I, xlvi, part 2, 701. On Feb. 25, 1865, 2:30 P.M., Maj. Gen. Philip H. Sheridan, Winchester, Va., telegraphed to USG. "I could not get off today as I expected in a privious despatch to you but will be off on monday. I was delayed in getting the brigade from Loudon Country and the canvas ponton bridge which was necessary for me to have as all the streams in the country are at present unfordable Where is Sherman aiming for can you give me any definite information as to the points he may be expected to move on this side of Charlotte? The Cav. officers say the cavalry was never in such good condition I will leave behind about 2000 men which will increase to 3000 in a short time." Telegram received, DNA, RG 108, Letters Received; copies (2), DLC-Philip H. Sheridan. *O.R.*, I, xlvi, part 2, 701. See following telegram.

To Abraham Lincoln

———

(Cipher)   City Point, Va, Feb.y 26th *1865* [6:30 P.M.]
A. LINCOLN, PRESIDENT, WASHINGTON.

It is 2.000 Cavalry and that to be increased to 3.000 besides all his Infantry, and that will to be increased to 3.000 is what Sheridan means. His movement is in the direction of the enemy and the tendency will be to protect the B. & O road and to prevent an attempt to invade Maryland and Pa.

U. S. GRANT

Lt. Gn.

ALS (telegram sent), James S. Schoff, New York, N. Y.; telegram received (at 8:00 P.M.), DLC-Robert T. Lincoln; DNA, RG 107, Telegrams Collected (Bound). *O.R.*, I, xlvi, part 2, 704. On Feb. 25, 1865, President Abraham Lincoln telegraphed to USG. "Gen. Sheridan's despatch to you of to-day, in which he says he 'will be off on Monday' and that he 'will leave behind about two thousand men' causes the Secretary of War and myself considerable anxiety. Have you well considered whether you do not again leave open the Shenandoah-valley entrance to Maryland and Pennsylvania?—or, at least, to the B & O. Railroad?" ALS (telegram sent—marked as sent on Feb. 26, 11:00 A.M.), DNA,

RG 107, Telegrams Collected (Bound); telegram received (marked as sent at
8:00 P.M., received on Feb. 26), *ibid.*, RG 108, Letters Received. *O.R.*, I, xlvi,
part 2, 685. Lincoln, *Works*, VIII, 316. See preceding telegram. On Feb. 27,
10:25 A.M., Lincoln telegraphed to USG. "Subsequent reflection, conference
with Gen. Halleck, your despatch, and one from Gen. Sheridan, have relieved
my anxiety; and so I beg that you will dismiss any concern you may have on my
account, in the matter of my last despatch." ALS (telegram sent), DNA, RG
107, Telegrams Collected (Bound); telegram received (at 10:25 A.M.), *ibid.*,
RG 108, Letters Received. *O.R.*, I, xlvi, part 2, 717. Lincoln, *Works*, VIII,
320–21.

To Edwin M. Stanton

City Point, Va, Feb.y 26th *1865*

HON. E. M. STANTON,
SEC. OF WAR,
SIR:

I regreted greatly when I learned that Gen. Gilmore had been
assigned to the command of the Dept. of the South. He probably
will be a suitable officer to have the general superintendence of the
fortifications on the Sea Coast. But on that duty he should be required to have all his requisitions approved by Gen. Delafield or he
will expend to much.

Foreseeing the fall of ~~Fort~~ Charleston I sent orders to Gn Gilmore, in advance of hearing of the event, to occupy the necessary
points on the Coast for us to hold, with Minimum garrisons, and
send the balace of his forces to the Cape Fear river, and to send
all White troops, leaving the Colored ones where they have been
raised and where their families are; Before he received that order I
suppose he sendt a letter calling for from 4.000 to 5.000 more
troops, one thousand mounted men, with which he expects, by
uniting the Civil with the Military, to feed and foster the Union
sentiment in Ga. I feel confidant that with Terry in command of
that Department instead of wanting an addition to his force he will
spare 10.000 men to be used elswhere and the balance will be
much more economically supported and usefuly employed. He
will administer the affairs of his Department with sense and judge-

ment and will not talk about expeditions and conquests where there
is no enemy to oppose him. He will also prove a most excellent man
to organize Colored troops.

Very respectfully
your obt. svt.
U. S. GRANT
Lt. Gn.

ALS, DNA, RG 94, Letters Received, 1809P 1865. *O.R.*, I, xlvii, part 2, 582.
On Sept. 16, 1865, Maj. Gen. Henry W. Halleck, San Francisco, wrote to Secre-
tary of War Edwin M. Stanton. "I enclose herewith an original letter of Genl
Grant in regard to Genl Gillmore which by some mistake was sent here with my
papers. It properly belongs to your files." ALS, DNA, RG 94, Letters Received,
1809P 1865. USG's letter has no endorsements, and what attention it received
before it was misplaced remains unclear.
On Feb. 26, USG telegraphed to Maj. Gen. John G. Parke. "Assign brevet
Bg Gen McKibbin to the command of a Brigade in Gen Potters Div with his
Brevet rank. Please send me the initials of McKibbin's name so that I may
telegraph to have him assigned to duty with his Brevet rank by the president."
Telegram received (at 10:15 A.M.), *ibid.*, War Records Office, Army of the
Potomac; copies, *ibid.*, RG 108, Letters Sent; *ibid.*, Letters Received; DLC-USG,
V, 46, 74, 108; Meade Papers, PHi. *O.R.*, I, xlvi, part 2, 706. At 10:48 A.M.,
Parke telegraphed to USG. "Brevet Brig. Gen'l. M'Kibben's initials are 'G. H.'—
He is a Capt: & A. A. G.—appointed from New York." ALS (telegram sent),
DNA, RG 393, Army of the Potomac, Miscellaneous Letters Received; copy,
ibid., Letters Sent. Also on Feb. 26, 11:00 A.M., USG telegraphed to Stanton.
"Will you please assign Brevet Brig, Gen, McKibbin (G. H.) to duty with his
Brevet Rank? He is very much wanted for the command of a Brigade in the 9th
Corps and cannot command it with his line rank" Copies, DLC-USG, V, 46, 74,
108; DNA, RG 108, Letters Sent. *O.R.*, I, xlvi, part 2, 705. At 9:00 P.M., Stanton telegraphed to USG. "Brevet Brigadier General McKibben is assigned to
duty on his brevet rank. To avoid delays you are hereby autherised to assign any
officer in the Service to duty on his brevet rank notifying the Adjutant General
so that it may be duly recorded." ALS (telegram sent), DNA, RG 107, Telegrams Collected (Bound); telegram received (at 9:30 P.M.), *ibid.*, RG 108,
Letters Received. *O.R.*, I, xlvi, part 2, 705. On Feb. 27, Lt. Col. Theodore S.
Bowers telegraphed to Parke. "Brevet Brig General G. H McKibben has been
assigned to duty by the President under his Brevet rank." Telegram received (at
11:30 A.M.), DNA, RG 94, War Records Office, Army of the Potomac; copies,
ibid., RG 108, Letters Sent; DLC-USG, V, 46, 74, 108; Meade Papers, PHi.
O.R., I, xlvi, part 2, 718.
On March 1, Maj. Gen. George G. Meade wrote to Bowers. "I find on my
return, the enclosed telegram from the Lieut General Commanding, and consider
it due to myself, to lay before him the following statement of facts. Under the
call made by me, upon Corps and subordinate Commanders, for nominations for
Brevet for distinguished and gallant services in the field in the recent campaign,
—Brig: Genl: Potter, Commanding Division in the 9th Corps, thought proper to
present the name of Captn McKibbin A. A. G for the successive Brevets of Major,

Lieut: Col:, Colonel, and Brig: General.—Owing to the large number of officers recommended, and relying on my subordinate officers not abusing the privilege given them to make nominations, particularly, as the Circular making the call, cautioned them to present no names, but such as had clearly earned the rewards proposed;—I did not critically inspect the list, but forwarded it to the Department of War, and it was not until the appointments were made and distributed, that my attention was called to the extraordinary, and as I think, improper use, General Potter had made of this privilege.—Upon learning the state of the case, I communicated verbally my views to General Potter, and stated to him, whilst, I would refrain from asking the Department to cancel the two higher grades conferred, as I conceived, improperly, yet, I should not approve, and would resist this Officer being asigned to duty with his grade of Brigadier General.—I, understanding General Potter's action to be predicated on his desire to obtain this Officer for a Brigade Commander. Accordingly, when General Potter applied for this Officer to be assigned to duty with his rank as Brigadier General,—I disapproved the application.—Subsequently, on Captain McKibbin being confirmed by the Senate, General Potter, notwithstanding my expressed views and action in the matter, renewed his application, which was forwarded to Washington, disapproved by me, for the reasons given above.—Now, I find, during my absence, and without any opportunity given me to explain my position, General Potter has thought proper, thro' some unofficial channel, to bring the case to the attention of the Lieut General Commanding, and has obtained the decision in his favor. I respectfully submit, that the whole of Gen'l Potter's course is not consistent with the respect due to me as his Commanding General, and I feel quite satisfied, had all the facts of the case been made Known to the Lieut General Commanding, he would have awaited explanation of my action, before deciding against me. My objections to the assignment of this Officer to a Brigade, are, 1st: The improper manner in which his appointment was procured. 2ndly—The injustice to this Army, which will be done, by assigning a Staff Officer, thus elevated, to the command of troops, when, there are at least six, if not more, Brevet Brigadier Generals who have been promoted for gallantry, whilst commanding Brigades and regiments, and, who are now awaiting assignment to commands. In making these objections, I am not governed by any personal considerations, for I have no Knowledge of Captain McKibbin, beyond what I have obtained in the progress of this affair, and have no reason to dispute General Potter's opinion that he is an officer of merit, and would make a good Brigade commander.—My objections are to the modus-operandi,—the injustice to other officers, and the injury to the whole Brevet system, which will result from its successful accomplishment. With the foregoing explanation of my motives and course in this matter,—I leave any further action to the judgment of the Lieut: General Commanding." LS, DNA, RG 108, Letters Received. O.R., I, xlvi, part 2, 771–72. See ibid., p. 967.

On Feb. 26, 5:00 P.M., Stanton telegraphed to USG. "I submit the following ~~enqui~~ accompanying enquiry of Governor Fenton for your judgment, whether it be expedient to accept such troops for the time and on the terms proposed. Please favor me with an early answer so that the offer cannot serve to delay the draft" ALS (telegram sent—misdated 1864), DNA, RG 107, Telegrams Collected (Bound); telegram received, ibid., Telegrams Collected (Unbound); (at 6:00 P.M.) ibid., RG 108, Letters Received. O.R., I, xlvi, part 2, 705. Stanton transmitted a telegram of Feb. 25 from Governor Reuben E. Fenton of N. Y. to Stanton. "Will you accept five to ten Regts of the state national Guard for one

hundred days to do garrison duty in Charleston Savannah Wilmington or other
ports to be applied on the state Quota three men for one, one year man" Copy,
DNA, RG 108, Letters Received. *O.R.*, I, xlvi, part 2, 705. On Feb. 26, 7:00
P.M., USG telegraphed to Stanton. "I do not think favorably of Governor Fenton's
proposition. The ~~true~~ value of 100 days men is more than absorbed in getting
them to where they are wanted and ~~either~~ in transferring men relieved by them
to where they will be needed, and again in releiving them when their time expires." ALS (telegram sent), Doheny Library, St. John's Seminary, Camarillo,
Calif.; telegram received (marked as sent at 8:00 P.M., received at 9:00 P.M.),
DNA, RG 107, Telegrams Collected (Bound). *O.R.*, I, xlvi, part 2, 705.

To Maj. Gen. Henry W. Halleck

City Point Va, Feby 26th 1865

MAJ, GEN, HALLECK
WASHINGTON

I approve of the assignment of Hancock to Sheridans command
during his absence   If Crocker can be reached he will make a fine
Officer to take Crook's place unless it is decided to retain Hancock,
In that event he would take Kelly's with advantage,

I can send troops from here to break up traffic on the Penin-
sulas—Augar need not send out,

U. S. GRANT Lt, Gen,

Telegram, copies, DLC-USG, V, 46, 74, 108; DNA, RG 108, Letters Sent.
Printed as sent at 7:00 P.M., received at 9:00 P.M., in *O.R.*, I, xlvi, part 2, 704.
On Feb. 26, 1865, 3:00 P.M., Maj. Gen. Henry W. Halleck had telegraphed to
USG. "Genl Augur, by direction of Genl Sheridan, is fitting out a cavalry expedition against the Rappahannock peninsula. To do this requires most of his cavalry, and Genl Sheridan has withdrawn his from the line of the Potomac. The
Secty of War thinks this will leave Alexandria & the Maryland line too much
exposed to rebel raids. I have therefore directed Genl Augur to wait till I could
hear from you as to the necessity of the Rappahannock expedition. Major Genl
Hancock has been assigned to the temporary command of West Va. & the troops
of the Middle Mil. Division, not with Genl Sheridan in the field. He will still
attend to his recruiting." ALS (telegram sent), DNA, RG 107, Telegrams Collected (Bound); telegram received, *ibid.*; *ibid.*, RG 108, Letters Received. *O.R.*,
I, xlvi, part 2, 704. At 1:30 P.M., Secretary of War Edwin M. Stanton had telegraphed to USG. "I propose to assign General Hancock temporarily to the
command of the Department of West Virginia and in General Sheridans absence
to command the Division—provided you approve" ALS (telegram sent), DNA,
RG 107, Telegrams Collected (Bound); telegram received, *ibid.*, RG 108,
Letters Received. *O.R.*, I, xlvi, part 2, 704.

To Lt. Col. John E. Mulford

———

City Point Va Feby 26th [*1865*]

LIEUT, COL, MULFORD
AG'T OF EX—JONES LANDING.

Please inform me how the matter of Exchange is coming on? We do not want to deliver faster than we recieve, When deliveries stop on James River, we will stop until it is known, that deliveries are to be made elsewhere, Two of my Staff Officers have returned from Wilmington, They say that Hoke sent a "Flag of Truce" proposing to exchange a certain number of prisoners without saying it was an agreement with me and before Schofield received my order, Schofield was advancing on Wilmington at the time and could not have stoped to receive them About 200 of our prisoners escaped and came into our lines, Whatever the number escaping in that way was, will be credited to the enemy and will be furloughed until exchanged, Why was it no prisoners were sent to us yesterday when they were still able to receive them?

U. S, GRANT
Lt, General

Telegram, copies, DLC-USG, V, 46, 74, 108; DNA, RG 108, Letters Sent; USG 3. On Feb. 26, 1865, Lt. Col. John E. Mulford, Varina, Va., telegraphed to USG. "Exchange is progressing slowly, no deliveres made today, the reason why no delivery of our men was made yesterday was because they could not get down with their boat on a/c of high water, I had taken thier men to a point where I expected to meet the boat beinng disappointed in this I deliverd them through the enemys picket line, I think the forwarding of prisonrs may be suspended a few days without ~~predjudice~~ prejudice to the exchange,—What shall I say to Mr Ould about the reception of our men at Wilmington Will they be received there now by Genl Schofield I have now on hand here about 2200 Confederate prisonrs, 700 of them sick & wounded" ALS (telegram sent), DNA, RG 107, Telegrams Collected (Unbound); telegram received (at 11:55 P.M.), *ibid.*, RG 108, Letters Received. *O.R.*, II, viii, 309–10.

On Feb. 27, Mulford twice telegraphed to USG. "I have received today & forwarded to Annapolis Md One Hundred and fifty ~~men~~, Officers & thirteen hundred enlisted men," ALS (telegram sent), DNA, RG 107, Telegrams Collected (Unbound). "I am informed that deliveries at the rate of two thousand per day are now being made at Wilmington & will continue to the number of ten or twelve thousand, I shall send a detachmt through tomorrow and receive some on Wednesday if the water & weather will permit" ALS (telegram sent), *ibid.*; telegram received (at 4:00 P.M.), *ibid.*, RG 108, Letters Received.

To Maj. Gen. Henry W. Halleck

City Point Va
3.30 p m Feby 27th 1865

MAJ GENL HALLECK
CHF OF STAFF

Among the Brevet promotions, I do not see the name of Genl
Robt Allen—

I think of all the Qr Mrs in the army he should be Breveted a
Brigadier first—Believing you agree with me in this, I telegraph
to you hoping you will ask the Secretary of War to make his the
more honored promotion   His date I think should place him next
to the Qr Mr Genl

U S. GRANT
Lt Genl

Telegram received, DNA, RG 94, ACP, 278 1875; copies, *ibid.*; (marked as sent
at noon) *ibid.*, RG 108, Letters Sent; DLC-USG, V, 46, 74, 108. Printed as sent
at noon, received at 3:30 P.M., in *O.R.*, I, xlviii, part 1, 989–90. See letter to
Edwin M. Stanton, Dec. 31, 1864. On Jan. 31, 1865, President Abraham Lincoln nominated Brig. Gen. Robert Allen as bvt. lt. col., bvt. col., and bvt. brig.
gen., U.S. Army, all as of July 6, 1864.

To Maj. Gen. Henry W. Halleck

(Cipher)   City Point, Va, Feb.y 27th *1865* [6:00 P.M.]
MAJ. GEN. HALLECK, WASHINGTON,

An expedition to destroy the Rapidann rail-road bridge would
serve as a diversion in favor of Sheridan. Unless he has directed it
however I would not order it. If he has directed it let the expedition go.

U. S. GRANT
Lt. Gen.

ALS (telegram sent), OClWHi; copies, DLC-USG, V, 46, 74, 108; DNA, RG
108, Letters Sent. *O.R.*, I, xlvi, part 2, 718. On Feb. 27, 1865, 4:00 P.M., Maj.
Gen. Henry W. Halleck telegraphed to USG. "It has been suggested that an

expedition be sent from here to destroy the Rapidann R. R. Bridge & the Railroad to Culpepper. Would the advantage equal the waste of horseflesh? ⁊Nine (9) regiments & three (3) companies of Infantry & 5 companies of artillery have been sent within the last twelve days to Nashville from Ill. Ind. Ohio & Wisconsin." ALS (telegram sent), DNA, RG 107, Telegrams Collected (Bound); telegram received, *ibid.*; (marked as sent at 3:00 P.M.) *ibid.*, RG 108, Letters Received. *O.R.*, I, xlvi, part 2, 718; *ibid.*, I, xlix, part 1, 777.

Also on Feb. 27, 3:30 P.M., USG telegraphed to Halleck. "Please direct Col, Ekin to consign houses [*horses*] for the Armies operating against Richmond as General Ingalls has requested him, When it is desired that any particular command shall have them they will be distributed according to the directions," Copies, DLC-USG, V, 46, 74, 108; DNA, RG 108, Letters Sent. *O.R.*, I, xlvi, part 2, 718.

To Maj. Gen. Edward R. S. Canby

City Point Va. Feb. 27 1865

MAJ. GEN E. R S. CANBY.
COMDG. MIL DIV WEST MISS.
GENERAL!

Brevet Brig General C B. Comstock, the bearer of this, will report to you for temporary service.[1] Relieve him and order him back to these Headquarters as soon as you commence a movement to the interior from Mobile, should that City fall into your possession soon, or when it is clearly ascertained that you are to have a protracted siege. Until recently I supposed that Mobile would probably be surrendered without a struggle. Since however, I have learned that orders have been given from Richmond to hold the place at all hazards. These orders are now but about a week old, and may have reached there too late. The great length of time that has elapsed since I have heard from you however, makes it impossible for me to judge whether your campaign had progressed far enough to interfere with a compliance with this order. I am extremely anxious to hear of your forces getting to the interior of Alabama. I sent Grierson, an experienced Cavalry Commander to take command of your cavalry. At the time he received his orders, I did not know that you were intending to send your cavalry from Vicksburg. He was therefore directed to report to you in person. I am afraid this will prevent his taking the command I intended, and interfere somewhat with the success of your cavalry. Forrest seems to be near Jackson, Miss., and if he is, none but the best of our cavalry commanders will get by him. Thomas was directed to start a cavalry force from Eastport, Miss, as soon after the 20th of February as possible, to move on Selma, Miss., which would tend to draw Forrest off. He promised to start it by that day, but I know he did not, and I do not know that he has yet started it.

It but rarely happens, that a number of expeditions, starting from various points to act upon a common centre, materially aid each other. They never do, except when each acts with vigor, and either makes rapid marches, or keeps confronting an enemy. Whilst one column is engaging any thing like an equal force, it is necessarily aiding the other by holding that force. With Grierson I am satisfied you would either find him at the appointed place in time, or you would find him holding an enemy, which would enable the other column to get there. I think you will find the same true of Wilson, who I suppose will command the forces starting from Eastport.

I directed that you should organize your forces in two Corps, one under Steele and the other under A J. Smith. Both these officers have had experience in subsisting off the country through which they are passing.

I write this now, not to give any instructions not heretofore given, but because I feel a great anxiety to see the enemy entirely broken up in the west, whilst I believe it will be an easy job. Time will enable the enemy to reorganize and collect in their deserters, and get up a formidable force. By giving them no rest, what they now have in their ranks will leave them. It is also important to prevent as far as possible the planting of a crop this year, and to destroy their railroads, machine shops &c.

It is also important to get all the negro men we can before the enemy put them in their ranks.

Stoneman starts from East Tennessee in a few days to make a raid as far up on Lynchburg road as he can get. Sheridan started this morning from Winchester Va., to destroy the Va Central road and James river canal, and to get to Lynchburg if he can. Each starts with cavalry forces alone.

I am not urging because of any, even supposed, delay, but because I feel a great anxiety to see every thing pushed, and the time it takes to communicate, leaves me in the dark, as to the progress you are making.

Please write to me fully on receipt of this. Gen. Comstock will give you detailed news from this quarter.

> Very Respectfully
> Your Obt Serv't
> U S. Grant
> Lieutenant General

Copies, DLC-USG, V, 46, 73, 108; DNA, RG 108, Letters Sent. *O.R.*, I, xlix, part 1, 780–81.

1. On Feb. 27, 1865, USG telegraphed to Maj. Gen. Henry W. Halleck. "Please notify Gen. Comstock to remain in Washington until he receives dispatches which will be sent to him by to-morrow's mail." ALS (telegram sent), Kohns Collection, NN; copies, DLC-USG, V, 46, 74, 108; DNA, RG 108, Letters Sent. See *O.R.*, I, xlix, part 1, 781–82. On March 1, Bvt. Brig. Gen. Cyrus B. Comstock telegraphed to USG. "Despatches received today. I leave for Cairo tonight." ALS (telegram sent), DNA, RG 107, Telegrams Collected (Bound); telegram received, *ibid.*, RG 108, Letters Received.

To Maj. Gen. Edward O. C. Ord

[Feb. 27, 1865]

Your note . . . enclosing one from General Longstreet is just received . . . I should like to meet him . . . this will depend on the result of your interview. It probably will be better for you to have another interview with Gen. Longstreet . . . before I agree to meet him . . . go tell him that you will try to arrange for an interview . . .

Charles Hamilton Auction No. 14, Sept. 22, 1966, p. 45. According to the catalogue description, the USG letter was accompanied by a commentary written by Maj. Gen. Edward O. C. Ord. ". . . In the interview—held with Genl Longstreet by me he evidently was impressed with the truth of my views . . . to try and convince Genl Lee—and through him Genl Davis, the Presid. of the Confed—of the great wrong of subjecting the South to further bloodshed . . . Longstreet . . . stated that Mr. Davis was the great obstacle to peace . . . that General Lee con-

sidered the cause of the South hopeless . . . That it was a great crime against the
Southern people and Army for the chief Generals to continue to lead their men
to hopeless and unnecessary butchery . . . [Ord's remarks conclude with the observation that, with a threat to resign, Lee could have forced Davis to secure a
peace] that could have given the South compensation for the loss of their slaves,
and an immediate share in the Gov't." *Ibid.* Also on Feb. 27, 1865, USG telegraphed to Ord. "I will not be able to go up to-morrow. I will write by your Staff
Officer." ALS (telegram sent), Ralph Geoffrey Newman, Inc., Chicago, Ill.;
telegram received (at 4:00 P.M.), Ord Papers, CU-B. On the same day, 7:00
P.M., Ord telegraphed to USG. "As the meeting is to arrange for the exchange
of Political prisoners—and their mutual release—had I not better have some
definite proposition—to cover ~~general~~ other cases—as well as that of Pryor and
Dent—" ALS (telegram sent), *ibid.*; telegram received, DNA, RG 108, Letters
Received. *O.R.*, I, xlvi, part 2, 722. On the same day, USG telegraphed to Ord. "I
thought the ostensible object of the meeting was to arrange for the release of prisoners improperly captured. You can arrange definitely for the exchange of all civilians confined within your Dept., and make such arrangements as you can for all
others subject to the approval of the highest authority both sides." Copies, DLC-
USG, V, 46, 73, 108; DNA, RG 108, Letters Sent. *O.R.*, I, xlvi, part 2, 722. Ord
noted on the reverse of the telegram received: ". . . had meeting with Longstreet
. . . but tho he & Genl Lee no doubt were anxious, nothing could be done with
J. Davis." Charles Hamilton Auction No. 14, Sept. 22, 1966, p. 45.

To Maj. Gen. George H. Thomas

(Cipher)   City Point, Va, Feb.y 27th *1865* [*11:00* A.M.]
MAJ. GEN. THOMAS, NASHVILLE TENN. COPY FOR GEN. STONE-
MAN KNOXVILLE TENN.

General Stoneman being so late in making his start from East
Tenn and Sherman having passed out of the state of South Carolina I think now his cours had better be changed. It is not impossible that in the event of the enemy being driven from Richmond
they may fall back to Lynchburg with a part of their force and
attempt a raid into East Tenn. It will be better therefore to keep
Stoneman between our garrisons in East Tenn. and the enemy.
Direct him to repeat his raid of last Fall destroying the rail-road as
far towards Lynchburg as he can. Sheridan starts to day from
Winchester for Lynchburg. This will vastly favor Stoneman.

Every effort should be made to collect all the surplus forage
and provisions of East Tenn. in Knoxville and to get there a large
amount of stores besides. It is not impossible that we may have to

use a very conciderable force in that section the coming Spring. Preparations should at once be made to meet such contingency.

If it had been possible to have got Stoneman off in time he would have made a diversion in favor of Sherman and would have destroyed a large amount of rail-road stock cut off and left in Northwest S. C. It is too late now to do any good except to destroy the stock.

U. S. GRANT

Lt. Gn.

ALS (telegram sent), Elkins Collection, Free Library of Philadelphia, Philadelphia, Pa.; telegram received (marked as sent at noon, received at 12:30 P.M.), DNA, RG 107, Telegrams Collected (Bound); *ibid.*, Telegrams Collected (Unbound). *O.R.*, I, xlix, part 1, 777. On Feb. 27, 1865, 8:00 P.M., Maj. Gen. George H. Thomas telegraphed to USG. "Your telegram of 11 A. M. today is recd. I am sorry that the expedition under Gen Stoneman could not get off sooner than this but he has not had time to prepare fully since I recd. your instructions I will direct him to throw his force into South West Va. as you direct and in anticipation of probable operations in East Tenn. this spring, have allready thrown into Knoxville over two millions (2.000.000) rations and have given orders to have the store houses filled to their full capacity; Orders were also given some weeks since to accumulate forage at Knoxville which order is now being complied with by the Q. M. dep. Unless you wish otherwise I shall send Gen Stanleys entire corps to East Tenn as soon as a sufficient number of new regiments report to enable me to withdraw it from Huntsville Ala. I shall also concentrate the surplus of new regts at Chattanooga as the most available point from which troops to reinforce the troops in East Tenn if necessary" Telegram received (on Feb. 28, 12:40 A.M.), DNA, RG 107, Telegrams Collected (Bound); *ibid.*, RG 108, Letters Received; copy, *ibid.*, RG 393, Dept. of the Cumberland, Telegrams Sent. *O.R.*, I, xlix, part 1, 778. On March 1, 3:00 P.M., Maj. Gen. George Stoneman, Louisville, telegraphed to USG. "Your telegram of 27th recd. yesterday You cannot be more anxious to have me get off than I am to go. The delay has been due entirely to the difficulty in collecting together the troops which were very much scattered over Ky & to the deficiency in horses to replace those entirely broken down and lost on their last trip into Va. The regts have been sent forward as fast as mounted, The last is now being fitted out and will be ready by day after tomorrow. All will go by railroad & water as this will be much the quickest route, will prevent the horses from becoming broken down by a long march over the mountains at this season of the year will enable them to procure plenty of forage en route, will ~~enable~~ obviate the necessity of taking a wagon train or pack mules for supplies & will desguise from the enemy our objects & destination and will enable us to make up for the unavoidable delay in vigor & dash I gave orders a month ago to collect all the forage & subsistence possible from East Tenn. for all animals to be subsisted from the Country outside of Knoxville I leave for Knoxville tomorrow" Telegram received, DNA, RG 108, Letters Received; copy, *ibid.*, RG 393, Dept. and Army of the Ohio, Telegrams Sent. *O.R.*, I, xlix, part 1, 810.

On Feb. 26, 10:30 A.M., USG had telegraphed to Thomas. "When did

Stoneman start on his expedition?" ALS (telegram sent), Ralph Geoffrey Newman, Inc., Chicago, Ill.; telegram received (at 8:00 P.M.), DNA, RG 107, Telegrams Collected (Bound); *ibid.*, Telegrams Collected (Unbound). *O.R.*, I, xlix,
part 1, 773. On Feb. 27, 2:00 P.M., Thomas telegraphed to USG. "Your telegram of 26th is just recd. Gen. Stoneman has not yet started but informed my
Chief of Staff a few days since at Louisville that he would ready to start about
the 1st of Mar. I will notify you as soon as he will gets off. He has been delayed
for want of horses   I have just returned from Eastport having completed the
arrangements for the Cavalry expedition from that point. Owing to the recent
stormy and rainy weather Gen Wilson will be delayed a few days for the roads
to dry up. He will be able to start in a few days with at least 10.000 men" Telegram received (at 7:30 P.M.), DNA, RG 107, Telegrams Collected (Bound);
ibid., RG 108, Letters Received; copy, *ibid.*, RG 393, Dept. of the Cumberland,
Telegrams Sent. *O.R.*, I, xlix, part 1, 777.

On Feb. 28, 11:30 P.M., USG telegraphed to Thomas. "I think your pre-
caution of in sending the 4th Corps to Knoxville a good one. I also approve of
sending the new troops to Chattanooga. Eastport will be m must be held particularly whilst troops are operating in Alabama." ALS (telegram sent), deCoppet
Collection, NjP; telegram received (marked as sent at 10:30 P.M., received on
March 1, 12:50 A.M.), DNA, RG 107, Telegrams Collected (Bound); *ibid.*,
Telegrams Collected (Unbound). *O.R.*, I, xlix, part 1, 783.

On Feb. 28, 9:00 P.M., Thomas telegraphed to USG. "Have just heard from
Canby that his cavalry will start from Vicksburg on the 5th of march   Gen
Wilson is now ready & I will give him instructions about the same date as the
cavalry from Vicksburg starts" Telegram received (at 11:50 P.M.), DNA, RG
107, Telegrams Collected (Bound); *ibid.*, RG 108, Letters Received; copy, *ibid.*,
RG 393, Dept. of the Cumberland, Telegrams Sent. *O.R.*, I, xlix, part 1, 783.
On March 1, 10:30 A.M., USG telegraphed to Thomas. "In view of the fact that
Hood is about Jackson Miss, it will be well for Wilson to start before the Vicks-
burg forces—The latter may not be able to make their way across Pearl river
until Wilson has created a diversion in their favor" Telegram received (at
noon), DNA, RG 107, Telegrams Collected (Bound); (at 12:05 P.M.) *ibid.*,
Telegrams Collected (Unbound); copies, *ibid.*, RG 108, Letters Sent; DLC-USG,
V, 46, 74, 108. *O.R.*, I, xlix, part 2, 805. At 2:00 P.M., Thomas telegraphed to
USG. "Your telegram of 10 30 A. M. today received. I will send your order to
Gen. Wilson to get off at once" Telegram received, DNA, RG 107, Telegrams
Collected (Bound); *ibid.*, RG 108, Letters Received; copy, *ibid.*, RG 393, Dept.
of the Cumberland, Telegrams Sent. *O.R.*, I, xlix, part 1, 805.

To Brig. Gen. Charles K. Graham

City Point Va, Feby 27th [*1865*]

BRIG, GEN, GRAHAM
BERMUDA 100—

Mrs, Graham is here and ask's to have you come over and see
her, You are authorized to do so,

I should like you to hold at your service the means of returning at any hour during the night in case of necessity

U. S. GRANT
Lieut, General

Copies, DLC-USG, V, 46, 74, 108; DNA, RG 108, Letters Sent. Charles K. Graham, born in New York City in 1824, served as midshipman, U.S. Navy (1841–48), and was an engineer at the Brooklyn Navy Yard who led some 400 workmen into the army. Appointed col., 74th N. Y., as of May 26, 1862, and brig. gen. as of Nov. 26, he was captured at Gettysburg, and later served under Maj. Gen. Benjamin F. Butler and his successor in the Army of the James. On Feb. 26, 1865, Lt. Col. Theodore S. Bowers telegraphed to Mary Graham. "You have permission to visit your husband at Bermuda." Telegram received (press), *ibid.*, RG 107, Telegrams Collected (Bound).

To Lt. Col. John E. Mulford

City Point Va, Feby 26th [27] 1865 [*1:00* A.M.]
LT, COL, MULFORD
AG'T OF EX—CARE GEN, ORD

Say to Col, Ould the prisoners sent to Wilmington will be received, if they have not been already, Gen, Schofield received my orders on the subject after Gen, Hoke proposed to deliver, Gen Schofield was advancing on the City at the time and could not stop, The notice he received did not say that it was by agreement that prisoners were sent there for ~~exchange~~ delivery but a proposition to exchange was made to him, or rather he received word that Hoke had 25,00 prisoners which he proposed to exchange, Gen, Schofield sent back in reply, that he was not authorized to make exchanges but he would receive any prisoners that might be delivered, This reply probably never reached Gen, Hoke as the town was evacuated before it could have got there, About two hundred of the prisoners escaped and come within our lines, What ever the number may be, will be credited and the men paroled and Furloughed until properly exchanged

U. S. GRANT
Lieut, General

Telegram, copies, DLC-USG, V, 46, 74, 108; DNA, RG 108, Letters Sent; USG 3. *O.R.*, II, viii, 310.

On Feb. 26, 1865, Lt. Col. John E. Mulford telegraphed to USG. "Charleston was evacuated by the enemy on the 16th inst—no fighting—it is not known ~~where~~ whether we ~~occupied~~ ocupy the city or not" Telegram received, DNA, RG 107, Telegrams Collected (Unbound).

To Lt. Col. John E. Mulford

By Telegraph from City Pt
Dated Feby 27 1864 5.

To LT COL MULFORD.
CARE GENL ORD.

R. A. Pryor is here on his way for exchange. I will not permit him to go further until J. C. Dent is released.[1] You can use your judgement about whether to use this with Col Ould or not. If Dent is released without it it will be better to say nothing about Pryor & let him go off parole same as any other prisoner.

U. S. GRANT
Lt Genl

Telegram received, Ord Papers, CU-B; copies, DLC-USG, V, 46, 74, 108; DNA, RG 108, Letters Sent. On Feb. 27, 1865, 8:00 P.M., Lt. Col. John E. Mulford telegraphed to USG. "Pryor arrived this evening, Shall I hold him, & inform Mr Ould how and Why—He has a pass from the President as follows 'Allow Roger A. Pryor to procede to Genl Grants Hd Qrs City Point for Exchg" ALS (telegram sent), *ibid.*, RG 107, Telegrams Collected (Unbound). *O.R.*, II, viii, 313. On the same day, USG telegraphed to Mulford. "Detain R. A. Prior and ascertain if John Dent is to be released, If he is, you need not say anything about the cause of detention, nor need you detain him after you know that fact, If you get no satisfactory reply send Prior back here under guard" Copies, DLC-USG, V, 46, 74, 108; DNA, RG 108, Letters Sent. On the same day, Mulford telegraphed to USG. "Two telegrams recvd. I will take care of Pryor" ALS (telegram sent), *ibid.*, RG 107, Telegrams Collected (Unbound).

On Feb. 28, USG telegraphed to Mulford. "You may send Prior through with the first prisoners sent off, Speak to him however about John Dent and say to him that he has been promised his freedom so often that I had thought of detaining him until Dent was released On reflection however I thought it better to trust and wait," Copies, DLC-USG, V, 46, 74, 108; DNA, RG 108, Letters Sent. *O.R.*, II, viii, 317. On March 1, 10:00 A.M., Mulford telegraphed to USG. "Your despatch received, I am glad of your decission, Pryor does not yet know that ~~I am de~~ he has been detained, I *pursuaded* him yesterday to remain & was waiting until I could hear from Ould to whom I wrote a private note yesterday in Dents case & I realey have strong hopes that it will result in the release of Mr Dent—I sent Capt Hewitt Lewis to you this morning," ALS (telegram sent), DNA, RG 107, Telegrams Collected (Unbound). *O.R.*, II, viii, 320. On March 2, 5:30 P.M., Mulford telegraphed to USG. "John Dent is with me will be on

board my boat by Four Oclock, He is well I have no boat to send him down"
ALS (telegram sent), DNA, RG 107, Telegrams Collected (Unbound).

Also on March 2, USG telegraphed to Mulford. "Transfer all the sick prisoners to the steamer New York and march the balance through so as to relieve
all the other transports." ALS (telegram sent), Kohns Collection, NN; copies,
DLC-USG, V, 74; USG 3. On the same day, Mulford telegraphed to USG. "The
New York is and has been filled with sick I have made arrangements to send
them through tomorrow and will release four steamers. I had fourteen hundred
sick & disabled men here this morning have sent about five hundred off today.
Shall send others tomorrow. I am doing all I can to relieve the transportation
sent me" Telegram received (at 11:00 P.M.), DNA, RG 108, Letters Received.

1. On Dec. 26, 1864, Lt. Col. Frederick T. Dent wrote to "W D W Barnard
or James O Fallon 5th Avanue Hotel New York." "An order from our Secretary
of War to Col Mulford to obtain the release of John C Dent has been given. All
has been done that can be—we may get him when the exchange takes place at
Aikins—I have written Amanda" ALS, PCarlA. On Jan. 8, 1865, Dent wrote
to C.S.A. Brig. Gen. William N. R. Beall. "Your note of 5th inst is just received.
Gen Grant was present when it was placed in my hands and on reading it I
handed it to him for his perusal—he desired me to say to you. 'that the order
was given to receive the cotton in Mobile bay—a note was received from Judge
Olds some time since saying that the cotton was at Mobile ready for the Ships
but no order had been received by the federal officers in Mobile bay to receive
and transport it—the General immediately telegraphed to the Sec of War and
received in answer 'that the order to receive and transport the cotton to New
York had been given—and a duplicate order had just been forwarded' the General desires me to further say that he thinks the cotton will soon arrive in New
York I regret that any thing should have occurred such as you relate in your
letter, and cannot see what could have influenced the Sec of War to give the order
for your going to Lafayette of course it is not my place to discuss the official
acts of my superiors—still I may regret that it was deemed necessary—thank you
for your kind offer in relation to my brother John C Dent—he is charged as being
the lesee of a plantation—which is not the case—a young man of Louisiana,
whose plantation was raided negroes & stock all gone came to my Brother and
proposed as he had no means to work the plantation conjointing—to this my
Brother consented and furnished the means and commenced to put in a crop—
when he was captured by a gurrilla party taken to Mobile and from there to
Columbia S C—where he has been placed in close confinement in the same cell
with negroes and convicts—I have had the power frequently to have retaliated,
but never the will—I imagine that had he not have been a brother-in law of Lt
Gen Grant he would have been exchanged long ago—every offer that could be
has been made until I despair effecting an exchange may I ask you to obtain
authority to have Major Norman Fitz Hugh paroled and take him as one of your
assistants—I learn he is suffering his lungs being affected—Cousin Loo I know
would be much pleased to see you she is living in Burlington New Jersey"
ALS, Museum of the Confederacy, Richmond, Va. On Feb. 23, Dent wrote to his
wife. "I have put Norman's and Carr's names on the list for exchange Mulford
will very soon order them down. he did not hesitate a moment when I told him
that my wife was anxious for the exchange of her brother in-law and an old
friend who had proved himself such in storm and fire on the Pacific—but said
you might regard it as settled and registered their names in the order of officers

to be sent down—are you satisfied   I do not know when the order will go up for
them but I am going up to Varina to meet John C Dent to morrow and will see
Mulford and learn when N & C will leave Fort Delaware—and let you know by
letter or telegraph—John has been in Richmond some four days   could not come
down on the Reb truce boat because it was overloaded with officers—so had to
wait until next boat   he will be down for certain tomorrow—is coming down with
Judge Olds   mulford telegraphed for me to come up tomorrow to meet him—
. . ." ALS, John D. Burt, Redwood City, Calif. See *O.R.*, II, viii, 381.

To Commanding Officer, Wilson's Wharf

City Point Va Feby 27th [*1865*]

Com'dg Officer
Wilson Wharf

Please send out a party of men to try and find Capt Mason who
left Harrisons Landing yesterday with a body of Cavalry, to scout
towards the Chickahominy and communicate to him the following
message

A ~~party~~ number of the enemy scouts are at Jones Bridge,   A
party of our prisoners escaped from Richmond. on Friday[1] and
Saturday night's and were closely pursued by the enemy,   The
impression among the people of Charles City C, H, is that our
men are concealed on the other side of the Chickahominy near the
"Forge"

U. S. Grant
Lieutenant General

Copies, DLC-USG, V, 46, 74, 108; DNA, RG 108, Letters Sent. *O.R.*, I, xlvi,
part 2, 723.

1. Feb. 24, 1865.

To Edwin M. Stanton

City Point, Va, Feb. 28th *1865*

Hon. E. M. Stanton,
Sec. of War,
Sir:

Col. Tal. P. Shaffner, the bearer of this, who has had great
experiance in recent European Wars in Mining, in the Manufac-

tory of fuses and in the use and application of Electricity to the explosion of Mines, torpedoes and &c. has spent a couple of days here in visiting our lines and in explaining his practice to our Engineer officers. They are much pleased with it and believe we may derive practical advantage from the use of his inventions.—I would respectfully recommend that Col. Shaffner be allowed to bring his Machinery to City Point for the purpose of experimenting under the direction of the Engineer and Ordnance Officers in the field.

Col. S. will explain to you that the Rebels have been using instruments for exploding torpedoes, fuses, and even guns, that are manufactured at no other place but the Government work shop in England. The fuses and instruments are the same he proposes to give us the benefit of, not to sell any patent.

I have sent orders to Gn. Schofield to send some fuses, identified as those captured at Wilmington, for the purpose of fixing the fact that shops in England, controlled entirely by the Govt. have been manufacturing for the Rebels.[1] I do not know but they may have the right but it is not in accordance with their professed neutrality. Private individuals might do this, but for the British Government to be aiding our enemies is a different thing.

Very respectfully
your obt. svt.
U. S. GRANT
Lt. Gn.

ALS, DLC-Edwin M. Stanton. Taliaferro P. Shaffner, born in Va. in 1818, was an inventor active in the development of telegraphic communication and conducted experiments with nitroglycerin. See *SMD*, 35-1-263. On Feb. 27, 1865, Shaffner, City Point, wrote to USG. "I have been requested by Maj. Michil, Chief Engineer &c to give a brief statement respecting my system of Artillery Mining, and with that view I transmit you this note. 1st The Apparatuses employed by me are Magneto-Electric, and ignite a mine at any desired number of miles. It is portable and can be carried with one hand and can be operated at any moment & in any weather. 2d The wires I have can be used at all times, in cold or hot weather and not liable to be damaged by handling 3d My fuses are exceedingly sensitive and will explode without the possibility of a failure to ignite at the precise moment. 4th The arrangement of my fuses will ignite any desired quantity of powder *at the same instant* & produce the combustion of *all* the powder. 5th An apparatus will explode instantly, at least six mines at the same instant. There are other advantages that need not be mentioned at present. The whole of these articles are now in New York, sufficient for the service before Richmond and can be brought here in a few days if desired. I desire to have the articles properly delivered to the Chief of the Engineers and will give all necessary information respecting the operating of them. In this matter I do not seek for any remuneration, and will be pleased to serve the government by giving full explanations respecting these modern inventions and discoveries, having fully developed them in Military services. I would respectfully request that this statement bᵧe transmitted to the Chief of Engineer, that he may inform you whether or not his department of the service requires the articles and information. . . . N B. I desire to remark, that I do not propose any plan for excavating for the mine, and I only contemplate the introduction of the plan for instantaneously igniting a mine in land or water, and for *burning all the powder* of any number of mines, & of any quantity of powder, for the greatest possible destruction of the objective point." LS, DNA, RG 108, Letters Received. On March 3, Secretary of War Edwin M. Stanton wrote to the "Secretary of the Treasury." "I respectfully request you will give orders for the release from the Custom House in New York, without payment of duties, of the articles enumerated in the list herewith enclosed, which are intended exclusively for the United States Military Service, by the owner, Colonel T. P. Shaffner & are desired by Lt. Gen Grant for experiments at City Pt. Va" Copy, *ibid.*, RG 94, Letters Received, 442W 1865.

On March 22, USG endorsed the report of a board of officers appointed to investigate Shaffner's "System of Artillery Mining." "The recommendations of the board of officers on Col. Tal. P. Shaffner's system of artillery mining—that it be adopted by the U. S. Government—is approved and respectfully forwarded for the action of the Secretary of War. In our ports and harbors this system can undoubtedly be made of incalculable value as a defence in case of war with foreign nations." Copies, DLC-USG, V, 58; (printed) DNA, RG 107, Letters Received from Bureaus. On March 28, Shaffner wrote to USG. "The articles that will be required by the Engineers of the armies before Richmond, to successly apply my system of military mining,—as approved by the Board of Officers appointed to examine the same,—will be: viz: 1st About fifteen miles of the india rubber insulated wire, 2d Four apparatus 3d About 1000 fuses 4th Materials for making joints, and a few tools. The above articles I can have procured for the Armies within this week, if authorised to do so. If acceptable I will be gratified to give my services to the Engineers in assisting them in practically applying the system in case of necessity before Richmond." LS, *ibid.*, RG 108, Letters Received. On the same day, Lt. Col. Theodore S. Bowers issued Special Orders No. 63 authorizing the supplies. Copies, DLC-USG, V, 57, 63, 65.

On April 9, 1866, Shaffner wrote to President Andrew Johnson. "For many years past, I have been experimenting in Europe and America, to determine a system for the application of Torpedoes and Military Mines for Offensive and Defensive measures in war. The most of my operations have been in Russia, Denmark and Sweden, always conditional that I should be at liberty to make known the results to my own country, though held by them as secrets and obtained by an expenditure of nearly a quarter of a million of dollars. Believing that I could be of service to my country and anxious to partake in some manner in its defense against the rebellion, other than the assistance given our Diplomatic Agents, I abandoned my great enterprises in Europe and purchased about ten thousand dollars ($10.000) worth of materials suitable for Torpedo and Military Mining purposes, and came home early last year, to enter the service during the war—having closed my business affairs and properly provided for my family. I did not wait for an appointment at Washington, nor did I seek for any, but went immediately to Lt. General Grant and offered myself as a useful man, subject to the orders of the officers in the service or otherwise, at my own expense, and my inventions I offered without price. A Board of Officers was appointed to examine the System, and the report (accompanying) recognized my inventions to be of *great value*. I was invited to co-operate with the officers of the two Armies, (James and Potomac) and I immediately prepared for the campaign. The early termination of the war prevented me from rendering the service that I have contemplated. Besides these inventions, applicable in the field, I have others of importance, for Harbor defenses, such for example (amongst others of equal value) as the determining the position of a vessel, three miles distant, within 30 seconds. I attain this end by the aid of electricity, a branch of physics developed by me in the art of war., more than, perhaps, all other men, and I am anxious to prove them by actual experiments, with apparatuses and materials in detail at my own expense. As an appreciation for my past services and other considerations, I would respectfully request that an official position be given me, with a proper and just Brevet rank; and I will then be pleased to serve under the orders of the Board of Officers in Harbor defenses, even with or without compensation." LS, DNA, RG 107, Letters Received from Bureaus. On April 10, USG endorsed this letter. "Respectfully forwarded to the Secretary of War. I think it would be desirable to have the information of Col. Shafner made available to the Board of officers, to which the matter of torpedoes and similar subjects has been referred; but I know of no way in which brevet rank can be conferred without a real rank on which to base it." ES, *ibid.*

1. On March 19, 1865, USG wrote to Secretary of State William H. Seward. "With this I have the honor of forwarding to you, specimens of fuse's captured at Fort Fisher N, C, together with the certificate of Lieut, Col, O, E, Babcock, A, D, C, on my Staff that they were so captured, and the statement of Col, Tal, P, Shaffner that the same were manufactured at the 'Woolwich Arsenal', England an Arsenal owned and run by the British Government" Copies, DLC-USG, V, 46, 75, 108; DNA, RG 108, Letters Sent. *O.R.*, I, xlvi, part 3, 38. On March 21, Seward wrote to USG. "I have received your letter of the 19th instant on the subject of certain fuses sapposed to have been furnished to the insurgents by Professor Abel who is said to be employed by the British government at Woolwich arsenal. In reply, I have to state that a copy of your communication and the samples of the fuses which accompanied it have been sent to Mr Adams at London, with an instruction directing him to ask the attention of Earl Russell to the matter and to express our expectation that, if the charge should prove to be well founded Professor Abel will be made sensible of the displeasure of that government." LS, DNA, RG 108, Letters Received.

To Bvt. Brig. Gen. William Hoffman

From City Point Va February 28 *1864*5.

BR GEN W HOFFMAN

We will have a large number of prisoners left after exchanging for all we have in the south   Hold all guerrillas and such other prisoners at it will be objectionable to turn loose to the last. When all our prisoners are released a settlement will be made showing how many men we owe and that number will be delivered only. I am now informed that deliveries are going on at Welmington at the rate of two thousand 2000 a day—

U S GRANT
Lieut Gen

Telegram received (at 7:20 P.M.), DNA, RG 107, Telegrams Collected (Bound); *ibid.*, Telegrams Collected (Unbound); *ibid.*, RG 249, Letters Received; copies, *ibid.*, RG 108, Letters Sent; DLC-USG, V, 46, 74, 108; USG 3. *O.R.*, II, viii, 317. Also on Feb. 28, 1865, USG telegraphed to Bvt. Brig. Gen. William Hoffman. "I have just learned that the rebels are delivering two thousand (2000) of our men daily at Welmington I shall probably know tomorrow if this is so—in which case I shall want the prisoners sent down I will let you know as soon as I can ascertain the truth of the report—" Telegram received (at 9:50 P.M.), DNA, RG 107, Telegrams Collected (Bound); *ibid.*, RG 249, Letters Received; copies, *ibid.*, RG 108, Letters Sent; DLC-USG, V, 46, 74, 108; USG 3.

On the same day, Hoffman telegraphed to USG. "Transportation has been provided for prisoners of war from Fort-Delaware, It is required elsewhere and if prisoners are not soon to be forwarded for exchange I will return it to the QurMaster" ALS (telegram sent), DNA, RG 107, Telegrams Collected (Unbound); telegram received, *ibid.*, RG 108, Letters Received.

On March 2, 6:30 P.M., USG telegraphed to Hoffman. "You may commence forwarding Rebel prisoners for Exchange." ALS (telegram sent), Kohns Collection, NN; telegram received (at 9:40 P.M.), DNA, RG 107, Telegrams Collected (Bound); *ibid.*, RG 249, Letters Received. *O.R.*, II, viii, 329.

To Maj. Gen. Henry W. Halleck

(Cipher)   City Point, Va, Feb.y 28th *1865* [*11:30* P.M.]
MAJ. GEN. HALLECK, WASHINGTON.

I do not know that there is any objection to Gen. Hancock having his Hd Qrs. at Martinsburg but nothing should be brought away from Winchester except in case on necessity until it is known that Sheridan will not return. The probabilities are decidedly in favor of Sheridan returning to Winchester with his command.

U. S. GRANT
Lt. Gn

ALS (telegram sent), IHi; telegram received (at 11:30 P.M.), DNA, RG 393, Middle Military Div., Telegrams Received. *O.R.*, I, xlvi, part 2, 728.

To Lt. Col. John E. Mulford

City Point Va, Feby 28th 1865

Lt, Col, Mulford

Care, Gen, Ord

If you have a Lt, Foote son of Senator Foote of Tenn—at Varina for exchange, detain him and send him here, His name is said to have appeared on the Rolls as Lt, Falls through mistake. If he should come with any other lot of prisoners hereafter the same order will be obsirved, His sister Mrs, Senator Stewart is desirous of seeing him before he goes back South,

U. S. Grant

L[ieu]t[.] G[en.]

Copies, DLC-USG, V, 46, 74, 108; DNA, RG 108, Letters Sent. On Feb. 28, 1865, Lt. Col. John E. Mulford telegraphed to USG. "Capt Hewitt is here will send him down today, Lieut Foot was passed through the lines this morning before your despatch reached me Have not seen Mr Ould today, nor do I expect to tomorrow, Delivered 1600 Confederate prisoners today" ALS (telegram sent), *ibid.*, RG 107, Telegrams Collected (Unbound).

At 10:40 a.m., Secretary of War Edwin M. Stanton had telegraphed to USG. "If Lieutenant Foote son of Senator Foote who recently came from Johnsons-island has not been exchanged please detain him so that his sister Mrs Stewart wife of the Senator of Nevada may [h]ave an interview with him. His name ~~may~~ is said to appear by mistake on the rolls as Lieutenant Falls." ALS (telegram sent), *ibid.*, Telegrams Collected (Bound); telegram received, *ibid.*, RG 108, Letters Received. *O.R.*, I, xlvi, part 2, 728. At 4:30 p.m., USG telegraphed to Stanton. "Lt, Foote was delivered to Rebel Authorities before the receipt of your dispatch, I regret to say," Copies, DLC-USG, V, 46, 74, 108; DNA, RG 108, Letters Sent.

On March 1, Stanton telegraphed to USG. "Mrs Stewart daughter of Mr Foote has by a series of accidents been prevented from seeing either her father or brother. Would there be any objection to giving Lt Foote notice to meet her ~~and to~~ at the place of exchange and allowing her to go there on the Flag of truce boat." ALS (telegram sent), *ibid.*, RG 107, Telegrams Collected (Bound); telegram received (at 12:20 p.m.), *ibid.*, RG 108, Letters Received. At 1:00 p.m., USG telegraphed to Stanton. "There will be no objection to Mrs, Stewart meeting her brother, I will send word at once to Lt, Foote that he will be allowed to visit our Flag of Truce Boat and will notify you when he will be there" Copies, DLC-USG, V, 46, 74, 108; DNA, RG 108, Letters Sent. On the same day, USG telegraphed to Mulford. "Please ask Col, Ould, to allow Lieut, Foote to visit our Flag Boat for the purpose of meeting his sister who is very anxious to see him and has been prevented doing so before by circumstances, Notify me if Foote may be expected" Copies, *ibid.* At 2:15 p.m., Mulford telegraphed to USG. "I will make application to Judge Ould tomorrow & notify you of his answer. I doubt if he can be brought down before the 3d o[r] 4th inst if at all" ALS (telegram sent), *ibid.*, RG 107, Telegrams Collected (Unbound); telegram received, *ibid.*, RG 108, Letters Received.

To Elihu B. Washburne

City Point, Va, Feb. 28th *1865*

DEAR WASHBURN,

Capt. A.[1] has arrived and for the present I assign him to duty with Gen. Ord who is badly off for Staff Officers and is very glad to secure his services.—Gratiot[2] has been every where and seems to enjoy himself very much   He is not atall in the way.—Mrs. Grant will remain here until some time after the 4th of March. She will be pleased to have Mrs. Washburn visit her here. I shall look for you down immediately after the 4th.

My regards to Mrs. W.—

Yours Truly
U. S. GRANT

ALS, MHi.
1. Capt. Charles B. Atchison. See letter to Elihu B. Washburne, July 23, 1864.
2. Gratiot Washburne, eldest son of Elihu B. Washburne.

To Edwin M. Stanton

City Point Va, March 1st 1865 [*1:30* P.M.]

HON, E, M, STANTON
SEC, OF WAR,
WASHINGTON

There are persons not connected with the Army who I have no objection to ~~having come~~ the visits of,   Any General Order on the subject would prohibit them,   Would it not answer to publish an order that all permits to visit the Armies must come from the Commanders themselves?

U. S GRANT
Lieut, General

Telegram, copies, DLC-USG, V, 46, 74, 108; DNA, RG 108, Letters Sent. *O.R.*, I, xlvi, part 2, 769. On March 1, 1865, 10:00 A.M., Secretary of War Edwin

M. Stanton telegraphed to USG. "If you will make an order that no persons male or female not connected with the service will be admitted within your lines from and after this date it will save you from an avalanch of visitors who will get down by hook or crook. I will on such order being made prohibit the issue of any passes Send me a copy of your orders" ALS (telegram sent), DNA, RG 107, Telegrams Collected (Bound); telegram received, *ibid.*, RG 108, Letters Received. *O.R.*, I, xlvi, part 2, 769.

To Maj. Gen. Henry W. Halleck

City Point Va, March 1st 1865 [*3:30* P.M.]

MAJ, GEN, HALLECK
WASHINGTON

Was not the order sent for Canby to organize two Corps, naming Steele and A, J, Smith as Commanders? I so understood, I am in receipt of a letter saying that Granger and Smith are the Commanders, If so, I despair of any good service being done,

U. S. GRANT
Lieut, Gen,

Telegram, copies, DLC-USG, V, 46, 74, 108; DNA, RG 108, Letters Sent. Printed as received at 4:15 P.M. in *O.R.*, I, xlviii, part 1, 1045. On March 2, 1865, 11:00 A.M., Maj. Gen. Henry W. Halleck telegraphed to USG. "Genl Canby was instructed to make Genl A. J Smith's command an Army corps; but no instructions, so far as I know, were given him in regard to Genl Granger. Your views in regard to the unfitness of Genls Hurlbut & Granger for an important command, as telegraphed to me, were forwarded to Genl Canby." ALS (telegram sent), DNA, RG 107, Telegrams Collected (Bound); telegram received, *ibid.*; *ibid.*, RG 108, Letters Received. *O.R.*, I, xlviii, part 1, 1055–56. At 12:30 P.M., USG telegraphed to Halleck. "I think orders should go to Canby to put Steele in Command of the new Corps formed which properly should be numbered 13th and A. J. Smith's 16th," Copies, DLC-USG, V, 46, 74, 108; DNA, RG 108, Letters Sent. Printed as received at 3:55 P.M. in *O.R.*, I, xlviii, part 1, 1056; *ibid.*, I, xlix, part 1, 864.

To Maj. Gen. George G. Meade

(Cipher)   City Point, Va, March 1st *1865* [*12:30* A.M.]

MAJ. GEN. MEADE,

If the report of the departure of two Divisions of Lee's Army can be verified we will try the assault in front of each Potter's &

Wilcox Divisions. I can bring over 15.000 men from North of the James to support them if necessary.

U. S. GRANT
Lt. Gen

ALS (telegram sent), Blumhaven Library & Gallery, Philadelphia, Pa.; copies, DLC-USG, V, 46, 74, 108; DNA, RG 108, Letters Sent; (2—dated March 2, 1865) Meade Papers, PHi. Dated March 2, 12:30 P.M., in *O.R.*, I, xlvi, part 2, 785. On March 1, 11:30 P.M., Maj. Gen. George G. Meade telegraphed to USG transmitting a copy of a telegram of 10:45 P.M. from Maj. Gen. Horatio G. Wright to Bvt. Maj. Gen. Alexander S. Webb. "Deserters just in report as follows. Lee gone south with Rhodes & Gordons Divisions leaving Johnson in command, Orders signed by latter having been published. No other troops moved. One a Sergeant was in Petersburg day before yesterday and saw six trains leave by S. S. Road loaded with Cotton & Tobacco   were hauling such property toward Depot   No artillery is known to have been moved from the lines in vicinity of their camp. They repeat the story of a new line which is now said to run from Drurys Bluff to some point on Roanoke River. Negroes employed on this line. This is camp rumor not traceable to any reliable source. Artillery horses said to be in very bad condition. Hardly able to draw the pieces. The shooting heard last night was done by order in their Brigade as stated by the Sergt who says he received the order for the men to cheer when the bands struck up. Reason not given. Could not have been in consequence of news rec'd or he should have heard of it. Says the only news from N C is a report that Sherman instead of marching on Charlotte is moving on Fayetteville and that Schofield was moving up the Cape Fear with troops and transports to form junction at that place. This report was brought by a man just returned to their army from N. C. who must have left about three days ago. The Sergt belongs to 11th N C and is worth examining"   Telegram received (at 11:50 P.M.), DNA, RG 108, Letters Received. *O.R.*, I, xlvi, part 2, 774.

At 11:00 P.M., Meade had telegraphed to USG. "Thirty deserters have been examined today—The only material information is that on the 27th Ulto Six guns were seen on the cars of the S. S. R. Rd marked Danville and 300 hogsheads of tobacco piled in one street, which informant undertood was to be destroyed—No change in position of troops, or movements reported." ALS (telegram sent), DNA, RG 393, Army of the Potomac, Telegrams Received; telegram received (at 11:00 P.M.), *ibid.*, RG 108, Letters Received. *O.R.*, I, xlvi, part 2, 770.

On March 2, 11:00 A.M. and 11:30 A.M., Meade telegraphed to USG. "A critical examination of the deserters reported last night by Gen Wright goes to show that the statement made by the Sergeant 11th N. C. amounts only to the fact the Rhodes Div. left its Camp north of the Appomattox prior to the 26th Ulto. & on that day the Sergeant was in the old Camp & saw some stragglers who said the Div had gone to N-C. on the 26th   We received positive information that Rhodes was encamped at Sutherland station on the S S R R   No deserter has been recd from Rhodes since the 26th, nor has any positive information in connection with this Div. or that of Gordons been received since that date & from all I can learn the three Divisions may have been sent away   That fact is as yet only based on camp rumors, founded on their known change of position to sutherland station. Thirty deserters are reported as coming in to our lines and received by Provost marshal Gen for the 24 hours preceeding 12 oclock of last night. No movements reported by them except the above rumor by the sergt 11th N-C. of the departure of Rhodes & Gordon" "I have sent you a despatch from which you will perceive the reported departure of two of Lees Divisions is not only not confirmed but is by no means reliable: neverthless I have directed the Chief Engr to visit the proposed point of attack and confer with Generals Potter & McLaughlin and shall make my preliminary arrangements to attack in case your orders should require it or my judgement justify my recommending it: This judgement will be based on the facts reported by the Chief Engr which I will lay before you as soon as recd. I am of the opinion I have force enough under my Comd. at present, as the question is not so much one of numbers as of the probability of carrying entrenched lines—These once carried and overcome I have men enough to meet the whole of Lees army" Telegrams received (the first at 11:30 P.M.), DNA, RG 108, Letters Received; copies, *ibid.*, RG 393, Army of the Potomac, Letters Sent; (2) Meade Papers, PHi. *O.R.*, I, xlvi, part 2, 784–85. At 9:00 P.M., Meade telegraphed to USG. "I forward report just received from Prov. Mar. Dept. of examination of deserters today." ALS (telegram sent), DNA, RG 94, War Records Office, Army of the Potomac; telegram received, *ibid.*, RG 108, Letters Received. *O.R.*, I, xlvi, part 2, 785. The enclosure, indicating no major movement of C.S.A. forces, is *ibid.*

To Charles W. Ford

City Point, Va, March 1st *1865*

DEAR FORD,

I have just heard that the land which I sent you $1500 00 to buy in at land sale is not to be sold until November next. I do not like to tax you too much but as I cannot attend to the matter myself will you do me the favor to enquire if this is so? If it is I would like you to return me the draft sent to you by J. R. Jones so that I can pay up and stop interest.

Mrs. Grant and Jesse have been with me for the last six weeks.

All that is now wanted to make the aspect of affairs look bright and cheering is good news from Sherman. I feel no doubt of the result with him but cut loose as he is I necessarily feel anxious. As long as Sherman is individually safe his Army will be. But an unlucky ball to touch him would materially mar the prospects of his Army. Sherman has immortalized his name and that of the Army he commands. It would be too unfortunate now to have anything to occur to prevent him, and those under him, enjoy their laurels. My anxiety will be intense until I hear directly from Sherman. That will be but a few days hence however I hope.

Yours Truly
U. S. GRANT

ALS, USG 3.

To Isaac N. Morris

City Point, Va, March 1st *1865*

HON. I. N. MORRIS,

Persons have been permitted to pass through our lines recently by higher authority than my own, and I presume without detriment to the public service. I can not therefore withold my permission for your friend, whose name I have forgotten, to have an equal privilege.

This letter will be his authority to visit these Hd Qrs. where he will receive the necessary pass to go his way.

Very Truly yours,
U. S. GRANT
Lt. Gn.

ALS, Mrs. F. C. Baumgart, Livingston, Mont. On March 8, 1865, Isaac N. Morris, Quincy, Ill., added an endorsement. "My friend to whom Gen'l Grant referrs in his letter is J. M. A Drake Esqr. of La Prairie, Adams County Illinois, to whom I have handed this as evidence of his identity" AES, *ibid.*

To Abraham Lincoln

City Point, Va, March 2d 1865 [*1:00* P.M.]

A. LINCOLN PRESIDENT, WASHINGTON,

Richmond papers are received daily. No bullitins were ~~sent~~ sent Teusday or Wednsday because there was not an item of either good or bad news in them. There is every indication that Sherman is perfectly safe. I am looking every day for direct news from him.

U. S. GRANT
Lt. Gen.

ALS (telegram sent), OClWHi; telegram received (marked as sent at 12:30 P.M., received at 3:55 P.M.), DNA, RG 107, Telegrams Collected (Bound); DLC-Robert T. Lincoln. *O.R.*, I, xlvi, part 2, 780. On March 2, 1865, 10:00 A.M., President Abraham Lincoln telegraphed to USG. "You have not sent contents of Richmond papers for Tuesday or Wednesday—Did you not receive them? If not, does it indicate anything?" ALS (telegram sent), DNA, RG 107, Telegrams Collected (Bound); telegram received, *ibid.*, RG 108, Letters Received. *O.R.*, I, xlvi, part 2, 780. Lincoln, *Works*, VIII, 329.

On March 3, 11:00 A.M., USG telegraphed to Secretary of War Edwin M. Stanton. "Although I am not possitively advised of the fact I think Sherman and Schofield are in communication and both therefore perfectly secure." ALS (telegram sent), OClWHi; copies, DLC-USG, V, 46, 74, 108; DLC-Edwin M. Stanton; DNA, RG 108, Letters Sent. *O.R.*, I, xlvii, part 2, 660.

To Edwin M. Stanton

(Cipher) City Point, Va, March 2d *1865* [*8:30* P.M.]
HON. E. M. STANTON, SEC. OF WAR, WASHINGTON
The reports shew in Dept. of Washington 25.442[1] effective men and Dept. of West Va, 13.946, exclusive of one Division of 19th Corps and 2000 effective mounted Cavalry left by Sheridan. The Rebels are receiving many valuable supplies from Northern cities by the Fredericksburg road no doubt and necessarily picket the Rappahannock to protect this trafic. Col. Wells[2] or Gen. Augur should find out what force there is on the Rappahannock. I shall clear out that country as soon as transports can be got to move the men and it stops raining for a day or two.

U. S. GRANT
Lt. Gn.

ALS (telegram sent), OClWHi; copies, DLC-USG, V, 46, 74, 108; DNA, RG 108, Letters Sent. *O.R.*, I, xlvi, part 2, 782. On March 2, 1865, Secretary of War Edwin M. Stanton twice telegraphed to USG, the second time at 4:00 P.M. "A telegraphic despatch received this morning that Bull town south of

Parkersburg was captured this morning and that our pickets were driven in at Elizabeth about forty miles from Parkersburg. I am not advised what forces ~~are~~ we have in that region if any." ALS (telegram sent), DNA, RG 107, Telegrams Collected (Bound); telegram received, *ibid.*, Telegrams Collected (Unbound); (at 7:10 P.M.) *ibid.*, RG 108, Letters Received. *O.R.*, I, xlvi, part 2, 781. "The following telegram has just been received. Every thing has been stripped so bare here that you may be runing great risk." ALS (telegram sent), DNA, RG 107, Telegrams Collected (Bound); telegram received, *ibid.*, RG 108, Letters Received. *O.R.*, I, xlvi, part 2, 781. The enclosure, reporting a brigade of C.S.A. cav. under Maj. Gen. Fitzhugh Lee picketing the Rappahannock, is *ibid*. See following telegram.

1. Numerals not in USG's hand written over his original numerals. The figure is 24,442 in USG's letterbooks.
2. Henry H. Wells, appointed col., 26th Mich., as of March 30, 1864, served as provost marshal, Defenses South of the Potomac, in the Dept. of Washington, Maj. Gen. Christopher C. Augur.

To Edwin M. Stanton

City Point Va, March 2d 1865 [*10:30* P.M.]

Hon, E, M, Stanton
Secy of War, Washington

My dispatch of this afternoon answers yours of 9.30 this evening, I do not think it possible for Lee to send anything towards, Washington unless it should be a Brigade of Cavalry, Augurs returns show a good force of Cavalry to meet anything of the kind besides a large Infantry force, The great number of deserters and refugees coming in daily enables us to learn if any considerable force starts off almost immediately as soon as it starts, Except in the neighborhood of Staunton there is not now North of the Chickahominy 5,000 rebel Soldiers including all the guards on the Central Rail road I have not sent a force to the Rappahannock, but shall do so as soon as possible

U., S, Grant
Lieut, Gen,

Telegram, copies, DLC-USG, V, 46, 74, 108; DNA, RG 108, Letters Sent. *O.R.*, I, xlvi, part 2, 782–83. On March 2, 1865, 9:00 P.M., Secretary of War Edwin M. Stanton telegraphed to USG. "~~D~~Have you sent any force towards the Rappahannock? If Lee has made any detachment in that direction ~~it~~ would it not be easy for him to put batteries on the Potomac to intercept transports, ~~with~~ ~~b~~ or even move on Alexandria and destroy the depots there. ~~I~~ Past disasters from stripping this Department of troops ~~from~~ ~~here~~ repeatedly have made me very solicitous in this matter and apprehensive of a surprise ~~ap~~ in our defenseless condition. [It] is a hazard to which the National Capitol should not again be exposed." ALS (telegram sent), DNA, RG 107, Telegrams Collected (Bound); telegram received (marked as sent at 9:30 P.M.), *ibid.*, RG 108, Letters Received. *O.R.*, I, xlvi, part 2, 782.

To Edwin M. Stanton

City Point, Va, March 2d *1865*

HON. E. M. STANTON,
SEC. OF WAR,
SIR:

If the returns I have of the troops in the Dept. of Washington are anything like correct there need not be the slightest apprehension for the safety of the Capital. At this time if Lee could spare any conciderable force it would be for the defence of points now threatened which are necessary for the very existence of his Army. He could not send off any large body without my knowing it. If they should move towards Washington that would be known also.

With the Cavalry Gen. Augur has at his command he can always have notice of the approach of any considerable body of men, and could dispose his force to meet their advance. The fact is I think the enemy are reaping such advantages by the way of the Fredericksburg road that they are anxious to avoid attracting attention in that direction.

I have ordered a force, mostly Infantry, to prepare to go up the Rappahannock, as soon as transportation can be got for them, for the purpose of breaking up this trade and shall try to have the road broken up at the same time. The force I sentd will draw everything the enemy has on the Potomac, below Alexandria, and on the Rappahannock, and will give General Augur a good opportunity of breaking the rail-road up to the Rapidann. I would direct the force sent from here to do that but it will be impossible for me to send any conciderable amount of Cavalry. Infantry cannot get there very well.

It will be necessary to have a good man in Command in West Va, and even then we cannot prevent occational parties getting in on the rail-road. I have recommended Gen. Crocker for that place but I believe he has not been ordered in from New Mexico. I wanted that done last Fall and supposed until a few days since that he had been ordered in.

Is there not a great mistake made in keeping a large number of Cavalrymen posted through the City of Washington? It seems to me one half the force of Cavalry in the Department is wasted in duties in no way tending to the protection of the place. I may be mistaken and only call attention to see whether this is not so.

At this time, ~~and~~ not until the roads get good, do I think there is ~~not~~ the slightest danger of the enemy attempting to blockade the Potomac. They have not got the Artillery horses nor men to spare for such an enterprise. On the whole I think there is not the slightest need of apprehension except from a dash of a few mounted men into Alexandria, and with proper watchfulness this ought not to occur.

> Very respectfully
> your obt. svt.
> U. S. GRANT
> Lt. Gen

ALS, DLC-Edwin M. Stanton. *O.R.*, I, xlvi, part 2, 781–82.

To Maj. Gen. Henry W. Halleck

City Point March 2d 1865 [*9:00* P.M.]

MAJ, GEN, HALLECK
WASHINGTON

Has, Gen, Crocker been ordered in from New Mexico? If he has not, please order him in at once,   He would be invaluable in the command of West Va, An active traveling General is wanted who would visit all his posts in the Department, I think it will be advisable to order Gen, Carroll to report to Gen, Hancock for the temporary command of that Department,

U. S. GRANT

Lieut, General

Telegram, copies, DLC-USG, V, 46, 74, 108; DNA, RG 108, Letters Sent. *O.R.*, I, xlvi, part 2, 784. On March 3, 1865, 11:00 A.M., Maj. Gen. Henry W. Halleck telegraphed to USG. "Genl Carroll was ordered with Genl Hancock on sunday last. Genl Crocker was ordered East some time ago, but probably has not been able to make the journey in the winter. Vessels sent from here to cape Fear River are sent back to discharge at Beaufort. If a change has been made in this respect, notice should be given to the Qr. Mr. Dept in order to save time & expense." ALS (telegram sent), DNA, RG 107, Telegrams Collected (Bound); telegram received, *ibid.*; *ibid.*, RG 108, Letters Received. *O.R.*, I, xlvi, part 2, 802; *ibid.*, I, xlvii, part 2, 660. On the same day, Maj. Gen. Winfield S. Hancock, Winchester, Va., twice telegraphed to USG, the first time transmitting a telegram from Brig. Gen. Samuel S. Carroll. "At Parkersburg is Fort Foreman [*Boreman*] with five pieces of artillery and a garrison of 170 men, have ordered down the river from Wheeling three companies 125 men and from this place a regt. of 500 men which will give a force of 790 men. At Grafton there are six (6) pieces of artillery and 150 men. I have ordered it reinforced by 300 men from Clarkesburg 22 miles off making the force four hundred & fifty men. The approaches to Clarkesburg are defended by 488 men at Bulltown 5 miles South of Clarkesburg, by 385 men at Phillippei 17 miles south of Grafton, by 600 men at Beverly 25 miles south of Phillippi, by 692 men at Buckhannon 28 miles south of Clarkesburg. I consider Grafton & Clarksburg safe, perfectly. Am informed by the Comdg officer at Clarkesburg that a force of 150 rebels are at Elizabeth 22 miles South of Parkersburg & a force of the same strength at Glennville 25 miles south of West Union on the Kanawha. The force at Bulltown have been notified of this fact and will be on the watch for them. I have sent Gen. Lightburn to Clarkesburg" "A scouting party I sent to strasburg has just returned. They saw no enemy & heard of none. Citizens report that sheridan entered Staunton yesterday having met no enemy in force on his march" Telegrams received (the second at 6:00 P.M.), DNA, RG 108, Letters Received. *O.R.*, I, xlvi, part 2, 819.

On April 22, Maj. Gen. Grenville M. Dodge, St. Louis, telegraphed to Brig. Gen. John A. Rawlins. "Gen Crocker has arrived here from New Mexico sick— He is ordered to report to Gen Thomas but can go no further Please change his order to report to me—I will send him home to wait dicision on his resignation which he will send on He will have to go out of the Service Would like to be mustered out if that is possible Answer" Telegram received (at 2:50 P.M.), DNA, RG 94, ACP, C733 CB 1863; *ibid.*, RG 107, Telegrams Collected (Bound). On the same day, Bvt. Col. Theodore S. Bowers endorsed this telegram. "Respectfully forwarded to the Adjutant General of the Army with the request that Gen Crocker's orders be changed—to report to Gen. Dodge instead of General Thomas." AES, *ibid.*, RG 94, ACP, C733 CB 1863. Brig. Gen. Marcellus M. Crocker died on Aug. 26, 1865.

To Maj. Gen. Henry W. Halleck

City Point, Va., March 2, 1865

MAJOR GENL H. W. HALLECK,
CHIEF OF STAFF.

Lieut Col C. B. Comstock and Lt Col O. E. Babcock were at the dates of their appointments as Aides-de-camp, Asst Inspectors General with the rank of Lt.-Col, and as such I am informed are announced in the army Register for 1864, instead of aides-de-camp on my staff. Will you please have this corrected in the Army Register if it is not too late, & if necessary to enable you to do so have an order issued relieving them from duty in the Inspector General's Dept. to date from the date of their appointment as aides-de-camp.

U. S. GRANT
Lt. Genl.

Telegram, copies, DNA, RG 94, ACP, C154 CB 1865; *ibid.*, RG 108, Letters Sent; DLC-USG, V, 46, 74, 108. Printed as received at 10:10 P.M. in *O.R.*, I, xlvi, part 2, 784.

On Feb. 17, 1865, 11:00 A.M., USG had telegraphed to Secretary of War Edwin M. Stanton. "I would respectfully ask whether Comstock is a Brevet Brigadier in the regular army or in the volunteer service? If the latter I would recommend him for promotion to the full rank of Brigadier Volunteers" Telegram received (at noon), DNA, RG 94, ACP, C860 CB 1863; copies, *ibid.*, RG 107, Telegrams Received in Cipher; *ibid.*, RG 108, Letters Sent; DLC-USG, V, 46, 74, 108. *O.R.*, I, xlvi, part 2, 574. On Feb. 18, Col. James A. Hardie telegraphed to USG. "Lieut. Col. Comstock was recommended nominated and confirmed for Brevet Brigadier General in the Volunteer Service. I fear there are no [v]acancies now in the full Brigadiers to which he could be appointed." ALS (telegram sent), DNA, RG 107, Telegrams Collected (Bound); copy, *ibid.*, RG 94, ACP, C860 CB 1863. *O.R.*, I, xlvi, part 2, 584.

On March 11, Bvt. Lt. Col. Samuel F. Chalfin, AGO, wrote to USG. "I have the honor to acknowledge the receipt of your telegram of the 2d instant referred by Major General Halleck to this office, and to inform you in reply that Lieut Cols C. B. Comstock and O. E. Babcock are borne on the records of this Office as Aides de-Camp on your staff, and also that no register for the year 1864 has yet been published." LS, DNA, RG 108, Letters Received.

To Brig. Gen. John W. Turner

City Point, 12 p m, March 2d 1865

GEN-TURNER

CHIEF OF STAFF, A. J.

I want an expedition to consist of one picked brigade of infantry and one regiment of cavalry prepared to send up the Rappahannock as soon as the Quarter Master Department can furnish water transportation for them. They will take ten days rations with them and with such supplies as they can collect from the country will be prepared to remain absent longer if necessary. The object is to break up the illicit trade of the Northern Neck, and if they can, to break up the Fredericksburg railroad. An officer of experience and reliability will be necessary to take command. When he is designated more particular instructions will be given from these Headquarters

U. S. GRANT
Lieut. Genl

Telegram received, DNA, RG 107, Telegrams Collected (Unbound); copies, *ibid.*, RG 94, Turner-Baker Papers, 3941T; *ibid.*, RG 108, Letters Sent; DLC-USG, V, 46, 74, 108. *O.R.*, I, xlvi, part 2, 790. John W. Turner, born in N. Y. in 1833, USMA 1855, appointed col. as of May 3, 1862, served as chief commissary for Maj. Gen. Benjamin F. Butler, Dept. of the Gulf, and as chief of staff for Maj. Gen. Quincy A. Gillmore, Dept. of the South, before appointment as chief of staff for Butler as of Nov. 20, 1864. He continued in that position under Maj. Gen. Edward O. C. Ord until assigned command of the 2nd Div., 24th Army Corps, as of March 20, 1865.

USG acted upon information supplied by Samuel Ruth, superintendent of the Richmond, Fredericksburg and Potomac Railroad, a U.S. secret agent, who disclosed C.S.A. plans to trade tobacco for bacon. Meriwether Stuart, "Samuel Ruth and General R. E. Lee," *Virginia Magazine of History and Biography*, 71, 1 (Jan., 1963), 102–3. On Feb. 22, Col. George H. Sharpe had written to Lt. Col. Theodore S. Bowers. "By our scouts and agents we have news from Richmond up to yesterday noon. . . . Another friend writes 'you are now feeding us with meal from Fredericksburgh and Port Royal; Mosby's five Companies on the Northern Neck have sent us bacon and beef by the way of Port Royal and the Fredericksburg Rail Road.' " Copy, DNA, RG 94, Turner-Baker Papers, 3113T.

On March 3, 2:00 P.M., USG telegraphed to Secretary of War Edwin M. Stanton. "I send an expedition ef up the Rappahannock to-morrow If Gen, Augur sends out to destroy the railroad his forces should start by the 6th"

Copies, DLC-USG, V, 46, 74, 108; DNA, RG 108, Letters Sent. *O.R.*, I, xlvi, part 2, 801. See letters to Col. Samuel H. Roberts, March 4, 1865; Bvt. Maj. Gen. Montgomery C. Meigs, June 27, 1865.

To Edwin M. Stanton

City Point Va, March 3d 1865 [*12:30* P.M.]

HON, E, M, STANTON
SEC, OF WAR, WASHINGTON

A great many deserters are coming in from the enemy bringing their Arms with them expecting the pay for them as the means of a little ready cash,   Would there be any objection to amending my order so as to allow this? Now that the sources of supply are cutt off from the enemy it is a great object to deprive the enemy of present supply of Arms

U. S. GRANT
Lieut, General

Telegram, copies, DLC-USG, V, 46, 74, 108; DNA, RG 108, Letters Sent. *O.R.*, I, xlvi, part 2, 800–1. On March 3, 1865, 2:00 P.M., Secretary of War Edwin M. Stanton telegraphed to USG. "There is no objection to your paying ~~deser~~ rebel deserters for their arms horses or any thing they bring in a full and fair price. That Kind of trade will not injure the service" ALS (telegram sent), DNA, RG 107, Telegrams Collected (Bound); telegram received (marked as sent at 1:30 P.M.), *ibid.*, RG 108, Letters Received. *O.R.*, I, xlvi, part 2, 801. At 11:30 A.M., Maj. Gen. George G. Meade telegraphed to USG. "Pro Mar Genl reports 36 deserters as received at these Hd Qurs up to mid night last night. Wright reports this morning 36 as coming into his lines last night. ~~Thse~~ these are not included in the above report of P M Genl as they have not yet reached these Hd Qurs. of these last—Wright reports 21 as bringing in their arms & as expecting pay for them under their construction of your order. I deem it of great impotance these arms should be paid for & would be glad to have authority to do so. Some price might be fixed say the contract prices of the Ordnance Dept for similar arms & Equipments—now that the sources of supply are cut off it is important to get away from the enemy all the arms we can" Telegram received (at 11:30 A.M.), DNA, RG 108, Letters Received; copies, *ibid.*, RG 393, Army of the Potomac, Letters Sent; Meade Papers, PHi. *O.R.*, I, xlvi, part 2, 803–4. On the same day, USG telegraphed to Meade. "The Ord. Dept. has no funds to pay for Arms but you may order the Provost Marshal to pay for them at such rate as you deem proper." ALS (telegram sent), Kohns Collection, NN; telegram received (at 12:20 P.M.), DNA, RG 94, War Records Office, Army of the Potomac. *O.R.*, I, xlvi, part 2, 804. At 1:40 P.M., Meade telegraphed to USG. "In addition to the thirty six deserters reported by Wright

as coming in last night Humphreys reports 18 p̶Parke 5 & Warren has just reported 3 making in all sixty two. Those reported by Warren have just come in
and they stated to Warren that a Brigade had been sent to Weldon about 3 days
ago. I will examine into this and report on their arrival at these Hd Qrs. I have
directed the P M Genl to pay for arms and accoutrements at the lowest Govt contract prices" Telegram received (at 1:45 P.M.), DNA, RG 108, Letters Received; copies, *ibid.*, RG 393, Army of the Potomac, Letters Sent; Meade Papers,
PHi. *O.R.*, I, xlvi, part 2, 804. On the same day, USG telegraphed to Meade and
Maj. Gen. Edward O. C. Ord. "You are authorized to order payment at a fair
valuation for Arms, Accoutrements or any other species of property brought in
by rebel deserters. Circulars to this effect may be distributed if if you desire it."
ALS (telegram sent), Scheide Library, Princeton, N. J.; telegram received, Ord
Papers, CU-B. Printed as received at 4:30 P.M. in *O.R.*, I, xlvi, part 2, 804. See
ibid., pp. 828–29.

On March 7, USG endorsed a letter of Brig. Gen. Alexander B. Dyer, chief
of ordnance, to Stanton concerning payment to deserters for arms. "Respy returned. It will be seen by reference to the enclosed order (S. O. 44 Mch. 4, 1865,
a u s) that payment has been ordered to deserters for arms & other property
brought into our lines by them. Previous to the date of said order, deserters were
not paid for arms, there being no authority for doing so. The Provost Marshal,
however, gave deserters memorandum reciepts for all arms delivered to him."
Copy, DLC-USG, V, 58.

To Edwin M. Stanton

City Point March 3d 1865 [3:00 P.M.]

HON, E, M, STANTON
SEC, OF WAR, WASHINGTON

Capt, Wilder[1] A, Q, M, has been ordered to report to the War
Dept, He is charged with receiving money from negroes for the
use of public property and giving no account of it, May he be
retained until an investigation can be had?

U, S, GRANT
Lieut, General

Telegram, copies, DLC-USG, V, 46, 74, 108; DNA, RG 108, Letters Sent. On
March 3, 1865, 12:30 P.M., Maj. Gen. Edward O. C. Ord, Fort Monroe, telegraphed to USG. "I find that Capt Wilder A. Q M has been receiving money
from negroes for the use of public property which money he denies any knowledge of. The order I gave Wilder to report for duty to Maj Plato has been
rescinded at the War Department and Wilder is directed to report in person at
the War Dep. This will prevent my holding him responsible or investigating
the fraud. Will you get authority from the Secretary to retain h̶i̶m̶ Capt. Wilder
until proper inquiry into his administration can be made" Telegram received,

ibid., Letters Received. On March 3, Secretary of War Edwin M. Stanton telegraphed to USG. "Captain Wilder will be detained here or sent back as you
prefer. I was not aware that there were any charges against him. His reputation
has been good" ALS (telegram sent), *ibid.*, RG 107, Telegrams Collected
(Bound); telegram received, *ibid.*, RG 108, Letters Received. USG drafted a
telegram to Ord at the foot of the telegram received. "The above dispatch just
received. Will you have Wilder sent back or will you send the charges." ADfS
(telegram sent), *ibid.*; telegram received (press), *ibid.*, RG 107, Telegrams
Collected (Bound); Ord Papers, CU-B. On the same day, Ord telegraphed to
USG. "Having now the time to do so I will examine carefully into the charges
against Capt Wilder—they may not turn out as represented and I will if the
matter is not serious send him to Washn to report ~~as the secretary directs—to
morrow~~ P. M—" ALS (telegram sent), *ibid.*; telegram received, DNA, RG
108, Letters Received.

On March 3, USG twice telegraphed to Ord, first at 10:00 A.M. "If Gordon's
Commission has not yet ~~been~~ adjourned I think it will be advisable to call before
it the Cashier of the National Bank Norfolk." "You can remain until to-morrow."
ALS (telegrams sent), Kohns Collection, NN; telegrams received (the first at
10:00 A.M.), Ord Papers, CU-B. The second is in *O.R.*, I, xlvi, part 2, 811.

1. Charles B. Wilder of Mass., appointed q. m. and capt. as of Feb. 19,
1863, was relieved as asst. superintendent of Negro affairs, District of the Peninsula, on Feb. 22, 1865. *Ibid.*, pp. 647–48. His finances received further attention
in *HED*, 42-3-27.

To Edwin M. Stanton

(Cipher)   City Point. Va. ~~Feby~~ Mar 3 *1864*[5]. [*6:00* P.M.]
HON. E. M. STANTON, SEC. OF WAR, WASHINGTON,

The following communication has just been received from
Gen. Lee. . . .[1]

Gen. Ord met Gen. Longstreet a few days since at the request
of the latter to arrange ~~to arrange~~ for the exchange of Citizen prisoners and prisoners of War improperly captured. He had my authority to do so and to arrange definitely for such as were confined
in his Dept. Arrangements for all others to be submitted for approval. A general conversation ensued on the subject of the War
and has induced the above letter. I have not returned any reply but
promised to do so at 12 m to-morrow. I respectfully request ~~this to
be laid before the President and for~~ his instructions.

U. S. GRANT
Lt. Gn.

ALS (telegram sent), Ritzman Collection, Aurora College, Aurora, Ill.; telegram received (at 8:30 P.M.), DLC-Robert T. Lincoln. *O.R.*, I, xlvi, part 2, 801–2. On March 3, 1865, midnight, Secretary of War Edwin M. Stanton twice telegraphed to USG. "The President directs me to say to you that he wishes you to have no conference with Gen Lee unless it be for the capitulation of Lees army, or on solely minor and purely military matters   He instructs me to say that you are not to decide, discuss, or confer upon any political question: such questions the President holds in his own hands; and will submit them to no military conferences or conventions—mean time you are to press to the utmost, your military advantages" Telegram received (on March 4), DNA, RG 108, Letters Received; copies (2), DLC-Edwin M. Stanton; DLC-William T. Sherman. *O.R.*, I, xlvi, part 2, 802; *ibid.*, I, xlvii, part 3, 263, 285. Printed as drafted by President Abraham Lincoln in Lincoln, *Works*, VIII, 330–31. "I send you a telegram ~~in a~~ written by the President himself in answer to yours of this evening ~~and signed~~ which I have signed by his order. I will add that General Ords ~~conduct~~ conduct in holding intercourse with General Longstreet upon political questions not committed to his charge is not approved. The same thing was ~~eo~~ done in one instance by Major Key when the army was commanded by General McClellan and he was sent to meet Howell Cobb on the subject of exchanges. ~~If you h~~ and it was ~~strongl~~ in that instance as in this disapproved. You will please in future instruct officers ~~having special matters~~ appointed to meet ~~the~~ rebel officers to confine themselves to the matters specially committed to them." ALS (telegram sent), DNA, RG 107, Telegrams Collected (Bound); telegram received, *ibid.*, Telegrams Collected (Unbound); (on March 4, 1:45 P.M.) *ibid.*, RG 108, Letters Received. *O.R.*, I, xlvi, part 2, 802.

1. Ellipses appeared in the telegram sent; the telegram received included a copy of a letter of March 2 from Gen. Robert E. Lee to USG concerning a military convention. See letter to Gen. Robert E. Lee, March 4, 1865.

To Maj. Gen. Henry W. Halleck

By Telegraph from City Point, Mar. 3rd *1865*.
To Maj. Genl. H. W. Halleck,
Chief of Staff.

I have not heard from Schofield since Genl. Comstock returned from him. It is likely he has concluded to open the road from Newberne alone; if so, he will want all accumulation of supplies taken there. I am now looking for the return of a staff officer sent to Wilmington and when he gets back will know whether transports are to be stopped at Beaufort or not and will direct accordingly.

U. S. Grant,
Lt. Genl.

Telegram, copies (marked as received at 6:00 P.M.), DLC-John M. Schofield; DLC-USG, V, 46, 74, 108; DNA, RG 108, Letters Sent. Printed as sent at 4:00 P.M. in *O.R.*, I, xlvii, part 2, 660–61.

To Maj. Gen. John Gibbon

By Telegraph from City Pt. 2 P M [*March 3*] 1865
To MAJ. GENL. GIBBON
COMDG. A OF J.
If there are any Army Gunboats that can accompany the expedition up the Rappahannock I want them to go with it—Some others should also go. Please communicate with Commodore Radford and ask him to send two or more of his light draft gun boats with the expedition[1]—There will be no ojbjection to taking any that are now guarding roads leading to the river any where from Jamestown Island to Varina. The boats he sends may start as soon as they can be got off to await the arrival of the troops in the Rappahannock

U. S. GRANT
Lt. Genl

Telegram received, DNA, RG 45, Area File; copies, *ibid.*, RG 108, Letters Sent; DLC-USG, V, 46, 74, 108. *O.R.*, I, xlvi, part 2, 813.

On March 3, 1865, USG telegraphed to Brig. Gen. John W. Turner, chief of staff for Maj. Gen. Edward O. C. Ord. "Transportation will be ready tomorrow for two thousand Infantry and three hundred Cavalry. Have the expedition ready to embark by twelve (12) M. at. Varina or Deep Bottom as may be most conveninentent No transportation except five 5 ambulances to one thousand men will be taken—" Telegram received (at 10:30 A.M.), DNA, RG 94, War Records Office, Miscellaneous War Records; copies, *ibid.*, RG 108, Letters Sent; DLC-USG, V, 46, 74, 108. *O.R.*, I, xlvi, part 2, 812. At 11:05 A.M., Maj. Gen. John Gibbon telegraphed to USG, then to Lt. Col. Theodore S. Bowers. "Twenty seven deserters from Bratton's So. Ca. Brig. came in last night. They say they had orders to be ready to move, but I think it was to send them to some place where they could not desert, as Eight came in from that Brig. the day before" Telegram sent, DNA, RG 107, Telegrams Collected (Unbound); telegram received (at 11:20 A.M.), *ibid.*, RG 108, Letters Received. *O.R.*, I, xlvi, part 2, 812. "In Gen Grants first telegram to Gen Turner no mention is made of an infantry force, the second dispatch 10.30 a. m. ~~two thousand infantry are mentioned~~, it is stated that transportation will be ready for two thousand Infantry and three hundred cavalry—I inferd the infantry also to come from this command —Will rations be put aboard of the steamers in addition to what the men carry on their persons" ALS (telegram sent), DNA, RG 107, Telegrams Collected

(Unbound); telegram received (at 11:20 A.M.), *ibid.*, RG 108, Letters Received. *O.R.*, I, xlvi, part 2, 812. On the same day, Bowers telegraphed to Gibbon. "Genl. Grants first telegram to Genl. Turner asks for one 1 picked brigade of Infantry and one 1 regime[nt] of Cavalry The omission was a Cipher mistake. It also directs that the men take ten 10 days rations with them—" Telegram received (at 12:10 P.M.), DNA, RG 94, War Records Office, Miscellaneous War Records. *O.R.*, I, xlvi, part 2, 812. At 12:30 P.M. and 1:10 P.M., Gibbon telegraphed to USG. "The force will be embarked from Deep Bottom" Telegram received, DNA, RG 108, Letters Received. *O.R.*, I, xlvi, part 2, 812. "The Richmond Despatch this morning says. We have nothing from Sherman. He is presumed to be still in the mud of South Carolina" Telegram sent, DNA, RG 94, War Records Office, Dept. of Va. and N. C.

On the same day, Gibbon twice telegraphed to USG, the second time at 6:00 P.M. "Two Army gun boats will go with the expedition and probably three, Pilots will be necessary for them, will you give the instructions [for] the Pilots" ALS (telegram sent), *ibid.*, RG 107, Telegrams Collected (Unbound). *O.R.*, I, xlvi, part 2, 813. "Henrys brigade of 1800 men under command of Col I. H. Roberts 139th New York Vols will go on the expedition. Will the transports be ready at Deep Bottom at noon tomorrow" Telegram received, DNA, RG 108, Letters Received. *O.R.*, I, xlvi, part 2, 813. On the same day, Bowers telegraphed to Gibbon. "The pilots are ready. Direct the boats to call on Colonel Bradley, depot quartermaster, for them." Printed as received at 7:45 P.M. *ibid.*, p. 814. On the same day, Gibbon telegraphed to Bowers. "The gun boats have gone down the pilots had better go down on mail boat" ALS (telegram sent), DNA, RG 107, Telegrams Collected (Unbound). On the same day, USG telegraphed to Gibbon. "Transports are ordered to be ready at Deep Bottom at 12 m to-morrow." ALS (telegram sent), Kohns Collection, NN; telegram received (at 8:00 P.M.), DNA, RG 94, War Records Office, Miscellaneous War Records. *O.R.*, I, xlvi, part 2, 814.

At 9:30 P.M., USG telegraphed to Bvt. Brig. Gen. George H. Sharpe, asst. provost marshal, Washington, D. C. "Send a good guide to Fort Monroe to accompany the expedition to the Northern Neck He must leave on the Baltimore boat so as to reach Fort Monroe on Sunday morning the 5th" Telegram received (at 10:30 P.M.), DNA, RG 94, War Records Office, Dept. of Va. and N. C.; *ibid.*, RG 107, Telegrams Collected (Bound); copies, *ibid.*, RG 108, Letters Sent; DLC-USG, V, 46, 74, 108.

At 10:00 [P.M.], Turner telegraphed to USG. "Your telegram received Col Sumner 1 Mtd Rifles would be the best officer to send,—He is now at Norfolk on four days leave. I will telegraph for him if you think there is time to get him up—" ALS (telegram sent—marked as sent at 10:00 A.M.), DNA, RG 107, Telegrams Collected (Unbound); telegram received (at 10:10 P.M.), *ibid.*, RG 108, Letters Received. *O.R.*, I, xlvi, part 2, 814. On the same day, Bowers telegraphed to Turner. "Gen, Grant directs me to say to you, that he thinks Sumner will be a good man, and that there will be time to send for him," Copies, DLC-USG, V, 46, 74, 108; DNA, RG 108, Letters Sent. Printed as received at 10:30 P.M. in *O.R.*, I, xlvi, part 2, 814.

At 11:50 P.M., Bowers telegraphed to Gibbon. "As fast as the Boats are loaded to morrow they will proceed to Fort Monroe, and there await orders from the Commanding Officer, Direct the Officer in Command to stop here on his way down, and receive his orders" Copies, DLC-USG, V, 46, 74, 108; DNA,

RG 108, Letters Sent. Printed as sent at 11:30 P.M. in *O.R.*, I, xlvi, part 2, 814.

On March 4, Bowers telegraphed to Gibbon. "Can you furnish me the names of the army gun-boats that will accompany the expedition?" Printed as received at 10:30 A.M. *ibid.*, p. 830. On the same day, Gibbon telegraphed to Bowers. "The Chamberlain, The Moss-Wood & The Jessup if Genl Patrick Can dispense with her." Telegram received (at 11:25 A.M.), DNA, RG 108, Letters Received. *O.R.*, I, xlvi, part 2, 830. At 7:00 P.M., Gibbon telegraphed to USG. "Troops are all embarked and the last of the ambulances now going on board" Telegram received, DNA, RG 108, Letters Received. *O.R.*, I, xlvi, part 2, 831.

1. On March 3, Gibbon endorsed the telegram received. "Respectfully referred to Com. Radford. Please let me know what boats you can send and when they will be ready to start. The expedition is to embark at noon tomorrow to go up the Rappahannock" AES, DNA, RG 45, Area File. On the same day, Commodore William Radford twice telegraphed to USG. "I will send 2 vessels to Co-operate from the lower post of the River" Telegram received, *ibid.*, RG 108, Letters Received; typescript (marked as sent at 4:50 P.M.), *ibid.*, RG 45, Area File. *O.R.*, I, xlvi, part 2, 807. "Telegraph to Foxhall A Parker at Point Lookout, Md. it is in his district and he has a number of light draft gunboats" ALS (telegram sent), DNA, RG 45, Area File; telegram received, *ibid.*, RG 108, Letters Received. *O.R.*, I, xlvi, part 2, 807. On the same day, USG telegraphed to Radford. "Your Two dispatches recd—Do you mean that you will send two (2) gunboats or do you still wish me to call on Capt Parker Your dispatches being both received at the same time without the hour being noted I cannot understand which of them I am to be governed by—I would prefer you should furnish them if Convenient." Telegram received, DNA, RG 45, Area File; copies (typescript), *ibid.*; *ibid.*, RG 108, Letters Sent; DLC-USG, V, 46, 74, 108. *O.R.*, I, xlvi, part 2, 807–8. At 7:30 P.M., Radford telegraphed to USG. "I have Sent two gunboats this afternoon, as requested. The 2nd telegraph was to let you know where others was to be obtained if required" ALS (telegram sent), DNA, RG 45, Area File; telegram received (at 7:30 P.M.), *ibid.*, RG 108, Letters Received. *O.R.*, I, xlvi, part 2, 808.

To Maj. Gen. George G. Meade

City Point, Va, March 3d *1865*

MAJ. GEN. G. G. MEADE,
COMD.G A. P.
GENERAL,

Colonel Duane's communication of this date to you, ~~and~~ with your endorsement, is just rec'd at the hands of Major Mason of your Staff. The proposed attack was based on the supposition that the enemy had detached largely from the Army about Petersburg. That supposition does not now seem to be sustained.

Whilst the enemy holds nearly all his force for the defence of Richmond and Petersburg the object to be gained by attacking intrenchments is not worth the risk to be run. In fact for the present it is better for us to hold the enemy where he is than to force him South. Sheridan is now on his way to Lynchburg and Sherman to join Schofield. After the junction of the two latter is formed they will push for Raleigh N. C. and build up the road to their rear. To drive the enemy from Richmond now would be to endanger the success of these two columns. Unless therefore the enemy should detach to the amount of at least two Divisions more than we know anything about as yet we will not attack his entrenchments and probably not then if the roads improve so as to admit of a flank movement.

It is well to have it understood where and how to attack suddenly if it should be found at any future time that the enemy are detaching heavily. My notion is that Petersburg will be evacuated simultaneously with such detaching as would justify an attack.

Very respectfully
your obt. svt.
U. S. GRANT
Lt. Gn

ALS, Meade Papers, PHi. *O.R.*, I, xlvi, part 2, 806. On March 3, 1865, Bvt. Col. James C. Duane, chief engineer, Army of the Potomac, wrote to Maj. Gen. George G. Meade. "In compliance with instructions contained in a letter from the Chief of Staff dated March 2nd I have the honor to make the following report The plan of attack proposed by Major Gen Potter is as follows—An Attacking column to be formed in our front line, to the left of the Jerusalem plank road— A supporting column a little in rear under cover of a ridge in front of Fort Davis The first column to move foward, carry the rebel works to the right of Fort Mahone Then without delay attack—the rear line on the hights—This column to be preceded by a pioneer party to clear away obstructions The supporting column to follow as soon as the first line of works is carried The plan of Gen McLaughlin is nearly the same—His column of attack is to push through the Rebel line in front of fort Hascall and from thence to the works on the crest of cemetary hill—In addition to this he proposes to destroy the dam built this winter by the enemy in front of fort Steadman—Overflow the ground in rear of the Rebel left—thus cut off the retreat of that portion of the line Both of these attacks must take place in the night—As by day light the attacking columns would be

exposed to a heavy artillery fire in front and on both flanks   There is great
danger of troops mooving in the night over ground—obstructed by Abattis en-
tanglements &c—falling into confusion firing into each other—or at least delay-
ing long enough to allow the enemy to bring up his reserves   In case of a reverse
—the returning troops must suffer severly—Particularly on Gen Potters front—
as they would be exposed for a long distance to a heavy Artillery fire   As an
isolated operation I consider the result of the proposed attack as *very* doubtful.
If however a moovement were made by our left, or by the Army of the James—
sufficiently serious to draw off the rebel reserves—I think the proposed assault
might be made with a fair chance of success"   ALS, DNA, RG 108, Letters
Received. *O.R.*, I, xlvi, part 2, 805. On the same day, Meade endorsed this letter.
"Respectfully forwarded for the information of the Lt. Genl. Comdg.—I consider
the success of the proposed attacks too doubtful, to advise their attempt—unless
strong evidence is obtained of the enemy's line being weakened by detachments.
Their success is entirely dependant on the enemy's being *surprised*, and his
works carried at all hazards, before he recovers from the surprise or can reinforce. My experience with this army does not lead to any sanguine hope of
success in a *coup-de main*—and tho I have every confidence in the judgement &
zeal of Genl. Potter & McLachlan I fear the matter is more dependant on the
views of the enlisted men—and I know among these, there is great indisposition
to attack entrenchments.—I concur with the Chief Engr that in case of any movements drawing away & occupying the bulk of the enemys forces & reserves—
these attacks could be made with hope of success but the difficulty here is that
to produce such a weakening of the enemys line we have to reserve the bulk of
our forces.—I think these attacks should be held in view—and the first favorable
opportunity for making them seized.—" AES, DNA, RG 108, Letters Received.
O.R., I, xlvi, part 2, 805–6.

   Also on March 3, 12:00 P.M., Meade telegraphed to USG. "I forward report
of todays examination of 72 deserters. You will perceive that Gordons Div. is
accounted for present and that Rhodes was on ~~yesterday~~ Tuesday last at Sutherland station reported under marching orders. It would appear that Lewis [*Lane's*]
Brigade Pegrams Div. had gone somewhere recently and as this is Hokes old
brigade of N-C. troops it is possible it has gone to join him. I see no positive
evidence of any other Command having left" Telegram received (at 12:55
P.M.), DNA, RG 108, Letters Received; copies, *ibid.*, RG 393, Army of the
Potomac, Letters Sent; (2) Meade Papers, PHi. Printed as sent at midnight in
O.R., I, xlvi, part 2, 806–7.

   On March 4, 1:00 P.M. and 1:25 P.M., Meade telegraphed to USG. "Sixteen (16) deserters on the 6th Corps front & 2 on The 2d Corps front. are all
that are reported as Coming last nigh[t]   No information of importance as yet
recievd from there from which I infer they have none to communicate as they are
examined at Divn and Corps Hd Qurs" "I forward despatch just recd from Gen
Davies Comdg Cavy. It would appear the reported departure of Troops for N C
via Weldon R R Could not be Correct or these men would have known it." Telegrams received, DNA, RG 108, Letters Received; copies, *ibid.*, RG 393, Army
of the Potomac, Letters Sent; Meade Papers, PHi. *O.R.*, I, xlvi, part 2, 826. The
enclosure is *ibid.*, pp. 829–30.

To Lt. Col. John E. Mulford

City Point Va, March 3d 1865

Lieut, Col, Mulford
Care Gen, Ord

Word has been sent to me that there is in Richmond 34 Boxes blankets 10 boxes Blouse's 18 boxes Shoes, 4 boxes Socks, 2 boxes Shirts and 2 boxes Pants,   Some measures I think should be taken to have these articles returned or cared for, for the benefit of future prisoners,   They had probably better be returned,

U, S, Grant
Lieut, General

Telegram, copies, DLC-USG, V, 46, 74, 108; DNA, RG 108, Letters Sent; USG 3. *O.R.*, II, viii, 336. On March 3, 1865, Lt. Col. John E. Mulford, Varina, Va., telegraphed to USG. "Genl Hayes holds Judge Oulds receipt for all packages public & private left in Richmond,   They were left subject to our order—,   I mentioned the matter to you, & on the understanding I had of the matter authorized the use under supervission of our own Officers thier, of such articles as might be needed by our men coming into Richmond from other points, they being mostly sick & wounded,   I will call on Mr Ould tomorrow to return what[ever] he may now have [o]n hand" ALS (telegram sent), DNA, RG 107, Telegrams Collected (Unbound); telegram received, *ibid.*, RG 108, Letters Received. *O.R.*, II, viii, 336.

Also on March 3, Mulford telegraphed to Lt. Col. Theodore S. Bowers. "I have only the New York & Leary in which to receive fifteen hundred sick men now in Richmond   I have made arrangements today for their immediate delivery —If you must have her I can send her to you as soon as I can transfer the Hospital Stores &c," Telegram received, DNA, RG 107, Telegrams Collected (Unbound); (at 6:40 P.M.) *ibid.*, RG 108, Letters Received. On the same day, USG telegraphed to Mulford. "I will try and send you one of the Hospital Steamers. If it cannot be sent you will have to keep the Leery." ALS (telegram sent), Kohns Collection, NN; copies, DLC-USG, V, 46, 74, 108; DNA, RG 108, Letters Sent.

On March 6, 7:30 P.M., USG telegraphed to Bvt. Brig. Gen. William Hoffman. "You may now discontinue sending rebel prisoners for exchange, except by the regular flag-of-truce boat, Stmr 'NewYork'" Telegram received (at 8:00 P.M.), *ibid.*, RG 107, Telegrams Collected (Bound); (at 8:20 P.M.) *ibid.*, RG 249, Letters Received; copies, *ibid.*, RG 108, Letters Sent; DLC-USG, V, 46, 74, 108. *O.R.*, II, viii, 359.

To Gen. Robert E. Lee

March 4th *1864*5.

GEN R. E. LEE
COMD'G C. S. A,
GENERAL,

Your two letters of the 2nd inst. were received yesterday. In regard to any apprehended misunderstanding in reference to the exchange of political prisoners, I think there need be none. Gen Ord and Gen Longstreet have probably misunderstood what I said to the former on the subject. Or I may have failed to make myself understood possibly. A few days before the interview between Gen Longstreet and Ord I had received a dispatch from Gen Hoffman, Com.ry. Gen. of Prisoners, stating in substance that all Prisoners of War, who were or had been in close confinement, or irons, whether under charges or sentence, had been ordered to City Point for exchange. I forwarded the substance of that dispatch to Lieut Col Mulford Asst. Agt. of Exchange, and presumed it probable that he had communicated it to Col Ro. Ould. A day or two after, an offender, who was neither a prisoner of War, nor a political prisoner, was executed, after a fair and impartial trial, and in accordance with the laws of War, and the usage of civilized Nations. It was in explanation of this class of cases, I told Gen Ord to speak to Gen Longstreet.

Reference to my letter of Feby. 16th will show my understanding on the subject of releasing political or citizen prisoners—

In regard to meeting you on the 6th inst. I would state, that I have no authority to accede to your proposition for a conference on the subject proposed. Such authority is vested in the President of the United States alone.

Gen Ord, could only have meant that I would not refuse an interview on any subject on which I have a right to act, which of course, would be such as are purely of a military character, and on the subject of exchanges which has been entrusted to me.

> I have the honor to be
> Very Respectfully
> Your Obt. Svt
> U. S. GRANT
> Lt. Gen

Copies, DLC-USG, V, 46, 75, 108; DNA, RG 94, Record & Pension Office, 520701; *ibid.*, RG 108, Letters Sent. *O.R.*, I, xlvi, part 2, 825. On March 2, 1865, Gen. Robert E. Lee twice wrote to USG. "Lt Gen Longstreet has informed me that in an interview with Maj Gen Ord, that officer expressed some apprehension lest the general terms used by you with reference to the exchange of political prisoners should be construed to include those charged with capital offences. Gen Ord further stated that you did not intend to embrace that class of cases in the agreement to exchange. I regret to learn that such is your interpretation, as I had hoped that by exchanging those held under charges by each party, it would be possible to diminish to some extent the sufferings of both without detriment to their interests. Should you see proper to assent to the interview proposed in my letter of this date, I hope it may be found practicable to arrive at a more satisfactory understanding on this subject." "Lt Gen Longstreet has informed me that in a recent conversation between himself and Maj Gen Ord as to the possibility of arriving at a satisfactory adjustment of the present unhappy difficulties by means of a military convention, Gen Ord stated that if I desired to have an interview with you on the subject, you would not decline, provided I had authority to act. Sincerely desiring to leave nothing untried which may put an end to the calamities of war, I propose to meet you at such convenient time and place as you may designate, with the hope that upon an interchange of views, it may be found practicable to submit the subjects of controversy between the belligerents to a convention of the Kind mentioned. In such event, I am authorised to do whatever the result of the proposed interview may render necessary or advisable. Should you accede to this proposition, I would suggest that, if agreeable to you, we meet at the place selected by Generals Ord and Longstreet for their interview, at 11 A M on Monday next." LS, DNA, RG 94, Record & Pension Office, 520701. *O.R.*, I, xlvi, part 2, 824–25.

On March 3 and 4, USG telegraphed to Maj. Gen. John Gibbon. "Say to Gen Longstreet that my reply to Gen Lee's communication, will be delivered to him at twelve M tomorrow." Telegram received (at 4:25 P.M.), Ord Papers, CU-B; copies, DLC-USG, V, 46, 74, 108; DNA, RG 108, Letters Sent. *O.R.*, I, xlvi, part 2, 813. "You may say to Gen. Longstreet that I will send my reply to Gn. Lee's communication as early as possible but may not be able to do so today." ALS (telegram sent), Williams College, Williamstown, Mass.; telegram received (at noon), Ord Papers, CU-B. *O.R.*, I, xlvi, part 2, 830.

To Edwin M. Stanton

———

(Cipher)   City Point, Va, March 4th *18645*. [*4:30* P.M.]
HON. E. M. STANTON, SEC. OF WAR, WASHINGTON.

Your dispatch of 12 p. m. the 3d received. I have written a
letter to Gen. Lee Copy of which will be sent to you by to-morrows
Mail. I can assure you that no act of the enemy will prevent me
prossing all advantages gained to the utmost of my ability. Neither
will I under any circumstances ~~accede~~ exceed my authority or in
any way ~~compromise~~ embarrass the Govt. It was because I had no
right to meet Gen. Lee on the subject proposed by him that I refered the matter for instructions. ~~Peace must Come some day and
I would regard it just as wrong to~~ I would regard it as wrong to
~~receive such reject such communications without refering them.~~

U. S. GRANT, Lt. G—

Telegram, copies, DLC-USG, V, 46, 74, 108; DNA, RG 108, Letters Sent;
CSmH; (typescript) Abraham Lincoln Book Shop, Chicago, Ill. *O.R.,* I, xlvi,
part 2, 823–24. On March 4, 1865, USG wrote to Secretary of War Edwin M.
Stanton. "I have the honor to transmit herewith, letters received from Gen. R. E.
Lee, and copy of my answer to the same, together with copy of a letter to Gen
Lee referred to in my answer." LS, DNA, RG 94, Record & Pension Office,
520701. *O.R.,* I, xlvi, part 2, 824.

To Col. Samuel H. Roberts

———

City Point, March 4th 1865
COL. S. H. ROBERTS
COMDG. 3D BRIG., 3RD DIV. 24TH A. C,
COL.

With your brigade and the cavalry ordered to report to you
will proceed up the Rappahannock river as far as you may deem
it safe and expedient to go on transports. You will then debark and
proceed by land as rapidly as possible to Fredericks burg, Va, and
capture the place if not too strongly defended. Two Army and two
Navy Gunboats are ordered to accompany the expedition. They

are authorized to assemble in the Rappahannock in advance of the expedition,   You will ascertain at Fort Monroe however, whether they have gone forward, and if they have not you will not proceed without them. In advancing up the river be careful that no transport precedes the leading convoy.

When you leave the transports you will place a small guard on the river bank for their protection in the absence of the expeditionary force. It is understood that a very considerable contraband trade is carried on across the Potomac by what is known as the "Northern Neck" and through Fredericksburg into Richmond. The object of your expedition is to break this up as far as possible. If you succeed in reaching Fredericksburg you seize or destroy all property which you have good reason to be lieve is being used in barter for unauthorized articles of trade between the rebel armies and the Northern cities. You will also destroy the rail road depot and as much of the road back towards Richmond as you can. After having accomplished this you are authorized to go to any point where information you may receive may lead you to suppose goods can be found which are in transit either North or South. All such will be either seized or destroyed. You will also arrest and bring with you all persons you know to be engaged directly or indirectly in smuggling or trading between the North and South. You will not unnecessarily disturb peaceful and quiet citizens, but you will take from the country such supplies and forage as may be necessary for your command. You will also destroy all accumulations of supplies of whatever description as you may have reason to believe are being collected for the use of the enemy

Having accomplished the object of the expedition you are sent upon you will return with your command to the place of starting. If you find that it would be advantageous after doing all you can from your first landing to go elsewhere on the Potomac or tributaries, you are authorized to use your transports for that purpose

Very respectfully
Your obedt servant
U. S. GRANT
Lieut. Genl

Copies, DLC-USG, V, 46, 74, 108; DNA, RG 94, Turner-Baker Papers, 3941T; *ibid.*, RG 108, Letters Sent. *O.R.*, I, xlvi, part 2, 832.

On March 5, 1865, Col. Samuel H. Roberts, 139th N. Y., telegraphed to Lt. Col. Theodore S. Bowers. "I cannot find the Scout that was to report to me this morning. Will be ready to proceed in two hours. Shall I go without him?" Telegram received (at 11:30 A.M.), DNA, RG 107, Telegrams Collected (Unbound). On the same day, USG telegraphed to Roberts. "Start as soon as possible with or without these guide who was to meet you at FtMonroe. He was expected down on the Baltimore boat." Telegram received (at 12:05 P.M.), *ibid.*, RG 94, War Records Office, Miscellaneous War Records; copies, *ibid.*, RG 108, Letters Sent; DLC-USG, V, 46, 74, 108. Printed as sent at 12:05 P.M. in *O.R.*, I, xlvi, part 2, 847. At noon, Bvt. Brig. Gen. George H. Sharpe, Washington, D. C., telegraphed to Bowers. "It was impossible to find any one here yesterday until night—Good guides for northern neck leave on todays boat to report ~~in the morning~~ to Lieut Col Conrad at Fortress Monroe with a letter of explanation." ALS (telegram sent), DNA, RG 107, Telegrams Collected (Unbound). Printed as sent at 12:30 P.M. in *O.R.*, I, xlvi, part 2, 842.

To Edwin M. Stanton

(Cipher)   City Point, Va, March 5th 1865 [2:00 P.M.]
HON. E. M. STANTON, SEC. OF WAR, WASHINGTON

Deserters from every part of the enemy's line confirm the capture of Charlottesville by Sheridan.[1] They say he captured Early and nearly his entire force consisting of 1800 men. Four Brigades ~~hare~~ reported as being sent to Lynchburg to get there before Sheridan if possible. I think there is no doubt now but Sheridan will at least succeed in destroying the James River Canal.

                              U. S. GRANT
                              Lt. Gen.

ALS (telegram sent), Harkness Collection, NN; telegram received (at 3:30 P.M.), DNA, RG 107, Telegrams Collected (Bound). *O.R.*, I, xlvi, part 2, 841. On March 5, 1865, 11:00 A.M. and 4:00 P.M., USG telegraphed to Secretary of War Edwin M. Stanton. "Deserters in this morning report that Sheridan had routed Early and captured Charlotteville. They report four regiments having gone from here to reinforce Early." ALS (telegram sent), OClWHi; telegram received (at 11:45 P.M.), DNA, RG 107, Telegrams Collected (Bound). *O.R.*, I, xlvi, part 2, 841. "Refugees confirm the statements of deserters as to the capture of Early and nearly his entire force. They say it took place on Thursday last between Staunton & Charlottesville and that the defeat was total." ALS (telegram sent), Columbia University, New York, N. Y.; telegram received (at 6:45 P.M.), DNA, RG 107, Telegrams Collected (Bound). *O.R.*, I, xlvi, part

2, 841. At 8:50 P.M., Stanton telegraphed to USG. "I congratulate you on Sheridans success. We are anxiously waiting intelligence from Sherman and Scofield. No apprehension is felt that you will ever exceed your authority and your object in applying for instructions was ~~fully~~ understood. The President ~~the knew~~ supposed you desired them to be explicit and made them so, not only to correspond with your wishes, but also because it was believed the enemy had a purpose in desiring to enter into political negotiations with ~~Military some of your~~ Military officers. The inauguration went off admirably without mishap of any kind. Rawlins nomination went in Friday but I [am] unable to ascertain until tomorrow whether it was acted on. I saw the Chairman of the Military Committe who said if they could get into Executive session it would be confirmed but he thought they would have no session until Monday. The commission will be forwarded ~~immediately~~ without delay." ALS (telegram sent), DNA, RG 107, Telegrams Collected (Bound); telegram received (at 8:50 P.M.), *ibid.*, RG 108, Letters Received. *O.R.*, I, xlvi, part 2, 841. An undated telegram from William S. Hillyer to USG was probably sent on Thursday, March 9. "Gen Rawlins has been confirmed as Brigadier General and Chief of Staff." ALS (telegram sent), DNA, RG 107, Telegrams Collected (Unbound).

On March 5, USG telegraphed to Maj. Gen. John M. Schofield. "Last Thursday Sheridan met Early between Staunton & Charlottesville, & defeated him cap[tur]ing nearly his entire commadnd Early & Staff are among the prisoners This news is brought by deserters Refugees [&] our own scouts." Telegram received (press), *ibid.*, Telegrams Collected (Bound); copies, *ibid.*, RG 108, Letters Sent; DLC-USG, V, 46, 74, 108. On March 6, 12:30 P.M., USG telegraphed to Schofield. "Sheridan will push on to Lynchburg and if information received there justifies it he will push on into N. C. and join you and Sherman with a Cavalry force of about 8000 men." ALS (telegram sent), OClWHi; copies, DLC-USG, V, 46, 74, 108; DNA, RG 108, Letters Sent. *O.R.*, I, xlvii, part 2, 706. On the same day, USG telegraphed to Capt. William L. James. "A cipher dispatch will be ready for Gen Schofield in a few minutes— When it is recd you can let the Oriental go" Telegram received (at 12:40 P.M.), DNA, RG 107, Telegrams Collected (Unbound).

On March 6, 2:30 P.M., USG telegraphed to Stanton. "Deserters to-day report that Sheridan has cut the James River Canal. As Richmond papers have determined not to give us news I will have to report such as is obtained through scouts ~~and~~ deserters, and refugees, to be taken for what it is worth." ALS (telegram sent), OClWHi; copies, DLC-USG, V, 46, 74, 108; DNA, RG 108, Letters Sent. *O.R.*, I, xlvi, part 2, 858.

On March 7, 10:00 P.M., USG telegraphed to Stanton. "I would respectfully renew my recommendation for the promotion of Capt, Geo, K, Leet A, A, Gen, in the Office in Washington to the rank of Maj, of Vols, in the Adj, Gen's Dept—" Copies, DLC-USG, V, 46, 74, 108; DNA, RG 108, Letters Sent. On March 8, Col. James A. Hardie telegraphed to USG. "Captain George K. Leet has been nominated and Confirmed as Major and A. A. G of Vol's" LS (telegram sent), *ibid.*, RG 107, Telegrams Collected (Bound); telegram received (at 11:00 A.M.), *ibid.*, RG 108, Letters Received. On the same day, Stanton telegraphed to USG. "General Crocker was ordered in some time ago. Major Leet was promoted & confirmed. Forty ~~of~~ rebel officers and Thirteen hundred enlisted men prisoners of war are ~~at~~ reported as having arrived at Winchester General Sheridan was at Waynesboro. Early made his escape, but his staff were captured." ALS (telegram sent), *ibid.*, RG 107, Telegrams Collected (Bound); telegram received (at 1:40 P.M.), *ibid.*, RG 108, Letters Received. *O.R.*, I, xlvi, part 2, 887. On March 8, Lt. Col. Theodore S. Bowers telegraphed to Maj. Gen. George G. Meade and all corps commanders transmitting the information about Maj. Gen. Philip H. Sheridan's victory at Waynesboro, and later that day Bowers transmitted Sheridan's telegram of March 2 to Maj. Gen. Henry W. Halleck reporting the victory. See *O.R.*, I, xlvi, part 2, 792.

On March 8, 11:15 A.M. and 12:20 P.M., Meade telegraphed to USG. "Pro Mar Gen reports 23 deserters yesterday up to Midnight   Corps commanders report this morning 16th as coming in during the night. No movements of troops reported   Defeat of Early confirmed & occupation of Raleigh rumored—Sharp picket firing with exchange of artillery shots took place at daylight this moring in front of fort Sedgewick. Began by the enemy who seemed nervous & as if anticipating an attack" "I forward despatch just recd. from 5th Corps Hd Qurs giving deserters report of rebel army rumors. By them you will note Early is reported Killed & Rosser wounded" Telegrams received, DNA, RG 108, Letters Received; copies, *ibid.*, RG 393, Army of the Potomac, Letters Sent; (2—one of the second) Meade Papers, PHi. *O.R.*, I, xlvi, part 2, 887–88. The enclosure in the second is *ibid.*, p. 889.

1. On March 5, 10:15 A.M., Brig. Gen. John W. Turner, chief of staff for Maj. Gen. Edward O. C. Ord, telegraphed to USG. "The following dispatch is received 'Hatchers House Mar 5th 65   Terrys and Stewart's Brigades of Picketts Division were relieved at four o'clock this morning by two Brigades of mahones Division   (signed)   CHAS K GRAHAM BR GENL' Deserters in at Dutch Gap Canal last night say that four Regiments of Stuarts Brigade Picketts Div. had gone to the Valley. Deserters from Brattons Brigade Fields Div. say that Charlotteville was captured by Sheridan and that Early had been routed" Telegrams received (2—one incomplete, the other received at 12:10 P.M.), DNA, RG 94, War Records Office, Miscellaneous War Records; (at 10:35 P.M.) *ibid.*, RG 108, Letters Received. *O.R.*, I, xlvi, part 2, 846. USG endorsed the telegram received. "Operator please send the above to Maj Gen Meade—" Copy, DNA, RG 108, Letters Received. On March 5, noon, Meade telegraphed to USG. "Sixteen [*Fifteen*] deserters are reported as coming in last night. They report Mahones & Grimes Divisions as under marching orders and some think that two of Mahones Brigades have gone   they state it was reported in their camp that Sheridan occupied Staunton and Charlottesville and had defeated Earlys troops. This last report comes from desterters on the extreme right and left showing the report existed all through the rebel army. The firing yesterday P. M. was on the 9th Corps front. The enemy opening when we were relieving a Battery in one of the works" Telegram received (at 12:30 P.M.), *ibid.*; copies, *ibid.*, RG 393, Army of the Potomac, Letters Sent; (2) Meade Papers, PHi. *O.R.*, I, xlvi, part 2, 843. On the same day, Ord telegraphed to USG transmitting a telegram of 12:40 P.M. from Maj. Gen. Godfrey Weitzel. "Intelligent deserters report That the medical Stores & machinery have been moved to Lynchburg   That Sheridan has captured Gen Early and his entire command numbering 1800 men—Four Brigades of Long-Streets Corps have been Sent to intercept Sheridan at Lynchburg if possible—Sheridan captured Saunton on Thursday last   These deserters left Richmond at 7 P m yesterday—" ALS (incomplete telegram sent), DNA, RG 107, Telegrams Collected (Unbound); telegram received (at 1:20 P.M.), *ibid.*, RG 108, Letters Received. *O.R.*, I, xlvi, part 2, 846.

To Maj. Gen. Henry W. Halleck

City Point Mch 5th 186[5, *10:30* A.M.]

MAJ, GEN, HALLECK
WASHINGTON

I have not heard whether it was still intended to send an expedition from Washington to break up the Orange and Alexandria Road,   An expedition over 2.000 strong left here to go up the Rappahannock to break up the trade carried on across the "Northern Neck"   They will go to Fredericksburg first

U. S. GRANT
Lieut, Gen,

Telegram, copies, DLC-USG, V, 46, 74, 108; DNA, RG 108, Letters Sent. *O.R.*, I, xlvi, part 2, 842. On March 5, 1865, 12:30 P.M., Maj. Gen. Henry W. Halleck telegraphed to USG. "No expedition was sent against the Rapidann R. R. bridge. Genl Sheridan did not ask it, and moreover all the troops were required here to preserve order & guard the public stores during the inauguration." ALS (telegram sent), DNA, RG 107, Telegrams Collected (Bound); telegram received, *ibid.*; *ibid.*, RG 108, Letters Received. Printed as sent at 12:50 P.M. in *O.R.*, I, xlvi, part 2, 842. At 3:30 P.M., USG telegraphed to Halleck. "I did not care to have an expedition go out from Washington. Simply wanted to know if they were out so that the Commanding officer of the one going up the Rappahannock could be informed if it was so." ALS (telegram sent), OClWHi; copies, DLC-USG, V, 46, 74, 108; DNA, RG 108, Letters Sent. *O.R.*, I, xlvi, part 2, 842.

To Maj. Gen. George H. Thomas

City Point Va
Mar 5th 1865 [*4:30* P.M.]

MAJ GEN GEO H. THOMAS
NASHVILLE TENN.

Have any of our prisoners been delivered to you at Eastport yet? Orders have gone from Richmond to deliver all to you that are convenient to send out that way—

Deliveries to the rebels are all made here

U S GRANT
Lt Genl

Telegram received (at 7:00 P.M.), DNA, RG 107, Telegrams Collected (Bound); *ibid.*, Telegrams Collected (Unbound); copies, *ibid.*, RG 108, Letters Sent; DLC-USG, V, 46, 74, 108; USG 3. *O.R.*, II, viii, 357. On March 6, 1865, 10:30 A.M., Maj. Gen. George H. Thomas telegraphed to USG. "I have an officer at Corinth miss. to recieve prisoners of war but none have been delivered to him yet I will report the moment I hear from him" Telegram received (at 1:40 P.M.), DNA, RG 107, Telegrams Collected (Bound); *ibid.*, RG 108, Letters Received; copy, *ibid.*, RG 393, Dept. of the Cumberland, Telegrams Sent. *O.R.*, II, viii, 361.

On March 31, 7:00 P.M., Thomas telegraphed to USG. "On my return from Memphis I find that Col J. G. Parkhurst my Pro. Mar Genl has returned without having recd any of our prisoners from Forrest—forrests excuse was that the prisoners were on the way but the heavy rains had so damaged the R R that he could not get them further north than West point & that he had since recd orders to send them to Vicksburg and Mobile. Col Watts was then the 13th Inst. delivering them to the U S authority" Telegram received (at 10:45 P.M.), DNA, RG 107, Telegrams Collected (Bound); (2) *ibid.*, RG 108, Letters Received; copy, *ibid.*, RG 393, Dept. of the Cumberland, Telegrams Sent. *O.R.*, II, viii, 448.

To Maj. Gen. Henry W. Halleck

(Cipher)   City Point, Va, March 6th *1865* [*8:00* P.M.]
MAJ. GEN. HALLECK, WASHINGTON,

In view of the large number of men sent to Gen. Thomas I think it will be better to send all new organizations yet left in the states where they were raised as follows: Those from Minnesota, Iow, & Wisconsin ~~and Illinois~~ to Mo. From Illinois to Thomas and from Ia. Ohio & Michigan to the Middle Div.

U. S. GRANT
Lt. Gn.

ALS (telegram sent), MH; copies, DLC-USG, V, 46, 74, 108; DNA, RG 108, Letters Sent; *ibid.*, Letters Received. Printed as received at 9:20 P.M. in *O.R.*, I, xlix, part 1, 848. On March 6, 1865, 4:00 P.M., Maj. Gen. Henry W. Halleck telegraphed to USG. "As directed by you, all new regiments east of Ohio have been ordered to Middle Military Division. Since January 1st we have sent to Genl G H. Thomas (2~~1~~2,~~6~~583) twenty ~~one~~ two thousand, ~~six~~ five hundred & eighty three men, which makes his army almost equal to what it was when he met Hood. Unless otherwise directed, we shall continue to send to Genl Thomas all new troops from the North western states." ALS (telegram sent), DNA, RG 107, Telegrams Collected (Bound); telegram received, *ibid.*; *ibid.*, RG 108, Letters Received. *O.R.*, I, xlix, part 1, 848.

To Maj. Gen. Winfield S. Hancock

(Cipher)   City Point, Va, March 6th 1865 [2:30 P.M.]
MAJ. GN. HANCOCK, WINCHESTER, VA,

Our own scouts from Richmond confirm the report of the capture of Early with most of his Staff and command. Those not captured have returned to Richmond without arms. These last, the skeedadlers, report Sheridan moving in two columns one down the Va. Central road towards Gordonsville and the other towards Scottsville, about 20.000 strong in all.

U. S. GRANT
Lt. Gen

ALS (telegram sent), PPRF; telegram received (at 3:00 P.M.), DNA, RG 107, Telegrams Collected (Bound); *ibid.*, RG 393, Middle Military Div., Letters Received. *O.R.*, I, xlvi, part 2, 863. On March 6, 1865, Maj. Gen. Winfield S. Hancock, Cumberland, Md., telegraphed to USG. "I came here from Winchester today since 11 a. m. to see what was doing here & to inspect the line. Sent 500 cavalry to Strausburg to attack 300 of Rossers disbanded men, said to be collecting there. I sent a scout to communicate if possible with Sheridan & to offer to take his prisoners off his hands. A detachment I directed Gen Augur to send to Rappahannock station returned today   no enemy there but few troops at Culpepper   Rapidan bridge carried away by freshet" Telegram received (at 11:35 P.M.), DNA, RG 107, Telegrams Collected (Bound); (on March 7) *ibid.*, RG 108, Letters Received. Printed as received on March 7, 11:35 P.M., in *O.R.*, I, xlvi, part 2, 863.

On March 9, Hancock, Winchester, Va., telegraphed to Maj. Gen. Henry W. Halleck, sending a copy to USG. "Dr Dubois Med Dir of Sheridans forces has written a note to Dr Ghisselson saying that they number of wounded in his command including thursday was but six (6) and that of the enemy twelve all of which were left at Waynesboro on account of the condition of the roads. There are rumors here of another capture of about one thousand prisoners at Gordonsville or elsewhere. I shall send a considerable cavalry force up the valley tomorrow & shall see what there is in the rumor and ascertain something of guerillas also" Telegram received (at 10:05 P.M.), DNA, RG 108, Letters Received. Printed as addressed to Halleck in *O.R.*, I, xlvi, part 2, 910.

To Bvt. Brig. Gen. William Hoffman

City Point Va
12.30 p m Mch 7th 1865

Br Gen H W Hoffman
C G Prisoners

The enemy are putting all their returned prisoners into the ranks of the Eastern army without regard to the organization to which they belong

As the men returned to us are unfit for duty I want all of the same class in our hands returned before any more well men are sent back

U S. Grant
Lt Genl

Telegram received (at 1:00 P.M.), DNA, RG 107, Telegrams Collected (Bound); *ibid.*, RG 249, Letters Received; copies, *ibid.*, RG 108, Letters Sent; DLC-USG, V, 46, 74, 108; USG 3. *O.R.*, II, viii, 363. On March 7, 1865, 3:20 P.M., Bvt. Brig. Gen. William Hoffman telegraphed to USG. "Telegrams of last Evening and today received, and will be observed" ALS (telegram sent), DNA, RG 107, Telegrams Collected (Unbound); telegram received (at 5:30 P.M.), *ibid.*, RG 108, Letters Received.

On March 9, Hoffman telegraphed to USG. "Do you wish exchanged prisoners armed and equipped before joining their regiments" ALS (telegram sent), *ibid.*, RG 107, Telegrams Collected (Unbound); telegram received, *ibid.*, RG 108, Letters Received. On the same day, USG telegraphed to Hoffman. "Send exchanged soldiers to their Regiments without arms & equipments. They can be armed and equipped to better advantage with their regiments" Telegram received (at 5:00 P.M.), *ibid.*, RG 107, Telegrams Collected (Unbound); *ibid.*, RG 249, Letters Received; copies, *ibid.*, RG 108, Letters Sent; DLC-USG, V, 46, 74, 108; USG 3.

To Maj. Gen. George G. Meade

City Point Mch 7th 1865 [*12:10* P.M.]

Maj, Gen, Meade

All of Mahone's Division is now reported to be on the Bermuda Front and Pickett's Division, which was there, at the Rail-Road Depot awaiting transportation it is spposed for Lynchburg

U. S. Grant
Lieut, General

Telegram, copies, DLC-USG, V, 46, 74, 108; DNA, RG 108, Letters Sent; (2) Meade Papers, PHi. *O.R.*, I, xlvi, part 2, 865. On March 7, 1865, noon, Maj. Gen. George G. Meade telegraphed to USG. "Despatch relative to Mahone and Pickett received. Only five deserters reported this morning. The information they bring not yet received. I think it probable if any troops are sent Lynchburg, Picketts being all Virginians are likely to go" Telegram received (at 12:30 P.M.), DNA, RG 108, Letters Received; copies, *ibid.*, RG 393, Army of the Potomac, Letters Sent; (2) Meade Papers, PHi. *O.R.*, I, xlvi, part 2, 865.

On March 6, 1:30 P.M., Meade telegraphed to USG. "Nothing particular to report 27 deserters rec'd by Pro Mar Genl up to midnight last night 28 are reported as having come since then by Corps Comdrs. I transmit the information obtained from such as have reported at these Hd Qrs. Their statements as to the movements of Mahones Div. are compared. Instead of this Div. going to the north bank of the James as reported yesterday you will now note it is stated it was going to Burgess Mill to relieve a Div of Earlys Corps ordered to the Valley—" Telegram received (marked as sent at 1:35 P.M., received at 2:00 P.M.), DNA, RG 108, Letters Received; copies, *ibid.*, RG 393, Army of the Potomac, Letters Sent; Meade Papers, PHi. *O.R.*, I, xlvi, part 2, 858.

On March 7, Maj. Gen. Edward O. C. Ord telegraphed to USG transmitting a telegram from Brig. Gen. Charles K. Graham, Hatcher, Va. "All of Mahones Div. is on this front this morning. Picketts Div. was at the railroad last evening waiting transportation. The report was that it was going to Lynchburg" Telegram received (at 10:45 A.M.), DNA, RG 108, Letters Received. Printed as transmitted at 10:35 A.M. in *O.R.*, I, xlvi, part 2, 880.

On March 9, 11:40 A.M. and 11:45 A.M., Meade telegraphed to USG. "54 deserters received up to midnight by Pro Mar Genl, only a few are reported this morning and no information of importance learned from them" Telegram received (at 12:25 P.M.), DNA, RG 108, Letters Received; copies, *ibid.*, RG 393, Army of the Potomac, Letters Sent; Meade Papers, PHi. *O.R.*, I, xlvi, part 2, 903. "25 deserters only reported yesterday by Pro. Mar. Genl.—A few reported this morning by corps comds—No news except a camp rumour that Lynchburgh had fallen.—" ALS (telegram sent), DNA, RG 393, Army of the Potomac, Miscellaneous Letters Received; telegram received (dated March 10), *ibid.*, RG 108, Letters Received. *O.R.*, I, xlvi, part 2, 903.

To Maj. Gen. Edward O. C. Ord

City Point Mch 7th 1865

MAJ, GEN, ORD

I would advise Michie by all means to accept the appointment of Asst, Inspector General, You can still retain him in charge as chief Eng—and in the mean time if anything can be done to advance him in the Regular Army I will be but too glad to do it, His services emenintly entitle him to substantial promotion and they will not in the end go unrewarded

U. S. GRANT Lieut Gen,

Copies, DLC-USG, V, 46, 74, 108; DNA, RG 108, Letters Sent. *O.R.*, I, xlvi, part 2, 880. On March 6, 1865, Maj. Gen. Edward O. C. Ord telegraphed to USG. "Lt Michie's nomination as Brevet Major is not confirmed, He is about accepting the appointment of Asst Insp'r Genl 25th A. C. to support his family, his services to this army ares chief Engr are not to be dispensed with. He is worth his weight in gold as an Engineer. Cannot he be promoted to Brevet Major, he richly deserves it by untiring industry exposing his life frequently and the practice of skill in the most important and responsible positions. I would only part with him as Chief Engineer to give him a Division as Brigadier" Telegram received (at 11:05 P.M.), DNA, RG 108, Letters Received. *O.R.*, I, xlvi, part 2, 861. On March 8, Maj. Gen. Godfrey Weitzel wrote to Brig. Gen. Lorenzo Thomas recommending Bvt. Maj. Peter S. Michie for inspector gen., 25th Army Corps. LS, DNA, RG 94, ACP, 1244 1871. On March 21, USG endorsed this letter. "Approved and respectfully forwarded to the Secretary of War." ES, *ibid.*

On March 7, USG telegraphed to Ord. "If it is possible to open the pontoon bridge today I wish you would have it done. There are transports above that it is important to get out as well as gunboats below to get above—" Telegram received (at 11:40 A.M.), Ord Papers, CU-B; copies, DLC-USG, V, 46, 74, 108; DNA, RG 108, Letters Sent.

On March 1, Ord telegraphed to USG. "There are at least One hundred fifty (150) good mechanics in the armory at Springfield Mass and in the various work shops in the manufacturing towns there that desire to enlist in the Engineers or Ponton Command of this army—provided they Can be assured of being retained in those branches of the service. We have frequent applications for such service and need these men sadly. Can authority be granted to raise one or two Companies for this duty with this army. One of the Companies of Pontoniers here is heavy artillery the men applied for Could be also an independent Company heavy artillery or Pontoniers" Telegram received, *ibid.*, Letters Received. *O.R.*, I, xlvi, part 2, 775.

On March 9, Ord telegraphed to USG. "The Engr force in this army is inadequate for the next Campaign. I respectfully request authority from washington to assign the 24th Mass Vols Infty as an Engineer Regt with permission to re-enlist it to its maximum Strength which I am informed can be done before May—" Telegram received (at 4:40 P.M.), DNA, RG 108, Letters Received. *O.R.*, I, xlvi, part 2, 905–6. On March 20, USG endorsed a letter of Mass. AG William Schouler concerning the raising of an engineer regt. "Respy forwarded to the Secetary of War. I recommend that under the condition herein proposed, the 24th Reg. Mass. Vols. be assigned to Engineers Gen Ord is very anxious to have this done. His army has but one small battalion of Engineer troops & requires more" Copy, DLC-USG, V, 58.

To Maj. Gen. John Pope

City Point, Va, March 7th *1865*

MAJ. GEN. J. POPE,
COMD.G MIL. DIV. OF MO.
GENERAL,

Your dispatch of this date in relation to securing for Col. F. Myers promotion, by brevet, to the rank of Brig. Gen. in the regular Army is received. I received also your letter of last December on the same subject. My recollection is that I answered your letter stating that recommendations for promotion, by brevet or otherwise, must come from officers under whom the recipient of such promotion has served and either go to the Adj. Gen. of the Army direct; an if it is desirable to have my recommendation then to me for endorsement.

The number of applications I receive to secure promotion for officers makes it necessary for me to adhere to this rule for all officers except those who have served directly under me.

I will be very happy to affix my approval to your recommendation of Col. Myers promotion. It will probably be too late now to secure his confirmation this extra session of the Senate; but his appointment can be made and held over to be acted on when Congress does meet.

Very respectfully
your obt. svt.
U. S. GRANT
Lt. Gen.

ALS, DNA, RG 94, Staff Papers. *O.R.*, I, xlviii, part 1, 1114. On March 7, 1865, Maj. Gen. John Pope, St. Louis, telegraphed to USG. "Will you please try and have Lt Col Fred Myers a. q. m nominated for Bvt Brig Genl in the regular Army before adjournment—For his services in Virginia and elsewhere see my letter to you dated some time in December" LS (telegram sent), DNA, RG 94, War Records Office, Army of the Potomac; telegram received, *ibid.*, RG 108, Letters Received. *O.R.*, I, xlviii, part 1, 1114.

On March 15, Pope wrote to USG. "I have the honor to recommend Lieut Col Fred Myers A. Q. M. and Chief Quartermaster of this Military Division for the Brevet of Brigadier in the Regular Army   Colonel Myers served during the Campaign in Virginia in 1862 as Chief Quartermaster of McDowell's Corps, but during the last days of that Campaign, his activity, efficiency and zeal were so manifest, and so essential to the situation, that I assigned him to duty as Chief Quarter Master of the Army of Virginia. In that position he rendered invaluable service during the last days of that Campaign, and it is not too much to say that, to him, more than to any other man, the safety of our large Army Trains was due—His indefatigable and intelligent services secured us from heavy losses of material, and he is eminently entitled to the promotion asked for him. He served for two years as Chief Quarter Master Department of the North West, with what fidelity to the Government and regard for the public interests, the records in the Office of the Quartermaster General, will abundantly show. He is an Officer of integrity, intelligence and sobriety, and entirely capable of discharging the duties of any position to which he may be assigned. I have the honor to request, General, that you will give this recommendation a favorable endorsement and forward it to the proper authority." Copy, DNA, RG 393, Military Div. of the Mo., Letters Sent. *O.R.*, I, xlviii, part 1, 1181–82.

To Maj. Gen. George H. Thomas

(Cipher)   City Point, Va. March 7th *1865* [*9:30* A.M.]
MAJ. GEN. THOMAS, NASHVILLE KY.

I think it will be advisable now for you to repair the rail-road in East Tenn. and throwgh a good force up to Bulls Gap and fortify there. Supplies at Knoxville could always be got forward as required. With Bulls Gap fotified you can occupy as outposts about all of East Tenn. and be prepared if it should be required of you in the Spring to make a Campaign towards Lynchburg or into North Carolina. I do not think Stoneman should break the road until he gets into Va. unless it should be to cut of rolling stock that may be caught West of that.

U. S. GRANT
Lt. Gn

ALS (telegram sent), OClWHi; telegram received (at 12:45 P.M.), DNA, RG 107, Telegrams Collected (Bound). *O.R.*, I, xxxiv, part 1, 48; *ibid.*, I, xxxvi, part 1, 51–52; *ibid.*, I, xxxviii, part 1, 40; *ibid.*, I, xlix, part 1, 854. On March 6, 1865, 10:00 A.M., Maj. Gen. George H. Thomas telegraphed to USG. "We have had a very heavy storm which has retarded the commencement of operations in this department by swellig the streams and distroying R R bridges but I am in hopes Wilson has started by this time—Stoneman will reach Knoxville by Saturday next the 11th with his expeditionary force and will start from there immediately—I will then adjust the ~~Infantry~~ available Infantry force to support Stoneman and repair the E Tennessee & Virginia R. R. as far as the Watauga bridge for the present—It will be necessary for Genl Hatch to remain at Eastport for horses to mount his division, and as his force is strong enough to hold that point for the present I have not ordered any Infantry there, but will await the developement of events in Miss & Ala." ALS (telegram sent), Duke University, Durham, N. C.; telegram received (at 1:30 P.M.), DNA, RG 107, Telegrams Collected (Bound); *ibid.*, RG 108, Letters Received. *O.R.*, I, xlix, part 1, 848.

To Edwin M. Stanton

(Cipher)   City Point, Va, March 8th *1865* [*11:00* A.M.]
HON. E. M. STANTON, SEC. OF W, WASHINGTON.
(Confidential)   I beleive Gen. Singleton[1] should be ordered to return from Richmond and all permits he may have should be revoked. Our friends in Richmond, and we have many of them there, send word that tobacco is being exchanged on the Potomac for bacon and they believed Singleton to be at the bottom of it. I am also of the opinion that all permits issued to Judge Hughes[2] should ~~also~~ be canseled. I think the same of all other permits heretofore granted. But in the case of Singleton and Judge Hughes I believe there is a deep laid plan for making millions and they will sacrifice every interest of the country to succeed. I do not know Huges personally never having seen him but once but the conviction here expressed is forced upon me

U. S. GRANT, Lt. Gn.

ALS (telegram sent), OClWHi; telegram received (at 2:00 P.M.), DLC-Robert T. Lincoln. *O.R.*, I, xlvi, part 2, 886. On March 8, 1865, 11:30 A.M., USG telegraphed to Secretary of War Edwin M. Stanton. "We have got supplies going out by Norfolk to the rebel army stopped, but information received shows that large amounts still go by way of the Blackwater—They no doubt go on the Treasury permits heretofore given under Act of Congress regulating trade with states in insurrection. I would respectfully recommend that orders be sent to the Army and Navy every where, to stop supplies going to the interior and annulling all permits for such trade heretofore given" Telegram received (at 2:00 P.M.), DLC-Robert T. Lincoln; copies, DLC-USG, V, 46, 74, 108; DNA, RG 108, Letters Sent. *O.R.*, I, xlvi, part 2, 886. At 9:30 P.M., Stanton telegraphed to USG. "In reply to your telegram in respect to trade with the enemy; I am unable to control the influences that procure permits; but I understand that the Presidents passes & permits are subject to your authority as Comdr in Chief, and that notwithstanding any permit given by the Secy of the Treasy or President himself, you as Commander may prohibit trade through your lines, and may seize goods in transit either way, and may also prohibit individuals crossing lines; This I understand is the effect of the instructions to you by the Presidents order through me of Feby 7th and the letter of same date   Military necessity is paramount to all other considerations and of that for [*you*] as Commander of the forces in the [*field*] are the absolute & paramount judges; This I believe to be the Presidents own view & that every one who procures a trade permit or pass to go through the lines from him does it impliedly subject to your sanction,   You are so instructed to act until further orders"   Telegram received, DNA, RG 107, Telegrams Collected (Bound); (on March 9) *ibid.*, RG 108, Letters Received. *O.R.*, I, xlvi, part 2, 886–87. The telegram received at USG's hd. qrs. had a postscript added by Maj. Thomas T. Eckert, March 9, 10:00 A.M. "The above despatch was handed me by the Secy War at his house last evening with the date of the Presidents letter left blank for me to fill up but owing to the absence of the Secys. confidential clerk I could not get it till this hour"   Telegram received, DNA, RG 108, Letters Received. *O.R.*, I, xlvi, part 2, 887. On March 8, 11:30 P.M., President Abraham Lincoln telegraphed to USG. "Your two despatches to the Secretary of War—one relating to supplies for the enemy going by the Blackwater, and the other to Gen. Singleton and Judge Hughes—have been laid before me by him. As to Singleton and Hughes, I think they are not in Richmond by any authority, unless it be from you. I remember nothing from me which could aid them in getting there except a letter to you as follows, towit: 'Executive Mansion Washington City Feb. 7, 1865   LIEUT GENL. GRANT City-Point, Va. Gen. Singleton who bears you this, claims that, ~~by your consent~~, he already has arrangements made, if you consent, to bring a large amount of Southern produce through your lines. For it's bearing on our finances, I would be glad for this to be done, if it can be, without injuriously disturbing your military operations, or supplying the enemy. I wish you to be judge and Master on these points. Please see and hear him fully; and decide whether anything & if anything, what can be done in the premises. Yours truly A. LINCOLN. I believe I gave Hughes a card putting him with Singleton, on the same letter. However this may be I now authorize you to get Singleton and Hughes away from Richmond, if you choose, and can. I also authorize you, by an order, or in what form you choose, to suspend all operations on the Treasury-trade-permits, in all places South Eastward of the Alleghanies. If you make such order, notify me of it, giving a copy, so that I can give corresponding direction to the Navy." ALS (telegram sent), DNA, RG 107, Telegrams Collected (Bound); LS, DLC-Robert T. Lincoln; telegram received (on March 9), DNA, RG 108, Letters Received. *O.R.*, I, xlvi, part 2, 885–86. Lincoln, *Works*, VIII, 343–44.

On Feb. 25, USG wrote to James W. Singleton. "Such Southern products as may be sent to Fredericksburg, Va. consigned to you, I will give directions to leave unmolested, by Military forces, from injury, or capture, so long as it remains there, or is in process of removal North, if done with authority of the Military commander of the Dept. of Washington and under Treasury regulations." ALS, Berkshire Museum, Pittsfield, Mass.

On Oct. 22, 1864, Lincoln wrote a letter of recommendation. "James Hughes of Indiana is a worthy gentlemen, and a friend whom I wish to oblige. He desires to trade in Southern products, and all officers of the army and Navy and other Agents of the Government will afford him and his Agents such protection and such facilities of transportation and otherwise, in such business as can be conveniently done with the Regulations of trade and with the public service—" Copy, Robertson Topp Papers, Southwestern at Memphis, Memphis, Tenn. Lincoln, *Works*, VIII, 73. At an unknown date, Lincoln wrote a permit. "Allow the bearer James Hughes to pass over lines with any Southern products, and go to any of our trading posts, there to be subject to the Regulations of the Treasury January 11th 1865." Copy, Topp Papers. On Feb. 25, 1865, USG endorsed a copy of the recommendation and permit. "So far as trade is allowed, under existing military Regulations or Regulations hereafter made Commanders will please extend to Judge James Hughes all the privileges given to authorized traders in Southern products" Copies, Topp Papers; Raymond Montgomery Johnson, Memphis, Tenn.

On March 13, Lincoln wrote to USG. "I think it will tend to remove some injurious misunderstanding for you to have another interview with Judge Hughes. I do not wish to modify anything I have heretofor said, as to your having entire control whether anything, in the way of trade shall pass either way through your lines—I do say, however, that having known Judge Hughes intimately during the whole of the rebellion, I do *not* believe he would knowingly betray any interest of the country, or attempt to deceive you in the least degree—Please see him again—" ALS, Morristown National Historical Park, Morristown, N. J. Lincoln, *Works*, VIII, 353. See Theodore Calvin Pease and James G. Randall, eds., *The Diary of Orville Hickman Browning* (Springfield, 1925–33), II, 10–11; telegram to Edwin M. Stanton, March 9, 1865; letter to James W. Singleton, March 20, 1865.

1. James W. Singleton, born in Va. in 1811, prominent in Ill. as physician, lawyer, and politician, took an active role in the peace movement in 1864–65, which led to his access to southern products. See letter to James W. Singleton, March 24, 1862.

2. James Hughes, born in Md. in 1823, a nongraduate of USMA, an Ind. lawyer, judge, and U.S. Representative (1857–59) and judge of the U.S. Court of Claims (1860–65), converted from Democrat to Republican during the Civil War.

To Edwin M. Stanton

City Point Va, March 8th 1865 [*6:30* P.M.]

HON, E, M, STANTON
SEC, OF WAR, WASHINGTON

I understand that Rebel prisoners in the North are allowed to take the oath of allegiance and go free, I think this is wrong, No one should be liberated on taking the oath of allegiance, who has been captured whilst bearing Arms against us, except where persons of known loyalty vouch for them, Men who desire to take the oath, are the best men to exchange They can afterwards come into our lines if they do not wish to fight,

U. S. GRANT
Lieut, General

Telegram, copies, DLC-USG, V, 46, 74, 108; DNA, RG 108, Letters Sent. Printed as received at 8:00 P.M. in *O.R.*, I, xlvi, part 2, 887. See following telegram.

To Abraham Lincoln

City Point Va

Mar. 9th 1865 5. P. M

His Excellency A. Lincoln
Prest U S.

Your despatch of this morning shows that prisoners of war are being discharged only in accordance with the rule I proposed. I questioned the officers from Camp Morton & Rock Island who arrived here yesterday in charge of prisoners for exchange and they told me that great numbers were being discharged on taking the oath of allegiance. They thought all who desired to do so are permitted to obtain their liberty in this way. I supposed this was in pursuance of a general policy which you knew nothing about and I wanted it changed so that none would be allowed to take the oath of allegiance except by special permission

U. S. Grant
Lt Genl

Telegram received (at 6:30 P.M.), DLC-Robert T. Lincoln; DNA, RG 107, Telegrams Collected (Bound); copies, *ibid.*, RG 108, Letters Sent; DLC-USG, V, 46, 74, 108; USG 3. *O.R.*, I, xlvi, part 2, 900. On March 9, 1865, 11:00 A.M., President Abraham Lincoln had telegraphed to USG. "I see your despatch to the Sec. of War, objecting to rebel prisoners being allowed to take the oath and go free. Supposing that I am responsible for what is done in this way, I think fit to say that there is no general rule, or action, allowing prisoners to be discharged merely on taking the oath—What has been done is that Members of Congress come to me from time to time with lists of names alleging that from personal knowledge, and evidence of reliable persons they are satisfied that it is safe to discharge the particular persons named on the lists, and I have ordered their discharge. These Members are chiefly from the border states; and those they get discharged are their neighbors and neighbors sons—They tell me that they do not bring to me one tenth of the names which are brought to them, bringing only such as their knowledge or the proof satisfies them about. I have, on the same principle, discharged some on the representations of other than Members of Congress, as, for instance, Gov. Johnson of Tennessee. The number I have discharged has been rather larger than I liked—reaching I should think an average of fifty a day, since the recent general exchange commenced. On the same grounds, last year, I discharged quite a number at different times, aggregating perhaps a thousand, Missourians and Kentuckians; and their Members returning here since the prisoner's return to their homes, report to me only two cases of proving false. Doubtless some more have proved false; but, on the whole I believe what I have done in this ways has done good rather than harm." ALS (telegram sent), DNA, RG 107, Telegrams Collected (Bound); telegram received, *ibid.*, RG 108, Letters Received. *O.R.*, I, xlvi, part 2, 900. Lincoln, *Works*, VIII, 347–48. See preceding telegram.

To Abraham Lincoln

City Point, Va, March 9th *1865*

HIS EXCELLENCY, A. LINCOLN,
PRESIDENT,
SIR:

I would respectfully recommend Jacob. Arnold Augur for the appointment of Cadet, at large, to West Point the coming year. He is the Son of Maj. Gen. C. C. Augur of the Army. Gen. Augur having served in the Army continuously since 1843 has no Congressional District, or delegate in Congress, to apply to for such appointment.

The young man will be, on the 1st day of July 1865, the date of his entry into West Point, if he is fortunate enough to receive the appointment here asked   years and   months old.—His father has always maintained a high character as a gentleman and a soldier. In the Mexican War he distingushed himself and in the present War he has risen, by his merit, to the position of Major General.

I will deem it a special favor if this appointment can be granted.

Very respectfully
your obt. svt.
U. S. GRANT
Lt. Gen.

ALS, DNA, RG 94, Cadet Applications. The first and middle names of Jacob Arnold Augur, USMA 1869, are not in USG's hand.

To Edwin M. Stanton

(Cipher)   City Point, Va, March 9th *1865* [*2:30* P.M.]
HON. E. M. STANTON, SEC. OF WAR, WASHINGTON.

My views about the operations of Mr. Singleton and Judge Hughes are merely suspicions based upon what is said in Richmond of the object of Singleton's visit and of the trade that is actually carried on. I recognized the importance of getting out Southern products if it ~~could~~ can be done without furnishing anything that ~~would~~ will aid in the support of the rebellion. I told Mr. Singleton that if the proposition was made I would agree that all Southern products should be brought to any of the ports held by us, the Government receiving one third and the balance should be stored and protected for the benefit of the owner at the end of the War; ~~and~~ that under no circumstances would I approve of supplies of any kind going in payment. I was not certain but I might consent to part payment being made in United States Currency but before doing so I would have to think of the matter. Judge Hughes has not been south of our lines and if my suspicions are correct it is not his interest to be there. I do not judge him to be worse than other men; but all who engage in trade promising such large rewards, and where the time it is likely to remain open to them is so limited, work themselves up to beleive that the small assistance they can give to the rebellion will not be felt. I will make an order ~~regulating or rather prohibiting, supplies going through the lines~~ Suspending the operations of all trade permits south east of the ~~Alleghanies~~ Alleghanies[1] and submit it. I will also notify Gen. Singleton that no agreement made by him will be regarded as binding upon Military Authorities without the approval of the President is obtained.

U. S. GRANT
Lt. Gn.

ALS (telegram sent), OClWHi; copies, DLC-USG, V, 46, 74, 108; DNA, RG 108, Letters Sent. Printed as received at 9:30 P.M. in *O.R.*, I, xlvi, part 2, 901–2.

On March 10, 1865, USG wrote to Secretary of War Edwin M. Stanton. "I have the honor to transmit herewith Special Orders No 48. If it meets with approval, please telegraph me, as I shall not send it out until I hear from you."

LS, DNA, RG 94, Letters Received, 1388A 1865. *O.R.*, I, xlvi, part 2, 913. Special Orders No. 48, March 10, read: "The operations on all Treasury Trade Permits within the State of Virginia, except that portion known as the Eastern Shore, and the States of North Carolina and South Carolina, and that portion of the State of Georgia immediately bordering on the Atlantic, including the city of Savannah, are hereby suspended until further orders. All contracts and agreements made under or by virtue of any Treasury Trade Permit within any of said States or parts of States, during the existence of this order, will be deemed void, and the subject of such contracts or agreements will be seized by the military authorities for the benefit of Government, whether the same is at the time of such contracts or agreements within their reach or at any time thereafter comes within their reach, either by the operations of war or the acts of the contracting parties or their agents. The delivery of all goods contracted for and not delivered before the publication of this order is prohibited. Supplies of all kinds are prohibited from passing into any of said States or parts of States, except such as are absolutely necessary for the wants of those living within the lines of actual military occupation, and under no circumstances will military commanders allow them to pass beyond the lines they actually hold." Copy (printed), DNA, RG 94, Letters Received, 1388A 1865. On March 11, 1:00 P.M., Stanton telegraphed to USG. "Special Order No 48 in relation to ~~Treasury~~ Trade permits has just been received and is approved. But have you not limited it too much by the specification of 'Treasury Trade permits'? So as to meet the whole mischief should it not include all 'Trade permits' by whomsoever granted, so as to cover every species of trade license ~~which~~ including unauthorised licenses by Military commanders as well as ~~by~~ the Treasury permits and also to prevent abuses under the Presidents permits. I am content however with the order in any form you choose." ALS (telegram sent), *ibid.*, RG 107, Telegrams Collected (Bound); telegram received (at 6:50 P.M.), *ibid.*, RG 108, Letters Received. *O.R.*, I, xlvi, part 2, 925. Following this, Special Orders No. 48 was amended by an insertion in the first sentence after the word "Permits." "and all other trade permits and licenses to trade, by whomsoever granted," Copy (printed), DLC-Robert T. Lincoln. Variant text in *O.R.*, I, xlvi, part 2, 915.

On March 28, Maj. Gen. Quincy A. Gillmore, Hilton Head, S. C., wrote to Brig. Gen. John A. Rawlins. "I have the honor to acknowledge the receipt of Special Orders No. 48, dated Headquarters Armies of the United States, City Point. Va, March 10th 1865, upon the subject of trade. The provisions of that order, do not, as I interpret it, in any way effect existing orders and regulations in this Department, for no traffic has been engaged in beyond the lines of actual military occupation since I assumed command, and the trade within the lines has been carefully restricted to the wants of the army and of the inhabitants depending on it for support. Several persons having authority to purchase cotton for the Treasury Department and bearing the order of the President to pass them, and their means of transportation, to and fro through the lines, are within my command, awaiting an opportunity to begin operations: thus far their efforts have been restricted to preliminary negotiations, in consequence of the delays they experience in finding the parties they sought, or pretended to seek, beyond the lines. An 'agent for the purchase of the products of insurrectionary States, on behalf of the government of the United States' has been sent here by the Treasury Department, with instructions to take post at Fernandina, Florida. All needful military restrictions, to prevent supplies reaching the enemy, shall be imposed upon trade in that quarter. I have been led to believe that it is the wish of our government, to get possession of as large a quantity, as possible, of the products of insurrectionary States,—especially cotton—so far as it can be done, without, in any degree, giving aid to the insurgents or compromising the success of military operations. It has been stated, also, on apparently good authority, that the confederate government is are equally desirous of getting rid of the cotton within their lines, and that since the fall of Wilmington and Charleston haves put a stop to blockade running on this coast, they are not very particular as to the terms upon which the owners dispose of it.—This is not altogether the case however; the military authorities keep a very careful watch upon all cotton operations, in order to secure to their government an immediate benefit for every pound that is disposed of—They are willing it should leave their lines, but want to be paid for it in supplies. A military officer is appointed to examine and approve all invoices of cotton sent out, as well as ofor the goods to be received for it—This I learn from intercepted correspondence between holders of cotton in the interior, and their agents and friends in Savannah and Charleston. The parties holding and controling large lots of cotton, as a general rule, believing that the war is near its close and that it behooves them to look out for their own interests while there is yet time, had much rather exchange it for United States currency than for supplies, upon which they would not be able to realize anything of greater value than confederate notes. I have reason to believe that there is a very considerable amount of cotton, held or controlled by persons entertaining these views, so located at the present time, that it can reach our lines without the knowledge of the rebel military authorities. It is more particularly with regard to cotton thus circumstanced and parties thus disposed, that I have thought it my duty to address you upon this subject. The question is, can Special Orders No 48, be so interpreted or amended, as to allow 'the purchase of the products of insurrectionary States' by treasury agents, for cash, in South Carolina and Georgia, excluding the seller from the privilege of taking any supplies whatever into the interior. I enclose copies of the only orders issued from these Headquarters, upon the subject of trade." LS, DNA, RG 108, Letters Received. *O.R.*, I, xlvii, part 3, 52–53.

1. The phrase "Suspending the operations of all trade permits south east of the Alleghanies Alleghanies" not in USG's hand.

To Edwin M. Stanton

City Point, Va, March 9 1865

HON. E. M. STANTON
SEC. WAR, WASHINGTON, D. C.

The following dispatch just received. I have ordered the expedition to finish up their work and break up supplying the rebel army from the North via Fredericksburg [*if I can*].

"Fort Monroe, Va, 10 p. m. March 8 1865

LIEUT COL BOWERS.

I have just got back from Fredericksburg. The transports are coming in. Had no fight. Captured and destroyed 28 cars, 18 loaded. Have some prisoners and refugees and about 400 cases of tobacco, 36 mules and wagons. The tobacco belonged to the Confederate Government, and I am informed was to have been exchanged for wheat through the agency of one M. C. Martin who was said to have authority from our Govt to make the exchange. It was consigned to Dr. L. B. Rose of Fredericksburg. I have brought him with me. The whole matter appears to me to be worthy of investigation. The transaction was to cover 4000 cases, and we would have caught it all in Frederickburg if we had been two days later. What shall I do with tobacco and prisoners?

sgd S. H. ROBERTS

Col. Comdg Expedition

U. S. GRANT

Lieut. Genl.

Telegram, copies, DLC-USG, V, 46, 74, 108; DNA, RG 94, Turner-Baker Papers, 3941T; *ibid.*, RG 108, Letters Sent. *O.R.*, I, xlvi, part 2, 900. The enclosure is printed as received on March 9, 1865, 11:30 A.M., *ibid.*, p. 891. On March 8, 10:00 P.M., Col. Samuel H. Roberts, Fort Monroe, telegraphed to Lt. Col. Theodore S. Bowers. "The guide for the lower counties of the Northern neck having reached me today I propose if the Lieut General permits to take my command to some point on the Potomac River & march down. There are some 500 cavalry in the country living upon the people & ready to collect conscripts & horses for the confederates. I think the greater part of the soldiers can be captured and a great many horses & cattle collected & the comd subsisted upon the country. I will wait here until tomorrow morning for reply It will take about five days to do the work well" Telegram received (on March 9, 10:30 A.M.), DNA, RG 108, Letters Received. *O.R.*, I, xlvi, part 2, 891. See *ibid.*, I, xlvi, part 1, 542–44.

On March 9, Roberts telegraphed to Bowers. "I am waiting for answer to my despatches sent last night. I have among my prisoners a Sergt. Shadbourne a notorious rebel scout well known to the Army of the Potomac. Had he better be sent to Genl Patrick." ALS (telegram sent), DNA, RG 107, Telegrams Collected (Unbound). At 11:10 A.M., USG telegraphed to Roberts. "Your dispatch of last night but just this moment received. Go back on the Potomac as you propose. Turn over your captures of property to the Quarter master at Fort Monroe to be held for further orders. Your prisoners may be turned over to the Provost Marshal at Fort Monroe." Copies, DLC-USG, V, 46, 74, 108; DNA, RG

94, Turner-Baker Papers, 3941T; *ibid.*, RG 108, Letters Sent. *O.R.*, I, xlvi, part 2, 907. On the same day, 12:30 P.M., Roberts telegraphed to Bowers. "Telegram from the Lieut. Genl. recd. Will be ready to leave here to-morrow morning. Can I have cooperation of the Navy. Can the mail of this Brigade, 3d Brig. 3d Div. 24 A. C. be sent down to-night, If it can be I should be glad to get it." ALS (telegram sent), DNA, RG 107, Telegrams Collected (Unbound); telegram received, *ibid. O.R.*, I, xlvi, part 2, 908. On the same day, USG telegraphed to Roberts. "You Will Call upon the Naval Commander at Fort Monroe and request him in my name to send the same boats to Cooperate with you that you had on the first expedition—Genl. Ord has been telegraphed to send your mail" Telegram received (at 10:00 P.M.), DNA, RG 107, Telegrams Collected (Unbound); copies, *ibid.*, RG 108, Letters Sent; DLC-USG, V, 46, 74, 108. *O.R.*, I, xlvi, part 2, 908.

Also on March 9, USG telegraphed to Commodore William Radford. "Please direct the Naval Vessels that accompanied the recent expedition up the Rappahannock to again return up the river and Cooperate with the forces under Col Roberts which returns for further Operations" Telegram received, DNA, RG 45, Area File; copies, *ibid.*, RG 108, Letters Sent; DLC-USG, V, 46, 74, 108. *O.R.*, I, xlvi, part 2, 903. At 11:50 P.M., Radford, Jones' Landing, telegraphed to USG. "Telegraph recd. The vessels will be Sent. I have not heard of their return" Telegram received, DNA, RG 108, Letters Received. *O.R.*, I, xlvi, part 2, 903.

On May 31, James W. Denver and James Hughes wrote to USG. "We request the discharge of D. W. Slye, and John Kendall, prisoners, confined at Point Lookout, and of Dr Rose, a prisoner in the Old Capitol, on the following grounds; Joseph H. Maddox, of Baltimore, who was the owner of certain tobacco, destroyed by your order at Fredericksburg Virginia, sent Slye and Kendall into Virginia, to purchase tobacco for sale to the United States Government, under the Act of Congress. He (Maddox) having a Treasury permit in the usual form. They were returning from Virginia, where they had been employed in the purchase of tobacco, when they were captured by Genl Sheridan's cavalry, and have since been held as prisoners. Soon after the capture of the Fredericksburg tobacco, Maddox was arrested, and after being confined for over sixty days, he was discharged, there being no charges preferred against him. Dr. Rose was the consignee of Maddox's tobacco, at Fredericksburg, and only consented to act in that capacity upon being assured that Maddox had proper authority for trading which was the fact. We also request an order for the delivery to Maddox, or his authorised agents, of any tobacco of his remaining in the custody of the United States forces." Copy, DNA, RG 94, Turner-Baker Papers, 3113T. On the same day, USG endorsed this letter. "Respectfully referred to the Sec. of War. I would recommend the release of these prisoners from confinement but the tobacco cannot be returned as the little which was taken I directed to be issued to the colored troops of the Dept of Va. who were without the means of purchasing" Copies, *ibid.*; DLC-Caleb Cushing. Further information concerning the activities of Joseph H. Maddox and others, who had a trade permit signed by President Abraham Lincoln on Nov. 17, 1864, is in Charles C. Nott and Archibald Hopkins, *Cases Decided in the Court of Claims at the December Term, 1872; and the Decisions of the Supreme Court in the Appealed Cases from October, 1872, to May, 1873* (Washington, 1874), VIII, 70–76.

To Gustavus V. Fox

City Point Va
Mch 9th 1865 [*midnight*]

G V Fox
ASST SECY NAVY

The James River is high enough for gunboats to ascend, Except in cooperation with the Army however I do not think any practical results could come from sending them up. If Admiral Porter comes down here, as I expect in a few days, I will consult with him on the subject & let you know the conclusion—

U S GRANT Lt Gen

Telegram received (on March 10, 1865, 2:40 A.M.), DNA, RG 45, Miscellaneous Letters Received; *ibid.*, RG 107, Telegrams Collected (Bound); copies, *ibid.*, RG 108, Letters Sent; DLC-USG, V, 46, 74, 108. *O.R.*, I, xlvi, part 2, 902; *O.R.* (Navy), I, xii, 62.

On March 8, Maj. Gen. John A. Dix, New York City, telegraphed to Secretary of the Navy Gideon Welles, sending a copy to USG. "The Schooner 'Ann Pickered left here on monday for Washington She has goods intended to be landed at Piankatank or Mob-Jack Bay in charge of J. Mackintosh Williamson believed to be a Rebel agent. He is a Scothman with Red hair whiskers & moustache Cannot the vessel be Stopped on entering Cheapeake Bay—" Telegram received, DNA, RG 107, Telegrams Collected (Unbound); (on March 9, 10:00 A.M.) *ibid.*, RG 108, Letters Received. On March 9, 10:30 A.M., USG telegraphed to Welles. "Would it not be advisable to have Gun Boats sent into York river, Mob Jack bay, Piankatank harbor and the Rappahannock frequently to capture or destroy vessels running into those harbors for the purpose of supplying the enemy?" Telegram received (at 2:00 P.M.), *ibid.*, RG 45, Miscellaneous Letters Received; *ibid.*, RG 107, Telegrams Collected (Bound); copies, *ibid.*, RG 108, Letters Sent; DLC-USG, V, 46, 74, 108. *O.R.*, I, xlvi, part 2, 902. At 8:30 P.M., Asst. Secretary of the Navy Gustavus V. Fox telegraphed to USG. "Naval force along the Va. shore of the Chesepeake will be increased Is the James high enough to make an attempt to go up? We have a very large naval force realeased & the sacrifice of some of them might open the way for others to get through" Telegram received, DNA, RG 108, Letters Received. *O.R.*, I, xlvi, part 2, 902; *O.R.* (Navy), I, xii, 62.

On March 4, 4:00 P.M., Fox had telegraphed to USG. "Two (2) monitors have been ordered to James River some eight days since. If the river is very high perhaps we had better send of to hurry them up" Telegrams received (2— at 2:00 P.M. and 4:15 P.M.), DNA, RG 107, Telegrams Collected (Bound); *ibid.*, RG 108, Letters Received. *O.R.*, I, xlvi, part 2, 826. At 7:00 P.M., USG telegraphed to Fox. "The James river is very high & will continue so as long as the weather of the past week lasts. It would be well to have at once all the iron-

clads that it is intended should come here." Telegram received (at 8:30 P.M.),
DNA, RG 45, Miscellaneous Letters Received; *ibid.*, RG 107, Telegrams Col-
lected (Bound); copies, *ibid.*, RG 108, Letters Sent; DLC-USG, V, 46, 74, 108.
O.R., I, xlvi, part 2, 826; (received at 8:20 P.M.) *O.R.* (Navy), I, xii, 59.

To Maj. Gen. Henry W. Halleck

City Point Va, Mch 9th 1865 [*10:30* A.M.]

MAJ, GEN, HALLECK

WASHINGTON

Persons friendly to the Union, living in Richmond have sent
out word that the Rebel Navy, liberated from duty in Charleston
Harbor by the evacuation of Charleston, have been sent West, for
the purpose of depredating upon our river transportation, It is
expected thaat they will operate most on the Ohio river, but it will
be well for us to guard particularly against their operations on
bothe the Ohio and the Miss—, Will you please put all Commanders on the Ohio and the Miss—on their guard against these men?

U. S. GRANT
Lieut, General

Telegram, copies, DLC-USG, V, 46, 74, 108; DNA, RG 108, Letters Sent. *O.R.*,
I, xlvi, part 2, 903.
    On March 8, 1865, 10:30 A.M., USG telegraphed to Maj. Gen. John M.
Palmer, Louisville. "AInformation from Richmond indicates that a Naval party
have gone to the Ohio river for some mischievous purpose. Look out for them
and if caught in disguise hang them up as fast as caught." ALS (telegram
sent), OClWHi; copies, DLC-USG, V, 46, 74, 108; DNA, RG 108, Letters Sent;
(2) *ibid.*, RG 393, Dept. of Ky., Telegrams Received. *O.R.*, I, xlix, part 1, 863;
O.R. (Navy), I, xxvii, 86.

To Maj. Gen. Edward R. S. Canby

(Cipher,   City Point, Va, March 9th *1865* [*midnight*]

MAJ. GEN. CANBY NEW ORLEANS, VIA CAIRO

I am in receipt of a dispatch from Gen. Meigs informing me
that you have made requisition for a constructi[on] Corps and
material to build 70 miles of rail-road.[1] I have directed that none

be sent.[2] Gen. Thomas Army has been depleted to send a force to you that they might be where they could act in the Winter and at least detain the force the enemy had in the West. If there had been any idea of repairing rail-roads it could have been done much better from the North where we already had the troops. I expected your movements to have been co-operative with Shermans last? This has now entirely failed. I wrote to you long ago urging you to push forward promptly and to live upon the country and destroy rail-roads, Machine-shops an&c not to build them. Take Mobile and hold it and push your forces to the interior to Mongtgomery & Selma. Destroy rail-road, rolling stock and everything useful for carrying on War and when you have done this take such positions as can be supplied by water. By this means alone you can occupy a positions from which the enemys roads in the interior can be kept broken.

U. S. GRANT
Lt. Gn.

ALS (telegram sent), Mr. and Mrs. Philip D. Sang, River Forest, Ill.; telegram received (on March 10, 1865, 3:00 A.M.), DNA, RG 107, Telegrams Collected (Bound); *ibid.*, Telegrams Collected (Unbound). *O.R.*, I, xlix, part 1, 875. On March 23, 5:30 P.M., Maj. Gen. Edward R. S. Canby, Fish River, Ala., telegraphed to USG. "Your dispatch of the 9th has just been received. Estimates for railroad material and construction had no reference to immediate operations, but was made with a view to the future, if we should not be able to open the navigation of the Alabama. You cannot regret more than I do the delays that have attended this movement. We have been embarrassed, and delayed by rain and windstorms that have not been paralleled in the last 40 years. The flood have been general, and embraced the whole section of the Southwest. It was impossible to bridge streams in order to move by land, because the overflow was so great that their banks could [*not*] be reached, and the weather on the gulf has been so tempestuous that our transports could not be used more than half the time, and the services of several has been lost by being driven ashore. We have now two consecutive bright days, the two in a month, and a footing upon fair ground. If the 13th Corps gets up to night, as I hope it will, we will move in the morning for Blakely, and will endeavor to open way for the gunboats into the Alabama" Telegrams sent (2), DNA, RG 107, Telegrams Collected (Unbound); telegram received (on April 1, 9:00 P.M.), *ibid.*, Telegrams Collected (Bound). *O.R.*, I, xlix, part 2, 66.

On March 10, Bvt. Brig. Gen. Cyrus B. Comstock, New Orleans, telegraphed to USG. "Gen Canby left here Mch 5th for Mobile Lt Bay where Grangers command &. Smiths command now are with the exception of two or three thousand men who are now getting off. Steele with about 8000 men is at Pensacola probably to move on Blakely. Grierson is here & his Cavalry coming.

He goes I am told to Canby and it will take him a week to get his command there. Much delay has been caused by a cipher clerks blunder, which made Smith land at Vicksburg & discharge his steamboats. Rebels are supposed to have 9000 men at Mobile & as many at Blakely ~~I leave for Mobile~~" ALS (telegram sent), DNA, RG 107, Telegrams Collected (Bound); telegram received (on March 18, 6:00 P.M.), *ibid.*; (on March 19) *ibid.*, RG 108, Letters Received. Printed as received March 16, 6:00 P.M., in *O.R.*, I, xlix, part 1, 884.

1. On March 9, 3:00 P.M., Bvt. Maj. Gen. Montgomery C. Meigs telegraphed to USG. "Gen Canby asks that construction corps, 800 experienced workmen, with material and stock to rebuild 70 miles of R. R from Pascagoula to Pollard and from and from Pensacola to Barrancas, may be sent from the North. The iron alone would cost in New York Eight hundred and seventy five thousand dollars; the other material & labor would carry the cost to two million subject to some deductions for rolling stock which Canby hopes to get from the Mobile & O. road. We are embarrassed to provide transportation to N. C. for R. R. stock and material to prepare to meet Sherman, and the fitting out of an expedition to establish a new R R construction centre at Pensacola would be a serious tax upon the resources of the commercial marine and upon the appropriations of this Dep. If we begin this R R construction at Pensacola it will inevitably extend & result in the expenditure up R Rs in that region of several millions. Consulting Gen Halleck he advises me to telegraph to you and ask your views upon the subject. Whatever is approved will be attempted & executed if possible, but I have doubts as to the necessity or expediency of commencing this great expenditure. The Ala. river is generally navigable & the miss. can furnish all needed steamboats. The southwestern roads are repaired in good navigable condition" Telegram received, DNA, RG 108, Letters Received. *O.R.*, I, xlix, part 1, 868.

2. At 11:30 P.M., USG telegraphed to Meigs. "You need not send an article of rail-road material or a man to Gen. Canby. We have no time for building rail-roads there now." ALS (telegram sent), deCoppet Collection, NjP; telegram received (on March 10, 12:50 A.M.), DNA, RG 92, Consolidated Correspondence; *ibid.*, RG 107, Telegrams Collected (Bound); *ibid.*, Telegrams Collected (Unbound). *O.R.*, I, xlix, part 1, 868.

To Edwin M. Stanton

By Telegraph from City Point, Va. Mar. 10th *1865.* [*8:20* P.M.]
To HON. E. M. STANTON,
SEC'Y OF WAR.

Schofield has been apparently slow in getting started on account of unprecedentedly stormy and bad weather. There has been but little time when vessels could run in over the bar and consequently he was without transportation and could go no farther than men could carry rations to supply them. When he wrote however, his waggons were arriving and he was going to start without waiting for full supplies.

U. S. GRANT,
Lt. Genl.

Telegram, copies, DLC-USG, V, 46, 74, 108; DNA, RG 108, Letters Sent; (marked as received at 9:00 P.M.) DLC-John M. Schofield. *O.R.*, I, xlvii, part 2, 753. On March 10, 1865, 4:00 P.M., Asst. Secretary of War Charles A. Dana telegraphed to USG. "Two telegraph operators who were in the rebel service at Wilmington up to its capture, and who ~~have~~ have arrived here, having left Wilmington on the 2nd inst. ~~report~~ state that it was officially ~~known~~ reported at Wilmington on the night of Feb. 21. that Sherman's advance had reached Chesterville S. C. on that day & that a body of his cavalry were at Camden. When these men left Schofield had not moved from Wilmington." ALS (telegram sent), DNA, RG 107, Telegrams Collected (Bound); telegram received, *ibid.*; *ibid.*, RG 108, Letters Received. *O.R.*, I, xlvii, part 2, 752.

On March 2, Lt. Col. Theodore S. Bowers telegraphed to Maj. Gen. John M. Schofield. "Owing to the scarcity of sea going transportation & the great necessity for it to keep our armies supplied, It is absolutely necessary that it be not detained one hour longer than it is required for unloading You will please instruct Quarter Masters & other officers of your Command Controlling it to this end & will see that the instructions are complied with—If you have any troops yet to move by water move them at once and send back the transportation without delay" Telegram received (press), DNA, RG 107, Telegrams Collected (Bound); copies, *ibid.*, RG 108, Letters Sent; DLC-USG, V, 46, 74, 108. *O.R.*, I, xlvii, part 2, 653. USG added a note: "Operator at Fort Monroe will please put up. and hand to Captain James A Q. M. to be forwarded by first boat." Copies, DLC-USG, V, 46, 74, 108; DNA, RG 108, Letters Sent. *O.R.*, I, xlvii, part 2, 653.

On March 5 and 7, Schofield wrote to USG. "I have sent several despatches to Genl Sherman, some of which I have no doubt will reach him. I have received nothing from him yet. The paroled officers who have arrived here and others all agree in the report that he was near Chesterville on the Columbia and Charlotte road on the 24th, and that he turned Eastward from that place. I presume he will march straight for Goldsboro, passing through or near Fayettville. We are having heavy and continuous rains here. If they extend into the interior his march will be slow. I have at length got teams enough to make a start from this point with a portion of my troops. I shall send Genl Couch with the two divisions of the 23d Corps to join Genl Cox beyond Newburn. He will take the coast road to about Onslow and then make straight for Kinston. I expect him to effect a junction with Cox in five or six days. I will go to Morehead City tomorrow. I have not heard from Cox since he went to Newburn, but I expect him to get Kinston before Couch joins him. I will then push for Goldsboro, and hold it until Genl Sherman arrives; or if I find he is keeping out further from the coast I will advance toward Raleigh and join him. I will be able to move against Goldsboro with about 20,000 effective men. Genl Terry will remain here with his command for the present, but will advance along the railroad as ~~soon~~ fast as Col. Wright can repair it or as soon as he can get the necessary transportation to move independently. Nothing has arrived here yet for the railroad. Indeed the weather has been so bad that we have had but little communication by sea since the capture of Wilmington. Much of the time no vessel whatever has been able to cross the bar. The delivery of prisoners by the enemy was completed yesterday, and I am sending them North as rapidly as practicable. The well ones can all be sent in a short time, but it will take much longer to dispose of the sick, as they can only be placed on hospital vessels. They have been made comfortable here and are doing well. The whole number of prisoners delivered is about ten thousand, one hundred and twenty colored troops among the number. I will send the rolls to the Adjt Genl of the Army for his disposition." "The troops under Genl Cox have reached South West Creek, three miles this side of Kinston, today. They find the enemy in considerable force behind the creek. Hokes command is said to be there. Whether any other troops is not ascertained. I arrived here today and will go to the front tomorrow. The repair of the railroad is now being pushed forward as rapidly as possible. Some iron arrived from the North this evening and no doubt it will now come as fast as it can be put down. The troops are several miles in advance of the present terminus of the road, and I think will be able to keep ahead of it. If Hokes command alone is in our front he can not detain us long. If a greater force, I may have to wait till Genl Couch arrives. But I shall make the attempt to take Kinston at once unless satisfied that it can not be done. Palmer's delay is unfortunate, since it has given the enemy time to concentrate and has kept the railroad workmen idle some time longer than necessary. Since Cox arrived he has pushed matters with all possible vigor, and I will do all I can to make up lost time. Col. Wright thinks he can repair the road to Goldsboro by the 20th if we are able to clear the way. I will write more fully as soon as I develop the real condition of affairs in front." ALS, DNA, RG 108, Letters Received. *O.R.*, I, xlvii, part 2, 693–94, 722.

On March 9, Schofield wrote to USG. "Yesterday the enemy assumed the offensive, recrossed South West Creek, some distance to the Left of Genl. Cox's position, and drove back a brigade which was reconnoitering for a crossing of the creek, but did not succeed in disturbing the main line. The enemy maintained his ground on this side of the creek, and is now entrenched in Cox's immediate front. The loss was not very large on either side. Hoke has been reenforced by troops from Johnson's Army, one division probably and I think more are expected. We can make no further progress until Genl. Couch arrives which should be within two or three days. Meanwhile Col. Wright will have all he can do to complete the road to where the troops now are. I enclose a letter just received from Genl. Terry giving the latest information of Genl. Sherman. Mr Richardson is a very reliable man, and derived his information from a source he fully credits. I fear Genl. Sherman is finding very bad roads. I sent today a despatch in cipher, to be forwarded from Wilmington, giving him the situation here, and stating that I did not think it at all certain that I would be able to get Goldsboro' before he arrives. My beleif is that all of Johnson's force will be concentrated here now that Sherman has turned toward the coast. In that case I will hardly be able to do more than hold my own with my present force. I cannot reduce Terry's command unless I give up the idea of opening the road from Wilmington, at least until I know where Genl. Sherman is going. If he moves for Goldsboro', Hardee, who appears to have been left in rear, will have nothing better to do than to interfere with Terry's operations. One steamer load of troops have arrived from Savannah, but I have not learned what others may be expected, nor when. These detachments do not amount to much, Palmer's command, including the fragments brought here by Meagher are little better than militia. I think more troops could be used here to advantage, if in view of your general plans they are not more needed elsewhere. As soon as Couch gets up I will test the question as to what can be done. It is raining almost constantly and the country is nearly covered with water. Fortunately the effect is not so bad here as in a clay soil but it makes some of the swamps and streams impassable. . . . P. S. Maj. Genl. Schofield left for the front this morning without signing the above, and has since directed me to forward it with this explanation Very Respectfully G. W. SCHOFIELD Brvt. Brig. Genl." LS, DNA, RG 108, Letters Received. *O.R.*, I, xlvii, part 2, 743–44. On March 13, USG endorsed a copy of this letter. "Respectfully forwarded for the information of the Secretary of War." ES, DNA, RG 94, Letters Received, 113N 1865. *O.R.*, I, xlvii, part 2, 744.

On March 10, Schofield, Wise's Forks, N. C., telegraphed to USG. "The Enemy made a heavy attack upon our Centre & left today but was decisively repulsed and with heavy loss. His dead and badly wounded men left upon the field we also took Several hundred Prisoners. Our loss is Small—Genl Couch is only twelve (12) miles from here tonight and will be up Early in the morning we took Prisoners from Lees & Stewarts Corps—They Say Two Corps are here and the rest of Johnsons Army Coming" Telegram received, DNA, RG 108, Letters Received. *O.R.*, I, xlvii, part 2, 766. USG transmitted copies of this telegram to Secretary of War Edwin M. Stanton on March 13 and to Maj. Gen. George G. Meade on March 14. Telegram received (at 4:15 P.M.), DNA, RG 107, Telegrams Collected (Bound); copy, Meade Papers, PHi.

On March 14, Schofield, Kinston, N. C., wrote to USG. "I have the honor to report that I occupied Kinston this morning without opposition. The bridge across the Neuse is burned, and the ironclad ram is partially sunk, and is still burning. The enemy left two heavy guns, and a large amount of ammunition in the works at the bridge. These works are as formidable as any I have yet seen. I have ordered up light steamers from NewBerne with supplies, and have put a large force upon the railroad to help the Construction Corps, to push the road through as rapidly as possible. My present information is that the enemy is moving his stores from Goldsboro to Raleigh, and preparing to concentrate all his force at that place. The general impression is that Sherman is moving from Fayetteville straight for Raleigh, and no doubt that will be the appearance, at least, of his movement. It is probable that I can occupy Goldsboro, at any time, when I can supply myself there; Yet the enemy will doubtless renew the attempt he made on the Eighth and tenth as soon as I get near enough for Johnson to strike me with his combined forces, and then recover his position in front of Sherman. This I will have to look out for, and yet I must push the enemy all I can to diminish the resistance in Sherman's front. My aim will be to occupy Goldsboro about the (20th) twentieth inst. and then open communication with Sherman. This will be easy if he, after threatening Raleigh, marches rapidly for Goldsboro, as seems to be his plan. Bragg had here, Hoke's Division; Lee's Corps, and a part of Stewarts Corps, I think about 15.000 men. The remainder of Johnson's Army including Hardee's force, I presume to be in front of Sherman. The whole, I suppose, amounts to about (30,000) thirty thousand, if Lee has not sent any troops from Richmond recently. Terry is ordered to join me with such force as can be spared from Wilmington, as soon as he can get wagons enough to bring him through. But he will hardly reach me before I unite with Sherman. I apprehend the greatest difficulty will be the matter of supplies. We can hardly do more than get the railroad done to Kinston by the 20th. How much damage is done beyond this place I have not learned, but it is no doubt considerable. If Sherman reaches Goldsboro by the 20th he will probably have to send his wagons to Kinston for supplies. I have barely teams enough to haul supplies for my troops three or four miles; and have to use the same teams to haul my pontoon train. I have not yet been able to get the latter to the river, but had to repair the tressel bridge before I could cross. Under these circumstances it seems impossible to make my junction with Sherman beyond Goldsboro, in any event; and I think I am right in making the reconstruction of the road, the primary object, instead of trying to push forward my troops more rapidly than the road progresses—A few days ago General Hoke sent a proposition to General Cox to exchange prisoners, which, by my direction, the latter declined. I do not understand that I am authorized to *deliver* prisoners, although I am to *receive* them,—and there are important reasons why it should not be done here. But I respectfully request to be informed of your wishes on the subject." LS, DNA, RG 108, Letters Received; ADfS, DLC-John M. Schofield. *O.R.*, I, xlvii, part 2, 833–34.

To Edwin M. Stanton

City Point Va, March 10th 1865

Hon, E, M, Stanton,
Sec, of War, Washington

Deserters continue to report the capture of Linchburg, They also say a report prevails that two bridges on the Danville road, North of Burksville have been destroyed by Union Cavalry

U. S. Grant
Lieut, General

Telegram, copies, DLC-USG, V, 46, 74, 108; DNA, RG 108, Letters Sent. *O.R.*, I, xlvi, part 2, 914. On March 10, 1865, 2:00 P.M., USG had telegraphed to Secretary of War Edwin M. Stanton. "Deserters in this morning report a Camp rumer that Lynchburg has been captured by Sheridan." ALS (telegram sent), OClWHi; copies, DLC-USG, V, 46, 74, 108; DNA, RG 108, Letters Sent. *O.R.*, I, xlvi, part 2, 913.

Also on March 10, Brig. Gen. John W. Turner telegraphed to USG transmitting a telegram of 10:45 A.M. from Bvt. Maj. Gen. August V. Kautz to Turner. "Two (2) deserters of the 47th Alabama just in report that the Union Cavalry penetrated into the suburbs of Manchester yesterday. Our own pickets heard firing in that direction yesterday morning a report prevails that the Union Cavalry have destroyed two (2) bridges between Burksville & Richmond on the Danville Road, There are but two (2) fleet creek & Mattox, Sheridan is reported to be in Lynchburg, Geary was sent off in big hurry yesterday to the other side of Richmond with all the Cavalry he could raise which cannot be much" Telegram received, DNA, RG 108, Letters Received. Printed as received at 4:00 P.M. in *O.R.*, I, xlvi, part 2, 917.

To Bvt. Brig. Gen. William Hoffman

City Point Va
9 30 p m Mch 10th 1865

BRIG GEN WM HOFFMAN
COM GEN PRIS—

I have received information from Genl Schofield that he has received about ten 10 thousand of our prisoners at Wilmington. Exchanges are also going on at Mobile, You may continue to send rebel prisoners on the "Leary" and "New York."

The former will be at Pt Lookout on Sunday—

U S GRANT
Lt Genl

Telegram received (at 11:30 P.M.), DNA, RG 107, Telegrams Collected (Bound); *ibid.*, RG 249, Letters Received; copies, *ibid.*, RG 108, Letters Sent; DLC-USG, V, 46, 74, 108; USG 3.

Speech

[*March 11, 1865*]

I accept the Medal and joint resolutions of Congress which the President has commissioned you to deliver to me. I will do myself the honor at an early day to acknowledge the receipt of the letter of the President accompanying them ~~Medal and resolution~~ and to communicate, in orders, to the officers & soldiers, ~~Armies that ha~~ who served under my Command prior to the passage of the resolution, the thanks so generously tendered to them by the Congress of the United States.

AD, DLC-Sylvanus S. Cadwallader. USG spoke in response to a speech made by U.S. Representative Elihu B. Washburne. "By a joint resolution of the Congress of the United States, approved on the 17th day of ~~January~~ December 1863, the thanks of Congress were presented to you, then a Major General in the ~~Volunteer services~~ Army ~~of the United States~~ of the United States, and the officers and ~~men~~ soldiers who had fought under your command during the rebellion for their gallantry and good conduct ~~during the rebellion~~ in the battles in which they had been engaged, and the President of the United States was requested to cause a gold medal to be struck, with suitable emblems, devices and inscriptions to be presented to you. And it was further resolved that when the said medal should have been struck the President should cause a copy of the joint resolution to be engrossed on parchment and transmit the same to you together with the medal to be presented to you in the name of the people of the United States of America. The medal provided for in the said resolution has been completed and the resolution engrossed, and the President has commissioned me to deliver the same to you. It only remains for me, therefore, to discharge the duty which has been devolved upon me. I first present you with the open letter of the President, which with your permission I will read: I now ~~present~~ deliver to you ~~with~~ a copy of the joint resolution of Congress engrossed on parchment. Having delivered the resolution, it is now my pleasure to place in your hand the medal." AD, *ibid.*

On March 7, 1865, President Abraham Lincoln wrote to USG. "In accordance with a Joint Resolution of Congress, approved December 17, 1863, I now have the honor of transmitting, and presenting to you, in the name of the People of the United States of America, a copy of said resolution, engrossed on parchment, together with the gold medal therein ordered and directed. Please accept, for yourself and all under your command, the renewed expression of my gratitude for your and their arduous and well-performed public service." LS, DLC-Robert T. Lincoln. Lincoln, *Works*, VIII, 339. See *PUSG*, 9, 503*n*–4*n*.

On March 3, Washburne telegraphed to USG. "The Chief of Staff bill has passed both Houses, and will be a law tomorrow. If you send your recommendation to me, it will be immediately attended to. We may start for City Point Tuesday or Wednesday next. Shall take medal. Will you send me a pass for self and friends." ALS (telegram sent), DNA, RG 107, Telegrams Collected (Unbound); telegram received, *ibid.*, RG 108, Letters Received. *O.R.*, I, xlvi, part 2, 803. On the same day, USG telegraphed to Washburne. "I have sent recommendation for Rawlins appointment to the Secretary of War Your pass will go up by mail in the morning—" Telegram received (at 6:00 P.M.), DNA, RG 107, Telegrams Collected (Bound); copies, *ibid.*, RG 108, Letters Sent; DLC-USG, V, 46, 74, 108. *O.R.*, I, xlvi, part 2, 803.

On March 9, Washburne telegraphed to USG. "Our party leaves for City Point this afternoon at four o'clock." ALS (telegram sent), DNA, RG 107, Telegrams Collected (Unbound).

On March 11, Brig. Gen. John A. Rawlins telegraphed to Maj. Gen. Edward O. C. Ord. "Hon E. B. Washburne will present to the Lt Genl the medal voted by Congress this evening at 9 Oclk on board the stmr 'M. Marten'. If you can do so come down with such officers as can be spared for an hour or two from the front" Telegram received, Ord Papers, CU-B. For the presentation ceremony, see *New York Herald*, March 14, 1865; Horace Porter, *Campaigning with Grant* (New York, 1897), pp. 393–94.

Brig. Gen. John A. Rawlins, Lt. Gen. Ulysses S. Grant, and Lt. Col. Theodore S. Bowers at City Point. Photograph attributed to Mathew B. Brady. *Courtesy National Archives.*

Rear view of Grant's cabin at City Point.
Courtesy Library of Congress.

To Edwin M. Stanton

City Point, Va.,
8.30 p. m. Mch. 11, 1865.

HON. EDWIN M STANTON,
SECTY. OF WAR,

I would like to have either Hartsuff[1] or Sykes ordered here to command, a division which has no general officer.

This is the division now commanded by Brevet Brig. Genl. Harris[2] who goes out of service.

U. S. GRANT
Lieut Genl

Telegram, copies, DNA, RG 94, Letters Received, 284A 1865; *ibid.*, RG 108, Letters Sent; DLC-USG, V, 46, 74, 108. *O.R.*, I, xlvi, part 2, 925.

1. George L. Hartsuff, born in N. Y. in 1830, USMA 1852, served on the staff of Brig. Gen. William S. Rosecrans in 1861–62. Appointed brig. gen. as of April 15, 1862, he fought with the Army of the Potomac until a severe wound received at the battle of Antietam virtually terminated his field service, though he was promoted to maj. gen. as of Nov. 29, 1862. See telegram to Edwin M. Stanton, March 12, 1865. On March 15, 1865, USG telegraphed to Maj. Gen. George G. Meade. "Genl. Hartsuff has reported here for duty. Do you want him to Command a Div in the 9th A C" Undated telegram received (at 8:15 P.M.), DNA, RG 94, War Records Office, Army of the Potomac; copies (2), Meade Papers, PHi. On March 16, 5:00 P.M., Meade telegraphed to USG. "I have now more officers to command divisions than divisions. Under these circumstances, although there is no officer I should be more glad to have than General Hartsuff, yet I can not, in justice to others, say I want him." Copies, *ibid.*; DNA, RG 393, Army of the Potomac, Letters Sent. Hartsuff was assigned to command the lines at Bermuda Hundred.

2. On March 6, Maj. Gen. Edward O. C. Ord telegraphed to USG. "The Breaking up of three (3) Companies of Col. I & Brevet Br. Gen. Harris' reg't will require that he be mustered out of service in about ten days. Gen Harris is a valuable officer. His Division from the army of West Virginia would have no General officer to Command it & I have no good one to replace him. besides on the eve of a Campaign Commanders should, if good be retained Gen. Gibbon recommends Gen Harris be made a full Brigadier If this Cannot be done I recommed he be assigned to duty according to his brevet & retained as such in service" Telegram received, *ibid.*, RG 108, Letters Received. On March 7, Lt. Col. Theodore S. Bowers wrote to Ord. "Your Telegram in relation to the case of Brevet Brig Gen Harris is recieved, please forward to these Head Qrs. a full statement of all the facts in his case, the date of his appointment by brevet, the date of the expiration of his term of service, the number of companies in his regiment and the date, that the term of service of each expires in order that his

case may be fully meet. In this connection your attion is called to the enclosed copy of a letter from the Adjutant Genl's Office (see Circular No 8 Hd Qrs Dept of Va series of 1865.) authorizing the remuster and retention of Colonels of regiments under certain circumstances. You will therefore make out and forward to these Head Quarters a statement in the case of such Colonels whose term of service have expired or is about to expire but whose regiment still continue in service without losing their regimental organization by companies thereof being mustered out that you desire to retain. You will state particularly the date of the expiration of the existing terms of service of each Colonel and the number of company organizations in each of their regiments, and the date of the expiration of each company in order that they may recieve the action of the Lieut General." Copies, DLC-USG, V, 46, 74, 108; DNA, RG 108, Letters Sent; *ibid.*, Letters Received. On March 10, Ord endorsed to Bowers a copy of the latter's letter with the information enclosed. ES, *ibid.* On March 10, USG telegraphed to Ord. "What are the initials of Col. Harris 10th West Va. Please answer" Telegram received (at 10:10 A.M.), Ord Papers, CU-B. At 11:30 A.M., USG telegraphed to Stanton. "I would respectfully recommend that Bvt, Brig, Gen, T, M, Harris be appointed full Brig. Gen, of Vols, Most of his Regiment goes out of service in the next ~~four~~ two days, and he is the only ~~man~~ Officer in his Division to Command it" Copies, DLC-USG, V, 46, 74, 108; DNA, RG 108, Letters Sent. *O.R.*, I, xlvi, part 2, 913. On March 11, Stanton telegraphed to USG. "There is no vacant Brigadiership to which Brevet Brig Harris can be appointed" ALS (telegram sent), DNA, RG 107, Telegrams Collected (Bound); telegram received (at 7:00 P.M.), *ibid.*, RG 108, Letters Received. *O.R.*, I, xlvi, part 2, 925.

To Maj. Gen. Henry W. Halleck

City Point Mch 11th 1865 [*8:30* P.M.]

MAJ, GEN, HALLECK
WASHINGTON

If Gen, Webster gives no better reason than his simple protest, against the removal of troops North, from the Dept. of the South I would have the order renewed, There is no necessity for detaining our Brigades[1] until transports are ready for the whole command, sent, Instruct Gillmore that if Sherman strikes the Sea coast at any other point than Wilmington before the execution of this transfer of troops then they will join him, wherever he may be

U. S. GRANT
Lieut. Gen,

Telegram, copies, DLC-USG, V, 46, 74, 108; DNA, RG 108, Letters Sent. Printed as received at 10:00 P.M. in *O.R.*, I, xlvii, part 2, 778. On March 11, 1865, 11:30 A.M., Maj. Gen. Henry W. Halleck telegraphed to USG. "I have

just recieved a letter from Genl Gillmore stating that he had ordered two brigades of Grover's command to Cape Fear river, but that he had transports for
only one. In the mean time, Genl Webster protests, as chief of Genl Sherman's
Staff, against sending any more troops north, till you were again consulted. I
do not know by what authority Genl Webster pretends to act in this matter for
Genl Sherman during his absence. Genl Gillmore thinks that the troops can be
spared, but says your decision will probably reach him by the time he can get
transports for the second brigade. What shall I say?" ALS (telegram sent),
DNA, RG 107, Telegrams Collected (Bound); telegram received, *ibid.*; *ibid.*,
RG 108, Letters Received. *O.R.*, I, xlvii, part 2, 778. See *ibid.*, pp. 658, 709, 804.

On March 29, Maj. Gen. Quincy A. Gillmore wrote to Brig. Gen. John A.
Rawlins. "I enclose herewith a copy of a letter from General Sherman from a
point 12 miles from Fayetteville. N. C. directing an expedition to be sent to
Florence & Sumpterville. The letter which the General says he sent General
Foster from Fayetteville was dated the 12th March & came safely to hand, after
considerable detention. The expedition is to start from Georgetown & would
have been off before now, if a heavy north-easter which is still raging, had not
delayed the concentration of the troops. It will probably start day after tomorrow
for Florence, and will then move on Sumpterville, returning by way of the
shortest route to transports on Santee River. I most heartily approve and shall
cordially carry out in good faith, the views of General Sherman, and the orders
of the Lieut. General in regard to the reduction to a minimum of the garrisons
on this coast. Between 800 & 900 of the 5000 white troops which I ordered to go
to North-Carolina, I shall detain until the expedition return." ALS, DNA, RG
108, Letters Received. *O.R.*, I, xlvii, part 3, 58.

1. Reads "one brigade" in other letterbook copies.

To Maj. Gen. George G. Meade

By Telegraph from City Pt [*March*] 11 *1865*

To MAJ GEN MEADE

I will go to the front this morning with Mr Washburne & a
small party consisting of six (6) ladies, & about an equal number
of gentlemen. We will leave here at twelve (12) M & go to the
extreme left at first. will you join us?

We would like to have two ambulances on the left when we
arrive.

U S GRANT
Lt Genl

Telegram received (at 11:10 A.M.), DNA, RG 94, War Records Office, Miscellaneous War Records; copy, Meade Papers, PHi. *O.R.*, I, xlvi, part 2, 925.
On March 11, 1865, 11:15 A.M., Maj. Gen. George G. Meade telegraphed to

USG. "I will be at Humphreys station by 1 p m. to meet you. I have asked Humphreys to parade a portion of his corps in the vicinity, that the ladies may see a review." Copy, DNA, RG 393, Army of the Potomac, Letters Sent. *O.R.*, I, xlvi, part 2, 926. On the same day, USG telegraphed to Meade. "owing to an accident on the Road no train will leave here until one P. M." Telegram received, DNA, RG 94, War Records Office, Miscellaneous War Records; copy, Meade Papers, PHi. *O.R.*, I, xlvi, part 2, 926.

To Edwin M. Stanton

City Point Mch 12th 1865 [*1:00* P.M.]

HON, E M, STANTON
SEC, OF WAR, WASHINGTON

There is no doubt but some prisoners were captured from Cox, or Palmers, near Kinston,   Col, Mulford has been notified that they have been ordered to Richmond to be immediately exchanged, I do not want them furloughed   They should be kept at Annapolis or Point Lookout until declared exchanged,   I do not suppose it to have been a defeat but a severe fight with our advance upon Kinston in which we have lost some prisoners,   On Thursday[1] morning before day light Kilpatrick was surprized near *cheraw* with a loss of Camp Equipage, one or two hundred men and a large number of Rebel prisoners previously captured by him. This is a Rebel account,[2]   No paper was published in Richmond yesterday or to day

U. S. GRANT
Lieut, General

Telegram, copies, DLC-USG, V, 46, 74, 108; DNA, RG 108, Letters Sent. Printed as received at 1:35 P.M. in *O.R.*, I, xlvii, part 2, 793. On March 12, 1865, 11:15 A.M., Secretary of War Edwin M. Stanton telegraphed to USG. "General Hartsuff is ordered to report to you immediately. What credit do you give Braggs report that he had captured fifteen hundred prisoners?" ALS (telegram sent), DNA, RG 107, Telegrams Collected (Bound); telegram received, *ibid.*, RG 108, Letters Received. *O.R.*, I, xlvi, part 2, 935. A notation on the telegram received: "Please Send to Grant at Gen Ord's Hdqrs." See telegram to Edwin M. Stanton, March 11, 1865.

1. March 9.
2. On March 11, 3:00 P.M., Maj. Gen. Edward O. C. Ord telegraphed to Brig. Gen. John A. Rawlins. "Col Mulford states that the rebel Secty of War

has official despatch of Kilpatricks having been surprised in his camp near cheraw S- C- day before yesterday at daylight—with loss of camp equipage all his guns—several hundred prisoners and the recapture of a large number of rebels who we had taken—The Rebels were unable to remove the guns & destroyed them—Genl S is reported ~~south~~ near cheraw—Kilpatrick fell back on him—and thus the rebels learned where Genl S- was" ALS (telegram sent), Ord Papers, CU-B; telegram received, DNA, RG 108, Letters Received. *O.R.*, I, xlvi, part 2, 928. On March 10, C.S.A. cav. under Maj. Gen. Joseph Wheeler and Lt. Gen. Wade Hampton surprised and overran the camp of Bvt. Maj. Gen. Judson Kilpatrick at Monroe's Cross-Roads, N. C. Kilpatrick recovered the camp with the remainder of his command. See John G. Barrett, *Sherman's March Through the Carolinas* (Chapel Hill, 1956), pp. 126–30; telegram to Charles A. Dana, March 16, 1865. On March 13, USG telegraphed to Stanton. "The following items are taken from todays Richmond papers. 'We have some good news this morning. News of a victory in South Carolina. It is announced in the following official despatch from General Lee. Though the despatch is rather scant in its particulars, enough is given to show that Kilpatrick was badly routed. "Head Qrs &c March 10th 1865 HON JOHN C. BRECKENRIDGE Secy of war Genl Hampton attacked Genl Kilpatrick at daylight this morning and drove him from his camp, taking his guns, wagons, many horses, several hundred prisoners and releasing a great number of our own men who had been captured. The guns and wagons could not be brought off for want of horses. Many of the Enemy were killed and wounded. Our loss not heavy. Lieut Col J. S. King was killed. Brig Genl Hume, Colonels Hagan & Harrison & Majors Lewis, Ferguson & others were wounded. (signed) R. E. LEE General" It will be observed that the locality of the fight is not named in the despatch, this is for prudential reasons. Sherman has no communication with the north and it would be imprudent to publish where he was, as it would only be giving news to ~~Government~~. Grant of his progress. Matters are beginning to look decidedly better for us in the South. In the last three days, we have had news of two victories, one in North Carolina and one in South Carolina. "From the Valley. We alluded in our last issue to a movement that was being made for the purpose of recapturing our prisoners who were taken from Early in the recent fight near Waynesboro and who were being conducted under guard to Winchester. The following official despatch tells of it. 'Head Qrs Mar 9th 1865. HON JNO C. BRECKENRIDGE Secy of war. Genl Rosser reports that on the 6th with a ~~force~~ few of his men he attacked the Enemy near Harrisonburg who were guarding prisoners taken at Waynesboro and captured a few prisoners. On the morning of the 7th he again attacked them near Rudes Hill having detained them for a day and night at the river. He caused them to retire in haste, abandoning the only piece of artillery they had and their ambulance. He annoyed them a good deal and enabled a good many of our men to escape (signed) R. E. LEE General' The northern papers claim to have captured about a thousand prisoners in the fight with Early and report that most of this number had reached Winchester. 'Charlotte Mar 8th The Southern Express Company's messenger from Augusta brings advices to 3rd inst. No news of interest had transpired West of the Savannah River. The Georgia Senate passed a resolution declaring that it does not concur in the recommendation of Gov'r Brown for a convention yeas 20. nays 8. Several extensive fires had occurred in Augusta supposed to be the work of an incendiary. About four hundred Yankee prisoners will leave Richmond this morning on their return home by flag of truce boat. Among the number are thirty three 33 officers including Genls Kelly & Crook recently captured' " Telegram received (at 3:45 P.M.), DNA, RG 107, Telegrams Collected (Bound). Incomplete in *O.R.*, I, xlvi, part 2, 946; (incomplete) *ibid.*, I, xlvii, part 2, 806–7.

To Edwin M. Stanton

City Point Mch 12th 1865 [*8:30* P.M.]

HON, E, M, STANTON
SEC, OF WAR WASHINGTON

The Scouts who brought Gen, Sheridan's dispatch represent having found forage and provisions in great abundan[ce.] He also found plenty of horses to re-mount his men where their horses failed, They say the command is better mounted now, than when they left, I start supplies and forage for Sheridan to-night I have also sent for the command that is now on th[e] Potomac to run up to White House and to remain there until they meet Sheridan,

U. S. GRANT
Lieut, Gen,

Telegram, copies, DLC-USG, V, 46, 74, 108; DNA, RG 108, Letters Sent. *O.R.*, I, xlvi, part 2, 935.

On March 12, 1865, Maj. Gen. Winfield S. Hancock, Winchester, Va., telegraphed to USG. "A scouting party have just returned from Mount. Jackson they could get nothing but rumors the most reliable of which is that a Sheridan crossed the James River at Hardwicksville time not known. it is also said that he captured two (2) trains near. Gordonsville containing in all about twenty three hundred (2300) men if this is so he has sent them up the other side of the Ridge. I have had frequent reports of firing in the direction of Page valley last week and have sent a cavalry force to Warrenton and sperryville to assist any party that may be coming in that direction" Telegram received, DNA, RG 108, Letters Received. Printed as received at 2:30 P.M. in *O.R.*, I, xlvi, part 2, 942.

On March 13, 1:50 P.M., Maj. Gen. John Gibbon telegraphed to USG. "A deserter who left the Bennings Brig. at 9 this morning brings a report from the rebel camp that Sheridan is within 5 miles of Richmond, & on the north of the city" ALS (telegram sent), DNA, RG 107, Telegrams Collected (Unbound); telegram received (at 2:20 P.M.), *ibid.*, RG 108, Letters Received. *O.R.*, I, xlvi, part 2, 953. At 2:30 P.M., USG telegraphed to Secretary of War Edwin M. Stanton. "Sheridan is reported to be within five miles of Richmond this morning, His route from Gouchland would bring him within about that distance of the City, and I think therefore the rumor may be correct," Copies, DLC-USG, V, 46, 74, 108; DNA, RG 108, Letters Sent. *O.R.*, I, xlvi, part 2, 946.

To Gustavus V. Fox

From City Point Va 9 30 A m Mar 12 *1864*5.

HON. G. V. FOX.
ASST SECY. NAVY,

Can you as conveniently as not spare a gunboat to go to Wilmington & Charleston and return? Mr Washburne and lady are here and would like to go down, They with one of my Staff would constitute the party going.

When is Adml. Porter coming down here?

U S GRANT
Lt Gen

Telegram received (at 11:20 A.M.), DNA, RG 45, Miscellaneous Letters Received; *ibid.*, RG 107, Telegrams Collected (Bound); copies, *ibid.*, RG 108, Letters Sent; DLC-USG, V, 46, 74, 108. *O.R.*, I, xlvi, part 2, 936. On March 12, 1865, 3:30 P.M., Asst. Secretary of the Navy Gustavus V. Fox telegraphed to USG. "Have telegraphed to enquire about gunboat to go south. The Arago fine ocean steamer fitted for lady passengers leaves New York tuesday, touches at Hampton Roads wednesday with a congressional party; that will be the most comfortable for Mrs Washburne Admiral Porter and I leaves here thursday evening for City Point" Telegram received, DNA, RG 108, Letters Received. On March 13, USG telegraphed to Fox. "Mr Washburn will go on the 'Fulton' " Telegram received (at 11:00 P.M.), *ibid.*, RG 45, Miscellaneous Letters Received.

On March 15, USG telegraphed to U.S. Representative Elihu B. Washburne. "The Senatorial party bound for Charleston are here They will be at Old Point about 6 P M" Telegram received (press), *ibid.*, RG 107, Telegrams Collected (Bound). Another telegram from USG to Washburne is dated only March. "The Senatorial party bound for Charleston are just leaving heare at 4.20. P. M, on steamer, Thos Collyer—" Telegram received, *ibid.*, Telegrams Collected (Unbound).

To Maj. Gen. Philip H. Sheridan

City Point, Va. March 12th 1865.

MAJ. GEN. P. H. SHERIDAN.
COMD'G MID, DIV.
GENERAL,

Your scouts from Columbia[1] giving the gratifying intelligence of your success up to that time have just arrived. The importance of your success can scarcely be estimated. I congratulate you and the command with you upon the skill and endurance displayed.

I have an expedition of one Brigade of Infantry now up on the Northern Neck attempting to break up a smuggling trade that is being carried on by that route between Richmond and Northern cities. I despatch immediately a Staff Officer to get the Expedition and to move it to the White House. I also send without delay 100.000 rations and ten days forage for ten thousand horses.

Remain with your command on the Pamunkey until further orders. I shall not probably keep you there many days. It is known that a large amount of tobacco has gone from Richmond to the neighborhood of Fredericksburg to be exchanged for bacon and other necessaries for Lee's Army. Northern men and rebel agents are concerned in this trade. If you can secure this tobacco, or can learn where it is, so that it can be secured hereafter do it.

Keep the Infantry I send to you, until you break up at White House, and then order it here in the absence of other orders.

Very Respectfully
Your Obt. Svt.
U. S. GRANT.
Lt. Gen.

Copies, DLC-USG, V, 46, 75, 108; DNA, RG 108, Letters Sent. *O.R.*, I, xlvi, part 2, 940. On March 10, 1865, Maj. Gen. Philip H. Sheridan, Columbia, Va., wrote to USG. "In my last dispatch dated Waynesboro I gave a brief account of the defeat of Genl Early by Custers Division. The same night this Division was pushed across the Blue ridge and entered Charlottesville at 2. O'clock P. M. the next day. The Mayor of the city & the principal inhabitants came out and delivered up the Keys of the public buildings. I had to remain at Charlottesville two (2.) days—this time was consumed in bringing over from Waynesboro our ammunition & pontoon trains. The mud was horrible beyond description and the rain incessant. The two divisions were during this time occupied in destroying the two large iron bridges, one over the Rivenna river, the other over Morses [*Moore's*] Creek near Charlottesville and the railroad for a distance of Eight (8.) miles in the direction of Lynchburg—On the 6th of March I sent the 1st division Genl Devin Comdg. to Scottsville on the James river with directions to send out light parties through the country & destroy all Merchant mills—Factories & Bridges on the Rivanna river—these parties to join the division at Scottsville. The division then proceeded along the Canal to Dunguidsvill fifteen miles from Lynchburg destroying evry Lock in and in many places the bank of the canal. At Dunguidsville we hoped to secure the bridge to let us cross the

river as our pontoons were useless on account of the high water—In this however we were foiled as both this bridge and the bridge at Hardwicksville were
burned by the enemy upon our approach. Genl Merritt accompanied this division. The 3d Division started at the same time from Charlottesville and proceeded down the Lynchburg railroad to Amherst CourtHouse destroying evry
bridge on the road and in many places miles of the track. the bridges on the
road were numerous and some.—of them five hundred feet in length Finding
I could not cross the James I concentrated at Newmarket and determined to
return along the canal and still further destroy it in the direction of Richmond.
We arrived here to night & will destroy the canal as far as Goochland tomorrow. I will then move on to the Central railroad and continue its destruction and
will then strike the Fredericksburg railroad and destroy it. We have found great
abundance in this country for our men and animals—in fact the canal has been
the great feeder of Richmond—At the Rockfish river the bank of the canal was
cut and at Newmarket, where the dam is, across the James the Aqueduct guard
Lock was destroyed and the James river let into the canal, carrying away the
banks and washing out the bottom of the canal, The Dam across the James at
this point was also partially destroyed, After finishing the Fredericksburg road
I will join you unless otherwise directed. Send forage and rations to the White
House also Pontoons in case I have to go around that far. I have had no opposition; Evry body is bewildered by our movements. I have had no news of any
Kind since I left—the latest Richmond paper was of the 4th but contained
nothing. I omitted to mention that the bridges on the railroad from Swoops
depot on the other side of Staunton to Charlottesville were utterly destroyed—
also all bridges for a distance of ten miles on the Gordonsville railroad, The
weather has been very bad indeed raining hard Evry day with the exception of
four (4.) days since we started, My wagons have from the state of the roads
detained me. Up to the present time we have captured fourteen (14.) pieces of
Artillery—Eleven at Waynesboro and three at Charlottesville. The party that I
sent back from Waynesboro started with six pieces but they were obliged to
destroy two of the six for want of animals. The remaining nine pieces were
thoroughly destroyed. We have captured up to the present time twelve canal
boats laden with supplies—Ammunition, rations, Medical Stores &c I cannot
speak in too high terms of Generals Merritt, Custer and Devin and the officers
and men of their commands: they have waded through mud & water during
this continuous rain and are all in fine spirits and health. Commodore Hollins of
the rebel Navy was shot near Gordonsville while attempting to make his escape
from our advance in that direction," LS, DNA, RG 108, Letters Received. *O.R.*,
I, xlvi, part 2, 918–19. On March 12, 7:00 P.M., USG telegraphed to Secretary
of War Edwin M. Stanton transmitting a copy of Sheridan's letter. Telegram
received (on March 13), DNA, RG 107, Telegrams Collected (Bound). On
March 13, Lt. Col. Theodore S. Bowers sent copies of Sheridan's letter to army
and corps commanders.

    1. See Horace Porter, *Campaigning with Grant* (New York, 1897), pp.
396–400.

To Col. Samuel H. Roberts

———

City Point, Va. March 12th *1865*

COL. S. H. ROBERTS,
COMD.G EXPEDITION,
COLONEL,

Immediately on receipt of this you will embark your command and proceed up the York and Pamunkey rivers to the White House, taking with you all your Infantry. The Cavalry may be returned to its place on the James. It is expected that Gen. Sheridan with a large force of Cavalry will arrive at the White House near the same time with you. If you find him there you will be subject to his orders.[1] If you do not you will remain there until he arrives. Take with you the Army Gunboats accompanying your expedition and also request the Navy Gunboats to go, and remain, with you. Rations and forage will be sent to you immediately not only for your force but for the command under Gen. Sheridan.

> Very respectfully
> your obt. svt.
> U. S. GRANT
> Lt. Gn.

ALS, DLC-USG, I, B. *O.R.*, I, xlvi, part 2, 939–40.

1. This sentence is omitted in the printed text, *ibid.*

To Lt. Col. Orville E. Babcock

———

City Point Mch 12th 1865

LIEUT, COL, O, E, BABCOCK
AID-DE-CAMP
COLONEL!

You will proceed without delay to the Potomac river and find the Expedition which left here under Col, S. H. Roberts, Having found Col, Roberts, you will deliver to him the dispatches to his address and urge upon him to lose no time in carrying out the instructions contained in them,   Order the Army Gunboats with the Expedition to continue with it and to remain subject to the orders of Col, Roberts,   You will also request the Navy Gun-Boat's now with the expedition to continue with it,

One hundred thousand rations for men and horses are ordered from here to White House for the Command of Gen, Sheridan, Col, Roberts will draw from this supply,   Request the Naval Commander at Fort Monroe to send two more Gunboats as a Convoy to these supplies,   You might mention to him at the same time the subject of ordering the boats now with Col, Roberts to remain with him,   Direct that the Vessels with the forage and rations go as high up York River as it is safe to go, without any delay,   They will then remain until the expedition under Col, Roberts arrives, when they will proceed under his orders,

As soon as you see Col, Roberts fairly under way, embarking his troops, return to Fort Monroe and ascertain whether the rations and forage have started,   If not give such directions as may be necessary to start them and proceed on up with the expedition and remain with it until you see Gen, Sheridan,   If you find that he is in want of any thing, take immediate steps to provide it telegraphing here for the necessary orders

Very Respectfully
Your obt svt
U. S. GRANT
Lt, Gen,

Copies, DLC-USG, V, 46, 75, 108; DNA, RG 108, Letters Sent. *O.R.*, I, xlvi, part 2, 939.

To Charles W. Ford

City Point, Va, March 12th *1865*

DEAR FORD,

I have just learned that the farm on which Mr. Dent is living is not to be sold until next Sept. I will be glad if you will hold

$50 00 to be paid to Mr. S. Sappington who I will direct to call on you for it and send me a draft for the balance. It may be that before you receive this you will have sent me the whole amount in your hands. If so may I ask you to give Sappington the $50 00 nevertheless and let me know so that I may return it to you.

It is late at night and I am very much fatigued so I will bid you good night.

Yours Truly
U. S. GRANT

ALS, USG 3. On March 24, 1865, Sebastian Sappington wrote a receipt. "Recd of Genl Grant by C W Ford Fifty Dollars as per order of Genl Grant in his letter dated City point March 12th 1865" ADS, *ibid.*

To Edwin M. Stanton

———

(Cipher)   City Point Va, March 13th *1865* [*1:00* P.M.]
HON. E. M. STANTON, SEC. OF WAR, WASHINGTON.

I am in receipt of a letter of the 7th from Gen. Schofield. At that time Cox was within three miles of Kinston and repairs on the rail-road were going on rapidly. Hokes Division was confronting him. Schofield was going out himself and expected to push out and take Kinston at once. Palmer was ordered and should have taken Kinston whilst Hoke was at Wilmington. I have not yet learned his excuse for his failure.

U. S. GRANT
Lt. Gen.

ALS (telegram sent), PHi; copies, DLC-USG, V, 46, 74, 108; DNA, RG 108, Letters Sent; (marked as received at 2:00 P.M.) DLC-John M. Schofield. *O.R.,* I, xlvii, part 2, 806. See telegram to Edwin M. Stanton, March 10, 1865.

On March 13, 1865, midnight, USG telegraphed to Secretary of War Edwin M. Stanton transmitting a telegram of March 12 from Maj. Gen. John M. Schofield to USG. "I have the honor to forward a despatch in cipher from Genl Sherman giving most gratifying information of his progress. Terry and Dodge at Wilmington are endeavoring to carry out Shermans wishes there and I hope to be able to fulfil his expectations here. On the night of the 10th near South west Creek Bragg was fairly beaten; during the night he retreated across the Neuse at Kinston he now holds the North bank of the river at that point"

Telegram received (on March 14, 8:30 A.M.), DLC-Robert T. Lincoln; DNA, RG 107, Telegrams Collected (Unbound); *ibid.*, RG 108, Letters Received; copy, DLC-John M. Schofield. *O.R.*, I, xlvii, part 2, 799. Schofield transmitted a telegram of March 8 from Maj. Gen. William T. Sherman, Laurel Hill, N. C., to commanding officer, Wilmington. "We are marching on Fayetteville will be there saturday, sunday and monday and then will march for Goldsboro. If possible send a boat up Cape Fear River and have word conveyed to Genl. Schofield that I expect to meet him about Goldsboro We are all well and have done finely; The rain makes our roads difficult and may delay me about Fayetteville; in which case I would like to have some bread sugar and coffee—We have an abundance of all else. I expect to reach Goldsboro by the 20th Inst." Telegram received (on March 13), DNA, RG 108, Letters Received. *O.R.*, I, xlvii, part 2, 735.

To Edwin M. Stanton

City Point, Va.
4 P. m. Mar. 13th 1865.

HON. EDWIN M. STANTON,
SECRETARY OF WAR.

Under agreement to release all prisoners in close confinement, or irons, we are getting all of our prisoners of that class.

From the number of cases still in irons in the north, it seems General Hoffman is not sending forward prisoners of this class according to the agreement. Will you please direct him to send forward those in Alton and at all other points where they are still left back.

U. S. GRANT
Lt. Genl.

Telegram, copies, DLC-USG, V, 46, 74, 108; DNA, RG 108, Letters Sent; USG 3; (marked as received at 10:40 P.M.) DLC-Edwin M. Stanton. *O.R.*, II, viii, 383. See telegram to Bvt. Brig. Gen. William Hoffman, March 14, 1865. On March 13, 1865, 4:00 P.M., USG telegraphed to Secretary of War Edwin M. Stanton. "Colonel Ould has requested to be informed of any prisoners that may be held in the south in close confinement or irons that we may learn of through returned prisoners and he will have them released at once. Some have already been released where his attention has been called in this way." Copies, DLC-USG, V, 46, 74, 108; DNA, RG 108, Letters Sent; USG 3; (marked as received at 7:30 P.M.) DLC-Edwin M. Stanton. *O.R.*, II, viii, 382.

On March 11, C.S.A. Agent of Exchange Robert Ould wrote to USG.

"Private E. M. Dotson, of Perrin's Miss. Regt. Ferguson's Brigade, was captured near Powder Spring in Ga., on the 4th of Nov. last. He, and three others of his Command, taken at the same time, were carried to Camp Douglas. A few weeks afterwards, he was remanded to Louisville. Maj. Steele, who arrived here some two weeks ago, left Priv. Dotson in close confinement at Louisville, on the 14th Ulto. He was then held subject to the orders of Gen'l. Thomas, as to the time and place of his execution. The pretext alleged for this course on the part of the Federal Military Authorities in Ky. was, that Dotson belonged to Perrin's Regt., which was recruited in a neighborhood where three Federal soldiers, 'had been murdered.' It is not alleged that these Federal soldiers were 'murdered' by Dotson, or even by Perrin's Command, nor is it suggested that Dotson and Perrin's Regt. are not regularly in the Confederate service. I feel confident that it is only necessary to bring this case to your attention, to insure the prompt release and delivery of this soldier." Copies, DNA, RG 109, Ould Letterbook; Ould Letterbook, Archives Div., Virginia State Library, Richmond, Va. *O.R.*, II, viii, 379. See *ibid.*, pp. 164, 291. On March 17, USG endorsed this letter. "Respy referred to Brig Gen W Hoffman, Com Gen of Prisoners who will if the facts prove as within stated forward this man for exchange" Copy, DLC-USG, V, 58. On March 27, Bvt. Brig. Gen. William Hoffman endorsed this letter. "Respectfully returned to Lt. Genl. U. S. Grant. Comd'g U. S. Army. Private Dotson is held as a prisoner of war at Louisville subject to the order of Maj. Genl Thomas but not in close confinement. Instructions have been given to forward him for exchange." Copy, DNA, RG 249, Letters Sent. Other papers in the same case, endorsed to USG by Maj. Gen. Henry W. Halleck on March 23, were endorsed by Lt. Col. Theodore S. Bowers on March 27. "Respy. returned. Retaliatory measures of this kind should, if ever proper, be carried into execution as nearly the place and time of the perpetration of the outrages they are intended to avenge and prevent as possible   From the within statement and endorsemnt thereon it appear that the murder was committed by guerillas, and that the man proposed to be executed in retaliation is a regular Confederate soldier,   Why he should have been selected especially, while so many of the class committing the offense were held by us, does not appear. The action of Gen Howard is therefore disappd. This man if in close confinement, should be forwarded at once to this point for exchange under the recent agreement for the delivery of all prisoners of war held in close confinement or in irons" Copy, DLC-USG, V, 58.

On March 11, Ould twice wrote to USG. "R. A. Blandford a Confederate soldier, was captured a short time since in Kentucky, while he was acting under written orders from Gen. Lyon. He had those orders on his person when he was captured. He was carried to Lexington in irons, and is now held there in close confinement. I will thank you to have him released and delivered to us." Copy, Virginia State Library. *O.R.*, II, viii, 380. "Lt. O. H. Lumpkin, 2d Tenn. Cav., who was captured in Mississippi, in April, 1863, and who was a prisoner at Johnson's Island for twenty months, was taken *in handcuffs* from the latter place, on the 20th Ulto., in charge of a detective officer, and carried to Washington. He was seen by one of our returned Officers, at Petersburg, on his way. Lt. Lumpkin was unable to ascertain the cause of this proceeding. It is said to have been done in pursuance of special orders from Washington. I will thank you for any information upon this subject. Will you not cause Lt. Lumpkin to be delivered to us?" Copies, DNA, RG 109, Ould Letterbook; Ould Letterbook, Virginia State Library. *O.R.*, II, viii, 380. On March 17, USG endorsed this letter. "Respy. referred to Brig Gen W. Hoffman, Com. Gen of Prisoners, who will please cause the within named parties to be sent forward for exchange" Copy, DLC-USG, V, 58. On March 27, Hoffman endorsed this letter. "Respectfully returned to Lt. Genl. U. S. Grant. Comd'g. U. S. Army. Lieut. Lumpkin was brought to this City as a witness in the case of a union Citizen. He is held and treated as a prisoner of War, and will be forwarded for exchange as soon as his testimony is taken." Copy, DNA, RG 249, Letters Sent.

On March 15, Hoffman wrote to USG. "Your telegram of the 13th inst. to the Sec'y. of War in reference to release of prisoners in close confinement or in irons has been referred to this office, and I am directed to carry out your instructions. I would respectfully beg leave to state in explanation that Gen. Orders No. 6, of the 18th Jan'y, which requires all prisoners of war in close confinement or in irons to be forwarded to Lt. Col. Mulford at Fort Monroe for Exchange, was generally distributed and it was expected it would fully meet the case. Whenever doubtful cases have been referred to this office, with the advice of Maj. Gen. Hitchcock, Comr. for Exchange, the broadest construction has been put upon the order, and under its terms, Spies, Murderers &c. &c, have been forwarded for exchange. On the 18th ult. pursuant to your telegram of the 17th, I sent an order to all stations in the North where prisoners have been so confined, 'to forward all rebel prisoners who are or have been in close confinement or in irons to Point Lookout for exchange.' Under this order a number of prisoners have been forwarded, and if any have been detained it is without my Knowledge. On March 2d, I gave the orders required by your telegram of the 23d Febry, directing that a certain class of citizen prisoners should be forwarded for exchange, but that those who were awaiting trial on grave charges, or who were undergoing sentence should be detained. Reports of the cases detained will be forwarded as soon as they are received. This last order would cover some of the cases discharged under the previous order. There may be some cases occurring since the date of these orders, of arrests as spies, or for violation of the laws of War, where the parties are still held as not coming within reach of the orders, and I would be glad to be informed whether such cases should be forwarded for exchange. On the 13th ult. under Genl. Orders No. 6, and your instructions of the 17th ult, I directed that S. H. Anderson a citizen prisoner in confinement at Fort Wyman, Mo, should be forwarded for exchange. In the meantime his sentence to be hung was announced and was commuted to confinement during the War at Alton, where he now remains as required by your telegram of the 23d ult. In reply to my telegram of the 18th ult, I have received reports from Commanders of prison stations from which it appears that there were no prisoners of war in close confinement, or in irons, at Fort Delaware Fort McHenry, Camp Chase or Alton, and those who were at Fort Warren, Johnsons Island, Louisville, Nashville and St. Louis have been forwarded. None have been reported at other northern stations, but to insure that none shall be so held, instructions have been sent to every station. I have communicated your instructions to Maj. Gen. Canby with the request that they may be carried out in the Milty. Div. of the West Mississippi." LS, *ibid.*, RG 108, Letters Received. *O.R.*, II, viii, 400–1.

To Edwin M. Stanton

City Point Va. Mar. 13th *1864*5.

HON. E. M. STANTON
SECRETARY OF WAR,
WASHINGTON, D. C.
SIR:

I would respectfully ask that Lieutenant Colonel Michael R. Morgan, United States Volunteers, Chief Commissary of the 25th Army Corps, be assigned to duty as Chief Commissary of the Armies operating against Richmond, under the late act of Congress entitled "An Act for the better organization of the Subsistence Department. He is now, and has been since the 16th day of June, 1864, on duty as Chief Commissary of said Armies, and has managed his department with great ability

Very Respectfully Your Ob't Serv't
U. S. GRANT
Lieutenant General.

LS, DNA, RG 94, ACP, 1330 ACP 1882. *O.R.*, I, xlvi, part 2, 947.
On March 1, 1865, Lt. Col. Theodore S. Bowers issued Special Orders No. 43. "Brevet Colonel M. R. Morgan, U S A., Chief Commissary Armies operating against Richm'd is, by authority of the Secretary of War, assigned to duty with his brevet rank." Copies, DLC-USG, V, 57, 63, 64, 65. *O.R.*, I, xlvi, part 2, 772.

To Maj. Gen. Henry W. Halleck

City Point Mch 13th 1865 [7:30 P.M.]

MAJ GEN, HALLECK
WASHINGTON

Were orders sent placing Steele in command of the 13th Corps, I recd a letter from Gen, Canby to day of the 1st of March, At that time he said nothing about starting for Mobile, Although I wrote to him he must go in command himself I have seen nothing from him indicating an interview [*intention*] to do so, In fact I

have seen but little from Canby to show that he intends to do, or
have anything done,

U. S. GRANT
Lieut, General

Telegram, copies, DLC-USG, V, 46, 74, 108; DNA, RG 108, Letters Sent.
Printed as received at 8:00 P.M. in *O.R.*, I, xlix, part 1, 907. On March 14,
1865, 12:30 P.M., Maj. Gen. Henry W. Halleck telegraphed to USG. "Your
despatch of March 1st was duly submitted to the Secty of War, but I am not
aware that any action was taken, Genl Canby having been previously instructed
to nominate his corps commanders, as has usually been done to other Generals."
ALS (telegram sent), DNA, RG 107, Telegrams Collected (Bound); telegram
received, *ibid.*; *ibid.*, RG 108, Letters Received. *O.R.*, I, xlviii, part 1, 1165. See
telegram to Edwin M. Stanton, March 14, 1865.

To Maj. Gen. George G. Meade

———

By Telegraph from City Point [*March*] 13 *1865*

To GEN MEADE

If you can possibly spare Gen McKenzie[1] I would like to order
him to take command of Ord's Cavalry.

I see nothing better than to send one of sheridan's officers to
command your Cavalry. McKenzie cannot very well command
your Cavalry because he is junior to Gen Davis[2] who is now with it

U S GRANT
Lt. Genl.

Telegram received (at 12:45 P.M.), DNA, RG 107, Telegrams Collected
(Bound); copies, *ibid.*, RG 108, Letters Sent; DLC-USG, V, 46, 74, 108; (2)
Meade Papers, PHi. *O.R.*, I, xlvi, part 2, 947. On March 13, 1865, 2:00 P.M.,
Maj. Gen. George G. Meade telegraphed to USG. "I transmit a despatch from
Maj Gen Wright to whom I referred your proposition in reference to Gen Mc-
Kenzie I have no objection beyond what Gen Wright states & if you think Gen
McKenzie ~~better~~ can do better service to the cause with Ord than with Wright,
I say take him" Telegram received (at 2:50 P.M.), DNA, RG 108, Letters
Received; copies, *ibid.*, RG 393, Army of the Potomac, Letters Sent; (2) Meade
Papers, PHi. *O.R.*, I, xlvi, part 2, 947. The enclosure is *ibid.*, p. 950. See *ibid.*,
p. 967.

On March 14, USG telegraphed to Maj. Gen. Edward O. C. Ord. "Gen
McKenzie is ordered to report to you to take command of the Cavalry provide
an Infy command for Kautz either under Turner of to take Harris place as you
deem best." Telegram received, DNA, RG 94, War Records Office, Miscella-

neous War Records; copies, *ibid.*, RG 108, Letters Sent; DLC-USG, V, 46, 74, 108. *O.R.*, I, xlvi, part 2, 977.

On March 18, 12:30 P.M., Meade telegraphed to USG. "Genl. McKenzie is on a board examining engineer officers There are a number of cases pending which can be finished in two days, but if he leaves will take weeks for a new Board to go over the same ground—Under these circumstances I have suspended the order relieving him from duty till these pending cases are closed." ALS (telegram sent), DNA, RG 94, War Records Office, Army of the Potomac; telegram received (at 12:30 P.M.), *ibid.*, RG 108, Letters Received. On the same day, USG telegraphed to Meade. "Your action in the case of Genl McKenzie is approved" Telegram received (at 12:40 P.M.), *ibid.*, RG 94, War Records Office, Army of the Potomac; copies (2), Meade Papers, PHi.

Also on March 18, Ord telegraphed to Brig. Gen. John A. Rawlins. "Is Gen McKenzie Coming to take Charge of my Cavalry any news of Gen Sheridans whereabouts" Telegram received, DNA, RG 108, Letters Received. On the same day, Rawlins telegraphed to Ord. "Gen McKenzie will report to you day after tomorrow. Sheridan arrived with his whole command at White House at 12 M today." Telegram received, Ord Papers, CU-B.

1. Ranald S. Mackenzie, born in New York City in 1840, USMA 1862, served as an engineer officer before appointment as col., 2nd Conn. Heavy Art., as of July 10, 1864. He commanded a brigade in the Shenandoah Valley and was appointed brig. gen. as of Oct. 19, 1864. On March 20, 1865, Mackenzie was assigned to relieve Bvt. Maj. Gen. August V. Kautz in command of the cav. div., Army of the James. *O.R.*, I, xlvi, part 3, 55. USG later characterized Mackenzie "as the most promising young officer in the army." *Memoirs*, II, 541.

2. Henry E. Davies, Jr., born in New York City in 1836, graduated from Columbia (1857) and practiced law before the Civil War. Appointed capt., 5th N. Y., as of May 9, 1861, he rose to col., 2nd N. Y. Cav., as of June 16, 1863, and was appointed brig. gen. as of Sept. 16. Davies drew on wartime experience in writing *General Sheridan* (New York, 1895).

To Col. Samuel H. Roberts

From City Point March 13 1864*5*. [*11:15* A.M.]

COL S H ROBERTS
PT LOOKS

I have sent an officer of my staff with instructions to you Start immedy and run into York River and await Your instructions The officer who went in search of your command left fort Monroe early this morning on Str Seneca & will run in close to the Va shore from the Mouth of the Rappahannock until he finds You You may keep your cavalry with You until You join ~~g~~Genl sheridan & then send it back here

U S GRANT
Lt Genl.

Telegram received, DNA, RG 107, Telegrams Collected (Unbound); copies, *ibid.*, RG 108, Letters Sent; DLC-USG, V, 46, 74, 108. *O.R.*, I, xlvi, part 2, 954. On March 13, 1865, Col. Samuel H. Roberts, St. Inigoes, Md., telegraphed to Lt. Col. Theodore S. Bowers. "I regret to report that my expedition to the northern neck has not been very successful so far I find the Enemy in stronger force than I expected & superior in Cavalry and a perfect knowledge of the country I can march through the country with my present force but I should probably lose a good many men & it would take several days more time In view of the probable results I do not feel justified in losing the men & time without further instructions I think the expedition should be stronger in cavalry & have a light artillery force My co[m]mand is now on transports a[n]d I shall proceed to point Lookout and wait for instructions from the Lt General by te[le]graph The neck is pretty well stripped of horses and beef cattle but there is a good deal small stock left yet If the Lt Gen[er]al directs me to continue my operations I propose t[o] land at Cone River I shall be at Point Looko[u]t in about two hours time My casualties are one (1) officer & five (5) men wounded send answer to Pt Lookout" ALS (telegram sent), DNA, RG 107, Telegrams Collected (Unbound); telegram received, *ibid.*, RG 108, Letters Received. *O.R.*, I, xlvi, part 2, 954.

At 6:30 A.M., Lt. Col. Orville E. Babcock, Fort Monroe, telegraphed to Brig. Gen. John A. Rawlins. "Capt Glisson says he will send gun boats as desired, at once. Convoy is now ready. I leave in a few moments with pilots for Col Roberts." ALS (telegram sent), DNA, RG 107, Telegrams Collected (Unbound); telegram received, *ibid.* At 4:30 P.M., Babcock, Point Lookout, Md., telegraphed to Rawlins. "Col Roberts will leave here in a short time, is taking in water, I shall start for Ft Monroe at once." ALS (telegram sent), *ibid.*; telegram received, *ibid.*; (press) *ibid.*, Telegrams Collected (Bound). Also at 4:30 P.M., Babcock telegraphed to Capt. William L. James, Fort Monroe. "Please send steamer called for by Col. Roberts soon as possible." Telegram received, *ibid.*; *ibid.*, Telegrams Collected (Unbound).

On March 14, 1:30 A.M. and 7:30 A.M., Babcock telegraphed to Rawlins. "Head of Col Roberts command entered York River about 10 P. M. last night. Supplies have left under charge of Capt Blunt. I have changed the Seneca for the Black Bird. Shall soon leave." "Col Roberts command started from here at sun rise. Supplies are with the fleet. No naval vessels have been sent up the river. One gun army boat, ~~Army~~ and the naval Convoy one boat are all we have now. Two more Army Gunboats are behind. The two Navy boats with Col R. were left at St Inegou. We shall wait at West Point for our other armed boats and go on as soon as we can." ALS (telegrams sent), *ibid.*; telegrams received (at 1:40 A.M. and 7:00 A.M.), *ibid.*, RG 108, Letters Received.

On March 15, 3:00 P.M., Babcock telegraphed to Rawlins. "Col Roberts command reached here ~~last~~ yesterday at 3.30 P M, and at once landed—Cavalry and scouts were sent out at once, and neither can find any definite information.

Rumors of a fight near Old Church, and then near Bottom's Bridge—is all we can learn. We have but three small Army gunboats here, and I have suggested to Col R. to keep the Cavalry until we can hear from you. Col Dent will telegraph from Yorktown. The Scouts have left for to try and find him." ALS (telegram sent), *ibid.*, RG 107, Telegrams Collected (Unbound). See *O.R.*, I, xlvi, part 1, 549–50.

To Henry Wilson

City Point Mch 13th 1865

HON, HENRY WILSON
CHAIRMAN OF COMMITTEE ON MILITARY AFFAIRS, U. S. SENATE,
CARE SEC, OF WAR,

Bvt, Major P. S. Michie thinks his nomination to Brevet, of Major U. S. Army has not been confirmed, He is one of the most deserving young Officers in the Service, and has been for several months Chief Engineer of the Army of the James, It is important to his holding his present post, from which he can hardly be spared, that his nomination should be confirmed

U. S. GRANT
Lieut, Gen,

Copies, DLC-USG, V, 46, 74, 108; DNA, RG 108, Letters Sent. *O.R.*, I, xlvi, part 2, 947.

To Gen. Robert E. Lee

March 14th 1865

GEN, R, E, LEE
COMDG, C, S, ARMY
GENERAL:

Enclosed I send you Copy of statement made by Lieut, G, W, Fitch 12th U. S. Colored Troops whose murder was attempted after his capture, and whose companions, who were captured at the same time, were murdered,

It is not my desire to retaliate for acts which I must believe are unauthorized by commanders of troops in Arms against the authority of the United States, but I would ask to have those barberous practices prohibited as far as they can be controlled,

Soon after the organization of the first Colored troops recieved into the Army of the United States a little skirmish took place between some of these troops and Confederate forces, at Milekens Bend, La in which there were captures on both sides, Information subsequently received, and which I believe reliable, convinced me that all the White Officers captured, were put to death, Although I have no reason for believing this course has been persistently followed towards the Officers of Colored troops since that time yet I believe it has been the practice, with many Officers and men in the Confederate Army, to kill all such Officers as may fall into their hands,

> Very Respectfully
> Your obt svt,
> U. S. GRANT
> Lieut, Gen

Copies, DLC-USG, V, 46, 74, 108; DNA, RG 108, Letters Sent. *O.R.*, II, viii, 393. On March 23, 1865, Gen. Robert E. Lee wrote to USG. "I have the honor to acknowledge the receipt of your letter of the 13th inst: with the enclosed paper relative to an alleged attempt to murder a Federal officer while a prisoner of war, and the murder of two others. In reply I beg leave to say that I know nothing of the facts stated in the communication, nor does it afford me the means of ascertaining them. The act complained of, if committed, was done without any authority, and is at variance with the rules by which the Confederate Government endeavors to conduct hostilities. It was probably one of those acts of unauthorised violence, proceeding from individual passions, which it is difficult to prevent, but which are not the less to be lamented. Many similar outrages committed upon the persons of Confederate soldiers and citizens by persons in the Federal service have been reported to me, which I trust admit of the same explanation. I endeavor by every means in my power to prevent such violations of the rules of civilized warfare, which only tend to inflame feelings already unfortunately too much embittered, and which unavoidably reflect upon the party to which the perpetrators belong." LS, NHi. *O.R.*, II, viii, 425. See *ibid.*, pp. 19–20, 64–65, 171.

On March 22, USG wrote to Lee. "I am informed that Colonel J, H, Ainsworth of the 1st U, S, Ga, Vols, a prisoner of war who was brought to Richmond with other prisoners to be exchanged, was then taken out and placed in 'Castle Thunder' where he is now detained, I would respectfully request to be informed of the cause of this detention and of the charges against Col, Ainsworth, if any exist," Copies, DLC-USG, V, 46, 75, 108; DNA, RG 108, Letters Sent.

To Edwin M. Stanton

City Point March 14th 1865 [3:00 P.M.]

HON, E, M, STANTON
SEC, OF WAR, WASHINGTON

I am very much dissatisfied with Canby, He has been slow beyond excuse, I wrote to him long since that he could not trust Gen, Granger in Command, After that he nominated him for the command of a Corps, I wrote to him too, that he must command the troops going into the field in person, On the 1st of March he is in New Orleans and does not say a word about leaving there, I would like now to have Steele, as I recommended, long since, in a dispatch addressed to Gen, Halleck, put in command of the 13th Corps, As soon as Sheridan can be spared I will want him to supercede Canby, and the latter put in command of the Dept, of the Gulf unless he does far better in the next few weeks than I now have any reason to hope for,

U. S. GRANT
Lieut, General

Telegram, copies, DLC-USG, V, 46, 74, 108; DNA, RG 108, Letters Sent. Printed as received at 5:00 P.M. in *O.R.*, I, xlviii, part 1, 1164. On March 14, 1865, 8:00 P.M., Secretary of War Edwin M. Stanton telegraphed to USG. "~~I the~~ If Canby has been ~~explicitly~~ distinctly notified of your wishes in respect to the command of the 13th Corps and disregarded them your disatisfaction would be well founded. But I think it will turn out differently. In that impression I forwarded him myself your last telegram to General Halleck last week. In respect to superseding him in command your ~~wi~~ views will be fully acquiesced in whenever you ~~are~~ choose to make ~~the~~ a change. I will start for City Point to see you on this & other matters tomorrow." ALS (telegram sent), DNA, RG 107, Telegrams Collected (Bound); telegram received, *ibid.*, RG 108, Letters Received. *O.R.*, I, xlviii, part 1, 1165.

Probably on March 15, USG telegraphed to Maj. Gen. Edward O. C. Ord. "The. Secy. of War will be here tomorrow If all is quiet on your front come down and see him—" Telegram received (on March 15, noon), Ord Papers, CU-B. On March 16, Brig. Gen. John A. Rawlins telegraphed to Ord. "Secretary Stanton is here." *O.R.*, I, xlvi, part 3, 10.

On March 18, Maj. Gen. George G. Meade wrote to USG. "Has the Secretary left City Point, if not at what time does he expect to leave? Does he return to Washington?" Copy, DNA, RG 393, Army of the Potomac, Letters Sent. *O.R.*, I, xlvi, part 3, 28. USG endorsed this letter. "Answer the Secretary of War left early this morning for Washington." *Ibid.*

To Bvt. Brig. Gen. Edward D. Townsend

City Point Va
4 30 p m Mch 14th 18[65]

BR GEN E D TOWNSEND
A A GENL

Dispatch of this date received. There may have been irregularities in allowing persons with passes to travel free on boats that were running on Govt service, but the practice will be discontinued.

Of the three parties recently visiting here, but one came on a boat furnished from here and that was coming any how—The Qr Master was with that boat and says he supposed the party had proper passes. I think Ingalls was not responsible

U S GRANT
Lt Genl

Telegram received (at 7:00 P.M.), DNA, RG 94, Letters Received, 287A 1865; _ibid._, RG 107, Telegrams Collected (Bound); copies, _ibid._, RG 108, Letters Sent; DLC-USG, V, 46, 74, 108. On March 14, 1865, Bvt. Brig. Gen. Edward D. Townsend telegraphed to USG, sending copies to Maj. Gen. George G. Meade, Maj. Gen. Edward O. C. Ord, Brig. Gen. Rufus Ingalls, Brig. Gen. Marsena R. Patrick, and to the chief q. m., Fort Monroe. "It is represented to the secy of War that officers in the Qr. Mr. Dept have given transportation to persons to visit the Army of the Potomac without authority from this Department. The Sec'y. orders that no passes or transportation be given to any one without authority from him, or Lt Gen Grant, and that in no case boats or transportation be furnished to any persons or parties not in the service without his express orders and Gen Rucker is directed to seize any Government transport that may without authority of the Sec'y of war or Lt Gen Grant be used for such unauthorized purpose and report the officers offending to the adjutant General Acknowledge receipt" Telegram received (at 4:20 P.M.), DNA, RG 108, Letters Received; copies, _ibid._; _ibid._, RG 107, Telegrams Collected (Unbound).

To Bvt. Brig. Gen. William Hoffman

City Point Va
Mar. 14th 1865 7 P. M

BRIG GEN W. HOFFMAN
COM'Y GEN PRISONERS

My despatch to the Secy of War applied to prisoners of War —Continuous reports of men being retained in irons are being brought by prisoners going forward for exchange—I made a proposition applying to citizens but recieved no reply. There is I believe a large number of prisoners in irons at Alton Illinois who have been sentenced by Military Commissions who should be released under the agreement made.

U. S. GRANT
Lt Genl

Telegram received (at 8:20 P.M.), DNA, RG 107, Telegrams Collected (Bound); *ibid.*, RG 249, Letters Received; copies, *ibid.*; *ibid.*, RG 108, Letters Sent; DLC-USG, V, 46, 74, 108. *O.R.*, II, viii, 392. See telegram to Edwin M. Stanton, March 13, 1865, 4:00 P.M. On March 14, 1865, Bvt. Brig. Gen. William Hoffman twice telegraphed to USG. "Please inform me if your telegram of yesterday to the Secretary of War in reference to prisoners in irons applies to Citizen prisoners." "Repeated orders have been issued directing all rebel prisoners in close confinement or in irons to be forwarded for exchange, It is not known that there are any now so held   Your telegram of the 23d Ult. directs that citizen prisoners awaiting trial, or under sentence, shall be held till further orders. I write by mail." ALS (telegrams sent), DNA, RG 107, Telegrams Collected (Unbound); telegrams received, *ibid.*, RG 108, Letters Received. *O.R.*, II, viii, 391, 392.

On March 15, USG telegraphed to Hoffman. "Please have Maj R C Taylor now confined at Fort Delaware and Lieut Jno C Taylor A D C confined at Fort Lafayette sent forward for exchange" Telegram received (at 11:30 A.M.), DNA, RG 249, Letters Received; copies, *ibid.*, RG 108, Letters Sent; DLC-USG, V, 46, 74, 108.

On March 16, 12:50 P.M., Hoffman telegraphed to USG. "A prisoner of war is in irons at Camp Douglas for the murder of another prisoner of war. Shall he be forwarded for Exchange" ALS (telegram sent), DNA, RG 107, Telegrams Collected (Unbound); telegram received (on March 17, 1:00 P.M.), *ibid.*, RG 108, Letters Received. *O.R.*, II, viii, 403. On March 17, USG telegraphed to Hoffman. "The agreement for the exchange of prisoners in close confinement or irons does not cover cases taken up after the agreement was entered into" Telegram received (at 12:00 P.M.), DNA, RG 107, Telegrams Collected (Bound); *ibid.*, RG 249, Letters Received; copies, *ibid.*, RG 108, Letters Sent; DLC-USG, V, 46, 74, 108; USG 3. *O.R.*, II, viii, 405.

On March 23, Hoffman wrote to USG. "I have the honor to report that I have to day been furnished with an authenticated copy of the proceeding of a Military Commission which sentenced Walter H. Pierson to be confined at Fort Delaware during the war. From these proceedings it appears that he was at the time of his capture in June 1863, a private in Co A, 1st Md Artillery, rebel army, and understanding your recent instructions in regard to prisoners of war of this class as requiring all held under such circumstances to be forwarded for exchange, I have directed that Pierson shall be sent to City Point with the first party from Fort Delaware. He is not confined in a cell nor is he in irons, but he is held in close confinement as prisoners under sentence usually are and not as a prisoner of war. He has heretofore been reported as a citizen prisoner. I understand your instructions to cover all prisoners of war, not citizens, who at the time of the agreement were under sentence or held under any special confinement, not as other prisoners of War. Some were in close confinement, not in cells, nor in irons, waiting trial; some were waiting sentence; some were under sentence but were not in irons nor in cells; others were under sentence and wearing ball and chain. All these classes I have considered to come within the spirit of your instructions, but to guard against misunderstanding I have directed that a history of each case should be sent with the rolls to City Point, so that the propriety of delivery might be decided on there. I presume it is desirable that Mr Ould should have no pretext for holding Union soldiers in special confinement on the plea that men of the rebel army are not released according to agreement. I will report in relation to the cases referred by Mr Ould as soon as I have obtained the necessary information." LS, DNA, RG 108, Letters Received. *O.R.*, II, viii, 423.

On March 25, Hoffman telegraphed to USG. "The rebel officers reported by Mr Ould as wearing ball and chain at Alton, are not in close confinement, they are not now nor have they been wearing ball and chain, but they are sentenced to confinement for various periods. Shall they be forwarded for Exchange" ALS (telegram sent), DNA, RG 107, Telegrams Collected (Unbound); telegram received (at 1:15 P.M.), *ibid.*, RG 108, Letters Received. Printed as sent at 1:15 P.M. in *O.R.*, II, viii, 428. On the same day, USG telegraphed to Hoffman. "Forward all men referred to in your dispatch of one fifteen (1 15) P. M. for Exchange" Telegram received (at 5:00 P.M.), DNA, RG 107, Telegrams Collected (Bound); *ibid.*, RG 249, Letters Received; copies, *ibid.*, RG 108, Letters Sent; DLC-USG, V, 46, 74, 108. *O.R.*, II, viii, 428.

To Maj. Gen. George G. Meade

City Point Va, Mch 14th 1865 [*10:30* A.M.]

MAJ, GEN, MEADE

From this time forward keep your command in condition to be moved in the very shortest possible notice, in case the enemy should evacuate or partially evacuate Petersburg taking with you the maximum amount of supplies, your trains are capable of carrying, It will not be necessary to keep wagons loaded as they can be loaded in a few hours at any time, If we do move, the line Southwest of the "Jones House" will be abandoned

U. S GRANT
Lieut, General

Telegram received (incomplete), DNA, RG 107, Telegrams Collected (Unbound); copies, *ibid.*, RG 108, Letters Sent; DLC-USG, V, 46, 74, 108; (2) Meade Papers, PHi. *O.R.*, I, xlvi, part 2, 962. On March 14, 1865, noon, Maj. Gen. George G. Meade telegraphed to USG. "Despatch in cipher received & will be attended to.—" ALS (telegram sent), DNA, RG 107, Telegrams Collected (Unbound); telegram received, *ibid.*, RG 108, Letters Received. *O.R.*, I, xlvi, part 2, 962.

To Maj. Gen. George G. Meade

By Telegraph from City Point 12 30 P M [*March*] 14th *1865*
To Major Gen Meade

Since telegraphing you in cipher I have seen a letter from a lady in Richmond in which she says that Fitz Lees Cavalry has been ordered on to the Danville road, private stores, tobacco cotton etc had been turned over to the Provost Marshall to be got out of the way and citizens were ordered to be organized no doubt to prevent plundering in the city when it was evacuated—The information clearly indicates an intention to fall back to Lynchburg—Sheridan will be at the White house today, if there is no falling back for four or five days he can have his Cavalry in the right place

U S Grant
Lt Gen

Telegram received, DNA, RG 107, Telegrams Collected (Unbound); copies (marked as sent at 2:30 P.M.), *ibid.*, RG 108, Letters Sent; DLC-USG, V, 46, 74, 108; (2) Meade Papers, PHi. Printed as sent at 2:30 P.M. in *O.R.*, I, xlvi, part 2, 963.

On March 14, 1865, 10:40 A.M., noon, and 2:30 P.M., Maj. Gen. George G. Meade telegraphed to USG. "Only 11 deserters reported yesterday by Prov. Mar. Genl—This morning corps comdrs report 15 as arriving—From these the only movement learned is a reported change of position between Johnstons Divn in our extreme right with Rodes Divn on our extreme left.—The signal officers report the enemy under arms & in line betwee in vicinity of the Lead works and to the left—which would seem to confirm deserters reports as this part of the line is held by Johnsons Division.—" ALS (telegram sent), DNA, RG 107, Telegrams Collected (Unbound); telegram received (at 11:45 A.M.), *ibid.*, RG 108, Letters Received. *O.R.*, I, xlvi, part 2, 962–63. "Warren telegraphs some deserters have just Come in from W. H. F. Lee's Div of Cavalry, who left their lines at 9 P. m. yesterday & who report a movement of Lee's Div yesterday at 9 a. m. towards Dinwiddie C. H. I have sent for these men to examine them more particularly and if Lee has moved his Cavalry, I think it would be well to send Davies out to find out what is going on. I have directed Davies to hold himself in readiness Signal officer reports Great activity and apparent excitement in the enemy's lines in the vicinity of fort Mahone near Jerusalem Plank road" Telegram received, DNA, RG 108, Letters Received; copies, *ibid.*, RG 393, Army of the Potomac, Letters Sent; (2) Meade Papers, PHi. *O.R.*, I, xlvi, part 2, 963. "I have examined the cavalry deserters, and they say positively that the two brigades of W. H. F. Lee's division hitherto, at Stoney Creek moved yesterday morning, with all their transportation towards Dinwiddie C. H—leaving no one at Stoney Creek The former picket line is still held—These men did not know where they were going or the object of the movement.—The signal officer report a brigade of Infantry of 9 regiments as passing this morning on the Cox road going in to Petersburgh.—It may be that Rodes Division hitherto at Sutherlands Station, which deserters last night said was to relieve Johnson in front of 9. corps, is moving in for that purpose & W. H. F. Lee's cavalry have been sent to hold the extreme right about Sutherland Stn or it may be they are concentrating the cavalry to meet anticipated movements of Sheridan.—I forward despatch of Prov. Mar with information obtained from 24 deserters who have come in this morning.—" ALS (telegram sent), DNA, RG 94, War Records Office, Miscellaneous War Records; telegram received (at 3:00 P.M.), *ibid.*, RG 108, Letters Received. *O.R.*, I, xlvi, part 2, 963–64. The enclosure is *ibid.*, p. 966. At 10:00 P.M., Meade telegraphed to USG. "No movement of the enemy has been noted today—except that previously reported, namely a column of 9 Regts moving into Petersburgh from the enemys extreme right on the Cox road. Two deserters have just come in from Wise Brigade, who state that Wallace's brigade Johnstons Division was relieved last night by a brigade of Gordon's Division, and that Wise is to be relieved tonight—It was reported that Johnston & Gordon were changing places—Today about 11. a m ~~what was supposed to be an~~ An officer & orderly in our uniform, are reported to have ridden out the Halifax road & passing outside of our Picket line, to have gone over to the enemy—The officer was mistaken by the pickets when he passed as the Division officer of the day.— On reaching the rebel lines they were dismounted & marched off under guard. It is impossible to say whether these men were deserters who had stolen horses or bold rebel scouts disguised in our uniform.—The affair will be thoroughly investigated, and any responsible parties found guilty punished.—" ALS (telegram sent), DNA, RG 94, War Records Office, Miscellaneous War Records; telegram received, *ibid.*, RG 108, Letters Received. *O.R.*, I, xlvi, part 2, 964.

To Maj. Gen. George G. Meade and Maj. Gen. Edward O. C. Ord

City Point, Va, March 14th 1865

Maj. Gen Ord & Meade,

I am in receipt of dispatch ~~of~~ from Sherman of the 8th and Schofield of the 12th.[1] Sherman was at Laurel Hill and said that he would reach Fayetteville on Saturday, Sunday & Monday. He found abundance of supplies and wanted nothing but Sugar, Cof-

fee & Hard bread. He says "We are all well and have done finely."
Schofield says that Bragg was fairly beaten in the battle of the
10th and retired during the night behind the Neuse river.

U. S. GRANT
Lt. Gn.

ALS (telegram sent), OClWHi; telegram received (at 10:00 A.M.), Ord Papers,
CU-B. *O.R.*, I, xlvi, part 2, 962. On March 14, 1865, 10:45 A.M., Maj. Gen.
George G. Meade telegraphed to USG. "Despatches from Sheridan Sherman &
Schofield received & circulated.—I am glad to hear Schofields account of Lee's
reported victory; & hope Killpatricks defeat as reported by Lee in yesterdays
Richmond papers, will prove of the same character." ALS (telegram sent),
DNA, RG 107, Telegrams Collected (Unbound); telegram received, *ibid.*, RG
108, Letters Received. *O.R.*, I, xlvi, part 2, 963.

On March 14, 11:10 A.M., Maj. Gen. Edward O. C. Ord telegraphed to
Brig. Gen. John A. Rawlins. "I have the honor to inform you that the Rebels
refuse to exchange papers to day, Capt Grednor [*Greaner*] informs me he
received an order this A. M. directing him to give us only such dates as we give
them, or in other words, ex changing date for date. He also informs me that Col
Elliott 25th Va, and editor of one of the Richmond papers (the 'Examinor' I
believe) ~~will~~ will to day make an effort to have this order countermanded.—"
ALS (telegram sent), DNA, RG 108, Letters Received; telegram received, *ibid.*
O.R., I, xlvi, part 2, 976. On the same day, USG telegraphed to Meade and Ord.
"Stop all exchanges of papers on the lines unless we get the latest dates pupb-
lished for those of the latest dates received from the North." ALS (telegram
sent), Kohns Collection, NN; telegrams received (2—one at 3:05 P.M.), DNA,
RG 107, Telegrams Collected (Unbound). *O.R.*, I, xlvi, part 2, 964.

1. See telegram to Edwin M. Stanton, March 13, 1865.

To Maj. Gen. Edward O. C. Ord

—————

By Telegraph from City Pt [*March 14*] 1865

To MAJ. GEN ORD

I will send orders to have Sumners[1] Cavalry stopped at Norfolk   It will not be there for a couple of days yet

U S GRANT
Lt Gen

Telegram received (at 11:25 P.M.), Ord Papers, CU-B. On March 14, 1865,
8:30 P.M., Maj. Gen. Edward O. C. Ord telegraphed to USG. "Gordon ~~R~~reports

that his expedition sent to Murfees depot might, according to refugees account —have gone to Weldon—perhaps the news of that scout will make the rebs look out from that quarter—If Sumners cavalry are on their way back I should like to have him—take his own cavalry and what he can raise at Ports mouth and try if he can reach Weldon he may get to the Nottoway and destroy the Bridge" ALS (telegram sent), *ibid.*; telegram received, DNA, RG 108, Letters Received. *O.R.*, I, xlvi, part 2, 977.

On the same day, USG telegraphed to the q. m., Fort Monroe. "Col. Dent left here about 7 p. m. on the Steamer 'Wilson Small' for the York River. Stop his boat and deliver to him the accompanying dispatchs." ALS (telegram sent), Kohns Collection, NN; telegram received, DNA, RG 107, Telegrams Collected (Unbound). *O.R.*, I, xlvi, part 2, 980. USG also telegraphed to Lt. Col. Frederick T. Dent. "Direct Col. Roberts at White House to send Col. ~~Sommers~~ Sumner's Cavalry to Norfolk Va. without delay. Col. S. will report by telegraph his arrival at Norfolk to Gen. Ord." ALS (telegram sent), Kohns Collection, NN; telegram received, DNA, RG 94, War Records Office, Miscellaneous War Records. *O.R.*, I, xlvi, part 2, 980.

Also on March 14, 10:20 A.M., Ord telegraphed to USG transmitting a telegram from Bvt. Brig. Gen. Benjamin C. Ludlow, Fort Magruder. "Picket post Number two (2) 'Queens Creek,' reports fifteen (15) transports having passed up York River last night with troops" ALS (telegram sent), DNA, RG 108, Letters Received; telegram received (at 11:05 A.M.), *ibid. O.R.*, I, xlvi, part 2, 976. At 4:00 P.M., Ord telegraphed to Brig. Gen. John A. Rawlins. "deserter from Brattons S. C. Brigade, who was in Richmond on sunday says that people came streaming in on the Brooks pike Sunday a m (it comes in from due north) stating that Sheridans Cavalry were in that road about Six miles out near 8 gun Battery there was a right smart scare, and local troops he thinks were being sent out—~~that same~~—on that Same morning I learn from other deserters that the rebels manned their works before daylight for an attack on this front—" ALS (telegram sent), DNA, RG 108, Letters Received; telegram received (at 4:00 P.M.), *ibid. O.R.*, I, xlvi, part 2, 976–77. On the same day, Ord telegraphed to USG. "Following from Richmond Whig of today . . . Men dressed in a little Confederate authority were rushing around yesterday, jumping fences, bursting into stables, peering into the backyards & houses of private residents in search of horses to impress for some purpose not made public. They preferred violence and used it. They got few animals not Candidates for 'horse heaven' except those belonging to Market Carts & wagons & Cavalrymen. such as they did get, it was Concluded to return to their owners before the Close of the day, either because the number obtained was too trifling to be of any avail or because the exigency supposed to exist in point of fact existed only in somebodys heated imagination. We would suggest that citizens of Richmond dispense with horse altogether & substitute thesem for Negroes with long poles after the manner of the Chinese Coolies'" Telegram received (at 4:15 P.M.), DNA, RG 108, Letters Received. *O.R.*, I, xlvi, part 2, 977.

1. Edwin V. Sumner (son of Maj. Gen. Edwin V. Sumner, who died in 1863), born in Pa. in 1835, 2nd lt., 1st Cav., as of Aug. 5, 1861, appointed col., 1st N. Y. Mounted Rifles, as of Sept. 8, 1864.

To Maj. Gen. Philip H. Sheridan

City Point, Va. March 14th 1865.

MAJ. GEN. P. H. SHERIDAN,
MID. MIL. DIVISION,
GENERAL,:

Enclosed with this I send you some information obtained by the Provost Marshal General about the "Northern Neck." I do not expect you to remain where you are, however, long enough to take advantage of it.

Information just received from Richmond indicates that everything was being sent from there to Lynchburg, and that the place would have been cleared out but for your interference. I am disposed now to bring your Cavalry over here, and to unite it with what we have and see if the Danville and South Side road cannot be cut. You could come by Long Bridge and Deep Bottom or Aikens Landing, at both of which places we have bridges. Troops can be thrown out from the Army of the James to protect you in crossing, and a bridge for the Chickahominy can be sent from here if you are not sufficiently provided. Write to me how soon you feel you could start and what assistance you would want from here. Do not start however until you hear from me again

You want to send a staff officer by the boat that takes this to have your supplies of forage and provisions distributed for your command all the way from the Chickahominy to Hatchers run. When you do start I want no halt made until you make the intended raid unless rest is necessary. In that case take it before crossing the James.

Very Respectfully
Your Obt. Sevt
U. S GRANT,
Lieut. General

Copies, DLC-USG, V, 46, 74, 108; DNA, RG 108, Letters Sent. *O.R.*, I, xlvi, part 2, 980.

On March 15, 1865, 1:30 P.M., Maj. Gen. Philip H. Sheridan, "Richd &

Potomac R. Rd Bridge—South Anna River," telegraphed to USG. "A messenger from the White House met me here this morning—After sending my dispatch to you from Columbia Col Fitzhughs brigade was advanced as far as Goochland destroying the canal to that point—We then moved up to the Virginia Central railroad at Tolesville and destroyed it down to Beaver Dam Station—totally destroying fifteen (15.) miles of the road, Genl Custer was then sent to Ashland and Genl Devin to the South Anna bridges, all of which have been destroyed There is not a bridge on the R Rd from South Anna to Lynchburg—This morning two (2) divisions of Infantry came out to near Ashland. Pickets and Corses and I have concluded to cross the North Anna & go to the white House on the North side—I think this force too large to fight and it may attempt to prevent my crossing over from the White House unless you can draw them back—They know that if this Cavalry force can join you that it will be bad for Richmond— The Ammount of Public property destroyed in our march is enormous—The enemy attempted to prevent our burning the ~~bridge~~ Central R Rd bridge over the South Anna, but the 5th U. S. Cav charged up to the bridge & about thirty men dashed across on foot driving off the enemy and capturing three (3.) pieces of Artillery 20 pdr Parrotts." LS (telegram sent), DNA, RG 107, Telegrams Collected (Unbound); telegram received (on March 17, 12:30 P.M.—sent via Yorktown, Va., 7:15 A.M.), *ibid.*; *ibid.*, Telegrams Collected (Bound); (on March 17, 10:40 A.M.) *ibid.*, RG 108, Letters Received. *O.R.*, I, xlvi, part 2, 993–94. See telegram to Maj. Gen. Philip H. Sheridan, March 17, 1865.

To Commodore William Radford

By Telegraph from City Pt. [*March 14*] *1865*

To COMMO. RADFORD

CARE GENL ORD,

Will you please have a few gun-boats say six 6 including four 4 already gone sent into the York & Pamunkey Rivers to keep open free navigation between White House and the mouth of York River I have a large force now on its way to White House when it is with drawn the navy can withdraw also

U. S GRANT
Lt Gen

Telegram received, DNA, RG 45, Area File; copies, *ibid.*, RG 108, Letters Sent; DLC-USG, V, 46, (2) 75, 108. *O.R.*, I, xlvi, part 2, 979. On March 14, 1865, 12:55 P.M., Commodore William Radford, "Flag Ship 'Dumbarton,'" telegraphed to USG. "Telegram rec'd. Will send vessels required immediately." ALS (telegram sent), DNA, RG 107, Telegrams Collected (Unbound); telegram received, *ibid.*, RG 108, Letters Received. *O.R.*, I, xlvi, part 2, 980.

To Mrs. Daniel P. Livermore and Mrs. Abraham H. Hoge

———

City Point, Va, March 14th *1865*

MRS. D. P. LIVERMORE[1]
MRS. A. H. HOGE,[2]
COR. SEC.s N. W. SAN. FAIR,
DEAR FRIENDS,

Your kind invitation for myself and Mrs. Grant to attend the
great N. W. Fair which is to be held in Chicago, commencing on
the 30th of May next, is received. My duties are such as to make
it impossible for me to promise anything ahead except continued
efforts to suppress the existing rebellion, and to render needless, as
soon as I can, the humane offices of the Sanitary Commission.

Mrs. Grant feels very much inclined to attend your Fair and
will do so if, when the time comes, it is practicable.

Hoping you success equal to your expectations, the greatness
of the cause and of the growing Northwest where the "Fair" is to
be held, I remain,

Very Truly Yours
U. S. GRANT
Lt. Gn. U. S. A.

ALS, DLC-USG, I, B.

1. Mrs. Daniel P. Livermore (Mary A.), born in Boston in 1820, married
in 1845, and moved with her husband (a Universalist minister) to Chicago in
1857. She worked with the Chicago (later the Northwestern) Sanitary Commission through the Civil War.
2. See *PUSG*, 7, 343n.

To William H. Seward

———

City Point, Va. March 15th 1865 [*3:00* P.M.]
HON. W. H. SEWARD, SEC. OF STATE, WASHINGTON.

Earl Russells Communication to Mason, Slidell & Mann was
received the evening of the 12th,[1] forwarded to Gen. Lee on the

13th[2] and his acknowledgement of the receipt of it received on the 14th.[3] I reported the whole to the Sec. of War[4] and sent him a copy of my letter to Gen. Lee.

U. S. GRANT

Lt

ALS (telegram sent), OClWHi; telegram received (at 5:00 P.M.), DNA, RG 107, Telegrams Collected (Bound). *O.R.*, I, xlvi, part 2, 986. On March 15, 1865, 2:00 P.M., Secretary of State William H. Seward telegraphed to USG. "I will think you to inform me whether the communication of Earl Russell to Mess. Mason & Slidell a copy of which was sent to you to be forwarded through the insurgent lines by flag of truce has been so forwarded, to whom it was addressed and delivered and when you complied with the request" Telegram received, DNA, RG 108, Letters Received.

On March 23, Gen. Robert E. Lee wrote to USG. "In pursuance of instructions from the Government of the Confederate States, transmitted to me through the Secretary of War, the documents recently forwarded by you are respectfully returned. I am directed to say 'that the Government of the Confederate States cannot recognize as authentic a paper which is neither an original nor attested as a copy; nor could they under any circumstances, consent to hold intercourse with a neutral nation through the medium of open dispatches, sent through hostile lines after being read and approved by the enemies of the Confederacy.'" Copies, *ibid.*; *ibid.*, RG 84, Great Britain, Instructions; DLC-James M. Mason. *O.R.* (Navy), II, iii, 1265. On March 25, USG wrote to Secretary of War Edwin M. Stanton. "I have the honor to forward herewith a communication of General R. E. Lee. 'Commanding Armies Confederate States,' of date 23d inst, with enclosures." Copies, DLC-USG, V, 46, 75, 108; DNA, RG 84, Great Britain, Instructions; *ibid.*, RG 108, Letters Sent.

1. On March 9, Asst. Secretary of War Charles A. Dana wrote to USG. "This Department has received from the Hon. William H. Seward, Secretary of State, a communication, a copy of which is hereto annexed for your information. The paper referred to therein is enclosed herewith. The Secretary of War directs me to request that you will please cause it to be delivered to General Lee, as requested, and report your action to this Department." LS, *ibid.*, Letters Received. *O.R.* (Navy), II, iii, 1265. The enclosed correspondence embodied a British protest against C.S.A. efforts to undermine British policy of neutrality. *Ibid.*, pp. 1267–70.

2. On March 13, USG wrote to Lee. "Enclosed with this I send you copy of communication from Earl Russell, Secretary of State for Foreign Affairs, England, to Messrs. Mason. Slidell and Mann. The accompanying copy of a note from the Hon. W. H. Seward, Secretary of State, to the Secretary of War, explains the reason for my sending it to you." Copies, DLC-USG, V, 46, 74, 108; DLC-James M. Mason; DNA, RG 107, Letters Received from Bureaus; *ibid.*, RG 108, Letters Sent. *O.R.* (Navy), II, iii, 1264.

3. On March 13, Lee wrote to USG. "I have received your letter of this date, enclosing the copy of a communication from Earl Russell, Secretary of State for Foreign Affairs, England, with the accompanying copies of letters from the Hon. Wm H. Seward and Hon. C. A. Dana." Copy, DNA, RG 107, Letters

Received from Bureaus. On March 14, USG endorsed this letter. "Respectfully forwarded to the Secretary of War, in connexion with papers on same subject forwarded yesterday" ES, *ibid.*

4. On March 13, USG wrote to Stanton. "I have the honor to acknowledge the receipt of your communication of date 9th inst. transmitting letter of Hon William H. Seward, Secretary of State, forwarding communication of Earl Russell; and to inform you that in compliance with your instructions I have this day forwarded the same by flag of truce to General R. E. Lee, commanding Confederate Armies." LS, *ibid.*

To Maj. Gen. George G. Meade

City Point Mch 15th 1865

MAJ, GEN, MEADE

Arrangements were made between Longstreet and Ord for mutual exchange of prisoners captured under circumstances such as you discribe and with my consent, We have delivered some on that arrangement, I do not know that Gen, Lee gave his sanction to it nor that we could claim the restoration of captures made South of the James river on it, You might address a note to the Officer commanding in front of where the capture was made asking the return of the ~~two men~~ two men so that if refused we will not feel under obligations to return men we may take hereafter under similar circumstances

U, S, GRANT Lt, Gen,

Copies, DLC-USG, V, 46, 74, 108; DNA, RG 108, Letters Sent; USG 3; (2) Meade Papers, PHi. *O.R.*, I, xlvi, part 2, 987. On March 15, 1865, 10:30 A.M. and 8:15 P.M., Maj. Gen. George G. Meade telegraphed to USG. "Fifty deserters yesterday—Fifteen are reported this morning by corps comdr—No news beyond the relief of Johnsons (Bushrod) Division in front of 9. corps by Gordons old Division of Gordons corps.—The idea seems to be that Johnson is to exchange places with Gordon but no evidence of this has yet been obtained.—" "A deserter from the enemy this morning, states that the two men reported by me as yesterday riding into the enemys lines, were our men, and that they asserted, they had gone there by mistake.—Did I not understand you to say that some arrangement had been made, by which such mistakes could be corrected on application.—" ALS (telegrams sent), DNA, RG 94, War Records Office, Miscellaneous War Records; telegrams received (at 11:20 A.M. and 9:00 P.M.), *ibid.*, RG 108, Letters Received. *O.R.*, I, xlvi, part 2, 986–87.

To Maj. Gen. Edward O. C. Ord

—

By Telegraph from City Point [*March 15*] 1865 [*10:30* A.M.]
To MAJ GEN E. O. C. ORD

I think it will pay to organize a force of cavalry to be followed
a portion of the way by Infantry supports to take Weldon and
destroy the stores collected there and the R R bridge if they can—

If they fail in this they may be able to strike the Hicksford
bridge—

Sumner's Cavalry is ordered to Norfolk

U. S. GRANT
Lt. Genl

Telegram received (at 10:50 A.M.), Ord Papers, CU-B; copies, DLC-USG, V,
46, 74, 108; DNA, RG 108, Letters Sent. *O.R.,* I, xlvi, part 2, 991.
On March 15, 1865, Maj. Gen. Edward O. C. Ord telegraphed to Brig. Gen.
John A. Rawlins. "Deserter in to day—stated that 4 or 5 regts of negros are near
Petersburg—Heard it from a captain in the 44th ala to which he belongs—Heard
firing in that direction & was told it was caused by drilling the negroes in firing
with blank catridges. Negroes were put in the field for the first time last week"
ALS (telegram sent), Ord Papers, CU-B; telegram received, DNA, RG 108,
Letters Received. *O.R.,* I, xlvi, part 2, 991.

To Lt. Col. Frederick T. Dent

—

By Telegraph from City Pt
Dated Mar 15 18645.

To COL F. T. DENT A D C

I sent orders to Fts Monroe after you left here for Col Roberts
to retain sumners Cavly until he had joined Sheridan then to send
sumners to Norfolk with orders to report his arrival there to Genl
Ord by telegraph.—If S is not heard from by saturday Col Roberts
may return. If it is ascertained elalier that he has gone elsewhere
then return as soon as the fact is known—

U. S. GRANT
M G

Telegram received, DNA, RG 107, Telegrams Collected (Unbound); copies,
ibid., RG 108, Letters Sent; DLC-USG, V, 46, 74, 108. *O.R.,* I, xlvi, part 2,

994. On March 15, 1865, 8:15 [P.M.], Lt. Col. Frederick T. Dent, Yorktown, Va., telegraphed to USG. "Arrived at White House at 2 P M and left at 3 P M Sheridan had not arrived—nor did the scouts learn where he was—sent out other scouts—Col B Col R & myself concluded it was best to retain Sumners Cavalry until S got in—unless you direct to the contry by telegraph—I await your order here as soon as S gets in Hudson will leave for this place & City Point" ALS (telegram sent), DNA, RG 94, War Records Office, Miscellaneous War Records; telegram received, *ibid.*, RG 108, Letters Received. *O.R.*, I, xlvi, part 2, 994.

On March 16, 7:00 A.M., Dent telegraphed to USG. "Your message is receved and will be given to Col Roberts in a few hours—I leave for White House at once" ALS (telegram sent), DNA, RG 107, Telegrams Collected (Unbound).

To Charles A. Dana

From City Point Va Mar. 16th *1864*5.

HON C. A. DANA
ASST SECY OF WAR.

I am just in receipt [o]f a letter from Gen Sherman of the 12th from Fayetteville. He describes his army as [i]n fine health and spirits, having met [w]ith no serious opposition. Hardee keeps [in] his front at a respectful distance. At Columbia he distroyed immense [A]rsenals and Rail Road Establishments [a]nd forty three (43) Cannon. At Cheraw [h]e found much machinery and war material including twenty five (25) cannon [a]nd thirty six hundred (3600) barrels of [po]wder. In Fayetteville he found twenty [(20)] pieces of Artillery and much other material. He says nothing about Kilpatrick's defeat by Hampton but the officer who brought his letter says that before daylight on the 10th Hampton got two brigades in rear of Kilpatrick's Head Quarters and surprised and captured all the Staff but two Officers. Kilpatrick Escaped, formed his men and drove the enemy with great loss recapturing about all that he had lost. Hampton lost Eighty six (86) left dead on the field

U S GRANT
Lt Gen

Telegram received (at 3:55 P.M.), DNA, RG 107, Telegrams Collected (Bound); copies, *ibid.*, RG 108, Letters Sent; DLC-USG, V, 46, 74, 108. *O.R.*, I, xlvii, part 2, 859. See letter to Maj. Gen. William T. Sherman, March 16, 1865.

To Maj. Gen. George G. Meade

By Telegraph from City Point [*March 16*] *1865*
To MAJ GENL MEADE

Make the Changes you deem proper in the garrison of City Point Have all the returns of troops here sent to you. In making Changes leave with Genl Patrick the regiment which he has always had with him. There are two Colored regiments at City Point, One under the Quarter Master This I will have retained but the others I will order back to the 25th Corps. It will be necessary to replace it with a Battalion

U S GRANT
Lt Genl

Telegram received, DNA, RG 94, War Records Office, Miscellaneous War Records; copies, *ibid.*, RG 108, Letters Sent; DLC-USG, V, 46, 74, 108; (2) Meade Papers, PHi. Printed as received at 11:00 A.M. in *O.R.*, I, xlvi, part 3, 4. See *ibid.*, p. 5. On March 16, 1865, 10:00 A.M., Maj. Gen. George G. Meade had telegraphed to USG. "Nothing new this morning.—No further or very precise information obtained of the change of position in Enemys troops in my front I think it likely some troops have been sent to hold the Northern defenses of Richmond against anticipated attacks from Sheridan. Prior to moving this army I desire to make certain changes in the troops at & around City Point—I should like to have the 11th U. S. Inft at these Hd Qrs where I propose to collect the regular regiments as they return & keep them for Provost duty & as a reserve—There are several fragments of regiments—viz 3 co's from Delaware—a Batn from Maine & one from N. Hampshire—that have been all winter at City Point & with Genl. Benham—as these organisations are not filled or likely to be I propose to attach them to organisations from the same states—of course any troops removed from City Point would first be relieved by others—I propose to make that portion of the garrison of City Point belonging to this army—a detachment under command of Bvt. Brig Genl. Collis—hitherto they have formed part of the Provost guard of this army—They can be returned thro' these Hd Qrs—or if deemed advisable thro' your Hd Qrs.—Please let me Know if you have no objection to the above which are submitted because I consider City Point as only partially under my command—" ALS (telegram sent), DNA, RG 94, War Records Office, Miscellaneous War Records; telegram received (at 10:35 A.M.), *ibid.*, RG 108, Letters Received. *O.R.*, I, xlvi, part 3, 3–4.

On March 17, 10:00 A.M., Meade telegraphed to USG. "Pro Mar Gen reports 39 deserters yesterday Corps Comdrs report 13 this morning No movements are reported but the relief of Johnstons though one man says he heard Rodes Division had gone to N. C" Telegram received, DNA, RG 108, Letters Received; copies, *ibid.*, RG 393, Army of the Potomac, Letters Sent; Meade Papers, PHi. *O.R.*, I, xlvi, part 3, 18.

To Maj. Gen. Edward O. C. Ord

By Telegraph from City Pt [*March 16*] 1865

To MAJ GEN ORD.

You can send a despatch to Ft Monroe & Norfolk directing that when Sumner reaches there he will come on up the river without debarking his troops   I think he will not ~~have~~ leave White House earlier than tomorrow noon. Last night Sheridan had not reached there.

U. S. GRANT
Lt Genl

Telegram received, DNA, RG 94, War Records Office, Miscellaneous War Records; copies, *ibid.*, RG 108, Letters Sent; DLC-USG, V, 46, 74, 108. *O.R.*, I, xlvi, part 3, 9. On March 16, 1865, 8:30 A.M., Maj. Gen. Edward O. C. Ord telegraphed to USG. "The Black~~wor~~water a Branch of the Chowan I am informed can not be ~~crossed~~ ~~exe~~ forded except near the Army of the Potomac—~~a~~ Cava[lry] would have to have a ferry or pontoons   the ferry is destroyed—hence a dash can not be made now—would it not be well to telegraph to Yorktown that a boat may be sent up notifying Sumner—~~to I think the S E gale~~" ALS (telegram sent), Ord Papers, CU-B; telegram received, *ibid.*, RG 108, Letters Received. *O.R.*, I, xlvi, part 3, 9.

On the same day, 10:00 A.M. and 11:25 A.M., Ord telegraphed to Brig. Gen. John A. Rawlins. "Deserter from Bartons Brig say there were rumors in camp that part of Pickets went on Sunday toward Lynchburg where Sheridan had cut the canal & another portion went to Hanover Junction and had a fight ~~yesterday~~ with some of Sheridans command—Heard that Pickett was driven back   Dont know the day the fight occurred—" "Twenty five (25) deserters have come in since yesterday. They report that Harris Brig, Mahones Div, has returned to our front near Howletts house and that Grimes Div has relieved Johnsons Div on lines at Petersburg, Johnson going to their extreme right." ALS (telegrams sent), DNA, RG 108, Letters Received; telegrams received (at 10:05 A.M. and 11:15 A.M.), *ibid. O.R.*, I, xlvi, part 3, 10.

To Maj. Gen. William T. Sherman

City Point, Va. March 16th 1865

MAJ. GEN. W. T. SHERMAN,
COMD.G MIL. DIV. OF THE MISS.
GENERAL.

Your interesting letter of the 12th inst. is just received. I have never felt any uneasiness for your safety but I have felt great anxiety to know just how you were progressing. I knew, or thought I did, that with the magnificent Army with you, you would come out safely some place. To secure certain sucsess I deemed the Capture of Wilmington of the greatest importance. Butler came near loosing that prize to us. But Terry and Schofield have since retrieved his blunders, and I do not know but the first failure has been as valuable a sucsess for the country as the Capture of Fort Fisher. Butler may may not see it in that light.—Ever since you started on the last campaign, and before, I have been attempting to get something done in the West, both to co-operate with you, and to take advantage of the enemy's weakness there, to accomplish results favorable to us. Knowing Thomas to be slow beyond excuse, I depleted his Army to reinforce Canby, so that he might act from Mobile Bay on the interior. With all I have said, he had not moved at last advices. Canby was sending a Cavalry force of about 7,000 from Vicksburg towards Selma. I ordered Thomas to send Wilson from Eastport towards the same point and to get him off as soon after the 20th of Feb.y as possible. He telegraphed me that he would be off by that date. He has not yet started, or had not at last advices. I ordered him to send Stoneman from East Tennessee into Northwest South Carolina, to be there about the time you would reach Columbia. He would either have drawn off the enemy's Cavalry from you, or would have sucseeded in destroying rail-roads, supplies and other material which you could not reach. At that time the Richmond papers were full of the accounts of your movements, and gave daily accounts of movements in West North Carolina. I supposed all the time it was Stoneman. You may judge my surprise when I afterwards learned that Stoneman was still in Louisville, Ky., and that the troops in N. C. were Kirk's[1] forces. In order that Stoneman might get off without delay I told Thomas that 3000 men would be sufficient for him to take. ᵀIn the mean time I had directed Sheridan to get his Cavalry ready and as soon as the snow in the Mountains melted sufficiently, to start for Staunton, and go on, and destroy the Va. Central road and Canal. Time advanced, until he set the 28th of Feb.y for starting. I informed Thomas, and directed him to change the course of Stoneman towards Lynchburg, to destroy the road in Va. up as near to that place as possib[le.] Not hearing from Thomas I telegraph[ed] to him about the 12th to know if Stoneman was yet off. He replie[d] not, but that he, (Thomas,) would start that day for Knoxville to get him of as soon as possible—Sheridan has made his raid and with splendid sucsess, so far as heard. I am looking for him at "White House" to-day.—Since about the 20th of last month the Richmond papers have been prohibited from publishing accounts of Army movements. We are left to our own resources therefore for information.—You will see from the papers what Sheridan has done. If you do not the officer who bears this will tell you all.

Lee has depleted his Army but very little recently, and I learn of none going South. Some regiments may have been detached but I think no Division or Brigade. The determination seems to be to hold Richmond as long as possible. I have a force sufficient to leave enough to hold our lines, (all that is necessary of them,) and move out with a plenty to whip his whole Army. But the roads are entirely impassable. Until they improve I shall content myself with watching Lee, and be prepared to pitch into him if he attempts to evacuate the place. I may bring Sheridan over,—think I will,—and break up the Danville & Southside rail-roads. These are the last avenues left to the enemy.

Recruits have come in so rapidly at the West that Thomas has now about as much force as he had when he attacked Hood. I have stopped all who, under previou[s] orders, would go to him except those from Ill.—Fearing the possibility of the enemy falling back to Lynchburg, I ~~directed~~ and afterwards attempting to go into East Tenn. or Ky., I have ordered Thomas to move the 4th Corps to Bulls Gap, and to fortify there, and to hold out to the Va. line if he can. He has accumulated a large amount of Supplies in Knoxville, and has been ordered not to destroy any of the rail-road West of the Va. line. I told him to get ready for a Campaign towards Lynchburg, if it became necessary. He never can make one there, or elsewhere, but the steps taken will prepare for any one else to take his troops and come East or go towards Rome, which ever may be necessary. I do not beleive either will.

When I hear that you and Schofield are to-gether, with your back upon the coast, I shall feel that you are entirely safe against anything the enemy can do. Lee may evacuate Richmond and he can not get there with force enough to touch you. His Army is now demoralized and deserting very fast, both to us and to their homes. A retrograde movement would cost him thousands of men even if we did not follow.

Five thousand men belonging to the Corps with you are now on their way to join you. If more reinforcements are necessary I will send them. My notion is that you should get Raleigh as soon as possible and hold the rail-road from there back. This may take more force than you now have. From that point all N. C. roads can be made useless to the enemy without keeping up communications with the rear.

Hoping to hear soon of your junction with the forces from Wilming[ton] & New Bern, I remain

> Very respectfully
> your obt. svt.
> U. S. GRANT
> Lt. Gen

ALS, DLC-William T. Sherman. *O.R.*, I, xlvii, part 2, 859–60. On March 12, 1865, Maj. Gen. William T. Sherman, Fayetteville, N. C., wrote to USG. "We reached this place yesterday at noon, Hardee as usual retreating across the Cape Fear burnig his Bridge, but our pontons will be up today, and with as little delay as possible I will be after him towards Goldsboro. A tug has just come up from Wilmigton and before I get off offrom here I hope to get up from Wilmigton some shoes & stockigs, some sugar coffee & flour. We are abundantly supplied with all Else, havig in a measure lived off the country. The Army is in Splendid health, condition and Spirit although we have had foul weather and roads that would have stopped travel to almost any other body of men I ever read of. Our march was substantially what I designed, straight on Columbia feignig on Branch ville & Augusta. We destroyed in passig the Rail road from the Edisto nearly up to Aiken, again from Orangeburg to the Congaree, again from Columbia down to Kingsville and the Wateree, and up towards Charlotte as far as the Chester Line. Thence I turned East on Cheraw, and thence to Fayetteville. At Columbia we destroyed immense arsenals & Railroad Establishmts, among which were 43 cannon. At Cheraw we found also machinery

& material of war from Charleston among which 25 guns, and 3600 barrels of Gun powder. And here we find about 21 guns, and a magnificent U. S. arsenal. We cannot afford to leave detachments, and I shall therefore destroy this valuable arsenal for the Enemy shall not have its use, and the United States Should never again confide such valuable property to a People who have betrayed a trust. I could leave here tomorrow but want to clean my columns of the vast crowd of refugees and negros that encumber me. Some I will send down the River in boats & the balance will send to Wilmigton by land under small escort as soon as we are across Cape Fear River. I hope you have not been uneasy about us, ~~but I hope~~ and that the fruits of this march will be appreciated. It had to be made, not only to secure the valuable ~~points~~ depots by the way, but its incidents in the necessary fall of Charleston, Georgetown and Wilmigton. If I can now add Goldsboro, without too much cost, I will be in position to aid you materially in the Sprig Campaign. Joe Johnston may try to interpose between me here and Schofield about New bern, but I think he will not try that but concentrate his scattered armies at Raleigh, and I will go straight at him as soon as I get my men reclothed and our wagons reloaded. Keep Evry body busy, and let Stoneman push towards Greensburg or Charlotte from Knoxville. Even a feint in that quarter will be most important. The Railroad from Charlotte to Danville is all that is left to the Enemy, and it wont do for me to go there on account of the 'Red clay' hills that are impassable to wheels in wet weather. I expect to make a junction with Schofield in ten days." ALS, DNA, RG 108, Letters Received. *O.R.*, I, xlvii, part 2, 794–95.

1. Lt. Col. George W. Kirk, 3rd N. C. Mounted Inf.

To Lt. Col. Orville E. Babcock

By Telegraph from City Pt. 17
Dated Mar 16th *1864.5*

To LT COL. BABCOCK
W. HOUSE

Your dispatch recd—I sent orders for Col Roberts to return if Sheridan does not arrive by saturday[1] of course this does not apply if Sheridan is heard from and it is known that he is going to White House   Dispatches are recd from Sherman himself from Fayettville   all was well with him

U S GRANT
Lt Genl

Telegram received, DNA, RG 107, Telegrams Collected (Unbound); copies, *ibid.*, RG 108, Letters Sent; DLC-USG, V, 46, 74, 108. *O.R.*, I, xlvi, part 3, 13.

On March 16, 1865, noon, Lt. Col. Orville E. Babcock, White House, Va., wrote to Brig. Gen. John A. Rawlins. "Scouts sent out last night returned this morning saying they went to within 4 miles of Hanover C. H. and conversed with the people in that vicinity—and all report a fight yesterday in vicinity of Ashland Station—though they say Sheridan had not crossed the South Anna. The people say Pickets Div. and a brigade of ~~infantry~~ cavalry went to Ashland to oppose Sheridan. The cavalry has gone out again to day, and will go as far as Bottoms Bridge. No other information known. The steamer with this goes to Ft Monroe for Stores for the Steam boats and will bring back any Dispatches for us." AL, DNA, RG 107, Telegrams Collected (Unbound). Printed as delivered to USG's hd. qrs. by Capt. Jesse J. Underhill at 7:45 P.M. in *O.R.*, I, xlvi, part 3, 13. At 7:15 P.M. and 8:00 P.M., Babcock telegraphed to Rawlins. "Two Scouts from Sheridan just in—and brings dispatches. They say he has some over 2000 negroes, and a number of captured waggons His horses are in good condition but foot Sore. I have telegraphed from ~~Y~~Yorktown for plank to plank the R R bridge here. It is ready for planking Scouts say the advance will be here in the morning. Please telegraph Capt James at Fort Monroe to Send the plank at once. ~~Dent is here.~~ Capt Hudson takes this to Yorktown, and will waits answer" ALS (telegram sent), DNA, RG 107, Telegrams Collected (Unbound); telegram received (press), *ibid.*, Telegrams Collected (Bound); (on March 17, 10:55 A.M.) *ibid.*, RG 108, Letters Received. The last sentence does not appear in the telegrams received or *O.R.*, I, xlvi, part 3, 14. "Capt. James can send what Genl Sheridan wants and send them within five hours. I will wait your answer." ALS (telegram sent), DNA, RG 107, Telegrams Collected (Unbound).

1. March 18.

To Maj. Gen. Philip H. Sheridan

———

City Point, Va, March 17th/65 [*1:50* P.M.]

MAJ. GN. P. H. SHERIDAN, WHITE HOUSE VA. TELEGRAPH TO YORKTOWN—.

GENERAL,

Your dispatch of the 15th is this moment received. A brigade of troops as gurd to supplies for your command have been at "White House" for two days to meet you. The evening of the 15th I sent all the Cavalry of the Army of the James except necessary Pickets to the Chickahominy to threaten in that direction and hold the enemy's Cavalry as far as possible. I have ordered them now to move up between Whiteoak Swamps and the Chickahominy to attract as much attention as they can and to go as far as they can.

It has been so long since your dispatch was written however I fear you will receive no material benefit from movements made here.

U. S. GRANT
Lt. Gn.

ALS (telegram sent), IHi; telegram received, DNA, RG 107, Telegrams Collected (Unbound). *O.R.*, I, xlvi, part 3, 24. See letter to Maj. Gen. Philip H. Sheridan, March 14, 1865. On March 17, 1865, 2:00 P.M., Lt. Col. Theodore S. Bowers telegraphed to Maj. Gen. William T. Sherman conveying the news received from Maj. Gen. Philip H. Sheridan. Telegram received (press), DNA, RG 107, Telegrams Collected (Bound); *ibid.*, Telegrams Collected (Unbound). *O.R.*, I, xlvii, part 2, 869. On the same day, Bowers issued Special Orders No. 53. "1st Lieut Wm M. Dunn, Jr., acting Aide deCamp, will proceed as bearer of dispatches to Maj. Gen. W. T. Sherman, comdg. Military Division of the Mississippi, upon the delivery of which he will rejoin these Headquarters. He will proceed from City Point to Fort Monroe on the mail-boat, and then take the first steamer for New Berne, N. C., from which point he will proceed by the most practicable means. The Quartermaster Department will furnish necessary transportation" Copies, DLC-USG, V, 57, 63, 64, 65. *O.R.*, I, xlvii, part 2, 869.

At 3:00 P.M., Lt. Col. Orville E. Babcock, White House, Va., telegraphed to Brig. Gen. John A. Rawlins. "Capts Moore and Allen of Genl Sheridans staff came in this morning. The Genl marched from Mangahick Church this morning. His advance will be within twelve miles tonight. I send his dispatch by Col Dent who will telegraph it from Yorktown. We have sent a squadron of Cavalry to new Castle today to see if they can hear from Longstreet. They have been gone some five hours and sent in no report yet. We have several Gunboats now and shall give them a handsome fight if they come here before Genl Sheridan Genl Sheridan has directed me what to do in case of an attack Hudson has not returned yet. Dent brings all of Sheridans dispatches I will see the Genl and then join you as soon as possible. Sheridan sends me word that he has plenty of supplies in case of trouble . . . P. S. Have just received note from Genl Sheridan he will camp at King Williams C. H. tonight 10 miles from here. His note was written 10 A M 17th He has no farther information about Longstreet" Telegram received, DNA, RG 108, Letters Received. *O.R.*, I, xlvi, part 3, 18. On the same day, Lt. Col. Frederick T. Dent, Yorktown, Va., telegraphed to Rawlins. "Sheridan will be in early tomorrow morning at White House. Our scouts up as far as Piping Tree were not able to find Longstreet, Think he has gone back but are on the watch for him, A cavalry scout to New Kent C. H. this morning ran into a rebel scouting party. We had two men wounded killed one private wounded and captured a Sergt Maj. of the rebels. Col Babcock will leave as soon as Genl Sheridan comes in will bring the staff officer of Sheridans directed, with him" Telegram received (at 9:35 P.M.), DNA, RG 108, Letters Received. *O.R.*, I, xlvi, part 3, 18.

To Maj. Gen. Edward O. C. Ord

(Cipher)   City Point, March 18th *1864*5. [*7:45* P.M.]
MAJ. GEN. ORD.

Gen. Sheridan reached White House to-day. He will remain there several days to shoe up his animals and then join the Armies here. I want you to hold the crossings of the Chickahominy but do not want to jeopardise the command there. It probably will be well for you to send a Division of troops to meet Sheridan. They need not start however until about the time Sheridan starts notice of which I will give you. If you deem a little Infantry necessary for the support of your Cavalry you may send it.

U. S. GRANT
Lt. Gn.

ALS (facsimile telegram sent), *The Flying Quill: Autographs at Goodspeed's* (May, 1975), p. 4; telegram received (at 8:00 P.M.), Ord Papers, CU-B. *O.R.*, I, xlvi, part 3, 32. On March 18, 1865, 9:00 P.M., Maj. Gen. Edward O. C. Ord telegraphed to USG. "To keep the cavalry and Infantry at between bottoms— and White oak bridge exposes them to easy attack while they are cut off from me by the white oak Swamp, would it not be better to have Sheridan cross lower down Say at Jones Bridge—and which is too far to our right rear for the enemy to atempt annoy parties at the bridge—feeding and foreging a party across White oak Swamp at Bottoms bridge will cost me Some loss and the roads are is reported very bad" ALS (telegram sent—misdated March 17), Ord Papers, CU-B; telegram received, DNA, RG 108, Letters Received. The phrase "and which is . . . at the bridge—" does not appear in the telegram received or *O.R.*, I, xlvi, part 3, 32–33. At 10:00 P.M., USG telegraphed to Ord. "Probably it will be better to bring your Cavalry in and when Sheridan moves we will send out again. I feel some alarm for the safety of the Cavalry where it is." ALS (telegram sent), deCoppet Collection, NjP; telegram received (at 10:15 P.M.), Ord Papers, CU-B. *O.R.*, I, xlvi, part 3, 33.

Also on March 18, Maj. Gen. Winfield S. Hancock, Winchester, Va., telegraphed to USG. "I have a report this morning that Sheridan is on the Ty River in Nelson Co followed by Fitz Lees Division & the remnant of Earlys troops about eleven hundred (1100.) Infantry I am disposed to disbelieve the whole story as it sounds improbable but if it should happen to be so I would render him assistance have you anything that would Corroberate the story It Comes through some loyal people who Came up the Valley this morning. Rosser has left the Valley and gone to the Ty River I had this information 2 or 3 days ago." Telegram received (press), DNA, RG 107, Telegrams Collected (Bound); (2) *ibid.*, Telegrams Collected (Unbound); *ibid.*, RG 108, Letters Received; copy, *ibid.*, RG 393, Middle Dept., Telegrams Sent. *O.R.*, I, xlvi, part 3, 36. On the same day, USG telegraphed to Hancock. "Gen Sheridan was last night ten (10) miles from White House north of the Pamunkey I had previously sent troops & supplies to White house & last evening the road between sheridan and that base was opened to travel. He is no doubt there now & all safe." Telegram received (at 12:00 P.M.), DNA, RG 107, Telegrams Collected (Unbound); (press) *ibid.*, Telegrams Collected (Bound); (on March 19) *ibid.*, RG 393, Middle Military Div., Letters Received; copies, *ibid.*, RG 108, Letters Sent; DLC-USG, V, 46, 74, 108. *O.R.*, I, xlvi, part 3, 37.

Also on March 18, Maj. Gen. George G. Meade telegraphed to USG transmitting a telegram of 10:00 A.M. from Bvt. Col. Frederick T. Locke to Bvt. Maj. Gen. Alexander S. Webb. "Th Two scouts from Gen Sheridan have just Come in. They left sheridans Army on the 10th inst They left him at Columbia They brought in one prisoner from 9th Va whom they Captured last night The party will be sent up at once. Gen Warren being temporarily absent I have the honor to send This" Telegram received (at 11:15 A.M.), DNA, RG 108, Letters Received. Printed as forwarded at 11:00 A.M. in *O.R.*, I, xlvi, part 3, 30.

On the same day, Lt. Col. Orville E. Babcock, Yorktown, Va., telegraphed to Brig. Gen. John A. Rawlins. "I left Gen sheridan at White House 12 M his Command is all there I have telegraphed to Capt James for twenty five (25) portable forges & shoeing tools &C if Capt James Cannot fill the order at once Gen. Ingalls had better send them Gen Forsyth is with me he shall be at Ft Monroe by 8 P. M & at City Point before morning" Telegram received, DNA, RG 108, Letters Received. *O.R.*, I, xlvi, part 3, 35. On the same day, Rawlins telegraphed to Babcock. "The articles you require will be sent from here, they will leave in an hour" Copies, DLC-USG, V, 46, 74, 108; DNA, RG 108, Letters Sent. *O.R.*, I, xlvi, part 3, 35.

Also on March 18, USG telegraphed to Asst. Secretary of War Charles A. Dana, sending a copy to Secretary of War Edwin M. Stanton, Fort Monroe. "Dispatches from White House of 12, M, announce the arrival of Sheridan there, with all his command," Copies, DLC-USG, V, 46, 74, 108; DNA, RG 108, Letters Sent. *O.R.*, I, xlvi, part 3, 27.

On the same day, USG telegraphed to Maj. Gen. Philip H. Sheridan. "Two (2) more scouts sent by you from columbia have just come in—This makes four (4) arrived from that place" Telegram received, DNA, RG 107, Telegrams Collected (Unbound).

To Edwin M. Stanton

City Point Mch 19th 1865 [*11:30* A.M.]

HON, E, M, STANTON
SEC, OF WAR, WASHINGTON

Will you please direct the Ordnance Dept, to send money here at once, to pay for Arms brought in by deserters, A great many are coming in now bringing their Arms with them,

U. S. GRANT
Lieut, Gen'l

Telegram, copies, DLC-USG, V, (marked as sent at 12:30 A.M.) 46, 75, 108; DNA, RG 108, Letters Sent. Printed as sent at 10:30 A.M. in *O.R.*, I, xlvi, part 3, 38. On March 20, 1865, Secretary of War Edwin M. Stanton telegraphed to USG. "The Chief of Ordnance reports that the ordnance officer ~~has some~~ [Lt] Dutten has twenty five hundred dollars of funds on hand for purchase of deserters arms and that ~~an adequate supply for all contingencies~~ ten thousand will be sent this ~~to~~ day." ALS (telegram sent), DNA, RG 107, Telegrams Collected (Bound); telegram received (at 11:30 A.M.), *ibid.*, RG 108, Letters Received. *O.R.*, I, xlvi, part 3, 50.

To Maj. Gen. Edward O. C. Ord

By Telegraph from City Point [*March*] 19 *1865*

To MAJ GEN ORD—

Gen Sheridan has brought in with him some two 2 or three 3 thousand Negroes   I have directed him to send them to the Pro Mar at Fort Monroe[1]   The Chief Qr Mr Gen Ingalls will give directions for the distribution and employment of the able bodied Men. The balance you may direct to be sent to such settlements as you may think can best employ them

U S GRANT

Lt Gen

Telegram received, Ord Papers, CU-B; copies, DLC-USG, V, 46, 75, 108; DNA, RG 108, Letters Sent. *O.R.*, I, xlvi, part 3, 41.

On March 19, 1865, Maj. Gen. Edward O. C. Ord twice telegraphed to Brig. Gen. John A. Rawlins, first at 9:20 A.M. "I have the honor to report the Safe return of my Cavalrys division to Camp. When I receive a report from it I will telegraph results   A prisoner reports that Picketts division returned to Richmond yesterday afternoon and encamped below Richmond" Telegrams received (2), DNA, RG 108, Letters Received. *O.R.*, I, xlvi, part 3, 41. "The cavalry report but one man wounded and three captured as casualties of the Division during the expedition" Telegram received (at 3:20 P.M.), DNA, RG 108, Letters Received. *O.R.*, I, xlvi, part 3, 42.

At 11:50 A.M., Ord telegraphed to USG. "Sumner is at Ft Monroe—has orders from Sheridan to send his transports back from Norfolk as soon as possible—I think I can make him useful—with other cavalry in a raid to winston from Suffolk and thence to—Halifax or Weldon—if there is a crossing at Winston—or I can send pontons   Shall I try it—~~would like to hav~~" ALS (telegram sent), Ord Papers, CU-B; telegram received (marked as sent at noon), DNA, RG 108, Letters Received. Printed as sent at noon in *O.R.*, I, xlvi, part 3, 41. At 2:00 P.M., USG telegraphed to Ord. "I think it will be advisable to Start Sumner from Suffolk to go to Weldon when Sheridan Starts from our left flank It will be well to leave him in Norfolk Portsmouth or Newport News until time to start About next Saturday will be the time for him to leave Suffolk" Telegram received (at 2:15 P.M.), Ord Papers, CU-B; copies, DLC-USG, V, 46, 75, 108; DNA, RG 108, Letters Sent. *O.R.*, I, xlvi, part 3, 41.

Also on March 19, Ord telegraphed to Rawlins. "Deserters from Brattons Brigade near Darbytown road state—was under marching orders last night— the rumor was that *we* were flanking the rebels line—heard that one Regt of negroes was on the Williamsburg road—a great many Georgians are going home —heard that 400—left last tuesday night—perhaps the secretary would like to hear that the enemy thought our review meant an attack *they* formed line of batte, and massed men from near the James in front of the review this accounts for the small number of them seen from Fort Harrison 46—deserters reported since yesterday morning—generally with their arms—the ordnance Dept—should send money to pay for them our quarter master has not the money and it is important to pay them here so that they can write or send word to their comrades of the fact—onely one of your orders just reached the company of palmetto sharpshooters and brought in 8—this morning—with their guns—" Telegrams received (2), DNA, RG 108, Letters Received. *O.R.*, I, xlvi, part 3, 42.

1. On March 19, USG telegraphed to Maj. Gen. Philip H. Sheridan. "Send all your colored people to the Pro' Mar at Ft Monroe I will have them cared for there—" Telegram received, DNA, RG 107, Telegrams Collected (Unbound); copies, *ibid.*, RG 108, Letters Sent; DLC-USG, V, 46, 75, 108. *O.R.*, I, xlvi, part 3, 47.

To Maj. Gen. Philip H. Sheridan

City Point, Va. March 19th 1865

MAJ GEN. P. H. SHERIDAN,
COMD'G MID. MIL. DIV.
GENERAL,

I have ordered Steamers to White House, to take your disabled horses and men back to Washington the men to return to Winchester. You may dismount one Brigade giving the servicable horses to dismounted men of the balance of the command and send the brigade back with the broken down horses; or you may send back broken down horses and men, keeping with you all your organizations as you deem best. We will probably be able to give you 1.000 horses when you arrive here. The dismounted men who you expect to take with you, had better come here by water. Whilst you remain at White House, you can retain a despatch boat to run between there and Yorktown. Yorktown and City Point are in telegraphic communication—

Start for this place as soon as you conveniently can but let me know as early as possible when you will start. I will send cavalry and Infantry to Chickahominy to meet you when you do start. Let me know whether you will wish to have them make Bottom's Bridge or Long Bridge, and whether you wish Pontoons taken from here.

When you start out from here, you will be reinforced with about 6.000 cavalry. I will also move out by the left at least 50.000 Infantry, and demonstrate on the Enemy's right and probably remain out. Your problem will be to destroy the South side and Danville roads, and then either return to this Army or go on to Sherman as you may deem most practicable.

I have a letter from Sherman of the 14th. at that time he had crossed Cape Fear River, at Fayetteville, and would start the next day for Goldsboro. Schofield had possession of Kinston at that time, and the Richmond Whig of yesterday contains an Extract from a Danville paper saying that he was in Goldsboro. After crossing the Dan River, I believe you would find no difficulty in keeping North of Johnston at Raleigh and making your way to sherman—This however I care but little about, the principal thing being the destruction of the only two roads left to the enemy at Richmond—

Very Respectfully
Your Obt. Svt
U. S. GRANT.
Lt. Gen.

P. S. Keep Col. Roberts with his Inft'y. with you to march across the country. The transports now with him can be used to Expedite getting off your men that return to the valley

U. S. G.

Copies, DLC-USG, V, 46, 75, 108; DNA, RG 108, Letters Sent. *O.R.*, I, xlvi, part 3, 46–47.

On March 16, 1865, Maj. Gen. Philip H. Sheridan, Mangohick Church, Va., telegraphed to USG. "After my dispatch of yesterday all but Col Penningtons brigade of Custers Division was withdrawn to the north side of the south Anna and Lt Col Maxwell comd'g the 1st Mich. Cavalry who was at Hanover C. H. was also withdrawn. Col Pennington was then directed to send forward from Ashland and develope the position of the enemy who was found occupying the line of the north Fork of the Chickahominy near Reyalls mill Pond. Both Cavalry and Infantry were here encountered and the following additional information obtained in reference to the Infantry force mentioned in my despatch of yesterday. The Adjt of the 15th Va Infantry who was captured yesterday says that Longstreets Corps marched out from Richmond, this is also stated by a colored man who came out from Richmond with Picketts Division. aAfter obtaining the above information I withdrew Penningtons Brigade and crossed my command to the north side of the north aAnna river. The enemy advanced with four Regiments as far as Ashland after Pennington withdrew and about seventy five men to the South Anna. I left two scouts in Ashland to watch the movements of the enemy. They report the main force of the enemy at the Chickahominy and that four (4) Regiments to Ashland and seventy five men to the South Anna river. Five railroad Bridges over the north Fand South Anna and Little river was totally destroyed also the trestle work over Sextons Swamp at the Junction. In the reconnoisance made by the 1st Conn Cavalry of Penningtons Brigade 3d Division we lost one officer killed and one officer and seven men wounded. I made a short march today as our horses are very tired most of them however are looking well. The majority of the horses lost was owing to the hoof rot caused by the mud. The roads since we reached Beaver Dam are very good the roads being sandy. The columns is encumbered by about two thousand negroes They have however rendered great assistance to our wagon train on the bad roads We have had to pass over. They have also helped to consume the supplies of the country which was abundant along the James River. We have not been pinched for food or forage up to the present time although we have only had of our own supplies Coffee Sugar and Salt for sixteen days—" Telegram received (on March 17, 9:15 P.M.), DNA, RG 108, Letters Received; copies (2—marked as sent at 9:15 P.M.), DLC-Philip H. Sheridan. *O.R.*, I, xlvi, part 3, 14. On the same day, Sheridan wrote to Lt. Col. Orville E. Babcock. "Information that seems to be reliable reached me this evening that Longstreet marched all last night and arrived with Picketts division at Peaks turnout near Hanover Court House and on the road to the White House. There is not much doubt but that Longstreet with two divisions and two Battallions of Artillery marched out from Richmond to meet me and the indications from all nights march last night is that they will try to prevent my crossing at the White House. I will march tomorrow morning to Ayletts near Dunkirk and will open connection communication with you. The enemy can get to the White House before I can in which case let the Provisions and Forage drop down to West Point under charge of one Gunboat. Let the other two remain at White House until we can settle the affair. Should they get the crossing at the White House I can cross the Mattapony & get rid of my 2000 negroes and other debris at West Point. I think that the enemy will risk greatly at Petersburg to keep me from getting to the South Side. It is possible that my information may be incorrect so do not leave the White House with anything until it is verified." LS, DNA, RG 108, Letters Received. *O.R.*, I, xlvi, part 3, 15.

To Maj. Gen. George H. Thomas

(Cipher)   City Point, Va, March 19th *1865* [*noon*]
MAJ. GN. G. H. THOMAS, KNOXVILLE TENN.

If Stoneman is not yet off on his expedition start him at once with whatever force you can give him. He will not meet with opposition now that cannot be overcome with 1500 men. If I am not much mistaken he will be able to come within fifty miles of Lynchburg.

U. S. GRANT
Lt. Gn.

ALS (telegram sent), OClWHi; copies, DLC-USG, V, 46, 75, 108; DNA, RG 108, Letters Sent; *ibid.*, RG 393, Dept. of the Cumberland, Telegrams Received. *O.R.*, I, xlix, part 2, 28. On March 20, 1865, Maj. Gen. George H. Thomas telegraphed to USG. "Your telegram of 11 A. M. 19th recd. I presume you had not recd. my telegram on the 18th from Chattanooga concerning Stonemans expedition. I think he has already started   Will forward your telegram to him" Telegram received (at 7:30 P.M.), DNA, RG 107, Telegrams Collected (Bound); *ibid.*, RG 108, Letters Received; copy, *ibid.*, RG 393, Dept. of the Cumberland, Telegrams Sent. *O.R.*, I, xlix, part 2, 34.

On March 4, Thomas telegraphed to USG. "I can now spare the detachments of fourteenth and twentieth Corps with me   Shall I send them to Genl Sherman and which way" Telegram received, DNA, RG 108, Letters Received; copy, *ibid.*, RG 393, Dept. of the Cumberland, Telegrams Sent. *O.R.*, I, xlix, part 1, 824.

On March 9, 1:30 P.M. and 6:00 P.M., Thomas telegraphed to USG. "Gen Canby telegd me March 1st from New Orleans that in consequence of the continuous heavy rains during the month of Feby that he cannot start the cavalry expedition from Vicksburg as he intended & has ordered Gen Knipe to New Orleans. These heavy rains having extended as far north as this state have also swollen the streams to an impassable condition & Gen Wilson will be somewhat delayed thereby, but will be able to move in time to cooperate with Canby in his operations against Mobile, Selma & Montgomery   Have just heard from my P. M. Gen. Col Parkhurst   he recd a communication from Forrest stating that owing to high water, bad roads & damage by high water to their R. R. that he will not be able to commence delivering our prisoners here before the 10th or 12th of this month. He claims to have about 7000 of our men. Col Parkhurst believes that he has ascertained pretty definitely that Cheathams & Lees corps' started for S. C. but that afterwards Lees corps was, with Stuarts, ordered to Selma & Mobile where they now are and that Forrest has between eight & Ten thousand cavalry in Miss. & Ala., stationed at Okolona, Verona, Tuscaloosa & Selma. Gen Hatch sends information obtained [*through his scouts that a telegram received*] at Rienzi, date not given, says Longstreet in front of Sherman, Hardee on his right flank, cheatham with his corps came upon Shermans rear who turned upon Cheatham & completely used him up" Telegram received (at

6:20 P.M.), DNA, RG 107, Telegrams Collected (Bound); *ibid.*, RG 108, Letters Received; copy, *ibid.*, RG 393, Dept. of the Cumberland, Telegrams Sent. Bracketed words appear in copy and *O.R.*, I, xlix, part 1, 869. "There are two or three thousand men at Chattanooga belonging to the 14th & 20th Corps' which can now be spared, Shall I send them to Newberne N. C. to be forwarded thence to Shermans army" Telegram received (misdated March 10), DNA, RG 108, Letters Received; copy, *ibid.*, RG 393, Dept. of the Cumberland, Telegrams Sent. The words "two or" do not appear in the copy or *O.R.*, I, xlix, part 1, 869. On March 10, 9:00 P.M., USG telegraphed to Thomas. "You can send all troops in your command belonging to the army with Sherman, that you can spare, to New Berne." Telegram received, DNA, RG 107, Telegrams Collected (Unbound); copies, *ibid.*, RG 108, Letters Sent; DLC-USG, V, 46, 74, 108. Printed as received on March 11 in *O.R.*, I, xlix, part 1, 881. On March 13, 9:30 P.M., Thomas telegraphed to USG. "Five thousand men under Brig Gen. Cruft started from Chattanooga at one oclock P M today for Sherman I am on my way to Kno[x]ville to arrange matters there" Telegram received (on March 14, 1:35 A.M.), DNA, RG 107, Telegrams Collected (Bound); *ibid.*, RG 108, Letters Received; copy, *ibid.*, RG 393, Dept. of the Cumberland, Telegrams Sent. *O.R.*, I, xlix, part 1, 907.

On March 14, noon, USG telegraphed to Thomas. "Has Stoneman started yet on his raid? Have you commenced moving troops to Knoxville and Bull's Gap?" ALS (telegram sent), OCIWHi; copies, DLC-USG, V, 46, 74, 108; DNA, RG 108, Letters Sent; (misdated March 12) *ibid.*, RG 393, Dept. of the Cumberland, Telegrams Received. Variant text in *O.R.*, I, xlix, part 1, 916. On March 14, 5:00 P.M., Thomas telegraphed to USG. "Gen Stoneman has not started yet. I am now on my way to Knoxville to get him off The heavy rains have delayed him up to this time. One Div. of Infy. is now on its way to Bulls Gap the others will follow as we get the transportation" Telegram received (at 9:40 P.M.), DNA, RG 107, Telegrams Collected (Bound); *ibid.*, RG 108, Letters Sent; copy, *ibid.*, RG 393, Dept. of the Cumberland, Telegrams Sent. *O.R.*, I, xlix, part 1, 916.

To Jesse Root Grant

City Point, Va, March 19th *1865*

DEAR FATHER,

I received your two letters announcing the death of Clara.[1] Although I had known for some time that she was in a decline yet I was not expecting to hear of her death at this time.—I have had no heart to write earlyer. Your last letter made me feel very badly. I will not state the reason and hope I may be wrong in my judgement of its meaning.

We are now having fine weather and I think will be able to

wind up matters about Richmond soon. I am anxious to have Lee hold on where he is a short time longer so that I can get him in a position where he must loose a great portion of his Army. The rebellion has lost its vitality and if I am not much mistaken there will be no rebel Army of any great dimentions a few weeks hence. Any great catastrophy to any one of our Armies would of course revive the enemy for a short time. But I expect no such thing to happen.

I do not know what I can do either for Will. Griffith's son or for Belville Simpson. I sent orders last Fall for John Simpson to come to these Hd Qrs. to run between here and Washington as a Mail Messenger. But he has not come. I hope this service to end now soon.

I am in excellent health but would enjoy a little respite from duty wonderfully. I hope it will come soon.

My kindest regards to all at home. I shall expect to make you a visit the coming Summer.

Yours Truly
ULYSSES.

ALS, PPRF.

1. Clara Rachel Grant, the oldest of USG's three sisters, died on March 6, 1865.

To Maj. Gen. Henry W. Halleck

City Point Mch 20th 1865 [8:00 P.M.]

MAJ, GEN, HALLECK
WASHINGTON

I think Arkansas should belong to the same Command as Mo, and Kansas, and that Gen, Pope should be instructed to commence preparations at once, for offensive operations against Price and should drive him across the Red River   Please lay this before the Secretary and if the change is authorized telegraph the order to Gen, Pope and inform me and I will then write to him fully,   By taking an early start, going light, Pope will be able at least to throw the enemy beyond the Red River not to return again,

U. S. GRANT
Lieut, Gen,

Telegram, copies, DLC-USG, V, 46, 75, 108; DNA, RG 108, Letters Sent. *O.R.*, I, xlviii, part 1, 1216. On March 21, 1865, 12:30 P.M., Maj. Gen. Henry W. Halleck telegraphed to USG. "Order has been issued placing the Dept of Arkansas in Genl Pope's command. I have notified him to expect instructions from you." ALS (telegram sent), DNA, RG 107, Telegrams Collected (Bound); telegram received, *ibid.*; *ibid.*, RG 108, Letters Received. *O.R.*, I, xlviii, part 1, 1225.

To James W. Singleton

City Point Mch 20th 1865

HON, J, W, SINGLETON
DEAR SIR

Your communication of the 16th inst, is just received, I see you labor under a mistake as to what I said I would authorize, I distinctly told you and Judge Hughes that if the proposition was made to me from the South, I would agree to permit them to bring into ports held by us all their products they might wish to dispose of, Government to take at once the portion required by law, The balance would be stored and reciepts given to the owners to be settled for after the war or when the Government could permit it without aiding the enemy in Arms against us, I further stated that I was not prepared to say but I might be willing to permit a percentage of the value to be paid in United States currency, but before agreeing to any thing of the kind, I would have to consider the matter, There were arguments in favor of such a course as well as against it,

I now have made up my mind to give no sanction, whatever to trade of any kind beyond the limits of our picket lines, I am satisfied that to do so would benefit the enemy and prove proportionally injurious to the country

Enclosed I send you copy of an order which I caused to be published on discovering a trade which seemed to be springing up between the North and South by way of Fredericksburg,

Very Respectfully

U. S. GRANT,

Lt. General

Copies, DLC-USG, V, 46, 74, 108; DNA, RG 108, Letters Sent. On March 16, 1865, James W. Singleton, Richmond, Va., wrote to USG. "By permission of his Excellency the President of the U S, and under the sanction of our laws and regulations I purchased in Richmond Petersburgh Wilmington other places (appearing of record in the Treasury Dept at Washington) a large amount of Tobacco rosin turpentine and cotton, which I contracted to deliver to Mr H A. Risley assistant secretary, and special agent of the Treasury Dept, for the states of Virginia & North Carolina. Nothing has been omitted on my part—to fulfill the requirements of the law and regulations—nothing has been done or attempted in violation of either. I have so far and shall continue in all respects to be guided strictly by the law and the spirit of my authority My advances have not exceed the *per centum* indicated by your conversation with judge Hughes and myself on the 25th ult I am of course greatly embarassed by the late unexpected raid on Fredricksburgh to which point under your Authority and assurance of protection I was industriously preparing to send my products. I had no connection with the contract under which the tobacco seized and burned at Fredricksburgh was sent there—I had no interest in the matter directly or indirectly—but under the impression made on the masses, by the erroneous newspaper statements— much indignation was unjustly aroused against me here—and is still very embarassing to me. As all communication with Fredricksburgh is now cut off or rendered impracticable in consequence of the destruction of the roads and bridges, I desire to know if there is any other point at which you can without interruption permit me to make the delivery to Mr Risley treasury agent for this Dept. I can obtain permission here to send to City Point either by the James the appomatox or by rail via Petersburgh—by your permission and protection of transports. If you thinke it impracticable for me to deliver at City Point or any other, within your lines at this time please advise me by Flagg of Truce, so that I may take the necessary steps to have it stored and protected here until such time as it may suit you to have it pass north." ALS, *ibid.*, Letters Received.

To Edwin M. Stanton

(Cipher)   City Point, Va, March 21st *1865* [*2:30* P.M.]

~~MAJ. GN.~~ HON. E. M. STANTON, SEC. OF WAR, WASHINGTON.

I would recommend releiving Gen. Crook from command of his Dept. and ordering him to command the Cavalry of the A. P.[1]

I would call attention to the fact that our White troops are being paid whilst the Colored troops are not. If paymasters could be ordered here immediately to commence paying them it would have a fine affect.[2]

U. S. GRANT

Lt. Gn.

ALS (telegram sent), OClWHi; copies, DLC-USG, V, 46, 75, 108; (misdated March 20) DNA, RG 94, Letters Received, 310A 1865; (incomplete) *ibid.*, Generals' Papers and Books, Crook; *ibid.*, RG 108, Letters Sent. *O.R.*, I, xlvi, part 3, 61. On March 21, 1865, 10:00 P.M., Secretary of War Edwin M. Stanton telegraphed to USG. "I have ordered Crook to be relieved and report to you for assignment to command & and have directed Paymasters to be sent down to pay the Colored troops. The reason for the difference is was that the request of the Secretary of the Treasury the troops were ordered to be paid by Corps in their numerical order. We have not money to pay all at once but can pay them progressively" ALS (telegram sent), DNA, RG 107, Telegrams Collected (Bound); telegram received, *ibid.*, Telegrams Collected (Unbound); (on March 22) *ibid.*, RG 108, Letters Received. *O.R.*, I, xlvi, part 3, 61.

At 7:45 A.M., Brig. Gen. John A. Rawlins telegraphed to Maj. Gen. George G. Meade. "Genl Grant desires to know the effective mounted strength of your Cavalry." Copies (2), Meade Papers, PHi. *O.R.*, I, xlvi, part 3, 62. At 7:50 A.M., Meade telegraphed to Rawlins. "The return of the Cavalry Division for March 10th showed six thousand (6000) men equipped & present." Copy, DNA, RG 393, Army of the Potomac, Letters Sent. *O.R.*, I, xlvi, part 3, 62.

At 5:30 P.M., USG telegraphed to Stanton. "There is part of companies A, B, C & D 4th Mass. Cavalry, in the Department of the South the remainder of the regiment being here. Will you please have Gillmore directed to send the men here so the regiment may be got together. He can retain the horses to mount Infantry or other cavalry." Copies, DLC-USG, V, 46, 74, 108; (marked as received at 9:20 P.M.) DNA, RG 94, Letters Received, 311A 1865; *ibid.*, RG 108, Letters Sent. At 9:35 P.M., Stanton telegraphed to USG. "The order has been issued to Gilmore as requested in your telegram" ALS (telegram sent), *ibid.*, RG 107, Telegrams Collected (Bound); telegram received, *ibid.*, Telegrams Collected (Unbound); (marked as sent at 10:00 P.M., received on March 22) *ibid.*, RG 108, Letters Received.

1. On March 18, 8:00 P.M., Meade telegraphed to USG. "Gen Wheaton suffers from piles and fears he would not be physically able to do cavalry service. You can therefore send for Gen Crook. Deserters say we occupy Goldsboro" Telegram received, *ibid.* *O.R.*, I, xlvi, part 3, 29. At 9:00 P.M., USG telegraphed to Bvt. Brig. Gen. Edward D. Townsend. "Please notify Genl Crook that his exchange has been effected and order him back to his Department. As soon as he goes on duty I will have him relieved and ordered to command the cavalry of the Army of the Potomac—" Telegram received (at 11:00 P.M.), DNA, RG 94, Letters Received, 313A 1865; *ibid.*, Generals' Papers and Books, Crook; *ibid.*, RG 107, Telegrams Collected (Bound); copies, *ibid.*, RG 108, Letters Sent; DLC-USG, V, 46, 74, 108. *O.R.*, I, xlvi, part 3, 28. On March 21, Town-

send telegraphed to USG. "General Crook is now at Cumberland and has received the order announcing his Exchange and directing him to assume command of his Department—" ALS (telegram sent), DNA, RG 107, Telegrams Collected (Unbound); telegram received (at 12:10 P.M.), *ibid.*, RG 108, Letters Received. *O.R.*, I, xlvi, part 3, 61. See *ibid.*, I, xlvi, part 2, 966; telegram to Maj. Gen. Henry W. Halleck, March 26, 1865.

On March 21, Brig. Gen. Samuel S. Carroll telegraphed to Maj. Gen. Winfield S. Hancock. "Genl Crook assumed Command of the dept today by order of Genl Grant" Telegram received, DNA, RG 94, Generals' Papers and Books, Crook. On the same day, Hancock wrote to USG. "I beg leave to invite your attention to the case of Brigadier General S. S. Carroll, which seems to me one of unusual hardship. This most gallant officer is well known to you by reputation. The Country has not had a more willing soldier, one more prodigal of his life when example was needed to troops. He is now crippled for life, and in infirm health, but proud of his reputation, is ready and anxious to devote his remaining strength to the service. He is however almost the only officer of distinction whose services have not been recognized by promotion by brevet or otherwise, and all the officers of his date with whom he served in the Army of the Potomac in the last campaign are Brevet Major Generals, though none were more distinguished. To add to his mortification he was some time since ordered to report to me as a Brevet Major General and I obtained permission from the Adjutant General to assign him to duty on his brevet rank. After he had been on duty for several days I was informed by the Adjutant General that he had no brevet, and by the order of Major General Halleck I was forced to announce in orders that there was a mistake, and had to relieve him from the duty to which I had assigned him. I may add that I cannot use him in the position his merit entitles him to, and the interest of service calls for unless he can get his brevet and I respectfully request your influence in his behalf. He is one of that class of soldiers the country most needs." Copy, *ibid.*, RG 393, Middle Military Div., Letters Sent. Resumption of command by Maj. Gen. George Crook provoked a quarrel with Hancock that culminated in Crook's arrest. See *O.R.*, I, xlvi, part 3, 59, 61, 69, 72, 81–83, 85–86. On March 22, 4:30 P.M., Stanton telegraphed to USG. "Your account of the way Crook talked on his return from Richmond, and other circumstances, induce me to suggest a careful consideration of the propriety of giving him a command so important as that of your cavalry. For that reason I ordered him to report to you without indicating any specific duty to which he was to be assigned. With this suggestion the matter is left entirely to your own judgment. Any thing you may do in regard to it will be approved." ALS (telegram sent), DNA, RG 107, Telegrams Collected (Bound); telegrams received (2), *ibid.*, Telegrams Collected (Unbound); *ibid.*, RG 108, Letters Received. *O.R.*, I, xlvi, part 3, 72. See *ibid.*, p. 198.

2. On March 20, Maj. Gen. Edward O. C. Ord telegraphed to USG. "The following recd from Gen Weitzel My officers and men are discouraged because the rest of the army have been paid and the Colored troops have not although repeated promises have been made—They have about Six (6) months pay due" Telegram received (at 5:10 P.M.), DNA, RG 108, Letters Received.

To Maj. Gen. John Pope

City Point Va. March 21st 1865.

MAJ. GEN. J. POPE,
COMD'G MIL DIV OF THE MO.
GENERAL.

Now that Arkansas has been added to your command I think you will be able to concentrate force enough to take the offensive against Price, where he is, or at least meet him before he makes any progress Northward.

I have not given the matter sufficient study to say how this should be done, but leave the details for you. I presume the great difficulty you will labor under will be getting your supplies in season to take the offensive.

I have directed that all ~~men~~ new organizations being raised in Iowa, Nebraska Minnesota and Wisconsin be ordered to report to you. This will give you some additional force but I am unable to say how much. Among the new troops thus added to your command there will undoubtedly be many veteran soldiers. But it can hardly be expected that they will equal, for the field, those now in the service. I would suggest therefore putting these new troops in garrison, as far as possible, and relieving the older troops for the front. Your present Mo. force I presume you will want to keep where they are.

If you can break up Price where he is you may find it practicable to make a campaign in Northeast Texas, subsisting entirely off the Country. If you can do so it is highly desirable. It ~~I~~ would let out thousands of negroes who would go into our army and many white people who are held in that country against their consent.

I do not know the number of men Canby may have taken from Reynolds recently, and cannot therefore tell exactly what force you will find in Arkansas to operate with. But there has been left what was deemed sufficient to hold the line of the Arkansas against all the enemy are supposed to have to bring against it. For an advance therefore, or to follow the enemy if he should advance, you must be able to raise quite an army from that quarter.

Movements now in progress may end in such results within a few weeks as to enable me to send you forces enough for any campaign you may want to make, even to the overrunning of the whole of Texas. If so, and you want them, they will be promptly sent.

Write me as soon as you can the moveable force, about, you can have, with your present resources, and what you propose. Also what you would propose doing if say 25.000 additional troops could be added.

> Very respectfully. your obe't Serv't
> U. S. GRANT
> Lieut. Genl.

Copies, DLC-USG, V, 46, 75, 108; DNA, RG 108, Letters Sent. *O.R.*, I, xlviii, part 1, 1228–29. On March 24, 1865, 3:00 P.M., USG telegraphed to Maj. Gen. Henry W. Halleck. "I wrote to Gen, Pope the day I rec'd notice of Ark— being attached to his Command, That letter will probably reach him to day, or to morrow, He had better recieve it before starting," Copies, DLC-USG, V, 46, 75, 108; DNA, RG 108, Letters Sent. Printed as received at 3:30 P.M. in *O.R.*, I, xlviii, part 1, 1247.

On March 9, Maj. Gen. John Pope wrote to USG. "Indian affairs in Kansas and in the Plains are so far settled as no longer to need the presence of Genl. Dodge at F Leavenworth—All troops except one Regiment in the Southern part of the State, have been sent out of Kansas—the Territories of Utah, Colorado & Nebraska have been formed into one District called the 'District of the Plains' & Genl Conner assigned to the command—He thus commands all the forces operating against the Indians & I think that no farther difficulties of a serious character are likely again to occur on the Overland Routes—The great mass of business in Genl Dodge's Dept is in Missouri—The Military Prisons are all here & in Alton—All the difficulties in his Dept are in Missouri & he has a great quantity of detailed daily business which it is exceedingly difficult if not impossible for him to attend to with his Head Quarters at F Leavenworth—I respectfully recommend that they be retransferred to St Louis or that authority be given me to retransfer them—I wrote to Genl. Halleck on the subject some time since, but he replied that the Head Quarters Dept of Missouri had been changed to F Leavenworth by your desire & that the Secretary of War, to whom he referred my letter, declined for the present to make any change—I think it will be better for the interests of the service & for the discharge of public business that Genl Dodge should be in St Louis—" ALS, DNA, RG 108, Letters Received. *O.R.*, I, xlviii, part 1, 1131.

On March 15, Pope wrote to USG. "I have the honor to invite your attention to my letter of the 6th (Int) to Genl Halleck in relation to an expected raid into Missouri or Kansas by the Rebel forces in southern & southwestern Arkansas & the Indian Country west of Arkansas—All indications point to such a raid & the son of Sterling Price who, you will remember, took the amnesty oath & returned to Missouri Eighteen months or so ago, called upon Genl Dodge privately & told him that he considered it a duty to give him information of great importance to the State—Young Price stated that he knew by letters received from his father's

Head Quarters that a raid in force would be attempted early in the Spring—He was very anxious to impress that belief upon Genl Dodge stating that of course he would be suspected and probably maltreated if such a raid were made & that he desired to place himself right with the authorities in advance—I do not know what force Genl Reynolds has in Arkansas, its character, nor how it is disposed Neither do I know what to expect from him in the way of resistance to a movement of the enemy north—It is needless to tell *you* that Arkansas properly belongs to the defense of Missouri & Kansas—If these States remain under different commands, it would seem diffcult if not impossible to ensure cooperation against any such anticipated movement of the enemy—The inaction of Steele during Price's last invasion, makes me feel very uncertain what I am to expect from that Quarter—I am left in the position either of depending upon Reynolds whose force I do not know & who is not under my command or of making all the preparations necessary, if he were not in Arkansas at all—Of course in the latter case I should need many more troops as is explained in my letter of the 6th (Inst) to Genl Halleck referred to,—I beg that you will consider the letter in question and give me your decision on the matter as early as you can—By the middle of April it is believed that Price will begin his movement—if he moves north at all—" ALS, DNA, RG 108, Letters Received. *O.R.*, I, xlviii, part 1, 1181.

On March 21, Pope wrote to USG. "I have the honor to transmit enclosed Special Order No 15 which is designed to carry out the purposes set forth in my letter of March 3d to the Governor of Missouri and his proclamation of the 7th (Inst) The only apprehension I have about the success of these measures, is another invasion or raid by Price from the direction of Arkansas—All indications point to such an attempt, General Dodge having been informed by Young Price who took the oath of allegiance some eighteen months ago, that it was certain such an attempt would be made—Our Scouts and Spies from Arkansas concur in this belief. I do not doubt from all I can learn that there are troops enough in Arkansas to prevent such a raid if they were properly equipped and posted. General Reynolds writes me that most of his Cavalry is dismounted, and that he is on a defensive footing. The term of service of the Missouri State Militia is about expiring and we will be left in Missouri with only four or five Regiments, mostly Infantry. I need not say that the proper defence of Missouri from invasion from the direction of Arkansas, is on the Arkansas River—I would be glad to be informed whether I am responsible for protecting Missouri against such a raid or whether I am to trust it to General Reynolds. In the former case it is manifest that as I have no control over the forces in Arkansas and cannot regulate their position or movements, I must require a much larger force in Southern Missouri. I cannot of course *safely* rely upon operations by the forces in Arkansas after the unexplainable inaction of General Steele during Price' raid of last year —Either the troops in Arkansas should be placed under my Command or troops sent me here to station in Southern Missouri. If this raid be made it will begin soon and we ought to be prepared—I think it proper to lay these facts and suggestions before you as they seem to me to indicate the best method of defending Missouri with the smallest force, and I have neither the desire nor the purpose to ask for other troops which are so much needed elsewhere—If all the troops in Arkansas and Missouri were in one Command it is probable that there would be a sufficient force for the purpose, If not, in view of what occurred last year, preparations ought immediately to be made to defend Missouri against invasion irrespective of any force in Arkansas—I wrote quite fully on this subject on the

6th (inst) to General Halleck but have received no reply and as the time is near at hand when some steps ought to be taken in the matter I write again and respectfully request that I may be informed what I am to expect" LS, DNA, RG 108, Letters Received. *O.R.*, I, xlviii, part 1, 1229–30. The enclosure is *ibid.*, pp. 1202–3. See *ibid.*, pp. 1131–32.

On March 27, 1:00 P.M., Pope telegraphed to USG. "I leave tomorrow for Ark. Will let you know in ten days every thing concerning men & means in Ark & elsewhere in this Div. for the purpose suggested in your letter of 21st" Telegram received (at 3:30 P.M.), DNA, RG 107, Telegrams Collected (Bound); *ibid.*, RG 108, Letters Received; copy, *ibid.*, RG 393, Dept. of Mo., Telegrams Sent. *O.R.*, I, xlviii, part 1, 1270. Also on March 27, Pope telegraphed to USG. "The following telegram just received relative to Rebel force in Louisiana and Arkansas. 'By telegraph from Hd Qrs District S. W. Missouri March 24th 1865 12 m. MAJ BARNES. a. a. G. Dept Mo. Five deserters from Gen Shelbys Division Came in last evening. They left their regiments and brigade at Camden on the 10th inst. and state that all the General officers of the Rebel army in Trans Mississippi Dept met at Shrevesport on the 1st inst and remained there about eight days. Shelby's Head Qrs. were at Louisville. The Army was stationed at Clarksville, Shreveport Louisville, Fulton & Camden. Was reported to number sixty thousand (60.000) men. Enough to eat. some deficiencies in shoes and clothing. Heard and knew of scarcity of Ammunition. Strong fortifications have been Constructed this winter on the north east side of Red river at Danley Ferry near Fulton. Col Green Commands the regiment to which they belonged. Said the day before they left that all the Infantry was ordered to march across the Mississippi river and the Armed Mounted Cavalry was ordered to Merville or Marksville on the Red river and would all move as soon as the force at Clarksville moved down to occupy Camden and Fulton and they were expected on the 11th or 12th inst Had seen but little artillery. Forage was scarce and stock poor. The Rebels had 3 steam boats that they had seen at Fulton One a Yazoo river packet & the othe two small boats. & were accustomed to run around the raft at Shreveport by the way of a buoy. The had heard of no Contemplated advance into this state this spring. Col Green said that ᵐMagruder was to cross the Mississippi with the Infantry & shelby was to remain this side with Cavalry. Price has not been with the army for 90 days signed JNO. T. SANBORN Br. Gen. Comdg'" Telegram received (at 9:25 P.M.), DNA, RG 108, Letters Received.

On April 8, Pope wrote to USG a lengthy letter discussing plans for an expedition from Ark. into Tex. LS, *ibid.* *O.R.*, I, xlviii, part 2, 50–53.

To Maj. Gen. Philip H. Sheridan

City Point, Va. March 21, 1865

MAJ. GEN. P. H. SHERIDAN
COM'DG MIDDLE MILITARY DIVISION
GENERAL:

I do not wish to hurry you, and besides fully appreciate the necessity of both having your horses well shod and well rested before starting again on another long march. But there is now such a possibility, if not probability of Lee and Johnston attempting to unite, that I feel extremely desirous not only of cutting the lines of communication between them but of having a large and properly commanded cavalry force ready to act with in case such an attempt is made. I think that by Saturday[1] next you had better start, even if you have to stop here to finish shoeing up

I will have a force moved out from north of the James, to take possession of Long Bridge crossing, and to lay a pontoon for you. Some of the troops will push up as far as Bottom Bridge if they do not meet with too much opposition. This move will not be made at the date indicated unless it is known that you are ready to start. It will be made earlier if you indicate a readiness to start earlier.

Stoneman started yesterday from Knoxville with a Cavalry force of probably 5000 men to penetrate S. W. Virginia as far towards Lynchburg as possible. Under his instructions he may strike from New river towards Danville. This however I do not expect him to do. Wilson started at the same time from Eastport towards Selma with a splendidly equipped Cavalry force of 12000 men. Canby is in motion and I have reason to believe that Sherman and Schofield have formed a junction at Goldsboro.

U. S. GRANT
Lieut. Genl.

Copies, DLC-USG, V, 46, 75, 108; DNA, RG 108, Letters Sent. Printed as received on March 22, 1865, in *O.R.*, I, xlvi, part 3, 67. On March 22, Maj. Gen. Philip H. Sheridan wrote to USG. "I will march from the White House on the morning of the 25th instant and will cross the Chickahominy at Jones bridge encamping that night between Charles City Court House and Westover. The next day, the 26th, I can cross at Deep Bottom and will require forage at some convenient point not far from the bridge. When the column reaches Harrisons Landing I will cross over to City Point to see you and make such preparations as may be necessary to carry out the views expressed in your communication of March 19th. I thin[k] the route by Charles City C. H. the best for me to take and the one which will give you no trouble by movement of troops. the road is good. the crossing of the Chickahominy not difficult. We have with us two hundred (200.) feet of bridging which I think sufficient. Tomorrow an Engineer Officer will be sent to Jones bridge to examine and if we have not bridging enough I will at once telegraph to you and pontoons can be sent to Long Bridge (crossing.)" LS, DNA, RG 108, Letters Received. *O.R.*, I, xlvi, part 3, 79–80. On March 23, Sheridan wrote to USG. "Your communication of the 21st instant by hands of Major Ord was received last night. I will certainly move from here on Saturday morning the 25th instant. I intended to go Via Jones Bridge & Charles City Court House and sent a communication to you yesterday by Capt Sheridan to that effect. the road Via Jones bridge and Charles City C. H. is good and the difference in distance will only be about four (4.) miles so that it will take about the same length of time to make the trip. If you wish me to go Via Long Bridge telegraph me at Yorktown. By going Via Jones Bridge I can make two crossings and you need not move any troops or send any Pontoon train. The horses are being shod night and day. No transportation has been detained here; the boats have been loaded day and night and notfication has been sent to General Ingalls of the boats leaving ~~and when loaded~~. I think they may have been detained by the storm and Genl Ingalls did not get the telegrams on account of the wires being down." ALS, DNA, RG 108, Letters Received. *O.R.*, I, xlvi, part 3, 90–91.

On March 21, Sheridan telegraphed to USG. "I will ship to City Point twelve hundred (1200.) men with equipments to be mounted on the animals you say can be furnished in your communication of yesterday—" Telegram sent, DNA, RG 107, Telegrams Collected (Unbound); telegram received (at 2:25 P.M.), *ibid.*, RG 108, Letters Received. On the same day, Sheridan wrote to Brig. Gen. John A. Rawlins. "I send to day to City Point under command of Col Coppenger 15th N. Y. Cav. Twelve hundred (1200.) Cavalrymen armed and equipped to be mounted on horses which the Lieutenant General notified me could be furnished. I find over Twenty one hundred (2100.) horses which had to be condemned and will be sent to Giesboro Point. Nearly all these horses are affected with the hoof rot and will not be servicable for some time to come: this of course dismounts that number of men, there ~~is~~ is to be added to this over One thousand (1000.) dismounted men who came in on foot and on mules so that my Cavalry force will be diminished over Three thousand (3000.) A great exertion should be made to get horses to City Point" LS, *ibid. O.R.*, I, xlvi, part 3, 67.

At 3:00 P.M., USG telegraphed to Sheridan. "I have ordered twenty-five additional forges to facilitate your horse shoeing. ~~and~~ I have ordered Crooke here to command the Division of Cavalry which will reinforce your column." ALS (telegram sent), Kohns Collection, NN; telegram received, *ibid.*, RG 107, Telegrams Collected (Unbound). *O.R.*, I, xlvi, part 3, 68. One sentence cut from the middle of the telegram sent is not recoverable from any copy.

On March 22, USG wrote to Sheridan. "Please give Col, Bradley Chief Q. M. of the Depot, facilities for getting off all the transportation now at the White House that can be spared from there, The detention of Boats is preventing the accumulation of horses for remounting your Cavalry," Copies, DLC-USG, V, 46, 75, 108; DNA, RG 108, Letters Sent. *O.R.*, I, xlvi, part 3, 80.

1. March 25.

To Maj. Gen. George H. Thomas

From City Point 4 p m Mch 21 *18645.*
MAJ GEN G H THOMAS
NASHVILLE

Has Cruft started yet with the detachments belonging to Shermans army? Your dispatches of 18th & 20th were received yesterday—[1]

Stonemans directions are satisfactory but Sheridan did not go to Lynchburg—If not too late inform Stoneman of the fact

U S GRANT
Lt Genl

Telegram received (at 9:30 P.M.), DNA, RG 107, Telegrams Collected (Bound); copies, *ibid.*, RG 108, Letters Sent; DLC-USG, V, 46, 75, 108. Printed as received on March 22, 1865, in *O.R.*, I, xlix, part 2, 43. On March 22, 8:00 P.M., Maj. Gen. George H. Thomas telegraphed to USG. "Your telegram of 4 P M 21st received—Genl Cruft embarked with his command here on the 14th. I learned through the newspapers that Genl Sheridan did not go to Lynchburg and so informed Genl Stoneman" Telegram received (on March 23, 10:30 A.M.), DNA, RG 107, Telegrams Collected (Bound); *ibid.*, RG 108, Letters Received; copy, *ibid.*, RG 393, Dept. of the Cumberland, Telegrams Sent. *O.R.*, I, xlix, part 2, 52.

On March 23, Thomas telegraphed to USG. "I will start for Memphis to day to see [w]hat policy has been heretofore adopted the[re] and to systemize the future policy. Shall be gone away ten 10 days." Telegram received (at 11:30 P.M.), DNA, RG 107, Telegrams Collected (Bound); copy, *ibid.*, RG 393, Dept. of the Cumberland, Telegrams Sent. Printed as sent at 8:10 A.M. in *O.R.*, I, xlix, part 2, 60.

On March 31, 5:30 P.M., Thomas telegraphed to USG. "Have heard of Stonemans Comd. at Watauga river on the 25th He is moving his main force down the valley of New River as I telegraphed you on the 18th from Chattanooga—Gen. Tiber [*Tillson*] with his infy. support will move in the direction of Ashville N. C. I ~~will order~~ will leave a force at Watauga bridge & at Kengsport thirty miles north of Carters station sufficiently strong enough to cover Stonemans rear & give him support should he be forced back by superior force—On the same day Wilson was on the Black Warrior in the Vicinity of Tuscaloosa He had captured some prisoners and many deserters from the rebels & also that he had heard that Forrest was moving so as to interpose between Gen Wilson & Selma I found the citizens of West Tenn very anxious to restore civil government" Telegram received (at 11:00 P.M.), DNA, RG 107, Telegrams Collected (Bound); (2—one on April 1) *ibid.*, RG 108, Letters Received; copy, *ibid.*, RG 393, Dept. of the Cumberland, Telegrams Sent. *O.R.*, I, xlix, part 2, 152.

1. On March 18 (Saturday), 9:30 P.M., Thomas telegraphed to USG. "Have reached this point on my return to Nashville from Knoxville. Stoneman starts on monday, he has been delayed by high water. Wilson will also start on monday; he has been delayed by the same cause. Stanleys command will be at Bulls Gap on tuesday and in good order. I have directed Stoneman to pass out of Tenn. by the lead of New River valley then move down that valley to Christian-burg about ten or fifteen miles where there are numerous trestles and small bridges but not to destroy the bridge over New River west of Christianburg. Should he ascertain that there is not a large force of the enemy in South-West-Va., and should he ascertain on reaching Christianburg that Sheridan has cap-tured Lynchburg as is now reported in the papers, he will not destroy any of the East Tenn. and Va. railroad, but to move in the direction of Danville and threaten that place should it be garrisoned by a large force, but if weakly garrisoned to attack, and destroy as much of the railroad as he can, then withdraw towards Tenn. and observe the movements of the enemy reporting to me at once all his operations" Telegram received (on March 20, 5:00 A.M.), DNA, RG 107, Telegrams Collected (Bound); *ibid.*, RG 108, Letters Received; copy, *ibid.*, RG 393, Dept. of the Cumberland, Telegrams Sent. *O.R.*, I, xlix, part 2, 17–18. See telegram to Maj. Gen. George H. Thomas, March 19, 1865.

To Bvt. Brig. Gen. John E. Mulford

City Point Mch 21st 1865

BRIG, GEN, MULFORD
CARE GEN, ORD

Have you information yet of our prisoners in the West being released? I have no information of any being sent by the way of Eastport or the Miss River, except from the West bank, Only News-paper report of those

U. S. GRANT
Lieut, Gen,

Copies, DLC-USG, V, 46, 75, 108; DNA, RG 108, Letters Sent; USG 3. *O.R.*, II, viii, 418. On March 21, 1865, Bvt. Brig. Gen. John E. Mulford wrote to USG. "I have no information on the subject of deliveries in the West. Mr. Ould informed me some time since that he had dispatched agents from Richmond to the different points where our prisoners were held, with full power and instruc-tions to deliver all prisoners in the shortest time possible. He informed me two days since that all communication with the South was cut off, in consequence of which he is unable to obtain any information, and expects to hear by way of our lines. I have been expecting our deliveries of Confederate prisoners at this point would fall off, but as yet there is no abatement. I would suggest that General Hoffman be requested to limit the shipments for the present to some 2,000 or

3,000 per week, at least until we learn what is being done at other points. Have you any information concerning the officers who were at Fort Pulaski?" *Ibid.*, pp. 418–19.

At 8:00 P.M., USG telegraphed to Bvt. Brig. Gen. William Hoffman. "You may reduce the number of prisoners forwarded here for delivery to 2000 per week until further notice." ALS (telegram sent), Kohns Collection, NN; telegram received, DNA, RG 107, Telegrams Collected (Unbound); (misdated March 22—received on March 23, 1:00 A.M.) *ibid.*, Telegrams Collected (Bound); *ibid.*, RG 249, Letters Received. *O.R.*, II, viii, 418.

On March 9, Mulford had telegraphed to USG. "I have received nine hundred sick men today, expect prisoners tomorrow, I am infered deliveries have commenced at Mobile & Red River" ALS (telegram sent), DNA, RG 107, Telegrams Collected (Unbound); telegram received (at 8:45 P.M.), *ibid.*, RG 108, Letters Received.

On March 21, Brig. Gen. John A. Rawlins wrote to Mulford. "You will please put in writing, and forward to these Headquarters, the terms and conditions of the existing agreement, entered into between you and Judge Ould, under which Prisoners of War are being exchanged and the number delivered on each side up to date under the present arrangement, You will also please put in writing and forward as above requested, the agreement entered into between you and Judge Ould on the enclosed correspondence between the Lieut, Gen'l, and Gen'l, R, E, Lee relating to certain Citizen prisoners alleged to have been held in Richmond, and a general Exchange of Citizen prisoners not under charges of being Spies, or under conviction for offences against the Laws of War, and if the prisoners referred to have been released, Please comply with the above request at the earliest possible moment," Copies, DLC-USG, V, 46, 75, 108; DNA, RG 108, Letters Sent; USG 3. *O.R.*, II, viii, 419. See *ibid.*, pp. 420, 424.

To Bvt. Brig. Gen. John E. Mulford

City Point Mch 21st 1865

BRIG, GEN, MULFORD
CARE GEN, ORD

I do not know what has been done with the Officers at Ft, Pulaski, I sent orders to have them delivered at Charleston, Before the orders was recieved Charleston had fallen into our possession, I then sent order to have them sent to the James River Before that order was recieved Gen, Gillmore wrote to me that having recieved my first order which had been directed to Gen, Foster he had sent a Flag to find an enemy to deliver the prisoners to, I have heard nothing since,[1]

U, S, GRANT Lt, Gen,

Copies, DLC-USG, V, 46, 75, 108; DNA, RG 108, Letters Sent; USG 3. *O.R.*,
II, viii, 419.

On March 22, 1865, Lt. Col. Theodore S. Bowers wrote to Maj. Gen. John
M. Schofield. "Your action thus far in the matter of Exchanges is satisfactory,
and is approved, You will continue to recieve and reciept for all Union Prisoners
of War, delivered to you by the Rebels, but you will make no deliveries in return,
All deliveries of prisoners to the Rebels will be made on the James River, An
Army Commander is authorized to exchange Man, for Man, all prisoners cap-
tured on the ground, with a view to their being immediately put into the ranks
If the Rebels desire and propose it, this course may be adopted in North Carolina, if you deem proper" Copies, DLC-USG, V, 46, 75, 108; DNA, RG 108,
Letters Sent; USG 3. *O.R.*, II, viii, 420–21.

1. On March 30, Maj. Gen. Quincy A. Gillmore telegraphed to USG. "Gen.
Howell Cobb of the Confederate Army desires to deliver to me over five thousand
5000 Union prisoners and I shall receive them on and after the eighth of ~~March~~
April unless I get other orders on the subject The papers relating to it are sent
by Mail." Telegram received (sent via New York, April 1—received in Washington on April 2, 1:30 P.M.), DNA, RG 107, Telegrams Collected (Unbound);
(2—on April 2, 6:00 P.M.) *ibid.*, RG 108, Letters Received. *O.R.*, II, viii, 446.
On April 3, Gillmore endorsed to USG communications relating to other C.S.A.
efforts to return prisoners. ES, DNA, RG 108, Letters Received. *O.R.*, II, viii,
445. The enclosures are *ibid.*, pp. 427, 436, 445, 465.

To Maj. Gen. Edward O. C. Ord

> *By Telegraph from* City Point, [*March 22*] *1865*
>
> *To* MAJ GEN ORD.
>
> The colored regt at City Pt has been ordered to your command
> also the colored cavalry from Pt Lookout numbering nine hundred
> horses & twelve hundred men. They bring their transportation
> with them. They are now armed with muskets
>
> U. S. GRANT
Lt Genl

Telegram received, DNA, RG 393, Dept. of Va. and N. C., 1st Military District,
Telegrams Received; copies, *ibid.*, RG 108, Letters Sent; DLC-USG, V, 46, 75,
108. See *O.R.*, I, xlvi, part 3, 75.

On March 20, 1865, 4:30 P.M., USG telegraphed to Maj. Gen. Christopher
C. Augur. "Is the 5th Mass (colored) Cavalry longer needed at Pt Lookout? If
not send it to the army of the James" Telegram received (at 7:40 P.M.), DNA,
RG 107, Telegrams Collected (Bound); copies, *ibid.*, RG 108, Letters Sent;
DLC-USG, V, 46, 75, 108. Printed as received at 8:40 P.M. in *O.R.*, I, xlvi,

part 3, 58. On March 21 and 22, Augur telegraphed to USG. "The fifth Mass. Cavalry, (colored,) will be sent as you have directed as soon as they can exchange their muskets for carbines, and transportation be obtained." "The 5th Mass. Cav number 1200. men. They have 900. horses. Shall I send them as they are, or supply them with complemet of horses? They are armed with muskets. Shall they be furnished with Carbines instead. Shall they take ~~horses~~ wagons with them." ALS (telegrams sent), DNA, RG 107, Telegrams Collected (Unbound); telegrams received, *ibid.* The first printed as sent at 4:30 P.M., the second received at 6:10 P.M., in *O.R.*, I, xlvi, part 3, 70, 83. On March 22, 7:00 P.M., USG telegraphed to Augur. "You may send the 5th Mass, Cavalry as it is transportation and all." ALS (telegram sent), Kohns Collection, NN; telegram received (on March 23, 12:30 A.M.), DNA, RG 107, Telegrams Collected (Bound). *O.R.*, I, xlvi, part 3, 83.

To Maj. Gen. William T. Sherman

City Point, Va. March 22d *1865*

MAJ. GEN. W. T. SHERMAN,
COMD.G MIL. DIV. OF THE MISS.
GENERAL,

Although the Richmond papers do not communicate the fact yet I saw enough in them to satisfy me that you occupied Goldsboro on the 19th inst. I congratulate you and the Army on what may be regarded as the sucsessful termination of the third Campaign since leaving the Tenn. river less than one year ago.

Since Sheridan's very sucsessful raid North of the James the enemy are left dependent on the South Side and Danville roads for all of their supplies. These I hope to cut next week. Sheridan is at "White House" shoeing up and resting his Cavalry. I expect him to finish by Friday[1] night and to start the following morning via Long Bridge, New Market, Bermuda Hundred and the extreme left of the Army around Petersburg. He will make no halt with the Armies operating here, but will be joined by a Division of Cav.y, 5500 strong, from the Army of the Potomac, and will proceed directly to the S. S. & Danville roads. His instructions will be to strike the S. S. road as near Petersburg as he can and destroy it so

that it cannot be repaired for three or four days, and push on to
the Danville road as near to the Appomattox as he can get. Then I
want him to destroy the road towards Burkesville as far as he can;
then push on to the S. S. road, West of Burkesville, and destroy it
effectually. From that point I shall probably leave it to his discretion either to return to this Army crossing the Danville road
South of Burkeville, or go and join you passing between Danville
and Greensboro?

When this movement commences I shall move out by my left
with all the force I can, holding present intrenched lines. I shall
start with no distinct view further than holding Lee's forces from
following Sheridan. But I shall be along myself and will take advantage of any thing that turns up. If Lee detaches I will attack or
if he comes out of his lines I will endeavor to repulse him and follow it up to the best advantage. It is most difficult to understand
what the rebels intend to do. So far but few troops have been detached from Lee's Army. Much Machinery has been removed and
materiel has been sent to Lynchburg showing a disposition to go
there. Points too have been fortified on the Danville road.

Lee's Army is much demoralized and are deserting in great
numbers. Probably from returned prisoners and such conscripts as
can be picked up his numbers may be kept up. I estimate his force
now at about 65.000 men.

Wilson started on Monday with 12.000 Cavalry from Eastport. Stoneman started on the same day from East Tenn. towar[d]
Lynchburg. Thomas is moving the 4th Corps to Bulls Gap. Canby
is moving with a formidable force on Mobile and the interior of
Alabama.

I ordered Gilmore, as soon as the fall of Charleston was known,
to hold all important posts on the Seacoast and to send to Wilmington all surplus forces. Thomas was also directed to forward
to New Berne all troops belonging to the corps with you. I understand this will give you about 5000 men besides those brought
East by Meagher.

I have been telegraphing Gen. Meigs to hasten up locomotives and cars for you.[2] Gen. McCallum he informs me is attending to it. I fear they are not going forward as fast as I would like.

Let me know if you want more troops or anything else.

> Very respectfully
> your obt. svt.
> U. S. GRANT
> Lt. Gn.

ALS, DLC-William T. Sherman. *O.R.*, I, xlvii, part 2, 948–49.

On March 14, 1865, Maj. Gen. William T. Sherman, "opposite Fayetteville," wrote to USG. "I am now across Cape Fear River with nearly all my army save a Division with orders to cross at day light tomorrow. I shall then draw out ten miles and begin my manoeuvers for the possession of Goldsboro, which is all important to our future purposes. I was in hopes that I could get some shoes & stockings at Wilmigton, but the tug 'Davidson' has returned with Brig Gen Dodge Chf Qr Mr with word that there is no clothing there, but he brings us some forage sugar & Coffee. I can get along for ten days having forced the army to collect plenty of Beef, and a good deal of Corn meal. I shall tonight move my Cavalry (5000) straight toward Raleigh and follow it with four Divisions without trains, & Keep the trains off toward the Right Rear. I will hold another 4 Divisions in close support, and move towards Smithland or to strike the Rail road half way between Goldsboro & Raleigh, then when my trains are well across toward the Neuse will move rapidly to Bennettsville and afterward at leisure move opposite Goldsboro, open direct communication with Schofield, who is ordered to press against Kinston & Goldsboro. I may cross Neuse about Cox's Bridge and move into Goldsboro, but will not attempt it till in close communication with Schofield. I have sent full orders to Schofield. It will not do to build any determinate plan further till I am in full possession of Goldsboro. I have ordered Schofield and Terry to press toward Goldsboro, as hard as possible from the East as I advance from the South West. The Enemy is Superior to me in Cavalry, but I can beat his Infantry man for man, and I dont think he can bring 40000 men to Battle. I will force him to guard Raleigh till I have interposed between it and Goldsboro. Weather is now good but threatens rain. We are all well Keep all parts busy and I will give the Enemy no rest." ALS, DNA, RG 108, Letters Received. *O.R.*, I, xlvii, part 2, 821–22.

On March 22, Sherman, "Cox's Bridge over Neuse River," wrote to USG. "I wrote you from Fayetteville N. C. on Tuesday the 14th Inst. that I was all ready to start for Goldsboro, to which point I had also ordered Genl Schofield from Newbern, and Genl Terry from Wilmigton. I knew that Genl Joe Johnston was supreme in command against me, and that he would have time to concentrate a respectable Army to oppose the last stage of this March. Accordingly Genl Slocum was ordered to send his main supply train under escort of two Divisions straight for Bentonville whilst he with his other four Divisions disencumbered of all unnecessary wagons should march toward Raleigh by way of threat as far as averasboro. Genl Howard in like manner sent his trains with the 17th Corps well to the Right and with the four Divisions of the 15th Corps took Roads which would enable to come promptly to the Exposed Left flank. We

started on the 15th but again the rains set in, and the road already bad enough
became horrible. On Thursday the 15th Gen Slocum found Hardees Army from
Charleston which had retreated before us from Cheraw, in position across the
narrow swampy neck between Cape Fear & North Rivers where the Road
branches off to Goldboro. There a pretty severe fight occurred in which Genl
Slocums troops carried handsomely the advanced Line held by a S. C. Brigade
~~held~~ commanded by a Col Butler. Its commander Col Rhett of Fort Sumpter
Notoriety with one of his Staff had the night before been captured by some of
Gen Kilpatricks scouts from his very skirmish Line.—The next mornig Hardee
was found gone and was pursued through & beyond Averasboro Genl Slocum
buried 108 dead rebels, & captured and destroyed three Guns. Some 80 wounded
Rebels were left in our hands, and after dressing the wounds we left them in a
house attended by a Confederate officer & 4 privates detailed out of our prisoners
& parolled for the purpose. We resumed the March toward Goldsboro. I was
with the Left Wing until I supposed all danger was passed, but when Gen
Slocums head of column was within 4 miles of Bentonville after skirmishing as
usual with Cavalry he became aware that there was Infantry at his front. He
deployed a Couple of Brigades, which on advancing sustained a partial repulse
but soon rallied and he formed a Line of the two leading Divisions, Morgans and
Carlins of Jeff. C. Davis Corps. The Enemy attacke[d] these with violence but
was repulsed. This was in the forenoon of Sunday the 19. Gen Slocum brough[t]
forward the two Divisions of the 20th Corps and hastily disposed of them for
Defense, and Genl Kilpatrick massed his Cavalry on the Left. Gen Joe Johnston
had the night before marched his whole Army, Bragg, Cheatham, S. D. Lee,
Hardee, and all the troops he had drawn from Evry quarter determined as he told
his men to crush one of our Corps and then defeat us in detail. He attacked
Slocum in position from 3 P m of the 19th till dark but was evry where repulsed
and lost fearfully. At the time I was with the 15th Corps marching on a Road
more to the Right, but on hearing of Slocums danger directed that Corps towards
Cox's Bridge, and that night brought Blairs Corps over, and on the 20th marched
rapidly on Johnstons flank & rear. We struck him about noon and forced him to
assume the defensive and to fortify. Yesterday we pushed him hard and came
very near crushing him. The Right Division of the 17th Corps Mower's having
broken in to within a hundred yards of where Johnston himself was at the Bridge
across Mill Creek. Last night he retreated leaving us in possessin of the Field,
dead and Wounded. We have ov[er] 2000 prisoners from this affair and the one
at Averasboro, and am satisfied that Johnstons army was so roughly handled
yesterday that we could march right on to Raleigh, but we have now been out
six weeks, living precariously on the collections of our foragers, our men, 'dirty
ragged and Saucy' and we must rest and fix up a little. Our Entire losses thus far
Killed wounded & prisoners will be covered by 2500. a great part of which are
as usual slight wounds. The Enemy has lost more than double as many, and we
have in prisoners alone full 2000. I limited the pursuit, this morig to Mill Creek,
and will forthwith march the Army to Goldsboro, to rest, reclothe and to get
some rations. Our Combinations were such that Schofield Entered Goldsboro,
from New bern, Terry got Cox's Bridge with pontoons laid and a Brigade across
Entrenched, and we whipped Joe Johnston all on the same day. After riding over
the Field of Battle today near Bentonville, and making the necessary orders I
have ridden down to this place Cox's Bridge to see Genl Terry, & tomorrow
shall ride into Goldsboro. I propose to collect there My army proper, shall put

Genl Terry about Faisons Depot, and Genl Schofield about Kinston partly to protect the Road but more to collect such food and forage as the Country affords until the Railroads are repaired leading into Goldsboro. I fear these have not been pushed with the vigor I expected, but I will soon have them both going. I shall proceed forthwith to organise the three Armies, into bodies of 25000 men each, and will try and be all ready to march to Raleigh or Weldon as we may determine by or before April 10. I enclose you a copy of my orders of today I would like to be more specific but have not the data. We have lost no Genl officer, or no organization. Slocum took 3 Guns at Averasboro, & lost 3, at the first dash on him at Bentonville. We have all our wagons & trains in good order." ALS, DLC-Edwin M. Stanton. *O.R.*, I, xlvii, part 2, 949–50. On March 27, USG endorsed this letter. "Respectfully forwarded to the Secretary of War." ES, DLC-Edwin M. Stanton.

On March 23, Sherman, Goldsboro, wrote to USG. "On reaching Goldsboro this morig I found Lt Dunn waiting for me with ~~his~~ your letter of March 16, and despatch of 17th. I wrote you fully from Bentonville yesterday, and since reaching Goldsboro have learned that my letter was sent punctually down to Newberne whence it will be despatched to you. I am very glad to hear that Sheridan did such good service between Richmond and Lynchburg, and hope he will Keep the ball moving. I know these raids and dashes disconcert our Enemy and discourage him. Slocum's two Corps 14th & 20th are now coming in and I will dispose them North of Goldsboro, between the Weldon Road and Little River. Howard today is marching South of the Neuse, and tomorrow will come in and occupy ground North of Goldsboro, and extending from the Weldon Railroad to that leading to Kinston. I have ordered all the provisional Divisions made up of troops belonging to other Corps to be broken up and the men to join their proper Regiments and organizations, and have ordered Schofield to Guard the Railroads back to Newberne & Wilmigton and make up a Moveable Column Equal to 25000 men with which to take the Field. He will be my Center as on the Atlanta Campaign. I don't think I want any more troops other than absentees & Recruits to fill up the present Regiments, but that I can make up an army of 80000 men by April 10. I will put Kilpatrick out at Mt Olive Station on the Wilmigton Road, and then allow the Army some rest. We have sent all our Empty wagons under Escort, with the proper staff officers to bring up Clothing and provisions. As long as we move we can gather food & forage, but the momt we stop trouble begins. I feel sadly disappointed that our Railroads are not done. I dont like to say that there has been any neglect until I make inquiries, but it does seem to me the Repairs should have been made and the road properly stocked. I can only hear of one Locomotive beside the 4 old ones on the New-berne Road, and two damaged locomotives found by Terry on the Wilmigton Road. I left Easton & Beckwith purposely to make arrangemts in anticipation of my arrival and I have heard from neither, though I suppose them both to be at Morehead City. At all events we have now made a junction of all the Armies and if we can maintain them will in a short time be in position to march against Raleigh, or Gaston, or Weldon, or Even Richmond as you may determine. If I get the troops all well placed, and the supplies working well I might run up to see you for a day or two, before diving again into the bowels of the Country again. I will make in a very short time accurate reports of our operations for the past two months." ALS, Ritzman Collection, Aurora College, Aurora, Ill. *O.R.*, I, xlvii, part 2, 969.

On March 24, Sherman wrote to USG. "I have kept Lt Dunn over today that I might report further. All the Army is now in save the Cavalry which I have posted at Mt Olive Station South of the Neuse, and Gen Terrys Command which tomorrow will move for Cox's ferry to Faisons Depot also on the Wilmigton Road. I send you a copy of my orders of this mornig the operation of which will I think soon complete our Roads. The telegraph is now done to Morehead City & by it I learn that Stores have been sent to Kingston in boats, and our wagons are there loading with rations and clothing. By using the Neuse as high up as Kingston and hauling from there 26 miles, and by equipping the two Roads to Morehead City and Wilmington I feel certain I can not only feed & equip the Army, but in a short time fill our wagons for another start. I feel certain from the character of the fighting that we have got Johnstons Army afraid of us. He himself acts with timidity & Caution. His cavalry alone manifests spirit, but limits its operations to our stragglers & foraging parties. My marching columns of Infantry dont pay the Cavalry any attention but walk right through it. I think I see pretty clearly how in one more move we can checkmate Lee, forcing him to unite Johnston with him in the defense of Richmond, or by leaving Richmond to abandon the cause. I feel certain if he leaves Richmond Virginia leaves the Confederacy. I will study my maps a little more before giving my clear views. I want all possible information of the Roanoke, as to navigability, how far up, and with what draft. We find the country here sandy, dry, and with good roads, and more corn & forage than I expected. The families remain but I will gradually push them all out to Raleigh or Wilmigton—We will need Evry house in the Town. Lt Dunn can tell you of many things of which I need not write" ALS, DNA, RG 108, Letters Received. *O.R.*, I, xlvii, part 3, 3–4.

1. March 24.
2. On March 21, 9:00 A.M., USG telegraphed to Bvt. Maj. Gen. Montgomery C. Meigs. "Has rolling stock sufficient to supply an Army of 100,000 men with the usual proportion of Cavalry, & transportation & Artillery, ~~been sent to New Berne?~~ over a distance of 130 miles, been sent to New Berne? If not more should be sent at once." ALS (telegram sent), Ritzman Collection, Aurora College, Aurora, Ill.; telegram received (at 3:00 P.M.), DNA, RG 92, Military Railroads, Letters Received; *ibid.*, RG 107, Telegrams Collected (Bound). *O.R.*, I, xlvii, part 2, 929. At 4:00 P.M., Meigs telegraphed to USG. "Despatch of 9 A M received Rolling stock is being sent to Newberne Gen McCallum who received his instructions directly from Gen Sherman at Savannah is attending to this. It is not going forward as fast as I could wish. Its embarkation is confined to certain docks at New York & Wilmington Delaware where alone the facilities are to be found & where the wide gauge engines & cars are collected. Gen McCallum was here last week & has gone back to NewYork to urge it forward. It requires many vessels & the ice interfered with the earlier shipments What ever is possible is being done to get forward a sufficient supply of rolling stock. Your despatch will be sent to him." ALS (telegram sent), DNA, RG 107, Telegrams Collected (Unbound); ADfS (marked as sent at 5:00 P.M.), *ibid.*; telegrams received (2), *ibid.*; *ibid.*, RG 108, Letters Received. Printed as sent at 5:00 P.M. in *O.R.*, I, xlvii, part 2, 930.

To Brig. Gen. Alexander B. Dyer

City Point Mch 23d 1865

BRIG, GEN, A, B, DYER
CHIEF OF ORDNANCE WASHINGTON D, C,
GENERAL!

Your letter of date March 15th in relation to Theadore J, Eckerson, has been recieved, I know him as a faithful and intelligent Officer, and recently forwarded his application for appointment as an Assistant Quartermaster in the Army, to the Secretary of War, with an earnest recommendation that he be appointed I have written him fully on the subject but presume he had not recieved my letter at the date of writing to you

I have to-day renewed my recommendation, but do not know whether there is a vacancy to which he can be appointed at present,

Very Respectfully
Your obt svt
U. S. GRANT
Lieut, Gen,

Copies, DLC-USG, V, 46, 75, 108; DNA, RG 108, Letters Sent. Alexander B. Dyer, born in 1815 in Richmond, Va., USMA 1837, served as ordnance officer before the Civil War and commanded the Springfield Armory from Aug. 22, 1861, until his appointment as brig. gen., chief of ordnance, as of Sept. 12, 1864. On March 15, 1865, Dyer wrote to USG. "At the request of Military Storekeeper Theodore J. Eckerson, now in charge of the U. S. Ordnance Depot at Vancouver W. T. I transmit the accompanying papers by which it will appear that he desires to be appointed Assistant Quarter Master in the Army. Mr Eckerson has been Mily Storekeeper in this Department since September 1853, previous to which he had served one or more enlistments in the Artillery, and his appointment was warmly urged by the Officers under whom he had served. His service in this Department has been entirely satisfactory and his correspondence with this office afford ample evidence of his capacity to fill with credit to himself and to the service the position which he desires to obtain." LS, *ibid.*, RG 94, ACP, 4943 ACP 1873. On March 23, USG endorsed this letter. "Respectfully forwarded to the Secretary of War, with the recommendation that Theodore J. Eckerson, Military Storekeeper, Ordnance Bureau, be appointed an Assistant Quarter Master of the Army." ES, *ibid.*

On Dec. 14, 1863, Sgt. Theodore J. Eckerson, Vancouver Arsenal, Wash. Territory, wrote to USG. "Although I am aware that you have enough to absorb your attention, yet I am confident you can spare a few moments to a communication from an old friend. Permit me therefore to present for your perusal the enclosed copies of letters in my favor, from Brigadier Generals Ripley, Wright and Alvord, and Deputy Paymaster General Ringgold, of the Army, also Hon. S. P. Chase, Secretary of the Treasury and His Excellency A. C. Gibbs, Governor of the State of Oregon, recommending me for promotion.—As I was largely indebted to you for my present commission, and as these recommendations go to show that I have fully borne you out in your recommendation by ten years of creditable service as a Military Storekeeper, I trust that I may now successfully ask you to add your recommendation in my favor, by a brief note to His Excellency the President, sent to me in order that I may use it in connection with the originals of those herewith enclosed. I should experience unbounded pride in being able to add your name to the list of those who have recommended me for promotion, and I trust I may receive it." ALS, USG 3. Eckerson enclosed letters recommending him for appointment as paymaster. Copies, *ibid.* On Dec. 17, 1864, Brig. Gen. George Wright, Sacramento, wrote to USG. "I take the liberty of writing you this, in behalf of Captain Theodore J Eckerson M. S. K. U. S. Ord. Dept. The Captain asks for the appointment of Asst. Quarter Master; he has served long & faithfully as Mil. Store keeper at Fort Vancouver; You know him well, and his prievous history: & I take great pleasure in asking your influence to procure him the appointment" ALS, CSmH. See letter to Capt. Theodore J. Eckerson, Feb. 6, 1866.

To Maj. Gen. Edward O. C. Ord

City Point, Va, March 23d *1865*

MAJ. GEN. ORD.

I see what appears to be large fires due North from here and also Northeast. Do you see what they are from your Hd Qrs.?

U. S. GRANT
Lt. Gen.

ALS (telegram sent), OClWHi; copies, DLC-USG, V, 46, 75, 108; DNA, RG 108, Letters Sent. *O.R.*, I, xlvi, part 3, 90. On March 23, 1865, Maj. Gen. Edward O. C. Ord telegraphed to USG. "The fires which you see are the woods burning inside my lines—I have given directions to have them extinguished as soon as possible" Telegram received (at 9:45 P.M.), DNA, RG 108, Letters Received. *O.R.*, I, xlvi, part 3, 90.

On the same day, USG telegraphed to Ord. "What is the matter with Gen. Heckman that made it necessary to relieve him from duty." ALS (telegram sent), Kohns Collection, NN; telegram received, Ord Papers, CU-B. At 6:30 P.M., Ord telegraphed to USG. "He did not find the expedition who were in plain sight on 27th Sept.; let the corps, or part of it, go without rations two days, with plenty of wagons and rations near by; had no control over the officers; and took no care of his men in camp. Besides, he ranks all the General officers in command of divisions; and is not fit to command." Telegram received, DNA, RG 108, Letters Received. See *O.R.*, I, xlvi, part 3, 87–88.

To Maj. Gen. Henry W. Halleck

City Point Mch 24th 1865 [*noon*]

MAJ, GEN H. W. HALLECK
WASHINGTON

I have no present purpose of making a Campaign with the forces in the Middle Department but want them in the best possible condition for either offensive or defensive operations, If Lee should retreat South, the surplus force under Hancock could be transferred to another field, If he should go to Lynchburg they will be required where they are, The 19th Corps ought to be discontinued or else all the new troops coming into the field added to it

We want here, all the Cavalry horses that can be delivered between now and next Wednesday,[1] Direct all the Cavalry horses to be sent to Canby that can be, His Cavalry ought however to remount itself in the Country where it is operating, Canby should be supplied from the West and by the Miss, River

U. S. GRANT
Lieut, Gen'l,

Telegram received, DNA, RG 107, Telegrams Collected (Unbound); copies, *ibid.*, RG 108, Letters Sent; DLC-USG, V, 46, 75, 108. *O.R.*, I, xlvi, part 3, 97. On March 23, 1865, noon, Maj. Gen. Henry W. Halleck had telegraphed to USG. "Genl Sheridan makes requisition for three thousand cavalry horses to be sent to him immediately. Only about six hundred on hand, & to fill this requisition no more can be sent, for some time to Armies of Potomac & James. Shall this be done?" ALS (telegram sent), DNA, RG 107, Telegrams Collected (Bound); telegram received, *ibid.*; *ibid.*, Telegrams Collected (Unbound); (on March 24) *ibid.*, RG 108, Letters Received. *O.R.*, I, xlvi, part 3, 87. In the telegram received by USG, the name "Canby" appears instead of "Sheridan."

1. March 29.

To Maj. Gen. George G. Meade

City Point. Va. March 24th *1865*

MAJ. GEN. GEO. G. MEADE,
COMD.G A. P.
GENERAL,

On the 29th inst. the Armies operating against Richmond will be moved, by our left, for the double purpose of turning the enemy out of his present position around Petersburg, and to insure the sucsess of the Cavalry under Gen. Sheridan, which will start at the same time, in its efforts to reach and destroy the South Side and Danville rail-road.

Two Corps of the Army of the Potomac will be moved at first, in two Columns, taking the two roads crossing "Hatcher's Run" nearest where the present line held by us strikes that stream, both moving towards Dinwiddie C. H.

The Cavalry under Gen. Sheridan, joined by the Division now under Gn. Davies, will move at the same time by the Weldon road and Jerusalem plank road, turning west from the latter before crossing the Nottoway, and West with the whole Column before reaching Stony Creek. General Sheridan will then move independently under other instructions which will be given him. All dismounted Cavalry belonging to the Army of the Potomac and the dismounted Cavalry from the Mid. Mil. Div. not required for guarding property belonging to their Arm of service, will report to Brig. Gn. Benham, to be added to the defenses of City Point.

Maj. Gen. Parke will be placed in command of all of the Army left for holding the lines about Petersburg and City Point, subject of course, to orders from the commander of the Army of the Potomac.

The 9th A. C. will be left in tact to hold the present line of works so long as the whole line now occupied by us is held. If however the troops to the left of the 9th Corps are withdrawn then the left of this Corps may be thrown back so as to occupy the position held by the Army prior to the Capture of the Welden road.

All troops to the left of the 9th Corps will be held in readiness to move at the shortest notice, by such route as may be designated when the order is given.

General Ord will detach three Divisions, two white and one Colored, or so much of them as he can, and hold his present lines, and march for the present left of the Army of the Potomac. In the absence of further orders, or until further orders are given, the White Divisions will follow the left Column of the A. P. and the Colored Division the right Column.

During this movement ~~Bvt.~~ Maj. Gen. Weitzel will be left in command of all the forces remaining behind from the Army of the James.

The movement of troops from the Army of the James will commence on the night of the 27th inst.

General Ord will leave behind the Minimum number of Cavalry necessary for picket duty, in the absence of the Main Army.

A Cavalry expedition will also be started ~~by~~ from Suffolk, to leave there on Saturday the 1st of Apl. under Col. Sumner, for the purpose of cutting the rail-road about Hicksford. This if accomplished will have to be a surprise and therefore from three to five hundred men will be sufficient. They should, however, be supported by all the Infantry that can be spared from Norfolk and Portsmouth, as far out as to where the Cavalry crosses the Blackwater. The crossing should probably be at Winton. Should Col. Sumner sucseed in reaching the Welden road he will be instructed to do all the damage possible to the triangle of roads between Hicksford, Welden and Gaston. The rail-road bridge at Welden being fitted up for the passage of carriages it might be practicable to destroy any accumulation of supplies the enemy may have collected south of the Roanoke.

All the troops will move with four days provisions in haversacks, and eight days in waggons. To avoid as much hawling as possible, and to give the Army of the James the same number of days supply with the Army of the Potomac, Gen. Ord will direct ~~dhis~~ Quartermaster and Com.y to have sufficient supplies delivered, by rail, at the terminous of the road to fill up in passing.

Sixty rounds of Ammunition per man will be taken in waggons, and as much grain as the transportation on hand will carry after taking the specified amount of other supplies.

The densly wooded country in which the Army has to operate making the use of much Artillery impracticable, the Amount taken with the Army may be reduced to six or eight guns to each Division at the option of the Army Commanders. All necessary preparations for carrying these directions into operation may be commenced at once.

The reserves of the 9th Corps should be massed as much as possible. Whilst I would not now order an unconditional attack on the enemy's line by them, they should be ready, and should make the attack if the enemy weakens his line in their front, without waiting for orders. In case they carry the line, then the whole of the 9th Corps could follow up so as to join or cooperate with the balance of the Army. To prepare for this the 9th Corps will have rations issued to them same as the balance of the Army.

General Weitzel will keep a vigilant watch upon his front, and if found atall practicable to break through at any point he will do so. A sucsess North of the James should be followed up with great promptness.—An attack will not be feasable unless it is found that the enemy has detached largely. ~~and~~ ɨIn that case it may be regarded as evident that the enemy are relying upon their ɨLocal Reserves principally for the defence of Richmond. Preparations may be made for abandoning all the line North of the James, except enclosed works, only to be abandoned however ɨafter a break is made in the lines of the enemy.

By these instructions a large part of the Armies operating against Richmond are left behind. The enemy knowing this may, as one only chance, strip their lines to the merest skeleton in the hope of advantage not being taken of it, whilst they hurls every thing upon the moving Column, and return. It can not be impressed too strongly upon commanders of troops left in the trenches not to allow this to occur without taking advantage of it. The very fact of the enemy coming out to attack, if he does so, might be regarded as almost conclusive evidence of such a weakening of his lines.

I would have it particularly enjoined upon Corps Commanders that in case of an attack from the enemy those not attacked are not to wait for orders from the commanding officer of the Army to which they belong, but that they will move promptly and notify the commander of their action. I would also enjoin the same action on the part of Division commanders when other parts of their Corps are engaged. In like manner I would urge the importance of following up a repulse of the enemy.

Very respectfully
your obt. svt.
U. S. GRANT
Lt. Gn.

ALS, Meade Papers, PHi. *O.R.*, I, xxxiv, part 1, 48–50; *ibid.*, I, xxxvi, part 1, 52–53; *ibid.*, I, xxxviii, part 1, 41–42; (incomplete) *ibid.*, I, xlvi, part 3, 202. Copies went to Maj. Gen. Edward O. C. Ord (LS, James S. Schoff, New York, N. Y.) and Maj. Gen. Philip H. Sheridan.

On March 21, 1865, 10:00 A.M., Maj. Gen. George G. Meade telegraphed to USG. "Only 12 deserters yesterday Some that came in late last night report that Johnstons and Heths Divisions were under marching orders with 2 days rations that it was rumored they were going N. Carolina the cars being ready on S S R R for them & that our troops were skirmishing within 10 miles of Raleigh. I will keep a sharp lookout & advise you the moment I am satisfied of any movement" Telegram received (at 10:45 A.M.), DNA, RG 108, Letters Received; copies, *ibid.*, RG 393, Army of the Potomac, Letters Sent; Meade Papers, PHi. *O.R.*, I, xlvi, part 3, 62.

On March 22, 10:30 A.M. and twice at 10:45 A.M., Meade telegraphed to USG. "22 deserters yesterday twenty one reported this morning no movements. The whole Confederate Army appear to have had 2 days cooked rations & told to be on the alert, I think due more to an expected attack from us than any projected movement on their part I regret to say that 8 desertions to the Enemy are reported last night 6 substitutes from the 9th Corps & 2 from the 6th ~~from the~~ sharp picket firing last night on 9th Corps front" Telegram received, DNA, RG 108, Letters Received; copies, *ibid.*, RG 393, Army of the Potomac, Letters Sent; (2) Meade Papers, PHi. *O.R.*, I, xlvi, part 3, 72. "In addition to the 19 deserters just reported as Coming in last night Humphreys reports 22 Coming in on his line which makes 41 in all no special Information reported." Telegram received, DNA, RG 108, Letters Received; copy, *ibid.*, RG 393, Army of the Potomac, Letters Sent. *O.R.*, I, xlvi, part 3, 73. "I shall leave here at 11 a m to meet Mrs Meade & party whom I expect at City Point this afternoon." ALS (telegram sent), DNA, RG 94, War Records Office, Army of the Potomac; copy, *ibid.*, RG 393, Army of the Potomac, Letters Sent.

To Maj. Gen. Edward O. C. Ord

City Point, Va, March 24th *1865* [2:00 P.M.]

MAJ. GEN. ORD,

I spoke to Commodore Radford about sending Gunboats up the ~~Appo~~ Chickahominy when Sheridan ~~wou~~ started to cross. I believe he made all the preparations to do so. It can have no special protecting advantage to have the Navy go up as they cannot ascend to the point of crossing but it may be desirable to make a reconnoisance up there[1] to see what is going on and whilst the troops are crossing it will be safe to make it. ~~Please~~ Sheridan will encamp to-morrow night on the Chickahominy. Please send this to Adml. Porter.

U. S. GRANT
Lt. Gen.

ALS (telegram sent), Slack Collection, Marietta College, Marietta, Ohio; telegram received, DNA, RG 107, Telegrams Collected (Unbound). *O.R.*, I, xlvi, part 3, 100.

On March 24, 1865, USG telegraphed three times to Maj. Gen. Edward O. C. Ord. "The President is expected but I do not know when When I know definitely will inform you" Telegram received (at 10:30 A.M.), Ord Papers, CU-B. "Before coming down here tomorrow wait to receive orders, which will be sent to you in the morning. You will probably want to give some directions before leaving the front." Telegram received (at 3:45 P.M.), DNA, RG 94, War Records Office, Dept. of Va. and N. C.; copies (dated March 25), *ibid.*, RG 108, Letters Sent; DLC-USG, V, 46, 75, 108. "Has Gen Meade and party started back. Mrs Grant is uneasy about Jesse. The President will be here tonight." Telegram received (at 8:45 P.M.), DNA, RG 94, War Records Office, Dept. of Va. and N. C. At 9:20 P.M., Bvt. Brig. Gen. Theodore Read, chief of staff for Ord, telegraphed to Lt. Col. Theodore S. Bowers. "In answer to a telegram from the Lieut Genl to Genl Ord please inform Gen Grant that Gen Ord & Gen Meade & party started from here ~~and~~ some time since for City Point" ALS (telegram sent), *ibid.*, RG 107, Telegrams Collected (Unbound).

On March 20, 10:00 A.M., USG had telegraphed to President Abraham Lincoln. "~~Could~~ Can you not visit City Point ~~as well as not~~ for a day or two? I would like very much to see you and I think the rest would do you good." ALS (telegram sent), CSmH; telegram received (at 3:20 P.M.), DLC-Robert T. Lincoln; DNA, RG 107, Telegrams Collected (Bound). *O.R.*, I, xlvi, part 3, 50. At 6:00 P.M., Lincoln telegraphed to USG. "Your kind invitation received. Had already thought of going immediately after the next rain—Will go sooner if any reason for it. Mrs L. and a few others will probably accompany me. Will notify you of exact time, once it shall be fixed upon." ALS (telegram sent), DNA, RG 107, Telegrams Collected (Bound); telegram received (on March 21), *ibid.*, RG 108, Letters Received. *O.R.*, I, xlvi, part

3, 50. Lincoln, *Works*, VIII, 367. On March 23, noon, Lincoln telegraphed
to USG. "We start to you at One P. M. to-day—May lie over during the dark
hours of the night. Very small party of us." ALS (telegram sent), DNA, RG
107, Telegrams Collected (Bound); telegram received, *ibid.*, Telegrams Collected (Unbound). *O.R.*, I, xlvi, part 3, 86. Lincoln, *Works*, VIII, 372.

1. The preceding six words were omitted in letterbook copies (DLC-USG,
V, 46, 75, 108; DNA, RG 108, Letters Sent) and *O.R.* although they appear in
the telegram received.

To Maj. Gen. Edward O. C. Ord

City Point, Va., March 24. 1865

MAJ. GEN. E. O. C. ORD
COM'DG ARMY OF THE JAMES
GENERAL:

A dispatch from General Sheridan of Tuesday[1] said that he
would be able to start from White House on Saturday, and that he
would come by Jones Bridge, if practicable. He had sent an officer
to examine the ~~road~~ route and would report to me. If he comes by
that route he thought he would require no cooperation from your
troops. I have not heard from him since and have deferred giving
you orders in consequence.

In the absence of further instructions you may move out tomorrow and open the route by Long Bridge in the manner proposed in your ~~route~~ note of this ~~morning~~ date As there is no intention of using Bottom's Bridge there is no necessity of risking
detachments of troops there

U. S. GRANT
Lieut. General

Copies, DLC-USG, V, 46, 75, 108; DNA, RG 108, Letters Sent. *O.R.*, I, xlvi,
part 3, 100. On March 24, 1865, Maj. Gen. Edward O. C. Ord wrote to USG.
"Shall I send out the Division—some Cavalry—and pontons to morrow to meet—
Genl—Sheridan I can occupy the Charles City Cross roads—(this side of White
oak bridge)—that bridge *also* and send the main body of my men to long bridge
—thus covering the crossing at those approaches—, and without sending any one
to bottoms bridge at all—the latter bridge being between the two swamps—and
its possession unnecessary to the purpose—besides being an ugly place to be
caught in by forces approaching from the north—" ALS, DNA, RG 108, Letters
Received. *O.R.*, I, xlvi, part 3, 99.

On March 24, Ord telegraphed to Brig. Gen. John A. Rawlins. "Gen Kautz Cannot be placed in Command of Gen Wilds Division unless assigned to duty according to his Brevet Rank,   Gen Turner deserves the same at least as much as any. ~~Can he not~~ Cannot Michie, Read & Draper also be placed on duty as Brevets" Telegram received, DNA, RG 108, Letters Received. On the same day, Rawlins telegraphed to Ord. "If you desire to place Generals Kautz and Turner in Command of Divisions on thei[r] Brevet Rank please forward application to that effect stating the necessity of immedia[te] action. It is only in cases of urgency and requiring immedia[te] action that the Lieut. General is authorized to assign officers to duty on their brevet rank   The assignment of the other officers named unless it is to command troops must come from the Secy. of War" Telegram received (at 12:50 P.M.), Ord Papers, CU-B; copies, DLC-USG, V, 46, 75, 108; DNA, RG 108, Letters Sent. On the same day, Ord wrote to Rawlins. "I respectfully request that General A. V. Kautz, be assigned to duty according to his Brevet Rank of Major General, to command the 1st Division of the 25th Army Corps and that General John W. Turner be assigned to his Brevet Rank to command the Independant Division of the 24th Army Corps, late a Division of the army of West Virginia. The necessity for these assignments is immediate" LS, *ibid.*, Letters Received. See *O.R.*, I, xlvi, part 3, 98, 1077. At 4:00 P.M., Ord telegraphed to USG. "I have ordered Genl—Turners Division—the Cavalry Ponton Trains—and Cavalry out to morrow to put the bridge across at Long Bridge   they start to morrow morning" ALS (telegram sent), Ord Papers, CU-B.

1. Actually Wednesday, March 22. See letter to Maj. Gen. Philip H. Sheridan, March 21, 1865.

To Edwin M. Stanton

City Point Va
1 30 P. M Mar 25, 1865.

HON. EDWIN M. STANTON,
SECRETARY OF WAR,

The following dispatch of Genl. Parke is received from Genl Meade.

sigd U. S. GRANT
Lt. Genl.

"The enemy attacked my front this morning at about 4 30 a m, with 3 divisions under command of Genl Gordon; by a sudden rush they seized the line held by the 3rd Brig. 1st. Div. at the foot of the hill to the right of Ft. Steadman, wheeled & overpowering the garrison took possession of the fort,   They established themselves on the hill turning our guns upon us,   Our troops on either

flank stood firm,   Soon after a determined attack was made on Ft.
Haskell held by part of McLaughlin's Brig. Wilcox' Divn. and
was repulsed with great loss to the enemy,   The 1st Brig. of
Hartranft's[1] Division held in reserve was brought up and a check
given to any further advance. One or two attempts to retake the
hill were made and were only temporarily successful, until the
arrival of the 2d Brig. when a charge was made by that brigade
aided by the troops of the 1st. Divn. on either flank, and the enemy
were driven out of the fort with the loss of a number of prisoners
estimated at about 1,600. Two battle flags have also been brought
in. The enemy also lost heavily in killed outside of our lines.
The whole line was immediately re-occupied, & the guns retaken
uninjured,

I regret to add that Genl McLaughlin was captured in Ft
Steadman, our loss was otherwise not heavy. Great praise is due
to Hartranft for the gallantry displayed in handling his Divn.
which behaved with great skill in this, its first engagement.

(signed) JNO. G. PARKE
Maj. Gen"

Telegram received (at 6:00 P.M.), DNA, RG 107, Telegrams Collected (Bound);
copies, *ibid.*, RG 108, Letters Sent; *ibid.*, RG 393, Middle Military Div., Letters
Received; DLC-USG, V, 46, 75, 108. *O.R.*, I, xlvi, part 3, 109–10. On March
25, 1865, USG drafted a telegram addressed to Secretary of War Edwin M.
Stanton. "The enemy attacked the 9th Corps this A. m.   The following dispatch
from Gen. Parke shows about the result." ALS, CtY. Perhaps this is the draft
for the message printed above, a message which USG decided not to send, or
(least likely) a message not recorded elsewhere.

At 6:10 A.M., Maj. Gen. John G. Parke wrote to USG. "The enemy have
attacked & broken through our lines near Fort Steadman—I have reported to
Gen'l. Meade but just learn that he is not present—" ALS, DNA, RG 108,
Letters Received. *O.R.*, I, xlvi, part 3, 145. On the same day, USG telegraphed
to Parke. "Call for such assistance as you may require from the troops on your
left,   Address dispatches to Gen, Hunt until Gen, Meade gets out" Copies,
DLC-USG, V, 46, 75, 108; DNA, RG 108, Letters Sent. *O.R.*, I, xlvi, part 3,
146. At 8:30 A.M., Parke telegraphed to USG. "~~I have just~~ Fort Steadman &
whole line reoccupied—No particular as yet—~~It is reported that Gen'l. Hartranft
is wounded~~—" ALS (telegram sent), DNA, RG 94, War Records Office, Miscellaneous War Records; telegram received (at 8:30 A.M.), *ibid.*, RG 108, Letters Received. *O.R.*, I, xlvi, part 3, 146.

Also on March 25, Maj. Gen. Horatio G. Wright telegraphed to Parke,
sending a copy to Maj. Gen. George G. Meade, City Point, received at 8:45 A.M.
"The corps officer of the day reports that the enemy's camps in front of Fort
Fisher are vacated, but their picket-line has been strengthened with intervals at

five paces and strong reserves." *Ibid.*, p. 139. USG endorsed this message, probably to Meade. "Will not Warren be in the right position to go in with Wright
if the enemy have weakened in front of the Sixth Corps?" *Ibid.*

On March 25, USG telegraphed to Maj. Gen. John Gibbon. "The Enemy
have attacked on Genl Parke's front & broken through his line This may be a
signal for leaving. Be ready to take advantage of it" Telegram received, DNA,
RG 393, 24th Army Corps, Letters Received; copies, *ibid.*, RG 108, Letters Sent;
DLC-USG, V, 46, 75, 108. *O.R.*, I, xlvi, part 3, 162.

On the same day, USG telegraphed to Bvt. Maj. Gen. Henry J. Hunt.
"SHave you sent troops to repel the enemy in front of 9th Corps? Assistance
should be sent them without delay." ALS (telegram sent), Kohns Collection,
NN; copies, DLC-USG, V, 46, 75, 108; DNA, RG 108, Letters Sent. *O.R.*, I,
xlvi, part 3, 114. At 7:55 A.M., Hunt telegraphed to USG. "Dis I sent down at
once. to Jones House the provisional brigade. and 5.th Corp Artilly near here req
and requested Genl Wright to send a division The division is passing down now
these Hd Qurs. The 5.th Corp. Crawfords division is also moving closely followed
by Ayres. Griffin follows as far as the Wyatt House, where he will await further
orders, . . . Genl Parke notified" ALS (telegram sent), DNA, RG 94, War
Records Office, Miscellaneous War Records; copies, *ibid.*, RG 393, Army of the
Potomac, Letters Sent; Meade Papers, PHi. *O.R.*, I, xlvi, part 3, 114.

Also on March 25, Bvt. Brig. Gen. Henry L. Abbot telegraphed to Brig.
Gen. John A. Rawlins. "Have just been informed by mounted orderly from my
chief of arty at Petersburg front that the enemy have captured Batteries no 12.
10. 9 and 8 on the right of the line" Telegram received (at 7:35 A.M.), DNA,
RG 108, Letters Received.

1. John F. Hartranft, born in 1830 in Pa., a graduate of Union College
(1853) in civil engineering, was active in law, politics, and the local militia
before the Civil War. Appointed col., 51st Pa., as of Nov. 16, 1861, and brig.
gen. as of May 12, 1864, he commanded the 3rd Div., 9th Army Corps, during
the battle of Fort Stedman. See *O.R.*, I, xlvi, part 1, 345–49.

To Edwin M. Stanton

City Point Va
Mar 25th 1865 7 30 P. M

HON EDWIN M STANTON
SECY OF WAR

I am not yet able to give the results of the day accurately but
the number of prisoners captured proves larger than at first reported. The slaughter of the enemy at the appoint where they entered our lines and in front of it was probably not less than three
thousand (3000). Our loss is estimated at eight hundred (800)
but may prove less.

Genl Humphreys attacked on the left with great promptness capturing near one hundred men and causing the enemy to return troops to that part of his line rapidly—

U. S. Grant

Lt Genl

Telegram received (at 8:20 P.M.), DNA, RG 107, Telegrams Collected (Bound); copies, *ibid.*, RG 108, Letters Sent; *ibid.*, RG 393, Middle Military Div., Letters Received; DLC-USG, V, 46, 75, 108. *O.R.*, I, xlvi, part 3, 110. On March 25, 1865, 8:00 P.M., USG telegraphed to Secretary of War Edwin M. Stanton. "The number of prisoners received by the Provost Marshal is twenty two hundred (2200) taken by the 9th Corps and five hundred (5.00) by the 2nd Corps. There may be still some more to be brought in" Telegram received (at 8:20 P.M.), DNA, RG 107, Telegrams Collected (Bound); copies, *ibid.*, RG 108, Letters Sent; *ibid.*, RG 393, Middle Military Div., Letters Received; DLC-USG, V, 46, 75, 108. *O.R.*, I, xlvi, part 3, 110. On the same day, USG telegraphed to Stanton. "The following dispatch just recieved from Gen, Meade will show the result of operations of to day in full, except the casualities in the 2d and 5th Corps, which I think will prove numerically small." Copies, DLC-USG, V, 46, 75, 108; DNA, RG 108, Letters Sent. *O.R.*, I, xlvi, part 3, 110. For the enclosed telegram of 8:30 P.M., see telegram to Maj. Gen. George G. Meade, March 25, 1865.

To Edwin M. Stanton

City Point Mch 25th 1865 [*10:00* P.M.]

Hon, E, M, Stanton

Sec, of War Washington

Gen, Cruft was ordered to Newberne, I think Steamers are now in readiness for him in Washington, but Gen, Halleck can advise you on this point, Col, Parsons was sent West to look after the transportation of Cruft's Command His excuse that he does not know where he is going is frivulous,

U. S. Grant

Lt, Genl,

Telegram, copies, DLC-USG, V, 46, 75, 108; DNA, RG 108, Letters Sent. *O.R.*, I, xlvii, part 3, 18. On March 25, 1865, Secretary of War Edwin M. Stanton telegraphed to USG. "General Crufts force is on the road between Parkersburg and Baltimore. Mr Garret complains that the transportation has been and is greatly delayed and endangered by Crufts [cont]inual interference with the arrangements made by the Company for the working the trains. Crufts excuse is that he does not know where he is to go. I have no knowledge on the subject.

Please let me know what you want done with him and I will see to it promptly"
ALS (telegram sent), DNA, RG 107, Telegrams Collected (Bound); telegram
received (at 8:35 P.M.), *ibid.*, RG 108, Letters Received. *O.R.*, I, xlvii, part
3, 18.

On March 23, 2:30 P.M., USG telegraphed to Maj. Gen. Henry W. Halleck.
"Have you heard anything from Gen. Cruft's command which left Nashville on
the 14th for New Berne?" ALS (telegram sent), Kohns Collection, NN; copies,
DLC-USG, V, 46, 75, 108; DNA, RG 108, Letters Sent. *O.R.*, I, xlvii, part 2,
969. On March 24, 3:50 P.M., Halleck telegraphed to USG. "Whereabouts of
crufts command not known. Have telegraphed to Genl Allen for information.
Col. Parsons has gone west to attend to it. Rail-roads in bad condition." ALS
(telegram sent), DNA, RG 107, Telegrams Collected (Bound); telegram received, *ibid.*; (marked as sent at 4:00 P.M.) *ibid.*, RG 108, Letters Received.
O.R., I, xlvii, part 3, 3. On March 25, 10:00 A.M., Halleck telegraphed to USG.
"The troops for Sherman's army passed Cincinnati on the 20th for Washington.
Have been delayed by loss of Railroad bridges. Vessels are here ready on their
arrival to take them to Beaufort N. C. The 19th corps has been discontinued—
As soon as it is determined what troops are to remain in West Va. I think they
should be consolidated as the 8th Corps." ALS (telegram sent), DNA, RG 107,
Telegrams Collected (Bound); telegram received, *ibid.*; *ibid.*, RG 108, Letters
Received. *O.R.*, I, xlvi, part 3, 111; *ibid.*, I, xlvii, part 3, 18–19. At 12:30
[P.M.], USG telegraphed to Halleck. "I think all the troops in West Va, should
constitute the 8th Corps and Gen, Hancock should be instructed to organize all
not necessary for holding the line of the B, and O, road into Brigades and Divisions and get them into condition to be used wherever required," Copies, DLC-
USG, V, 46, 75, 108; DNA, RG 108, Letters Sent. *O.R.*, I, xlvi, part 3, 111.

To Edwin M. Stanton

By Telegraph from City Point, Mar. 25th *1865.* 10 30 P. M.
To HON. E. M. STANTON,
SEC'Y OF WAR.

Schofield recommends and I approve the appointment of Genl.
Cox to the command of the twenty third (23d) Corps.[1] He also
asks the organization of the balance of the troops in his Department into a Corps under Genl. Terry.[2] This will be of great advantage to his command. I would suggest that Terry's Corps be called
the Tenth (10th).

U. S. GRANT,
Lt. Genl.

Telegram, copies, DLC-USG, V, 46, 75, 108; (marked as received at 11:00
P.M.) DLC-John M. Schofield; DNA, RG 108, Letters Sent. *O.R.*, I, xlvii, part
3, 18.

On March 21, 1865, Maj. Gen. John M. Schofield, Goldsboro, telegraphed to USG. "I have the honor to report that I occupied Goldsboro this afternoon with but slight opposition. Genl Terry's column from Wilmington was at Faisons Depot Last night and should be near this place tonight. Genl Shermans Left was engaged with the enemy near Bentonsville on Sunday. The artillery firing was quite rapid during the day and for a short time Monday morning. Genl Sherman's Right (the 17th Corps) was near Mt. Olive Sunday night. There has been some artillery firing during today which indicates a gradual approach of Genl Sherman's army toward this place. All this being strictly in accordance with Genl Sherman's plans I have no doubt all is well. I hope to have more definite and later information from Genl Sherman very soon, and will forward it to you without delay. I find the railroad bridges burned but otherwise the road is not injured, and the depot facilities here are very fine. I captured here seven cars and Genl Terry has captured two locomotives and two cars which he is now using." ALS (telegram sent), DNA, RG 107, Telegrams Collected (Unbound); telegrams received (2), *ibid.*; (2—transmitted via Fort Monroe, March 25, 7:00 P.M., received at 8:30 P.M.) *ibid.*, Telegrams Collected (Bound); *ibid.*, RG 108, Letters Received. *O.R.*, I, xlvii, part 2, 941.

1. On March 22, 1:30 P.M., Schofield telegraphed to USG incorporating an endorsement by Maj. Gen. William T. Sherman. "Near a month ago I wrote you a letter requesting that Maj Gen J. D. Cox be assigned to the command of the 23d Army Corps and that the remaining troops in this Dep. be organized into a Corps under command of Maj Gen. A H Terry. Having recd no reply I presume my letter did not reach you, therefore I beg leave to renew the request but if it be not deemed advisable to organize a corps for Gen Terry I nevertheless respectfully request that Maj Gen Cox may be assigned to the Command of the 23d Corps . . . I approve this—I know that Gen Cox is a good officer & Gen Terry has the best possible reputation—Gen Schofield will want two Corps organizations quick as possible" Telegram received (on March 25, 7:30 P.M.), DNA, RG 107, Telegrams Collected (Bound); (2) *ibid.*, Telegrams Collected (Unbound); *ibid.*, RG 108, Letters Received; copy, *ibid.* *O.R.*, I, xlvii, part 2, 960–61.

2. On March 25, Schofield wrote to USG. "I would like very much to have the ballance of Genl Terry's Old Division of the 24th Corps (one brigade of which is now here) sent to join his command, so that he may have a full Corps. If it is not desired to create a new Corps, Genl Terry might then be announced as Commander of the 24th Corps." ALS, DNA, RG 108, Letters Received. *O.R.*, I, xlvii, part 3, 23.

To Rear Admiral David D. Porter

City Point Mch 25th 1865

ADMIRAL D, D, PORTER
JONES LANDING

I have just returned from the A, P, front and find your dispatch of this morning,   Quiet is entirely restored and there is now no necessity of sending Boats up the Appomattox, Sheridan will leave the Chickahominy to morrow morning so that if Boats have not gone up it will be to late, Everything went off well, We captured about 2,000 prisoners and killed and wounded a large number of the enemy

U. S. GRANT
Lieut, General

Telegram, copies, DLC-USG, V, 46, 75, 108; DNA, RG 108, Letters Sent. *O.R.*, I, xlvi, part 3, 112; *O.R.* (Navy), I, xii, 81.

On March 25, 1865, USG telegraphed to Rear Admiral David D. Porter. "The enemy have attacked and broken through the right of our line at Petersburg, If they are permitted to get through they may march towards City Point, I would suggest putting one or two Gunboats on the Appomattox up as high as the Pontoon Bridge," Copies, DLC-USG, V, 46, 75, 108; DNA, RG 108, Letters Sent. *O.R.*, I, xlvi, part 3, 111; (printed as sent at 8:00 A.M.) *O.R.* (Navy), I, xii, 79. On the same day, Porter twice telegraphed to USG. "The Gunboats will go up the appomattox at once" Telegram received (at 10:00 A.M.), DNA, RG 108, Letters Received. *O.R.*, I, xlvi, part 3, 111. "I sent one or two gun boats down the river to City Point yesterday. Others are on their way now—Will you please direct any commander of gun boat there to proceed to any point you wish to protect—I am ready to send light draft gun boats up the Chickahominy—Do you wish them sent?" LS (telegram sent), DNA, RG 45, Area File; telegram received (at 10:20 A.M.), *ibid.*, RG 108, Letters Received. *O.R.*, I, xlvi, part 3, 111; *O.R.* (Navy), I, xii, 79.

To Maj. Gen. George G. Meade

By Telegraph from City Point [*March*] 25 *1865*
To MAJ GEN MEADE
Your last despatch was forwarded as received[1]—It reflects great credit on the Army for the promptness with which it became the attacking force after repelling an unexpected attack from the enemy. Do we now hold the entrenched picket line captured from the enemy? I would like to know as soon as you ascertain the losses outside of the 9th Corps

U S GRANT
Lieut Genl

Telegram received (at 10:15 P.M.), DNA, RG 107, Telegrams Collected (Unbound); (at 10:30 P.M.) William C. Banning, Silver Spring, Md.; Humphreys Papers, PHi; copies, DLC-USG, V, 46, 75, 108; DNA, RG 108, Letters Sent;

(incomplete) *ibid.*, RG 393, 5th Army Corps, 3rd Div., 3rd Brigade, Letters Received; (3) Meade Papers, PHi. Printed as sent at 10:15 P.M. in *O.R.*, I, xlvi, part 3, 113.

On March 25, 1865, [noon], Maj. Gen. George G. Meade telegraphed to USG. "The Enemy at daylight this Morning attacked the right of my line held by the 9th a c succeeding in surprising & temporarily occupying a small portion of it till Hartranft's Division in reserve was brought up when the Enemy was handsomely driven out of & the line reoccupied I forward Maj Gen Parkes detailed despatch.   immediately on learning of the attack Wheatons Division 6th Corps the small brigade at these Hd Qrs & at a brigade of Cavalry were ordered up, to Parkes support but the affair was decided before any reached the scene of action 2 Divisions of the 5th Corps were also immediately put in Motion but were halted at these Hd Qrs, on learning repulse of the Enemy   instructions were also sent to Maj Gen Wright & Humphreys to push forward their skirmishers and feel the Enemys strength & in Case he was found weakened to attack. Griffins Division 5th Corps was ordered to support Humphreys,   The last dispatch from Gen Humphreys reported he had anticipated his orders had driven in the Enemys skirmishers & would attack so soon as he Could ascertain how strongly the lines in his front were Manned"   Telegram received, DNA, RG 108, Letters Received. *O.R.*, I, xlvi, part 3, 112.

Probably on the same day, Meade telegraphed to USG. "Wrights holds his captured line   Humphreys had all of his at 8 P. M. but I authorized his retaining only such positions as in his judgement it would be advantageous to hold. Parke sends in the return of casualties in his artillery Brigade to be added to his previous return   4 killed 14 wounded and 25 missing total 43   Humphreys estimates his killed and wounded at about 450   very few missing   thinks enemys losses in killed and wounded more than double his. Wright reported his loss small"   Telegram received (dated March 26—received on March 26, 12:50 A.M.), DNA, RG 108, Letters Received; copies (dated March 25), *ibid.*, RG 393, Army of the Potomac, Letters Sent; (2—one dated March 25, one dated March 26) Meade Papers, PHi. Dated March 25, sent on March 26, 12:50 A.M., in *O.R.*, I, xlvi, part 1, 155; *ibid.*, I, xlvi, part 3, 113.

1. On March 25, 8:30 P.M., Meade telegraphed to USG. "Since my report of 12 m no further operations have taken place in the 9th Corps front. Maj Gen Parke reports his Casualties as 64 killed 323 wounded & 481 missing   his Captures amount to 8 battle flags & 1800 prisoners. The Enemy was permitted under a flag of truce to carry away from our lines 120 dead & 15 very severely wounded,   under the orders sent Maj Gen. Wright to feel the Enemy the skirmishers of the 6th Corps were advanced but found the Enemys pickets strongly intrenched   Maj Gen Wright supported his skirmishers by his 2d Division 1. brigade of the 3d Division & 2 Brigades of the 1st Division & after a spirited Contest under a sharp fire of Artillery & Musketry the enemys entrenched picket line was carried capturing 416 prisoners   this line is now held   Maj Gen Humphreys Comdg 2d Corps likewise advanced his skirmishers well supported by his 1st & 3d Divisions & Carried the Enemys entrenched skirmish line taking over 200 prisoners   subsequently the Enemy was reinforced & made several vigorous & determined attacks all of which were repulsed Humphreys capturing in these last affairs 2 battle flags & over 400 prisoners   the fighting on this part of the line continued till near 8 oclock. Numerous deserters have been reported since dark   total captures reported today 10 battle flags & 2800

prisoners, Griffins Division 5th Corps was sent to support Humphreys & was engaged with the 2d Corps, Crawfords & Ayres Divisions of the 5th Corps & the Cavalry Division were held in reserve & promptly moved to different parts of the line" Telegram received (at 9:15 P.M.), DNA, RG 108, Letters Received; copies, *ibid.*, RG 393, Army of the Potomac, Letters Sent; (2) Meade Papers, PHi. Printed as sent at 9:05 P.M. in *O.R.*, I, xlvi, part 1, 155; *ibid.*, I, xlvi, part 3, 112–13.

To Maj. Gen. Edward O. C. Ord

City Point, Va. March 25th/65

MAJ. GN. ORD.

Gen. Sheridan crossed at Jones Ferry and is now going into camp at Harrison's Landing. You may send and bring back your troops from the Chickahominy.

In the fight to-day we captured 2700 of the enemy and killed and wounded a great number.

U. S. GRANT
Lt. Gn

ALS (telegram sent), DNA, RG 94, War Records Office, Miscellaneous War Records; copies, *ibid.*, RG 108, Letters Sent; DLC-USG, V, 46, 75, 108. *O.R.*, I, xlvi, part 3, 160. USG wrote his telegram on the docket of a telegram of March 25, 1865, 8:35 P.M., from Maj. Gen. Edward O. C. Ord to Lt. Col. Theodore S. Bowers. "The following dispatch has just been received from Genl Turner. Long Bridge March 25—3. P. M. On my arrival here I Sent a Staff Officer down to Jones Bridge, not finding Sheridan here. There were signs of a large Cavalry force having Crossed at Jones Bridge this P. M. which is also confirmed by negroes who Said it was Grants Cavalry. I think Sheridan must have arrived at Jones Bridge. The ponton Bridge is finished." ALS (telegram sent), DNA, RG 108, Letters Received; telegram received, *ibid.*, RG 94, War Records Office, Miscellaneous War Records. *O.R.*, I, xlvi, part 3, 162. On the same day, Bowers telegraphed to Ord. "Gen Benham has been ordered to move the ponton bridge at Deep Bottom early in the morning to a point below 4 mile creek & to return it to its present position tomorrow, as soon as Gen. Sheridan has crossed over," Telegram received (at 10:35 P.M.), DNA, RG 94, War Records Office, Miscellaneous War Records; copies, *ibid.*, RG 108, Letters Sent; DLC-USG, V, 46, 75, 108. *O.R.*, I, xlvi, part 3, 162.

On March 25, Bvt. Brig. Gen. Theodore Read telegraphed to Bowers. "The Signal Officer ~~from~~ at Cobbs Hill Signal Tower reports that at 7 A M a train of twelve cars heavily loaded passed Port Walthall Junction going toward Petersburg. Rapid Artillery firing on Petersburgh Front" ALS (telegram sent—misdated March 24), DNA, RG 107, Telegrams Collected (Unbound); telegram received (at 9:25 A.M.), *ibid.*, RG 108, Letters Received. Ord sent an almost

identical message to Brig. Gen. John A. Rawlins. Telegram received (at 1:25
P.M.), *ibid. O.R.*, I, xlvi, part 3, 161. At 12:15 P.M., Ord telegraphed to Rawlins.
"Capt DeKalb 2d Va Reserves left Richmond yesterday was piloted through the
line between the Darbytown & Charles City road by a member of Greggs Texas
brigade—Says Pickett was encamped between Fields Div & the intermediate line
—Guide told him ~~that~~ last night after 9 oclock that both Pickett & Field were
under orders to march this morning He said furthermore that it might amount
to nothing for they had had several such orders lately. Rumors in Richmond were
that Sherman had been defeated after a hard battle—but it was not generally
believed—The Armory is being moved The Naval works are all packed up—
Boxes are being sent by the Danville road—All the men who are not engaged in
boxing up are making Spikes The men think for the purpose of spiking guns—
People in Richmond are descouraged—~~All~~ Many supposed three weeks ago it
would be evacuated before this time—Very few believe it will hold out three
weeks longer—Provisions are scarce—Flour is $1500 pr bbl since Sheridan cut
the canal—" ALS (telegram sent), DNA, RG 108, Letters Received; telegram
received (at 12:30 P.M.), *ibid. O.R.*, I, xlvi, part 3, 160–61. The telegram received has a notation: "Please send to Gen Grant at Meades Hdqrs.—" At 3:30
P.M., Ord telegraphed to Rawlins. "at 2 15 P m forty four wagons and 7 ambulances with a guard of about 100 men passed the Junction on Turnpike ~~Junction~~
~~on~~ going towards Richmond Signed THOS S. BAIRD Sergt Sig Corps Respy
forwarded for the information of Genl Commanding From Cobbs Hill Tower"
LS (telegram sent), DNA, RG 107, Telegrams Collected (Unbound); telegram
received (at 3:45 P.M.), *ibid.*, RG 108, Letters Received. *O.R.*, I, xlvi, part 3,
161. On the same day, Ord transmitted to USG a telegram received by Ord at
5:45 P.M. "~~The following just rec'd in answer to inquiry~~ Cobbs Hill Sig Stan
'GEN HARTSUFF. The troops came from direction of Richmond I think they
were not taken from this front, as I cannot notice any change. a train of nine
cars partly loaded with troops just passed towards Richmond. Some of the troops
were dressed in our uniform. THOS H. BAIRD Sig officer' I inquired as to the
character of the reconnoissance directed because an advance beyond the picket
posts in any place would bring on an engagement along the whole line. I desire
to know whether it is the intention of the Genl Comdg that I should make such
an reconnoissace or whether only extra watchfulness & attention along the picket
line is required for information. G. L. HARTSUFF M. G. ~~Reconn~~ Quiet reconnoissance ordered to night" LS (telegram sent), DNA, RG 94, War Records
Office, Miscellaneous War Records. Printed as received at 5:45 P.M. in *O.R.*, I,
xlvi, part 3, 165.

On March 26, 10:30 A.M., Ord telegraphed to Rawlins. "One or two brigades of Picketts are reported moving yesterday from enemies left towards their
right and bridge over the James—I should like to know when Genl Sheridan
gets over, or if the deep bottom bridge will be ready for my ~~men~~ use to morrow
morning—I shall require it" ALS (telegram sent), DNA, RG 108, Letters Received; telegram received (at 10:30 A.M.), *ibid. O.R.*, I, xlvi, part 3, 187. On
the same day, Bowers twice telegraphed to Ord, the second time at 5:30 P.M.
"Gen, Sheridan will cross all his men to day and the Bridge will be returned and
be ready for your use by midnight to night" Copies, DLC-USG, V, 46, 75, 108;
DNA, RG 108, Letters Sent. Printed as sent at 10:50 A.M. in *O.R.*, I, xlvi, part
3, 188. "I am now starting a tug to the pontoon bridge with maps for you. Please
send some one down to the bridge, where Sheridan is crossing, to receive them."
Ibid. At 9:00 P.M., Ord telegraphed to USG. "I shall leave my wood pontons on

the river. Will I want any canvas pontons or Engineer troops" Telegram received, DNA, RG 108, Letters Received. *O.R.*, I, xlvi, part 3, 188. On March 27, 10:00 A.M., USG telegraphed to Ord. "You will want to take your Canvass pontoons and Engineer troops with you. As early as possible on Wednsday morning get your troops in the position now held by the 2d Corps and relieve their pickets that will be left until you arrive." ALS (telegram sent), deCoppet Collection, NjP; telegram received (at 10:30 A.M.), Ord Papers, CU-B. *O.R.*, I, xlvi, part 3, 207. At 11:15 A.M., Ord telegraphed to USG. "I shall send 15 pontons with Sumner—have 15 left—I shall ~~I~~ send the pontons for sumner without ~~waggons~~ mules as I have only mules enough for 15 canvas pontons to go with column here" ALS (telegram sent), Ord Papers, CU-B; telegram received (marked as sent at 11:00 A.M.), DNA, RG 108, Letters Received. *O.R.*, I, xlvi, part 3, 207.

To Maj. Gen. Philip H. Sheridan

City Point Va Mch 25th 1865

MAJ, GEN, P, H, SHERIDAN
COMDG MID—MIL—DIV—
WESTOVER CHURCH VA
GEN'L,

You will find a Pontoon Bridge at the point where Hancock crossed last summer below Four Mile Creek instead of Deep Bottom, The Bridge at Deep Bottom will be dropped down to this position before 8, A, M, tomorrow,

Gen'l, Roberts Command will move by the most direct route to their position in the Army of the James

U. S. GRANT
Lieut, Gen,

Copies, DLC-USG, V, 46, 75, 108; DNA, RG 108, Letters Sent. *O.R.*, I, xlvi, part 3, 166. On March 25, 1865, 7:20 P.M., Maj. Gen. Philip H. Sheridan, Harrison's Landing, Va., telegraphed (and signaled) to Brig. Gen. John A. Rawlins. "I am here with my cavalry & Genl Roberts infantry. They are going into camp at Westover Church." Signal, DNA, RG 108, Letters Received; telegram received (at 7:50 P.M.), *ibid.*; copies (2), DLC-Philip H. Sheridan. *O.R.*, I, xlvi, part 3, 165.

On the same day, Lt. Col. Orville E. Babcock wrote to Brig. Gen. Henry W. Benham. "The Lieut Gen'l, directs that the Bridge at Deep Bottom be dropped down to the position where Hancock crossed last summer, as we agreed this morning, A Tug has been ordered to report at Strang's Wharf for you, and will be in readiness, The Gen, will be pleased to have the Bridge in at daylight or as near then as possible," Copies, DLC-USG, V, 46, 75, 108; DNA, RG 108, Letters Sent. *O.R.*, I, xlvi, part 3, 116. See *ibid.*, p. 173.

To Edwin M. Stanton

From City Point Va Mar. 26th 10. P. M *18645*

HON EDWIN M. STANTON
SECY OF WAR.

I respectfully request that Major General Humphreys be announced in orders as commander of the 2nd Corps and Maj Genl Parke as the Commander of the 9th corps. I would also recommend that Brig Genl Hartranft be brevetted a Major General for conspicuous gallantry in repulsing and driving back the enemy from the lodgement which he made yesterday on our lines

U. S. GRANT
Lt Genl

Telegram received (at 11:30 P.M.), DNA, RG 94, Letters Received, 330A 1865; copies, *ibid.*, 328A 1865; *ibid.*, RG 108, Letters Sent; DLC-USG, V, 46, 75, 108. *O.R.*, I, xlvi, part 3, 170. On March 27, 1865, Secretary of War Edwin M. Stanton telegraphed to USG. "The annexed order has been made. General Hartranft appointment as Brevet has been made & forwarded to you by mail. Crufts command is embarking." ALS (telegram sent), DNA, RG 107, Telegrams Collected (Bound); telegram received, *ibid.*, RG 108, Letters Received. *O.R.*, I, xlvi, part 3, 195; *ibid.*, I, xlvii, part 3, 32. The enclosure is *ibid.*, I, xlvi, part 3, 195; *ibid.*, I, xlvii, part 3, 34.

On March 26, 10:00 A.M., Maj. Gen. George G. Meade telegraphed to USG. "I take advantage of the visit of the President to recall to your attention the fact that neither Parke or Humphreys have been assigned by the President to the command of their respective corps. I do this with the less hesitation because I understand Maj Gen Gibbon who has been in command a much shorter time and is junior to both these officers has been at Gen. Ords request assigned. I would also suggest the immediate breveting of Brig Gen Hartranft and his assignment to the permanent command of the Div. he so handsomely commanded yesterday. I consider the re-taking of Fort Steadman under the circumstances a meritorious service that should be promptly acknowledged" Telegram received (at 11:45 A.M.), DNA, RG 108, Letters Received; copies, *ibid.*, RG 393, Army of the Potomac, Letters Sent; Meade Papers, PHi. *O.R.*, I, xlvi, part 3, 170–71. On the same day, USG telegraphed to Meade. "I have telegraphed to the Secy of War asking to have orders published announcing Humphreys & Parke as the Commanders of their respectiv[e] Corps also asked to have Hartranft brevetted will probably receive answer in the morning" Telegram received (at 9:25 P.M.), DNA, RG 94, War Records Office, Miscellaneous War Records; copies, *ibid.*, RG 108, Letters Sent; DLC-USG, V, 46, 75, 108; Meade Papers, PHi. *O.R.*, I, xlvi, part 3, 171.

On March 27, Maj. Gen. John G. Parke wrote a letter recommending Brig. Gen. John F. Hartranft for appointment as bvt. maj. gen. LS, DNA, RG 108, Letters Received. *O.R.*, I, xlvi, part 3, 205. On the same day, Meade endorsed this letter. "Respectfully forwarded to Lieut General Grant, and a reference made to my telegram of yesterday, upon this subject, to which a reply was received that the nomination had been made to the Secretary of War, and information returned, that the appointment would be made. I forward this communication approved, in order that the facts may be placed on record in a more enduring form." ES, DNA, RG 108, Letters Received. *O.R.*, I, xlvi, part 3, 205.

To Maj. Gen. Henry W. Halleck

City Point, Va., Mch 26, 1865. [*10:30* P.M.]

MAJOR GENL H. W. HALLECK.

CHIEF OF STAFF.

Genl Barlow, an excellent officer is for duty, and can be assigned to Genl Hancock.[1] If there is any other unemployed generals he wants, let him have them. I will see if any can be sent from here. I would advise that no permanent commander be named for the eighth corps for a few days. I may be able to send Crook back soon,

U. S. GRANT

Lt Genl

Telegram, copies, DLC-USG, V, 46, 75, 108; (incomplete) DNA, RG 94, ACP, B583 CB 1866; *ibid.*, RG 108, Letters Sent; (incomplete) *ibid.*, Letters Sent by Halleck (Press). *O.R.*, I, xlvi, part 3, 170. On March 26, 1865, 1:00 P.M., Maj. Gen. Henry W. Halleck telegraphed to USG. "I will send you by mail a detailed report from Genl Hancock showing that he can take into the field about twenty five thousand (25,000) men, moving from Winchester as his base. No one has been named as commander of the 8th corps, when organized. Would not Genl Crook be the best man for it? Genl Hancock says he is very much in want of good Division & brigade commanders for his new troops. Could not some of the Brevet Genls in the Armyies of the Potomac & the James be spared for that purpose? Genl Gillmore has sent about four thousand of his own and seven thousand of Sherman's troops to North Carolina. Sherman has directed him to send two thousand five hundred men to destroy R. R. stock & stores at Sumpterville & Florence. A part of Crufts troops are expected to-day & will be sent forward at once." ALS (telegram sent), DNA, RG 107, Telegrams Collected (Bound); telegram received, *ibid.*; *ibid.*, RG 108, Letters Received. *O.R.*, I, xlvi, part 3, 170.

1. On March 23, USG telegraphed to Maj. Gen. George G. Meade. "What is the objection to giving Barlow the Division commanded now by Seymour?" ALS (telegram sent), Kohns Collection, NN; copies, DLC-USG, V, 46, 75, 108; DNA, RG 108, Letters Sent; (2) Meade Papers, PHi. On March 26, 3:45 P.M., Meade telegraphed to USG. "Your despatch of 24th in relation to Genl. Barlow, has just been seen by me—I being absent when it came. I prefer giving Barlow,

if he is assigned to this Army—Hays Division for the reasons that Hays has less claim than Seymour, but particularly because if Ricketts returns & I understand he is expected back he will consider himself entitled to Seymours Division, which he commanded before.—" ALS (telegram sent), DNA, RG 94, War Records Office, Army of the Potomac; telegram received (at 4:00 P.M.), *ibid.*, RG 108, Letters Received.

On March 28, USG telegraphed to Bvt. Maj. Gen. Francis C. Barlow, Brevoort House, New York City. "~~I wrote to Washington that you could be assigned to command~~ I telegraphed to Washington relative to your assignment. I suppose a Division may be given you in the Valley." ALS (telegram sent), Kohns Collection, NN; copies, DLC-USG, V, 46, 75, 108; DNA, RG 108, Letters Sent. On March 29, Barlow telegraphed to USG. "Am Coming to See Genl Meade about a Division." Telegram received, *ibid.*, RG 107, Telegrams Collected (Unbound).

To Maj. Gen. George G. Meade

(Cipher)   City Point, Va, March 26th 1865 [*10:00* P.M.]
MAJ. GEN. MEADE,

I made the changes to-day suggested in your dispatch of 4 p. m. in Ord movement. Humphrey's should of course leave pickets from Wrights left until their place is filled by Ord's troops. One regiment of Cavalry in addition to that with Gen. Collis[1] had better be left to report to Gen. Parke in case the 6th Corps moves and subject to your directions until it does move. About 1500 Cavalry from Ord's Command will be with the Army.

U. S. GRANT
Lt. Gn.

ALS (telegram sent), James S. Schoff, New York, N. Y.; telegram received, DNA, RG 107, Telegrams Collected (Unbound). *O.R.*, I, xlvi, part 3, 172. On March 26, 1865, 4:00 P.M., Maj. Gen. George G. Meade telegraphed to USG. "I would suggest a modification of your instructions of the 24th inst. viz—instead of placing Ords command on the two roads used by Warren & Humphreys —let Ord mass on the Halifax road in rear of our works, and when Humphreys moves out on the Vaughn road, let Ord move to the crossing of Hatchers run by this road & await developments   This will keep up communications with Wright, and will cover my supply trains which I shall order to park at the crossing of Hatchers run by the stage road the one Warren takes—There are so few roads & the country so little open—I do not deem it advisable to bring these trains nearer until we either move from Dinwiddie C. H or have exhausted our 4 days supplies.—I propose also to leave Humphreys pickets from Hatchers run to Wrights left to be relieved by Ord unless you direct otherwise.—Do you wish any of the cavalry left on picket on our rear line or shall Davis take it all—Collis has some 300 cavalry that might be sent to Parke & a small regiment left with Wright, to watch the roads coming from the south & keep off guerillas & scouts. —Let me know your views on these points at your earliest convenience—" ALS (telegram sent), DNA, RG 94, War Records Office, Miscellaneous War Records; telegram received, *ibid.*, RG 108, Letters Received. *O.R.*, I, xlvi, part 3, 171.

At 10:45 A.M., Meade telegraphed to USG. "All has been quiet since 8. P M last evening. Wright and Humphreys hold and have entrenched all the advanced line captured yesterday as far as the Armstrong House which includes all but a small portion on the extreme left near Hatchers Run which there was no military advantage in retaining. Humphreys now estimates his casualties at 700 Wright at 400 which will make our total casualties from all parts of the line about 2.000 Deserters report the fighting very severe and the result as having a depressing and demoralizing affect on their army" Telegram received (at 11:35 P.M.), DLC-Robert T. Lincoln; copies, DNA, RG 393, Army of the Potomac, Letters Sent; (2) Meade Papers, PHi. Printed as sent at 11:30 A.M. in *O.R.*, I, xlvi, part 1, 155–56; *ibid.*, I, xlvi, part 3, 171.

At 10:00 P.M., Meade telegraphed to USG. "Official returns from the several Corps show the Casualties of yesterday as follows   2d Corps killed 51 wounded 462 missing 177, 6th Corps killed 47 wounded 402 missing 30   9th Corps killed 68 wounded 337 missing 506   total killed 166 wounded 1201 missing 713; or, a grand total of 2080 which is 80 larger than my approximate estimate of this morning   of prisoners the account now stands 2d Corps 365, 6th Corps 469, 9th Corps 1949 total 2783 or 13 less than reported last night   of this number some 200 are wounded in our hospitals   It has been quiet along the lines today   permission was granted the Enemy on application to remove their dead & wounded under flag of truce both on the 2d & 6th Corps fronts" Telegram received, DNA, RG 108, Letters Received; copies, *ibid.*, RG 393, Army of the Potomac, Letters Sent; (2) Meade Papers, PHi. *O.R.*, I, xlvi, part 1, 156; *ibid.*, I, xlvi, part 3, 172. At 11:20 P.M., USG telegraphed to Meade. "Is the loss of the enemy in killed and wounded infront of the 2d and 6th Corps supposed to be as great as ours," Copies, DLC-USG, V, 46, 75, 108; DNA, RG 108, Letters Sent; (2) Meade Papers, PHi. Printed as received at 11:20 P.M. in *O.R.*, I, xlvi, part 3, 172. At 11:30 P.M., Meade telegraphed to USG. "Gen Humphreys estimates the Enemys losses in killed & wounded in his front as fully 3 times his & I have no doubt from the character of the fighting the heaviest being repulsing their attacks that their losses were much greater   Wright also thinks they lost much heavier than we did   On Parkes front they loss was quite severe from the Artillery fire of Adjacent batteries not only when their supports were moving up but when they were withdrawing   On the whole I think it would be reasonable to estimate the Enemys losses in killed & wounded as 50 per cent greater than ours   this would make them about 2000 which added to prisoners would give 4800   taking in stragglers & deserters I think it safe to estimate Lees loss for the day not less than 5000 men" Telegram received, DNA, RG 108, Letters Received; copies, *ibid.*, RG 393, Army of the Potomac, Letters Sent; Meade Papers, PHi. *O.R.*, I, xlvi, part 1, 156; *ibid.*, I, xlvi, part 3, 172–73.

1. Charles H. T. Collis, born in Ireland in 1838, served as capt., Pa. Zouaves, as of Aug. 17, 1861; col., 114th Pa., as of Sept. 1, 1862; and bvt. brig. gen. as of Oct. 28, 1864. During the Appomattox campaign, Collis commanded at City Point.

To Edwin M. Stanton

_____

City Point Va
10.30 a m March 27th 1865

HON EDWIN M STANTON
SECY OF WAR

The battle of the 25th resulted in the following loss on our side.

2nd Corps killed 51 wounded 462 missing 177—6th Corps killed 47 wounded 401 missing 30—9th Corps killed 68 wounded 337 missing 506—

Our captures were, by the 2nd Corps—365—6th Corps 469 9th Corps ~~1949~~—1949

The 2nd and 6th Corps pushed forward and captured the enemy's strong entrenched picket line, and turned it against him and still hold it. In trying to retake this, the battle was continued until eight oclock at night. The enemy losing very heavy.

Humphreys estimates the loss of the enemy in his front at three times his own and Gen Wright estimates it in his front as double. The enemy sent a flag of truce yesterday for permission to collect his wounded and bury his dead which were between what had been their picket line and their main line of fortifications. The permission was granted

U S GRANT
Lt Genl

Telegram received (at noon), DNA, RG 107, Telegrams Collected (Bound); copies, *ibid.*, RG 108, Letters Sent; DLC-USG, V, 46, 75, 108. *O.R.*, I, xlvi, part 3, 194–95.

To Edwin M. Stanton

_____

City Point Va
11 a m March 27th 1865

HON EDWIN M STANTON
SECY OF WAR

I am in receipt of Shermans report of operations from the time he left Fayetteville, up to the 22d inst. ~~I forward it by mail~~ this

~~morning~~ It shows hard fighting, resulting in very heavy loss to the enemy in killed and wounded and over two thousand prisoners in our hands—His own loss he says will be covered by twenty five hundred men since he left Savannah, many of them are but slightly wounded

U S GRANT
Lt Genl

Telegram received (at 12:20 P.M.), DNA, RG 107, Telegrams Collected (Bound); copies, *ibid.*, RG 108, Letters Sent; DLC-USG, V, 46, 75, 108. *O.R.*, I, xlvii, part 3, 32.

To Bvt. Brig. Gen. William Hoffman

City Point Va
Mar 27th 1865 3. P. M.

BR GEN'L W. HOFFMAN
COMY GENL PRISONERS.

I presume a large number of our prisoners are yet to arrive from Wilmington and also from the Mississippi river, you may however discontinue the deliveries of rebel prisoners except so fast as the Steamer New York can bring them—Discharge all other vessels engaged in the business—

U S GRANT
Lt Genl

Telegram received, DNA, RG 107, Telegrams Collected (Bound); *ibid.*, RG 249, Letters Received; copies, *ibid.*, RG 108, Letters Sent; DLC-USG, V, 46, 75, 108. *O.R.*, II, viii, 435–36. On March 27, 1865, Bvt. Brig. Gen. William Hoffman telegraphed to USG. "Since the 1st of Feby. sixteen thousand seven hundred (16700) paroled prisoners of war have arrived at Annapolis. Twenty four thousand two hundred [(242]00) rebel prisoners of war have been delivered through Genl. Mulford. Shall I continue to send them forward" ALS (telegram sent), DNA, RG 107, Telegrams Collected (Unbound); telegram received (at 2:50 P.M.), *ibid.*, RG 108, Letters Received. *O.R.*, II, viii, 435.

Also on March 27, Maj. Gen. Ethan A. Hitchcock wrote to USG. "I find, through General Hoffman, Commy Gen. of Pris: that we have been delivering many more prisoners of war than we have any account of having received; towit —24200 to 16700. I understand from Gen. Hoffman that in all cases, the prisoners we send are accompanied by proper rolls duly authenticated; but that many parties of prisoners arrive at Annapolis without any rolls whatever, and their number is there ascertained by our own inspections. Here, as it appears to me, are two sources of difficulty; the correction of one of them is to suspend farther deliveries until we receive equivalents; the other is to require rolls to be delivered with the prisoners, and in failure to receive them, Judge Ould should be given to understand that we must claim the right to appeal to our own *inspections* in determining the number sent from the other side." ALS, DNA, RG 108, Letters Received. *O.R.*, II, viii, 435.

On March 26, Bvt. Brig. Gen. John E. Mulford telegraphed to USG. "Received thirteen hundred prisoners including Sixty Officers today, also thirty Negroes, Expect one thousand more in 2 or three days—One thousand more have been delivered to Schofield." ALS (telegram sent), DNA, RG 107, Telegrams Collected (Unbound); telegram received (at 4:50 P.M.), *ibid.*, RG 108, Letters Received.

On March 30, Mulford telegraphed to Lt. Col. Theodore S. Bowers. "I have received today from Richmd Va Fifteen hundred & Sixty ~~three~~ Six paroled prisnrs Expect more in a day or two" ALS (telegram sent), *ibid.*, RG 107, Telegrams Collected (Unbound); telegram received, *ibid.*, RG 108, Letters Received. On the same day, Bowers telegraphed to Mulford. "How many prisoners are you receiving from the ~~n~~North on an average daily. Are they coming too fast. Hitchcock and Hoffman represent that we have delivered over four thousand more than we have received" Copies, DLC-USG, V, 46, 75, 108; DNA, RG 108, Letters Sent. *O.R.*, II, viii, 446. On the same day, Mulford telegraphed to Bowers. "Arrivals of late have been slow less than sixteen hundred (1600) during the past week Genl Hitchock & Hoffman ~~ta~~ do not take into account the balance of near 8000 due the Enemy on the savanah & Charleston delivery which were ~~to~~ to be made up here deliveries are also being made in the south by the Enemy though to what extent I am unaware" Telegram received, DNA, RG 108, Letters Received. *O.R.*, II, viii, 447.

On March 31, Hoffman wrote to USG. "In the accompanying note, Maj Gen'l Hitchcock, Commissioner for Exchange, request me to bring to your notice certain irregularities and neglects that appear to exist in the performance of the duties of the Ass't Agent for Exchange at City Point to which I have called the General's attention, and with a view to remedy this defective practice, if it exists, I beg leave to lay the following matter before you. It is reported by Officers who have conducted prisoners of War to City Point, that they are delivered to the rebel agent by count and not by calling the roll which is sent with them. The consequence is, many having died by the way, escaped, or been left sick in hospital, it is impossible to say who of the prisoners have been delivered and who have not, and as many are non-commissioned Officers it will not be practicable to reduce them to their equivalent numbers, in privates, which is necessary in arranging an exchange. Duplicate rolls are sent with every party of prisoners forwarded to City Point. One of them is to be delivered with the prisoners, with a note opposite the name of every man not delivered, and the duplicate noted in the same manner, is to be forwarded to this Office, that every prisoner may be accounted for. By the plan pursued by the Agent this regulation of the War Department is wholly lost sight of. It is also reported that the Ass't Agent declines to give to Officers who deliver rebel prisoners to him, receipts for them according to grades, but will give a receipt only for the total number without regard to rank. It is required of Commanders of these parties that on their return to the station to which they belong, they shall make to the Commanding Officer a report of their service, accounting for all the prisoners placed in their charge and giving the names of all not delivered for exchange. By the course pursued by the Ass't Agent it is not in their power, in many cases, to do more than give the number for which they are responsible and the total number delivered. The rebel agent has delivered on the James river a good many Federal prisoners, in mass, without rolls or, as far as I am informed, writing of any Kind. These prisoners are sent to Annapolis where they are distributed to the Camp and the Hospital, and it is only after much delay and trouble that I can get any accurate reports of their names or numbers. While deliveries are made in this irregular way on both sides it will not be possible for the Agents to make an exchange based on accurate numbers. I have had frequent occasion, while the matter of exchanges was under the direction of Maj Gen'l Butler and since that time, to refer papers in relation to exchanges and other subjects to the Ass't Agent for Exchange and with rare exceptions these papers have never been returned to me, or replied to. My impression is that few books or files are Kept in the exchange office, and the records are in such a condition that it would be very difficult, if not impossible, to recover any paper once laid aside there. I would therefore respectfully suggest that an Officer be directed to inquire into the manner in which the duties are performed and the records Kept, in connection with exchanges, and that where it is found necessary, such reforms be ordered as the good of the service demands." LS, DNA, RG 108, Letters Received. *O.R.*, II, viii, 447–48. The enclosure is *ibid.*, p. 444.

To Maj. Gen. George G. Meade

City Point Mch 27th [*1865, 3:00* P.M.]

MAJ. GEN, MEADE

Gen, Ord draws his troops out of the position they now occupy to-night,   They cannot march at night however the whole distance without losing a great number of men by stragling and as they will be in view of the Enemy most of the time after they reach Broadway Landing I do not think it possible to conceal his movements His instructions are to get up so as to relieve the 2d Corps Pickets as early on Wednesday[1] as possible,   I will also instruct Ord to conceal his movements from the enemy if he can,   It is only the place of the pickets of 2d Corps that Ord will replace and the Command will be in compact marching order near to Hatchers Run

U. S. GRANT
Lieut, Gen,

Telegram, copies, DLC-USG, V, 46, 75, 108; DNA, RG 108, Letters Sent; (2) Meade Papers, PHi. *O.R.*, I, xlvi, part 3, 196. On March 27, 1865, 1:00 P.M., Maj. Gen. George G. Meade telegraphed to USG. "Gen Ord telegraphs he is directed to take position occupied by the 2d Corps & his command will be at

Broadway by noon tomorrow ready to move   This would indicate his crossing the bridge by daylight and making known his movement to the enemy; Do you intend this & do you design he should occupy Humphreys line? I do not know of any objection to the latter except his troops will not be quite so well in hand as if moved near Hatchers Run   I think however his movements ought to be concealed from the enemy if practicable" Telegram received, DNA, RG 108, Letters Received; copies, *ibid.*, RG 393, Army of the Potomac, Letters Sent; (2) Meade Papers, PHi. *O.R.*, I, xlvi, part 3, 195–96. See telegram to Maj. Gen. Edward O. C. Ord, March 27, 1865.

Also on March 27, USG wrote to Meade. "A Prisoner who returned from Richmond makes the following statement, 'I saw Gen, McLaughlin yesterday morning in Richmond, He wished me to communicate with Gen, Grant that the works in front of Battery five were not strong enough. The enemy intended to make another demonstration on that point and was strengthening his own works on that line' " Copies, DLC-USG, V, 46, 75, 108; DNA, RG 108, Letters Sent. *O.R.*, I, xlvi, part 3, 196. The information came from a telegram of March 27 from Col. Frederick D. Sewall, Annapolis, to Bvt. Brig. Gen. William Hoffman. Telegram received (at 5:55 P.M.), DNA, RG 108, Letters Received.

1. March 29.

To Maj. Gen. George G. Meade

City Point, Va, March 27th *1865*

MAJ. GN. MEADE,

Gen. Sherman is here and will remain until about noon tomorrow. I did not ask you to come in to-night because I did not know but you might be needed where you are in the morning. If all is quiet suppose you come in to-morrow morning.

U. S. GRANT
Lt. Gn.

ALS (telegram sent), CSmH; copies, DLC-USG, V, 46, 75, 108; DNA, RG 108, Letters Sent. *O.R.*, I, xlvi, part 3, 196. On March 27, 1865, 10:00 P.M., Maj. Gen. George G. Meade telegraphed to USG. "I will be at City Point by 9. a m tomorrow & will be most happy to see Genl. Sherman & beg leave to thank you for the opportunity to do so.—" ALS (telegram sent), DNA, RG 94, War Records Office, Miscellaneous War Records; telegram received (at 10:00 P.M.), *ibid.*, RG 108, Letters Received. *O.R.*, I, xlvi, part 3, 196. At 12:30 P.M., Maj. Gen. William T. Sherman, Old Point Comfort, Va., telegraphed to USG. "All well at Goldsboro. I am coming up to see you but must get back as soon as possible. Therefore get all the Maps ready that illustrate the Roanoke & Chowan Rivers. If Admiral Porter is there I should like to meet him." ALS (telegram sent), CSmH; telegram received, DNA, RG 108, Letters Received. *O.R.*, I, xlvii, part 3, 33. Sherman noted in his diary that he arrived at City Point on March

27, 6:00 P.M., and left on March 28, 4:00 P.M. DLC-William T. Sherman.

On March 27, Maj. Gen. Philip H. Sheridan telegraphed to Brig. Gen. John A. Rawlins. "I have established my Head quarters at this place (Gregg's Station)." Copies (2), DLC-Philip H. Sheridan. *O.R.*, I, xlvi, part 3, 215. On the same day, USG telegraphed to Sheridan. "Gen, Sherman will be here this evening to spend a few hours, I would like to have you come down" Copies, DLC-USG, V, 46, 75, 108; DNA, RG 108, Letters Sent. *O.R.*, I, xlvi, part 3, 215. On the same day, Sheridan telegraphed to USG. "I will be down on the first train" Telegram received (at 6:00 P.M.), DNA, RG 108, Letters Received; copies (2), DLC-Philip H. Sheridan. *O.R.*, I, xlvi, part 3, 215.

On March 26, Rear Admiral David D. Porter, Jones' Landing, Va., telegraphed to USG. "I hear the President is at City Point and likely to come here. please inform me about what time he will leave City Point" Telegram received, DNA, RG 108, Letters Received. *O.R.*, I, xlvi, part 3, 173. On the same day, USG telegraphed to Porter. "The President will start up the river about 11 o'clock this morning." *Ibid.* On March 27, USG telegraphed to Porter. "General Sherman has left Fortress Monroe on his way up here and will probably arrive about 6 P. M. Cant you come down and see him. He will probably return tonight and I know will be disappointed if he does not meet you." Copies, DLC-USG, V, 46, 75, 108; DNA, RG 108, Letters Sent. *O.R.* (Navy), I, xii, 84.

To Maj. Gen. George G. Meade

City Point Mch 27th 1865

MAJ, GEN, MEADE

The Chronicle of yesterday gives my dispatches differently from what they were written, at the time they were written[1] I had no estimate of our losses except in the 9th Corps, and placed our loss there at about 800, probably less, The enemys loss in front of that Corps I estimated at 3000 all told, killed, wounded and captured, I was not aware at the Time the published dispatches were written that the 6th Corps had accomplished anything or lost any thing, Subsequent dispatches which will probably be published in to days papers, give the latest information corrected so far as I know it,

U S GRANT
Lieut, Gen,

Copies, DLC-USG, V, 46, 75, 108; DNA, RG 108, Letters Sent. *O.R.*, I, xlvi, part 3, 197.

1. The preceding six words do not appear in letterbook copies (with the exception of DLC-USG, V, 75) and *O.R.*

To Maj. Gen. Edward O. C. Ord

In the Field, March 27 1865. [*3:00* P.M.]

To MAJ GEN ORD
Where, COMDG ARMY OF JAMES

It is only the pickets of the 2d Corps I want you to replace. Your Command will be moved up in Compact marching order near to Hatchers Run on the left of our lines. This is the ground occupied by the 2d Corps only. They are Scattered to cover a long line If you can possibly get to the ground which you are to occupy tomorrow night without being observed by the enemy I would like you to do it

U S GRANT
Maj Gen

Telegram received, DNA, RG 94, War Records Office, 24th Army Corps; copies, *ibid.*, RG 108, Letters Sent; DLC-USG, V, 46, 75, 108. *O.R.*, I, xlvi, part 3, 208. On March 27, 1865, 3:30 P.M., Maj. Gen. Edward O. C. Ord telegraphed to USG. "I am to start tonight, cross two rivers—one has but single bridge. Can I march new troops 30 miles by tomorrow night & relieve ~~two~~ Secondd corps next morning at 6 a m—Should not second corps hold their line till relieved if their line is important? The route Gen Meade sends me is 30 miles from my camp" Telegram received, DNA, RG 108, Letters Received. *O.R.*, I, xlvi, part 3, 208. At 5:30 P.M., USG telegraphed to Ord. "It is not particularly necessary that you should relieve the pickets of 2d Corps at 6 a. m. on the 29th. Marke your marches so as not to overfatigue your men and when you get up relieve them. Starting to-night and then early Wednsday you will be at Hatchers Run at an early hour on that day." ALS (telegram sent), deCoppet Collection, NjP; telegram received (at 5:45 P.M.), Ord Papers, CU-B. *O.R.*, I, xlvi, part 3, 208. At 5:30 P.M., Ord telegraphed to USG. "Will try to get Turners division up Do not expect to get more as it would scatter them for miles Sumner reports river at Winton 900 feet. All my ~~pontons~~ canvas pontons together reach but 600 feet; he will have to get the Admiral to send up & occupy Winton & ferry him over or give up the expidition" Telegram received, DNA, RG 108, Letters Received. *O.R.*, I, xlvi, part 3, 208.

On March 28, 7:40 A.M., Ord telegraphed to USG. "My men are all across. Gen Turner about six miles ahead of this. May get to Fort Sampson tonight Trains much delayed & not across bad roads &c. Fosters & Birney's Divisions must rest till 10 or 12 & cannot make more than ten miles today been up all night & march poorly" Telegram received (at 8:00 P.M.), DNA, RG 108, Letters Received. *O.R.*, I, xlvi, part 3, 236.

To Sidney S. Jerman

City Point Va March 27. 1865.

SIDNEY S JERMAN ESQ
SIR

I have received your proposition to run three large steamers, now on the Upper Red River, to New Orleans, and to take them laden with Cotton, on condition that the boats and Cotton will not be subject to seizure when they arrive in New Orleans

If you, or any other person having charge of these boats, choose to run them to New Orleans, loaded as proposed, you may do so, and the boats shall be exempt from seizure if belonging to parties now loyal, or parties who will conform to existing orders, law and proclamations on the subject, The parties having the cotton in charge will be allowed to sell it to ~~parties~~ the United States Government in accordance with Sec 8th of the Act of Congress regulating trade with insurrectionary States, published in General Orders, No 257. of September 15th 1864, and to have the full benefits of all proceeds so accruing.

Very Respectfully, Your Obt Servant
U S GRANT.
Lieut General.

Copies, CSmH; DLC-USG, V, 46, 75, 108; DNA, RG 108, Letters Sent; *ibid.*, RG 366, Seventh Special Agency. Variant text in *O.R.*, I, xlviii, part 1, 1267. Sidney S. Jerman had written an undated letter to USG. "I am a citizen of St Louis Mo and a loyal citizen of the United States and represent the owners of three steamboats now within the rebel lines and subject to the control of the rebel army. These boats are of large tonnage and capable of transporting a large number of troops, and munitions of war. I can make an arrangement to run these steamboats out of the rebel lines into the port of New Orleans laden with cotton, if I can get the assurance of the Federal authorities that the boats and Cotton shall be exempt from seizure on their arrival within our lines, and that the boats and cargoes shall be the absolute property of the owners without any other restrictions than is placed upon boats and cotton belonging to loyal owners within loyal ports. I have seen your order inviting deserters from the rebel lines to bring with them their arms and promising to purchase the same from them at a fair price Every loyal man sees and ~~approves~~ applauds the wisdom of your order I propose to bring these steamboats within our lines without asking ~~our~~ the Government to purchase them, and to bring with them the Cotton which will cheapen exchanges and gold, and thereby reduce the cost of the material of war to our Government. I dont ask, nor wish to take provissions, clothing or anything else within the rebel lines to pay for these boats or this cotton. Whatever is paid there will be paid in Confederate money. I respectfully submit this proposition to you, hoping that it will commend itself to your approval." Copies, CSmH; DNA, RG 366, Seventh Special Agency. On March 19, 1865, Jerman had written a virtually identical letter to President Abraham Lincoln. ALS, DLC-Robert T. Lincoln.

To Edwin M. Stanton

City Point, Va, March 28th *1865*

HON. E. M. STANTON, SEC. OF WAR, WASHINGTON.

Gen. Sherman requests that the 14th & 20th Army Corps be constituted the Army of Ga. Maj. Gen. Slocum commanding. As his Army now stands Gn. Howard commands an Army and can sign discharges, grant furloughs &c. whilst Slocum with an equal command can not. Will you please telegraph the order so that Sherman can take it with him.

U. S. GRANT
Lt. Gn.

ALS (telegram sent), James S. Schoff, New York, N. Y.; copies, DLC-USG, V, 75, 108; (dated March 27, 1865) *ibid.*, V, 46; DNA, RG 108, Letters Sent. Dated March 27 in *O.R.*, I, xlvii, part 3, 32. On March 29, Secretary of War Edwin M. Stanton telegraphed to USG. "By an oversight in my office your telegram of yesterday relative to the Army of George did not reach my attention until this morning. Subjoined you have the official order requested" ALS (telegram sent), DNA, RG 107, Telegrams Collected (Bound); telegram received, *ibid.*, RG 108, Letters Received. *O.R.*, I, xlvii, part 3, 54. On March 28 or 29, Bvt. Brig. Gen. Edward D. Townsend telegraphed to USG transmitting General Orders No. 51, March 28. Telegram sent (undated), DNA, RG 107, Telegrams Collected (Bound); telegram received (dated March 29), *ibid.*, RG 108, Letters Received; copy (dated March 28), *ibid.*, RG 94, Letters Sent. See *O.R.*, I, xlvii, part 3, 43.

To Maj. Gen. Henry W. Halleck

City Point Mch 28th 1865 [*3:00* P.M.]

Maj, Gen, Halleck
Washington

If orders have been made relieving Sheridan from the Command of the Middle Division I would ask to have it revoked, I understand that Gen, Hancock was temporarily in Command of the troops in the Division in Sheridans absence, Hancock might be assigned to the command of the Dept, of W, Va, permanently and succeed Sheridan in Command of the Div, when the latter is absent,

U. S. Grant
Lt, General

Telegram, copies, DLC-USG, V, 46, 75, 108; DNA, RG 108, Letters Sent. *O.R.*, I, xlvi, part 3, 218. On March 28, 1865, Maj. Gen. Henry W. Halleck had telegraphed to USG. "Orders have been recieved here issued by Genl Sheridan March 20th at White-House, as commanding Middle Military Division. The Head Quarters of that Division is Winchester & Major Genl Hancock has commanded the Division since Genl Sheridan left, by the assignment of the President. There cannot be at the same time two commanders of the same Division. Please call General Sheridan's attention to this in order to avoid conflict of orders." ALS (telegram sent), DNA, RG 107, Telegrams Collected (Bound); telegram received, *ibid.*; (at 2:50 P.M.) *ibid.*, RG 108, Letters Received. *O.R.*, I, xlvi, part 3, 218.

On the same day, Secretary of War Edwin M. Stanton telegraphed to USG. "The assignment of Hancock to the Middle Division and the Department of West Virginia is only temporary during Sheridans absence and with the express understanding that it ceases whenever Sheridan returns. Hancock was reluctant to take the command until I assured him it should only be temporary and that Crocker would take the Department and Sheridan relieve him of the Division ~~there is~~ no order was made releiving Sheridan. ~~S~~Hancock wants field duty. ~~and~~ [bu]t ~~but~~ I thought the command safer with him in Sheridans absence than it would be with any one else." ALS (telegram sent), DNA, RG 107, Telegrams Collected (Bound); telegram received (at 7:35 P.M.), *ibid.*, RG 108, Letters Received. *O.R.*, I, xlvi, part 3, 217–18.

To Maj. Gen. George G. Meade

City Point, Va, March 28th *1865*

MAJ. GEN. MEADE,

Does your order require all the troops at City Point to report to Gen. Benham? I have not seen the order but have seen the amendment made to the original.

U. S. GRANT
Lt. Gn.

ALS (telegram sent), Kohns Collection, NN; copies, DLC-USG, V, 46, 75, 108; DNA, RG 108, Letters Sent. *O.R.*, I, xlvi, part 3, 219. On March 28, 1865, 3:00 P.M., Maj. Gen. George G. Meade endorsed a copy of revised orders for the advance of his army. "I send you the within modifications based on our conversation this a m & the position to be occupied by Ord's command—If there is any thing that does not meet your approval, please let me know by bearer— Gillems [*Griffin's*] column is now passing—I think Humphreys will be able to move by 7. a. m if not earlier—" AES, DNA, RG 108, Letters Received. *O.R.*, I, xlvi, part 3, 224. The orders are *ibid.*; the original orders are *ibid.*, pp. 198–99. At 8:45 P.M., Meade telegraphed to USG. "The order for tomorrows movement was sent in this mornings mail to City Point, under cover to Col Bowers.—Parke was directed to take command of all the troops in the trenches & those garrisoning & defending City Point.—These order constituting the garrison of City Point a separate command specified, that when necessity required, this garrison would be moved to the line of outer defences & the commander would then report to Brig Genl Benham.—" ALS (telegram sent), DNA, RG 94, War Records Office, Miscellaneous War Records; telegram received (at 9:10 P.M.), *ibid.*, RG 108, Letters Received. *O.R.*, I, xlvi, part 3, 219.

At noon, Meade telegraphed to USG. "I would suggest if there are any operators telegraphic of the Army of the James to spare they be sent over here, as in extending our telegraph, we do not reduce the number of stations—" ALS (telegram sent), DNA, RG 94, War Records Office, Army of the Potomac; telegram received (at 12:15 P.M.), *ibid.*, RG 108, Letters Received. On the same day, USG telegraphed to Maj. Gen. Edward O. C. Ord. "Gen Meade suggests that if you have any telegraphic operators to spare they be sent over to him as in extending the telegraph the number of stations on this side are not reduced." Telegram received, *ibid.*, RG 393, Dept. of Va. and N. C., 1st Military District, Telegrams Received; copies, *ibid.*, RG 108, Letters Sent; DLC-USG, V, 46, 75, 108. *O.R.*, I, xlvi, part 3, 236. At 1:35 P.M., Maj. Gen. Godfrey Weitzel telegraphed to Lt. Col. Theodore S. Bowers. "I will send two (2) operators to night." Copy, DNA, RG 393, 25th Army Corps, Telegrams Sent.

At 4:30 P.M., Meade telegraphed to USG. "I desire to have Brvt. Major Andrew. S. Cowan 1st N. Yk Indp. Battery—assigned to duty with his Brevet rank to enable him to act as chief of artillery 6. A. C—Can you so assign him pending the orders of the President.—" ALS (telegram sent), *ibid.*, RG 94, War Records Office, Army of the Potomac; telegram received (at 4:45 P.M.), *ibid.*, RG 108, Letters Received.

To Maj. Gen. Philip H. Sheridan

City Point. Va., March 28. 1865

MAJ. GEN. P. H. SHERIDAN
COM'DG MID. MIL. DIV.
GENERAL:

The 5th Army Corps will move by the Vaughn road at 3 A. M., tomorrow morning. The 2d moves at about 9 A. M. having but about three miles to march to reach the point designated for it to have on the right of the 5th Corps after the latter reaching Dinwiddie C. H.

Move your Cavalry at as early an hour as you can, and without being confined to any particular road or roads. You may go out by the nearest roads in rear of the 5th Corps, pass by its left and passing near to or through Dinwiddie reach the right and rear of the enemy as soon as you can.

It is not the ~~at~~intention to attack the enemy in his intrenched position but to force him out if possible. Should he come out and attack us, or get himself where he can be attacked, move in with your entire force, in your own way, and with the full reliance that the army will engage or follow the enemy as circumstances will dictate.

I shall be on the field and will probably be able to communicate with you. Should I not do so, and you find that the enemy keeps within his main entrenched line, you may cut loose and push for the Danville road. If you find it practicable I would like you to cross the South side road between Petersburg and Burkesville and destroy it to some extent. I would not advise much detention however until you reach the Danville road which I would like you to strike as near to the Appomattox as possible. Make your destruction on that road as complete as possible. You can then pass on to the South-side road. west of Burkesville, and destroy that in like manner.

After having accomplished the destruction of the two railroads, which are now the only Avenues of supply to Lee's Army, you may return to this army selecting your road further South, or you may go on into North Carolina and join General Sherman.—Should you select the latter course get the information to me as early as possible so that I may send orders to meet you at Goldsboro.

> Very respectfully, your obed't Serv't
> U. S. GRANT
> Lieut. General

Copies, DLC-USG, V, 46, 75, 108; DNA, RG 108, Letters Sent. *O.R.*, I, xxxiv, part 1, 51; *ibid.*, I, xxxvi, part 1, 54–55; *ibid.*, I, xxxviii, part 1, 43–44; *ibid.*, I, xlvi, part 3, 234. In his *Memoirs* (II, 437–38), USG stated that the final paragraph was "a blind" inserted so that if the movement were not entirely successful, it would not be misinterpreted as "a disastrous defeat." USG told Maj. Gen. Philip H. Sheridan privately that "I intended to close the war right here . . ."

To Maj. Gen. Godfrey Weitzel

City Point Mch 28th 1865

MAJ, GEN, WEITZEL
ARMY JAMES

The information which you telegraph is the same that I got from other sources, except as to the location of Corse's[1] Brigade, Deserters to the A. P. report three Brigades of Picketts Division as confronting our left and I understood the other Brigade to be between Swift Creek and the Appomattox,   Fields Div—and three Brigades of Kershaw's are North of the James, besides the City Battalion,   Your informant may be right about the location of Corse

> U. S. GRANT
> Lieut, General

Telegram, copies, DLC-USG, V, 46, 75, 108; DNA, RG 108, Letters Sent. *O.R.*, I, xlvi, part 3, 238.

On March 28, 1865, 3:30 P.M., Maj. Gen. George G. Meade telegraphed to USG. "Deserters report Terrys, Huntons, & Steuarts brigades of Picketts division as in my front—in addition to Gordons corps—Heth & Wilcox's Divisions of Hills corps—& Bushrod Johnstons Division—It has also been reported that Thomas brigade, hitherto north of the Appomatox is also here.—This leaves Kershaw & Mahon north of the James & between it & the Appomatox.—" ALS (telegram sent), DNA, RG 94, War Records Office, Miscellaneous War Records; telegram received, *ibid.*, RG 108, Letters Received. *O.R.*, I, xlvi, part 3, 218. On the same day, USG telegraphed to Maj. Gen. Godfrey Weitzel. "Reports of deserters on the Petersburg front shows that ~~Corps~~, Johnson's, Division Heths and Wilcoxs Divisions are now south of the Appomattox, This leaves only Kershaw's and Mahone's Divisions North of the James and between the two Rivers" Copies, DLC-USG, V, 46, 75, 108; DNA, RG 108, Letters Sent. *O.R.*, I, xlvi, part 3, 237. At 5:35 P.M., Weitzel telegraphed to USG. "Deserters of last night on my front report the same thing. But that leaves Mahone's division between the Appomattox and James. and Custis Lee's command, three brigades of Kershaw's division and Field's division north of the James. The total force of the enemy at this moment north of the James is as follows. Custis Lee's command about 2000. composed of the following. 18th Ga. and and 18th, 19th 20th, 10th, 25th 40, 55th 47th 22nd Va. batallions. Kershaws three brigades about 1450. Woffords brigade 600. Bryant's brigade 450 and Humphrey's brigade 400. Field's division. 3935 men. Bratton's brigade 1325—Benning's brigade 700, Laws brigade 710, Anderson's brigade 900. Gregg's brigade 300. Total North of the James 7385 men." ALS (telegram sent), DNA, RG 107, Telegrams Collected (Unbound); telegram received (at 5:40 P.M.), *ibid.*, RG 108, Letters Received. Printed as sent at 4:40 P.M. in *O.R.*, I, xlvi, part 3, 237. On the same day, Weitzel twice telegraphed to USG. "A most intelligent deserter, who says he only came in because he punched his captain, who insulted him down says that he saw Corse's brigade of Pickett's division this morning. That it was then on their left. That three brigades of Pickett's division crossed on ~~Satur~~ Friday night and were to support Gordon's attack. That Pickett is blamed because he was late. That he loitered on the way at his old headquarters. This deserter belonged to Humphrey's brigade of Kershaw's division. He says the whole of Field's division is still over here." ALS (telegram sent), DNA, RG 107, Telegrams Collected (Unbound). Printed as sent at 10:10 P.M. in *O.R.*, I, xlvi, part 3, 237. "A deserter from Wofford's brigade of Kershaw's division who sits before me now says that he bought a ring from some of Pickett's division this morning He says he is sure that some of Pickett's division was there when he came in. I have no doubt that this is Corse's brigade." ALS (telegram sent), DNA, RG 107, Telegrams Collected (Unbound); copy, *ibid.*, RG 393, 25th Army Corps, Telegrams Sent.

Also on March 28, USG wrote to Weitzel. "Please send Mrs, M. S. McLean now in Richmond a pass to enter our lines and go North, Send it this evening by Flag of Truce to Care of Gen, Longstreet" Copies, DLC-USG, V, 46, 75, 108; DNA, RG 108, Letters Sent.

1. Montgomery D. Corse, born in D. C. in 1816, a banker in Alexandria, Va., before the Civil War, served as col., 17th Va., before appointment as brig. gen. as of Nov. 1, 1862. While commanding a brigade in the div. of Maj. Gen. George E. Pickett, he was captured at Sayler's Creek on April 6, 1865.

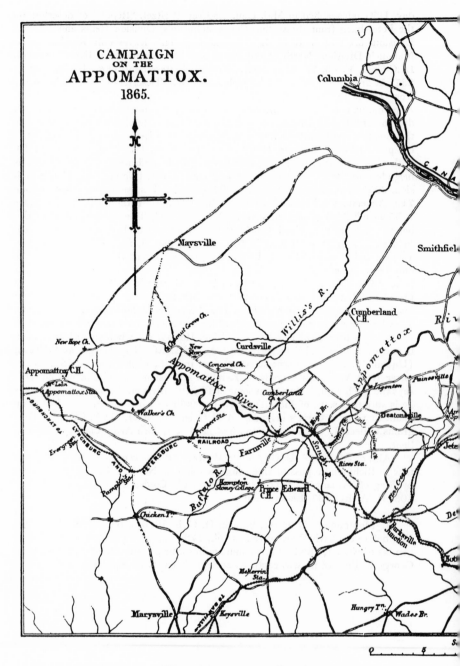

The Appomattox Campaign

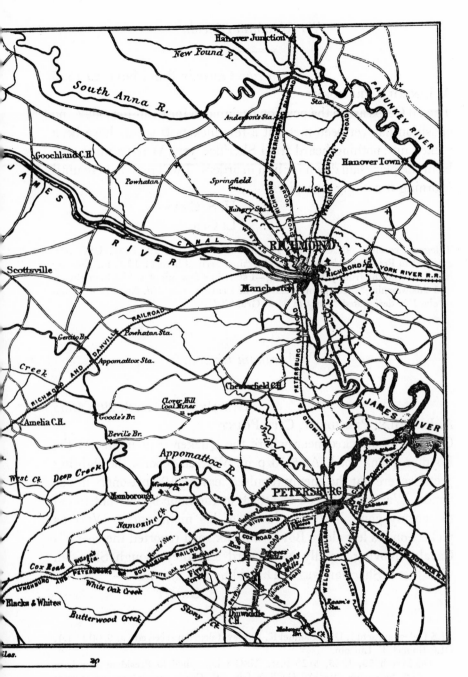

To Abraham Lincoln

From Gravelly Run March 29 *1865*

A. LINCOLN PRESIDENT

The 2d Corps are in the position designated for them for today   no oposition has yet been met but a few pickets & scouts have been picked up   nothing heard from Sheridan yet   Warren must now be in the place laid down for him in orders   I will remain here until Morning if nothing transpires

U. S. GRANT
Lt Gen

Telegram received, DLC-Robert T. Lincoln. On March 29, 1865, USG telegraphed to President Abraham Lincoln. "Just arrived here 11 12 a. m. Nothing heard of from the front yet—No firing—I start in a few minutes. Sheridan got off at 3 this Morning" Telegram received (at 11:15 A.M.), *ibid.* Another telegram received is designated "Copy to Mrs. Grant." *Ibid.*

To Abraham Lincoln

Gravely Run, March 29th *1865*

A. LINCOLN, PRESIDENT, CITY POINT

Griffin was attacked near where the Quaker road intersects the Boydton plank road. At 5.50 p m. Warren reports the fighting pretty severe but the enemy repulsed leaving 100 prisoners in our hands. Warren advanced to attack at the hour named but found the enemy gone, he thinks inside of his main works. Warrens pickets on his left along Boydton plank road reported the enemy's Cavalry moving rapidly Northward and they though Sheridan after them. Sheridan was in Dinwiddie this afternoon—

U. S. GRANT
Lt. Gn—

ALS (telegram sent), DLC-Samuel K. Rupley; telegram received (at 9:00 P.M.), DLC-Robert T. Lincoln.

On March 29, 1865, 5:20 P.M., USG telegraphed to President Abraham Lincoln. "The enemy attacked Griffin's Div. 5th Corps near where the Quaker road intersects the Boydtown road about 4 p. m. The enemy were repulsed leav-

ing about 60 prisoners in our hands. There was some loss of life on both sides."
ALS (telegram sent), DLC-Samuel K. Rupley; telegram received (at 5:10 P.M.),
DLC-Robert T. Lincoln. On the same day, Lincoln telegraphed to USG. "Your
three despatches received. From what direction did the enemy come that attacked
Griffin? How do things look now?" Lincoln, *Works*, VIII, 376.

To Rear Admiral David D. Porter

City Point, Va, March 29th *1865*

ADM.L D. D. PORTER,
COMD.G N. A. B. SQUADRON,
ADMIRAL:

In view of the possibility of the enemy attempting to come to
City Point, or by crossing the Appomattox at Broadway Landing
getting to Bermuda Hundred, during the absence of the greater
part of the Army, I would respectfully request that you direct one
or two gunboats to lay in the Appomattox, near the Pontoon bridge,
and two in the James River near the mouth of Bailey's Creek, the
first stream below City Point emptying into the James.

Very respectfully
your obt. svt.
U. S. GRANT
Lt. Gn.

ALS, DNA, RG 45, Area File. *O.R.*, I, xlvi, part 3, 245; *O.R.* (Navy), I, xii, 88.

To Maj. Gen. George G. Meade

Gravely Creek, March 29th *1865*

MAJ. GN. G. G. MEADE,
COMD.G A. P.
GENERAL,

General Warre[n]'s report of 5.50 p. m, looks as if the enemy
may fall back behind Hatchers Run during the night leaving the
road open to us to Burges Tavern. If so we will want to wheel to
the right so as to cover all the crossings of the run as soon as we

can. If the enemy does not fall back we will then push up close to him and feel out to our left and endeavor to force him to this course.

Sheridan has received orders to push for the enemy's right rear in the morning, unless the position of their cavalry ~~modifies~~ makes a different course necessary, and not to leave us until [h]e receives further orders.

Respectfully &c.
U. S. GRANT
Lt. Gn.

ALS, DNA, RG 107, Telegrams Collected (Unbound). *O.R.*, I, xlvi, part 3, 243. On March 29, 1865, 6:50 or 6:55 P.M., Maj. Gen. George G. Meade wrote to USG. "A despatch of 5.50 P. M from Maj Genl. Warren reports that on advancing to attack the enemy was found to have retired, ~~as~~ & is supposed to have withdrawn to his main line of works—Maj. Genl. Warren is following him—The fighting was quite severe for a while—casualties not yet reported—Brvt. Brig Genl. Sickels wounded—Genl. Warrens left is on the Boydtown Pike—he ~~reports~~ states his skirmishers ~~are~~ on the left report the Enemys Cavalry moving rapidly north from Dinwidie—undoubtedly before Sheridan." ALS (incomplete—marked as written at 6:50 P.M.), DNA, RG 108, Letters Received; copies (marked as written at 6:55 P.M.), *ibid.*, RG 94, War Records Office, Army of the Potomac; *ibid.*, RG 393, Army of the Potomac, Letters Sent; (2) Meade Papers, PHi. Printed as written at 6:55 P.M. in *O.R.*, I, xlvi, part 3, 243.

At 8:30 P.M., Meade wrote to USG. "Genl—Humphreys line of battle occupies Dabneys mill—There has been some sharp skirmishing about sunset at that point the enemy evidently feeling for our position—Humphreys right is now in advance of Ords left—Ords line is however a good one to retain for the present, but as it can be held with two divisions I would suggest his third division being sent across Hatchers run to take position on Humphrey right & advance with him in the morning, when if any appreciable advance is made Ord can throw forward his left—If this suggestion is approved Genl—Ord should send a staff officer to Genl. Humphreys who will designate the ground to be occupied.—" ALS, DNA, RG 108, Letters Received. *O.R.*, I, xlvi, part 3, 243–44. On the same day, USG wrote to Meade. "I ordered Ord to move one Division at 5 a. m. South of Hatchers Run to the support of Humphreys right—Also [to] send a staff officer to report to Genl Humphreys at the same hour to learn where the Divn should be posted" Copies, Humphreys Papers, PHi; DNA, RG 393, 2nd Army Corps, Letters Received. *O.R.*, I, xlvi, part 3, 244. At 9:15 P.M., Meade wrote to USG. "The enclosed order for tomorrow's movement, was written prior to the receipt of your views—I think it embodies them.—Since writing it the enclosed despatch from Warren has been received—I judge from it that Griffin at J. Strouds (intersection of Quaker & Boydtown roads) is up to the enemys line of works these works as I understand extending in front of the White Oak road & *south* of Hatchers run—I have written to Warren that if this is the case, that Griffin is up to these works then he must deploy to the left as far as he can securing his flank—and develop their line Humphreys will push up to Warrens right & between that & Hatchers run—the enemys line crosses the run about on the prolongation of the White oak road—If they have not got a continuos line Humphreys movement will develop the fact & will turn their works on the Boyd-town plank in front of Griffin if these are detached.—This order has been issued but can be modified if you wish it" ALS, DNA, RG 108, Letters Received. *O.R.*, I, xlvi, part 3, 244. The enclosures are *ibid.*, pp. 244–45. On the same day, USG wrote to Meade. "Your order is in conformity with the views I had and does not need any alteration that I See . . . P. S. Ord is only just getting his Cavalry started to guard our wagon train It looks to me that if the enemy at stony Creek find out the position of affairs they may try to destroy it in the morning." Copies (2—one incomplete), Meade Papers, PHi.

At 8:50 A.M., Meade had telegraphed to USG. "Humphreys moved at 6 a. m. & is now taking position Warren crossed Hatchers Run at 8 a. m. few shots exchanged No opposition. The telegraph is being extended across Hatch-ers to Humphreys Hd Qrs. I will be found there Deserters just in report no movement or any information of importance" Telegram received (at 8:55 A.M.), DNA, RG 108, Letters Received. *O.R.*, I, xlvi, part 3, 242. At 5:30 P.M., Meade wrote to USG. "Maj—Genl—Warren reports that Griffin when advancing on the Quaker road, was met & attacked by the enemy—Griffin handsomely re-pulsed the attack taking 100 prisoners representing portions of Johnsons & An-dersons divisions—Maj. Genl. Warren reports hes is bringing up Crawford & Ayres and as soon they are in position or by 6. P—M—if not again attacked he will attack the enemy. Maj. Genl. Humphreys, reports the 2d corps in posi-tion, but no enemy in his front as yet he still advancing—orders have been sent to him to push his nearest division to the support of Warren—" ALS, DNA, RG 108, Letters Received. *O.R.*, I, xlvi, part 3, 242–43.

To Maj. Gen. Edward O. C. Ord

By Telegraph from Gravelly Run [*March*] 29th *1865*
To GEN ORD

did your cavalry Get off this afternoon—How do things look in your front—does the enemy seem to be drawing off any forces from there—if he weakens much you might try to make a hole through his lines & move up the north side Hatchers run

U. S. GRANT.
Lt Genl.

Telegram received (at 9:20 P.M.), Ord Papers, CU-B; copies, DLC-USG, V, 46, 75, 108; DNA, RG 108, Letters Sent. Printed as received at 5:30 P.M. in *O.R.*, I, xlvi, part 3, 268. The printed time received may have been extrapolated from the telegraphic reply of March 29, 1865, from Maj. Gen. Edward O. C. Ord to USG. "Your dispatch calling for cavalry came about five & half 5½ McKenzie was a mile off he came here about 7. Knew nothing of the road asked for a guide too dark without one. The Guide has just come & McKenzie will be off in a few minutes. The Enemy show a stronger line than mine. Do not think they

have drawn troops from here" Telegram received (at 9:45 P.M.), DNA, RG
108, Letters Received. *O.R.*, I, xlvi, part 3, 268.
    Earlier on March 29, USG telegraphed to Ord, Humphrey's Station. "Send
your Cavalry by the road taken by the 5 Corps to the crossing of Hatcher's Run
to guard the Army trains wich are now insufficiently protected." ALS (telegram
sent), Scheide Library, Princeton, N. J.; telegram received, Ord Papers, CU-B.
O.R., I, xlvi, part 3, 268. On the same day, Ord telegraphed to USG. "Which is
the road the Fifth Corps took to Hatcher's Run? Is it the one by Perkins'?" *Ibid.*,
p. 269. On the same day, USG telegraphed to Ord. "The road taken by Warren's
Corps is the next one East of the Vaughn road. I believe it does go by Perkins
House." ALS (telegram sent), Scheide Library, Princeton, N. J.; copies, DLC-
USG, V, 46, 75, 108; DNA, RG 108, Letters Sent. *O.R.*, I, xlvi, part 3, 269.

To Maj. Gen. Edward O. C. Ord

         ~~Stony~~ Gravely Creek March 29th *1865* 10, p. m.
MAJ. GN. ORD, HUMPHREYS STATION.
    Throw one Division of your troops South of Hatcher's Run ~~an~~
to the support of the 2d Corps in the morning starting at 5 a. m.
Send a Staff officer at the same hour to Gen. Humphreys to learn
the position the Div. sent will occupy. Answer.

U. S. GRANT
Lt. Gn

    Did McKinzie move out this afternoon to guard the wagon
train?

U. S. G.

ALS (telegram sent), CtY; telegram received (at 10:00 P.M.), Ord Papers,
CU-B. Incomplete in *O.R.*, I, xlvi, part 3, 269. On March 29, 1865, Maj. Gen.
Edward O. C. Ord telegraphed to USG. "Dispatch rec'd and orders issued The
guide for Genl McKenzie was not obtained until 10 Oclock when he started off."
Telegram received, DNA, RG 108, Letters Received. *O.R.*, I, xlvi, part 3, 269.

To Maj. Gen. John G. Parke

             Gravely Creek Mar 29th/65
MAJ. GEN. PARKE, 9TH CORPS
    A large body of Cavalry were reported to have gone southeast
yesterday. It may be barely possible that Sheridan will pass out

West of them leaving them to annoy your rearr. You had better send a scouting party of Cavalry far out to the rear to watch.

U. S. GRANT
Lt. Gn

ALS, DLC-Samuel K. Rupley; Scheide Library, Princeton, N. J. *O.R.*, I, xlvi, part 3, 263.
On March 29, 1865, Maj. Gen. John G. Parke telegraphed to USG. "Two of Sherman's men 79th. Penna, 38th Ind. taken prisoners near Fayetville, and escaped from their guard at Roanoke Station, have just come in. They crossed the Nottoway below the R. R. Bridge. Saw and heard nothing of any large body of cavalry. The negroes told them that the Rebel Cavalry had gone to Dinwiddie to meet an expected raid from us. I sent out scouts, but have not elicited nothing as yet" Copy, DNA, RG 393, 9th Army Corps, Telegrams Sent. Printed as sent at 10:45 P.M. in *O.R.*, I, xlvi, part 3, 263.

To Maj. Gen. Philip H. Sheridan

Hd Qrs. Armies in field
Gravely Creek, March 29/65

MAJ. GEN. SHERIDAN.

Our line is now unbroken from the Appomattox to Dinwiddie. We are all ready however to give up all from the Jerusalem plank road to Hatchers Run when ever the forces can be used advantageously

After getting into line, south of Hatchers, we pushed forward to find the enemy's position. Gen. Griffin was attacked near where the Quaker road intersects the Boydtown road but repulsed it easily capturing about 100 men—Humphreys reached Dabneys Mill early and was pushing on when heard from.

I now feel like ending the mat[ter] if it is possible to do so before going back. I do not want you therefore to cut loose and go after th[e] enemy's roads at present. In the morning push round the enemy if you can and get on to his right rear. The movements of th[e] enemy's Cavalry may of course modify your action—We will act altogether as one Army here unt[il] it is seen what can be done with the enemy.

The signal officer at Cobbs Hill reported at 11.30 a. m. a Cav-

alry Column had passed that point from Richmond towards Petersburg taking 40 minuets to pass.

U. S. GRANT

Lt. Gn

ALS, Scheide Library, Princeton, N. J. *O.R.*, I, xlvi, part 3, 266.
    On March 29, 1865, Lt. Col. Ely S. Parker issued Special Orders No. 64.
"Major General P H Sheridan, commanding Middle Military Division, will order
the detachment of Co. "D" 5th U. S. Cavalry, now serving with him, to report
immediately to these Headquarters, wherever they may be in the field." Copies,
DLC-USG, V, 57, 63, 64, 65. *O.R.*, I, xlvi, part 3, 248.

To Maj. Gen. Godfrey Weitzel

————

Gravely Creek
Vaughn road Mar. 29/65

MAJ. GN. WEITZEL, A JAMES.

Keep me informed of any movements in your front so long as
telegraphic communication is kept up.

U. S. GRANT

Lt. Gn

ALS (telegram sent), Scheide Library, Princeton, N. J.; telegram received
(undated), DNA, RG 107, Telegrams Collected (Unbound). *O.R.*, I, xlvi, part
3, 271. On March 29, 1865, 1:00 P.M., Maj. Gen. Godfrey Weitzel telegraphed
to USG. "Dispatch received. I will." Copy, DNA, RG 393, 25th Army Corps,
Telegrams Sent.
    On the same day, Weitzel telegraphed three times to USG. At 1:00 P.M.
"The following despatch has just been received from Cobbs Hill tower, 11 a m
a Column of about four thousand (4000) Cavalry passed On the turpike going
towards Petersburg and are still passing" Telegram received, *ibid.*, RG 94,
War Records Office, Miscellaneous War Records; copy, *ibid.*, RG 393, 25th
Army Corps, Telegrams Sent. *O.R.*, I, xlvi, part 3, 272. At 1:25 P.M. "The following dispatch just recd from Cobbs Hill Tower 11 25 a. m. About one thousand (1000) more Cavalry passed in same direction the whole Column occupied
fifty minutes in passing. Were marching fast. Their wagons are now passing"
Telegram received, DNA, RG 94, War Records Office, Miscellaneous War Records; *ibid.*, RG 107, Telegrams Collected (Unbound); copy, *ibid.*, RG 393, 25th
Army Corps, Telegrams Sent. *O.R.*, I, xlvi, part 3, 272. "Thorton [*Hunton's*]
brigade of Picketts Div. is on this side James instead of Corses. Three Brigades
of Fitz Hugh Lee's Cavalry went through Richmond yesterday towards south
side road" Telegram received, DNA, RG 94, War Records Office, Miscellaneous

War Records; *ibid.*, RG 108, Letters Received; copy, *ibid.*, RG 393, 25th Army Corps, Telegrams Sent. *O.R.*, I, xlvi, part 3, 272.

At 5:00 P.M., Weitzel telegraphed to Lt. Col. Theodore S. Bowers. "What news?" Copy, DNA, RG 393, 25th Army Corps, Telegrams Sent. On the same day, Bowers telegraphed to Weitzel. "About four (4) P M the enemy attacked Griffins Div of the fifth A C at the point where the Quaker ~~road~~ road intersects the Boydtown plank   Griffin repulsed him capturing sixty (60) prisoners   No further particulars   Will furnish you all the news I receive" Telegram received, *ibid.*, RG 107, Telegrams Collected (Unbound); copies, *ibid.*, RG 108, Letters Sent; DLC-USG, V, 46, 75, 108. *O.R.*, I, xlvi, part 3, 272. At 11:15 P.M., Weitzel telegraphed to Bowers. "What does all the firing amount to?" Telegram received, DNA, RG 107, Telegrams Collected (Unbound); copy, *ibid.*, RG 393, 25th Army Corps, Telegrams Sent. On the same day, Bowers telegraphed to Weitzel. "I donot know what the fireing means on the 9th corps front—Have not heard from Gen Parke on the subject" Telegram received, *ibid.*, RG 107, Telegrams Collected (Unbound).

To Lt. Col. Theodore S. Bowers

Gravely Run, March 29th/65

LT. COL. BOWERS, CITY POINT

Give Col. Sumner extract from Gen. Ords orders which directs the movement against the Welden road. Ord should have given him orders and can do so yet. He is at Humphreys station.

U. S. GRANT

Lt. Gen

ALS (telegram sent), Scheide Library, Princeton, N. J.; copies, DLC-USG, V, 46, 75, 108; DNA, RG 108, Letters Sent. *O.R.*, I, xlvi, part 3, 242. On March 29, 1865, Lt. Col. Theodore S. Bowers telegraphed to Brig. Gen. John A. Rawlins. "Col, Sumner has gone down with his Cavalry, He has no orders, Please telegraph me his orders that I may forward them to him" Copies, DLC-USG, V, 46, 75, 108; DNA, RG 108, Letters Sent. *O.R.*, I, xlvi, part 3, 241. On the same day, Bowers telegraphed to Maj. Gen. Edward O. C. Ord. "Please send to me the orders you have to give to Col, Sumner, and I will forward them to him, He passed down to-day, and says he has no definate orders" Copies, DLC-USG, V, 46, 75, 108; DNA, RG 108, Letters Sent. *O.R.*, I, xlvi, part 3, 269. On March 30, Bowers wrote to Col. Edwin V. Sumner. "Herewith I send you a copy of the general instructions from Gen. Grant to General Ord in relation to the movement to be made by you. Genl. Grant expected General Ord to furnish you detailed instructions. I have telegraphed to Gen. Ord on the subject and received from him the enclosed dispatch." Copies, DLC-USG, V, 46, 75, 108; DNA, RG 108, Letters Sent.

On March 29, Lt. Col. Ely S. Parker telegraphed to Bowers. "The two

Corps moved out meeting with no serious opposition until quite late in the afternoon. When Griffins Div of Warrens Corps struck the enemy and had quite a fight. Griffin captured about 100 of the enemy, his loss not reported. Warren promptly brought up his whole Corps and upon advancing he found that the enemy had retired to his main works. Humphrey met with no opposition in his advance. Warrens left is across the plank road. Humphreys right is on Hatchers. Sheridan is at Dinwiddie and no enemy to oppose him." Telegrams received (2—one at 9:15 P.M.), *ibid.*, RG 107, Telegrams Collected (Unbound); copies, *ibid.*; *ibid.*, RG 393, 25th Army Corps, Telegrams Sent. *O.R.*, I, xlvi, part 3, 242. At 11:00 P.M., USG telegraphed to Bowers. "Warren reports his loss this afternoon at about 300 killed & wounded. He does not estimate the loss of the enemy but says his dead and badly wounded are in our hands. Also about 100 prisoners." ALS (telegram sent), CSmH; copies, DLC-USG, V, 46, 75, 108; DNA, RG 108, Letters Sent. *O.R.*, I, xlvi, part 3, 242.

   An undated telegram from USG to Bowers, sent from "Gravelly Run," may also have been sent on March 29. "Send One of the City Point Telegraph Operators out by the Morning train if one Can be spared"   Telegram received, DNA, RG 108, Miscellaneous Papers.

To Abraham Lincoln

———

                    Gravely Run, March 30t *1865* [2:00 P.M.]
A LINCOLN, PRESIDENT, CITY POINT,

   I understand the number of dead left by the enemy yesterday for us to bury was much greater than our own dead. The captures were larger than reported also amounting to about 160. This morning our troops have all been pushed forward and now occupy a line from what you will see marked on the map as the Crow House across the Boydton plank road North of where the Quaker road intersects it. Sheridan's Cavalry is pushing forward towards the White Oak road and I think this afternoon or to-morrow may push on to the South side road.

                                U. S. GRANT
                                Lt. Gn.

ALS (telegram sent), PPRF; telegram received, DLC-Robert T. Lincoln. *O.R.*, I, xlvi, part 3, 280–81. On March 30, 1865, 2:00 P.M., USG telegraphed to President Abraham Lincoln. "Gen. Warren reports having buryed 126 dead rebels including 12 officers   His own ~~casualties are dead~~ killed is 5 officers & 46 men. ~~killed, wounded~~" ALS (telegram sent), Kohns Collection, NN; telegram received, DLC-Robert T. Lincoln. *O.R.*, I, xlvi, part 3, 281.

To Maj. Gen. George G. Meade

Gravely Run March 30th/65

MAJ. GN MEADE,

As Warren and Humph[r]eys advances thus shortning their line I think the former had better move by the left flank as far as he can strech out with safety and cover the White Oak road if he can. This will enable Sheridan to reach the South Side road by Ford's road and it may be double the enemy up so as to drive him out of his works South of Hatcher's Run.

U. S. GRANT

Lt. Gn

ALS, Scheide Library, Princeton, N. J.; DNA, RG 107, Telegrams Collected (Unbound). *O.R.*, I, xlvi, part 3, 282. On March 30, 1865, 9:00 A.M., Maj. Gen. George G. Meade wrote to USG. "I forward despatch received from Maj-Genl. Warren—I have directed him not to advance on the Boydtown road, but to develop to the left—securing his flank independantly of Sheridans movements—I also transmit report from Prov. Mar. Dept—showing it was only Bushrod Johnstons Divn. ~~represented~~ in the fight yesterday ~~They~~ Deserters again report Picket as here or coming.—Maj. Genl. Parlke—reports numerous signal rockets last night, and a heavy cannonading on their part from 8 to 10 P M—Not feeling secure about the trains at the lower crossing of Hatchers run I ordered them up to the Vaughn road—The movement commenced about 2 a m but the rain has involved delay making the roads impassible & requiring the Engineers to repair them. Whilst writing the foregoing your despatch per Col. Dent received—You will perceive your suggestions of extending Warren have been attended to—The enemy *cover* the White oak road & I understand you to mean Warren to confront them. I forward another despatch from Warren—he seems a little anxious about his position till Humphreys gets up—but I think H.'s movements will protect Warren's right flank.—" ALS, DNA, RG 108, Letters Received. *O.R.*, I, xlvi, part 3, 282. The enclosures are *ibid.*, pp. 282–83, 298, 299.

On the same day, USG wrote to Meade. "My idea was that we should try to extend our left so as to cross the White Oak road, say at W. Dabney's, or as near up to the enemy as we can. This would seem to cover all the roads up to Ford's road by which Sheridan might then move and get onto the South Side road and possibly double up the enemy and drive him North of Hatcher's Run." ALS, Scheide Library, Princeton, N. J.; (received at 10:57 A.M.) DNA, RG 107, Telegrams Collected (Unbound). Variant texts in *O.R.*, I, xlvi, part 1, 807; *ibid.*, I, xlvi, part 3, 283. At 11:15 [A.M.], Bvt. Maj. Gen. Alexander S. Webb endorsed this letter to Maj. Gen. Gouverneur K. Warren. "This dispatch is forwarded to you for your information sim[p]ly. Your despatch has been recd The Comd Genl sees no reason for any change in his previous orders to you. He has no information of Genl Sheridans movements beyond the general statement that Genl S— is to turn the enemys right." AES, DNA, RG 107, Telegrams Collected (Unbound). Printed as received at noon in *O.R.*, I, xlvi, part 1, 807; *ibid.*, I, xlvi, part 3, 283. For telegrams from Warren to Webb, forwarded to USG, see *ibid.*, pp. 301, 303, 304.

To Maj. Gen. George G. Meade

~~Stony~~ Gravely Creek, March 30th/65

MAJ. GN. MEADE,

Gen. Merritt[1] met the enemy's Cavalry at J. Boisseaus and drove him on the right and left roads and pushed on himself, driving the enemy, and now occupies the White Oak road at Five Forks, and also where the righthand branch intersects it. Merritt lost 15"[2] men wounded.

U. S. GRANT

Lt. Gen—

Copy to Gn. Warren.

U. S. G.

ALS, Scheide Library, Princeton, N. J.; OClWHi. *O.R.*, I, xlvi, part 3, 283. A copy is marked sent (or received) at 5:25 P.M., Meade Papers, PHi. Maj. Gen. Gouverneur K. Warren stated that he received a copy about 5:30 P.M. *O.R.*, I, xlvi, part 1, 809.

On March 30, 1865, 12:10 P.M., Lt. Col. Ely S. Parker wrote to Brig. Gen. John A. Rawlins, sending a copy to Maj. Gen. George G. Meade. "A messenger just in from General Merritt with despatches for Sheridan. Merritt says that the reconnoissance Sent out from near Boisseaus encountered the enemy in considerable force. They went to about 2 miles of the Five Forks & found the enemy occupying the road. Those going north proceeded to about a mile of the White Oak road also occupied by the enemy. Nearly all the forces met were Cavalry. All the roads leading to the White oak road are covered by the enemy. No engagement reported." Copies (2), Meade Papers, PHi. Variant text in *O.R.*, I, xlvi, part 3, 281.

1. Wesley Merritt, born in New York City in 1834, raised in Ill., USMA 1860, appointed brig. gen. as of June 29, 1863, and bvt. maj. gen. as of Oct. 19, 1864, served through most of the Civil War with the cav., for the final year under Maj. Gen. Philip H. Sheridan. Merritt's report of the operations of the cav. div., Army of the Shenandoah, during the Appomattox campaign is *ibid.*, I, xlvi, part 1, 1116–21.

2. The figure 150 given in one *O.R.* printing and discussed in the other apparently resulted from a contemporary clerical error.

To Maj. Gen. George G. Meade

March 30. 1865

MAJ. GEN. MEADE

Would not the trains be in a better position and nearer the troops if they were west of the Vaughn road and between here and Hatchers Run than where they are? Do you know of any troops between where my Headquarters are and Stony Creek Station? I have but about 40 men at Headqrs and half of them are orderlies. I have just been thinking it a limited protection if the enemy should have any enterprising scouts about.

U. S. GRANT
Lieut. Genl.

Copies, DLC-USG, V, 46, 75, 108; DNA, RG 108, Letters Sent; (2) Meade Papers, PHi. Printed as written at 7:00 P.M., received at 10:30 P.M., in *O.R.*, I, xlvi, part 3, 284.

On March 30, 1865, Maj. Gen. George G. Meade telegraphed to USG transmitting a telegram from Maj. Gen. Gouverneur K. Warren to Bvt. Maj. Gen. Alexander S. Webb. "This despatch just recd   Wires hard to work over. . . . A portion of Wilcox's Division made a demonstration against Griffin about 20 minutes ago and were easily driven back into their lines. We took a few prisoners broken down men lately forced in to the service. They dont know much but think Johnson's Div moved to their right when they came down this morning. Genl Heth is here but they do not think his Division is. They think Heth commands the Corps & Hill all the defenses south of the James." Telegram sent, DNA, RG 94, War Records Office, Army of the Potomac; telegram received, *ibid.*, RG 108, Letters Received. *O.R.*, I, xlvi, part 3, 284. At 7:30 P.M., Meade telegraphed to USG. "I send despatch just received from Warren—line working badly. I think his suggestion the best thing we can do under existing circumstances—that is let Humphrey relieve Griffin & let Warren move on to the White oak road & endeavor to turn enemys right—As I understand Warren Ayres is now between S & W Dabneys liable to be isolated   he must either be supported or with drawn—by adopting the proposed plan he will be supported by the whole of the 5th corps & they ought to overcome any opposition the enemy can make, except from strong entrenchments." ALS (telegram sent), DNA, RG 94, War Records Office, 16th Army Corps; telegram received (at 7:30 P.M.), *ibid.*, RG 108, Letters Received. *O.R.*, I, xlvi, part 3, 284. The enclosure is *ibid.*, p. 304. At 8:30 P.M., Meade telegraphed to USG. "I send despatch from Parke   Wright also reports no change visible in his front—I should like to know at the earliest moment whether they are to attack tomorrow—I also would like to have as much time as possible to night for Humphreys to relieve Griffin in case this is decided on. Parke reports his casualties in the affair of pickets last night as 9 killed 40 wounded 2 missing" ALS (telegram sent), DNA, RG 94, War Records Office,

Miscellaneous War Records; copies, *ibid.*, RG 393, Army of the Potomac, Letters Sent; (2) Meade Papers, PHi. *O.R.*, I, xlvi, part 3, 284. The enclosure is *ibid.*, p. 317. See following telegram.

To Maj. Gen. George G. Meade

Gravely Run, March 30th/65 [*8:30* P.M.]

MAJ. GEN. MEADE,

You may notify Parke[1] & Wright that they need not assault in the mornig. They should of course watch their fronts and go in if the enemy strips to attack on our left. But the idea of a general attack by them is suspended. I have pretty much made up my mind on the course to pursue and will inform you in the morning. what it is.

Humphrey's and Warren may simply make secure their present positions & until await further orders.

U. S. GRANT

Lt. Gn

P. S. Since writing the above your dispatch of 7.30 received. Warren's dispatch alluded to not received, It will just suit what I intended to propose however to let Humphries relieve Griffin's Division and let that move further to the left. Warren should get himself strong to-night.

U. S. GRANT

Lt. Gn

ALS (incomplete telegram sent), Scheide Library, Princeton, N. J.; OClWHi; telegram received (at 8:35 P.M.), DNA, RG 107, Telegrams Collected (Unbound). *O.R.*, I, xlvi, part 3, 285. See preceding letter. On March 30, 1865, USG telegraphed to Maj. Gen. George G. Meade. "Warren proposes if Griffin can be relieved by Humphreys to get possession of the White Oak road at W. Dabneys, and to enable him to carry out his proposition, Humphreys has been directed to relieve Griffin at once." Copies, DLC-USG, V, 46, 75, 108; DNA, RG 108, Letters Sent. *O.R.*, I, xlvi, part 3, 285. At 8:45 P.M., Meade telegraphed to USG. "I have sent orders to Humphreys to at once relieve Warrens troops holding the Boydtown plank road. I have directed Warren to reinforce & strengthen Ayres, and to hold his whole corps ready to move at daylight under orders that will be sent him.—I have not given him orders what to do because I infer from your despatch you will send them to me—I have directed Parke & Wright not to attack tomorrow morning, but to be prepared to assume a threatening attitude & eventually attack, if any opportunity presents itself or orders are sent to them.—I am at a loss to account for the delay in the transmission of my despatch of 7.45—this delay will account for my last despatch—" ALS (telegram sent), DNA, RG 94, War Records Office, Miscellaneous War Records; telegram received (at 8:45 P.M.), *ibid.*, RG 108, Letters Received. *O.R.*, I, xlvi, part 3, 285. On the same day, USG telegraphed to Meade. "Your orders to Warren are right. I do not expect to advance him in the morning. I supposed however that he was now up to White Oak road. If he is not I do not want him to move up without further orders." ALS (telegram sent), CSmH; telegram received, DNA, RG 94, War Records Office, Miscellaneous War Records. *O.R.*, I, xlvi, part 3, 285.

At 4:30 P.M., Maj. Gen. Horatio G. Wright had telegraphed to Lt. Col. Theodore S. Bowers. "Everything is quiet on my front but there is sharp firing on my left Either from the force beyond Hatchers Run or from Genl Ord's line. I will report on getting further information," ALS (telegram sent), DNA, RG 107, Telegrams Collected (Unbound); telegram received (at 4:35 P.M.), *ibid.* *O.R.*, I, xlvi, part 3, 311.

1. On March 30, 8:12 A.M., USG telegraphed to Maj. Gen. John G. Parke. "Did you get any deserters last night? If so do they report any changes in your front—" Telegram sent, DLC-Samuel K. Rupley. At 8:55 A.M. and 10:10 A.M., Parke telegraphed to USG. "Deserters from the 5th. 6th & 9th La, came in last night. They know of no changes or movement of troops in our immediate front." Copy, DNA, RG 393, 9th Army Corps, Telegrams Sent. "Two—2—deserters from 12st Ala came in on Gen Potters front—They know of no movements or change in their line—Had a camp rumor of an attack upon us—As far as can be observed this a. m. no change is discoverd in the enemys lines—" Telegram received (at 9:30 A.M.), *ibid.*, RG 108, Letters Received; copy, *ibid.*, RG 393, 9th Army Corps, Telegrams Sent. *O.R.*, I, xlvi, part 3, 316. At 11:05 A.M., Parke telegraphed to Bowers. "The enemy drove in our pickets on line in vicinity of steadman & made demonstration on other portions of the line. Signal Rockets were thrown up by enemy & ~~Genl C~~ general cannonading ensued accompanied with heavy musketry on both sides The main line was not touched, & the picket line re established. The casualties not yet reported. Maj of the 18th N. H. killed" Telegram received (at 11:10 A.M.), DLC-Robert T. Lincoln; copy, DNA, RG 393, 9th Army Corps, Telegrams Sent. Printed as sent at 1:05 A.M. in *O.R.*, I, xlvi, part 3, 316. At 6:35 P.M., Parke telegraphed to Bowers. "I have just returned and find your dispatch. I have no news whatever from the left. Colonel Loring informed you of the heavy cannonading in the distance, probably in front of General Ord. There is now light cannonading in the same direction." Printed as received at 7:50 P.M. *ibid.*

To Maj. Gen. George G. Meade

Gravely Run, March 30th/65

MAJ. GEN MEADE,

From what Gen Sheridan reports of the enemy on White Oak road and the position of his cavalry tonight I do not think an attack on Warren's left in the morning improbable. I have notified Sheridan of this and directed him to be prepared to push on to his assistance if he is attacked. Warren I suppose will put himself in the best possible position to defend himself ‡ with the notice he has already received, but in addition to this I think it will be well to notify him again of the position of Sheridan's cavalry, what he reports the enemys position on White Oak road, and the orders he has rec'd if the enemy does attack. I think it will be well to instruct Humphries allso to help Warren if he is attacked either by sending troops to him or by a direct attack on his own front.

U. S. GRANT

Lt. Gen

ALS (telegram sent), Scheide Library, Princeton, N. J.; OClWHi; telegram received (at 9:50 P.M.), DNA, RG 107, Telegrams Collected (Unbound). Printed as sent at 9:50 P.M., received at 9:55 P.M., in *O.R.*, I, xlvi, part 3, 286. On March 30, 1865, 9:55 P.M., Maj. Gen. George G. Meade telegraphed to USG. "Despatch of 9.50. rceived.—I sent Warren Sheridans despatches—told him to put Ayres on his guard as he might be attacked at Daylight directed he should move Crawford up at once to his support if not already there, and move Griffin into supporting distance as soon as relieved—Warren by day light should have his whole corps in hand ready for the defensive or offensive, and ought to be secure in either contingency particularly as he can always fall back on Humphreys, but I can not see how the enemy can have a sufficient force to do him any damage   The orders to Humphreys will be sent as you suggest—I presume you understand Warren has no orders to advance, but simply to strengthen & secure his position—He will not be allowed to advance unless you so direct." ALS (telegram sent), DNA, RG 94, War Records Office, Miscellaneous War Records; telegram received (at 9:55 P.M.), *ibid.*, RG 108, Letters Received. *O.R.*, I, xlvi, part 3, 286.

To Maj. Gen. George G. Meade

———

~~Stony Creek~~

Gravely Run, March 30th/65

MAJ GEN. MEADE,

I think now it has got to be so late for getting out orders that it will be doubtful whether Wright could be fully co-operated with by all parts of the Army if he was to assault as he proposes. I dislike too checking him when he thinks sucsess will attend his efforts.

You might notify him to arrange his preliminaries and see if Parke can get ready also and if so give him definite orders as soon as it is known. I will telegraph to Ord and ascertain if he can get ready.

Warren & Humphries would have nothing to do but to push forward where they are, possibly the latter might have to move by his right flank across Hatchers Run if the attack was sucsessful.

U. S. GRANT
Lt. Gn

ALS, Scheide Library, Princeton, N. J.; (marked as received at 1:10 A.M.) DNA, RG 107, Telegrams Collected (Unbound). *O.R.*, I, xlvi, part 3, 286–87. On March 31, 1865, 1:00 A.M., Bvt. Maj. Gen. Alexander S. Webb, chief of staff for Maj. Gen. George G. Meade, endorsed this letter. "Major Genl. Wright in accordance with the abo[ve] will make all the necessary arrngments—preliminary to an attack and orders will be sent you if any thing deffinate be determined upon— . . . Major Genl Parke will make preperati[ons] to co operate with Genl Wright should an assault be orderd of which he will be notified" AES, DNA, RG 107, Telegrams Collected (Unbound). *O.R.*, I, xlvi, part 3, 287.

On March 30, 11:50 P.M., Meade telegraphed to USG. "This is referred to you for your information—There are so many other movements involved that I have not ordered any attack but have merely directed that the troops be massed & prepared to attack when ordered—" Telegram sent, DNA, RG 94, War Records Office, Miscellaneous War Records; copies (marked as sent at 11:30 P.M.), *ibid.*, RG 393, Army of the Potomac, Letters Sent; Meade Papers, PHi. *O.R.*, I, xlvi, part 3, 286. The enclosure may be Maj. Gen. Horatio G. Wright to Meade, 10:35 P.M., *ibid.*, p. 313.

On March 31, 12:30 A.M., Meade telegraphed to USG. "Gen McKenzie is at W Perkins house at Hatchers run with pickets out to Reams station also down to cuttail creek   the 5th corps trains guarded by the 11th & 14th U. S. Infty are at the Junction of the Vauhn & old stage roads and in park there   Three hundred (300) cavalry are at the junction of Quaker & Vaughn roads   tomorrow the trains will move at daylight down to the junction of the stage & Quaker roads thence north cross gravelly run & be parked in the neighborhood of the meeting house   It might be well to order up some of McKenzies Cavalry to picket east & southeast of your camp" Telegram received (at 12:30 A.M.), DNA, RG 108, Letters Received; copies, *ibid.*, RG 393, Army of the Potomac, Letters Sent; (2) Meade Papers, PHi. *O.R.*, I, xlvi, part 3, 334.

At 1:55 A.M. (sent at 2:05 A.M.), USG telegraphed to Meade. "Gen. Ord replies to my dispatch that he can not be ready for assault at daylight. It will be postponed therefore." ALS (telegram sent), Kohns Collection, NN; Scheide Library, Princeton, N. J.; copies, DLC-USG, V, 46, 75, 108; DNA, RG 108, Letters Sent; Meade Papers, PHi. Printed as received at 2:10 A.M. in *O.R.*, I, xlvi, part 3, 334.

On March 30, Meade wrote to Brig. Gen. John A. Rawlins. "I enclose herewith a communication received this a m from Col. Duane Acg. Chief Engineer of this army—Numerous complaints have been made to me from time to time by Col Duane, of the difficulty he was under of complying with the orders received from Bvt. Maj- Genl. Barnard Chief Engr. of the Armies operating against Richmond—A desire to avoid raising points & to act harmoniously has hitherto restrained my taking any notice of these complaints—but at the present moment when every minute of Col Duanes time is taken up in the duties under my orders—I do not think he should be subject to any other persons control, nor indeed can he properly perform his duties if so subjected.—I am not aware of the object Genl Barnard has in view in enquiring where the Engineer troops & trains are—if it is to give any orders to them I should feel myself called upon to object to his doing so—if it is for information only, I beg leave to say that I do not think the present a suitable time for calls for information as every one is extremely busy & there are but limited means in the shape of [clerks] for answering such calls.—" ALS, DNA, RG 108, Letters Received. On the same day, USG endorsed the enclosed note of Bvt. Maj. Gen. John G. Barnard. "Gen Barnard asks simple questions for information and very proper ones. Col Duanes endorsement is improper & uncalled for in this instance. It would have taken no longer to have given a civil answer to the questions asked than it has done to complain of serving two commanders, which he has not been called on to do, I have a right to information from Gen Barnard & he must get it from the other Engr officers. Gen Barnard will not give Col Duane improper orders. If he does they need not be regarded. I will direct Gen Barnard to send nothing in the shape of an order unless he sends them to you & with my knowledge. But for information it is not necessary that either you should know it—" Copy, *ibid.*; DLC-USG, V, 58.

To Maj. Gen. Edward O. C. Ord

By Telegraph from Gravelly Run [*March*] 30 1865 [*1:20* P.M.]
To MAJ. GEN ORD

deserters Just in to Humphreys Corps report Heth & Wilcox divisions this side of Hatchers run if this is so It only leaves Gordons corps confronting Parke wright & you I do not want to change the orders previously sent to you but send this for your Information—

U. S. GRANT
Lt Genl

Telegram received, Ord Papers, CU-B; copies (misdated March 20, 1865), DLC-USG, V, 46, 75, 108; DNA, RG 108, Letters Sent. Misdated March 29 in *O.R.*, I, xlvi, part 3, 267–68.

On March 30, Maj. Gen. Edward O. C. Ord telegraphed to USG. "I ~~placed~~ placed old soldiers on piquect last night one of them is reported this a. m as having deserted No changes discoverable since the movement reported yesterday afternoon from Gen. Wrights front of adivision of Infantry and some cavalry along enemies line towards their right—Six—6—deserters in last night left the lines on 29th   No changes then—" Telegram received (at 10:15 A.M.), DNA, RG 108, Letters Received. Printed as sent at 10:15 A.M. in *O.R.*, I, xlvi, part 3, 318–19.

To Maj. Gen. Edward O. C. Ord

Gravelly Run, March 20. [*30*] 1865 [*1:20* P.M.]
MAJ. GEN. ORD. HUMPHREY'S STATION

I think the movement of Humphreys south of Hatchers Run, up to the Crow House, must have moved the enemy back from the front of your left next to the run. If you can push up on the North side of the run to the Armstrong House, or further it will release a whole Division on the south side.

U. S. GRANT
Lt. Genl.

Copies (misdated March 20, 1865), DLC-USG, V, 46, 75, 108; DNA, RG 108, Letters Sent. Misdated March 29 in *O.R.*, I, xlvi, part 3, 268. The time sent may also be incorrectly entered in USG's letterbooks. On March 30, 1:00 P.M., Maj. Gen. Edward O. C. Ord telegraphed to USG. "Your despatch informing me of Gen Humpheys move to CrowHouse is just rec'd   Tis the first notice I have had of any move not in my command   I have ordered a brigade to swing round from my left & try to get up as far as Armstrongs The Picket line moving forward to cover it & feel enemy   I should like to know more definitely what force is on my left & if the Crow House is the one laid down on the maps at ¼ mile from Hatchers Run about one & half miles up the Run from my left   the brigade will not get forward for sometime as the ground is marshy wooded & unknown & will have to be reconnoitred" Telegram received (at 12:55 P.M.), DNA, RG 108, Letters Received. *O.R.*, I, xlvi, part 3, 319. At 1:20 P.M., USG twice telegraphed to Ord. "Gen. Turner is now near the Crow House and is relieved and directed to join you. He will probably be able to cross Hatchers Ru[n] at the Armstrong Mill. If so it will enable you to push your line up." ALS (telegram sent), Kohns Collection, NN; copies, DLC-USG, V, 46, 75, 108; DNA, RG 108, Letters Sent. *O.R.*, I, xlvi, part 3, 319. "Send an officer to Turner to see if he cannot cross hatchers run at the Crow House & if so let him cross there & push out & establish yourself as High up the run as you can & Entrench—you can start your new line from Such point of your ~~previous~~ present line as you deem best—" Telegram received, DNA, RG 94, War Records Office, 24th Army Corps; copies, *ibid.*, RG 108, Letters Sent; DLC-USG, V, 46, 75, 108. *O.R.*, I, xlvi, part 3, 319. Also on March 30, Ord telegraphed to USG. "I have advanced my line on the left—north of ~~to~~ R Armstrong House—to Crow House making it nearly Straight to little north of Thorns—we did not get very near ~~enough~~ to enemies works ~~too~~ encounter too much resistance—returns of casualties not in—

I am entrenching on the new line—I connect with 2d Corps—" ALS (telegram sent), DNA, RG 94, War Records Office, Miscellaneous War Records. *O.R.*, I, xlvi, part 3, 320.

To Maj. Gen. Edward O. C. Ord

Gravely Run, March 30th/65 [7:20 P.M.]

MAJ. GN. ORD, HUMPHREY'S STATION,

It is reported by deserters that Wilcox's Heth's & Picket's Divisions are here. I do not beleive that all of them are but deserters have been received from one Brigade of each of two of these Divisions. In case this information proves true, or even if it is found that the enemy have considerably weakened North of Hatcher's Run, Parke and Wright will be ordered to assault. They have been ordered to prepare accordingly. If they do assault I want you to go in at the same time. Make your preparations for receiving such an order.

Where does your left strike Hatcher's Run now.

U. S. GRANT
Lt. Gn

ALS (telegram sent), Scheide Library, Princeton, N. J.; OClWHi; telegram received, Ord Papers, CU-B. *O.R.*, I, xlvi, part 3, 320. On March 30, 1865, Maj. Gen. Edward O. C. Ord telegraphed to USG. "Your dispatch notifying me to prepare to assault is received. What time is it to take place?" *Ibid.* On the same day, USG telegraphed to Ord. "The attack on your front will not be made tomorrow morning. Keep up your preparations so that if the enemy withdraw from your front you can push forward in the absence of orders." ALS (telegram sent), Scheide Library, Princeton, N. J.; telegram received, Ord Papers, CU-B. *O.R.*, I, xlvi, part 3, 320. On the same day, Ord telegraphed to USG. "Despatch recd—deferring attack—and to keep up preparations—will do so—" ALS (telegram sent), DNA, RG 108, Letters Received; telegram received, *ibid. O.R.*, I, xlvi, part 3, 321.

To Maj. Gen. Edward O. C. Ord

Gravely Run March 30th *1865* [*10:58* P.M.]

MAJ. GEN. M̶E̶A̶D̶E̶, ORD,

If you have not already got it have a road made across Hatchers Run at your left near the Crow House so that troops can be moved rapidly from your position to this side of the run. Also spread your troops out so as to have one Div. in reserve.

U. S. GRANT

Lt. Gn—

I notified you some hours ago that the order for assault in the morning had been suspended.

U. S. G.

ALS (telegram sent), OClWHi; copies, DLC-USG, V, 46, 75, 108; DNA, RG 108, Letters Sent. *O.R.*, I, xlvi, part 3, 321.

On March 30, 1865, 9:00 P.M., Maj. Gen. Edward O. C. Ord telegraphed to USG. "despatch recd postponing attack the thick weather and timber prevented our seeing any thing of the enemies line to day—Swamps quite bad in his front we want a couple of days to learn their line and in the mean time the ground should dry—become more practicable for getting Artillery and Infantry into position—the Arty is necessary to open way through their abatis—now the whole country is reported a quick Sand on my left & over the only approach I can find to Enemy—It strikes me that if an attack is contemplated—my right and ~~that~~ front of the ~~enemy~~ other corps next to me should be pushed up closer—now it is a mile to my piquet line on the right and pretty bad marching to get there—" ALS (telegram sent), Ord Papers, CU-B. There is no record that USG received this telegram, and the text above indicates that he did not.

At 11:00 P.M., USG telegraphed to Ord. "Do you know where McKenzies Cavalry is to-night?" ALS (telegram sent), Kohns Collection, NN; telegram received (at 11:02 P.M.), Ord Papers, CU-B. *O.R.*, I, xlvi, part 3, 321.

On the same day, Ord telegraphed to USG. "A Lt of Rebel Infantry left their line tonight belongs to Jo Davis Brigade heths division says that 2 brigades of the division are still on this front & that only two brigades have crossed to south of Hatchers Run That a portion of picketts division went up towards Lynchburg but dont know if it remained there says the rebel rifle pits are 15 yards apart & five men in each that the men go on once every three or four days this would give a line of one ~~mile~~ man to the yard —Gen Michie corroborates the report as to distance & contents of their rifle pits" Telegram received, DNA, RG 108, Letters Received. *O.R.*, I, xlvi, part 3, 320–21. USG endorsed this telegram. "Forward for Gn. Meades information." AES, DNA, RG 108, Letters Received; telegram received (on March 31, 1:00 A.M.), *ibid.*

To Maj. Gen. Philip H. Sheridan

Gravely Run, March 30th/65

MAJ. GEN. SHERIDAN,

Your positions on the White Oak road are so important that they should be held even if it prevents sending back any of your

Cavalry to Humphreys station to be fed. The fifty wagon loads of forage ordered will be increased if you think it necessary. Let the officer who goes back to conduct it to your Cavalry call on Gn. Ingalls at my Hd Qrs.

U. S GRANT

Lt. Gn

P. S. Can you not push up towards Burgess Mills on the White Oak road?

U. S. G.

ALS, Scheide Library, Princeton, N. J. *O.R.*, I, xlvi, part 3, 324.

On March 30, 1865, Maj. Gen. Philip H. Sheridan, Dinwiddie Court House, Va., wrote four times to USG, second at 2:45 P.M., last at 7:00 P.M. "Genl: Merritt is moving out this morning on the road leading from Dinwiddie C. H. to the Five Forks—He will not go as far west as the five forks, but will if there is no opposition take the right hand road at J. Boisseau's, & get on to the White Oak road—Genl W. H. F. Lees Div: was still at Stoney Creek last night   Our trains did not get up last night, the road at the Crossing of the swamps was very bad—" "Genl. Merritt met th[e] Enemy Cavalry with (1) one Div: of Cavly at J. Boisseau's on the Ford Church Road, and drove them right, and left, on the right and left forks of the road, and now has possession of the White Oak Road, ~~and~~ at Five Forks ~~roads.~~ also where the right hand road intersects the White Oak road —Our loss was slight, fifteen or twenty wounded." "The Enemy has moved out Infantry on the White Oak Road—Picketts Division drove back a small Cavalry force which was at the Five Fork Cross roads—A prisoner from Picketts Div: reports a Concentration of the Enemys Cavly: there—We have Captured forty or fifty prisoners—I will be able to give you more detailed accounts this Evening —Picketts Div. came up from Burkesville" "Picketts Division is deployed along the White Oak Road, its right at Five Forks, and Extending towards Petersburg —After the small force at Five Forks was driven back, no attempt was made to follow up—and the Enemy did not appear to be in strong force—There is no doubt but that Picketts Division is on the White Oak road, his right Extending as far as Five Forks. Prisoners report the Enemys Cavalry concentrated at Five Forks, I have however no positive information of this—Genl: Merritts pickets nearly up to the White Oak—and is Encamped at J. Boisseau' house—" ALS, DNA, RG 108, Letters Received. *O.R.*, I, xlvi, part 3, 323–24. The last is also (incomplete) *ibid.*, I, xlvi, part 1, 811. USG endorsed the third and fourth of these messages, the fourth to Maj. Gen. George G. Meade. "Forward to the President at City Point and Gen. Meade." "The above dispatch just received. Warren will not from this dispatch have the Cavalry support on his left flank that I expected. ~~He~~ This information had better be sent to him with instructions to watch closely on his left flank." AES, DNA, RG 108, Letters Received. *O.R.*, I, xlvi, part 3, 324.

To Maj. Gen. Philip H. Sheridan

————

Gravely Run, March 30th/65

MAJ. GEN. SHERIDAN,

The heavy rain of to-day will make it impossible for us to do much until it dries up a little or we get roads around our rear repaired. You may therefore leave what Cavalry you deem necessary to protect the left and hold such positions as you deem necessary for that purpose and send the remainder back to Humphrey's Station where they can get hay and grain.

Fifty wagons loaded with forage will be sent to you in the morning. Send an officer back to direct the wagons to where you want them.

Report to me the Cavalry you will leave back and the positions you will occupy.

Could not your Cavalry go back by the way of Stony Creek Depot and destroy or capture the store of supplies there.

U. S. GRANT
Lt. Gn

ALS, Scheide Library, Princeton, N. J. *O.R.*, I, xlvi, part 3, 325.

To Maj. Gen. Philip H. Sheridan

————

Gravely Run, Mar. 30th/65

MAJ. GN. SHERIDAN,

From the information I have previously sent you of Warren's position you will see that he is in danger of being attacked on his left flank in the morning. I such occurs be prepared to push up with all your force to his assistance. Do not send any of your Cavalry to Humphries Station to-morrow.

U. S. GRANT
Lt. Gn—

ALS, Scheide Library, Princeton, N. J. *O.R.*, I, xlvi, part 3, 325.

To Maj. Gen. Philip H. Sheridan

Gravelly Run. March 30. 1865

MAJ. GEN. SHERIDAN

If your situation in the morning is such as to justify the belief that you can turn the enemys' right with the assistance of a corps of Infantry entirely detached from the balence of the army, I will so detach the 5th Corps and place the whole under your command for the operation—Let me know as early in the morning as you can your judgment in the matter, and I will make the necessary orders. Orders have been given Ord. Wright and Parke to be ready to assault at daylight tomorrow morning—They will not make the assault however without further directions—The giving of this order will depend upon receiving confirmation of the withdrawal of a part of the enemy's forces on their front. If this attempt is made, it will not be advisable to be detaching troops at such a distance from the field of operations. If the assault is not ordered in the morning, then it can be directed at such time as to come in cooperation with you, on the left—

Picketts entire Division cannot be in front of your cavalry. Deserters from Stewarts[1] Brigade of that Div., came into Humphrey's front this afternoon.

U. S. GRANT
Lt. Genl

Copies, DLC-USG, V, 46, 75, 108; DNA, RG 108, Letters Sent. *O.R.*, I, xlvi, part 3, 325.

1. George H. Steuart, born in Baltimore in 1828, USMA 1848, resigned from the U.S. Army as of April 22, 1861. Appointed C.S.A. brig. gen. as of March 6, 1862, he was captured on May 11, 1864, and, after exchange, commanded a brigade in the div. of Maj. Gen. George E. Pickett.

To Lt. Col. Theodore S. Bowers

Gravely Run, March 30th/65

LT. COL, BOWERS, CITY POINT

Warren and Humphreys have pushed forward until the enemy now occupy the same possition about Burgess Mill they did when Gen. Hancock had his battle last Fall. There has been some pretty sharp fighting but I do not know the result further than that the enemy were forced back.

Merritts Div. of Cavalry met the enemy's Cavalry at J. Boisseaus and drove them back on both roads from that point. Merritt followed up his sucsess and now holds Five Forks on the White Oak road and also where the right hand road from Boisseaus house intersects the same road.

U. S. GRANT
Lt. Gn

ALS (telegram sent), Scheide Library, Princeton, N. J.; OClWHi; telegram received (at 8:45 P.M.), DNA, RG 94, War Records Office, Miscellaneous War Records. *O.R.*, I, xlvi, part 3, 281.

On March 30, 1865, 12:45 P.M., 8:10 P.M., and 10:00 P.M., Maj. Gen. Godfrey Weitzel telegraphed to USG. "A reconnaissance on my left this morning, where it was reported the enemy had withdrawn forces, developed no change. No change observed or reported any where else in my front." ALS (telegram sent—misdated March 29), DNA, RG 94, War Records Office, Miscellaneous War Records; telegram received, *ibid.*, RG 108, Letters Received. Dated March 29 in *O.R.*, I, xlvi, part 3, 272; (dated March 30) *ibid.*, p. 327. "Signal officers report that only the regular trains ran to-day between Richmond and Petersburg." ALS (telegram sent), DNA, RG 107, Telegrams Collected (Unbound); copy, *ibid.*, RG 393, 25th Army Corps, Telegrams Sent. *O.R.*, I, xlvi, part 3, 328. "Up to this hour the enemy ~~does not seem to~~ on my front does not seem to have comprehended your movement. Deserter just in. No change All seem to think it a raid of Sheridan on South Side road." ALS (telegram sent), DNA, RG 107, Telegrams Collected (Unbound); telegram received, *ibid.*, RG 108, Letters Received. *O.R.*, I, xlvi, part 3, 328.

At 4:10 P.M., Weitzel telegraphed to Lt. Col. Theodore S. Bowers. "I hear many rumors of the fight last night on the 9th Corps front. What is the truth about it?" ALS (telegram sent), DNA, RG 107, Telegrams Collected (Unbound); copy, *ibid.*, RG 393, 25th Army Corps, Telegrams Sent. On the same day, Bowers twice telegraphed to Weitzel. "Have no definite information of the affair on front of the 9th corps last night. The enemy opened upon us and scared a portion of our picket line   This was recovered & the firing of artillery and musketry became general   Our loss is reported at nine (9) killed & about forty

(40) wounded Enemys loss unknown—Both sides appear to have been some
what stampeded" "Warren & Humphrey have pushed forward until the enemy
now occupy the same portion about Burgess Mill that they did when Hancock
had his battle last fall There has been some pretty sharp fighting but I have
no details further than that the enemy were pushed back. sheridan has driven
the Cavalry & now holds the five fork roads The mud is deep In the affair of
yesterday our men done handsomely Johnson Div attacked griffin & were
promptly repulsed we lost forty two killed & several hundred wounded we
buried 25 of enemy the army is in fine spirits over the result" Telegrams
received, *ibid.*, RG 107, Telegrams Collected (Unbound). *O.R.*, I, xlvi, part 3,
326, 327. On the same day, Weitzel had telegraphed to Bowers transmitting
information for President Abraham Lincoln. *Ibid.*, pp. 327–28.

To Lt. Col. Theodore S. Bowers

————

Gravely Run, March 30th/65

Lt. Col. T. S. Bowers, City Point.

There is nothing to communicate since my last dispatch. The
rain of to-day has made the roads horrible and our operations have
been confined to advancing our lines closer to the enemy and in
making corduroy roads. There has been some skirmishing all along
the lines resulting in a few casualties on both sides. We have captured and also lost a few men by capture. Tonight the enemy seem
to be consentrating a force on our left and I do not think an attack
upon us there in the morning improbable. All the orders that I can
give to prepare for it have been given.

U. S. Grant
Lt. Gn

ALS (telegram sent), OClWHi; telegram received (at 12: 10 p.m.), DLC-Robert
T. Lincoln. *O.R.*, I, xlvi, part 3, 281–82. Context indicates that the telegram
was received on March 31, 1865, 12: 10 a.m.

To Julia Dent Grant

————

By Telegraph from Hd Qurs A P Mar 30 *1865*

To Mrs Grant

I wrote to you today—Tell Mrs Rawlins that the Genl is not
going much in the rain.

This weather is bad for us but it is Consoling to know that it rains on the enemy as well

U S GRANT
Lt Genl

Telegram received, DLC-USG.

To Abraham Lincoln

Gravely Run, March 31st/65 12.50 p. m.

A. LINCOLN, PRESIDENT CITY POINT

There has been much hard fighting this morning   The enemy drove our left from near W. Dabney's House back well towards the Boydton plank road. We are now about to take the offensive at that point and I hope will more than recover the lost ground. The heavy rains and horrid roads have prevented the execution of my designs, or attempting them, up to this time. Gen. Ord reports the capture of some prisoners this morning but does not say how many.

U. S. GRANT
Lt. Gn

ALS (telegram sent), Scheide Library, Princeton, N. J.; telegram received (at 4:00 P.M.), DLC-Robert T. Lincoln. *O.R.*, I, xlvi, part 3, 332.

To Abraham Lincoln

From Boydtown Road [*March 31*] *1865.*

A. LINCOLN

Our troops after being driven back on to Boydton plank Road turned & drove the Enemy in turn & took the White Oak Road which we now have. This gives us the ground occupied by the Enemy this morning   I will send you a rebel flag Captured by Our troops in driving the Enemy back. There has been four (4) flags

Captured today. The one I send you was taken from a Va Regiment of Hunters[1] Brigade

U. S. GRANT
Lt Gen

Telegram received (at 7:00 P.M.), DLC-Robert T. Lincoln. Incomplete in *O.R.*, I, xlvi, part 3, 332.

1. Eppa Hunton, born in Va. in 1822, was a lawyer in Va., active in the militia, before the Civil War. He commanded the 8th Va. before appointment as brig. gen. as of Aug. 9, 1863. While commanding a brigade in the div. of Maj. Gen. George E. Pickett, he was captured at Sayler's Creek on April 6, 1865. On March 31, U.S. forces captured the flag of the 56th Va., Hunton's brigade. *Ibid.*, p. 350.

To Abraham Lincoln

————

Dabney Mills, March 31st *1865* [*9:30* P.M.]
A. LINCOLN, PRESIDENT CITY POINT.

Sheridan has had hard fighting to-day. I can only communicate with him by Courrier. At dark he was hotly engaged near Dinwiddie. I am very anxious to hear the result. Will let you know when I do hear. All else is apparently favorable at this time and I ~~th~~ hope that will prove so also. Infantry has been sent down the Boydton road to his assistance.

U. S. GRANT
Lt. Gn

ALS (telegram sent), David S. Light, M.D., Miami Beach, Fla.; telegram received, DLC-Robert T. Lincoln. *O.R.*, I, xlvi, part 3, 332–33.

To Maj. Gen. George G. Meade

————

Gravely Run, March 31st/65 [*12:15* P.M.]
MAJ. GN. MEADE, 5TH CORPS HD QRS.

If the enemy ~~haves~~ been checked in Warren's front what is to prevent him from pitching in with his whole Corps and attacking before giving him time to intrench or return in good order to his old intrenchments? I do not understand why Warren permitted his Corps to be fought in detail. When Ayres was pushed forward he should have sent other troops to their support.

U. S. GRANT

Lt. Gn

ALS (telegram sent), Scheide Library, Princeton, N. J.; OClWHi; telegram received (at 1:00 P.M.), DNA, RG 107, Telegrams Collected (Unbound). Printed as sent at 1:00 P.M. in *O.R.*, I, xlvi, part 3, 337. On March 31, 1865, Maj. Gen. George G. Meade twice telegraphed to USG, the second time at 1:00 P.M. "Tell Genl Humphreys that Miles is driving the enemy, a Brigade is moving out to support him & to push him   Another is held in readiness to move out, fire in front of Warren is receding" Telegram received (at 12:45 P.M.), DNA, RG 108, Letters Received. Printed as sent at 12:45 P.M. in *O.R.*, I, xlvi, part 3, 336. "Genl Warren reports by Staff Off that Ayres' advance to White Oak Road was repulsed   Ayres fell back to Crawford the enemy following & attacking both Ayres & Crawford & compelling both to fall back to Griffin. Here the enemy was checked the fighting still continuing   Genl Warren expresses confidence in his ability to hold his present position   Miles has been ordered to be prepared to support Warren   Humphreys will be ordered to attack as soon as I can communicate with him by telegraph if the affair is not over by that time" ALS (telegram sent), DNA, RG 107, Telegrams Collected (Unbound); telegram received, *ibid.*, RG 108, Letters Received. *O.R.*, I, xlvi, part 3, 337.

At 1:30 P.M., Meade telegraphed to USG. "In answer to your telegram of enquiry about Warren pushing ahead I send you a report just received from him —which will explain itself—I infer that both Ayres & Crawfords Divisions can not be relied on for a great deal today—We will push all we can.—" ALS (telegram sent), DNA, RG 94, War Records Office, Miscellaneous War Records; telegrams received (2—at 1:30 P.M.), *ibid.*, RG 108, Letters Received. *O.R.*, I, xlvi, part 3, 337. The enclosure is *ibid.*, p. 362.

At 7:40 A.M., USG had telegraphed to Meade. "Owing to the heavy rains this morning, the troops will remain substantially as they now are, but the 5th Corps should to day draw three days more rations—" Telegram sent, Scheide Library, Princeton, N. J.; telegram received (at 7:40 A.M.), DNA, RG 107, Telegrams Collected (Unbound). *O.R.*, I, xlvi, part 3, 334. At 7:45 A.M., Meade telegraphed to USG. "Your despatch of 7 40 received—Is there any reason the 2d Corps should not draw 3 days rations together with 5th—The Commissary supply wagons Can be sent to the RRoad terminus & refilled" Telegram received (at 7:45 A.M.), DNA, RG 108, Letters Received; copies, *ibid.*, RG 393, Army of the Potomac, Letters Sent; (2) Meade Papers, PHi. *O.R.*, I, xlvi, part 3, 335. At 8:20 [A.M.], USG telegraphed to Meade. "The 2d Corps can also draw their rations the same as the 5th" Copies, DLC-USG, V, 46, 75, 108; DNA, RG 108, Letters Sent. *O.R.*, I, xlvi, part 3, 335.

At 8:05 A.M. and 8:40 A.M., Meade telegraphed to USG. "I send a despatch just received from Maj. Genl. Warren which will show the position of his troops & gives topographical information—additional tools will be sent to him as soon as they can be gotten up, so that the road he is on can be made passable for artillery & wagons at the earliest moment.—" "Firing is heard apparently on left & left center of 2d corps   No report yet—Orders have been sent to Warren to support Humphreys, if necessary—Perhaps it would be well to send same to Ord —Orders for rations issued but I fear the condition of the roads will make their execution almost impossible." ALS (telegrams sent), DNA, RG 94, War Records Office, Miscellaneous War Records; telegrams received (at 8:05 A.M. and 8:40 A.M.), *ibid.*, RG 108, Letters Received. Printed as received at 8:25 A.M. and 8:50 A.M. in *O.R.*, I, xlvi, part 3, 335. The enclosure in the first is *ibid.*, p. 361. On the same day, USG telegraphed to Meade. "Rations must be got forward to Warren & no exertions must be spared to to execute your orders for the same" Telegram received (at 10:15 A.M.), DNA, RG 94, War Records Office, Army of the Potomac; copies, *ibid.*, RG 108, Letters Sent; DLC-USG, V, 46, 75, 108; (2) Meade Papers, PHi. *O.R.*, I, xlvi, part 3, 335.

On March 31, Maj. Gen. Edward O. C. Ord telegraphed to Meade. "The cannonading is, I think, to shell our working parties. The musketry is, I think, from our own men mostly." Printed as received at 10:35 A.M. and transmitted by Meade to USG at 10:38 A.M. *ibid.*, p. 375.

To Maj. Gen. George G. Meade

Gravely Run, March 31st/65 12.40 p m

MAJ. GN. MEADE, 5TH CORPS HD QRS.

It will take so long to communicate with Sheridan that he can not be brought up in co-operation unless he comes up in obedience to orders sent him last night. I understood Gen. Forsythe[1] to say however that as soon as another Div. of Cavalry got up he would push it forward with Merritt. It may be there now. I will send to him again ~~as soon~~ at once. I will also direct Ord to keep the enemy busy in his front and go through if he can.

U. S. GRANT.
Lt. Gn

ALS (telegram sent), Scheide Library, Princeton, N. J.; OClWHi; telegram received (at 12:40 P.M.), DNA, RG 107, Telegrams Collected (Unbound). *O.R.*, I, xlvi, part 3, 336. On March 31, 1865, noon, Maj. Gen. George G. Meade telegraphed to USG. "Genls Crawford & Ayers have been driven back on Griffins—Griffin is about to resume the offensive supported by an attack of Humphreys left. Humphreys will with draw from his right all he can spare to attack with miles since the enemy are trying to turn our left I deem it important to attack with sheridan to let Ord assume the offensive if practicable" Telegram received (at 12:15 P.M.), DNA, RG 108, Letters Received; copies, *ibid.*, RG 393, Army of the Potomac, Letters Sent; Meade Papers, PHi. *O.R.*, I, xlvi, part 3, 336.

At 11:50 A.M., USG telegraphed to Meade. "Humphries should not push to the front without a fair chanc[e] and full determination to go through." ALS

(telegram sent), Scheide Library, Princeton, N. J.; CSmH; telegram received
(at 11:50 A.M.), DNA, RG 94, War Records Office, Army of the Potomac. *O.R.*,
I, xlvi, part 3, 336. At 1:15 P.M., Meade telegraphed to USG. "Your despatch
11.40 relative to Humphreys advancing on his front recieved—as soon as I
reached the field I met Genl. Humphreys on the Boydtown plank, & it was determined between us not to attack on his front, but to push all his available
troops under Miles, to move forward from his left & attack the enemy in front of
Warren in flank—This was done & the enemy compelled to fall back—Warren
is preparing to advance his whole force in conjunction with Miles, and will endeavor to drive the enemy back to & across the White Oak road—Any movement
of the Cavalry on his left will materially aid this operation—" ALS (telegram
sent), DNA, RG 107, Telegrams Collected (Unbound); telegrams received (2
—at 1:15 P.M.), *ibid.*, RG 108, Letters Received. *O.R.*, I, xlvi, part 3, 337. At
1:40 P.M., Meade telegraphed to USG transmitting a telegram of 1:05 P.M.
from Maj. Gen. Andrew A. Humphreys. *Ibid.*, p. 348.

At 1:50 P.M., USG telegraphed to Meade transmitting a telegram of 1:00
P.M. from Lt. Col. Orville E. Babcock to Brig. Gen. John A. Rawlins. "Enemy
completely checked & warren is now pushing his command after them. They seem
to be falling away from his centre, & reported going both ways—He will attack
them [with] all his force. Prisoners from each Division of Hills corps & Bushrod
Johnson's Div." Telegram received (at 1:00 P.M.), DNA, RG 94, War Records
Office, Miscellaneous War Records; copy, Meade Papers, PHi. *O.R.*, I, xlvi, part
3, 334. At 8:00 A.M., Babcock had written to Rawlins. "Genl Warren finds
enemies works well manned in front of his skirmishers, not more than 150 yards,
His pickets are across the Boydton Road, Crawford at Gravelly Run, Ayers in
reserve,   Genl W. has sent his es cort down the Bdt Plank Road to Dinwiddie
No report from or ~~information~~ from Sheridan,   No firing has been heard,   I
will wait to hear from the escort,   Warrens Connec~~tions~~ with Humphrie" ALS,
DNA, RG 108, Letters Received.

1. James W. Forsyth of Ohio, USMA 1856, served as chief of staff for Maj.
Gen. Philip H. Sheridan during the last year of the Civil War, and was appointed
bvt. brig. gen. as of Oct. 19, 1864.

To Maj. Gen. George G. Meade

Dabney Mills March 31st/65

MAJ. GN. MEADE,

The operators at my Hd Qrs. have gone to the wrong place or
are still back. If at your Hd Qrs. will you please have them sent
here to-night.

I think Warren should be instructed to send well down the
White Oak road and also Southwest from his left to watch and see
if there is an enemy in ~~that~~ either direction. I would much rather

have Warren back on the plank road than to be attacked front and rear where he is.

He should intrench front and rear of his left at least and be ready to make a good fight of it if he is attacked in the morning.

We will make no offensive move ourselves to-morrow. If rations were not got up to-day they should be in the morning.

U. S. GRANT
Lt. Gn

ALS, Scheide Library, Princeton, N. J. *O.R.*, I, xlvi, part 3, 338. On March 31, 1865, 5:00 P.M., Maj. Gen. George G. Meade telegraphed to USG. "Sheridans firing was heard soon after you left   I have sent word to Warren to push a force down the White Oak road to co-operate with Sheridan—I will send you a list of casualties as soon as possible—At present 2d corps hospitals report 200 wounded —5th corps 600   I think the casualt[ies] for this day of killed [&] wounded in both corps will be under 1000—Some 60 prisoners have been reported by the 2d corps and 70 by the 5th corps—this will doubtless be increased as all have not yet come in—2d corps report 2 battle flags & 5th corps 1.—" ALS (telegram sent), DNA, RG 94, War Records Office, Miscellaneous War Records; copies (marked as sent at 5:30 P.M.), *ibid.*, RG 393, Army of the Potomac, Letters Sent; (2—one marked as sent at 5:00 P.M., one at 5:30 P.M.) Meade Papers, PHi. Printed as sent at 5:30 P.M. in *O.R.*, I, xlvi, part 3, 338.

To Maj. Gen. George G. Meade

Dabney Mills March 31st/65 8.45 p. m.

MAJ. GN. MEADE,

Your dispatch of 6.35 and your note of 7.30 are just received.[1] Capt Sheridan[2] has reported to you the situation of affairs with Sheridan. Let Warren draw back at once to his position on Boydton road and send a Div. of Infantry. to Sheridans relief. The troops to Sheridan should start at once, and go down Boydton road.

U. S. GRANT
Lt. Gn

ALS (telegram sent), Scheide Library, Princeton, N. J.; telegram received (at 8:45 P.M.), DNA, RG 107, Telegrams Collected (Unbound). *O.R.*, I, xlvi, part 3, 340. On March 31, 1865, 8:45 P.M. (sent at 9:00 P.M.), Maj. Gen. George G. Meade telegraphed to USG. "Orders have been sent to Genl. Warren to draw in at once to the Boydtown plank road & send on receipt of orders Griffin's Division to report to Genl. Sheridan they to move down the Boydtown road." ALS (telegram sent), DNA, RG 107, Telegrams Collected (Unbound); telegram received (at 8:45 P.M.), *ibid.*, RG 108, Letters Received. *O.R.*, I, xlvi, part 3, 340.

At 8:00 P.M. and 8:45 P.M., Meade wrote to USG. "From what Col Kellogg the bearer says it is evident Sheridan can not hold Dinwidie & will have to fall back tomorrow—If I do not contract my lines, can not Turner be sent at once out the Vaughn road to Support Sheridan—I think this will be the quickest thing that can be done.—" ALS, DNA, RG 108, Letters Received. *O.R.*, I, xlvi, part 3, 340. "For your information   March 31st 1865, 8.30 P. M. MAJOR GEN'L WEBB Chief of Staff   General   Lt Col Walsh reports, that an order ly from Gen'l Sheridan, reported to Gen'l Warren 'that he had been fighting Infantry' and had taken prisoners from the 58th Va. (Lillys Bragade, Walkers. Div. Gordons. Corps)   Very Respectfully Your Obt. Servt   (signed) J. C BABCOCK" Copy, CtY.

At 9:00 P.M., Meade wrote to USG. "I have ordered my medical Director to send the ambulances of the 6th Corps for Sheridans wounded.—" ALS, DNA, RG 94, War Records Office, Army of the Potomac, Cav. Corps. *O.R.*, I, xlvi, part 3, 340.

1. At 6:35 P.M. and 7:40 P.M., Meade telegraphed to USG. "A staff Officer from Genl Merritt was cut off by what is reported to be Brigades of Picketts Div. these are the Brigades reported to be on our left but not in our fight today   the firing has receded towards to Dinwiddie C. H. If Genl Sheridan reports that he cannot overcome the force now opposed to him I will be obliged to contract my lines & I must do it tonight. I have directed Warren to send a force down Boydton Plank road to try & open communication with Sheridan   under the present state of affairs it was impossible to send down the White Oak road as first ordered. Please let me know in regard to Sheridans report as soon as convenient my disposition against these Brigades should be made shortly   I leave for my Hd Qrs at old Camp" Telegram received, DNA, RG 108, Letters Received. *O.R.*, I, xlvi, part 3, 338. "Capt Sheridan from Sheridans Cavalry is here—And is directed to you by a Staff Office   He reports that Gnl Sheridan is just north of Dinwiddie [C.] H having been repulsed by the Enemy's infantry on the dirt road running north, and also on the road running ~~south~~ north west from north of Dinwiddie—Genl Sheridan states that if he ~~returns~~ is forced to return it will be on the Vaughn road—~~He~~ The Staff officer leave here to report to you—" ALS (telegram sent), DNA, RG 107, Telegrams Collected (Unbound); telegram received (at 7:40 P.M.), *ibid.*, RG 108, Letters Received. *O.R.*, I, xlvi, part 3, 340. A notation on the telegram sent of receipt at 8:40 P.M., combined with USG's wording, indicates that this message may have been delivered directly to USG.

2. Michael V. Sheridan, born in Ohio in 1840, who served his brother Philip as vol. aide early in the war, was appointed 1st lt., 2nd Mo., as of Sept. 7, 1863, and capt., aide to Maj. Gen. Sheridan, as of May 18, 1864.

To Maj. Gen. George G. Meade

Dabney Mills March 31st/65 9.45 p. m.

MAJ. GN. MEADE,

If you can get orders to McKenzie to move his Cavalry to the support of Sheridan, by way of the Vaughan road, do so. I have sent the same directions to Gn. Ord. Please let me know when Griffin gets started. If he pushes promptly I think there may be a chance for cutting up the Infantry the enemy have entrusted so far from home. Urge prompt movement on Griffin.

U. S. GRANT
Lt. Gn

ALS (telegram sent), CSmH; telegram received, DNA, RG 107, Telegrams Collected (Unbound). *O.R.*, I, xlvi, part 3, 341. On March 31, 1865, 9:15 P.M., USG telegraphed to Maj. Gen. George G. Meade. "I wish you would send out some Cavalry to Dinwiddie to see if information can be got from Sheridan   it will only take about half the time to go from your Head Qrs it will from mine & I have no one to send"   Telegram received (at 9:10 P.M.), DNA, RG 94, War Records Office, Army of the Potomac, Cav. Corps; copies, *ibid.*, RG 108, Letters Sent; DLC-USG, V, 46, 75, 108; (2) Meade Papers, PHi. Printed as sent at 9:10 P.M. in *O.R.*, I, xlvi, part 3, 341. At 10:00 P.M., Meade telegraphed to USG. "The only disposable cavalry I have is my escort—I will send an officer & 40 men to communicate with Sheridan   I believe the road is all open to him.—I have sent the orders to McKenzie"   ALS (telegram sent), DNA, RG 107, Telegrams Collected (Unbound); telegram received (at 10:00 P.M.), *ibid.*, RG 108, Letters Received. Printed as received at 10:20 P.M. in *O.R.*, I, xlvi, part 3, 342. At 10:30 P.M., USG telegraphed to Meade. "As you are sending to Sheridan Send him word of all the dispositions making to aid him & tell him to take General direction of the forces sent to him until the emergency for which they are sent is over"   Telegram received, DNA, RG 107, Telegrams Collected (Unbound); copies, *ibid.*, RG 108, Letters Sent; DLC-USG, V, 46, 75, 108; (2) Meade Papers, PHi. *O.R.*, I, xlvi, part 3, 342.

To Maj. Gen. George G. Meade

By Telegraph from Dabneys [*March 31*] 1865 [*9:45* P.M.]
To MAJ GENL MEADE

Ord has driven in the enemys pickets & sharp shooters near Hatchers Run & got possession of a knoll which takes the enemys works on Humphreys right in reverse   he is building a battery there tonight. This will drive the enemy out & give H. an opportunity of advancing his right & possibly of gaining a position which will take the works north of the Run in reverse so as to let Ord through, Humphrey has been notified of this but has no orders

U S GRANT
Lt Genl

Telegram received, DNA, RG 107, Telegrams Collected (Unbound); copies, *ibid.*, RG 108, Letters Sent; DLC-USG, V, 46, 75, 108; (2) Meade Papers, PHi. *O.R.*, I, xlvi, part 3, 341.

On March 31, 1865, 9:45 P.M., Maj. Gen. George G. Meade telegraphed to USG. "Would it not be well for Warren to go down with his whole corps & smash up the force in front of Sheridan—Humphreys can hold the line to the Boydtown Plank road & the refusal along it.—Bartletts brigade is now on the road from J. Boisseau running north, where it crosses Gravelly run, he having gone there down the White Oak road—Warren would move at once that way, & take the force threatening Sheridan in rear or he could send one division to support Sheridan at Dinwiddie & move on the enemys rear with the other two.— Warren suggests this." ALS (telegram sent), DNA, RG 107, Telegrams Collected (Unbound); telegram received (at 9:45 P.M.), *ibid.*, RG 108, Letters Received. *O.R.*, I, xlvi, part 3, 341. At 10:15 P.M., USG telegraphed to Meade. "Let Warren move in the way you propose and urge him not to stop for anything. Let Griffin go on as he was first directed." ALS (telegram sent), Kohns Collection, NN; telegram received, DNA, RG 107, Telegrams Collected (Unbound). *O.R.*, I, xlvi, part 3, 342. At 10:45 P.M., Meade telegraphed to USG. "Warren was ordered some time since to push Griffin promptly down the plank road to Sheridan I have now allowed him to move with the rest of his corps as light as possible, and push down the road running South from the White Oak road to Dinwiddie to attack the enemy in rear & look out to get over to the plank road, if they turn on him too strongly.—The messenger to Sheridan had not left when these orders were sent & Sheridan was notified of them—The officer has gone now so that I can not add what you desire about his taking command, but I take it for granted he will do so as he is the senior I will instruct Warren to report to him.—I find it reported that among Sheridans prisoners, is one from Lilleys brigade Walkers Divn Gordons corps—Formerly Hoke commanded a brigade in this Division from whence I think has arisen the rumour that Hoke is in front of Sheridan the men often giving the old names of their organisations—" ALS (telegram sent), DNA, RG 107, Telegrams Collected (Unbound); telegram received (at 10:45 P.M.), *ibid.*, RG 108, Letters Received. Printed as sent on April 1, 2:25 A.M., in *O.R.*, I, xlvi, part 3, 342. At 11:45 P.M., Meade wrote to USG. "A despatch just received from Warren reports bridge on Boydtown plank road across Gravelly run destroyed, and that it will take considerable time to rebuild—Orders have been sent to him if this is the case to send troops to Sheridan by the Quaker road or by both roads if necessary even if he gives up the rear attack Every exertion to reinforce Sheridan at the earliest moment & the vital importance of it, has been impressed on him—He has been informed Sheridan if not reinforced & compelled to retire will with draw by the Vaughn road.—I think it is possible the enemy may retire from Sheridans front tonight fearing an attack from the rear.—I have sent orders to Humphreys to co-operate with Ord

& take the work in his front, if Ords artillery fire renders it practicable—" ALS (marked as received on April 1, 1:30 A.M.), DNA, RG 108, Letters Received. *O.R.*, I, xlvi, part 3, 342–43.

On April 1, 6:00 A.M., Meade telegraphed to USG. "The officer sent to Sheridan returned between 2 & 3 a m without any written communication, but giving Genl. S's. opinion that the enemy were retiring from his front—The absence of firing this morning would seem to confirm this. I was asleep, at the time this officer returned & did not get the information till just now. Should this prove true Warren will be at or near Dinwiddie soon with his whole corps—& will require further orders—" ALS (telegram sent), DNA, RG 107, Telegrams Collected (Unbound); telegram received, *ibid.*, RG 108, Letters Received. Printed as received at 6:25 A.M. in *O.R.*, I, xlvi, part 3, 395.

To Maj. Gen. George G. Meade

Dabney's Mill
March 31st/65

MAJ. GEN. MEADE,

I send you copy of a report just sent by Sheridan. You will see that he reports Hoke's Div. which we know was in N. C.

Since this was rec'd Col. Porter has returned from Sheridan. He says that Devins had been driven back in considerable confusion South of J. Boisseaus house. Crooke was then going up west of the road and expected to turn the enemy and drive him back.

The effort has been to get our Cavalry on to the White Oak road West of Dabneys house. So far this has failed and there is no assurance that it will succeed. This will make it necessary for Warren to watch his left all round. The Cavalry being where it is will probably make the enemy very careful about coming round much in his rear but he can not be too much on his guard.—Let your provost question prisoners as to whether troops from N. C. have come up.

U. S. GRANT
Lt. Gn

ALS, Scheide Library, Princeton, N. J.; DNA, RG 107, Telegrams Collected (Unbound). *O.R.*, I, xlvi, part 3, 338–39. On March 31, 1865, 2:30 P.M., Maj. Gen. Philip H. Sheridan wrote to USG. "Hokes Division and (3) three brigades of Picketts Division are at the Five Forks—or were there last night. Their picket line is now in front of Devines Division. W. H. F. Lee attack Smiths brigade of

Crooks Div: on Chamberlains Creek and got cleaned out. I will now attack him, and push the 1st Cavly: Division against their Infantry line. I have ordered up one (1) brig: of Custers Div: which is yet back with our ammunition train—It has been impossible to get up this train on account of the swamps—" ALS, DNA, RG 108, Letters Received. *O.R.*, I, xlvi, part 3, 339. On the same day, USG wrote to Maj. Gen. George G. Meade. "The following dispatch forwarded for your information" Copies, DNA, RG 108, Letters Received; (2) Meade Papers, PHi. *O.R.*, I, xlvi, part 3, 339. At 7:10 P.M., Meade wrote to USG. "It is not impossible troops may have been sent up from the South, tho' I have heard nothing of it before—One prisoner said he heard Pickets Division had come up from Burksville, but as I knew Pickett had not been there I presumed he had been down the S—Side R. Rd to watch for our Cavalry—If Hoke or any considerable force of infantry is in sheridans front, it opens the rear of our army, as I understand from Capt Sheridan the bearer of this, that the road from J. M. Brock to Boiseau's to the Boydtown plank is now open to the enemy—Genl sheridan I think from the account of Capt. sheridan will be pressed tomorrow—He will either have to come in, or support must be sent to him—My line is so extended & flank in air, that I dont see how I can detach for this purpose, unless I contract my lines, when I shall have troops to spare. ~~Can Ord~~ Let me hear as soon as possible what you desire done." ALS, DNA, RG 108, Letters Received. *O.R.*, I, xlvi, part 3, 339.

To Maj. Gen. Edward O. C. Ord

Gravely Run March 31st/65 12.50 a. m.

MAJ. GEN. ORD, HUMPHREYS STATION.

Gen. Wright reports that he thinks he can assault at daylight in the morning with a good prospect of sucsess. I had suspended the order but authorized Gen. Meade to direct him to make the preliminary preparations. Are your men so arranged as to enable you to assault at the same time? It will require the massing of your troops at point where you intend attacking. Answer and I will give definite orders.

U. S. GRANT, Lt. Gn

ALS (telegram sent), Scheide Library, Princeton, N. J.; telegram received (dated "30"), Ord Papers, CU-B. Dated March 30, 1865, in *O.R.*, I, xlvi, part 3, 321. On March 31, Maj. Gen. Edward O. C. Ord telegraphed to USG. "Despatch on assault recd my men are not arranged so that they can assault at the same time—none of my officers have yet seen the enemies line on account of swamp and woods and the quick Sand on the only approachable place on their front is reported impracticable as yet for artillery required to open a passage—men are hard at work—loss pretty severe to day—" ALS (telegram sent—mis-

dated March 30), DNA, RG 108, Letters Received; telegram received, *ibid.*
O.R., I, xlvi, part 3, 377.

At 1:55 A.M., USG telegraphed to Ord. "The assault will not take place in
the morning. Did you inflict loss on the enemy to-day equal to your own?" ALS
(telegram sent), Scheide Library, Princeton, N. J.; Kohns Collection, NN; telegram received (at 1:55 A.M.), Ord Papers, CU-B. *O.R.,* I, xlvi, part 3, 374. On
the same day, Ord telegraphed to USG. "I think the enemys loss was considerable
though not as great as ours on account of nature of woods & swamps through
which we approached" Telegram received (at 2:00 A.M.), DNA, RG 108,
Letters Received. Printed as sent at 2:00 A.M. in *O.R.,* I, xlvi, part 3, 374.

To Maj. Gen. Edward O. C. Ord

Gravelly Run., March 31. 1865

MAJ. GEN. ORD.

No one here has ordered your operators forward. Please order
them forward at once—

Gen. Meade reports firing on Humphreys left and left center.
Hold yourself in readiness to support him in case he is attacked.

U. S. GRANT
Lt. Gen.

Copies, DLC-USG, V, 46, 75, 108; DNA, RG 108, Letters Sent. *O.R.,* I, xlvi,
part 3, 374. On March 31, 1865, 9:50 A.M., Maj. Gen. Edward O. C. Ord telegraphed to USG. "The enemy appear to be makeing an attack on my left in some
force perhaps to drive Turner and Foster from their position near Crows & R
Armstrongs ~~and the Barn~~—the ~~Arm~~ 2d Corps should be ready to attack on there
flank promply—if necessary" ALS (telegram sent), DNA, RG 108, Letters
Received; telegram received, *ibid.* Printed as sent at 9:30 A.M. in *O.R.,* I, xlvi,
part 3, 374. At 10:40 A.M., USG telegraphed to Ord. "Gen. Humphries and
Wright have been ordered to assist you if you are attacked either by making a
direct attack or by sending their reserves to you." ALS (telegram sent),
OCIWHi; telegram received, Ord Papers, CU-B. *O.R.,* I, xlvi, part 3, 375. At
11:00 A.M., Ord telegraphed to USG. "The following from the front—~~Genl Gibbons sends me the following from Battery~~ a on the ~~Old line~~—date—10—20—
a m—'sharp firing still going on in front of Foster—Foster is in centre to left—
the firing is going off towards our right Genl Turner has pushed his skirmishers forward a number of Prisoners are coming in—Signed GIBBON ~~It app
firing~~ I am in communication with Wright who holds a Division ready—I think
my new line Strong enough to be held—~~heavy firing to right is subsiding~~" ALS
(telegram sent), DNA, RG 107, Telegrams Collected (Unbound); telegram
received, *ibid.,* RG 108, Letters Received. *O.R.,* I, xlvi, part 3, 375. At 11:30
A.M., Ord telegraphed to USG. "Prisoners in this a m mostly N C report the line
in my front strongly reinforced from their left" Telegram received, DNA, RG
108, Letters Received. *O.R.,* I, xlvi, part 3, 375.

To Maj. Gen. Edward O. C. Ord

Gravely Run, March 31st/65 12.50 p m

MAJ. GN. ORD, HUMPHRIES STATION,

Ayres Division has been driven from near W. Dabneys back to the Boydton road. The 5th Corps is now preparing to take the offensive in turn aided by the 2d Corps. Keep the enemy busy in your front and if a chance presents itself for attacking do so.

U. S. GRANT.
Lt. Gn

ALS (telegram sent), Scheide Library, Princeton, N. J.; OClWHi; copies, DLC-USG, V, 46, 75, 108; DNA, RG 108, Letters Sent. *O.R.,* I, xlvi, part 3, 376. On March 31, 1865, 2:00 P.M., Maj. Gen. Edward O. C. Ord telegraphed to USG. "Your dispatch to occupy the enemy receivd and orders issued—They have been kept petty busy since 9. a m by Turner & Foster   all my men are still occupying them so that deserters in this a. m report they have strongly reinforced their line   where it is seen it is reported by Gen Turners as much cut up heavily slashed and deserters say has two—2—or three 3 lines of abattis   we will soon learn more of it." Telegram received, DNA, RG 108, Letters Received. *O.R.,* I, xlvi, part 3, 376.

To Maj. Gen. Edward O. C. Ord

By Telegraph from Butlers House [*March*] 31 *1865*

To MAJ. GEN ORD

you may adviance your picket if you deem it advisable   I do not ~~wait~~ want you to make an assault unless it becomes necessary to make it General at Different parts of the lines   at present I want the enemy to Keep ~~to~~ the force he now has north of hatchers Run where it is—Warren has advanced—since his repulse and now holds the white oak road   my Hd Qrs will be tonight at Dabneys mills—

U. S. GRANT
Lt Genl

Telegram received, Ord Papers, CU-B; copies, DLC-USG, V, 46, 75, 108; DNA, RG 108, Letters Sent. *O.R.,* I, xlvi, part 3, 376. On March 31, 1865, 3:00 P.M., Maj. Gen. Edward O. C. Ord telegraphed to USG. "I have recd. report from

Turners front of that part of enemys line which is near him   it is not favorable
to an assault by his men this afternoon because his men have been up all night
entrenching & engaged last P M & all day today & the ground is very difficult.
The rest of the enemies line is too far & too covered with woods for me to find
it out until I can drive their Pickets in   if you let me do this & establish my line
with Picquets near their sharp shooters in front & artilley in Position to silence
to their batteries I can then advance with some idea of what is before me"   Telegram received, DNA, RG 108, Letters Received. *O.R.*, I, xlvi, part 3, 376.

On the same day, Ord telegraphed to USG. "A boys, one of Gen Sheridans
Scouts who was captured on the Chickahominy and escaped from the enemy
yesterday morning reports that the enemy had at Stony Creek near Dinwiddie
C. H. two brigades of Cavalry, one of infantry and two peices of Artillery"
Telegram sent, DNA, RG 108, Letters Received; telegram received, *ibid*. *O.R.*,
I, xlvi, part 3, 377.

To Maj. Gen. Edward O. C. Ord

<del>Maj</del>. Dabney Mills, March 31st 1865 9.45 p m.
Maj. Gn. Ord, Humphries station

Send McKenzie at once to Dinwiddie to the support of Sheridan   He has been attacked by Cavalry and Infantry and driven
into Dinwiddie. Fighting was still going on when I last heard
from him which was after dark. He will probably be back on the
Vaughan road.

U. S. Grant
Lt. Gn

ALS (telegram sent), CSmH; telegram received, Ord Papers, CU-B. *O.R.*, I,
xlvi, part 3, 378. On March 31, 1865, Maj. Gen. Edward O. C. Ord telegraphed
to USG. "General McKenzie reports that the trains he has been guarding with
his cavalry Command have crossed the Creek and there is no apparent necessity
for his remaining longer. Have you any orders to give in regard to his command"
ALS (telegram sent), DNA, RG 108, Letters Received; telegram received (at
9:12 p.m.), *ibid*. *O.R.*, I, xlvi, part 3, 377.

At 10:00 p.m., Ord telegraphed to USG. "Your despatch recd   have sent
orders to McKenzie to get off as Soon to in the morning as possible—copy of your
despatch sent him to go by—" ALS (telegram sent), DNA, RG 108, Letters
Received; telegram received (at 10:30 p.m.), *ibid*. Printed as sent at 10:30
p.m. in *O.R.*, I, xlvi, part 3, 378. On the same day, USG telegraphed to Ord. "I
want McKenzie to go to-night. It may be to late to-morrow morning." ALS (telegram sent), OClWHi; copies, DLC-USG, V, 46, 75, 108; DNA, RG 108, Letters
Sent. *O.R.*, I, xlvi, part 3, 378.

Also on March 31, Ord telegraphed to USG. "Have <del>g</del> moved my centre line
of skirmish & sharp shooters & driven enemies picket in   shall establish batteries

tonight,   189 Prisoners 2 officers and 18 deserters one (1) a Lieut in So far   the enemies battery nearer & south of Hatchers run is so situated that it can be taken in reverse from my left where Miche proposes erecting a battery   We can render it untenable so that Genl Humphreys can take it. Prisoners state there is continuous lines of works, along Heths division & on his left with strong lines of abatis in rear of Heths division was this a m   Mahon & Cooks right rests on the run & they are on the extreme right of Heths division   they say their lines is well stretched but their reserve is good"   Telegram received (at 9:30 P.M.), DNA, RG 108, Letters Received. Printed as sent at 9:30 P.M. in *O.R.*, I, xlvi, part 3, 377. At 10:30 P.M., USG telegraphed to Ord. "Humphery has been informed of the Battery which you are building to take the enemys Line south of Hatches run in reverse and made disposition to take advantage of it   if Successfull he will endeavor to post up the south side high enough to take the worke in your front in reverse and return"   Telegram received, Ord Papers, CU-B; copies, DLC-USG, V, 46, 75, 108; DNA, RG 108, Letters Sent. *O.R.*, I, xlvi, part 3, 378.

To Maj. Gen. Philip H. Sheridan

Gravely ~~Bottoms~~ Run March 30th [*31*]/65 12.50 [P.M.]
MAJ. GN. SHERIDAN,
    The enemy have driven Ayres & Crawford's Divisions back to near the Boydton road. The whole 5th Corps is now about to attack the enemy in turn. It is desirable that you get up as much of your Cavalry as you can and push towards the White Oak road on the right Branch taken by Merritt yesterday. If the enemy does not go back to his old position by turning to the right you may be able to hit the enemy in the rear.
                                        U. S. GRANT
                                        Lt. Gn

ALS, Scheide Library, Princeton, N. J. *O.R.*, I, xlvi, part 3, 380.

To Maj. Gen. Philip H. Sheridan

Gravely Run, March 31st 1865
MAJ. GEN. SHERIDAN,
    It will be impossible to give you the 6th Corps for the operation by our left. It is in the center of our line between Hatcher's Run at

the Appomattox. Besides Wright thinks he can go through the line where he is and it is advisable to have troops and a commander there who feels so to co-operate with you when you get around.

I could relieve the 2d with the 5th Corps and give you that. If this is done it will be necessary to give the orders soon to have the troops ready for to-morrow morning.

U. S. GRANT
Lt. Gn.

ALS, Scheide Library, Princeton, N. J. *O.R.*, I, xlvi, part 3, 380. On March 31, 1865, Maj. Gen. Philip H. Sheridan wrote to USG. "My scouts report the enemy busy all last night in constructing breastworks at Five Forks, and as far as one mile west of that point. There was great activity on the Railroad; trains all going west. If the ground would permit, I believe I could with the 6th Corps, turn the enemy's left or break through his lines; but I would not like the 5th Corps to make such an attempt. The ground is very soft west of the Boydton Plank Road. Scouts report no reinforcements from Johnson." Copies (2), DLC-Philip H. Sheridan. *O.R.*, I, xlvi, part 3, 380.

To Maj. Gen. Philip H. Sheridan

Gravelly Run. March 31. 1865., ~~1 55~~ A M

MAJ. GEN. SHERIDAN

I am now at Mrs. Butler's House on Boydton plank road. My Headqrs will be at Dabney's Saw Mill to night.—Warren and Miles Division of 2d Corps are now advancing. I hope your Cavalry is up where it will be of assistance. Let me know how matters stand now with the Cavalry, where they are, what their orders &c

If it had been possible to have had a Div or two of them well up on the right hand road taken by Merritt yesterday they could have fallen on the enemy's rear as they were pursuing Ayers and Crawford

I would like you to get information from the Weldon road. I understand the enemy have some Infantry and a brigade of Cavalry at Stony Creek Station. I think it possible too that Johnston may be brought up that road to attack us in rear. They will see now that Sherman has halted at Goldsboro and may think they can leave Raleigh with a small force.

Word has just been brought in that Warren has got possession of White oak road.

U S GRANT
Lt Genl

Copies, DLC-USG, V, 46, 75, 108; DNA, RG 108, Letters Sent. *O.R.*, I, xlvi, part 3, 380–81.

To Maj. Gen. Philip H. Sheridan

Dabney Mills, March 31st/65 10.45 p. m

MAJ. GN. ~~MEADE~~, SHERIDAN

The 5th Corps has been ordered to your support. Two Divisions will go by J. Boissous and one down the Boydton road. In addition to this I have sent McKenzies Cavalry which will reach you by the ~~Boydton~~ Vaughan road. All these forces, except the Cavalry, should reach you by 12 to-night. You will assume command of the whole force sent to operate with you and use it to the best of your ability to destroy the force which your command has fought so gallantly to-day.

U. S. GRANT
Lt. Gn

ALS (telegram sent), Scheide Library, Princeton, N. J.; copies, DLC-USG, V, 46, 75, 108; DNA, RG 108, Letters Sent. Printed as sent at 10:05 P.M. in *O.R.*, I, xlvi, part 1, 1111; (at 10:45 P.M.) *ibid.*, I, xlvi, part 3, 381.

On March 31, 1865, Maj. Gen. Philip H. Sheridan wrote to USG. "The Enemys Cavly: attacked me about 10. oclock. A. M. to day on the road comming in from the west and little north of Dinwiddic C. H. This attack was very handsomely repulsed by Genl: Smith's brigade of Crook's Division, and the Enemy driven across Chamberlain Creek. Shortly afterwards, the Enemy's Infantry attack on the same Creek in heavy force, and drove in Genl Davies brigade, and advancing rapidly gained the ~~Five~~ Forks of the roads at J. Boisseau. This forced Devines, ~~and~~ who was in advance and Davies to cross to the Boydton Road—Genl: Greggs brigade & Genl: Gibbes brigade, which were towards Dinwiddie C. H. then attacked the Enemy in rear very handsomely. this stopped their march towards the left of ~~the~~ our Infantry—and finally caused them to turn towards Dinwiddie, and attack us in heavy force—the Enemy then again attacked at Chamberlain Creek, and forced Genl: Smiths position; at this time Pennington and Capeharts brigades of Custers Div: came up—and a very handsome fight occurred. The Enemy have gained some ground, but we still hold in front of Dinwiddie C. H. and Devines with Davies are coming down the Boydton

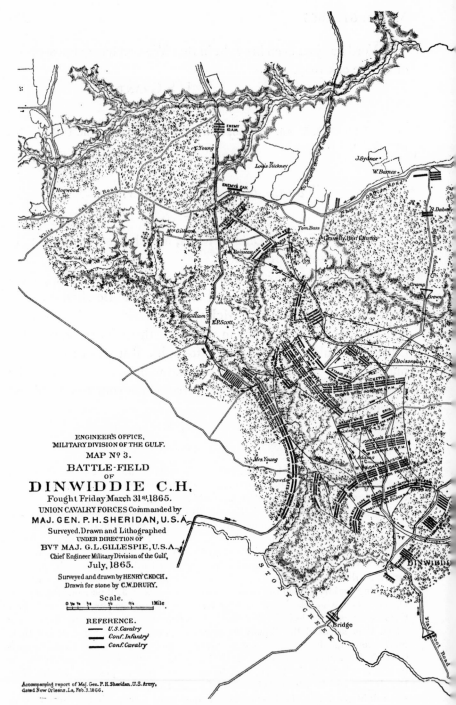

ENGINEER'S OFFICE,
MILITARY DIVISION OF THE GULF.

MAP Nº 3.

BATTLE-FIELD
OF
DINWIDDIE C.H.
Fought Friday March 31ˢᵗ, 1865.
UNION CAVALRY FORCES Commanded by
MAJ. GEN. P. H. SHERIDAN, U.S.A.
Surveyed, Drawn and Lithographed
UNDER DIRECTION OF
BVᵗ MAJ. G. L. GILLESPIE, U.S.A.,
Chief Engineer Military Division of the Gulf,
July, 1865.

Surveyed and drawn by HENRY C. KOCH .
Drawn for stone by C. W. DRURY.

Scale.
0 ⅛ ¼   ½   ¾   1 Mile

REFERENCE.
——— U.S. Cavalry
——— Conf. Infantry
——— Conf. Cavalry

Accompanying report of Maj. Gen. P. H. Sheridan, U.S. Army,
dated New Orleans. La, Feb. 3. 1866.

The Battle of Dinwiddie Court House, March 31, 1865

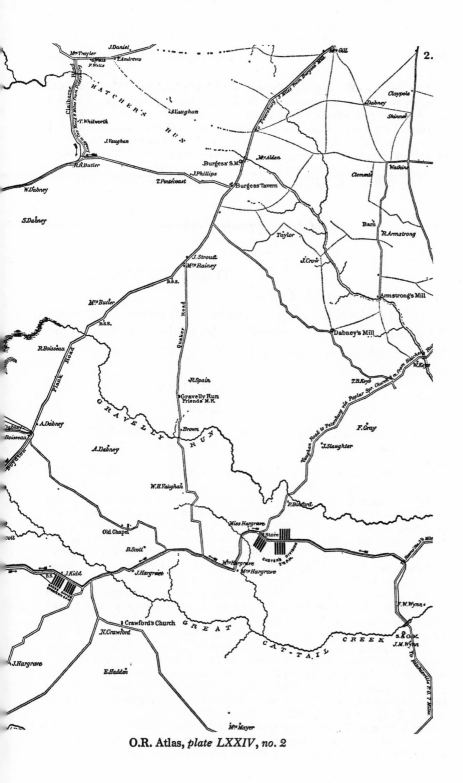

O.R. Atlas, *plate LXXIV*, no. 2

road to join us—The opposing force was Pickett's Division, Wise's Indepnt: Brigade, and Fitz Lees, Rossers, and W. H. Lees Cavly: Commands—The men have behaved spendidly. Our loss in Killed, and Wounded, will probably number 450 men. Very few men were lost as prisoners—We have of the Enemy a number of prisoners—This force is too strong for us—I will hold on to Dinwiddie C. H. until I am compelled to leave—We have also some prisoners from Johnsons Division— . . . P. S. Our fighting to day was all dismounted—" ALS, DNA, RG 108, Letters Received. *O.R.*, I, xlvi, part 1, 1110; *ibid.*, I, xlvi, part 3, 381.

To Maj. Gen. Godfrey Weitzel

Dabney Mills Mar. 31st *1865*

MAJ. GN. WEITZEL, A. JAMES

All of Picketts Div. is here. We have prisoners from Huntons Brigade and I beleive all other Brigades of the Div. Nothing has been seen of any of Fields or Kershaw's Div's. nor of ~~Majones~~ Mahone—[1]

U. S. GRANT
Lt. Gn

ALS (telegram sent), Kohns Collection, NN; telegrams received (2), DNA, RG 94, War Records Office, Miscellaneous War Records. *O.R.*, I, xlvi, part 3, 383.

On Friday, March 31, 1865, USG telegraphed to Maj. Gen. Godfrey Weitzel. "Prisoners captured near Hatchers Run this morning report that part of their line strongly reinforced from their left. What news do you get from your front?" ALS (telegram sent), Scheide Library, Princeton, N. J.; Kohns Collection, NN; telegram received, DNA, RG 94, War Records Office, Miscellaneous War Records; *ibid.*, RG 107, Telegrams Collected (Unbound). *O.R.*, I, xlvi, part 3, 382. At 1:20 P.M., Weitzel telegraphed to USG. "There is no evidence ~~to the moment~~ of any kind up to this moment, that any thing but three brigades of Pickett's Division have left my front since Monday. I have a scouting party out on my right now and will send you report as soon as it returns. Richmond papers rec'd a few moments ago say that Sheridan with cavalry infantry and artillery is evidently trying to get to the South Side Railroad. I have sent you the papers. ~~By~~ I am using every method to get informants and as soon as I can report any change I will do so at once. The lines in my front here show no change whatever, and Genl Hartsuff reports none on his. Please let me know if you hear any thing of Hamptons Brigade Picketts Division or of Fields Division" ALS (incomplete telegram sent), DNA, RG 107, Telegrams Collected (Unbound); telegram received, *ibid.*, RG 94, War Records Office, Miscellaneous War Records. *O.R.*, I, xlvi, part 3, 383.

At 7:25 P.M., Weitzel telegraphed to USG. "The 9 O'clock train to Petersburg did not run to day. Only the other regular trains ran." ALS (telegram sent), DNA, RG 107, Telegrams Collected (Unbound); telegram received, *ibid.*

At 10:45 P.M., USG telegraphed to Weitzel. "Mahone's Division is reported here this evening. This leaves, as I understand, Field, Kershaw and Bratton holding in front of you including your Bermuda front—" ALS (telegram sent), OClWHi; telegrams received (2—one at 10:45 P.M., one on April 1, 1:40 A.M.), DNA, RG 94, War Records Office, Miscellaneous War Records. Printed as received at 10:45 P.M. in *O.R.*, I, xlvi, part 3, 383.

At 10:45 P.M., Weitzel telegraphed to USG. "My scouting party has just returned. It reports the enemy's line unchanged as far as Charles City Road. Could not get across White Oak swamp to Williamsburg road on account of high water in swamp. I have nothing further new." ALS (telegram sent), DNA, RG 107, Telegrams Collected (Unbound); telegram received (at 10:45 P.M.), *ibid.*, RG 94, War Records Office, Miscellaneous War Records; copy (marked as sent on March 30, 12:20 A.M.), *ibid.*, RG 393, 25th Army Corps, Telegrams Sent. *O.R.*, I, xlvi, part 3, 383.

At 1:10 P.M. and 8:45 P.M., Weitzel telegraphed to Lt. Col. Theodore S. Bowers. "Richmond papers of to-day just rec'd. speak of the move as a raid of Sheridan" ALS (telegram sent), DNA, RG 107, Telegrams Collected (Unbound); copy, *ibid.*, RG 393, 25th Army Corps, Telegrams Sent. See *O.R.*, I, xlvi, part 3, 334. "What news from the left tonight." Telegram received, DNA, RG 107, Telegrams Collected (Unbound); copy, *ibid.*, RG 393, 25th Army Corps, Telegrams Sent. On the same day, Bowers telegraphed to Weitzel. "There has been very heavy fighting to day Enemy drove us back a mile—We in turn drove him back and took possesion of the ground he occupied yesterday—Have no particulars Will send them to you as soon as received" Telegram received, *ibid.*, Telegrams Received; copies, *ibid.*, Telegrams Sent; (2) *ibid.*, RG 107, Telegrams Collected (Unbound).

1. Word not in USG's hand.

To Abraham Lincoln

Dabney Mills Apl. 1st *1865* [*9:15* A.M.]

A. LINCOLN, PRESIDENT, CITY POINT.

Yesterday, as reported, the left of the 5th Corps attempted to push North so as to cross the White Oak road about W. Dabney's House but were driven back. Sheridan at the same time was pushing up the right branch of the two roads from J. Boisseaus North to the same road. He was at the same time holding Dinwiddie C. H. and the line of Chamberlain Creek. He was met by all the enemy's Cavalry and four or five Brigades of Infantry and gradually forced back until at 8 p. m. last evening he was holding a line from Chamberlains Creek to the Boydton road probably not more than one mile from the C. H. After the falling back of two Divisions of the

5th Corps they again pushed forward and gained the position on the White Oak road first sought. Finding however the situation Sheridan was in orders were sent Warren after dark to leave the position he held and to push two Divisions down by J. Boisseaus and one down the Boydton road to his relief. I had much hopes of destroying the force detached by the enemy so far to our rear. I have not yet heard the result but I know that Sheridan took the offensive this a. m.

Ord yesterday pushed the enemys pickets from the left of his, Ord's, line, next to Hatcher's run, Capturing 189 men and 2 officers, with but very little loss to us. This puts Ord so close to the enemy that he can not put out pickets in front. This morning before day the enemy attempted to drive him from this position but was repulsed without loss on our side and leaving over 60 prisoners in our hands.

~~There was a gooddeal of fighting at different points during the day yesterday resulting in heavy losses to the enemy~~

U. S. GRANT
Lt. Gn.

ALS (telegram sent), OCIWHi; telegram received (at 9:15 A.M.), DLC-Robert T. Lincoln. *O.R.*, I, xlvi, part 3, 393.

To Abraham Lincoln

―――――

From Dabneys Mills Apl 1st *1865*. 10.40 a. m

A LINCOLN PRESIDENT

In my despatch this morning I made a mistake in saying Ord lost nothing in the attack made on him this A m   his Casualties were about 30 killed & wounded   he reported no Casualties in Turners Division which led me into the Error,   The quicksand of this section exceeds anything I have ever seen   roads have to be Corduroyed in front of teams and Artillery as they advance   we were 56 hours moving 600 teams 5 miles with 1200 men to help them through the woods where it is perfectly dry for infantry horses will go through so deep as to scarcely be able to extricate themselves   I have nothing special to report at this hour,

U. S. GRANT
Lt, Gen

Telegram received (at 11:24 A.M.), DLC-Robert T. Lincoln; copies (marked as sent at 10:30 A.M.), DLC-USG, V, 46, 75, 108; DNA, RG 108, Letters Sent. *O.R.*, I, xlvi, part 3, 393.

To Abraham Lincoln

From Grant's Hd Qrs April 1st *1865.*

A LINCOLN PREST

The following dispatch is just recd from Col Porter of my staff who was sent to communicate with Gen Sheridan.

You remember I told you the 5th Corps was sent to him last evening—

U. S. GRANT Lt. Gen.

"Gen Sheridan's Hd Qrs J. Bousseau's Cross roads
April 1st 1865 2 P. m.

GEN RAWLINS CHF OF STAFF

Devins Div of Cavalry has just Carried the barricade at the five forks Held by Pickett's Div Capturing about two hundred prisoners. The enemy now seem to hold a line across the ford & white Oak roads   The whole 5th Corps is now moving from here up to five forks & Gen S. will attack the enemy with every thing the Head of warren's Column is now about a mile & ahalf from five forks moving up rapidly   Our men have never fought better. All are in excellent spirits and anxious to go in   The enemy is said by all the officers to be fighting badly giving away constantly before our dismounted cavy   The enemys loss yesterday was very heavy many of their dead are lying in the woods & several old men with heads perfectly balds   The enemy threw away many arms in their retreat & seem to have been pretty much demoralized

H. PORTER
Lt Col a. D. C

Telegram received (at 5:05 P.M.), DLC-Robert T. Lincoln. On April 1, 1865,
President Abraham Lincoln telegraphed to USG. "Yours showing sheridans
sucess of today is just recd & highly appreciated—Having no great deal to do
here I am still sending the substance of your dispatches to the Secy of War"
Telegram received, DNA, RG 108, Letters Received. *O.R.*, I, xlvi, part 3, 394.
Printed as sent at 5:45 P.M. in Lincoln, *Works*, VIII, 379.

At 11:10 A.M., USG telegraphed to Bvt. Col. Theodore S. Bowers. "I understand the Sec. of War is at City Point. Present my respects to him and say we
would have had Petersburg before this but for the rain which unfortunately set
in the first night we were out." ALS (telegram sent), IHi; copies, DLC-USG,
V, 46, 75, 108; DNA, RG 108, Letters Sent. *O.R.*, I, xlvi, part 3, 393. On the
same day, Lincoln telegraphed to USG. "Yours to Col Bowers about the secretary
of war is shown to me. He is not here nor have I any notice that he is coming. I
presume the mistake comes of the fact that the secy of state was here. He started
back to Washington this morning I have your two despatches of this morning
and am anxious to hear from sheridan" Telegram received, DNA, RG 108,
Letters Received. *O.R.*, I, xlvi, part 3, 394. Lincoln, *Works*, VIII, 379.

To Maj. Gen. George G. Meade

Dabneys Mills April 1st *18645*, *o'clock, M.* [*11:30* A.M.]
MAJ GEN MEADE 2D CORPS HD QRS

Gen Barnard has been out examining the left of Ord's & right
of Humphreys lines and says that Ord is farthest in advance and
that he thinks Humphreys can be thrown up even with it without
difficulty—I am in hopes Humphrey will be able to carry the enemys line next to the creek when Ord's Battery is established—The
Engineer officer thinks this will be done by 2 P M

U. S. GRANT
Lt Gen.

Telegram received, Humphreys Papers, PHi; copies (2), Meade Papers, *ibid.*;
DLC-USG, V, 46, 75, 108; DNA, RG 108, Letters Sent. *O.R.*, I, xlvi, part 3, 395.
On April 1, 1865, USG twice telegraphed to Maj. Gen. George G. Meade,
the second time at 5:35 P.M. "Gen. Ord's Eng. Officer did not get the guns in his
new battery opposite Hays right to-day. They will be in however to-night and
Hays movement on this side the run can be made in the morning with the other
movement." ALS (telegram sent), CSmH; copies, DLC-USG, V, 46, 75, 108;
DNA, RG 108, Letters Sent. *O.R.*, I, xlvi, part 3, 396. "The Guns have not been
put into the Battery opposite Hays right but will be put in tonight you will
therefore order that Hays ~~to~~ attack be made simultaneously with the other Corps
on the north side in the morning" Telegram received, DNA, RG 107, Telegrams Collected (Unbound); copies, *ibid.*, RG 108, Letters Sent; DLC-USG, V,

46, 75, 108; (2) Meade Papers, PHi. *O.R.*, I, xlvi, part 3, 396. USG apparently sent two similar messages to Meade because he learned that the first had not been received.

To Maj. Gen. George G. Meade

Dabney's Mills Apl. 1st *1865* 5.40 p. m.

Maj. Gen. Meade,

McKenzie is now on White Oak road where the right branch from J. Boisseau's intersects it. Sheridan with his Cavalry and the 5th Corps are about assaulting at the Five Forks and feel no doubt of sucseeding in carrying it. I think Miles Division should be wheeled by the right immediately so as to take the position ~~Ayres~~ Griffin had yesterday and to prevent reinforcing against Sheridan. Miles will be in position where he can fight or resume his present position as may become necessary.

U. S. Grant
Lt. Gn

ALS (telegram sent), CSmH; telegram received (at 5:50 P.M.), DNA, RG 107, Telegrams Collected (Unbound). *O.R.*, I, xlvi, part 3, 396. On April 1, 1865, 6:00 P.M. (sent at 6:10 P.M.), Maj. Gen. George G. Meade telegraphed to USG. "Your despatch in regard to Humphreys to be sent to him with orders in case the enemy turn his left & rear which will now be in the air, he must return & I send you a telegram just received from him—Two of the brigades reported in front of Sheridan are in his front Wise & Huntons—Humphreys reports the enemy about 3.30 made a demonstration on him with about a brigade but retired before at[tacking.]" ALS (telegram sent), DNA, RG 107, Telegrams Collected (Unbound); copies, *ibid.*, RG 393, Army of the Potomac, Letters Sent; (2) Meade Papers, PHi. *O.R.*, I, xlvi, part 3, 396.

To Maj. Gen. George G. Meade

Apl. 1st *1865*

Maj. Gn. Meade,

Capt. Hudson has just returned from Sheridan. Sheridan has captured every thing before him. He has Stewarts and two other Brigades, a wagon train &c, and is pushing now. Humphries must

~~now~~ push now or everything will leave his front and be consentrated against Sheridan. Inform Parke of this and tell him to be on the watch to go in.

U. S. GRANT
Lt. Gn

ALS (telegram sent), OClWHi; telegram received (at 8:35 P.M.), DNA, RG 107, Telegrams Collected (Unbound). *O.R.*, I, xlvi, part 3, 397. On April 1, 1865, 8:40 P.M., Maj. Gen. George G. Meade telegraphed to USG. "Despatch giving Capt Hudsons report received—Genl Humphreys was ordered to push his left out to the White oak road, and at 7 p. m he reported Miles moving out to place his Division across that road—Mott has 1 and ½ brigades of his division extended in single rank keeping up connection with Miles—In pursuance of your instructions, orders have been sent to Humphreys to assault at 4. a m tomorrow the Crow House battery, & he was authorised at the same time to assault from any point near his center or left, where he deemed it practicable to do so   If successful he is to push up the Boydtown road—Your despatch says Humphreys is to push now   do you mean he is to attack tonight?—Orders were sent both to Wright & Parke to attack tomorrow at 4. a m—These orders were peremptory no discretion being left to the~~ir~~m except as to point of attack & formation of troops—Your last despatch says Parke should be notified to watch—Do you mean his orders are to be changed?—" ALS (telegram sent), DNA, RG 107, Telegrams Collected (Unbound); telegram received (erroneously marked as received at 8:40 A.M.), *ibid.*, RG 108, Letters Received. *O.R.*, I, xlvi, part 3, 397.

To Maj. Gen. George G. Meade

~~Apl. Apl.~~ Dabney Mill, Apl. 1st/65

MAJ. GN. MEADE,

~~I neglected~~ Gen. Wright and Parke should both be directed to feel for a chance to get through the enemy's lines at once and if they can get through should push on to-night. All our batteries might be opened at once without waiting for preparing assaulting columns.

Let the Corps commanders know the result on the left and that it is still being pushed. Several batteries were captured and over 4000 prisoners.

U. S. GRANT
Lt. Gn

ALS (telegram sent), OClWHi; telegram received (at 8:56 P.M.), DNA, RG 107, Telegrams Collected (Unbound). Printed as sent at 8:40 P.M. in *O.R.*, I, xlvi, part 3, 397.

To Maj. Gen. George G. Meade

Dabney Mills Apl. 1st *1865* [*9.05* P.M.]

MAJ. GN. MEADE,

My dispatch to which yours of 8.40 is a reply was not sufficiently distinct. One sent since though gives my wishes more distinctly. Col. Porter left Sheridan since 7 p. m. At that time Sheridan was pushing West from Five Forks driving the remninant of the enemy before him. ~~Merritt~~ McKenzie pushed North on the Ford road. I believe with a bombardment beforehand the enemy will abandon his works. If not pursued Sheridan may find everything against him. Humphrey can push every reserve he has to his left and if he finds the enemy breaking in his front then push the single line left directly to the front. If there is no break made by the enemy then Miles Division can be pushed directly down the White oak road. Parke & Wright can open with Artillery and feel with skirmishers and sharpshooters and if the enemy is giving way push directly after him. Ord has been instructed the same way.

~~Sheridan~~

U. S. GRANT
Lt. Gn

ALS (telegram sent), OClWHi; telegram received (at 9:24 P.M.), DNA, RG 107, Telegrams Collected (Unbound). *O.R.*, I, xlvi, part 3, 397–98.

On April 1, 1865, 9:25 P.M. and 9:40 P.M., Maj. Gen. George G. Meade telegraphed to USG. "I have sent you copy of order to Humphreys Wright & Parke Humphreys has gone to him but the line being down between here & Ords I have sent Wright & Parkes to be telegraphed from Humphreys Station by the R. Rd line to those officers.—I am truly delighted with the news from Sheridan—What part did Warren take I take it for granted he was engaged.—" "I have modified my orders to conform with your despatch of 9.25—viz—ordered Humphreys to push out at once from his left—if the enemy yields follow with every thing, if he can not make any impression move Miles at once down the White Oak road.—Parke & Wright to open with artillery, feel with skirmishers & sharp shooters & follow up any success.—Telegraphic communication now with all" ALS (telegrams sent), DNA, RG 107, Telegrams Collected (Unbound); telegrams received, *ibid.*, RG 108, Letters Received. Printed (with the first as received at 9:45 P.M.) in *O.R.*, I, xlvi, part 3, 398–99. The enclosure in the first is *ibid.*, p. 407. At 9:50 P.M., USG telegraphed to Meade. "Your despatch to Corps comdrs rec'd—I did not mean that attack should be made without forming assaulting columns but that batteries should open on receipt of orders they can feel out with skirmishrs & sharp shooters if the enemy is leaving &

attack in their own way" Telegram received (at 10:00 P.M.), DNA, RG 107, Telegrams Collected (Unbound); copies, *ibid.*, RG 108, Letters Sent; DLC-USG, V, 46, 75, 108; William C. Banning, Silver Spring, Md.; (2) Meade Papers, PHi. *O.R.*, I, xlvi, part 3, 399.

To Maj. Gen. George G. Meade

Dabney Mills Apl. 1st *1865* 9.30 P. m.

MAJ. GN. MEADE,

I would fix 12 o'clock to-night for starting Miles Division down White Oak road to join Sheridan if the enemy is not started by that time and the 2d Corps in pursuit. With Miles Division and what he already has I think Sheridan could hold all of Lee's Army that could be got against him until we could get up.

U. S. GRANT
Lt. Gn.

ALS (telegram sent), OClWHi; telegram received (at 10:05 P.M.), DNA, RG 107, Telegrams Collected (Unbound); Humphreys Papers, PHi. *O.R.*, I, xlvi, part 3, 398. On April 1, 1865, 10:10 P.M., Maj. Gen. George G. Meade telegraphed to USG. "Your despatch of 9.30 has been sent to Genl Humphreys—At what time would you like the Second Corps to follow Miles—to join Sheridan— For if this movement is made it will be necessary to remove the Hospitals & wagon trains to the other side of Hatchers Run" Telegram sent, DNA, RG 107, Telegrams Collected (Unbound); copies, *ibid.*, RG 393, Army of the Potomac, Letters Sent; (2) Meade Papers, PHi. *O.R.*, I, xlvi, part 3, 399.

At 10:05 P.M., Meade telegraphed to USG. "I forward you wrights despatch. The preparations are in accordance with my Original Order I approve of his plans & if authorized will give him the Order to carry them out. . . . 'Hd Qrs. 6th A C Apl 1st BVT MAJ GEN WEBB C O. S. Your despatch by Capt Worth is Recd—Everything will be ready—The Corps will go in solid & I am sure will make the "Fur Fly" the General place being understood will by the Various Commanders there will be no hesitation from want of Knowledge of what is Expected and if the Corps does half as well as I expect We will have broken ~~the~~ through the Rebel lines in fifteen minutes from the word go signed H G WRIGHT Maj Genl Comdg'" Telegram received, DNA, RG 108, Letters Received. Printed as sent at 11:05 P.M. (incorporating telegram of 11:00 P.M.) in *O.R.*, I, xlvi, part 3, 399, 423. On the same day, USG telegraphed to Meade. "I like the way Wright talks it argues success. I heartily approve" Telegram received (at 11:10 P.M.), DNA, RG 107, Telegrams Collected (Unbound); copies, *ibid.*, RG 108, Letters Sent; DLC-USG, V, 46, 75, 108; Meade Papers, PHi. *O.R.*, I, xlvi, part 3, 399. According to David Homer Bates, *Lincoln in the Telegraph Office* (New York, 1907), pp. 345–46, about this time USG sent a telegram to Meade, Maj. Gen. Philip H. Sheridan, and corps commanders: "Let the fur fly." Although Bates learned of this from a man who claimed to have seen the original in USG's handwriting, the absence of copies indicates that Maj. Gen. Horatio G. Wright's words were wrongly attributed to USG.

Also on April 1, USG telegraphed to Meade. "The 5th Corps was in and did splendidly. But Sheridan had to releive Warren on the field after the fight began." ALS (telegram sent), OClWHi; telegram received (at 11:10 P.M.), DNA, RG 107, Telegrams Collected (Unbound). *O.R.*, I, xlvi, part 3, 399. See *ibid.*, pp. 462, 501, 536.

To Maj. Gen. George G. Meade

April 1. 1865. 11.50 p. m.

Maj. Gen. Meade

I do not know that the battery in front of the Crow House is the best place for Humphries to attack. Wherever he thinks he stands the best chance for breaking through will satisfy all conditions. If he is satisfied ~~that~~ on feeling that the enemy has not weakened his lines then I do not care to have him attack but to send Miles' Division as previously directed and look out for his left with what remains. I do not want him to attack and send Miles off both.

Before starting Miles he had better wait now until say 2 a. m. until we have a further opportunity of seeing what the enemy is doing. If the enemy are now leaving it is not impossible that he may be going on the White oak road the very one Miles will have to move on.

U. S. Grant
Lieut. Gen

Copies, DLC-USG, V, 46, 75, 108; DNA, RG 108, Letters Sent. *O.R.*, I, xlvi, part 3, 400. On April 1, 1865, 11:35 P.M., Maj. Gen. George G. Meade telegraphed to USG. "Humphreys enquires whether he is to attack the Crow house battery now, or at 4. a m tomorrow as previously ordered or at all in case Miles fails to break through on the left—What do you say." ALS (telegram sent), DNA, RG 107, Telegrams Collected (Unbound); telegram received, *ibid.*, RG 108, Letters Received. *O.R.*, I, xlvi, part 3, 400.

At 11:45 P.M., Meade telegraphed to USG. "Genl Humphreys enquires if Miles is to move down the White Oak road promptly at ~~do~~ 12 Oclock without reference to whether he has been able by that time to attack the Enemy I have informed him the order was predicated on the supposition that that Genl. Miles would by that time have made his attack & settled this question—& I consider an hour or two of less importance—than settling the question of the Enemys strength in Miles front—Am I right or must Miles move down promptly at 12— in case by that time he has not attack—Please answer as soon as possible—" Telegram sent, DNA, RG 107, Telegrams Collected (Unbound); telegram received, *ibid.*, RG 108, Letters Received. *O.R.*, I, xlvi, part 3, 400. On April 2, 12:15 A.M. and 12:30 A.M., USG telegraphed to Meade. "Has Miles possession of the White Oak road? If he has let him move down it at once and join Sheridan as rapidly as possible without awaiting anything. ~~This ignores my dispatch saying he may wait until 2 A. m before starting~~" ALS (telegram sent), OClWHi; telegram received (at 12:17 A.M.), DNA, RG 94, War Records Office, Army of the Potomac; Humphreys Papers, PHi. *O.R.*, I, xlvi, part 3, 451. "If Miles has not got possession of White Oak so as to follow up he might move by J Boisseau & from there to Five Forks" Telegram received, Humphreys Papers, PHi; copies, DLC-USG, V, 46, 75, 108; DNA, RG 108, Letters Sent; *ibid.*, RG 393, 2nd Army Corps, Telegrams Received; (2) Meade Papers, PHi; CtY.

To Maj. Gen. Edward O. C. Ord

Apl. 1st 1865 [8:55 P.M.]

MAJ. GN. ORD, HUMPHREY STATION.

I have just heard from Sheridan. He has Captured three Brigades of the enemy and is pushing him still. Everything the enemy has will probably be pushed against him. Get your men up and feel the enemy and push him if he shows signs of giving way.

U. S. GRANT
Lt. Gen.

ALS (telegram sent), Mr. and Mrs. Philip D. Sang, River Forest, Ill.; telegram received, Ord Papers, CU-B. *O.R.*, I, xlvi, part 3, 431. On April 1, 1865, 10:40 P.M., Maj. Gen. Edward O. C. Ord telegraphed to USG. "despatch recieved announcing Sheridans victory have ordered my men to mass—and will obey the order—" ALS (telegram sent), DNA, RG 94, War Records Office, Dept. of Va. and N. C.; telegram received, *ibid.*, RG 108, Letters Received. *O.R.*, I, xlvi, part 3, 431.

Earlier on April 1, Ord telegraphed to USG. "The firing you heard this a m was an attack of the enemy on my new line having notified my Commad to be ready the Rebels were handsomely repulsed—60 prisoners taken & a number Killed Rebels in front of our lines on Foster front—Our pickets give way & we lost eight 8 men Turner men behaved handsomely lost none our picket is reishtablished" Telegram received, DNA, RG 108, Letters Received. *O.R.*, I, xlvi, part 3, 429–30. On the same day, Ord telegraphed to Bvt. Col. Theodore S. Bowers. "Nothing new since the rebel attempt this morning to reestablish their picket line which we had driven in to their works the attempt handsomely repulsed & we Captured sixty one (61) prisoners Killed & wounded a number and lost but four (4) men their prisoners state that Gen Heth Commanding the

Corps was present at work there from One to till 4 a m arranging to recover this
line which he looked upon as of the utmost importance   we are errecting batteries with a view to further advance   my loss so far about 240 Killed & wounded
gain so far about 300 prisoners not counting rebel Killed & wounded"   Telegram
received (at 3:15 P.M.), DLC-Robert T. Lincoln. Printed as sent at 3:00 P.M.
in *O.R.*, I, xlvi, part 3, 430.

To Maj. Gen. Edward O. C. Ord

Dabney Mills, Apl. 1st/65

MAJ. GN. ORD.

Your dispatch of this evening received. You have received my
dispatch announcing Sheridans Victory since writing yours. If it
is impracticable for you to get through in your front I do not want
you to try it. But you can in that case draw out of your lines more
men as a reserve and hold them to throw in where some one else
may penetrate. My opinion is you will have no enemy confronting
you in the morning. You may find them leaving now. Understand:
I do not wish you to fight your way over difficult barriers, against
defended lines. I want you to see though if the enemy is leaving
and if so follow him up.

U. S. GRANT
Lt. Gn

ALS, Scheide Library, Princeton, N. J.; (incomplete) Ord Papers, CU-B. *O.R.*,
I, xlvi, part 3, 431. On April 1, 1865, Maj. Gen. Edward O. C. Ord wrote to
USG. "I have made arrangements to have an artillery fire and sharp shooters do
their best to keep reinforcements from the work south of Hatchers run   I have
ordered the Engineers to push the Battery that is to counterbatter those of the
enemy covering the approach to their work which I spoke of as appearing feasable
—since then I learn from Genl Foster on whose front it is that deserters from
the enemy have to cross an entervening bay gall on logs—which I presume is
what delayed Genl Heths party last night—I shall mass a column any how in
front of the place—Send out several scouts to reconnoitre the bay gall or morass
—and if it is found practicable shall try it—I am very sorry General that I find it
necessary to report these obstacles—and wish very much you would let some one
else take this line and put my Command out in the open country—I have no
doubt my officers and men can give a good account of the Enemies works as any
one but—I think they could give a better account of the enemy in an open and
I would not be compelled to report so many impracticable ~~approach~~ lines of rebel
works"   ALS, DNA, RG 108, Letters Received. *O.R.*, I, xlvi, part 3, 430.
    At 10:30 P.M., USG telegraphed to Ord. "Gen. Wright speaks with great

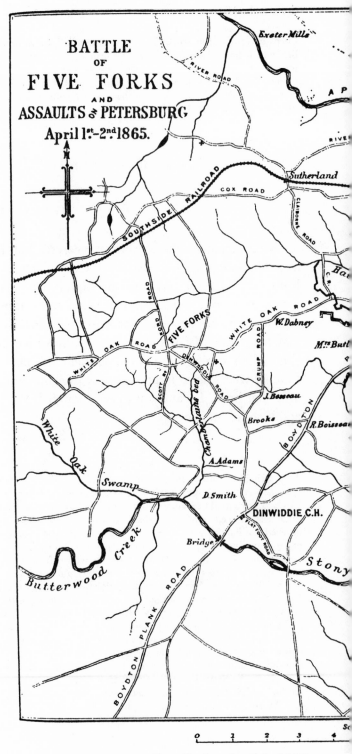

The Battle of Five Forks, April 1, 1865

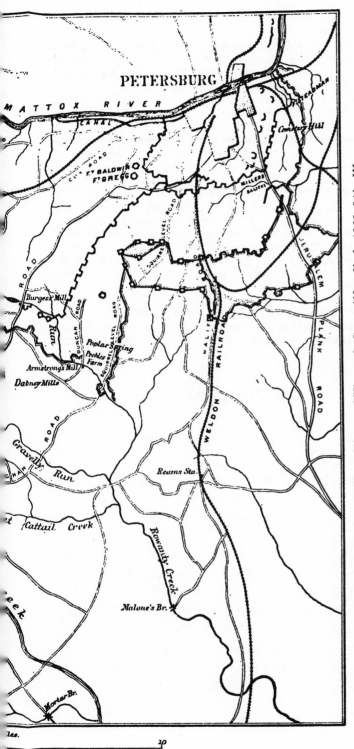

PETERSBURG

MATTOX RIVER

CANAL

CITY ROAD

FT BALDWIN

FT GREGG

Cemetery Hill

STEADMAN

MILLERS
SALIENT

SQUIRREL LEVEL ROAD

JERUSALEM

Burgess Mill

Run

DUNCAN ROAD

Poplar Spring

Peebles
Farm

SQUIRREL LEVEL ROAD

HALIF

WELDON RAILROAD

PLANK ROAD

Armstrongs Mill

Dabney Mills

ROAD

Gravelly Run

MA N

Reams Sta.

Cattail Creek

Rowanty Creek

eek

Malone's Br.

Mortar Br.

les.   10

From Adam Badeau, Military History of Ulysses S. Grant (*New York, 1868–81*), III

confidence of his ability to go through the enemy's lines. I think as you have such difficult ground to get over your reserves had better be ~~well~~ pushed well over to the right so that they can help him or go in with you as may be required." ALS (telegram sent), OClWHi; telegram received, Ord Papers, CU-B. *O.R.*, I, xlvi, part 3, 431. At 11:00 P.M., Ord telegraphed to USG. "Your despatch to following Wright is Recd I think if the enemy concentrates on Sheridan I am near enough to be of service to him & if Wright gets in he is strong enough to stay there without my help I agree with you that it is probable the enemy has given up the line in our immediate front & I hope to be able to send you the first reliable information on the subject as my scouts & pickets are feeling his main line now my men are massing on my left a mile & half from your HdQrs had I not better hold them there subject to your orders" Telegram received, DNA, RG 108, Letters Received. *O.R.*, I, xlvi, part 3, 431–32. At 11:20 P.M., USG telegraphed to Ord. "Your despatch of 11 P M recd. You can follow the course proposed in your despatch of that hour, has the enemy returned the fire along our line with any vigor?" Telegram received, Ord Papers, CU-B; copies, DLC-USG, V, 46, 75, 108; DNA, RG 108, Letters Sent. *O.R.*, I, xlvi, part 3, 432. At 11:40 [P.M.], Ord telegraphed to USG. "Dispatch recd of 11 20 the Enemy returned fire of musketry on my front but rarely this P m & it seems to have ceased tonight this the wind from the north I cannot tell you are only five hundred yards from Turners right & can hear any firing better. the cessation of firing is not a reliable sign & so I have sent out scouts who will soon report" Telegram received, DNA, RG 108, Letters Received. *O.R.*, I, xlvi, part 3, 432.

To Maj. Gen. Philip H. Sheridan

Dabney Mills Apl. 1st/65

Maj. Gn Sheridan.

~~Griffins~~ Miles' Div. has been ordered to swing round on to the White Oak road. It was so late however before I learned of Mc-Kenzie's position that I do not think he will reach there before 9 this evening.

An attack is ordered for 4 a. m. in the morning at three points on the Petersburg front, one by the 9th Corps between the Appomattox and Jerusalem P. road; one West of the Weldon road and the third between that and Hatcher's run. From your isolated position I can give you no specific directions but leave you to act according to sircumstances. I would like you however to get something down to the S. S. road even if they do not tear up a mile of it.

U. S. Grant
Lt. Gn

ALS, Scheide Library, Princeton, N. J. *O.R.*, I, xlvi, part 3, 434.

On April 2, 1865, Maj. Gen. Philip H. Sheridan, Five Forks, wrote to USG. "I have the honor to make the following report of our operations of yesterday: At daylight yesterday morning, I moved out with all the Cavalry against the enemy's infantry in front of Dinwiddie Court House. On our advance, they fell back rapidly in line of battle, this sudden withdrawal was, in part, due to the advance of Ayer's Division of the Fifth Army Corps from the Boydton Plank road. General Ayers was unable to get into the enemy's rear in time to attack as expected, owing to the darkness and bad roads, but his movements was sufficient to turn the enemy from the Five Fork's road, and force him to cross Chamberlain's bed, Custer's and Devin's Divisions of Cavalry, under General Merritt followed up the enemy with a gallantry that I have never seen exceeded, charging his their infantry and driving them from two lines of works, capturing prisoners from Pickett's and Johnson's Divisions of infantry, as well as from the enemy's Cavalry. The enemy made a last stand at the Five Forks, behind a strong line of earth works along the White Oak Road. After forcing him to this position I directed General Merritt to push his dismounted Cavalry well up to the enemy's works, drive in his skirmishers, and make him believe that our main attack would be made on his right flank. In the meanwhile I had ordered up the Fifth Corps to within a mile of the Five Forks, on the Dinwiddie Court House Road, for the purpose of attacking the enemy's left flank and rear, Between 4 and 5 o'clock, in accordance with these dispositions, the Fifth Corps moved out across the White Oak Road, swinging round to the left as they advanced, and struck the enemy in flank and rear. Simultaneously with this attack the Cavalry assaulted the enemy's works in front, in compliance with my orders to General Merritt, and the result of this combined movement was one the complete rout of the enemy, with the loss of five pieces of artillery and caissons, a number of wagons and ambulances, and I think at least Five thousand prisoners, and several battle flags. Gregg's brigade of General Crook's Division operated upon our left and rear, skirmishing with the enemy's Cavalry, the two other brigades of this Division remained in the vicinity of Dinwiddie Court House, guarding the trains and the crossings of Stoney Creek. I ordered General McKenzie's Division of Cavalry which reported to me in the morning, to the White Oak Road, by the way of J Boisseau's house with instructions to advance in the direction of Five Forks. When the Fifth Corps reached the White Oak Road, General McKenzie joined its right, and in the attack swept round over the Ford Church Road, cutting off this avenue of retreat to the enemy. After the enemy broke, our cavalry pursued them for six miles down the White Oak Road." Copies (2), DLC-Philip H. Sheridan. *O.R.*, I, xlvi, part 1, 1100–1.

To Maj. Gen. Godfrey Weitzel

Dabney's Mill, Apl. 1st/65 [*7:00* P.M.]

MAJ. GEN. WEITZEL, A. JAMES,

The only information we have of the presence of Mahones Div. south of the Appomattox is from prisoners who say they understand it is in reserve on this side. I do not think it has moved unless it was this afternoon. Prisoners just in say they understand 12,000 men are coming from North side.

U. S. GRANT

Lt. Gn

ALS (telegram sent), Kohns Collection, NN; telegrams received (2), DNA, RG 94, War Records Office, Miscellaneous War Records. *O.R.*, I, xlvi, part 3, 438.

On April 1, 1865, 9:30 A.M. and 2:50 P.M., Maj. Gen. Godfrey Weitzel telegraphed to USG. "Genl Hartsuff's reports no discernible change in his front. I have tried every thing here to ascertain any but have found none or little. Is it certain that Mahone's division is in your front. You say that it is so reported." ALS (telegram sent), DNA, RG 107, Telegrams Collected (Unbound); telegram received, *ibid*. *O.R.*, I, xlvi, part 3, 437. "Hartsuff has captured a man from Mahone's Div & has carefully observed his front. He says he is morally certain that Mahone's Div has not moved. I have directed him to open all his artillery on the enemy if this developes anything to advance & feel the position   I wish I had a little brigade to send him. There is no change on my front" Telegram received, DNA, RG 107, Telegrams Collected (Unbound); copy, *ibid.*, RG 393, 25th Army Corps, Telegrams Sent. *O.R.*, I, xlvi, part 3, 438. At 4:25 P.M., USG telegraphed to Maj. Gens. George G. Meade, Edward O. C. Ord, John G. Parke, and Horatio G. Wright. "Gen Weitzel reports that Hortsuff has captured a man from Mahones div. Hortsuffs says that the is morally certain that Mahone has not moved" Telegram received, Ord Papers, CU-B; DNA, RG 94, War Records Office, Army of the Potomac; copies, *ibid.*, RG 108, Letters Sent; DLC-USG, V, 46, 75, 108; (2) Meade Papers, PHi. *O.R.*, I, xlvi, part 3, 395.

At 7:15 P.M., Weitzel telegraphed to USG. "All the regular trains between Richmond & Petersburg Ran today excepting the 3 & 5 oclock trains." Telegram received, DNA, RG 107, Telegrams Collected (Unbound); *ibid.*, RG 108, Letters Received; copy, *ibid.*, RG 393, 25th Army Corps, Telegrams Sent. *O.R.*, I, xlvi, part 3, 438.

At 9:40 P.M., Weitzel telegraphed to Bvt. Col. Theodore S. Bowers. "Genl Grant having telegraphed this morning early that Mahones Division was reported on his front, I ordered a demonstration on Bermuda Front and found it still there. There is not the least discernable change as yet here. Something may turn up yet" Copy, DNA, RG 393, 25th Army Corps, Telegrams Sent.

To Maj. Gen. Godfrey Weitzel

Dabney Mills Apl. 1st/65 9.50 p. m.

MAJ. GN. WEITZEL. A. JAMES,

I have directed Col. Bowers to send you the report of Sheridans sucsess this afternoon. I have since ordered an attack to-night and pursuit. Communicate the result to your troops. Be ready also to push any wavering that may be shown in your front.

U. S. GRANT
Lt. Gn

ALS (telegram sent), deCoppet Collection, NjP; telegrams received (2), DNA, RG 94, War Records Office, Miscellaneous War Records; *ibid.*, RG 107, Telegrams Collected (Unbound). *O.R.*, I, xlvi, part 3, 438. On April 1, 1865, Bvt. Col. Theodore S. Bowers telegraphed to Maj. Gen. Godfrey Weitzel. "Sheridan & Warren pushed the enemy sharply today   Devins Div. of cavalry charged and carried the barricade at the five forks   Everything is reported to be progressing favorably   Have no particulars yet   what news have you"   Telegram received, DNA, RG 393, 25th Army Corps, Telegrams Received; copy, *ibid.*, RG 94, War Records Office, Dept. of Va. and N. C.

To Bvt. Col. Theodore S. Bowers

Apl. 1st *1865* [*7:45* P.M.]

COL. T. S. BOWERS
CITY POINT

Sheridan with his Cavalry and the 5th Corps has evidently had a big fight this evening. The distance he is off is so great however that I shall not probably be able to report the result for an hour or two. Except that there is nothing to report.

U. S. GRANT
Lt. Gn

ALS (telegram sent), OClWHi; telegram received (at 11:00 P.M.), DNA, RG 107, Telegrams Collected (Unbound). *O.R.*, I, xlvi, part 3, 394.

To Bvt. Col. Theodore S. Bowers

Dabney Mills Apl. 1st *1865* [*9:30* P.M.]

COL. T. S. BOWERS, CITY POINT

I have just heard from Sheridan. He has carried every thing before him. Capt. Hudson has just returnd from him and reports that he has captured three Brigade of Infantry and a train of wagons and is now pushing up his sucsess. I have ordered every thing else to

advance and prevent a consentration ~~of~~ of the enemy against Sheridan, ~~I hope to finish up the~~ ~~The whole job South of the Appomattox will be finished up by 10 a. m to-morrow,~~ Several batteries
were captured. The prisoners captured will amount to several
thousands,

U. S. GRANT
Lt, Gn

ALS (telegram sent), OClWHi; copies, DLC-USG, V, 46, 75, 108; DNA, RG
108, Letters Sent. *O.R.*, I, xlvi, part 3, 394. On April 2, 1865, 1:30 A.M., Bvt.
Col. Theodore S. Bowers telegraphed to Secretary of War Edwin M. Stanton. "A
dispatch from Genl Grant states that Gen Sheridan Commanding cavalry and
Infantry has carried everything before him He captured three Brigades of Infantry, a wagon train and several batteries of Artillery—The prisoners captured
will amount to several thousand. I will forward you the dispatches in cipher in
the morning with such other information as may come in—" Telegrams received (2—at 5:30 A.M.), DNA, RG 107, Telegrams Collected (Unbound);
copies (marked as sent at 1:00 P.M.), *ibid.*, RG 108, Letters Sent; DLC-USG,
V, 46, 75, 108.
    On April 1, Lt. Col. Ely S. Parker telegraphed to Bowers. "As to past events
you are posted Orders have been issued for all the Corps to attack at once or as
soon as the assaulting columns can be formed. All this will be preceded by an
artillery attack. Wright feels confident that 15 minutes from the time he starts
he will have the enemys works and he says he can and will hold them. Great
enthusiasm and confidence of success seem to exist among the officers and men.
Mile's Division goes to Sheridan at 12- tonight." Telegram received (on April 2,
12:00 A.M.), DNA, RG 107, Telegrams Collected (Unbound). *O.R.*, I, xlvi,
part 3, 394.

To Julia Dent Grant

———

Dabney's Mill Apl. 1st *1865*

DEAR JULIA,
    Another day has passed without anything decisive as to the
final result so far as I have heard. This morning the enemy attacked
Gn. Ord's picket line but a short distance from where I now write
but got repulsed with a loss of about 60 prisoners left in our hands
besides a number killed and wounded. We lost but four captured.
Gn. Sheridan, far to the left, about ten miles off, has been driving
the enemy all day and has killed and wounded a great number besides capturing about 200 prisoners,   Since I last heard from him

he has had quite a battle the result of which I have not heard. I am feeling very well and full of confidence. Love and kisses for you & Jess.

Ulys,

ALS, DLC-USG.

To Maj. Gen. George G. Meade

12.50 a. m. Apl. 2d/65

Maj. Gn. Meade,

The attack on Crow House battery may be suspended altogether. It was ordered at 4 a. m, in conjunction with other attacks that had then been orderd but which have been ordered earlyer and under a state of facts that were not then known. If they are successful there will be no necessity for the attack   if they are not it can not be told that we will be in a condition to make it.

U. S. Grant
Lt. Gn

ALS (telegram sent), OClWHi; telegram received (marked as received on April 1, 1865), DNA, RG 107, Telegrams Collected (Unbound). *O.R.*, I, xlvi, part 3, 451. On April 2, 12:32 a.m., Maj. Gen. George G. Meade telegraphed to USG. "What say you to my despatch about the attack on the Crow House By Hays on right of 2nd Corps   Shall it be at 4 a. [m.] or not." Telegram sent, DNA, RG 107, Telegrams Collected (Unbound); telegram received, *ibid.*, RG 108, Letters Received. *O.R.*, I, xlvi, part 3, 451.

At 12:34 [a.m.], Meade telegraphed to USG transmitting a telegram from Maj. Gen. Andrew A. Humphreys, April 1, 11:55 p.m., to Meade. "I have recd no report from Gen Miles since I sent him your first orders to attack   I hear firing now on his front by fitz & Starts   he must have advanced   the Officer who took him the last order has not returned   he was directed to wait & bring back a report of the Condition of things   their artillery has opened on miles   they Cheer from time to time in their works but the Cheering is not Extensive" Telegram received, DNA, RG 108, Letters Received; copy (misdated April 2), CtY. *O.R.*, I, xlvi, part 3, 409. At 12:55 a.m., Meade telegraphed to USG transmitting a telegram of 12:35 a.m. from Humphreys to Meade. "Miles has possession of the White Oak road   I have ordered him to move out it at once & join Gen Sheridan as rapidly as possible" Telegram sent, DNA, RG 107, Telegrams Collected (Unbound); telegram received, *ibid.*, RG 108, Letters Received. *O.R.*, I, xlvi, part 3, 462–63.

At 1:00 a.m., Meade telegraphed to USG. "I doubt very much any of the corps comdrs making their attacks before 4 a. m. since their columns are not yet formed I have ordered Humphreys to attack the Crow Battery at 4 a. m. and he will do so & probably in conjunction with the other attacks unless the order shall be countermanded." Telegram sent, DNA, RG 107, Telegrams Collected (Unbound); telegram received, *ibid.*, RG 108, Letters Received. *O.R.*, I, xlvi, part 3, 451–52. At 1:25 A.M., USG telegraphed to Meade. "Direct the attack of the Corps Comdrs to be made promptly at 4 oclock this A M as first ordered if they have not already been made. As one div of the 2d Corps is now ordered away Gen Humphreys need not attack at the Crow house but be in readiness to take advantage of any weakening of the enemy in his front" Telegram received, DNA, RG 107, Telegrams Collected (Unbound); (marked as received at 12:50 A.M.) Humphreys Papers, PHi; copies, DLC-USG, V, 46, 75, 108; DNA, RG 108, Letters Sent; (marked as received at 12:50 A.M.) *ibid.*, RG 393, 2nd Army Corps, Letters Received; Meade Papers, PHi; CtY. *O.R.*, I, xlvi, part 3, 452. At 2:10 A.M., Meade telegraphed to USG. "The following dispatches just recd from 9th Corps—Parke is ordered to attack at 4. a. m." Telegram sent, DNA, RG 107, Telegrams Collected (Unbound); telegram received, *ibid.*, RG 108, Letters Received. *O.R.*, I, xlvi, part 3, 452. The enclosures are *ibid.*, pp. 463, 482, 483.

On the same day, Meade twice telegraphed to USG, first at 4:05 A.M. "Genl Parke telegraphs that reports from 1s & 2n Div of 9n Corps indicate the enemys line as far as developed consists only of skirmishers & that a heavy Explosion occurred a little after 3 a m in heart of Petersburg Genl Park further states that he is ascertaining whether the Enemy have retired I have communicated this information to Genls Ord & Wright & Directed Genl Parke & Wright to push forward strong lines of skirmishers & use every effort to ascertain the condition of the enemy" Telegram received, DNA, RG 108, Letters Received. *O.R.*, I, xlvi, part 3, 452. "The Sixth Corps has carried the enemy's works. Parke is ordered to send up his reserves if he is not now using them." *Ibid.*, p. 453. At 5:30 A.M., Bvt. Maj. Gen. Alexander S. Webb telegraphed to USG. "Genl Wright has carried the enemy's works. Gen. Parke has been ordered to support Wright with his reserves if he is not now using them." Copies, DNA, RG 393, Army of the Potomac, Letters Sent; (2) Meade Papers, PHi; CtY. *O.R.*, I, xlvi, part 3, 453. Also, Meade telegraphed to USG transmitting a signal of 6:00 A.M. from Maj. Gen. Horatio G. Wright to Webb. "We have captured two guns & three Caissons Three flags & Several hundred prisoners. Have also cut Telegraph wire on Boydton Road this only for one Division wheatons" Telegram received, DNA, RG 108, Letters Received. *O.R.*, I, xlvi, part 3, 453. At 6:20 [A.M.], Meade telegraphed to USG. "forwarded. Parke is to push on if possible. . . . 9th A C 5.55 a m MAJ GEN WEBB We have carried lines opposite Fort Sedgwick but the enemy still hold works in the Rear JNO G PARKE Maj Gen" Telegram received, DNA, RG 108, Letters Received. *O.R.*, I, xlvi, part 3, 453.

At 6:40 A.M., USG telegraphed to Meade. "Is Humphreys engaged yet" Telegram received, DNA, RG 107, Telegrams Collected (Unbound); copies, *ibid.*, RG 108, Letters Sent; DLC-USG, V, 46, 75, 108; CtY. *O.R.*, I, xlvi, part 3, 453. At 6:45 A.M., Meade telegraphed to USG. "Humphreys attack was suspended last night but as soon as I heard of our success on the right I ordered him to push out & to do all he could. I presume his skirmishers are engaged by this time" Telegram sent (misdated April 1), DNA, RG 107, Telegrams Collected (Unbound); telegram received (at 6:45 A.M.), *ibid.*, RG 108, Letters Received. *O.R.*, I, xlvi, part 3, 454.

To Maj. Gen. George G. Meade

By Telegraph from Grants 6 45 P. M. [A.M.]
Dated Apl 2 *1864.* [*1865*]

To GENL MEADE

Wright can put in everything he has except the garrisons of enclosed works   Ord is pushing by the shortest road to help Wright. I heard from Sheridan at 12 30 this a m   He intended to start at daybreak & sweep the White Oak road & all north of it down to Petersburg

U S GRANT
Lt Genl

Telegram received, DNA, RG 94, War Records Office, Army of the Potomac; (addressed to Maj. Gen. Andrew A. Humphreys) Humphreys Papers, PHi; copies, Meade Papers, *ibid.*; DLC-USG, V, 46, 75, 108; DNA, RG 108, Letters Sent; *ibid.*, RG 393, 2nd Army Corps, Telegrams Received; CtY. *O.R.*, I, xlvi, part 3, 454. On April 2, 1865, 6:55 A.M., Maj. Gen. George G. Meade telegraphed to USG. "I presume that the best way for Ord to assist Wright will be for him to make a vigorous attack on his front if there is any hope of his carrying them—I forward Parke's last despatch." Telegram sent, DNA, RG 107, Telegrams Collected (Unbound); copies, *ibid.*, RG 393, Army of the Potomac, Letters Sent; (2) Meade Papers, PHi. *O.R.*, I, xlvi, part 3, 454.

To Maj. Gen. George G. Meade

Apl. 2d 1865, 7.10 a. m.

MAJ. GEN. MEADE,

There is more necessity for care on the Ppart of Parke than either of the others of our Corps Commanders. As I understand it he is attacking the main line of works around Petersburg whilst the others are only attacking an outter line which the enemy might give up without giving up Petersburg. Parke should either advance rapidly or cover his men and hold all he gets.

U. S. GRANT
Lt. Gn.

ALS (telegram sent), OClWHi; telegram received, DNA, RG 107, Telegrams Collected (Unbound). *O.R.*, I, xlvi, part 3, 454. On April 2, 1865, 6:57 A.M.,

Maj. Gen. George G. Meade telegraphed to USG. "Genl Park reports the capture of two redans—two forts & twelve guns opposite fort Sedgwick—but the Enemy have a line in the rear—" Telegram sent, DNA, RG 107, Telegrams Collected (Unbound); telegram received, *ibid.*, RG 108, Letters Received. *O.R.*, I, xlvi, part 3, 454.

At 7:50 A.M. and 8:00 A.M., Meade telegraphed to USG. "The following is Just received from Humphreys who is ordered to do all he can to help Sheridans movement— . . . 2nd A. C. 7.40 a. m 2nd GEN WEBB Gen McAllister Captured the picket line of the enemy & still holds it taking (120) prisoners from Scales and McCreas Brigades—Genl Mott reports that the prisoners state that they came on pocket at 4 oclock this morning at which time their brigades were ordered to moved to their right the prisoners will soon be here & I will examine & report A. A. HUMPHREYS Maj Gen" Telegram received, DNA, RG 108, Letters Received. *O.R.*, I, xlvi, part 3, 465. "Orders have been sent to Parke to Hold all he is got & to proceed cautiously in advancing—Wright if Ord can not penetrate should not go too far forward until sheridan has broken through or humphreys or Ord if he does he will be Isolate[d.] I have not sent him any orders relyin[g] on his Judgement & the fact of his Knowin[g] the operations on his right & left—" Telegram received, DNA, RG 108, Letters Received; copies, *ibid.*, RG 393, Army of the Potomac, Letters Sent; (2) Meade Papers, PHi. Printed as received at 8:05 A.M. in *O.R.*, I, xlvi, part 3, 455. On the same day, Meade twice telegraphed to USG, first at 8:10 A.M. "Forwarded . . . Tower 7.15 a. m. GEN WEBB—Gen Seymour third div reports eight (8) guns captured this is in addition to those already reported the 40th Vols is now tearing up the S. S. R R—H. G. WRIGHT Maj Gen" "This report which I hope will be confirmed is from A A G at Parkes HdQrs . . . 9th A C 6 05 CAPT BARROWS An officer just from fort Rice reports that the enemy's line of works in front of the 2d Div have been Captured & are held. Have heard nothing from Gen Parke as staff Gen Potter is mortally wounded JNO C YOUNGMAN A A G" Telegrams received, DNA, RG 108, Letters Received. Both printed as sent at 8:10 A.M. in *O.R.*, I, xlvi, part 3, 455.

At 8:35 A.M., USG telegraphed to Meade. "We have the forts next to Hatcher's run on both sides. I think there will be no difficulty in Humphries Marching forward now towards Petersburg or towards the retreating foe." ALS (telegram sent), OClWHi; telegram received (at 8:42 A.M.), DNA, RG 107, Telegrams Collected (Unbound). *O.R.*, I, xlvi, part 3, 455. At 8:45 A.M., Meade drafted his response at the foot of the telegram received. "Humphreys has already been ordered forward I being aware of the capture of the Forts. He will try & connect with Wright" ADfS, DNA, RG 107, Telegrams Collected (Unbound). *O.R.*, I, xlvi, part 3, 456.

At 8:35 A.M., Meade telegraphed to USG. "Forwarded . . . (From) 2n A C 8.30 GENL WEBB Genl Hays has just reported to me that he has taken the redoubt of the enemy near the Row House he is pushing forward his division. has captured a number of men Does not say how many nor does he say whether the enemy occupies the works on the other side of the run I expect more information soon A A HUMPHREYS MaG" Telegram received, DNA, RG 108, Letters Received. Printed as sent at 8:40 A.M. in *O.R.*, I, xlvi, part 3, 465.

At 9:00 A.M., Meade telegraphed to USG. "the Enemy has abandoned Humpherys front. I am pushing Humpherys troops up the Boydton plank road & Claiborne road to try to connect on the right & left Miles has returned here—

if we hear firing on left from sheridan I shall attack there with Humpherys corps the em. is moving apparently to his right & may be confronting Sheridans" Telegram received, DNA, RG 108, Letters Received; copies (marked as sent at 9:30 A.M.), *ibid.*, RG 393, Army of the Potomac, Letters Sent; (2) Meade Papers, PHi. Printed as sent at 9:30 A.M. in *O.R.*, I, xlvi, part 3, 456. The earlier time appears preferable in view of a statement sent at 9:15 A.M. that USG and Meade had gone to the front together. *Ibid.*

At 10:30 A.M., Meade telegraphed to USG. "Gen. Humphreys reports Miles moving up the Cox road and the enemy flying before him. The 5th I understand, is following Miles. I have sent an officer to Sheridan suggesting his force should move by the Cox and river roads, and, if he pushes the cavalry rapidly, he ought to cut some of them off, if they are going across the Appomattox, as I suppose. I have ordered up the pontoon train in Wright's rear. Humphreys has reassumed the command of Miles. 5th Corps left with Sheridan till your orders return it." Telegram sent, DNA, RG 94, War Records Office, Army of the Potomac; telegram received, *ibid.*, RG 108, Letters Received; William C. Banning, Silver Spring, Md. *O.R.*, I, xlvi, part 3, 456.

On the same day, Lt. Col. Ely S. Parker telegraphed to Meade. "The following received . . . BRIG: GEN'L RAWLING'S Genl Sheridan desired me to inform you that the 2nd Corps is marching up the Boydton Road towards Petersburg, and that Lee and his forces are moving this direction We have come up with their rear guard about 2 miles on the Clairborne Road from their works in front of that Road probably; but few stragglers. S HUDSON A D. C." Copies (2), Meade Papers, PHi; (2—incomplete) DLC-Philip H. Sheridan. *O.R.*, I, xlvi, part 3, 457.

Also on April 2, 10:00 P.M., Maj. Gen. John G. Parke telegraphed to Lt. Col. Orville E. Babcock. "I have just come from Potter's—He is doing well— And in good spirits. Shot through the body—low—down—probably escaped the intestines, but passed through the bladder. He is at the Jones House—And well cared for—I ~~presume~~ We have lost Gowen. Killed instantly at the head of his Reg't. All our people did splendidly today—" ALS (telegram sent), DNA, RG 107, Telegrams Collected (Unbound). *O.R.*, I, xlvi, part 3, 486.

To Maj. Gen. George G. Meade

April 2. 1865. 7.40 P. M.

MAJ. GEN. MEADE

I would send Humphreys no orders further than to report to Sheridan and return or cross the Appomattox as he wishes—

I have just heard from Sheridan. Lee himself escaped up the river. Sheridan thinks that all of the rebel army that was outside the works immediately around the City are trying to make their escape out that way. He is making dispositions to cut them off if he can.

The 5th Corps is now with or near the 2d and should not be moved in this direction to night. I think there is nothing in Petersburg except the remnant of Gordon's Corps and a few men brought from the North side to day.

I believe it will pay to commence a furious bombardment at 5 A M. to be followed by an assault at 6. only if there is good reason for believing the enemy is leaving.

Unless Lee reaches the Danville road tonight he will not be able to reach his army to command here.

U. S. GRANT

Lieut. Gen

Copies, DLC-USG, V, 46, 75, 108; DNA, RG 108, Letters Sent; (2) Meade Papers, PHi; CtY. *O.R.*, I, xlvi, part 3, 458. On April 2, 1865, 7:15 P.M., Maj. Gen. George G. Meade wrote to USG. "An officer who accompanied Genl. Humphreys has returned Humphreys affected a junction with Miles, but the enemy had withdrawn—H. was in pursuit—Miles had a very brisk engagement this afternoon was severely pressed and at one time a part of his command gave way—He however stubbornly maintained his position till Humphreys arrived— Both Divisions must be greatly fatigued from constant marching & Miles with fighting I expect therefore that the enemy will get away—Nothing was heard of Sheridan when this officer returned—What orders shall be sent Humphreys?" ALS, DNA, RG 108, Letters Received. *O.R.*, I, xlvi, part 3, 457.

At 8:00 P.M., Meade telegraphed to USG. "I understand the enemy have had a ponton bridge at Exeter Mills about 4 miles north of Sutherland station and they were fighting this afternoon to get their trains off on that road—It is a pity Sheridan did not move as I suggested on the Cox & River roads for had he have done so these fellows would have been cut off—Had I not better send our ponton train to Humphreys at Sutherland station & authorise his advancing by the Exeter Mills & crossing the river, if in his judgement or from the information he obtains he thinks he can do any thing.—G̶e̶o̶. ̶G̶. ̶M̶e̶a̶d̶e̶ ̶M̶a̶j̶. ̶G̶e̶n̶l̶. I have just received your note by Capt. Dunn—the information I send you of the crossing of Heth & Wilcox at exeter Mills is inconsistent with Genl. Sheridans theory. You say not to send orders to the 5th corps—I shall of course not do so till that corps is returned to my command but I would suggest Humphreys taking the 5th corps & the two divisions of the second & crossing at Exeter Mills, I sending him a bridge train He can when across co-operate with or take orders from Sheridan.— . . . I will give orders about bombardment & preparations to assault.—" ALS (telegram sent), DNA, RG 107, Telegrams Collected (Unbound); telegram received (at 8:30 P.M.), *ibid.*, RG 108, Letters Received. *O.R.*, I, xlvi, part 3, 458. See following telegram.

To Maj. Gen. George G. Meade

Apl, 2d 1865 9.30 p. m.

MAJ. GN. MEADE,

Miles has made a big thing of it and deserves the highest praise for the pertinacity with which he stuck to the enemy until he wrung from him victory. As the Cavalry was coming down the Cox and River roads I am very much in hopes we will hear to-night of the capture of the balance of the Heth's & Wilcox Divisions. I think a Cavalry force had been thrown to the very bridge over which they expected to escape in advance.

U. S. GRANT
Lt. Gn.

ALS (telegram sent), PPRF; telegram received, DNA, RG 94, War Records Office, Army of the Potomac. *O.R.*, I, xlvi, part 3, 459. On April 2, 1865, 8:30 P.M., Maj. Gen. George G. Meade wrote to USG. "I send Maj. Rosencrantz just from Miles. Brev. Maj. Gen Miles reports that he made three assaults on the enemy's position, the last being made about 3.30 P. M. One brigade attacked on their flank and succeeded in completely routing them capturing about from 600 to 1000 prisoners 2 guns and 2 colors. Gen. Miles has formed connection with Maj. Gen. Humphreys, but it was found that the enemy had retired, but Miles is still pursuing them. Maj. Rosencrantz will give you any further details. Miles has about 400 rebel wounded, which are included in the 1000—" Copies, DNA, RG 107, Telegrams Collected (Unbound); *ibid.*, RG 108, Letters Received. *O.R.*, I, xlvi, part 3, 457.

Also on April 2, Lt. Col. Ely S. Parker telegraphed to Meade. "Hd Qrs armies U. S. will be at Banks House north of [F]ort Fisher and near the Boydton plank road" Telegram received, DNA, RG 94, War Records Office, Army of the Potomac; copies (2), Meade Papers, PHi; CtY. *O.R.*, I, xlvi, part 3, 459.

To Maj. Gen. George G. Meade

Apl. 2d 9.45 [P.M.] *1865*

MAJ. GN. MEADE,

Direct Gen. Parke to use his seige Artillery upon the rail-road bridge during the night. If we can hit the bridge once it will pay. It will be well to send the Pontoon train up to Humphries but the troops not to cross until Sheridan gets there. Sheridan now has his

Cavalry out after trains of the enemy which he has heard of and will probable collect them to-night and be with Humphrey by 8 a. m. to-morrow. I sent him orders to-day to cross the river which he will do as soon as the enemy on this side is captured or driven off. He is marching on the Cox and river roads.

U. S. GRANT
Lt. Gen.

AL (facsimile telegram sent—signature not in USG's hand), Lloyd Lewis-Bruce Catton Collection, USGA; telegram received, DNA, RG 94, War Records Office, Army of the Potomac. Printed as sent at 9:00 P.M. in *O.R.*, I, xlvi, part 3, 458–59. On April 2, 1865, 9:00 P.M., Maj. Gen. George G. Meade telegraphed to USG. "The pontoon train has already been ordered to the left Maj. Gen. Humphreys has been ordered to report to Maj. Gen. Sheridan" Telegram sent, DNA, RG 94, War Records Office, Army of the Potomac; telegram received, *ibid.*, RG 108, Letters Received. *O.R.*, I, xlvi, part 3, 459.

To Maj. Gen. Edward O. C. Ord

———

Apl. 2d 1865

MAJ. GN. ORD:

Maj. Gn. Miles attacked what was left of Heth's & Wilcox Divisions in a strongly intrenched position at Southerland Station this afternoon and utterly routed them capturing about 1000 prisoners and two field pieces. As the Cavalry was coming down the road on which they retreated I am in hopes of hearing yet to-night of the balance being bpicked up.

U. S. GRANT
Lt. Gn.

ALS (telegram sent), OClWHi; telegram received, Ord Papers, CU-B. *O.R.*, I, xlvi, part 3, 495.

On April 2, 1865, 1:25 A.M., USG telegraphed to Maj. Gen. Edward O. C. Ord. "The attack on the enemys by Parke & Wright will be made promptly at 4 oclock this a m if they have not been before you receive this" Telegram received (misdated April 1), Ord Papers, CU-B; copies, DLC-USG, V, 46, 75, 108; DNA, RG 108, Letters Sent. *O.R.*, I, xlvi, part 3, 492. On the same day, Ord telegraphed to USG. "have my men ready to move in case 26th or 2d corps get in—" ALS (telegram sent), DNA, RG 107, Telegrams Collected (Unbound); telegram received, *ibid.*, RG 108, Letters Received. *O.R.*, I, xlvi, part 3, 492.

At 5:50 A.M., USG telegraphed to Ord. "Wright has carried the enemy's line and is pushing in ~~now~~ Now is the time to push your men to the right leaving your line very thin and go to his assistance—" Copies, DLC-USG, V, 46, 75, 108; DNA, RG 108, Letters Sent. *O.R.*, I, xlvi, part 3, 492. At 6:00 A.M., Ord telegraphed to USG. "I have ordered my men to move up to Wrights support by the shortest line" Telegram received, DNA, RG 108, Letters Received. *O.R.*, I, xlvi, part 3, 492.

At 7:00 A.M., 8:10 A.M., and 8:30 A.M., Ord telegraphed to USG. "Just heard from Gibbin who must have before this recd my order to ~~Giveo~~ to support Wright he says I advanced my skirmish line well supported and drew a heavy fire of infantry and shots from three or four guns at Different points along the line some of the skirmishers got across the swamp in front of Dandy but fell back to their pits since the above I hear Gen Gibbon has moved to wrights support" Telegram received, DNA, RG 108, Letters Received. *O.R.*, I, xlvi, part 3, 493. "Harris' brigade has taken the works on north side Hatcher's Run, and is moving up on north side. Colored troops are being put in also near the barn. The fort south of run reported evacuated. Second Corps should take possession and man it. All my white troops, except Harris' brigade, have gone to help Wright." *Ibid.* "Firing in my new front all most ceased think I have the enemys work opposite armstrongs prisoners are coming in deserters says that when Wright went in their picket Line moved off towards our left" Telegram received, DNA, RG 108, Letters Received. *O.R.*, I, xlvi, part 3, 493.

At 9:40 A.M., Ord telegraphed to Bvt. Col. Theodore S. Bowers. "I have several hundred prisoners in & more coming want a guard immediately of two hundred men to take them to city Pt My people are all out in trenches one enemys line. Have taken all their line in my front. A Number of guns & perhaps one thousand prisoners with Colors &c. Our loss not heavy" Telegrams received (2—at 10:20 A.M.), DNA, RG 108, Letters Received; copy, *ibid. O.R.*, I, xlvi, part 3, 494. On the same day, Bowers telegraphed to Ord. "Have all your prisoners been sent down. I have more marines here that I will send up to bring prisoners down if you want them, I cannot send them today as guards for stores, Please answer." Copies, DLC-USG, V, 46, 75, 108; DNA, RG 108, Letters Sent. *O.R.*, I, xlvi, part 3, 494. On the same day, Ord telegraphed to Bowers. "Colonel Washburn, or the officer commanding at Humphreys' Station, can inform you in regard to prisoners." Printed as received on April 3, 12:20 A.M., *ibid.*, p. 495. At noon, Ord telegraphed to Bowers. "All my men were sent from this neighborhood to aid General Wright who reported himself in danger of being driven back. They have followed the rebs. I remained here waiting orders from Gen Grant as to final disposition, but the Gen has gone towards Petersburg, and the 2d Corps has gone out to Genl Sheridan, so that the nearest troops to this place are some five miles off towards Petersburg—This is the depot for Sheridan Army; there is a large amount of ammunition and supplies here about 1000 prisoners and no troops except about 100 men and my Hdqr guard. Send up a regiment at least and at once." Telegrams received (2—at 2:40 P.M.), DNA, RG 108, Letters Received. *O.R.*, I, xlvi, part 3, 494.

At 7:15 P.M., Bowers telegraphed to USG. "General Ord telegraphed me at noon that he had a large number of prisoners and no troops to guard them, and asked for a regiment to be sent him. As there are not over a hundred men at City Point, and they are on duty, I applied to Admiral Porter for marines. He kindly furnished five hundred, which I sent to the front. They have returned with over 3000 prisoners, whom they are now guarding. If Collis Brigade is not to return I will have to call on the Admiral for all guards for prisoners." Copies, DLC-USG, V, 46, 75, 108; DNA, RG 108, Letters Sent. *O.R.*, I, xlvi, part 3, 450.

Also on April 2, Ord telegraphed three times to USG, first at 10:00 A.M., second at 10:40 A.M. "Is Genl Humpheris in the Enemis line & will he protect my rear if I move my force in connection with Wrights. towards Petersburg & try to reach the Appomattox   I have ~~just~~ large number of Prisoners in say one thousand" Telegram received, DNA, RG 108, Letters Received. *O.R.*, I, xlvi, part 3, 494. "I want to move my head ~~Quarters to follow my~~ with my command which has ~~been ordered to~~ moved as I suggested in my despatch to you towards Petersburg—in connection with Wright,   the Appomattox may have bridges between Humphreys rear and my rear—& the trains—Some ammunition at Depot—and prisoners are here with but small guard—if some of the city point force could come here ~~I would~~ it would be well—or will 2d Corps look after any such bridges" ALS, Ord Papers, CU-B. "Genl Gibbon reports that he has possession of the line from fort Welsh down to Hatcher's run with seven 7 pieces artillery two 2 ~~Batteryle~~ flags & a large number of prisoners is forming in Genl Wrights left with a view of sweeping towards Petersburg" ALS (telegram sent), DNA, RG 107, Telegrams Collected (Unbound). *O.R.*, I, xlvi, part 3, 493. The second telegram does not include an addressee and may not have been sent.

To Maj. Gen. Philip H. Sheridan

April 2nd *1865*

MAJ GEN SHERIDAN

Wright and Parke attacked at daylight thi[s] morning, and carried the Enemys works in their front,   Wrights troops some of them pushed through to the Boydton road and cut the telegraph line. Ord is now going on to reinforce Wright and Humphrey is feeling for a soft place in the line south of Hatchers Run. I think nothing now is wanting but the approach of your force from the West to finish up the job on this side—

U. S GRANT
Lt Gen

ALS, IHi. *O.R.*, I, xlvi, part 3, 488.

On April 2, 1865, 10:30 A.M., Lt. Col. John Kellogg, commissary and act. aide, telegraphed to Brig. Gen. John A. Rawlins. "Maj. Genl Sheridan instructs me to inform the Lt Genl Comdg that he has taken the line of the enemies works on the Claiborne and White oak roads—These works are very strong—He is pushing rapidly towards Petersburg—" ALS (telegram sent), DNA, RG 107, Telegrams Collected (Unbound). *O.R.*, I, xlvi, part 3, 488. At 11:00 A.M., Maj. Gen. Philip H. Sheridan telegraphed to Rawlins. "Miles has carried all the main works on the Claiborn road. we are following the enemy up that road. The enemy evacuated the works about 10 o'clock. Will send particulars as soon as heard." Copies (2), DLC-Philip H. Sheridan.

To Maj. Gen. Philip H. Sheridan

Richie House, Apl. 2d 1865 12.30 p. m

MAJ. GN. SHERIDAN,

I would like you to get the 5th Corps and all the Cavalry except McKenzie across the Appomattox as soon as you can. You may cross when you please. The position and movements of the enemy will dictate your movements after you cross. All we want is to capture or beat the enemy.

There is a pontoon train with the Army. If you want it send an officer to conduct it where it will be required.

U. S. GRANT
Lt. Gn

ALS, Scheide Library, Princeton, N. J. *O.R.*, I, xlvi, part 3, 488.
On April 2, 1865, Maj. Gen. Philip H. Sheridan wrote to USG. "I have the honor to inform you that I am now at Mrs Williamsons (on the map. R. Williams) situated on the river road, with the 5th Army Corps. Genl Miles Div. 2d A. C. is near Sutherlands Depot. the Cavalry is working up on the enemys flank towards the intersection of Fords road with the Namoizine road. A. P. Hills Corps passed by here this afternoon. his troops were in position on the Railroad near Sutherlands. our flank movement on Fords road stampeded them and they fled in disorder towards the Appomattox river. From what has transpired here I think beyond a doubt that the enemys troops, wagons & in fact evrything that is left of them have moved off south of the Appomattox. and are moving towards Burkesville Junction. with these impressions and your instructions I am in some doubt as to the result of my moving north of the Appomattox. I think evrything has left Petersburg or is leaving it. My Cavalry is now heavily engaged with the enemy some distance from here beyond the Namoizine road. Crawfords Div of the 5th Corps is now moving up to them. The Cavalry struck the Railroad early this morning some miles west of the intersection of Fords road with the Railroad cutting off a locomotive and two trains loaded with wounded. & destroyed the track in several places." ALS, DNA, RG 108, Letters Received. *O.R.*, I, xlvi, part 3, 489.

To Maj. Gen. Godfrey Weitzel

By Telegraph from Gen Grant HdQrs [*April 2*] *1865*
To MAJ GEN WEITZEL

Wright & Parke attacked the enemy this morning and carried the works on their front capturing guns & prisoners number not stated   Wrights men have cut the telegraph wire on the Boydtown Road. Ord is reinforcing Wright ~~to~~ no report from Ord but he has ~~appeared~~ apparantly taken the works on his front. Humphrey's advanced and the only report from him says he captured the enys picket & 120 prisoners this a m at 7:40   He has evendntly carried everything in his front as his firing ~~repe~~ rapidly advances. Sheridan has been reinforced by Miles Division of infy & from five forks is sweeping west towards towards Petersburg—The Greatest vigilance is necessary on your part that the enemy donot cross the appomattox to overwhelmn and drive Gen ~~p~~Parke   Wright is now tearing up the South Road

U S. GRANT
Lieut Gen

Telegram received, DNA, RG 94, War Records Office, Miscellaneous War Records; *ibid.*, RG 393, 25th Army Corps, Telegrams Received; copies, *ibid.*, RG 108, Letters Sent; DLC-USG, V, 46, 75, 108. *O.R.*, I, xlvi, part 3, 495. An undated telegram from Maj. Gen. Godfrey Weitzel to USG, 11:30 A.M., may have been sent on April 2, 1865. "Your dispatch rec'd" ALS (telegram sent), DNA, RG 107, Telegrams Collected (Unbound).

On April 2, 8:40 A.M., Weitzel telegraphed to USG, and, at 9:10 A.M., to Bvt. Col. Theodore S. Bowers. "I directed Heartsuff to attack this morning. He carried the picket line. but could not get any further. Prisoners captured say Mahone is still there" "How do matters stand now? On this front we ~~could'n~~ tried the Bermuda front, but Mahone was there and we only got the picket line. From prisoners, deserters and observation ~~no change~~ we learn that there is no change as yet." ALS (telegrams sent), *ibid.*; telegrams received, *ibid.*, RG 108, Letters Received. *O.R.*, I, xlvi, part 3, 496, 498.

An undated telegram from Weitzel to Bowers of 6:45 P.M. may have been sent on April 2. "How do matters stand at Petersburg now" ALS (telegram sent), DNA, RG 107, Telegrams Collected (Unbound). On April 2, Bowers telegraphed to Weitzel. "Referring to your dispatch of this P M I beg to say that the work goes bravely on   Our troops are now well up and we have a continuaes line from the appomattox below Petersburg to the ~~to the rear~~ river above and will intrench tonight   our prisoners are estimated at over 12000 with

50 pieces of artilley   a portion of ₤Foster division made a gallant charge cap-
tureing an important Fort & its garrison   Everything looks well—"   Telegram
received, *ibid.*, RG 94, War Records Office, Miscellaneous War Records; *ibid.*,
RG 393, 25th Army Corps, Telegrams Received; copies, *ibid.*, RG 108, Letters
Sent; DLC-USG, V, 46, 75, 108. *O.R.*, I, xlvi, part 3, 498. *O.R.* has "boats"
rather than "troops" in the second sentence, as does one of USG's letterbooks
(V, 75) and one telegram received.

To Maj. Gen. Godfrey Weitzel

T. Banks House, Apl. 2d./65 10.45 a. m.
MAJ. GEN. WEITZEL A. JAMES.
The enemy have been driven from all their works outside of the line
immediately enveloping Petersburg. We are now enveloping them
and will be able to enclose them to the Appomattox. I think The
whole amount of captures will amount to 10.000 men since we
started and many guns. One Brigade of Mahones Division is here
and no doubt more will sbe here soon.

Keep in a condition to assault when ordered or when you may
fell the right time has come.

U. S. GRANT
Lt. Gn

ALS (telegram sent), Scheide Library, Princeton, N. J.; telegram received,
DNA, RG 107, Telegrams Collected (Unbound); *ibid.*, RG 393, 25th Army
Corps, Telegrams Received. *O.R.*, I, xlvi, part 3, 496. On April 2, 1865, Maj.
Gen. Godfrey Weitzel telegraphed to USG. "Your dispatch rec'd. I know now
positively that there wer[e] some of Pickett's division still in my front last night.
These men and Gregg's and Benning's brigades of Field's division left to day
and were the troops who went to Petersburg to day. They were replaced on the
line near the Williamsburg road by Richmond militia. This leaves six thousand
three hundred and eighty five soldiers and the militia in my front. I can move
by leaving my lines in charge of the pickets and dead beats about eight thousand
men. I would rather that their line be a little more denuded of soldiers before
I make the attempt. But I am ready to assault whenever you order it, or whenever under your instructions I think there is the least chanc[e] of winning. You
know they have a very strong line in my front as far as engineering goes. I congratulate you on the success of to day" ALS (telegram sent), DNA, RG 107,
Telegrams Collected (Unbound); telegram received, *ibid.*; *ibid.*, RG 108, Letters
Received. *O.R.*, I, xlvi, part 3, 496.

To Maj. Gen. Godfrey Weitzel

Apl. 2d 1865 12.50 [P.M.]

MAJ. GN. WITZEL,

Rebel troops are pouring over the Appomattox rapidly it is reported. Direct Gen. Hartsuft to demonstrate against them in his front and if there is a good showing attack. The enemy evidently will leave your front very thin by night. I think I will direct you to assault by morning. Make your preparations accordingly.

U. S. GRANT
Lt. Gn

ALS (telegram sent), Scheide Library, Princeton, N. J.; telegram received, DNA, RG 107, Telegrams Collected (Unbound); *ibid.*, RG 393, 25th Army Corps, Telegrams Received. *O.R.*, I, xlvi, part 3, 496. On April 2, 1865, 2:20 P.M., Maj. Gen. Godfrey Weitzel telegraphed to USG. "Your dispatch rec'd. I have made the preparations. A battery of four guns, 13 cars loaded with troops and about 300 cavalry passed to Petersburg this morning and I have been trying to ascertain ever since where they went from. Hartsuff says it was not from his front. I think it was from the Williamsburg road, and I have sent out to see. Deserters up to three O'clock this morning report no movement in my front" ALS (undated telegram sent), DNA, RG 107, Telegrams Collected (Unbound); telegram received (at 2:10 P.M.), *ibid.*, RG 94, War Records Office, Miscellaneous War Records; *ibid.*, RG 108, Letters Received. Printed as sent at 2:10 P.M. in *O.R.*, I, xlvi, part 3, 497.

At 2:20 P.M., 2:50 P.M., 6:40 P.M., and 7:20 P.M., Weitzel telegraphed to USG. "My scouts report that there troops moved from near the Williamsburg road. I see every body that passes down the road to Petersburg. Unless I get different orders from you, as soon as they take enough away there to give a chance of success, I will attack. ~~the~~" "I suppose you are fully aware that troops can be taken away by the enemy between the Appomattox and Swift Creek and ~~the~~ on Curl's Neck, and that both places ~~are cannot be attacked excepting by crossing the Streams between us.~~ are practically unassallable by me." ALS (telegrams sent), DNA, RG 107, Telegrams Collected (Unbound); telegrams received, *ibid.*, RG 94, War Records Office, Miscellaneous War Records; *ibid.*, RG 108, Letters Received. *O.R.*, I, xlvi, part 3, 497. "In all to day there have passed to Petersburg by the railroad and turnpike about (1400) fourteen hundred infantry, a four gun battery and about three hundred cavalry. This does not decrease the force sufficiently to warrant an assault, in my opinion, with the force I have here." ALS (telegram sent), DNA, RG 107, Telegrams Collected (Unbound); telegram received, *ibid.*; *ibid.*, RG 108, Letters Received. *O.R.*, I, xlvi, part 3, 497. "The following just recd . . . Bermuda front To GEN WEITZEL. firing was delayed this afternoon by flag of truce to bring in our dead and Wounded between the lines. Truce was asked this morning but not replied to until nearly 4 p m   reply was signed by mahone   enemy has as strong picket line as ever & considerable more than the usual of number of men along his main line   during continuance of truce he has put some field guns in position on the right of Howlett House battery outside his main lines   one deserter from right of enemys line came in today   reported no change on that portion of line I think the brigade of Mahones division referred to by Gen Grant must be Coxs which has not manned the main line for sometime but has been in reserve on their right   signed   G. L. HARTSUFF Maj Genl." Telegram received, DNA, RG 108, Letters Received. *O.R.*, I, xlvi, part 3, 497–98.

On the same day, USG telegraphed to Weitzel. "You need not assault in the morning unless you have good reason for believing the enemy are leaving. We have a good thing ɨof it now and in a day or two I think I will be able to send you all the troops necessary." ALS (telegram sent), Charles Norton Owen, Glencoe, Ill.; telegrams received (2), DNA, RG 107, Telegrams Collected (Unbound); (2) *ibid.*, RG 393, 25th Army Corps, Telegrams Received. *O.R.*, I, xlvi, part 3, 498. At 7:50 P.M., Weitzel telegraphed to USG. "Your dispatch recd   I will watch them as closley as I can"   Telegram received, DNA, RG 94, War Records Office, Miscellaneous War Records; copy, *ibid.*, RG 393, 25th Army Corps, Telegrams Sent. *O.R.*, I, xlvi, part 3, 498.

To Bvt. Col. Theodore S. Bowers

By Telegraph from Dabneys Mill *1865* [*6:40* A.M.]

Ap. 2

To COL BOWERS

Both Wright and Parke got through the enemy's lines. The battle now rages furiously. Sheridan with his cavalry, the 5th Corps and Miles Div of the 2d Corps, which was sent to him since 1 this A M is now sweeping down from the west. All now looks highly favorable. Ord is engaged but I have not yet heard the result in his front.

U. S. GRANT
Lt Genl.

Telegrams received (2), DNA, RG 107, Telegrams Collected (Unbound); *ibid.*, RG 393, 25th Army Corps, Telegrams Received; copies, *ibid.*, RG 94, War Records Office, Miscellaneous War Records; *ibid.*, RG 108, Letters Sent; DLC-USG, V, 46, 75, 108. *O.R.*, I, xlvi, part 3, 448.

To Bvt. Col. Theodore S. Bowers

———

April 2d 8.25 a. m. *1865*

L̶t̶ Col. Bowers, City Point.

Wright has gone through the enemy's line and now has a regiment tearing up the track on the S. S. road West of Petersburg. Humphrey with two Divisions is W̶e̶s̶t̶ south of Hatchers run crossing the Boydton road. Sheridan with his Cavalry, the 5th Corps and one Division of the 2d Corps is moving from the West towards Petersburg. Ord has gone in with Wright. I do not see how the t̶r̶o̶o̶p̶s̶ ⅃ portion of the rebel army south o̶f̶ L̶u̶d̶ where Wright broke through, (̶f̶r̶o̶n̶t̶ o̶f̶ J̶o̶n̶e̶s̶ H̶ (Oak Grove) are to escape. Dispatch just received from Ord states that some of his troops have just captured the enemys works next to Hatcher's Run, North side, and are pushing on. This is bringing our troops rapidly to a focus with a portion of the rebels in the Center.

U. S. Grant.

Lt. Gn

ALS (telegram sent), Munson-Williams-Proctor Institute, Utica, N. Y.; telegram received (at 8:45 A.M.), DNA, RG 107, Telegrams Collected (Unbound). *O.R.*, I, xlvi, part 3, 448.

To Bvt. Col. Theodore S. Bowers

———

T. Banks House Apl. 2d 1865 10.45 a. m.

Col. Bowers, City Point

Everything has been carried from the left of the 9th Corps The 6th Corps alone captured more than 3000 prisoners. The 2d & 24th Corps both captured Forts, guns and prisoners from the enemy but I can not yet tell the number. We are now closing around the works of the City imediately enveloping Petersburg. All looks remarkably well. I have not yet heard from Sheridan.

U. S. Grant

Lt. Gn

ALS (telegram sent), Scheide Library, Princeton, N. J.; telegram received, DNA, RG 107, Telegrams Collected (Unbound). *O.R.*, I, xlvi, part 3, 449.

To Bvt. Col. Theodore S. Bowers

Boydton Road, Near Petersburg
Apl. 2d 4.40 [P.M.] 1865

COL. T. S. BOWERS. CITY POINT

We are now up and have a continuous line of troops, and in a few hours will be intrenched, from the Appomattox, ~~above~~ below Petersburg to the river above. Heths & Wilcox Divisions, such part of them as were not captured, were cut off from town either designedly on their part or because they could not help it. Sheridan with the Cavalry & 5th Corps is above them. Miles Division, 2d Corps, was sent from the White Oak road to ~~Southside~~ Sutherland station on the South Side R R. where he met them and at last accounts was engaged with them. Not knowing whether Sheridan would get up in time Gen. Humphrey was sent with another Division from here. ~~I~~ The whole captures since ~~we~~ the Army started out gunning will not amount to less than 12000 men and probably 50 pieces of Artillery. I do not know the numbers of men and guns accurately however. A portion of Gen. Foster's Div. 24th Corps made one of the most gallant charges and captured a very important fort from the enemy, with its entire garrison.

All seems well with us and everything quiet just now.

I think the President might come out and pay us a visit to-morrow.[1]

U. S. GRANT
Lt. Gn

ALS (telegram sent), Scheide Library, Princeton, N. J.; copies, DLC-USG, V, 46, 75, 108; DNA, RG 108, Letters Sent. *O.R.*, I, xlvi, part 3, 449.

1. On April 2, 1865, President Abraham Lincoln telegraphed to USG. "Allow me to tender to you and all with you the nations grateful thanks for this additional & magnificent success. At your Kind suggestion I think I will meet you tomorrow" Telegram received, DNA, RG 108, Letters Received. *O.R.*, I, xlvi, part 3, 449. Lincoln, *Works*, VIII, 383. On the same day, USG telegraphed to Bvt. Col. Theodore S. Bowers. "If the President will come out on the 9 a. m. train to Patrick Station I will send a horse and an escort to meet him It would afford me much pleasure to meet the President in person at the Station but I know he will excuse me for not doing so when my services are so liable to be needed at any moment. If 9 is an inconvenient hour telegraph me the hour when

the President will start and he will find his escort awaiting him when he arrives."
Copies, DLC-USG, V, 46, 75, 108; DNA, RG 108, Letters Sent. *O.R.*, I, xlvi,
part 3, 450.

To Bvt. Col. Theodore S. Bowers

April 2. 1865. 8:40 [P.M.]

COL. T. S. BOWERS. CITY POINT

I have just heard from Gen. Miles. He attacked what was left
of Heth's & Wilcox' Divs at Southerlands Station and routed them
capturing about 1.000 prisoners. The enemy took the route North
towards the Appomattox. As Sheridan was in above them I am in
hopes but few of them will escape. Genl. Miles also captured two
field pieces in this attack

U. S. GRANT
Lt. Gen

Telegram, copies, DLC-USG, V, 46, 75, 108; DNA, RG 108, Letters Sent.
O.R., I, xlvi, part 3, 450.

To Bvt. Col. Theodore S. Bowers

Apl. 2d *1865*

COL. T. S. BOWERS, ~~PETERSBURG~~, CITY POINT,

Notify Col. Mulford to make no more deliveries of rebel prisoners whilst the battle is going on.[1]

Parke captured two Forts and two Redouts this morning with
their guns. I have not yet heard from Sheridan but I have an
abiding faith that he is in the right place and at the right time.

U. S. GRANT
Lt. Gen

ALS (telegram sent), OCIWHi; telegram received, DNA, RG 107, Telegrams
Collected (Unbound). *O.R.*, I, xlvi, part 3, 449.
    Also on April 2, 1865, USG telegraphed to Bvt. Col. Theodore S. Bowers.
"Instruct Benham to get the men at City Point out to the outer lines and have
them ready. While all our forces are going in some enterprising Rebels may
possibly go through and down there in a fit of desperation to do what damage

they can." ALS (telegram sent), PPRF; copies, DLC-USG, V, 46, 75, 108; DNA, RG 108, Letters Sent. *O.R.*, I, xlvi, part 3, 448.

1. On April 2, 5:15 P.M., Bvt. Brig. Gen. John E. Mulford telegraphed to Bowers. "I must have transportation immediately for Eighteen hundred, or two thousand men, they are at the line now & I have no guard to take care of them. Send boats at once, with an Officer & ten men on each Have rations ready for the boats on their downward passage, they can stop & take them on, Answer at Hd Qrs Army of James" ALS (telegram sent), DNA, RG 107, Telegrams Collected (Unbound); telegram received, *ibid.*, RG 108, Letters Received. At 5:25 P.M., Bowers telegraphed to Mulford. "Boats will leave in a few minutes for Varina. Rations will be ready by the time they get down here." Copies, DLC-USG, V, 46, 75, 108; DNA, RG 108, Letters Sent. At 5:30 P.M., Bowers telegraphed to USG. "The enemy has just delivered 2,000 prisoners to Col. Mulford. I have sent boats for them" Copies, *ibid.* At 9:35 A.M., Bowers telegraphed to Mulford. "General Grant orders that you make no more deliveries of Rebel Prisoners whilst the battle now going on lasts." Copies, *ibid. O.R.*, II, viii, 462. Context indicates that the time sent, as entered in letterbooks, may be incorrect.

On March 29, Bvt. Brig. Gen. William Hoffman telegraphed to USG. "Mr Ould thinks he has ten thousand (10,000) prisoners to deliver at Mobile, and two thousand (2,000) in Richmond and N Carolina. Since the 25 Nov. 64, when the last declaration of exchange was made, we have delivered of all grades four thousand more prisoners than we have received. I respectfully suggest that no more be delivered until the balance is made up" ALS (telegram sent), DNA, RG 107, Telegrams Collected (Unbound); telegram received (at 5:50 P.M.), *ibid.*, RG 108, Letters Received. *O.R.*, II, viii, 444.

To Bvt. Col. Theodore S. Bowers

April 2. 1865

COL. T. S. BOWERS. CITY POINT

Send all my dispatches that have gone concerning operations to Sherman. What you receive hereafter send to Fort Monroe by telegraph to be forwarded by first steamer to Morehead City.

Have you stopped Mulford from delivering prisoners?[1] If he has any on hand for delivery tell him to hold on to them.

U. S. GRANT
Lt. Genl

Telegram, copies, DLC-USG, V, 46, 75, 108; DNA, RG 108, Letters Sent. *O.R.*, I, xlvi, part 3, 450; *ibid.*, I, xlvii, part 3, 82. On April 2, 1865, 4:30 [P.M.], Bvt. Col. Theodore S. Bowers telegraphed to USG. "A letter of date 31st from Gen Sherman is just received. He says the enemy is inactive in his front. He will move at the time stated to you. Thinks Lee will unite his and Johnstons army, and will not coop himself up in Richmond   Would like to be informed if Sheridan swings off that he may go out and meet him. Does not believe Sheridan can cross Ronoake for a month. Will send letter by mail." Copies, DLC-USG, V, 46, 75, 108; DNA, RG 108, Letters Sent. *O.R.,* I, xlvii, part 3, 82. See letter to Maj. Gen. William T. Sherman, April 3, 1865.

1. On April 3, Bowers telegraphed to USG. "Immediately on receipt of your telegram yesterday morning all deliveries by Mulford were stopped. The Rebels delivered to us about 2000 men." ALS (telegram sent), DNA, RG 107, Telegrams Collected (Unbound).

To Julia Dent Grant

———

~~City~~ P Apl. 2d *1865*

DEAR JULIA,

I am now writing from far inside of what was the rebel fortifications this morning but what are ours now. They are exceedingly strong and I wonder at the sucsess of our troops carrying them by storm. But they did do it and without any great loss. We have captured about 12,000 prisoners and 50 pieces of Artillery. As I write this news comes of the capture of 1000 more prisoners. Altogether this has been one of the greatest victories of the war. Greatest because it is over what the rebels have always regarded as their most invincable Army and the one used for the defince of their capitol. We may have some more hard work but I hope not.

Love and kisses for you and Jess.

ULYS.

ALS, DLC-USG.

To [*Abraham Lincoln*]

———

[*April 3, 1865*]

General Sheridan picked up 1,200 prisoners to-day, and from 300 to 500 more have been gathered by other troops. The majority of the arms that were left in the hands of the remnant of Lee's army are now scattered between Richmond and where his troops are. The country is also full of stragglers; the line of retreat marked with artillery, ammunition, burned or charred wagons, caissons, ambulances, &c.

O.R., I, xlvi, part 3, 545. Quoted in a telegram received (partly illegible), DNA, RG 107, Telegrams Collected (Bound), of April 4, 1865, 7:30 A.M., from President Abraham Lincoln to Secretary of War Edwin M. Stanton. "Weitzel telegraphs from Richmond that of Railroad stock, he found there twenty-eight (28) Locomotives, forty-four passenger & baggage cars, and two hundred and six freight cars. At 3/20 this morning Grant, from Southerland station, ten miles from Petersburg towards Burkesville, telegraphs as follows, towit:" Lincoln, *Works*, VIII, 385. Variant text as sent at 8:00 A.M., received at 8:45 A.M., in O.R., I, xlvi, part 3, 544–45, with a note stating that Lincoln's telegram was probably written on April 3. Since Lincoln's original telegram refers to the receipt of the telegram from USG in the morning, while the O.R. text puts it in the evening, the Lincoln editors believe that the O.R. editors erred. Whether USG's telegram was sent late on April 3 or early on April 4, and whether addressed to Lincoln cannot be determined.

USG apparently sent a similar message to Julia Dent Grant on April 3, Monday, from Sutherland Station, Va., received on April 4, 3:15 [A.M.]. ". . . We are progressing nicely, Sheridan picked up 1200 more prisoners today and 4 pieces of artillery. I will probably be in Richmond on Friday next." Parke-Bernet Sale 3655, June 11, 1974, no. 224. The same text of a telegram received, without indication of a recipient, appeared in the papers of Adam Badeau. John Anderson, Jr., Catalogue, May 19, 1902, no. 136. On April 5, Stanton telegraphed to Julia Dent Grant. "I pray you to accept for yourself & ~~Mrs~~ General Grant my congratulations upon the great and crowning glory of his achievements in the overthrow of Lees army & the Capture of Richmond. I send ~~your~~ by mail this day to your brother an appointment as full Brigadier." ALS (telegram sent), DNA, RG 107, Telegrams Collected (Bound); copy, *ibid.*, RG 108, Letters Received. On the same day, Mrs. Grant, City Point, telegraphed to Stanton. "your congratulations are received with pleasure and pride. ~~shall~~ Shall we not look for yourself and Mrs Stanton at Richmond   Genl Grant will be there friday" Telegram received (at 11:20 P.M.), *ibid.*, RG 107, Telegrams Collected (Bound).

To Maj. Gen. George L. Hartsuff

Petersburg Apl 3d/65

MAJ. GN. HARTSUFF, BERMUDA HUNDRED.

What do you learn of the position of the enemy in your front If the enemy have moved out try to connect pickets with the forces

from Petersburg on Swift Creek. Forces have been sent from here
to the North side of the Appomattox and I suppose are now on
Swift Creek.

U. S GRANT

Lt. Gn

ALS (telegram sent), Scheide Library, Princeton, N. J.; telegram received,
DNA, RG 94, War Records Office, Miscellaneous War Records; (at 1:35 P.M.)
ibid., RG 107, Telegrams Collected (Unbound). *O.R.*, I, xlvi, part 3, 537. On
April 3, 1865, Maj. Gen. George L. Hartsuff telegraphed to USG's adjt. "Dispatch directing me to Connect pickets with troops on swift Creek & asking information Concerning Enemy in my front received—I Had just previously sent
a dispatch stating that I occupied Chester Station on the Rail road & giving such
information about Enemy as I had obtained—Have waited reply to this before
Connecting pickets as directed because the station I hold is already some miles
in advance of what the picket line would be when Connected & my force is so
small that I would be obliged to abandon the position to make the picket Connection—As the Lt. Genl. did not know of this when the direction was given I
supposed the information I gave ~~would~~ might make it unnecessary to make the
Connection—I therefore request a reply & instructions soon as possible—The
Infty division is the only mobile part of this Command & that not fully supplied
with transportation   It is Commanded by Bvt. Maj. Genl. Ferrero & if ordered
to move I would be either supernumerary or be left in Command of the artillery
Brigade—I mention this only because it is possible Genl. Grant may not know
the orga[niza]tion & Condition of this Command & it might influence him in any
disposition he might desire to make of it or me." ALS (telegram sent), DNA,
RG 107, Telegrams Collected (Unbound); telegrams received (2), *ibid.*, RG
108, Letters Received. *O.R.*, I, xlvi, part 3, 537.

On the same day, USG telegraphed to Hartsuff. "Has the Enemy left your
front" Telegram received, DNA, RG 107, Telegrams Collected (Unbound).
O.R., I, xlvi, part 3, 536. On the same day, Hartsuff telegraphed three times to
USG's adjt. "the enemy is reprted moving in the direction of Chesterfield
Court House—it is the impression among deserters that they are going to Lynchburg—" Telegram received, DNA, RG 107, Telegrams Collected (Unbound);
ibid., RG 108, Letters Received. *O.R.*, I, xlvi, part 3, 536. "The following dispatch just recd from Gen Weitzel—25th A C 3d apl   To MAJ GEN HARTSUFF
await orders from Gen Grant. I am moving ~~today~~ towards Richmond   Signed
G. WEITZEL *M Genl*   The Enemy has Evacuated & I am in possession of his
line in my front—If Gen Warren assumes Command here under his order. Am
I relieved or placed under his Comd? I am his Senior" "The enemy in my front
evacuated his line at 4 a m   I moved my infantry Division on to their line &
have advanced a column of about twelve thousand 12000 [*1200*] as far as
Chester Station on the RR—One light 12 pdr gun & several Caisons with ammunition were found here   Refugees from Richmond this A M say it is evacuated   Other accounts represent the enemys line to extend from Drury Bluff to
Chester C H—I have no doubt of its evacuation   I only learned positively of the
evacuation of Petersburg from Refugees after I had reached the RR   I have
advanced thus far without any Knowledge of the condition of affairs except what
I have picked up & without any instructions whatever   I would liked to have

gone on to Richmond but did not feel authorized I have directed the column at the station to await further orders there Have picked up about 50 prisoners I respectfully request instructions" Telegrams received (2 of the second), DNA, RG 108, Letters Received. *O.R.*, I, xlvi, part 3, 536–37. Also on April 3, USG telegraphed to Hartsuff. "Your dispatch not recd at the time of sending my dispatch this morning I was not aware that Richmond was in our possession I have no orders to give now" Telegram received (on April 4, 3:20 A.M.), DNA, RG 94, War Records Office, Miscellaneous War Records; (on April 4, 3:10 A.M.) *ibid.*, RG 107, Telegrams Collected (Unbound). Printed as received at 3:10 A.M. in *O.R.*, I, xlvi, part 3, 538. At 9:30 P.M., Hartsuff telegraphed to USG's adjt. "I still Keep at Chester Station the force of about twelve hundred (1200) I reported as taking there this morning—Reconnoisance by ~~them~~ it this afternoon in ~~their~~ its front covering the wagon road to Chesterfield Court House developed a line of videttes & probably pickets about two or three miles from it, whether temporary to ~~recover~~ cover a halt or permanent & how far it extends not ascertained. Deserters coming to & men captured by this command today amount to over two hundred (200). Enemy took all his guns from his line in my front except the heavy ones at the Howlett Battery on the James & one (1) rifled field piece," Telegram sent, DNA, RG 107, Telegrams Collected (Unbound); copy, *ibid.*, RG 393, Dept. of Va. and N. C., Defenses of Bermuda Hundred, Letters Sent. *O.R.*, I, xlvi, part 3, 538.

To Maj. Gen. George G. Meade

Apl. 3d *1865*

MAJ. GN. MEADE,

Send Gn. Collis command immediately back to City Point. ~~All troops left in our old line can now be brough~~

Do you hear anything of the condition of the rail-road and bridges in Petersburg?

U. S. GRANT
Lt. Gn

ALS (telegram sent), Kohns Collection, NN; telegram received (at 6:25 A.M.), DNA, RG 94, War Records Office, Army of the Potomac. *O.R.*, I, xlvi, part 3, 511. On April 3, 1865, 6:35 A.M., Maj. Gen. George G. Meade telegraphed to USG. "Orders issued for troops from City Point to return—I have sent to enquire about the bridges in Petersburgh—No report yet—" ALS (telegram sent), DNA, RG 94, War Records Office, Miscellaneous War Records; telegram received, *ibid.*, RG 108, Letters Received. *O.R.*, I, xlvi, part 3, 512.

At 4:05 A.M., Meade had telegraphed to USG. "Gen Parke telegraphs ~~that~~ that reports from 1st & 2d div of corps indicate the enemy's line as far as developed Consists only of skirmishers—and that heavy explosion occurred a lit[tle] after 3. A. M. in the heart of Petersburg—Gen Parke further states that he is ascertaining whether the enemy have retired. I have communicated this information to Generals Ord and Wright, and directed Gens. Parke and Wright to push forward strong lines of skirmishers and use every effort to ascertain the condition of the Enemy—" Telegram sent, DNA, RG 107, Telegrams Collected (Unbound); copies, *ibid.*, RG 393, Army of the Potomac, Letters Sent; (2) Meade Papers, PHi. *O.R.*, I, xlvi, part 3, 511. There is no evidence that USG received this telegram. At 5:10 A.M., Meade twice telegraphed to USG. "The following dispatch is just received from Gen Parke— . . . Gen Griffin Commanding 2nd Div. reports 4.20 a. m. that Gen Collis has taken possession of the Entire line of the Enemy's works in his front—No Enemy appears to be in his front." "The 2d Brigade 1st Division 9th Corps, Col. Ely is in possession of Petersburg." Telegrams sent, DNA, RG 94, War Records Office, Miscellaneous War Records; telegrams received, *ibid.*, RG 108, Letters Received. Both printed, with the first as sent at 4:40 A.M., in *O.R.*, I, xlvi, part 3, 511. At 5:50 A.M., Meade telegraphed to USG. "From Both Parke & Wright I have the report—no enemy in their front & Petersburg evacuated—" Telegram sent, DNA, RG 107, Telegrams Collected (Unbound); telegram received, *ibid.*, RG 108, Letters Received. *O.R.*, I, xlvi, part 3, 511.

On the same day, USG telegraphed to Meade. "You will march immediately with your army up the Appatmattox taking the river road leaving one 1 division to hold Petersburg & the Railroad" Telegram received, DNA, RG 94, War Records Office, Army of the Potomac; copies, *ibid.*, RG 108, Letters Sent; DLC-USG, V, 46, 75, 108; (2) Meade Papers, PHi; CtY. *O.R.*, I, xlvi, part 3, 512. At 3:00 P.M., Meade, "River road near Sutherland's Stn," telegraphed to USG. "I have directed Genl—Wright with the 6th corps to proceed on the River road till he crosses the road leading from Sutherlands station to Exeter Mills & then to halt—Genl—Parke with two divisions of the 9th corps will be moved in rear of Wright The supply trains of the 2d 6th & 9th corps I have directed to come after us on the Cox road because the river road is very bad & I doubt if the trains could be gotten over it—I understand the 2d corps has crossed the Appomatox at Exeter Mills I was under the impression I was to follow the infantry now under the command of Maj. Genl. Sheridan My Hed Qrs will for the night be at Sutherlands stations where I will await your further orders—" ALS (telegram sent), Humphreys Collection, PHi; telegram received, DNA, RG 94, War Records Office, Miscellaneous War Records; *ibid.*, RG 108, Letters Received. *O.R.*, I, xlvi, part 3, 512. At 9:15 P.M., Meade wrote to USG. "I send you a despatch just received from Maj. Genl. Humphreys—He is on the Namozin road has not crossed the Appomattox & is moving under Genl. Sheridans orders—and has received no notification from Genl. Sheridan that he is returned to my command He is rationed till tomorrow night—I will send 3 days rations up to him ahead of the 6. corps—I understand the 5th corps trains are on this road—if this is the case, I can not get off till these trains have cleared the road—If Genl. Sheridan has not been advised of the 2d corps being returned to my command I would suggest its being done, or an order from your Hd Qrs being sent to Genl. Humphreys, as confusion may arise from a conflict of authority.—" ALS, DNA, RG 108, Letters Received. *O.R.*, I, xlvi, part 3, 512. The enclosure is *ibid.*, p. 516. On the same day, Lt. Col. Ely S. Parker wrote to Meade. "You will furnish to Gen Humphreys the rations called for by him at the earliest moment possible in accordance with your suggestion of 9.15 this evening—Enclosed are orders for Gen Humphreys to report to you hereafter, except, that on tomorrow he will follow the route of march designated for him by Gen Sheridan . . . P. S. Please forward to Gen Humphreys the order by one of your officer" ALS, DNA, RG 94, War Records Office, Army of the Potomac. *O.R.*, I, xlvi, part 3, 513. The enclosure is *ibid.*

To Maj. Gen. Edward O. C. Ord

Hd. Qrs. Gen Grant
4.30 A. M April 3d [*1865*]

GENL. ORD

Gen Parke reports but a thin line of skirmishers in his front and thinks this enemys leaving. Parke & Wright are pushing forward a strong skirmish line. I wish you to do the same.

U. S. GRANT,
Let. Genl,

Telegram received, Ord Papers, CU-B; copies, DLC-USG, V, 46, 75, 108; DNA, RG 108, Letters Sent. *O.R.*, I, xlvi, part 3, 532. On April 3, 1865, 4:30 [A.M.], 5:30 A.M., and 6:15 A.M., Maj. Gen. Edward O. C. Ord telegraphed to USG. "Prissoner just in states enemy ~~have~~ were ready to evacuated and packd up." ALS (telegram sent), Ord Papers, CU-B. "Genl Birney reported his Div: as having gone into town at 4 30 a m" Telegram received, DNA, RG 108, Letters Received. *O.R.*, I, xlvi, part 3, 532. "Just received the following from Lieutenant West, General Birney's aide-de-camp: PETERSBURG, *April 3.* GENERAL: The citizens inform me that General Lee intends to flank us on the right after our army enters the town." *Ibid.*

To Maj. Gen. Edward O. C. Ord

Apl. 3d 1865

MAJ. GN. ORD,

Gen. Sheridan is in your front on both roads you will travel but from seven to ten miles in advance. The Army of the Potomac will move on the North ~~side~~ side of the river parallel with it.

I will be on the Cox ł road.

U. S. GRANT
Lt. Gn.

ALS, Ord Papers, CU-B. *O.R.*, I, xlvi, part 3, 532.

Also on April 3, 1865, USG wrote to Maj. Gen. Edward O. C. Ord. "Efforts will be made to intercept the enemy who are evidently pushing toward Danville, push Southwest with your command by the Cox road; The A. P. will push up the river road." Copies, Ord Papers, CU-B; DLC-USG, V, 46, 75, 108; DNA, RG 108, Letters Sent. *O.R.*, I, xlvi, part 3, 532. On the same day, Lt. Col. Ely S. Parker wrote to Ord. "You will halt your rear Division at the point where it may be when this reaches and let them rest there until further orders from these Hdqrs." ALS, Scheide Library, Princeton, N. J.

To Maj. Gen. Philip H. Sheridan

Petersburg. Apl. 3d 1865 10.20 a. m.

MAJ. GEN SHERIDAN,

Lt. Allen[1] of your Staff has just reached. I have no special orders to send further than those taken by Maj. Hudson of my staff this morning. The troops got off from here early marching by the River and Cox roads. It is understood that the enemy will make a stand at Amelia C. H. with the expectation of holding the road between Danville and Lynchburg.

The first object of present movement will be to intercept Lee's Army and the 2d second to secure Burkesville. I have ordered the road to be put in order up to the latter place as soon as possible. I shall hold that place if Lee stops at Danville and shall hold it anyhow until his policy is indicated. Make your movements according to this programme.

U. S. GRANT
Lt. Gn

P. S. I shall move by the Cox road. Will start from here about 12 m.
U. S. G.

ALS, Scheide Library, Princeton, N. J. *O.R.*, I, xlvi, part 3, 528. On April 3, 1865, 1:45 P.M. and 4:10 P.M., Maj. Gen. Philip H. Sheridan wrote to USG, the second time from Namozine Church. "Before receiving your dispatch I had anticipated the evacuation of Petersburg, and had commenced moving West. My Cavalry is 9 miles beyond Namozine Creek and is pressing the Enemy's trains—I shall push on to the Danville Rail Road as rapidly as possible—" "A 11. o'clock A. M. the Cavalry advance was three (3.) miles beyond Namozine Creek on the main road pushing forward: Up to that hour Genl Custer had captured one Gun and ten (10.) Caissons. the resistance made by the Enemies rear guard was very feeble—the Enemy threw their Artillery ammunition on the sides of the road and into the woods & then set fire to the fences and woods through which the shells were strown. at one o'clock P. M. our advance was at Deep Creek on the direct road to Bevils Bridge. we captured the Enemies Rear guard numbering between two and three hundred men, with one battle flag. Bvt Brig Genl Wells Cavalry brigade was on the direct road to Amelia C. H. seven miles beyond Namozine Church—prisoners report quite a force of the Enemies Cavalry on this road—the roads are strown with burning and broken down Caissons, Ambulances, Wagons and debris of all descriptions—Up to this hour we have taken about twelve hundred (1200.) prisoners mostly of A. P Hills Corps & all accounts report the woods filled with deserters & stragglers principally of this Corps—One of our men recaptured reports that not more than one in five of the rebels have arms in their hands." ALS, DNA, RG 108, Letters Received. *O.R.*, I, xlvi, part 3, 529.

1. Vanderbilt Allen of N. Y., USMA 1864, 1st lt., Corps of Engineers, as of June 13, 1864, was appointed to Sheridan's staff as of Sept. 5, 1864. See telegram to Maj. Gen. George G. Meade, Aug. 29, 1864.

To Maj. Gen. Philip H. Sheridan

Southerland Station
Apl. 3d 1865

MAJ. GEN. SHERIDAN,

Tomorrow Gen. Ord will move forward by the Cox road Meade by the River road until after crossing Namozine Creek he will follow the road up the North side of the Creek. The 2d Corps, now North of the Appomattox will return to the South side at Bevel's Bridge. I will follow the A. P. to-morrow. Ord is on our left flank without any Cavalry to watch it. I wish you would order McKenzie to meet him to-morrow at White Oak Ch. to-morrow or in that vicinity.

Do you hear of any movement on the part of Johnston? I have heard from a variety of sources that he had been ordered up to unite with Lee. I[f] you can get scouts through to Burkesville to ascertain what is there I wish you would do it.

U S GRANT
Lt Gn

ALS, Scheide Library, Princeton, N. J. *O.R.*, I, xlvi, part 3, 529.
On April 3, 1865, Surgeon James T. Ghiselin telegraphed to Bvt. Brig. Gen. James W. Forsyth, chief of staff for Maj. Gen. Philip H. Sheridan. "I have the honor to report that the wounded of the Cavalry and 5th Corps were left at the following places for want of transportation to Send them to the rear namely— Dinweddie C H—Union 25 Confederate 5—There may be more at this place but

these are all that have been officially reported—5th Corps Hospital Southerland Station on South Side Rail Road about 100 and perhaps 15 ~~Coaval~~ Cavalry-men wounded in Skirmishes & left in Houses in that vicinity 12 Confederate wounded were Captured in Cars and left at Ford Station on South Side R R. Medical officers were left with all these wounded and they were Supplied with Everything Sufficient to last them 3 days. I respectfully Suggest that the wounded remining at the places mentioned be Sent for at once and the battle fields near Dinweddie C H and Gravelly Run Church and the Houses in their immediate vicinity be thouoghly Searched for any wounded who may have been left in Consequence of the rapid movemts of the army & the very limited trans-portation—" Telegram received, DNA, RG 108, Letters Received. *O.R.*, I, xlvi, part 3, 530. Sheridan endorsed this telegram. "Respy referred to Lt. Gen Grant Comdg Armies of U. S with a request that the wounded men of the Cavy now in the vicinity of Dinwiddie be Collected and Sent to City Point in the ambu-lances belonging to the troops now at City Point" Copy, DNA, RG 108, Letters Received. *O.R.*, I, xlvi, part 3, 530.

To Maj. Gen. William T. Sherman

Southerland Station S. S. Rail-road, Apl. 3d *1865*

MAJ. GEN. W. T. SHERMAN,
COMD.G MIL. DIV. OF THE MISS.
GENERAL,

The movement of which I spoke to you when you was here commenced on the 28th inst. and notwithstanding two days of rain which followed, rendering roads almost impassable, even for Cav-alry, terminated in the fall of both Richmond and Petersburg this morning. The Mass of Lee's Army was whipped badly South of Petersburg and to save the remnant he was forced to evacuate Richmond. We have about 12,000 prisoners and straglers are being picked up in large numbers.

SFrom all causes I do not estimate his loss at less than 25,000. Sheridan with his Cavalry and one Corps of Infantry was on our extreme left. The attack which ended the contest was made in the Center. All to the right of the point of attack were forced into Petersburg or killed or captured. Those to the left of it were cut off (our left) and forced to retreat up the Appomattox. Sheridan pushed in and intercepted them forcing them to the North side of the river and with great loss. The troops from Petersburg as well as those from Richmond retreated between the two rivers and there is every indication that they will endeavor to secure Burkesville and Danville. I am pursuing with five Corps and the Cavalry and hope to capture or disperse a large number more. It is also my intention to take Burkesville and hold it until it is seen whether it is a part of Lee's plan to hold Lynchburg & Danville. The rail-road from Petersburg up can soon be put in condition to supply an Army at that place. If Lee goes beyond Danville you will have to take care of him with the force you have for a while.

It is reported here that Johnston has evacuated Raleigh and is moving up to join Lee. Should he do so you will want either to get on the rail-road South of him, to hold it, or destroy it so that it will take him a long time to repair damages. Should Lee go to Lynchburg with his whole force, and I get Burkesville, there will be no special use in you going any further into the interior of North Carolina. There is no contingency that I can see, except my failure to secure Burkesville, that will make it necessary to for you to move on to the Roanoke as proposed when you were here. In that case it might be necessary for you to operate on the enemy's lines of communication between Danville and Burkesville whilst I would act on them, from Richmond, between the latter place and Lynchburg.

This Army has now won a most desicive Victory and followed the enemy. This is all that it ever wanted to make it as good an Army as ever fought a battle.

> Yours Truly
> U. S. GRANT
> Lt. Gn.

ALS, Schoff Collection, MiU-C. *O.R.*, I, xlvi, part 3, 510; *ibid.*, I, xlvii, part 3, 89–90.

On March 31, 1865, Maj. Gen. William T. Sherman wrote to USG. "I reached Goldsboro last night and find all things working well. The Enemy has manifested no activity hereabouts, and only some cavalry simply moving across our front from West to East. The Railroad to the Sea Coast at Morehead City is working well and is doing good work, but the Wilmigton Branch is not yet done. I have concluded arrangemts for the Barges to be loaded, brought to Kinston where our wagons will be loaded, and afterwards will be reloaded and moved up to the Chowan to await our arrival north of Roanoke. I shall keep things movig and be all ready by the date fixed April 10. In the mean time I expect to hear from your moving by the Left Flank. I will Keep you daily advised of progress. I must now set to work to make a Report of our March from Savannah to Goldsboro, before it fades from Memory or gets lost in the rush of Events. John Sherman came with me here, and will return with this to Old Point. I think Lee will unite his & Johnstons Army. I cannot think he will Coop himself in Richmond. If he do, he is not the General he is reputed to be, but we must go straight for him and fight him in open ground, or Coop him up where starvation will tame him. If Sheridan swings off and is likely to come down towards me, get me word that I may meet him. I doubt if he can cross the Roanoke for a month yet unless he has pontoons with him, but he cannot be better employed than in raiding the Road about Burkesville." ALS, DNA, RG 108, Letters Received. *O.R.*, I, xlvii, part 3, 65.

To Maj. Gen. Godfrey Weitzel

By Telegraph from Grants Hd Qrs [*April 3*] 1865
To MAJ GEN WEITZEL

I donot doubt that you will march into Richmond unoppoed— Take possession of the city and establish Guards and preserve order until I get there   permanit not man leave Town after you get possessin. The ~~firing~~ army here will endeavor to cut off the retreat the enemy.

U S GRANT
Lt Gen

Telegram received, DNA, RG 94, War Records Office, Miscellaneous War Records; *ibid.*, RG 107, Telegrams Collected (Unbound); copies, *ibid.*, RG 108, Letters Sent; DLC-USG, V, 46, 75, 108. *O.R.*, I, xlvi, part 3, 534.

On April 3, 1865, 4:30 [A.M.], Maj. Gen. Godfrey Weitzel telegraphed to USG. "I believe ~~Rich~~ the lines in my front are evacuated and I propose to see at once" ALS (undated telegram sent), DNA, RG 107, Telegrams Collected (Unbound); telegram received, *ibid. O.R.*, I, xlvi, part 3, 533. At 5:25 A.M. and 5:55 A.M., Weitzel telegraphed to USG. "Continual explosions and fires in enemy's lines. Large number of deserters. All report evacuation. I will move at daybreak" "We have possession of the enemy's works and are moving along." ALS (undated telegrams sent), DNA, RG 107, Telegrams Collected (Unbound); telegrams received (the second at 5:58 A.M.), *ibid.*; *ibid.*, RG 108, Letters Received. *O.R.*, I, xlvi, part 3, 533–34.

An undated telegram of 5:25 A.M. from Weitzel to USG may have been sent on April 3. "Deserters say it was common talk in camp that they were going to Danville" ALS (telegram sent), DNA, RG 107, Telegrams Collected (Unbound).

On April 3, 10:30 A.M., Bvt. Col. Theodore S. Bowers telegraphed to Secretary of War Edwin M. Stanton. "Gen. Weitzel telegraphs as follows: 'We took Richmond at 8:15 this morning. I captured many guns. Enemy left in great haste. The city is on fire in two places. Am making every effort to put it out. ~~Many people~~ The people received us with enthusiastic expressions of joy' Genl Grant started early this morning with army toward the Danville road to cut off Lee's retreating army if possible. President Lincoln has gone to the front." ALS (incomplete telegram sent), *ibid.*; telegram received (marked as sent at 11:00 A.M., received at 11:30 A.M.), *ibid.*, Telegrams Collected (Bound); (2) *ibid.*, RG 94, War Records Office, Miscellaneous War Records. Printed as sent at 11:00 A.M. in *O.R.*, I, xlvi, part 3, 509.

On the same day, USG twice telegraphed to Bowers. "Petersburg was evacuated last night. Pursuit will be immediately made. ~~of the rebel force which is suppos~~" ALS (telegram sent), OClWHi; copies, DLC-USG, V, 46, 75, 108; DNA, RG 108, Letters Sent. *O.R.*, I, xlvi, part 3, 509. "Say to the President that an officer and escort will attend him but as to myself I start towards the Danville road with the Army. I want to cut off as much of Lee's army as possible." ALS (telegram sent), CSmH; copies, DLC-USG, V, 46, 75, 108; DNA, RG 108, Letters Sent. *O.R.*, I, xlvi, part 3, 509. At 5:15 P.M., Bowers telegraphed to USG. "I have been unable to get a dispatch to you since 9 this morning. I regretted to ~~hear~~ learn from the President who has just returned that you did not receive Weitzel's dispatch announcing that he took possession of Richmond at 8.15 this morning. I have not heard from him since. Am sending prisoners as fast as they come in to Pt Lookout" Copies, DLC-USG, V, 46, 75, 108; DNA, RG 108, Letters Sent. *O.R.*, I, xlvi, part 3, 510.

On April 3, W. W. Townes, mayor of Petersburg, and others wrote to USG or "The Maj. Genl Comdng U. S. Forces in front of Petersburg—" "The City of Petersburg having been evacuated by the Confederate Troops, We, a Committee authorized by the Common Council, do hereby surrender the City to the United States Forces, with a request for the protection of the persons and property of its inhabitants." LS, DNA, RG 108, Letters Received. *O.R.*, I, xlvi, part 1, 1048.

To Maj. Gen. Godfrey Weitzel

Petersburg Apl. 3d 1865 12.30 p. m.

MAJ. GN. WEITZEL A. JAMES.

How are you progressing? Will the enemy try to hold Richmond? I have detained the Div. belonging to your Corps and will send it back if you think it will be needed. I am waiting here to hear from you. The troops moved up the appomattox this morning.

U. S. GRANT
Lt. Gn.

ALS (telegram sent), Scheide Library, Princeton, N. J.; telegram received, DNA, RG 94, War Records Office, Miscellaneous War Records; *ibid.*, RG 107, Telegrams Collected (Unbound). *O.R.*, I, xlvi, part 3, 534. On April 4, 1865,

Maj. Gen. Godfrey Weitzel telegraphed to USG. "I just recd your despatches of yesterday   all have been attended to. Quite now reigns" Telegram received, DNA, RG 94, War Records Office, Miscellaneous War Records. *O.R.*, I, xlvi, part 3, 566.

An undated telegram from Bvt. Col. Theodore S. Bowers to Weitzel may have been sent on April 3. "Please direct the Pontoon Bridges to be opened to enabled the wooden gun boats to come down." Telegram received, DNA, RG 393, 25th Army Corps, Telegrams Received. On April 4, Weitzel telegraphed to Bowers. "Your dispatch of yesterday only received this morning. Nothing new here. The fires are out and perfect quiet reigns." *O.R.*, I, xlvi, part 3, 566.

On April 3, 6:15 P.M., Weitzel twice telegraphed to USG. "I am informed that Gen Lee at half past 3 P M yesterday telegraphed to the War Dept that he had been driven by you with heavy loss—That he had taken a position which he could not possibly hold—and that they had better give up this City at 12 O'clock —It is further said that Hardie with 10000 men has been detached from Johnson to give you one more fight at Danville if he can reach it" "General Shepley has information that several millions of dollars in gold left by railroad Saturday and Sunday for Danville   This is probably the gold from New Orleans banks and the Mint" ALS (telegrams sent), DNA, RG 107, Telegrams Collected (Unbound); telegrams received (2), *ibid.*, RG 108, Letters Received. *O.R.*, I, xlvi, part 3, 534, 535. At 9:00 P.M., Weitzel telegraphed to USG. "We have in our possession the following rolling stock found at the rail road depots in this City. Twenty eight (28) locomotives. Two (2) stationery engines. Forty four (44) passenger and baggage cars. Two hundred and six (206) freight cars." ALS (telegram sent), DNA, RG 107, Telegrams Collected (Unbound); telegram received, *ibid.*; *ibid.*, RG 108, Letters Received. *O.R.*, I, xlvi, part 3, 534.

To Edwin M. Stanton

———

Wilson's Station Va
Apl. 4. 1865.

Hon. Edwin M. Stanton.
Secretary of war.

The army is pushing forward in the hope of overtaking or dispersing the remainder of Lee's army. Sheridan with his cavalry and the 5th corps is between this and the Appomattox, Genl meade with the 2d & 6th, following. Gen Ord is following the line of the Southside Railroad   All of the enemy that retains anything like organization have gone north of the Appomattox & are apparently heading for Lynchburg

Their losses have been very heavy—Houses through the country are nearly full all used as hospitals for wounded men,

In every direction I hear of rebel soldiers pushing for home some in large, some in small squads and generally without arms,

The cavalry have pursued so closely that the enemy have been forced to destroy probably the greater part of their transportation caissons, & munitions of war.

The number of prisoners captured yesterday will exceed 2.000.

From the 28th of march to the present time our loss in killed, wounded and captured will not probably reach 7000, of whom from 1.500 to 2.000 were captured & many but slightly wounded. I shall continue the pursuit as long as there appears to be any use in it.

U S GRANT Lt Gen

Telegram received (at 10:30 P.M.), DNA, RG 107, Telegrams Collected (Bound); copies, DLC-USG, V, 46, 108. *O.R.*, I, xlvi, part 3, 545. The telegram was sent originally to Bvt. Col. Theodore S. Bowers and Secretary of War Edwin M. Stanton. Telegram received (at 6:30 P.M.), DLC-Robert T. Lincoln; copies, DLC-USG, V, 75; DNA, RG 108, Letters Sent. Bowers sent this message to Maj. Gen. William T. Sherman. Copy, DLC-William T. Sherman.

To Maj. Gen. George G. Meade

W Potts House Apl. 4th 1865

MAJ. GEN. MEADE,

Direct the 9th Corps to turn to the Cox road by the 1st cross road leading to it and to leave detachments of not less than one Brigade at a place to protect the rail-road to the rear of the Army back to Southerland station.

I send you copy of a despatch just received from Gen. Sheridan. If you can not find roads free from trains let your troops pass them and press on making as long a march to-day as possible

U. S. GRANT
Lt. Gn

P. S. Wilcox Div. coming up from Petersburg will protect the road at Southerland Station.

U. S. G.

ALS, DNA, RG 94, War Records Office, Army of the Potomac; Scheide Library, Princeton, N. J. *O.R.*, I, xlvi, part 3, 546. On April 4, 1865, 7:15 A.M. and 2:30 P.M., Maj. Gen. George G. Meade wrote to USG. "I find Ord's colored

Division has taken the Namozine road instead of the Cox road—I have sent forward & directed the commander to take the first left hand cross road & get on to the Cox road again—Please send out one of your officers to him to confirm this order—This officer should be held accountable for not knowing ~~where h~~ how to follow his own column" "Your despatch by Capt Wolsey received The necessary orders have been sent to Genl Parke who has now one Division on the Cox road guarding my supply trains I have also directed Genl Wright to push ahead as far today as is consistent with its efficency and if necessary turning the 5th Corps & Cavalry trains out of the road until he has passed—" ALS, DNA, RG 108, Letters Received. *O.R.*, I, xlvi, part 3, 545, 546.

At 1:30 P.M., Meade, "Namozine road at Cozzens house Hd Qrs of Genl—Sheridan last night," wrote to USG. "I do not expect the 6th corps will be able to get beyond this point today some 15 miles, and hardly reach here—for the road is in a terrible condition and it has been with great difficulty that the trains of the 5th corps & Cavalry have been able to move—Not being able to find any paralell roads—I directed Genl. Wright to let these trains precede him, and to send a force, if necessary a division to repair the road & keep them moving—The rations of the 6th & 9th corps are out tomorrow—At this point there is a road which strikes the S. S. R R near Wilsons Stn it is called the Wells road—I have ordered rations to replenish the 6th & 9th corps to be brought across tonight which they will draw tomorrow.—The 2d Corps left here early this morning & as it has an unobstructed road—I presume it will make a long march—it was 10 miles distant when I last heard of it—I shall proceed & join Genl. Humphreys & will be found on ~~thise~~ Namozine road beyond this point—I have had no report from the front.—I do not believe the trains of the 5th & Cavalry would ever have reached them but for the assistance being rendered by the 6th" ALS, DNA, RG 108, Letters Received. *O.R.*, I, xlvi, part 3, 545–46.

To Maj. Gen. Philip H. Sheridan

Wilsons Station, Apl., 4th/65

MAJ GEN SHERIDAN

An Engineer from the S. S. rail road is just in from Burkesville. He reports that Davis and Cabinet passed there about 3. A, M. yesterday going South. There was no accumulation of supplies there except two train loads which had been cut off from Petersburg— These were run up the road to Farmville It was understood that Lee was accompanying his troops and that he was bound for Danville by way of Farmville—Unless you have information more positive of the movements of the enemy push on with all dispatch to Farmville, and try to intercept thes ~~the~~ enemy there—

U. S GRANT Lt Gen.

P. S., I will push two Div. of Ord's troops as far towards Burkesville tomorrow as possible. If you have not already done so, send some Cavalry over to him. It will be highly essential when he reaches Burkesville to throw down the Danville road and out towards the Farmville and Danville pikes—

U. S. Grant Lt Gen.

Copies, Scheide Library, Princeton, N. J.; DLC-USG, V, 46, 75, 108; DNA, RG 108, Letters Sent. *O.R.*, I, xlvi, part 3, 557. On April 4, 1865, Lt. Col. Ely S. Parker, who wrote out the message to Maj. Gen. Philip H. Sheridan, wrote to Maj. Gen. George G. Meade. "The Lt Gen forwards to you his dispatch to Gen Sheridan which after you have read he desires you will send by some of your men to Gen Sheridan" ALS, Scheide Library, Princeton, N. J.

On April 4, Sheridan twice wrote to USG, the second time at noon. "Genl. Merritt encamped last night at Deep Creek. He met there a strong force of Infantry. There is a large train on the West side of the creek. Everything was in confusion yesterday—the enemy moving to the No side of the Appomattox as if ignorant of the evacuation of Richmond—If we press on we will no doubt get the whole army. I will make for a point on the Rail Road intermediate between Amelia C. H. and Burkesville. Genl Crook will cover Genl Ord's front. Maj. Young of my scouts captured Genl Barringer yesterday—The River Road is bad; no bridge over creeks—" "Genl Merritt's reports that the force of the Enemy in his front have all crossed to the North Side of the Appomattox River and from the best information he can obtain Genl. Merritt is of the opinion that the Enemy is retreating towards Lynchburg—Genl. Crook has no doubt reached the Danville Rail Road before this and I am now moving out the 5th Corps from Deep Creek as rapidly as possible in the direction of Amelia C. H. . . . The number of prisoners captured yesterday will be nearly two thousand—" ALS, DNA, RG 108, Letters Received. *O.R.*, I, xlvi, part 3, 556–57.

To Maj. Gen. Godfrey Weitzel

Sutherland Station Apl. 4th/65

Maj. Gen. Weitzel, Richmond, Va,

Arrest all editors and proprietors of Richmond papers still remaining in the City and send them to Ft. Monroe for confinement subject to my orders. Do not let your intention get out but give this job to the Provost Marshal with instructions to be quiet about it and not to let them escape if they still remain in town.

U. S. Grant

ALS (telegram sent), OClWHi; Scheide Library, Princeton, N. J.; telegram received, DNA, RG 107, Telegrams Collected (Unbound). *O.R.*, I, xlvi, part 3,

567. On May 12, 1865, Bvt. Brig. Gen. Cyrus B. Comstock telegraphed to Maj. Gen. Godfrey Weitzel. "Lt. Gen. Grant directs me to ask for an explanation of a Richmond Editor, a Mr Tyler, recieving your pass to visit New York after you had been directed to arrest him." ALS (telegram sent), DNA, RG 107, Telegrams Collected (Unbound); telegrams received (2), *ibid.* On the same day, Weitzel telegraphed to Comstock. "I believed Genl Grants order to have been fully executed. I especially enjoined it upon my Provost Marshal and recollect now that many people in Richmond were much terrified at some of the arrests. Until I received your dispatch just now it did not strike me for a moment that Mr Tayler ~~of~~ was one of them as he was going around perfectly freely and boldly. I gave him the pass because he said he wanted to get material for a union Paper. He was in my office & all around and it seems strange to me now that as I did not in the hurry of other matters remember him some one did not call my attention to it. It never even struck me until the moment I read your dispatch. I am astonished at myself for not having recollected his name—But the few days I was there I was nearly run to death by everybody & everything" Telegram received (at 10:45 P.M.), *ibid.*, Telegrams Collected (Bound); *ibid.*, RG 108, Telegrams Received; copies, *ibid.*, RG 393, 25th Army Corps, Telegrams Sent; DLC-USG, V, 54. On May 15, Weitzel telegraphed to Comstock. "All is right. Can explain everything. Will be in Washington day after tomorrow—" Telegram received (press), DNA, RG 107, Telegrams Collected (Bound).

On April 4, USG telegraphed to Weitzel. "Send troops and a suitable commander for the city of Petersburg to relieve ~~Peter~~ the troops now there. I think you had better send Hartsuff for this duty." ALS (telegram sent), OCIWHi; telegram received, DNA, RG 94, War Records Office, Miscellaneous War Records; *ibid.*, RG 107, Telegrams Collected (Unbound). *O.R.*, I, xlvi, part 3, 567. On April 5, Brig. Gen. John A. Rawlins telegraphed to Maj. Gen. Gouverneur K. Warren. "Since the making of Gen Meade's order assigning you Gen Ord has been directed to relieve all the Army of the Potomac remaining at Cit Point, Petersburg ~~to~~ and on the S. S. R. R. to Sutherland Statio[n] as Gen Hartsuff is your senior, you will turn over to him the command of these places, and await further orders from the Lt Gen Comd'g" Telegram sent, Scheide Library, Princeton, N. J.; copies, DLC-USG, V, 46, 75, 108; DNA, RG 108, Letters Sent; *ibid.*, RG 393, Dept. of Va. and N. C., District of the Nottoway, Telegrams Received. *O.R.*, I, xlvi, part 3, 585.

To Edwin M. Stanton

Nottoway C. H. Apl. 5th/65

HON. E. M. STANTON, WASHINGTON.

Last night Gen. Sheridan was on the Danville road South of Amelia C. H. and sent word to Gen. Meade who was following with the 2d & 6th Corps by wahat is known as the River road that if the troops could be got up in time he had hopes of capturing or dispersing the whole of Lee's Army. I am moving with the Left wing commanded by Gen. Ord by the Cox, or direct Burkesville road. We will be to-night in or near Burkesville. I have had no communication with Gen. ~~Lee~~ Sheridan or Meade to-day but hope to hear very soon that they have come up with and captured or broken up the balance of the Army of N. Va. In every direction we hear of the men going home generally without Arms.

U. S. Grant
Lt. Gn

ALS (telegram sent), Scheide Library, Princeton, N. J.; copies, DLC-USG, V, 46, 75, 108; DNA, RG 108, Letters Sent. *O.R.*, I, xlvi, part 3, 572.

To Edwin M. Stanton

Nottoway C. H. Apl. 5th/65

Hon. E. M. Stanton, Washington

The following dispatch is just received from Gn. Sheridan. Gen Meade was following the same road pursued by Sheridan and Lt. Dunne of my staff who brought the dispatch met the 2d Corps within five miles of Amelia. Gn. Ord will push forward by Burkesville and endeavor to intercept the outlet South.

U. S. Grant
Lt. Gn

ALS (telegram sent), Scheide Library, Princeton, N. J.; copies, DLC-USG, V, 46, 75, 108; DNA, RG 108, Letters Sent. *O.R.*, I, xlvi, part 3, 572–73. USG appended a copy of a letter of April 5, 1865, from Maj. Gen. Philip H. Sheridan, Jetersville, Va., to USG. "The whole of Lees Army is at or near Amelia C. H. and on this side of it. General Davies whom I sent out to Painsville on their right flank has just captured six pieces of artillery and some wagons. We can capture the Army of Northern Virginia if force enough can be thrown to this point and then advance upon it. My cavalry was at Burksville yesterday and six miles beyond on the Danville road last night. Generall Lee is at Amelia C. H in person. They are out or nearly out of rations. They were advancing up the rail road towards Burksville yesterday when we intercepted them at this point" ALS, DNA, RG 108, Letters Received. *O.R.*, I, xlvi, part 3, 573. USG also transmitted a copy to Maj. Gen. Edward O. C. Ord. Copies, Scheide Library, Princeton, N. J.; Ord Papers, CU-B.

On the same day, Brig. Gen. Seth Williams, Burkeville, Va., telegraphed to Secretary of War Edwin M. Stanton. "Lieutenant General Grant received the following dispatch at 6 30 P, M, to-day while on his way to this point and at once proceeded to General Sheridan's Head Quarters,   General Grant directed me to transmit the dispatch to you on the opening of the telegraph Office at this place and to say that the 6th Corps without doubt reached General Sheridans position within an hour or two after the dispatch was written,   two Divisions of the Twenty-fourth (24) Corps, will encamp here to night, and one Division of the twenty fifth (25) Corps at Beach's [*Blacks*] and White's Station South Side R. R." Copies, DLC-USG, V, 46, 76, 108; DNA, RG 108, Letters Sent. Printed as sent at 10:00 P.M., received on April 6, 11:30 A.M., in *O.R.*, I, xlvi, part 3, 573. Williams enclosed a copy of a letter of 3:00 P.M. from Sheridan to USG. "I send you the enclosed letter which will give you an idea of the condition of the enemy & thereeir whereabouts. I sent Genl Davies brigade this morning around on my left flank—he captured at Fames Cross Roads Five (5.) ps Artillery—About 200 wagons and eight or nine battle flags & a number of prisoners —The 2d A—C. is now coming up—I wish you were here yourself—I feel confident of capturing the Army of Northern Va. if we exert ourselves—I see no escape for Lee—I will put all my Cavalry out on our left flank except McKenzie who is now on the right—"   ALS, DNA, RG 108, Letters Received. *O.R.*, I, xlvi, part 3, 582. The enclosure is *ibid.* The delivery of the message from Sheridan is described in Horace Porter, *Campaigning with Grant* (New York, 1897), p. 454. On the same day, Sheridan wrote to USG. "From present indications the retreat of the enemy is rapidly becoming a *route*. We are shelling their trains & preparing to attack their Infantry immediately   Their troops are moving on their left flank & I think we can break & disperse them—*Evrything* should be hurried forward with the utmost speed—If General Ord can be put in below it will probably use them up—"   ALS, DNA, RG 108, Letters Received. *O.R.*, I, xlvi, part 3, 582.

Also on April 5, Stanton telegraphed to USG. "I have directe It is desirable that all the letters papers & correspondence [p]rivate or public found at Richmond in the Post office or elsewhere should be immediately sent to Mr Seward by Special Messenger   I have ordered Weitzel to do so but if you can spare an intelligent & trusty officer to see that it is done please give the order. I would greatly prefer some other person that Shepley for Military Governor,   please remove him immediately & appoint some good man of your own selection who has not been connected with Butlers administration,   Had not Weitzel had better have duty elsewhere than Richmond?" ALS (telegram sent), DNA, RG 107, Telegrams Collected (Bound); telegram received, *ibid.*, RG 108, Letters Received. *O.R.*, I, xlvi, part 3, 573. On the same day, Bvt. Col. Theodore S. Bowers wrote to Bvt. Brig. Gen. Edward D. Townsend. "I have the honor to forward herewith twenty two Sacks of Rebel Mail, Captured on the evening of the 2d inst. by Sergeant Major Garrett and six men, of the 50th Penna. Vols., whilst being sent from Petersburg and Richmond." ALS, DNA, RG 94, Letters Received, 358A 1865. See *O.R.*, I, xlvi, part 3, 642. On April 8, Stanton telegraphed to USG. "In the mail Petersburg mail [*is*] found the following acknowledgement of ammunition received on the 3d inst at Amelia Court House. It may still be there." ALS (telegram sent), DNA, RG 107, Telegrams Collected (Bound); telegram received, *ibid.*, Telegrams Collected (Unbound); *ibid.*, RG 108, Letters Received. *O.R.*, I, xlvi, part 3, 641. Stanton appended a copy of a message of March 3 printed *ibid.*

To Maj. Gen. George G. Meade

Williams [*Wilson's*] Station
Apl. 5th 1865 4 a. m

MAJ. GEN MEADE,

Your note of 10.45 p m. last night and order for movement this morning is received. The note alluded to from Gen. Sheridan is not among the papers. Its purport however I suppose I get from Maj. Jay[1] and from the tenor of your note and orders.

I do not see that greater efforts can be made than you are making to get up with the enemy. We want to reach the remnant of Lee's Army wherever it may be found by the shortest and most practicable route. That your order provides for and has my hearty approval. Ord will make a forced march with Gibbons two Divisions and will come near reaching Burkeville.

U. S. GRANT
Lt. Gn

ALS, DNA, RG 94, War Records Office, Army of the Potomac; Scheide Library, Princeton, N. J. *O.R.*, I, xlvi, part 3, 575–76. On April 4, 1865, 10:45 P.M., Maj. Gen. George G. Meade wrote to USG. "I send you a despatch from Gen Sheridan and my order predicated thereon. Gen. Humphreys is partly across Deep Run within 9 miles, as I understand, of Jetersville. Gen Humphreys reached this point between 7 & 8 P M. where he halted, he having been since 5 A. M. endeavoring, under Gen. Sheridan's orders, to push forward after the 5th corps, but being prevented from doing so by obstacles in the form of trains, though principally by nearly the whole cavalry force cutting his column and taking the same road, interposing between him and the 5th Corps. Having read Gen Sheridan's despatch to you reporting the enemy retreating on Lynchburg and crossing the Appomattox—not hearing any guns—Gen. Humphreys having no communication from Gen Sheridan urging haste, and having cavalry right in his front, I considered the emergency requiring a night march as past—And Humphreys reporting his men considerably fatigued, having been moving working, and standing for 14 hours, out of rations tonight and expecting to receive them so as to be issued tonight, I did not consider it necessary to order him on, as he was going into bivouac when I joined him. I have now ordered him to move at all hazards at 3 A M tomorrow, but, if his rations can be issued to them prior to that, to march so soon as issued or, if the temper of the men, on having the despatch of Gen Sheridan communicated to them, leads to the belief that they will march with spirit, then to push on *at once*, as soon as they can be got under arms. I send you a copy of the order issued by me, and you may rest assured that every exertion will be made by myself and subordinate commanders to reach the point with the men in such condition that they may be available for immediate action. From all I can gather Humphreys has from 8 to 9 miles to march and Wright from 21 to 22." Copies, DNA, RG 107, Telegrams Collected (Unbound); *ibid.*, RG 108, Letters Received; *ibid.*, RG 393, Army of the Potomac, Letters Sent; DLC-Philip H. Sheridan; (2) Meade Papers, PHi. *O.R.*, I, xlvi, part 3, 547. The last sentence in other copies has "9 to 10" in place of "8 to 9." The enclosures mentioned are *ibid.*, pp. 549, 557. See following letter.

1. William Jay of N. Y., appointed capt. and aide as of Aug. 28, 1861, and bvt. maj. as of Aug. 1, 1864.

To Maj. Gen. George G. Meade

Nottoway C. H. Apl. 5th 1865 5.10 p m.

MAJ. GN. MEADE.

Your dispatch of 8.30 a. m. received. Your movements are right. Lee's Army is the objective point and to capture that is all we want. Ord has marched 15 miles to-day to reach here and is going on. He will probably reach Burkesville to-night My Hd Qrs. will be with the advance.

U. S GRANT

Lt. Gen

ALS, Scheide Library, Princeton, N. J. *O.R.*, I, xlvi, part 3, 576. On April 5, 1865, 8:30 A.M., Maj. Gen. George G. Meade wrote to USG. "Humphreys moved between 1 & 2—this morning without rations After proceeding about 2 miles, he found the cavalry, again ~~taking~~ occupying the road—being thus detained, he had his rations brought up & distributed—& moved on again between 7 & 8—Wright reached this point by 7. a m without having received his rations —I have directed 3 days to be issued to him from the 5th corps train which is here—Wright will move on as soon as his rations are issued—I send copy of despatch from Genl. Sheridan which should have been enclosed in my despatch of 2—a m Sheridan moving his cavalry would indicate the situation of affairs at Jettersville changed I have sent forward to enquire & if it is not necessary to go to Jettersville I will move on the most direct road to Farmville—" ALS, DNA, RG 108, Letters Received. *O.R.*, I, xlvi, part 3, 576. The enclosure is *ibid.*, p. 557. See preceding letter.

To Maj. Gen. George G. Meade

[*April 5, 1865*] 10.30 p. m.

MAJ. GN. MEADE,

I have just arrived here ~~leavin~~ having left the Hd of Gn. Ord's Column at about 7.30 p. m some 4 miles West of Nottoway   He will reach Burkesville to-night after a march of about 28 miles to-day.

Ords orders now are to move West at 8 a. m. and take up a position to watch all the roads leading South crossing between Burkesville and and Farmville.

Your orders for to-morrow morning will hold in the absence of others. It is my impression however that Lee will retreat during the night and if so we will pursue with vigor,

I would go over to see you this evening but it is late and I have roade a long distance to-day.

U. S. GRANT
Lt. Gn

ALS, Scheide Library, Princeton, N. J. Printed as received at 11:30 P.M. in *O.R.*, I, xlvi, part 3, 577. On April 5, 1865, 11:30 P.M., Maj. Gen. George G. Meade wrote to USG. "Your despatch of 10.30 received—I send you copy of despatch forwarded to you at 8. P. M.—" ALS, DNA, RG 108, Letters Received. *O.R.*, I, xlvi, part 3, 577. At 8:00 P.M., Meade had written to USG. "I reached this point in advance of the 2d Corps at 2 P. M. The 2d Corps reached here at 3.30. The Sixth 6th Corps could not get here until about 6 P. M. The second Corps arrived here in time to take position on the right & left of the 5th Corps found entrenched to meet an anticipated attack by the enemy. Owing to the late arrival of the 6th Corps I was unable to attack to night but I will do so with the three Corps in conjunction with Genl Sheridan at 6. A. M. tomorrow" LS, DNA, RG 108, Letters Received. *O.R.*, I, xlvi, part 3, 576.

To Maj. Gen. Edward O. C. Ord

Jetersville Apl. 5th/65 10.10 p. m

MAJ. GN. ORD, BURKESVILLE

In the absence of further orders move West at 8 a. m to-morrow morning and take position to watch the roads runing

South between Burkesville and Farmville. I am strongly of opinion Lee will leave Amelia to-night to go South   He will be pursued from here at 6 a. m. if he leaves   Otherwise an advance will be made upon him where he is.

\ U. S. GRANT
Lt. Gn

ALS, Scheide Library, Princeton, N. J. *O.R.,* I, xlvi, part 3, 583. USG wrote this message at least twice; one version was captured. ALS (variant), ViHi; Douglas Southall Freeman, *R. E. Lee* (New York, 1935), IV, 78–79.

To Maj. Gen. William T. Sherman

———

Wilson's Station Apl. 5th *1865*
MAJ. GN. SHERMAN, CARE COL. T. S. BOWERS CITY POINT.

All indications now are that Lee will attempt to reach Danville with the remnant of his force. Sheridan who was up with him last night reports all that is left, *Horse Foot* and *Dragoons*, at 20.000 much demoralized. We hope to reduce this number ~~fully~~ one half. I shall push on to Burkeville and if a stand ~~at~~ is made at Danville ~~is made~~ will in a very few days go there. If you can possibly do so push on from where you are and let us see if we can not finish the job with Lee's & Johnston's Armies. Whether it will be better for you to strike for Greensboro, or nearer to Danville, you will be better able to judge when you receive this. Rebel Armies now are the only strategic points to strike at.

U. S. GRANT, Lt. Gn

Col. Bowers will have this put in ~~Cyp~~ Cipher.

ALS, PPRF. *O.R.,* I, xxxiv, part 1, 53–54; *ibid.,* I, xxxvi, part 1, 57; *ibid.,* I, xxxviii, part 1, 46; *ibid.,* I, xlvii, part 3, 99–100. This message, as telegraphed, reached Maj. Gen. William T. Sherman on April 8, 1865. *Memoirs of Gen. W. T. Sherman* (4th ed., New York, 1891), II, 343. On April 5, Maj. George K. Leet was ordered to carry messages to Sherman. *O.R.,* I, xlvii, part 3, 99.

On April 4, Bvt. Col. Theodore S. Bowers telegraphed to Sherman. "On Sunday Morning the second we Charged & Carried the enemys entire line south of the Appomattox defeated & drove back Lees army & the same evening enveloped Petersburg from the Appomattox above to the river below—About one (1) oclock Monday Morning Petersburg was evacuated & we took possession of it—at 8.15 Weitzel took possession of Richmond from his position North of the

James—Jeff. Davis & his Cabinet & Lee with most of his army are retreating in hot haste towards Danville—The other Column is falling back on Lynchburg, We are pursuing Vigorously—Our prisoners will number from twelve thousand (12.000) to Fifteen thousand (15.000) with Several hundred pieces of artillery—Much of the Tobacco and Cotton in Petersburg & Richmond was burned by the enemy—He also attempted to burn Richmond—Weitzel succeeded in putting out the fires but not until several districts were in ruins. Everything is quiet there now & the people receive our army with great rejoicing—" Telegrams received (2—one received in Washington at 3:40 P.M., the other, retransmitted from New Berne, N. C., received on April 6), DNA, RG 107, Telegrams Collected (Unbound); (press) *ibid.*, Telegrams Collected (Bound); copies, *ibid.*, RG 108, Letters Sent; DLC-USG, V, 46, 75, 108. Printed as sent at 3:40 P.M. in *O.R.*, I, xlvi, part 3, 547; *ibid.*, I, xlvii, part 3, 95.

On April 5, Sherman, Goldsboro, N. C., wrote to USG. "I now enclose you a copy of my orders prescribing the movemt hence for a position on the Roanoke. The movemt begins on the 10th as I promised and by the 12th we will be fairly under way. Our Railroad have worked *double* what I calculated because the track is so level that a locomotive can haul 25 cars instead of 10 or 12 as in Upper Georgia. We now have enough bread & small stores for our wagons and I am hurrying up Crufts Provisional Division from Tennessee also the men who belonged to this Army who had been sent to Savannah & Charleston. We can use the Railroad to bring up the last, the others are marching. I get nothing from you not a word since I left you and am of course impatient to Know what Lee proposes to do. I hear nothing satisfactory from Johnston. We find Wade Hamptons cavalry on the Road to Weldon and Raleigh but evidently only watching us. They have made no effort to strike our Railroad anywhere. I shall expect to hear the effect of your move on Dinwiddie before I get off but shall not wait." ALS, DNA, RG 108, Letters Received. *O.R.*, I, xlvii, part 3, 100. The enclosure is *ibid.*, pp. 102–3.

On April 8, Sherman wrote to USG. "I have just received your letter of the 5th from Wilsons station and although I have written you several letters lately will repeat. On Monday at day-light all my army will move straight on Joe Johnston, supposed to be between me and Raleigh, and I will follow him where ever he may go. If he retreats on Danville to make junction with Lee, I will do the same though I may take a course round him bending toward Greensboro, for the purpose of turning him north. I will bear in mind your plain and unmistakeable point that 'the Rebel Armies are now the strategic points to strike at.'—. I will follow Johnston, presumig that you are after Lee or all that you have left to him and if they come together, we will also. I think I will be at Raleigh on Thursday the 13, and shall pursue Johnston toward Greensboro, unless it be manifest that ~~Johnston~~ he has gone toward Danville. I shall encourage him to come to Bay, or to move toward Danville, as I dont want to race all the way back through South Carolina and Georgia. It is to our interest to let Lee & Johnston come together, just as a billiard player would nurse the balls when he has them in a nice place. I am delighted and amazed at the result of your move to the South of Petersburg, and Lee has lost in one day the Reputation of three years, and you have established a Reputation for perseverance and pluck that would make Wellington jump out of his Coffin. I wish you could have waited a few days, or that I could have been here a week sooner, but it is not too late yet, and you may rely with absolute certainty, that I will be after Johnston with about 80000 men, provided for 20 full days, which will last me

40,—and I will leave a small force here at Goldsboro, & repair the Railroad up to Raleigh. If you have a spare division, you might send it to Schofield to help him hold this Line of Railroad out from Morehead City to Goldsboro, but I will not hesitate to let go Railroad and evry thing if I can get at Joe Johnston in an open field. If Sheridan dont run his horses off their legs, and you can spare him for a week or so, let him feel down for me, and I think he can make a big haul of horses. Tell him I make him a free gift of all the blooded stock of North Carolina including Wade Hampton whose pedigree and stud are of high repute. Dont fail to have Stoneman break through the mountains of west North Carolina. he will find plenty of Union men who will aid him to reach either your army or mine; and Canby should if he takes Mobile, get up the Alabama River about *Selma*, from which place he can catch all fragments passing towards Texas. I have an idea that he can get up the Alabama River, even if he do not take Mobile. I have a Report from Wilson who will I think break up all Railroad Lines in Alabama." ALS, DNA, RG 108, Letters Received. *O.R.*, I, xlvii, part 3, 128–29.

On April 10, Leet, Fort Monroe, telegraphed to Bowers. "I left Goldsboro on Saturday at three P. M. with dispatch from Gen. Sherman in which he says—'On Monday at daylight all my Army will move straight on Joe Johnston, supposed to be between here and Raleigh, and I will follow him wherever he may go.' On reaching Moorhead City yesterday morning I found the following telegram. 'Goldsboro Apl. 8th 7.45 P. M. GEN. MEIGS Am just in receipt of a cipher dispatch from Gen. Grant at Burkville of 6th. Tell Maj. Leet, who comes down today, to get to Old Point as quick as possible and get a message to Grant at any cost, that I will push Joe Johnston to the death W. T. SHERMAN Maj. Genl.' I will proceed immediately to Richmond" ALS (telegram sent), DNA, RG 107, Telegrams Collected (Unbound); telegram received, *ibid. O.R.*, I, xlvii, part 3, 150.

To Maj. Gen. George G. Meade

Burkesville Apl. 6th 1865 8.30 p. m.

MAJ. GEN. MEADE,

It was wright for Wright to remain after he had come up with the enemy. Your orders for the [5]th Corps to move to the left will answer the purpose. I understand the North Carolinians are all leaving Lee. If we press him with vigor for a couple of days more I do not beleive he will get off with 5000 men.

U. S. GRANT
Lt. Gn.

ALS (telegram sent), Meissner Collection, Washington University, St. Louis, Mo.; signal received (on April 7, 1865, 1:30 A.M.), DNA, RG 94, War Records Office, Army of the Potomac. *O.R.*, I, xlvi, part 3, 596. On April 6, 7:00 P.M., Maj. Gen. George G. Meade telegraphed to USG. "Maj Genl Wright reports that on receipt of my despatch to move on farmville he was actually engaged with the emeny & driving him. The Staff officers who brings the despatch states that prisoners were taken from ~~f~~Field and Kershaws Divisions. This will prevent wright moving as ordered to Farmville but I will direct Griffin to start as early as possible in the morning so that he will be on hand to assist Wright or move to Farmville   Sheridan was cooperating with Wright—Humphreys & Wright are pretty close together" Telegram received (marked as sent at 9:00 P.M.), DNA, RG 108, Letters Received; copies (2), Meade Papers, PHi. *O.R.*, I, xlvi, part 3, 596.

At 6:00 P.M., Meade telegraphed to USG. "Gen Humphreys reports that he has pursued the enemy 3 miles beyond Deatonsville   Has captured One gun & reports the Road literally strewn with tents Baggage & Camp equipage—He is still pushing on—no report from Griffin or Wright since you left" Telegram received (at 7:15 P.M.), DNA, RG 108, Letters Received; copies, *ibid.*, RG 393, Army of the Potomac, Letters Sent; (2) Meade Papers, PHi. *O.R.*, I, xlvi, part 3, 595.

At 10:00 P.M., Meade wrote (and telegraphed the same message) to USG. "At day light this morning I moved the ~~62d~~ 5th & 6 corps along the R. Rd. in the direction of Amelia C. H.—~~with~~ Soon after moving reliable intelligence was received that the enemy was moving towards Farmville—The direction of the 2d & 5—corps was immediately changed from a Northerly to a Northwesterly direction—the directing corps the 2d, moving on Deatonville the 5th hitherto the centre moving on the right of the 2d and the 6th faced about & moving by the left flank taking position on the left of the 2d—It was understood the cavalry would operate on the extreme left—These changes were promptly made the 2d corps soon becoming engaged with the enemy near Deatonville and driving him by night across Sailor creek to the Appomatox—The 5th corps made a long march but its position prevented its striking the rear of the enemys column before it had passed.—The 6th corps came up with the enemy about 4 P. M & in conjunction with the 2d on its right and the cavalry on its left—attacked and routed the enemy capturing many prisoners among them Lt. Genl. Ewell & Genl. Custis Lee—I transmit despatches both from Maj. Genl. Humphreys & Wright—which in justice to these distinguished officers and the gallant corps they command, I beg may be sent to the War Dept for immediate publication— It is impossible at this moment to give any estimate of the casualties on either side, or of the number of prisoners taken, but it is evident todays work is not going to be one of the least important in the recent brilliant operations—The pursuit will be continued so soon as the men have a a little rest.—Griffin with the 5th will be moved by the left & Wright & Humphreys continue the direct pursuit as long as it promises success." ALS, DNA, RG 108, Letters Received; telegram received (on April 7, 3:20 A.M.), *ibid.*; *ibid.*, RG 107, Telegrams Collected (Bound); *ibid.*, Telegrams Collected (Unbound). *O.R.*, I, xlvi, part 3, 596–97.

Also on April 6, USG telegraphed to President Abraham Lincoln. "The following Telegrams respectfully forwarded for your Information" Telegram received, DLC-Robert T. Lincoln. USG appended a copy of Meade's letter of 10:00 P.M., a telegram of 7:30 P.M. from Maj. Gen. Andrew A. Humphreys to Bvt. Maj. Gen. Alexander S. Webb, and a telegram of 9:10 P.M. (forwarded as sent at 10:00 P.M.) from Maj. Gen. Horatio G. Wright to Webb. Copies, *ibid.* The additional enclosures are in *O.R.*, I, xlvi, part 3, 600, 604–5. See Lincoln, *Works*, VIII, 390–92. At noon, Lincoln wrote to USG. "Secretary Seward was thrown from his carriage yesterday and seriously injured. This, with other matters, will take me to Washington soon. I was at Richmond yesterday and the day before, when and where Judge Campbell (who was with Messrs. Hunter and Stephens in Februay) called on me and made such representations as induced me to put in his hands an informal paper, repeating the propositions in my letter of instructions to Mr Seward (which you remember) and adding that if the war be now further persisted in by the rebels, confiscated property shall, at the least, bear the additional cost; and that confiscations shall be remitted to the people of any State which will now promptly, and in good faith, withdraw its troops and other support, from resistance to the government. Judge Campbell thought it not impossible that the rebel Legislature of Virginia would do the latter, if permitted; and accordingly, I addressed a private letter to Gen. Weitzel (with permission for Judge Campbell to see it) telling him, Gen. W. that if they attempt this, to permit and protect them, unless they attempt something hostile to the United States, in which case to give them notice and time to leave, and to arrest any remaining after such time. I do not think it very probable that anything will come of this; but I have thought best to notify you, so that if you should see signs, you may understand them. From your recent despatches it seems that you are pretty effectually withdrawing the Virginia troops from opposition to the government. Nothing I have done, or probably shall do, is to delay, hinder, or interfere with you in your work." ALS, PPRF. *O.R.*, I, xlvi, part 3, 593. Lincoln, *Works*, VIII, 388.

To Maj. Gen. Edward O. C. Ord

Jettersville Apl. 6th/65

MAJ. GN. ORD.

The enemy evacuated Amelia last night or this morning and are now apparently moving Southwest to get on the Farmville and Danville road. The 2d Corps moved from here towards Deatonville and have struck the flank of the enemy. The 5th & 6th Corps are moving, parallel with the 2d the 5th to the right of it and the 6th to the left. The Cavalry is still further southwest

You will move out to intercept them if possible. Taking roads according to the information you may get, recollecting that the capture of the enemy is what we want. McKenzie started to join you with the Cavalry this morning. Set your provost Marshal, or some one, to ascertain if there is any movement from Danville this way.

U. S. GRANT
Lt. Gn

ALS, Scheide Library, Princeton, N. J. *O.R.*, I, xlvi, part 3, 611. On April 6, 1865, Maj. Gen. Edward O. C. Ord twice wrote to USG, first from Burke's Station, second at 12:45 P.M. "Turners and Fosters divisions are here, have sent two Regts of Infantry and ~~what~~ 50 cavalry ~~I can~~ to destroy a span of high bridge near farmville—if ~~it~~ not too strongly guarded—and am tearing up ~~the~~ one rail of the two R. Roads towards Danville & Lynchburg—will throw up a line of rifle pits to cover from Cavalry—~~tr~~ my trains are nearly all up—" "I am now moving over fosters division to stike the enemy on the flank—have knowledge of but one road coming in from side of Deatonville—am moving Foster out on that road if I find other roads shall use them—I hope Washburn was in time to break the Farmville bridge to his force I have sent word, to look out on their left coming in and if it can be done take roads south of S. S—Rail Rd—" ALS, DNA, RG 108, Letters Received. *O.R.*, I, xlvi, part 3, 611.

To Maj. Gen. Edward O. C. Ord

Jeterville Apl. 6th 1865 4.20 p m

MAJ. GN. ~~SHERIDAN~~ ORD.

Send Gibbon with his two Divisions to Farmington to hold that crossing. The 6th Corps is also ordered. The Colored Division will be sufficient to retain at Burkeville.

The enemy are evidently making for Ligonton and Stony Point bridges. Indications are that the enemy are all most in a route. They are burning wagons, Caissons &c.

U. S. GRANT
Lt. Gn

ALS, Scheide Library, Princeton, N. J.; Ord Papers, CU-B; telegram received, DNA, RG 107, Telegrams Collected (Unbound). *O.R.*, I, xlvi, part 3, 611. In telegraphing this message, USG added a postscript addressed to Brig. Gen. Seth Williams. "If Gen Ord is absent let Gen Turner read this despatch & move at once with his divisions to the turnpike crossing at Farmville—" Telegram received, Ord Papers, CU-B; DNA, RG 107, Telegrams Collected (Unbound). *O.R.*, I, xlvi, part 3, 612.

To Maj. Gen. Philip H. Sheridan

Jetersville, Apl. ~~5~~6 1865 2.05 p. m.

MAJ. GN. SHERIDAN.

From this point Gen. Humphrey's Corps could be seen advancing over Truly Vaughan's farm. The enemy occupied that

place two hours ago with Artillery and Infantry. Griffin is further
to the right and has been urged to push on. He is no doubt doing
so. Wright is pushing out on the road you are on and will go in
with a vim any place you dictate. Ord has send two regiments out
to Farmville to destroy the bridge and is intrenching the balance
of his command at Burkes Station. If your information makes it
advisable for him to move out notify him and he will do so.

U. S. Grant
Lt. Gn

ALS, Scheide Library, Princeton, N. J. *O.R.*, I, xlvi, part 3, 609.
   On April 6, 1865, in the morning from Flat Creek and at 12:10 P.M., Maj.
Gen. Philip H. Sheridan wrote to USG. "The Enemys trains are moving on the
pike through Deatons-ville in the direction of Burkesville station   I am just
getting ready to attack it—I have notified Genl Ord—" "My information is that
the Enemy are moving to our left with their trains, and whole army—The trains
and army were moving all last night and are very short of provisions, and very
tired indeed—I think that now is the time to attack them with all your Infantry
—They are reported to have begd provisions from the people of the country all
along the road as they passed—I am working around farther to our left—" LS,
DNA, RG 108, Letters Received. *O.R.*, I, xlvi, part 3, 609–10. On the same day,
Sheridan, "Sailors Creek," wrote to USG. "I have the honor to report, that the
enemy made a stand ~~on~~ at the intersection of the Burkes station road, with the
road on which he was retreating. I attacked him with two Divisions of the 6th
Army Corps & routed him handsomely, making a Connection with the Cavalry.
I am still pressing on, with both Cavalry, & Infantry. Up to the present time we
have captured Genls Ewell, Kershaw, Barton, Corse, De Foe [*Du Bose*] & Custis
Lee—several thousand prisoners—fourteen pieces of artillery with caissons, &. a
large number of wagons. If the thing is pressed I think that Lee will surrender"
ALS, ICHi. *O.R.*, I, xlvi, part 3, 610. At 11:15 P.M., USG telegraphed to Presi-
dent Abraham Lincoln. "The following despatch just rec'd is respectfully for-
warded for your information." Telegram received, DLC-Robert T. Lincoln. See
Lincoln, *Works*, VIII, 389. On April 7, 11:00 A.M., Lincoln telegraphed to
USG. "Gen. Sheridan says 'If the thing is pressed I think that Lee will surren-
der.' Let the *thing* be pressed." ALS (telegram sent), ICHi; telegram received,
USMA. Lincoln, *Works*, VIII, 392. USG wrote at the foot of the telegram sent.
"The original dispatch sent by Mr Lincoln to me, Apl. 7th 1865." AES, ICHi.

To Bvt. Col. Theodore S. Bowers

Burkesville. April 6. 1865

Col. T. S. Bowers. City Point
   Please have the following dispatch put in cipher and ask Admiral Porter to send it to Moorehead City

Burkesville April 6. 1865
Maj. Gen. Sherman. Goldsboro N. C.

We have Lee's army pressed hard, his men scattering and going to their homes by the thousands. He is endeavoring to reach Danville where Davis and his cabinet have gone. I shall press the pursuit to the end. Push Johnston at the same time and let us finish up this job all at once.

U. S. Grant
Lt. Genl

Telegram, copies, DLC-USG, V, 46, 75, 108; DNA, RG 108, Letters Sent. *O.R.*, I, xlvii, part 3, 109. The telegram received (on April 8, 1865) by Maj. Gen. William T. Sherman is in PPRF.

On April 6, Sherman, Goldsboro, N. C., telegraphed to USG. "I have just heard of the occupation of Richmond and Petersburg—I expect orders from you but in the ~~meantime~~ absence of any I will hold on to Goldsboro and the two railroads and move on Raleigh I think Johnston still remains about Smithfield—I will strike him anyhow moving out on the 10th—In the meantime will expect orders via Newborn from you as I dont know the line of Lees retreat" Telegram received (on April 8, 10:30 A.M.), DNA, RG 107, Telegrams Collected (Unbound); *ibid.*, RG 108, Letters Received. *O.R.*, I, xlvii, part 3, 109.

On April 6 (sent via Fort Monroe, April 7, 1:00 A.M.), Bvt. Brig. Gen. Daniel C. McCallum, Norfolk, superintendent of military railroads, telegraphed to USG. "Genl. Sherman has directed me to furnish Rolling Stock, and put the Seaboard & Roanoke Railroad in running order to Weldon. with your approval. This order was given on monday last, and before the fall, of Richmond—~~Shall I was known at Goldsboro'~~ Shall I proceed with the work." ALS (telegram sent), DNA, RG 107, Telegrams Collected (Unbound); telegram received, *ibid.*; *ibid.*, RG 108, Letters Received. On April 8, USG, Farmville, Va., telegraphed to McCallum. "In my Opinion it is not necessary to stock and put in repair the Seabord and Roanoke R. R. as there is plenty of rolling stock in Richmond which can be used—You will however carry out Gen Sherman's wishes—" Telegram sent, Scheide Library, Princeton, N. J.; telegrams received (2), DNA, RG 107, Telegrams Collected (Unbound).

To Bvt. Col. Theodore S. Bowers

Headquarters Armies of the U. S.
Burkesville. April 6. 1865
Col. T. S. Bowers, City Point

The enemy left his position at Amelia C. H., during the night last night and attempted to get to Danville by the roads west of this place. The cavalry, 2d 5th and 6th Corps lay in the vicinity of Jetersville ready to attack this morning had he not moved. Their position was admirable for attacking in flank. Accordingly this morning these troops were moved out on roads nearly parallel, the cavalry and 6th Corps on the left, the 2d in the centre and the 5th on the right. The latter got upon the road after the enemy had passed but pushed after him with great vigor, picked up many of the enemy's stragglers and forced him to burn many of his wagons. All the others struck the enemy, but the country being open and roads numerous have not so far made as large captures of prisoners as I had hoped. They however forced the enemy to abandon much of his train, ammunition &c. and are still pushing: Genl. Gibbon with Foster's and Turner's Divisions of the 24th Corps reached here last night after a march of 28 miles for the day. These troops were sent out to Farmville this afternoon and I am in hopes will head the enemy and enable us to totally break up the Army of Northern Virginia. The troops are all pushing now though it is after night and they have had no rest for more than one week. The finest spirits prevails among the men and I believe that in three days more Lee will not have an army of 5,000 men to take out of Virginia, and no train or supplies. I have just returned from the right.

U. S. GRANT
Lt. Genl

Copies, DLC-USG, V, 46, 75, 108; DNA, RG 108, Letters Sent. *O.R.*, I, xlvi, part 3, 594–95.

On April 6, 1865, Bvt. Col. Theodore S. Bowers telegraphed to USG. "The 11 and 14th Regulars are here. Shall I send them back to Gen Meade   There are several hundred of Sheridans men here mounted. Shall they go to the front. I will start from here at 4 in the morning for your Headquarters, on business if there is no objection. The President is in the office anxious for any news you may have leisure to send him." ALS (telegram sent), DNA, RG 107, Telegrams Collected (Unbound). *O.R.*, I, xlvi, part 3, 595. On the same day, Lt. Col. Ely S. Parker wrote to Bowers. "You will direct the Commanding Officers of the 11th and 4th U S Infantry to report to Genl. Meade for orders   Sheridans remounted men can be retained to be sent out only as guards for cattle to the front when required. Upon their arrival at the front they will join their proper commands without delay." Copies, DLC-USG, V, 46, 75, 108; DNA, RG 108, Letters Sent. *O.R.*, I, xlvi, part 3, 595.

To Gen. Robert E. Lee

Apl. 7th 1865

GEN. R. E. LEE
COMD.G C. S. A.
GENERAL,

The result of the last week must convince you of the hopelessness of further resistance on the part of the Army of Northern Va. in this struggle. I feel that it is so and regard it as my duty to shift from myself, the responsibility of any further effusion of blood by asking of you the surrender of that portion of the C. S. Army known as the Army of Northern Va.

Very respectfully
your obt. svt
U. S. GRANT
Lt. Gn

ALS, Scheide Library, Princeton, N. J. *O.R.*, I, xxxiv, part 1, 54; *ibid.*, I, xxxvi, part 1, 58; *ibid.*, I, xxxviii, part 1, 47; (as sent at 5:00 P.M.) *ibid.*, I, xlvi, part 3, 619. On April 7, 1865, Gen. Robert E. Lee wrote to USG. "I have recd your note of this date. Though not entertaining the opinion you express of the hopelessness of further resistance on the part of the Army of N. Va. I reciprocate your desire to avoid useless effusion of blood & therefore before Considering your proposition ask the terms you will offer on condition of its surrender" ALS, DNA, RG 94, Treasure Room. *O.R.*, I, xxxiv, part 1, 54–55; *ibid.*, I, xxxvi, part 1, 58; *ibid.*, I, xxxviii, part 1, 47; *ibid.*, I, xlvi, part 3, 619.

Ely S. Parker, who copied and annotated the surrender correspondence in later years, commented: "The above was written and sent out from Farmville. Genl Seth Williams A. A. G. was the messenger accompanied by his orderly. Williams flag of truce was fired upon. The orderly deserted Williams, but Williams went through, narrowly escaped being shot. No apology was made for this violation of the flag. Williams, I believe, making no formal complaint on account of its being near dark and the enemy might not have distinguished the flag." ICN. See Horace Porter, *Campaigning with Grant* (New York, 1897), pp. 459–60.

To Maj. Gen. Andrew A. Humphreys

Farmville Apl. 7th/.65 5 p. m.

Maj. Gn. Humphreys,

Your note of 1.20 p. m. to Maj. Gn. Meade is just seen. Motts Div. of your Corps and Crooks Cavalry are both across the river at this point   The 6th & 24th Corps are both here. The enemy can not cross at Farmville.

U. S. Grant
Lt. Gn.

ALS, Humphreys Papers, PHi; Scheide Library, Princeton, N. J. *O.R.*, I, xlvi, part 3, 622.

On April 7, 1865, probably in the evening, Maj. Gen. Horatio G. Wright wrote to Brig. Gen. John A. Rawlins. "I have the honor to report that the Infantry of the Corps has crossed the River and are now in Camp—but owing to the difficulty in fording the River—the Artillery and Trains are obliged to wait until the Ponton Bridge is laid—My Hd. Qrs. are near a small house—in the vicinity of the burnt Bridge—and near the Road—" ALS, DNA, RG 108, Letters Received. Printed as addressed to Bvt. Maj. Gen. Alexander S. Webb in *O.R.*, I, xlvi, part 3, 631.

To Maj. Gen. George G. Meade

Burkesville, Apl. 7th 1865 12.10 a. m.

Maj. Gn Meade,

Sheridan and Wright have struck the enemy, captured a great many of their Gen Officers, and from ten to twelve thousand men. Every moment now is important to us. Communicate this to Gen. Griffin. Direct him to move at once to our left taking the most direct open road to Prince Edward C. H.   McKinzie's Cavalry is ordered there and will be off from here by 2 a. m

U. S. Grant
Lt. Gn

ALS (telegram sent), OClWHi; telegram received, DNA, RG 94, War Records Office, Army of the Potomac. *O.R.*, I, xlvi, part 3, 620.

On April 7, 1865, noon, Maj. Gen. George G. Meade, "High bridge," wrote to USG. "Maj. Genl—Humphreys About 9. a m crossed the appomatox at this point—driving in the Enemys rear guard skirmishers—The Enemy abandoned 8 guns on this side of the river & 10 are reported as left on the other side— Humphreys has advanced 4 miles on the R. Rd towards Farmville, and will continue to push them on that road—Wright is moving towards Farmville on this side the river—I understand Mahones Division is between him & Farmville and that he is after him.—Griffin is moving rapidly to Prince Edwards C. H. [&] will pass the Rices Station   you will find him on that road if neces[s]ary to send him orders" ALS, DNA, RG 94, War Records Office, Miscellaneous War Records. *O.R.*, I, xlvi, part 3, 620. At 5:30 P.M., Meade signaled to USG. "As soon as the operations of the day shall be over, I will remove my Head quarters to Rices Station, from which point I hope to have telegraphic Communication with Burks Station." Signal received, DNA, RG 108, Letters Received. *O.R.*, I, xlvi, part 3, 620.

At 3:30 P.M., Lt. Col. Adam Badeau, "Burksville Junction," wrote to Brig. Gen. John A. Rawlins. "I enclose Gen. Meade's despatch just received.—Col. Kellog of Sheridan's staff has just arrived with 7 (seven) generals and 5000 or 6000 prisoners. The supply trains of 2d (Second) and 6 (Sixth) corps are moving from Jettersville along Danville road, and will strike by cross road to Jenning's Ordinary on Lynchburg R. road; so reported by Lt Col. Pierce, Com 9th corps. . . . P. S. I enclose a telegram from the President" ALS, DNA, RG 108, Letters Received.

To Maj. Gen. George G. Meade

Farmville [*April*] 7th 1865 9.30 p. m.

MAJ. GEN. MEADE,

I enclose you copy of a dispatch sent to you this evening by signal.[1] The 5th[2] Corps is here. I will send copy of the dispatch to Gen. Griffin & Wright. Sheridan with the Cavalry is at prospect Station.

The enemy cannot go to Lynchburg possibly. I think there is no doubt but that Stoneman entered that City this morning. I will move my Hd Qrs. up with the troops in the morning, probably to Prospect Station.

Have the prisoners been sent to City Point yet? If not they should go at once under strong escort.

U. S. GRANT
Lt. Gn

ALS, DNA, RG 94, War Records Office, Army of the Potomac; Scheide Library, Princeton, N. J. *O.R.*, I, xlvi, part 3, 621.

On April 7, 1865, 7:00 P.M., Maj. Gen. George G. Meade wrote to USG.

"There has been heavy firing in the direction of Humphreys but no report as yet.—I send the bearer for any orders you may have for tomorrow   The 5th corps is at or near Prince Edward C. H—The 6th at Farmsville & the 2d across the Appomatox on the road from Farmsville to Lynchburgh.—As far as I can judge the Enemy is making for Lynchburgh—Perhaps only making a greater detour than he originally designed to get around us & he yet meditates going to Danville—Since writing the foregoing the following despatch has been recieved from Genl—Humphreys—Had I have been advised of the state of affairs at Farmsville I would either have crossed the 6th after the 2d or detained the 5th for that purpose—I never knew till 4. p. m that the Enemy had destroyed the bridges there nor did I know till late in the afternoon the causes of the delay in the advance of the 6th corps.—" ALS, DNA, RG 108, Letters Received. *O.R.*, I, xlvi, part 3, 620–21.

On April 8, 8:45 A.M., Meade, Piedmont coal mines, wrote to USG. "Maj. Genl—Humphreys is following the Enemy on the dirt road from this point to Appomatox C. H—The difficulty in obtaining in advance knowledge of roads & the time lost in ascertaining the position of troops—leads me to the conclusion time will be gained & a more prompt concentration can be made by keeping the 6 Corps on the same road   I have therefore ordered Maj. Genl—Wright to follow the 2d corps—I shall be found on this road with the 2d corps—Genl—Humphreys is satisfied that all of Lees army was here last night—He thinks the infantry moved in the direction he H is taking having their cavalry on their right flank & their trains on their left—This is what he gets from the country people   The confed Genl—Lewis is in our hands being wounded—" ALS, DNA, RG 108, Letters Received. *O.R.*, I, xlvi, part 3, 642.

1. On April 7, USG signaled to Meade. "Order The 5th Corps ~~will~~ to follow the 24th at 6 a. m. up the Lynchburg road. The 2d & 6th ~~will~~ to follow the enemy North of the river." ALS, Scheide Library, Princeton, N. J.; signal received (marked as sent at 7:45 P.M.), DNA, RG 94, War Records Office, Army of the Potomac. *O.R.*, I, xlvi, part 3, 621. What appears to be a tracing of USG's original is reproduced in facsimile in J. Willard Brown, *The Signal Corps, U. S. A. in the War of the Rebellion* (Boston, 1896; reprinted, New York, 1974), opposite p. 398.

2. USG probably meant "2nd."

To Maj. Gen. Edward O. C. Ord

Burkeville Apl. 7th *1865*

MAJ. GN. ORD.

Your troops are the nearest to Prince Edward C. H. unless the 5th Corps is between you and there. That Corps was ordered to Pr. Edward last night and on receipt of the news of our captures at 12 p. m. the order was reitterated for them to push on without waiting for morning. McKenzie is probably there now.

U. S. Grant

Lt. Gn.

ALS, Ord Papers, CU-B. *O.R.*, I, xlvi, part 3, 635. On April 7, 1865, 7:00 A.M., Maj. Gen. Edward O. C. Ord wrote to USG. "Gibbon has just reported the enemy has left his front   he is pushing after them—& I will follow with my whole force—turning to the the left if I find they have taken that direction beyond the river—better send infantry towards Pr Edward—fast" ALS, DNA, RG 108, Letters Received. *O.R.*, I, xlvi, part 3, 634.

To Maj. Gen. Philip H. Sheridan

———

Farmville Apl. 7th 1865

Maj. Gn. Sheridan,

The 2d Corps & Crooks Cavalry are North of the river at this place. I have no report yet of appearances in their front but hear contradictory reports, one that Lee is going to Maysville, another that he will strike South by roads further up the river. I think on the whole you had better throw your Cavalry up the river towards Chickentown to watch the different crossings. The 24th Corps will move up the South bank of the river. Just as this was written some of our men who were captured last night have returned. They state that just as they left about one thousand Cavalry was thrown out towards the crossings above here. You may be able to get in rear of the enemy possibly. It is reported among the citizens here that Lynchburg was evacuated last night. I do not doubt but Stoneman is there.

U. S. Grant

Lt. Gn

ALS, Scheide Library, Princeton, N. J. *O.R.*, I, xlvi, part 3, 633.

To Maj. Gen. Philip H. Sheridan

Farmville Apl. 7th/65

MAJ. GN. SHERIDAN,

The 2d & 6th Corps will press the enemy's rear to-morrow, on the North side of the river, the 6th Corps keeping in next to the river. The 5th & 24th will push up by Prospect Station and will be ready to turn upon the enemy at any time. I will move my Hd Qurs up by the South bank in the morning.

U. S. GRANT
Lt. Gn

ALS, Scheide Library, Princeton, N. J. *O.R.*, I, xlvi, part 3, 633–34. On April 7, 1865, 6:45 P.M., Maj. Gen. Philip H. Sheridan, Prince Edward's Court House, Va., wrote to USG. "On arriving at Prince Edwards Court House this P. M. I sent McKenzie's Division of Cavalry to Prospect Station on the Lynchburg RailRoad; ~~the~~ his advance should have reached there before this. I am following with the First and Third Cavalry Divisions and will reach the vicinity of Prospect Station tonight, if I do not go to Chickentown." Copies (2), DLC-Philip H. Sheridan. *O.R.*, I, xlvi, part 3, 633. On the same day, Sheridan, Prospect Station, Va., wrote to USG. "I am moving the Cavalry column on Appomattox Depot. There are Eight trains of cars at that point to supply Lee's army. Everything is being run out of Lynchburg towards Danville—Our troops are reported at Liberty—This must be Stoneman—One of my scouts reports this—possibly it may not be true—" LS, DNA, RG 108, Letters Received. *O.R.*, I, xlvi, part 3, 633.

To Julia Dent Grant

By Telegraph from Burkeville [*April 7*] 1865

To MRS U S GRANT

I think you had better return home as it may be 10 or 12 days before I return   I shall probably go on to Danville before returning & will try in conjunction with Sherman to break up the only thing remaing to be done with Johnson

U S GRANT
Lt Genl

Telegram received, DLC-USG. Julia Dent Grant noted on the reverse: "I did not obey I waited and returned with the victorious Genl's" AE, *ibid.*

To Gen. Robert E. Lee

Apl. 8th 1865

GEN. R. E. LEE
COMD.G C. S. A.
GENERAL,

Your note of last evening, in reply to mine of same date, asking the conditions on which I will accept the surrender of the Army of N. Va. is just received. In reply I would say that *peace* being my great desire there is but one condition I insist upon, namely: that the men and officers surrendered shall be disqualified for taking up arms again, against the Government of the United States, until properly exchanged.

I will meet you or will designate Officers to meet any officers you may name for the same purpose, at any point agreeable to you, for the purpose of arranging definitely the terms upon which the surrender of the Army of N. Va. will be received.

> Very respectfully
> your obt. svt.
> U. S. GRANT
> Lt. Gn

ALS, Scheide Library, Princeton, N. J. *O.R.*, I, xxxiv, part 1, 55; *ibid.*, I, xxxvi, part 1, 58–59; *ibid.*, I, xxxviii, part 1, 47; *ibid.*, I, xlvi, part 3, 641. USG wrote to Gen. Robert E. Lee during the morning of April 8, 1865, before leaving Farmville. *Memoirs*, II, 626; Horace Porter, *Campaigning with Grant* (New York, 1897), p. 460. On the same day, Lee wrote to USG. "I recd at a late hour your note of today—In mine of yesterday I did not intend to propose the Surrender of the Army of N. Va—but to ask the terms of your proposition. To be frank, I do not think the emergency has arisen to call for the Surrender of this Army, but as the restoration of peace should be the Sole object of all, I desired to know whether your proposals would lead to that end. I cannot therefore meet you with a view to Surrender the Army of N—Va—but as far as your proposal may affect the C. S. forces under my Command & tend to the restoration of peace, I should be pleased to meet you at 10 A m tomorrow on the old stage road to Richmond between the picket lines of the two armies—" ALS, DNA, RG 94, Treasure Room. *O.R.*, I, xxxiv, part 1, 55; *ibid.*, I, xxxvi, part 1, 59; *ibid.*, I, xxxviii, part 1, 48; *ibid.*, I, xlvi, part 3, 641.

On April 8, USG wrote to Secretary of War Edwin M. Stanton. "The enemy so far have been pushed from the road towards Danville and are now pursued towards Lynchburg. I feel very confidant of receiving the surrender of Lee and what remains of his Army by to-morrow." ALS, Scheide Library, Princeton,

N. J. Printed as written at noon in *O.R.*, I, xlvi, part 3, 640. Stanton later presented the letter to a friend. See W. J. Holland, "An Autograph Letter of Lieutenant-General U. S. Grant to the Hon. Edwin M. Stanton, Secretary of War," *Annals of the Carnegie Museum*, VIII, 1 (Dec., 1911), 188–89; (facsimile) plate XII.

To Maj. Gen. John G. Parke

Farmville, Apl 8th 1865

GEN PARKE

Send forward troops Enough to make a full Division at Burkesville for the purpose of furnishing Escorts to prisoners and guards to public property—

~~B~~

U. S. GRANT
Lt. Gen

Operator at Burkesville will remain until further orders

U. S. GRANT
Lt Gen

Telegram sent (at 12:40 P.M.), DNA, RG 107, Telegrams Collected (Unbound); (incomplete) Scheide Library, Princeton, N. J.; copies, DLC-USG, V, 46, 75, 108; DNA, RG 108, Letters Sent. *O.R.*, I, xlvi, part 3, 649.

On April 8, 1865, 9:00 A.M., Bvt. Col. Theodore S. Bowers telegraphed to Maj. Gen. John G. Parke. "Some six thousand (6000) [pri]soners are now starting from [her]e. The regular guard is insufficient. [Gen]l Curtin will send an additional [gu]ard to Nottoway C. H. Have a [thou]sand men in readiness to [re]lieve Curtins guard & to go forward [wi]th the regular guard & prisoners until you meet the ~~regular~~ force now coming from City [P]oint who in turn will relieve [y]our guard—The prisoners [h]ave no rations" Telegram received, DNA, RG 393, 9th Army Corps, 2nd Div., Letters Received.

At 1:00 P.M., Parke, Nottoway Court House, Va., telegraphed to USG. "I have telegraphed twice to Maj. Genl. Hartsuff at Petersburg requesting him to relieve my garrison at Sutherlands but get no reply. My command is now stretched out from Sutherland's to Burks. I would like to have it so arranged that the command from Petersburg would extend this way as far as possible so that I might concentrate the divisions and furnish the guard for prisoners and trains." Telegram received, *ibid.*, RG 108, Letters Received.

To Maj. Gen. Philip H. Sheridan

Farmville Apl. 8th/65

Maj. Gn. Sheridan

Make a detail from your own command to go with the Ambulances of the 5th Corps to collect in your wounded.

I think Lee will surrender to-day. I addressed him on the subject last evening and received a reply this morning asking the terms I wanted.

We will push him until terms are agreed upon.

U. S. Grant
Lt. Gn

ALS, Scheide Library, Princeton, N. J. *O.R.*, I, xlvi, part 3, 652.
On April 8, 1865, Maj. Gen. Philip H. Sheridan, Buffalo River, wrote to USG. "I respectfully Enclose a dispatch from Genl Merritt—If this is correct the Enemy must have taken the fine road north of the Appomatx River—I will move on Appmatx C. H. Should we not intercept the Enemy, and he be forced into Lynchburg, his surrender then is beyond question—" LS, DNA, RG 108, Letters Received. *O.R.*, I, xlvi, part 3, 652. The enclosure is *ibid*. At 9:20 P.M. and 9:40 P.M., Sheridan wrote to USG. "I marched Early this morning from Buffalo Creek and Prospect Statn on Appomattox Statn where my scouts had reported trains of cars with supplies for Lee's army. A short time before dusk Genl Custer who had the advance made a dash at the Station Capturing four trains of supplies with locomotives—One of the trains were burned and the others were run back towards Farmville for security—Custer then pushed on towards Appomattox C. H. driving the Enemy who Kept up a heavy fire of artillery, charging them repeatedly and capturing, as far as reported, twenty five pieces of artillery and a number of prisoners and wagons—The 1st Cavlry Division supported him on the right—A reconnoissance sent across the Appomattox reports the Enemy moving on the Cumberland road to appomattox Statn where they Expected to get supplies—Custer is still pushing on. If Genl Gibbon and the 5th Corps can get up to-night we will perhaps finish the job in the morning —I do not think Lee means to Surrender until compelled to do so." LS, DNA, RG 108, Letters Received. *O.R.*, I, xlvi, part 3, 653. "Since writing the accompanying dispatch General Custer reports that his command has captured in all, thirty pieces of Artillery, One thousand prisoners, including one General Officer and from One hundred and fifty to two hundred wagons." Copies (2), DLC-Philip H. Sheridan. *O.R.*, I, xlvi, part 3, 653.

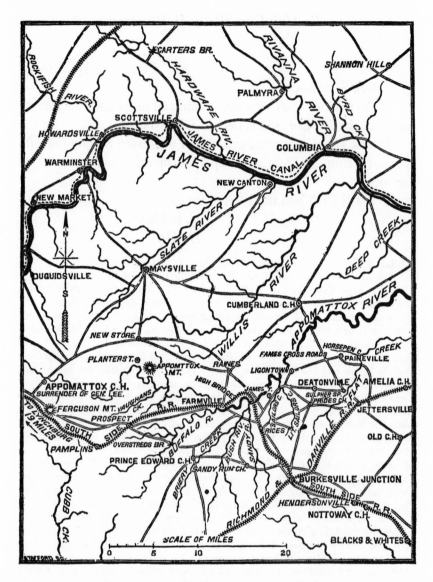

Appomattox Court House and Vicinity

From Henry Coppée, Grant and his Campaigns: A Military Biography
(*New York, 1866*), *p. 445*

To Gen. Robert E. Lee

Apl. 9th 1865

GN. R. E. LEE
COMD.G C, S, A,
GENERAL,

Your note of yesterday is received. As I have no authority to treat on the subject of peace the meeting proposed for 10 a. m. to-day could lead to no good. I will state however General that I am equally anxious for peace with yourself and the whole North entertains the same feeling. The terms upon which peace can be had are well understood. By the South laying down their Arms they will hasten that most desirable event, save thousands of human lives and hundreds of Millions of property not yet destroyed.

Sincerely hoping that all our difficulties may be settled without the loss of another live I subscribe myself

> very respectfully
> your obt. svt.
> U. S. GRANT
> Lt. Gn

ALS, Scheide Library, Princeton, N. J. *O.R.*, I, xxxiv, part 1, 55; *ibid.*, I, xxxvi, part 1, 59; *ibid.*, I, xxxviii, part 1, 48; *ibid.*, I, xlvi, part 3, 664. On April 9, 1865, Gen. Robert E. Lee wrote to USG. "I received your note of this morning on the picket line whither I had come to meet you and ascertain definitely what terms were embraced in your proposal of yesterday with reference to the surrender of this army. I now request an interview in accordance with the offer contained in your letter of yesterday, for that pu[r]pose." ALS, DNA, RG 94, Treasure Room. *O.R.*, I, xxxiv, part 1, 56; *ibid.*, I, xxxvi, part 1, 60; *ibid.*, I, xxxviii, part 1, 48; *ibid.*, I, xlvi, part 3, 664.

Also on April 9, 9:30 A.M., USG, "Clifton's House," telegraphed to Secretary of War Edwin M. Stanton. "The following correspondence has taken place between Gen Lee & myself. There has been no relaxation in the pursuit during its pendency—" Telegram sent, DNA, RG 107, Telegrams Collected (Unbound); telegram received (at 11:00 A.M.), *ibid.*, Telegrams Collected (Bound); *ibid.*, RG 94, War Records Office, Army of the Potomac. *O.R.*, I, xlvi, part 3, 663. The enclosures embraced the correspondence through USG's first message to Lee of April 9; variant texts in USG's letterbooks include correspondence through the surrender. At 1:00 P.M., Stanton telegraphed to USG. "Your telegram of this morning received. The rebel mails show that the [en]emies supplies to from Richmond were nearly if not quite all sent to Danville so that there can be no Lee can can have nothing there to hold out on. I hope you you will have

~~the scalps to your belt~~" ALS (telegram sent), DNA, RG 107, Telegrams Collected (Bound). *O.R.*, I, xlvi, part 3, 663.

At 10:00 A.M., Maj. Gen. George G. Meade wrote to USG. "I send you a despatch from Humphreys—his advance is now between 8 & 9 miles of Appomatox C. H & pushing on as fast as possible—I also send a letter from Genl— Lee, which I opened thinking time & some ~~th~~ good might result from so doing I sent the accompanying answer—Whilst I fully agree with you in the only terms, as stated in your letter, to be granted, I think it would be well for you to see Genl. Lee, as he may accept them after an interview—" ALS, DNA, RG 108, Letters Received. *O.R.*, I, xlvi, part 3, 667–68. At 1:10 P.M., Maj. Gen. Edward O. C. Ord wrote to Meade. "I have received two letters addressed to Genl Grant from Genl Lee each requesting an interview to arrange terms for the surrender of his Genl Lees Army. the appearance of the troops and train of Genl Lees—army indicates no preparations for a battle—and in my personal interview with Genl Longstreet I tacitly assented to the proposed cessation of Hostilities—made in the letter to Genl Grant—until the interview could be held —I Supposed Genl Grant was present with your Army—and hence my assent I am quite sure tnat Genl Grant if present would grant the cessation asked for and hence agreed to it and hope you will do the same on this assurance of Genl Lee that no move will be made by his troops or others cooperating therewith" ALS, Ord Papers, CU-B. For the enclosures, see following letter. At 2:00 P.M., Ord, "in the field near Appomattox Ct House," wrote to USG. "In obedience to orders The Army of James and Genl Griffins Corps, both under my command after a forced marchs of 33 miles yesterday reached upper End of this valley—and this A M at 6 oclock came in upon Genl Lees forces ~~which were~~ then trying to force a passage through Sheridans Cavalry which could not hold the ground; Gibbons and Griffins corps were deployed and Genl Lees force ~~artillery infantry~~ was driven back towards Genl Meade until 10 A M when Lee asked a cessation of Hostiltities to confer with you—I have sent you two notes from him asking an interview to arrange for a surrender, his ~~force~~ Army is almost surrounded ~~except by one difficult outlet~~ and I am about to ~~Say~~ write to him a joint note with Genl Sheridan that unless he surrenders on the terms you offered we must renew the fight" ALS, DLC-Edwin M. Stanton.

To Gen. Robert E. Lee

Apl. 9th 1865

GEN. R. E. LEE,
COMD.G C. S. A.
GENERAL,

Your note of this date[1] is but this moment, 11.50 a. m. rec'd. in consequence of my having passed from the Richmond and Lynchburg road to the Farmersville & Lynchburg road. I am at this writing about four miles West of Walker's Church and will push forward to the front for the purpose of meeting you. Notice sent to me on this road where you wish the interview to take place will meet me.

> Very respectfully
> your obt. svt
> U. S. GRANT
> Lt. Gn

ALS, Scheide Library, Princeton, N. J. *O.R.*, I, xlvi, part 3, 665.

On April 9, 1865, Gen. Robert E. Lee twice wrote to USG. "I ask a suspension of hostilities pending the adjustment of the terms of the surrender of this army, in the interview requested in my former communication today." "I sent a communication to you today from the picket line whither I had gone in hopes of meeting you in pursuance of the request contained in my letter of yesterday. Maj Gen Meade informs me that it would probably expedite matters to send a duplicate through some other part of your lines. I therefore request an interview at such time and place as you may designate, to discuss the terms of the surrender of this army in accordance with your offer to have such an interview contained in your letter of yesterday" ALS, DNA, RG 94, Treasure Room. *O.R.*, I, xlvi, part 3, 664–65. See *ibid.*, p. 666.

1. See preceding letter.

To Gen. Robert E. Lee

> Appomattox C. H. Va.
> Apl. 9th 1865

GEN. R. E. LEE,
COMD.G C. S. A.
GEN.

In accordance with the substance of my letter to you of the 8th inst. I propose to receive the surrender of the Army of N. Va. on the following terms: towit:

Rolls of all the officers and men to be made in duplicate One copy to be given to an officer designated by me, the other to be retained by such officer or officers as you may designate. The officers to give their individual paroles not to take up arms against the Government of the United States until properly exchanged and each company officer or regimental commander sign a like parole for the men of his men their commands.

The Arms, Artillery and public property to be parked and stacked and turned over to the officer appointed by me to receive them. This will not embrace the side Arms of the officers nor their ~~This~~ private horses or baggage.—This done each officer and man will be allowed to return to their homes not to be disturbed by United States Authority so long as they observe their parole and the laws in force where they may reside.

Very respectfully

U. S. GRANT Lt. Gn

ALS, NHi; (2) Scheide Library, Princeton, N. J.; LS, Stratford Hall, Stratford, Va. *O.R.*, I, xxxiv, part 1, 56; *ibid.*, I, xxxvi, part 1, 60; *ibid.*, I, xxxviii, part 1, 48–49; *ibid.*, I, xlvi, part 3, 665. On April 9, 1865, Gen. Robert E. Lee wrote to USG. "I have received your letter of this date containing the terms of surrender of the army of northern Virginia as proposed by you—As they are substantially the same as those expressed in your letter of the 8th inst, they are accepted— I will proceed to designate the proper officers to carry the stipulations into effect—" Copy, PPRF. *O.R.*, I, xxxiv, part 1, 56; *ibid.*, I, xxxvi, part 1, 60; *ibid.*, I, xxxviii, part 1, 49; *ibid.*, I, xlvi, part 3, 666. On the same day, Lee issued unnumbered special orders through Lt. Col. Walter H. Taylor, addressing a copy to USG. "Lieut. Genl. J. Longstreet, Major Genl. J. B. Gordon, and Brig. Genl. W. N. Pendleton are hereby designated to carry into effect the stipulations this day entered into between Lieut. Genl. U. S. Grant, Comd.g Armies of the United States, and General R. E. Lee, Comd.g Armies of the Confederate States in which Genl. Lee surrendered to Genl Grant, the Army of Northern Va." DS, DNA, RG 108, Letters Received; (printed) CtY. *O.R.*, I, xlvi, part 3, 666–67. On the same day, Lt. Col. Ely S. Parker issued Special Orders No. 72. "Major General John Gibbon, Brevet Major General Charles Griffin and Brevet Major General Wesley Merritt are hereby designated to carry into effect the stipulations this day entered into between Genl. R. E. Lee, Commanding C. S. Armies and Lieut Genl. U. S. Grant commanding Armies of the United States in which General Lee surrenders to General Grant the Army of Northern Virginia. Brevet Brig. Gen. George H. Sharpe, Assistant Provost Marshal General will receive and take charge of the rolls called for by the above mentioned stipulations." Copies, DLC-USG, V, 57, 63, 65; DNA, RG 108, Letters Received; (printed) CtY. Unnumbered in *O.R.*, I, xlvi, part 3, 666. On April 20, Bvt. Brig. Gen. George H. Sharpe wrote to Bvt. Col. Theodore S. Bowers reporting in detail the paroling of the Army of Northern Va. ALS, DNA, RG 94, Record & Pension Office, 52058. *O.R.*, I, xlvi, part 3, 851–53. On June 17, USG endorsed this report. "Respectfully forwarded to the Secretary of War together with the Rolls of officers & men of Lees Army" ES, DNA, RG 94, Record & Pension Office, 52058. *O.R.*, I, xlvi, part 3, 853.

USG wrote his letter to Lee in a Philp & Solomons' Manifold Writer, creating three copies. The first and second were corrected separately, the first by USG, the second by Parker; the third was not corrected. The second copy became the property of Parker and, on Oct. 21, 1880, USG certified its authenticity. "The document below is one of the original impressions [in] the manifold on which I wrote the terms of surrender of Gen [Lee a]rmy at Appomattox Court House, Apl. 9th 1865. It is one of the three [im]pressions taken by the Manifold." AES, NHi. This copy appears in facsimile in *Memoirs*, II, between pp. 496–97. Parker wrote the official copy, which USG signed and gave to Lee. See Lloyd A. Dunlap, "The Grant-Lee Surrender Correspondence: Some Notes and Queries," *Manuscripts*, XXI, 2 (Spring, 1969), 78–91.

On April 9, 4:30 p.m., USG telegraphed to Secretary of War Edwin M. Stanton. "Gen. Lee surrendered the Army of Northern Va this afternoon on terms proposed by myself. The accompanying additional correspondence will show the conditions fully." ALS (telegram sent), PPRF; telegram received, DNA, RG 107, Telegrams Collected (Bound). *O.R.*, I, xlvi, part 3, 663. USG appended copies of all communications of April 9 between himself and Lee except the first. A telegram of 3:00 p.m. from USG to Stanton may not be authentic. "Gen R. E. Lee Surrendered the Army of Northern Virginia to me *upon my own terms*." Copy, Eleutherian Mills Historical Library, Wilmington, Del. On April 10, USG, Prospect Station, wrote to an unnamed correspondent. "Gen. R. E. Lee surrendered the Army of N. Va. at Appomattox C. H. Va. on yesterday. The force surrendered was the remnant left from an Army of about 70.000 men who defended Richmond ten days ago." ALS (facsimile), Lloyd Lewis-Bruce Catton Collection, USGA. This message may have been written as a souvenir.

On April 9, 9:30 p.m. and 11:00 p.m., Stanton telegraphed to USG. "Thanks be to Almighty God for the great victory with which he has this day crowned you and the gallant army under your command. The thanks of this Department and of the Government and of the people of the United States ~~for all time~~ their reverence and honor ~~for all time~~ have been deserved and will be rendered to you and ~~your g~~ the brave & gallant officers & soldiers of your army for all time." ALS (telegram sent), DNA, RG 107, Telegrams Collected (Bound); telegram received, *ibid.*, Telegrams Collected (Unbound). *O.R.*, I, xlvi, part 3, 663–64. "Some thousands of our ~~so~~ prisoners in the hands of the rebels are still undelivered. Can any arrangements be made to hasten their release?" ALS (telegram sent), DNA, RG 107, Telegrams Collected (Bound); telegram received, *ibid.*, RG 94, War Records Office, Miscellaneous War Records. *O.R.*, I, xlvi, part 3, 664.

On April 9, Bowers transmitted the surrender correspondence to Maj. Gen. William T. Sherman. Telegrams received (4—one at 11:15 p.m., two misdated April 11), DNA, RG 107, Telegrams Collected (Unbound); *ibid.*, Telegrams Collected (Bound); *ibid.*, RG 393, 23rd Army Corps, Telegrams Received; DLC-William T. Sherman. *O.R.*, I, xlvii, part 3, 140. An appended "endorsement" of 9:00 p.m. may be a variant of USG's telegram to Stanton of 4:30 p.m. *Ibid.*

On April 12, 5:00 a.m., Sherman, Smithfield, N. C., wrote to USG adding instructions for transmitting the message. "By telegraph & mail. Telegraph from Goldsboro & steamer to Old Point & telegraph from there. This original send to Genl Easton Chf Q. M. who will forward to Genl Grant." "I have this momnt received your telegram announcing the Surrender of Lee's Army. I hardly know how to express my feelings, but you can imagine them. The terms you have given Lee are Magnanimous and liberal. Should Johnston follow Lee's Example, I shall of course grant the Same. He is retreating before me on Raleigh, and I shall be there tomorrow. Roads are heavy, but under the inspiration of the news from you we can march 25 miles a day. I am now 27 m from Raleigh but some of my army is 8 miles behind. If Johnston retreats south I will follow him to Ensure the Scattering his force, and capture of the locomotives & cars at Charlotte, but I take it he will surrender at Raleigh. Kilpatrick's Cavalry is 10 *m* to the South and west of me viz on Middle Creek and I have sent Maj Audenried with orders to make for the South & West of Raleigh to impede the Enemy if he goes beyond Raleigh. All the Infantry is pointed straight for Raleigh by five different Roads. The Railroad is being repaired from Goldsboro to Raleigh, but I will not Aim to carry it further. I shall expect to hear of Sheridan in case Johnston do not surrender at Raleigh. With a little more Cavalry I would be sure to capture the whole Army." ALS, DNA, RG 108, Letters Received; telegram received (on April 14, 2:30 P.M.), *ibid.*, Telegrams Received; (at 2:20 P.M.) *ibid.*, RG 107, Telegrams Collected (Bound); (2) *ibid.*, Telegrams Collected (Unbound). *O.R.*, I, xlvii, part 3, 177. USG endorsed Sherman's letter. "Have this telegraphed to Sheridan." AE, DNA, RG 108, Letters Received. *O.R.*, I, xlvii, part 3, 177. See *ibid.*, I, xlvi, part 3, 793.

On April 13, Sherman, Raleigh, N. C., telegraphed to USG. "I entered Raleigh this morning. Johnston has retreated westward. I shall move to Ashville & Salisbury or Charlotte. I hope Sheridan is coming this way with his Cavalry.—. If I can bring Johnston to a stand can soon fix him. The people here had not heard of the surrender of Lee, & hardly credit it. All well.—" Telegram received (on April 15, 7:00 P.M.), DNA, RG 108, Telegrams Received; *ibid.*, RG 107, Telegrams Collected (Bound); (2—one misdated April 14) *ibid.*, Telegrams Collected (Unbound); copy, DLC-USG, V, 54. *O.R.*, I, xlvii, part 3, 191. USG endorsed this telegram. "Forward for information of Maj. Gn. Sheridan, Burkeville." AES, DNA, RG 108, Telegrams Received. *O.R.*, I, xlvii, part 3, 191. See *ibid.*, I, xlvi, part 3, 761.

To Maj. Gen. Napoleon J. T. Dana

Appomattox C. H. Apl. 9th/65

N. J. T. DANA, CAIRO ILL.

All settlements for exchanged prisoners ₳were to be made with Col. Ould Confederate Agt. and the agreement to receive them at various points was for the accomodation of the South their railroads being so broken that they could not conveniently deliver all on the James. Say to the officer who has our prisoners for delivery that any that are due to the South will be delivered at Vicksburg or any place Col. Ould desires.

U. S. GRANT
Lt. Gn

ALS (telegram sent), Lincoln Memorial University, Harrogate, Tenn.; telegram received (on April 10, 1865, 12:40 A.M.), DNA, RG 107, Telegrams Collected (Bound); (undated) *ibid.*, Telegrams Collected (Unbound). The last six words of USG's telegram do not appear in the telegrams received or in *O.R.*, II, viii, 481–82. On April 5, Maj. Gen. Napoleon J. T. Dana, Vicksburg, telegraphed to USG. "The Confederates have about five thousand 5000 of our men in Camp under Flag of truce about four 4 miles from here which they refuse to deliver to us on parole unless they receive an Equivalent here notice of one having been delivered to them on the James River will you please order five Thousand Confederates or their Equivalent sent here from Western prisons or delivery to be made on the James & send official notice here. Capt. G A Williams Commissary of Musters will await your answer at Cairo & be able to make such Explanations as you may require—" Telegrams received (2—one on April 8, 4:45 P.M.), DNA, RG 107, Telegrams Collected (Unbound); *ibid.*, RG 108, Letters Received; copies, *ibid.*, RG 94, Letters Received, 735W 1865; *ibid.*, RG 393, Dept. of the Miss., Letters Received, Two or More Name File. *O.R.*, II, viii, 483–84.

On April 10, USG telegraphed to Capt. George A. Williams, Cairo, Ill. "Please take the preceeding dispatch to Gen. Dana Vicksburg for delivery to the Confederate Officer in charge of Federal prisoners near that point." Telegram received (at 4:15 P.M.), DNA, RG 107, Telegrams Collected (Bound); *ibid.*, RG 393, Dept. of the Miss., Letters Received, Two or More Name File. *O.R.*, II, viii, 489. USG transmitted a telegram of the same day from C.S.A. Agent of Exchange Robert Ould to "Confederate Officer having charge of prisoners Vicksburg—via Cairo." "All Federal officers and men who are held as prisoners by the Confederate authorities must be delivered at Vicksburg or any other Point where the Federal Military authorities are willing to receive them. No equivalents are to be demanded there. By agreement with Gen Grant equivalents are to be given in James River." Telegram received (at 4:10 P.M.), DNA, RG 107, Telegrams Collected (Bound); *ibid.*, RG 393, Dept. of the Miss., Letters Received, Two or More Name File. *O.R.*, II, viii, 489. On April 9, Ould, "Mrs Jone's House (near Lynchburg Road) Appomatox County," had written to USG. "I deem it [my] duty to inform you that I am here with fou[r] officers and attaches of the Exchange Bur[eau] personal baggage and material records of [my] office in which the U. S. Government and people are interested. I am here under flag [of] truce for the purpose of meeting any question[s] connected with the delivery and exchange [of] prisoners, and with no other view whatever—I am now I believe within your lines, and [have] been only since the morning. I avail mysel[f] of the first opportunity to notify you of this s[tate] of facts—I am ready to obey any direction [you] may give with reference to myself and par[ty.] If agreeable to you, I will thank you for either a Safeguard, or some writing which may serve as a protection— . . . At the suggestion of Capt McGinley I have come to the front and am now with the Army train—6th Corps" ALS, DNA, RG 109, Ould Letterbook. *O.R.*, II, viii, 482.

To Maj. Gen. George G. Meade

Appomattox C. H.
April 9th 1865.

Agreement having been made for the Surrender of the Army of North Va. hostilities will not be resumed. General Lee desires that

during the time the two Armies are laying near each other, the
men of the two Armies be Kept separate, the sole object being to
prevent unpleasant individual rencontres that may take place with
a too free intercourse.

U. S. GRANT.

Copies (2—one misdated April 7, 1865), Meade Papers, PHi. *O.R.*, I, xlvi, part
3, 668. On April 9, Lt. Col. Ely S. Parker wrote to Maj. Gen. George G. Meade.
"The 5th Corps of the Army of the Potomac and the 24th Corps of the Army
of the James, will remain here, until the stipulations of the surrender of the
C. S Army Known as the Army of Northern Virginia entered into by Gen'l
R. E. Lee and the Lieut General Commanding have been carried into effect. and
the captured and surrendered public property have been secured. All the other
forces will be moved back to Burkeville starting tomorrow where they will go
into camp. The Chief Ordnance Officer of the Army of the Potomac will collect
and take charge of all captured and surrendered Ordnance and Ordnance Stores.
and removed them to Burksville, The Acting Chief Quarter Master of the Army
of the James will collect and take charge of. all the Captured and surrendered
Quarter Masters Property & Stores and remove them to Burksville. You will
please give such orders to your troops and officers of the Staff Departments as
will secure the execution of the foregoing instructions The troops going to
Burksville will turn over to those remaining here all the Subsistence Stores they
may have, save a bare sufficiency to take them back." Copies, DNA, RG 393,
24th Army Corps, Letters Received; (2) Meade Papers, PHi. *O.R.*, I, xlvi, part
3, 668. At 11:30 P.M., Meade wrote to USG. "The order in cipher is received
and will be executed at once." *Ibid.*
   On April 10, Parker wrote to Meade. "The Lt. Genl requests that you will
furnish him with a brief summary of the operations of the several Corps in your
command since the last report made to him at Burkesville Station—This for
publication—" ALS, Scheide Library, Princeton, N. J.; DNA, RG 94, War
Records Office, Miscellaneous War Records. *O.R.*, I, xlvi, part 3, 687. On the
same day, Meade wrote to USG. "At early day light on the morning of the 7th
inst, the 2d & 6. corps were moved forward with orders to continue the direct
pursuit of the retreating enemy—The 5th corps was moved from the extreme
right with orders to proceed to Prince Edward's C. H.—The 2d corps overtook
the enemy at High bridge, where a rear guard stand was made & the high
bridge & common bridge set on fire The 2d corps promptly advanced forced
the passage of the river causing the enemy to retire & leaving in our hands 18
guns. The enemy having withdrawn on the roads to Farmville & Lynchburgh—
Barlow's Division was sent in pursuit on the former, whilst Maj. Genl. Humphrey with Miles & De Trobriand moved on the latter road. Maj. Genl Barlow
found the enemy in possession of Farmville burning the bridges & covering a
wagon train moving on the Lynchburgh road—Barlow promptly attacked compelling the enemy to evacuate, the town burning over 130 wagons, & retiring
on the Lynchburgh road. I regret to report that in this affair Brig Genl Thos.
A Smyth a gallant & distinguished officer was mortally wounded Maj—Genl
—Humphreys moving on the road from High Bridge found the enemy, in a
strongly entrenched position covering the intersection of the roads from Cumberland C. H. & Farmville Maj. Genl Humphreys immediately formed line of battle,

developping the enemys position which was found too strong to attack in front, and he was not able to outflank them with only two divisions. Barlow was withdrawn from Farmsville   Whilst waiting the return of Barlow, hearing firing on the left & perceiving the enemy to be shortening his right flank Maj. Genl Humphreys presuming the enemy was being attacked from Farmsville by troops known to be in that neighborhood—ordered an attack from his extreme right—which was repulsed with heavy loss.—Learning from prisoners that the whole of the Confederate army was in his front entrenched, he desisted from any further offensive movement, till the arrival of Barlow which did not occur till near dark.—The 6th corps moved on Farmsville but found the road obstructed first by the 24th corps & afterwards by the cavalry, so that it was late in the day, before Maj. Genl Wright reached that place, where the bridges were found burned. Maj. Genl Wright immediately commenced the construction of a foot bridge, over which after night he crossed his infantry, and a ponton bridge having been thrown he crossed his artillery & trains.—On the 8th the direct pursuit was continued by the 2d corps on on the Lynchburgh pike & the 6th on the plank road—the 5th was ordered to follow the 24th corps on the southside of the Appomatox.—Maj. Genl. Wright ~~on the~~ finding 15 guns abandoned on the road he was pursuing—On the 9th Maj. Genl Humphreys with the 2d corps having march nearly all night, came up with the enemy about noon, at a point 3 miles from Appomatox C. H.—Preparations were being made to attack, when I received a letter from Genl Lee to the Lt. Genl comd.g asking a suspension of hostilities—Understanding a truce had been agreed to by Maj. Genl. Ord, on the other side of the C. H.—I acceded to one till 2. P. M, by which time I received the orders of the Lt. Genl. comd.g to cease hostilities till further notice, and later in the afternoon I was advised by the Lt. Genl. comd.g that the Army of Northern Virginia had surrendered.—" ALS, DNA, RG 107, Telegrams Collected (Unbound). *O.R.*, I, xlvi, part 3, 687–88.

To Edwin M. Stanton

Prospect Station, Apl 10th, *1865* 7:30 P. M.
HON. E. M. STANTON, SEC. OF WAR, WASHINGTON
I am at this point on my return. The 2d & 6th Corps and the Cavalry are on their way back to Burkes Station. The 5th ~~Corps~~ and 24th Corps remain at Appomattox Station to arrange the paroles of ~~the~~ Gen. Lee's Army. When this is done the 5th Corps will join the ~~balance~~ other Corps of the A. P. If ~~proper~~ advantage is taken of the present feeling in the South I am greatly in hopes ~~of~~ an early peace will be secured.

U. S. GRANT
Lt. Gn

ALS (telegram sent at 8:20 P.M.), PPRF; telegram received (at 10:30 P.M.), DNA, RG 94, War Records Office, Miscellaneous War Records; *ibid.*, RG 107, Telegrams Collected (Unbound). *O.R.*, I, xlvi, part 3, 684–85.

On April 10, 1865, USG began a letter to Gen. Robert E. Lee. "In accordance with agreement of yesterday I have named Maj. Gens. Gibbon, Griffin and Merritt to carry out the stipulations" ADf, Scheide Library, Princeton, N. J. Perhaps USG abandoned this letter because the details of the surrender were developed by the officers assigned. See *O.R.*, I, xlvi, part 3, 685–86. The aborted message might also arise from USG's decision to change his plans to leave early in the morning for Washington in order to meet again with Lee to discuss peace efforts. *Memoirs*, II, 496–98; Horace Porter, *Campaigning with Grant* (New York, 1897), 489–92. On the same day, USG wrote a pass. "All officers commanding posts pickets or detachments will pass Genl. R. E. Lee through their lines north or south on presentation of this pass. Genl. Lee will be permitted to visit Richmond at any time unless otherwise ordered by competent authority, and every facility for his doing so will be given by officers of the U. S. Army to whom this may be presented." Copy, DNA, RG 108, Letters Sent. *O.R.*, I, xlvi, part 3, 686.

Also on April 10, Lt. Col. Ely S. Parker issued unnumbered special orders, later designated Special Orders No. 73. "All Officers and men of the Confederate service paroled at Appomattox C. H. Va., who, to reach their homes are compelled to pass through the lines of the Union Armies, will be allowed to do so, and pass free on all Government Transports and Military Rail Roads." Copies, DLC-USG, V, 57, 63, 65; DNA, RG 94, Record & Pension Office, Document File, 52058; *ibid.*, RG 107, Telegrams Collected (Unbound); CSmH; (printed) CtY. *O.R.*, I, xlvi, part 3, 687.

To Edwin M. Stanton

Prospect Station Va. Apl. 10th *1865* [*9:05* P.M.]

HON. E. M. STANTON, SEC. OF WAR, WASHINGTON

The surrender was only of the men left with the pursued Army at the time of surrender. All prisoners captured in battle previous to the surrender stand same as other prisoners of war and those who had escaped are were detached at the time are not included. I think however there will be no difficulty now in bringing in on the terms voluntarily given to Gen. Lee all the fragments of the Army of N. Va. and it may be the Army under Johnston also. I wish Hancock would try it with Mosby.[1]

U. S. GRANT
Lt. Gen.

ALS (telegram sent), PPRF; telegram received (at 10:15 P.M.), DNA, RG 94, War Records Office, Miscellaneous War Records; *ibid.*, RG 107, Telegrams Collected (Bound); *ibid.*, Telegrams Collected (Unbound). *O.R.*, I, xlvi, part 3, 685. On April 10, 1865, 3:50 P.M., Secretary of War Edwin M. Stanton had telegraphed to USG. "Rosser, and the troops operating about Loudon form part of the Army of Northern Virginia reporting to Lee. ~~Who~~ Are they included in the surrender or only those under Lees immediate personal command. The troops in Western-Virginia have also gone as part of the Army of Northern Virginia" ALS (telegram sent), DNA, RG 107, Telegrams Collected (Bound); telegram received, *ibid.*, RG 108, Letters Received. *O.R.*, I, xlvi, part 3, 685.

1. On April 10, Maj. Gen. Godfrey Weitzel telegraphed to USG. "The people here are anxious that Moseby should be included in Lee's surrender. They say he belongs to that army." ALS (undated telegram sent), Boston Public Library, Boston, Mass.; telegram received, DNA, RG 109, Documents Printed in *O.R. O.R.*, I, xlvi, part 3, 697.

To Maj. Gen. John Gibbon

Hd. Qrs. Armies of the U. States
Appomattox C. H. Va. Apl. 10th/65

MAJ. GN. GIBBON
COMD.G 24TH A. C.
GENERAL,

On completion of the duties assigned you at this place you will proceed with the two Divisions of your command now here, and the Cavalry under Brig. Gn. McKenzie to Lynchburg Va. It is desirable that there shall be as little destruction of private property as possible. If you find Lynchburg has been already occupied by our forces you can return to Burkes Station so soon as the fact is known to you.

On reaching the vicinity of Lynchburg send a summons for the city to surrender. If it does so respect all private property and parole officers and men garrisoning the place same as has been done here. If resistance is made you will be governed by your own judgement about the best course to pursue.

If the city is surrendered as it will in all probability be take possession of all public stores. Such as may be of use to your command appropriate to their use. The balance distribute among the poor of the city. Save all the rolling stock of the rail-roads and if you find it practicable to do so bring it to Farmville and destroy a bridg[e] to the rear of it. Destroy no other portion of the road.

All the warlike material you find destroy or carry away with you.

This accomplished return to Burkes station with your command and report your arrival to the Dept. Commander by telegraph

U. S. GRANT
Lt. Gn

ALS, Scheide Library, Princeton, N. J. *O.R.*, I, xlvi, part 3, 694–95. On April 10, 1865, Maj. Gen. John Gibbon wrote to USG. "Are our officers & men prisoners in the enemys hands & Captured with their army to return to duty or are they to await a regular exchange I think they ought to be returned to duty at once" ALS, DNA, RG 108, Letters Received. *O.R.*, I, xlvi, part 3, 695. At 9:20 P.M., USG, Prospect Station, Va., telegraphed to Gibbon. "I suppose our men held by the enemy at the time of surrender could properly be claimed as recaptured and that Genl Lee would not have objected to it. But he asked me what I proposed in the matter and I told him that I would regard them as prisoners of war delivered up to us to be paroled until exchanged." Copies, DLC-USG, V, 46, 75, 108; DNA, RG 108, Letters Sent. *O.R.*, I, xlvi, part 3, 695.

To Maj. Gen. John Gibbon

Apl. 11th *1865*
By Telegraph from Burke Station *1865*
To MAJ. GN. GIBBON, APPOMATTOX STATION

Owing to the excessive state of the roads I think you had better load your supplies so far as possible on the captured trains and move them up by rail as you progress. Returning the same means of transportation might be used. I expect you will find the captured teams too weak to bring back all the Artillery, Arms &c. If so destroy the Caissons and such small arms as can not be moved. Leave wagons for the country people to pick up and double team so as to send back the Artillery and as many of the waggons as you can loaded with small Arms.

U. S. GRANT
Lt. Gn

ALS (telegram sent), PPRF; copies, DLC-USG, V, 46, 76, 108; DNA, RG 108, Letters Sent. *O.R.*, I, xlvi, part 3, 710. On April 11, 1865, Maj. Gen. John Gibbon telegraphed to USG. "Your dispatch received. I have picked up in addition to the pieces surrendered fifty-four pieces of artillery. I do not know whether the Army of the Potomac will have teams enough to take everything back. The captured teams will do very well if we can get forage for them. I expected to leave here to-morrow, but the surrender goes on slowly, and questions come up which I have to decide. If it is important I should start soon please telegraph." *Ibid.*

At midnight, Gibbon telegraphed to USG. "A delegation of citizens has just reached here from Lynchburg with a letter from the Prest of the city Council proposing to surrender the town,   Gen Turner with his Div & McKenzies Cavy will start in the morning to Carry out your instructions   There is a large amount of RR stock in the city, which Cannot be brought off but I think should not be destroyed for it will assist the peopl in getting in provisions which are scarce. Please instruct me what to do in regard to it" ALS (telegram sent), DNA, RG 107, Telegrams Collected (Unbound); telegram received, *ibid.*, RG 108, Letters Received. *O.R.*, I, xlvi, part 3, 711. USG drafted his reply of April 12 at the foot of the telegram received. "Do not destroy rail-road, stock shops or anything connected with the rail-road. It is only warlike material that I want destroyed or carried off." ADfS, DNA, RG 108, Letters Received; copies, *ibid.*, Letters Sent; DLC-USG, V, 46, 76, 108. *O.R.*, I, xlvi, part 3, 722. A communication from Gibbon to USG dated April 11 may have been sent on April 12. "A lieutenant sent out as a scout by my direction has just come in from Lynchburg, where the mayor of the city delivered over the town to him. I have directed General Mackenzie to at once proceed there and carry out your instructions in regard to the public property found there." *Ibid.*, p. 710.

On April 11, Gibbon wrote to Bvt. Col. Theodore S. Bowers. "By the arrangement made between the officers appointed by Genls. Grant and Lee each officer and man after being paroled is furnished with a printed certificate stating the fact that he is a paroled prisoner of war, signed by his own Commanding officer or a staff officer of the same. A copy of the form of this certificate is enclosed, as also my order on the subject making the possession of this certificate the proof that the holder is a paroled prisoner. As these paroled prisoners will in order to reach their homes be scattered all over the country I respectfully suggest that an order similar to mine be published by authority of Lt. Genl. Grant requiring all officers and soldiers of the armies of the U. States to respect & recognise these certificates so that the officers and soldiers surrendered at this place may remain undisturbed by the U. States authorities in accordance with the stipulations of the surrender, and that the order be generally published in the newspapers throughout the country." ALS, DNA, RG 94, Record & Pension Office, Document File, 52058. *O.R.*, I, xlvi, part 3, 709. One of the enclosures is *ibid.*, pp. 709–10.

On April 13, Gibbon twice telegraphed to USG. "Gen McKenzie occupied Lynchburg at One thirty P M yesterday   he reports an immense quantity of public property there   Turners Division will be there today   I have directed him not to destroy the RR stock although he will not be able to bring it away on account of the bridges being broken." ALS (telegram sent), DNA, RG 107, Telegrams Collected (Unbound); telegram received (misdated April 14, received at 6:00 P.M.), *ibid.*; *ibid.*, Telegrams Collected (Bound); (misdated

April 14, received at 7:30 P.M.) *ibid.*, RG 108, Telegrams Received. *O.R.*, I,
xlvi, part 3, 734. "The surrender of Gen Lees army was finally Completed today. we have parold from 25 to 30,000 men One hundred & forty seven (147)
pieces of Artillery have been received about ten thousand small arms & seventy
one flags I received On the 11th a deputation from Lynchburg proposing to
surrender that place & asking for our protection I started Turners Division &
McKenzies Cavalry for that point yesterday Morning I have Conversed with
many of the surrendered officers & satisfied by that by announcing at once terms
a liberal merciful policy on the part of the Govt we can once more have a happy
united Country I believe all reasoning Men on both sides recognize the fact
that slavery is dead." ALS (telegram sent), DNA, RG 107, Telegrams Collected (Unbound); telegram received (on April 14, 6:00 P.M.), *ibid.*, Telegrams
Collected (Bound); *ibid.*, RG 108, Telegrams Received. *O.R.*, I, xlvi, part
3, 734.

On April 15, 1:00 P.M., Maj. Gen. George G. Meade telegraphed to USG.
"A despatch yesterday received from Maj Gen Gibbon stated that owing to the
large amount of property found at Lynchburg & the Condition of the roads It
would require at least a week before it Could be all removed. Today we have a
very heavy rain storm which will prevent this operation & render the transmission of supplies at Farmville very difficult" Telegram received (at 7:00 P.M.),
DNA, RG 107, Telegrams Collected (Bound); (2) *ibid.*, Telegrams Collected
(Unbound); *ibid.*, RG 108, Telegrams Received; copies, *ibid.*, RG 393, Army
of the Potomac, Letters Sent; DLC-USG, V, 54; Meade Papers, PHi. *O.R.*, I,
xlvi, part 3, 758.

To Maj. Gen. George G. Meade

Apl. 11th *1865*

By Telegraph from Burke Station *1865*

To MAJ. GN. MEADE FARMVILLE

I think it will be advisable for you to direct supplies to be un-
loaded at Farmville to be issued to troops as they return. Take your
own time in returning to Burke Station. When you get here let the
troops go into camp and await further orders.

U. S. GRANT
Lt. Gn

ALS (telegram sent), DNA, RG 94, War Records Office, Miscellaneous War
Records; copies, *ibid.*, RG 108, Letters Sent; DLC-USG, V, 46, 76, 108; Meade
Papers, PHi. *O.R.*, I, xlvi, part 3, 703.

On April 11, 1865, Bvt. Col. Theodore S. Bowers wrote to Maj. Gen. George
G. Meade. "You will please leave a garrison of at least one Brigade at Farmville,
until all the troops and trains in the neighborhood of the Appomattox have moved
forward to Burksville or to points South of there, when it will break up the Post

at Farmville and join its command." ALS, DNA, RG 94, War Records Office, Miscellaneous War Records; Scheide Library, Princeton, N. J. *O.R.*, I, xlvi, part 3, 703–4.

On April 12, USG telegraphed to Meade. "I start this evening for Washn to be gone several days; If you are so inclined you can visit Richmond whilst your army is collecting about Burksville" Telegram received (dated "12"), DNA, RG 107, Telegrams Collected (Unbound). At 4:15 P.M., Meade telegraphed to USG. "In accordance with your instructions the 6th & 2d corps were yesterday put en route for this place—The 6th will reach here today, & the 2d tomorrow.— Last evening at Farmsville Maj. Genl—Fitz hugh Lee of the confederate army with 5 officers of his staff—surrendered themselves to me & were by my directions sent to report to Maj. Genl Gibbon at Appomatox C. H—Maj. Genl. Lee stated that on learning of the surrender of the Confed. Army, he ordered his command to disperse & return to their homes & came in himself.—" ALS (telegram sent), *ibid.*, RG 94, War Records Office, Miscellaneous War Records; telegram received, *ibid.*, RG 107, Telegrams Collected (Unbound); *ibid.*, RG 108, Telegrams Received. *O.R.*, I, xlvi, part 3, 719. On April 11, Bowers issued Special Orders No. 74. "The Comdg Officer of U S Forces at Farmville, Va., will parole all prisoners of war at that place, and permit them to go to their homes, not to take up arms against the United States until properly exchanged. II Par. I of Special orders No 48 of date March 10 1865, from these Headquarters suspending 'trade operations within the State of Virginia, except that portion known as the Eastern Shore, and the States of NorthCarolina and SouthCarolina and that portion of the State of Georgia immediately bordering on the Atlantic, including the City of Savannah, until further orders' is hereby revoked." Copies, DLC-USG, V, 57, 63, 65. *O.R.*, I, xlvi, part 3, 703.

On April 13, Meade telegraphed to USG. "I find it impossible to have your orders to withdraw the troops belonging to this Army at City Point Executed in consequence of the interference of Brig Genl Patrick who continues to exercise control over them in face of my orders. Genl Patrick has also assumed to retain a battalion of the 14th Infy which I had ordered to the front   I understood the duties heretofore Executed by these troops would now be Performed by troops of the Army of the James   I have therefore to request you will instruct Brig Genl Patrick to this Effect and request him not to detain troops under my orders or in case circumstances may have rendered it necessary that I be relieved from the Command of these troops, that is, those formerly at City Point   the 14th Infantry —I desire to join me" Telegram received, DNA, RG 107, Telegrams Collected (Unbound); (at 4:00 P.M.) *ibid.*, RG 108, Letters Received. Printed as sent at 1:30 P.M. in *O.R.*, I, xlvi, part 3, 728. On April 12, Bowers wrote to Maj. Gen. Edward O. C. Ord. "As most of the State of Virginia is within your Command, Lieutenant General Grant desires to transfer to you Brig. Gen. M. R. Patrick, at present Provost Marshal General of the 'Armies operating against Richmond' for the purpose of having you appoint him Provost Marshal General of the Department of Virginia, with the view of giving him special and immediate control and management of affairs in Richmond. The 20th New York Regiment his present Provost Guard has also been ordered to report to you for the use of General Patrick in his new position. Gen. Patrick's integrity and purity of character; his familiarity with the people and affairs of Virginia, and his experience and business qualifications, it is believed, will make him invaluable to you and to the Government in the position indicated   He is therefore fully commæended to you, as an able, useful, honest, & moderate officer." ALS, DNA, RG 94, Generals' Papers and Books, Marsena R. Patrick. *O.R.*, I, xlvi, part 3, 724. On April 13, Brig. Gen. Marsena R. Patrick telegraphed to Bowers. "Have just returned from Richmond Genl Ord places me on duty at once as Marshal for his Department I am to take the 20th New York with me Please cause such order to be issued as will authorize my Removal and to take the 20th so soon as I can close out here" Telegram received (at 5:00 P.M.), DNA, RG 107, Telegrams Collected (Unbound); *ibid.*, RG 108, Letters Received. *O.R.*, I, xlvi, part 3, 729. On the same day, Bowers issued Special Orders No. 76. "I Brig Gen M. R. Patrick, Provost Marshal General Armies operating against Richmond, and his staff, will report to Maj. Gen. E. O. C. Ord, for assignment to duty as Prov Mar Genl Dept of Va. II The 20th Regt New York Infantry is transferred from the Army of the Potomac to the Department of Virginia, and will report to Maj Gen E O C. Ord, for assignment to duty with Gen Patrick. III Lieut Col. F. T. Dent, Aide de Camp to the Lieut General, having been appointed a Brigadier General of Volunteers, is hereby relieved from duty on the staff, and will report in person to Maj. Gen. E. O. C. Ord, Comdg Department of Virginia, for orders. . . . VI . . . Brevet Brig Gen Jno E. Mulford Agent of Exchange will as soon as practicable take station in Richmond, Va., until further orders." Copies, DLC-USG, V, 57, 63, 65. *O.R.*, I, xlvi, part 3, 728.

On May 1, USG issued a pass. "Pass Mrs. ₣Gen. F. T. Dent and family from Baltimore or Washington to Richmond, Va, free, on Govt. boats." ADS, Mrs. Gordon Singles, Arlington, Va.

To Maj. Gen. Henry W. Halleck

April 12. 1865. 1 P. M.

MAJ. GEN. HALLECK, WASHINGTON

I thought of sending Pope a full Corps of Ords troops. You may send him all the cavalry horses from the west until he is supplied. I shall be in Washington tomorrow.

U. S. GRANT
Lt. Gen

Telegram, copies, DLC-USG, V, 46, 76, 108; DNA, RG 108, Letters Sent. Printed as received at 3:00 P.M. in *O.R.*, I, xlvi, part 3, 718; *ibid.*, I, xlviii, part 2, 76. On April 12, 1865, 11:00 A.M., Maj. Gen. Henry W. Halleck had telegraphed to USG. "The *new* regiments sent to Genl Hancock since March 9th number 17,500 men. This is in addition to the 1st Veteran Corps which has about 5 full regiments. Shall I continue to send him other new regiments nearly ready at the north? Considering Genl Pope's apprehensions of an advance of Kirby Smith, would it not be well to send to Arkansas all new regiments raised in the West? Over six thousand cavalry horses have been sent to Genl. Canby between Oct 20th & March 31st. As Genl Reynolds is very destitute of horses, would it not now be well to supply him?" ALS (telegram sent), DNA, RG 107, Telegrams Collected (Bound); telegram received, *ibid.*; (marked as sent at 11:30 A.M.) *ibid.*, RG 108, Letters Received. *O.R.*, I, xlvi, part 3, 718; *ibid.*, I, xlviii, part 2, 76.

Also on April 12, Secretary of War Edwin M. Stanton telegraphed to USG. "I desire very much to consult with you on some important matters. Do you contemplate being at Washington soon or can you meet me at Point Look out or Fortress Monroe" ALS (telegram sent), DNA, RG 107, Telegrams Collected (Bound); telegram received, *ibid.*, RG 108, Letters Received. *O.R.*, I, xlvi, part 3, 718. On the same day, USG telegraphed to Stanton. "I shall leave here for Washington this afternoon." *Ibid.*

On April 13, Bvt. Brig. Gen. William A. Nichols issued AGO General Orders No. 64. "The Headquarters of the Armies of the United States are established at Washington, D. C." Copy (printed), NjP. *O.R.*, I, xlvi, part 3, 728. On the same day, USG wrote to Stanton. "The following dispatches detailing the last days operations are respectfully transmitted for your information." LS, DLC-Edwin M. Stanton.

To Maj. Gen. Edward R. S. Canby

Cipher   *Washington, D. C.*, April 13th 18645.
Maj. Gen. E. R. S. Canby
Mobile, Ala. Via New York, and Cairo, Ills.

The following dispatches from Judge J. A. Campbell, to myself and to Lieut. Gen. R. Taylor, C. S. A., Mobile, Ala., you will please forward to Lieut. Gen. Taylor without delay

U. S. Grant
Lieut. Gen.

Telegram sent, DNA, RG 108, Telegrams Sent; copy, DLC-USG, V, 54. *O.R.*, I, xlix, part 2, 346. On April 11, 1865, John A. Campbell, Richmond, wrote to USG. "The Events of the last few days in my Judgement are of a nature to require the cessation of Hostilities throughout the Confederate States On the part of those Who Command their forces—My impression is that the Military Commanders will adopt the same Conclusion—I have prepared a telegram to Gen Taylor who is in Command at Mobile ~~requesting~~ acquainting him with the facts which I request may be forwarded as fast as possible if not incompatable with your views of propriety—My object is to prevent the further effusion of blood & distruction of property—" Copies, DNA, RG 108, Letters Received; *ibid.*, Telegrams Sent; *ibid.*, RG 107, Telegrams Collected (Unbound); DLC-USG, V, 54; DLC-Edwin M. Stanton. *O.R.*, I, xlvi, part 3, 723; *ibid.*, I, xlix, part 2, 322. On April 12, Maj. Gen. Edward O. C. Ord telegraphed to USG transmitting Campbell's letter to USG and a letter addressed by Campbell to C.S.A. Lt. Gen. Richard Taylor. Telegram received, DNA, RG 107, Telegrams Collected (Unbound); *ibid.*, RG 108, Letters Received. *O.R.*, I, xlvi, part 3, 723.

To Maj. Gen. Edward O. C. Ord

Washington, D. C., Apl. 13st *1865* [*6:15* P.M.]

MAJ. GN. ORD, RICHMOND VA.

~~Change~~ Change the word "Call" and substitute the word "permission" for it in your notice which is to be published to-morrow morning, and add, that any of the persons named in the call signed by R. M. T. Hunter and others who are found in the City twelve hours after the publication of this notice will be subject to arrests unless they are residents of the City.

U. S. GRANT
Lt Gn.

ALS (telegram sent), DNA, RG 107, Telegrams Collected (Bound); telegram received, *ibid.*, Telegrams Collected (Unbound); Ord Papers, CU-B. *O.R.*, I, xlvi, part 3, 735. USG apparently responded to a telegram of April 13, 1865, from Maj. Gen. Edward O. C. Ord to President Abraham Lincoln. "Copy of order to be published in the city paper to-morrow, April 14: Owing to recent events the call for the reassembling of the gentlemen recently acting as the legislature of Virginia is rescinded. Should any of the gentlemen come to the city under the notice of the reassembling, already published, they will be furnished with passports to return to their homes." *Ibid.* At 9:30 P.M., Ord twice telegraphed to USG. "Your telegram regarding notice in tomorrows paper received—It will be carried out" "I find no call for a meeting signed by R M T Hunter—has been published—Do you not mean the call signed by J A Campbell" Telegrams received (on April 14, the first at 9:20 A.M., the second at 9:15 A.M.), DNA, RG 107, Telegrams Collected (Bound); *ibid.*, RG 108, Telegrams Received; copies, DLC-USG, V, 54. *O.R.*, I, xlvi, part 3, 736.

On the same day, Ord telegraphed to USG. "There are many Confederate Surgeons here who were found in charge of Hospitals   The Hospitals are broken up and all the inmates who could be removed have been sent away   Shall I parole the medical officers and let them go home,   ~~a~~A few may be necessary to take care of the Remaining patients" Telegram received (at 3:30 P.M.), DNA, RG 107, Telegrams Collected (Bound); *ibid.*, RG 108, Letters Received. *O.R.*, I, xlvi, part 3, 736. On the same day, USG telegraphed to Ord. "You may parole all surgeons left in Richmond whose services are no longer required." ALS (telegram sent), DNA, RG 107, Telegrams Collected (Bound); telegram received, *ibid.*, Telegrams Collected (Unbound). *O.R.*, I, xlvi, part 3, 736.

On the same day, USG telegraphed to Ord. "Notify Gen. Casey to suspend recruiting until I reach Richmond." ALS (telegram sent), DNA, RG 107, Telegrams Collected (Bound); telegram received, *ibid.*, Telegrams Collected (Unbound); Ord Papers, CU-B. *O.R.*, I, xlvi, part 3, 736.

To Maj. Gen. George G. Meade

———

Washington, D. C., Apl. 14th *1864*5

Maj. Gen. Meade Burke's Station Va.

Say to Lt. Col. Smith and W. D. Coleman that they can return to Danville. At present I have no reply to make to the questions ~~of~~ propounded by Mr. Smith. Should I have hereafter they will be forwarded by special Messenger.

U. S. Grant
Lt. Gn.

ALS (telegram sent), DNA, RG 107, Telegrams Collected (Bound); telegrams received (2), *ibid.*, RG 94, War Records Office, Miscellaneous War Records. *O.R.*, I, xlvi, part 3, 745. On April 13, 1865, 2:45 P.M., Maj. Gen. George G. Meade telegraphed to USG. "I forward communication just received—Col Smith & Mr Coleman await at these Hd Qrs such reply as you may think proper to give.—" ALS (telegram sent), DNA, RG 94, War Records Office, Army of the Potomac; telegram received (at 4:00 P.M.), *ibid.*, RG 107, Telegrams Collected (Bound); (at 3:30 P.M.) *ibid.*, RG 108, Telegrams Received. Meade transmitted a letter of April 11 from Governor William Smith, Danville, Va., to USG. "The government of Virginia of which I am the Executive head is for the present located in this town. Elected by the people under a recognized state Constitution, and in conformity to the laws of the Country, it is my duty to look to the interest of her people to the best of my ability. In view of the reported surrender of Genl Lee, and in ignorance of its terms, I respectfully propound the following interrogatories: Will the state government represented by me, be superseded by a military or civil organization under your authority or that of the Federal government. Will the State officials of the Virginia government be subject to Military arrest? and will they be allowed peaceably leave the state for Europe should they desire to do so? I send this despatch in charge of my aid Lt. Col. P. B. Smith and Wm D. Coleman Esq of this town, who will receive your reply, which I respectfully ask." Copies, *ibid.*; DLC-USG, V, 54; (2) Webb Papers, CtY. *O.R.*, I, xlvi, part 3, 704.

To Maj. Gen. Henry W. Halleck

———

Baltimore, April 15. 1865

Maj Gen Halleck

Please direct Gen. Hancock to send a regiment of infantry to Havre de Grace bridge without delay. one company of Cavalry should also be sent there for the present. If you can bring down from the north a regiment, sooner than it can be got from Hancock, you may direct one from there to Havre-de-Grace.

U. S. GRANT
Lt. Genl.

Telegram, copies, DLC-USG, V, 46, 76, 108; DNA, RG 108, Letters Sent. Printed as sent from Camden Station, Baltimore, received at 12:15 P.M., in *O.R.*, I, xlvi, part 3, 757–58.

On April 14, 1865, midnight (sent on April 15, 12:20 A.M.), Maj. Thomas T. Eckert telegraphed to USG "On night Train to Burlington." "The President was assassinated at Fords Theatre at 10 30 tonight & cannot live. the wound is a Pistol shot through the head. Secretary Seward & his son Frederick, were also assassinatd at their residence & are in a dangerous condition. The Secretary of War desires that you return to Washington immediately. please answer on receipt of this." ALS (telegram sent), DNA, RG 107, Telegrams Collected (Bound). *O.R.*, I, xlvi, part 3, 744–45. On April 15, 12:50 A.M., Asst. Secretary of War Charles A. Dana telegraphed to USG, Philadelphia. "Permit me to suggest to you to Keep a close watch on all persons who come near you in the cars or otherwise, also that an Engine be sent in front of the train to guard against anything being on the track." Telegram received, DNA, RG 107, Telegrams Collected (Bound). *O.R.*, I, xlvi, part 3, 756. On April 15, USG, Newark, N. J., telegraphed to commanding officer and provost marshal, Baltimore. "Have a guard at President street depot on arrival of train an Officer & ten (10) men of the party to go on to Washington with it. the train will be at the Depot by (11) eleven A M" Telegram received (at 9:22 A.M.), DNA, RG 393, Middle Military Div., Telegrams Received; *ibid.*, 8th Army Corps and Middle Dept., Letters Received.

On April 15, USG telegraphed to Bvt. Col. Orville E. Babcock, New York City. "No orders for you at present" ALS (telegram sent), *ibid.*, RG 107, Telegrams Collected (Bound); telegram sent, *ibid.* On the same day, USG telegraphed to Bvt. Col. Horace Porter. "The President died this morning. Join me here by end of next week." Elsie Porter Mende, *An American Soldier and Diplomat: Horace Porter* (New York, 1927), p. 95.

Also on April 15, Secretary of War Edwin M. Stanton wrote to USG. "I beg to call your attention to the security of this City, and especially to the large number of rebel officers and privates prisoners of war, and rebel refugees and deserters that are among us, and ask you to see that adequate force and vigilance are employed. Directions were given Major General Augur on this subject last night, and also instructions to look to the condition of the forts and defences. Adequate provision may have been made, but at the present deplorable juncture I feel it my duty to ask you to consider yourself specially charged with all matters pertaining to the security and defence of this National Capital. Please acknowledge the receipt of these instructions." ALS, DNA, RG 108, Letters Received. *O.R.*, I, xlvi, part 3, 757.

On April 16, Stanton wrote to USG. "The distressing duty has devolved upon the Secretary of War to announce to the armies of the United States, that at twenty-two minutes after seven o'clock on the morning of Saturday the fifteenth day of April, 1865; Abraham Lincoln, President of the United States, died of a mortal wound inflicted upon him by an assassin. The armies of the United States will share with their fellow citizens the feelings of grief and horror inspired by this most atrocious murder of their great and beloved President and Commander-in-Chief, and with profound sorrow will mourn his death as a national calamity. The Head Quarters of every Department, post and station will be draped in mourning for thirty days and appropriate funeral honors will be paid by every army, and in every Department and at every military post, and at the Military Academy at West Point, to the memory of the late illustrious Chief Magistrate of the nation and Commander-in Chief of its armies. Lieutenant General Grant will give the necessary instructions for carrying this order into effect." LS, DNA, RG 108, Letters Received; ADf (partly by Stanton), IHi. *O.R.*, I, xlvi, part 3, 788. This message was embodied in War Dept. General Orders No. 66, April 16. *Ibid.* On the same day, Stanton wrote to USG. "You will please announce by General Order to the armies of the United States that on Saturday the 15th. day of April 1865, by reason of the death of Abraham Lincoln, the office of President of the United States devolved upon Andrew Johnson, Vice President, who on the same day took the official oath prescribed for the President and entered upon the duties of that office." LS, DNA, RG 108, Letters Received. *O.R.*, I, xlvi, part 3, 786. See *ibid.*, p. 789.

To Maj. Gen. Edward O. C. Ord

(Cipher)   Apl. 15th *1865* [*4:00* P.M.]
MAJ. GEN. ORD, RICHMOND VA.

Arrest J. A. Campbell, Mayor Mayo[1] and [t]he members of the old Council of Richmond, who have not yet taken the oath of Allegiance, and put them in Libby prison. ~~and h~~Hold them guarded beyond the possibility of escape until further orders. Also arrest all paroled officers and surgeons until they can be sent beyond our lines unless they take the oath of Allegiance. The oath need not be received from any one who you have not good reason to believe will observe it, and from none who are excluded by the Presidents proclamation without authority of the President to do so. Extreme rigor will have to be observed whilst assassination remains the order of the day with the rebels.

U. S. GRANT
Lt. Gn.

ALS (telegram sent), DNA, RG 107, Telegrams Collected (Bound); telegram sent, *ibid.*; telegrams received (2), *ibid.*, Telegrams Collected (Unbound); (at 5:00 P.M.) Ord Papers, CU-B. *O.R.*, I, xlvi, part 3, 762. On April 15, 1865, 7:30 P.M., Maj. Gen. Edward O. C. Ord telegraphed to USG. "~~Your~~ Cypher telegram

directing certain parties to be arrested is received   the two citizens I have seen
they are [old nearly helpless] and I think incapable of harm   Genl Lee and Staff
are in town among the Paroled prisoners—Should I arrest them under the circumstances I think the rebellion here would be reopened—I will risk my life that
the present paroles will be kept—and if you will allow me to do so, trust the
people here who I believe are ignorant of the assassin[ation]s—done I think by
some insane brutus o̶r̶ with but few accomplices—p̶l̶e̶a̶s̶e̶ a̶n̶s̶w̶e̶r̶, Mr Campell
and Hunter pressed me earnestly yesterday to Send them to Washington to see
the President   would they have done so if guilty—please answer" ALS (telegram sent), Ord Papers, CU-B; telegram received (at 8:45 P.M.), DNA, RG
107, Telegrams Collected (Bound); *ibid.*, RG 108, Telegrams Received. *O.R.*,
I, xlvi, part 3, 762. At 8:00 P.M., USG telegraphed to Ord. "On reflection I will
withdraw my dispatch of this date directing the arrest of Campbell, Mayo and
others so far as it may be regarded as an order and leave it in the light of a suggestion to be executed only so far as you may judge the good of the service demands." ALS (telegram sent), DNA, RG 107, Telegrams Collected (Bound);
telegram sent, *ibid.*; telegram received (at 8:45 P.M.), Ord Papers, CU-B. *O.R.*,
I, xlvi, part 3, 762. At 9:30 P.M., Ord telegraphed to USG. "Second telegram
leaving the subject of arrests in my hands—is recieved—" ALS (telegram sent),
Ord Papers, CU-B; telegram received (at 10:20 P.M.), DNA, RG 107, Telegrams Collected (Bound); *ibid.*, RG 108, Letters Received. *O.R.*, I, xlvi, part
3, 763.

 At 2:00 P.M., Maj. Gen. George G. Meade telegraphed to USG. "I see by
an order in the Richmond Whig of Maj Gen Ords that passes to visit Richmond
are not to be respected unless signed by the Secy of War. Yourself or Maj General
Ord. I have to request that you will authorize my giving passes to such officers of
this army as can be spared who desire to visit Richmond & if I am so authorized
that you will notify Maj Gen Ord to that effect." Telegram received (at 7:00
P.M.), DNA, RG 107, Telegrams Collected (Bound); (2) *ibid.*, Telegrams
Collected (Unbound); *ibid.*, RG 108, Telegrams Received; copies, *ibid.*, RG
393, Army of the Potomac, Letters Sent; DLC-USG, V, 54; Meade Papers, PHi.
O.R., I, xlvi, part 3, 758. On the same day, Brig. Gen. John A. Rawlins tele-
graphed to Ord. "In your orders specifying the passes to be respected in visiting
Richmond, please embrace those of Maj. Gen's Meade and Sheridan. Gen. Grant
has informed them that these passes will be good for this purpose" Telegram
sent, DNA, RG 107, Telegrams Collected (Unbound); telegram received, *ibid.*
On April 16, Rawlins telegraphed to Meade, sending a copy to Maj. Gen. Philip
H. Sheridan. "Gen ord has been directed to respect your passes for persons to visit
Richmond" Telegram received (at 11:41 A.M.), *ibid.*, RG 94, War Records
Office, Miscellaneous War Records; (2—one dated April 15) *ibid.*, RG 107,
Telegrams Collected (Unbound); copy, Meade Papers, PHi. *O.R.*, I, xlvi, part
3, 787.

 1. Joseph Mayo, born in Va. in 1795, commonwealth attorney in Richmond
(1823–53) and mayor (1853–65).

To Maj. Gen. Philip H. Sheridan

(Cipher)   Washington Apl. 15th *18645*. [*7:00* P.M.]
Maj. Gn. Sheridan Burkesville Va.

Gen. Sherman is in motion after Johnston's Army. It may be
that instead of surrendering Johnston may follow his usual tactics
of falling back whenever too hard pressed. If so Sherman has not
got Cavalry enough to head off and capture his Army. I want you
to get your Cavalry in readiness to push South and make up this
deficiency if it becomes necessary. Sherman expected to occupy
Raleigh on the 13th but does not say which way the enemy is
moving. I hope to hear further from him almost any hour and will
inform you when I do.

U. S. Grant
Lt. Gn.

ALS (telegram sent), DNA, RG 107, Telegrams Collected (Bound); telegram
sent, *ibid.*; copies, *ibid.*, RG 108, Letters Sent; DLC-USG, V, 46, 76, 108. *O.R.*,
I, xlvi, part 3, 760.

On April 13, 1865, Maj. Gen. Philip H. Sheridan, Nottoway Court House,
Va., twice telegraphed to Brig. Gen. John A. Rawlins. "My Head Quarters is
here also the three (3) Divisions of cavalry. it is excellent place to refit the
command" Telegrams received (2—at 8:00 P.M.), DNA, RG 107, Telegrams
Collected (Unbound); *ibid.*, RG 108, Telegrams Received; copy, DLC-USG, V,
54. *O.R.*, I, xlvi, part 3, 733. "The Officers & Men of the 1st & 3d Divisions of
Cavalry brought with them from Winchester Only the Clothes they wore On their
persons & are badly off   all the trains & baggage of these Divisions Are at
Harpers Ferry   Would it be best to Order them down" Telegrams received (2—
at 8:00 P.M.), DNA, RG 107, Telegrams Collected (Unbound); (2) *ibid.*, RG
108, Letters Received; copies (2), DLC-Philip H. Sheridan. *O.R.*, I, xlvi, part
3, 733.

On April 14, Sheridan telegraphed to Rawlins. "Genl Grant said to me that
when he got to Richmond he would have ₲Genl Irwin Gregg exchanged,   as he
did not go there will you have the kindness to have it done if possible" Telegram
received, DNA, RG 107, Telegrams Collected (Unbound); (at 8:50 P.M.) *ibid.*,
RG 108, Telegrams Received; copy, DLC-USG, V, 54. *O.R.*, I, xlvi, part 3, 747.

To Maj. Gen. John Pope

(Cipher)   Washington Apl. 16th *1864*5. [*9:00* P.M.]
MAJ. GEN. POPE, ST. LOUIS MO.

Make your prepaprations for carrying out the campaign proposed in your communication of the 8th. I will direct Gn. Allen to
commence shipping wagons to Little Rock.¹ You may exercise
your judgement about sending to Kirby Smith for a surrender. I
believe by judicious management he might be induced to give up
the contest. He might want to get out of the country himself.

                                              U. S. GRANT
                                              Lt. Gen.

ALS (telegram sent), DNA, RG 107, Telegrams Collected (Bound); telegram
sent, *ibid.*; telegram received (on April 17, 1865, 9:30 A.M.), *ibid.*, Telegrams
Collected (Unbound); *ibid.*, RG 393, Dept. of the Mo., Telegrams Received.
O.R., I, xlviii, part 2, 106.

On April 10, Maj. Gen. John Pope wrote to USG. "I have sent you under
date of the 8th inst a plan of operations into Texas.—The glorious result of your
operations in Virginia and the surrender of Lee's Army may make such a movement unnecessary.—It is more than likely that when this news reaches Kirby
Smith' Army in an authentic form, they will disperse to their homes.—Would
you consider it advisable for me to send it to Kirby Smith under flag of truce and
demand the surrender or dispersion of his Army?" LS, DNA, RG 108, Letters
Received. *O.R.*, I, xlviii, part 2, 64.

1. On April 16, 9:00 P.M., USG telegraphed to Brig. Gen. Robert Allen.
"You may send all the surplus transportation in ~~the~~ Gen. Thomas' and Pope's
commands to Little Rock as fast as it can go. Bringing away Schofields & A. J.
Smith's forces without their teams must make a large surplus. All through
Tennessee the number of teams can be greatly reduced ~~also~~." ALS (telegram
sent), DNA, RG 107, Telegrams Collected (Bound); telegram sent, *ibid.*; copies,
ibid., RG 108, Letters Sent; DLC-USG, V, 46, 76, 108; DLC-John M. Schofield.
O.R., I, xlviii, part 2, 107. On April 17, Allen, Louisville, telegraphed to USG.
"Dispatch recd & instructions are given accordingly—The supplies of transporta-
tion may not be so large as you count on—A portion of Gen Schofields transportation followed him to Washn & a large number of wagons have recently been
shipped East as I understood your dispatch everything is to be shipped to Little
Rock" Telegram received (on April 18, 10:45 P.M.), DNA, RG 107, Telegrams
Collected (Bound); *ibid.*, RG 108, Telegrams Received; copy, DLC-USG, V, 54.

To Maj. Gen. Philip H. Sheridan

(Cipher)   Washington Apl. 16th 1865 [*3:30* P.M.]
MAJ. GEN. SHERIDAN, NOTTOWAY C. H. VA,

Your dispatch of this date received. Can you not move with from six to eight thousand cavalry to join Sherman? I have sent you two dispatches on the subject besides two from Sherman directed to Burkesville which I judge from yours you have not received. Telegraph up for them and if they are not there let me know and I will have them repeated.

U. S. GRANT
Lt. Gn.

ALS (telegram sent), DNA, RG 107, Telegrams Collected (Bound); telegram sent, *ibid.*; telegrams received (2—one marked as sent at 3:00 P.M.), *ibid.*, Telegrams Collected (Unbound). *O.R.*, I, xlvi, part 3, 794. On April 16, 1865, USG again telegraphed to Maj. Gen. Philip H. Sheridan, and the message was received as a note to the telegram printed above. "If you have no Cipher operator send to Gen. Meade for one." ALS (telegram sent), DNA, RG 107, Telegrams Collected (Bound); telegrams received (2), *ibid.*, Telegrams Collected (Unbound). *O.R.*, I, xlvi, part 3, 794. On the same day, Sheridan, Nottoway Court House, Va., telegraphed to USG. "I was about to move the Cavalry to City Point to refit and feed the horses. It is impossible to get the command in good condition at this place. The Railroad is in such bad condition that it not cannot furnish the necessary allowance of forage and other supplies. Thus far I have not been able to get anything. I will not move until I hear from you." Telegram received (at 11:50 A.M.), DNA, RG 107, Telegrams Collected (Bound); (3—two misdated April 15) *ibid.*, Telegrams Collected (Unbound); *ibid.*, RG 108, Telegrams Received; copies, DLC-USG, V, 54; (3) DLC-Philip H. Sheridan. *O.R.*, I, xlvi, part 3, 794.

On the same day, Sheridan, City Point, telegraphed to USG. "After sending my dispatch to you this morning I came down to this place to find the true condition of the RR I am satisfied that the Command cannot be supplied and refitted at Nottoway in any reasonable time If I could drop back to the vicinity of Petersburg forage could be sent up the river I am anxious to make the march you spoke of yesterday in your telegram and will gain time by coming back to Petersburg or this place" Telegram received (at 9:00 P.M.), DNA, RG 107, Telegrams Collected (Bound); (at 7:40 P.M.) *ibid.*, RG 108, Telegrams Received; copies, DLC-USG, V, 54; (2) DLC-Philip H. Sheridan. *O.R.*, I, xlvi, part 3, 794–95. At 10:00 P.M., USG telegraphed to Sheridan. "You may bring your cavalry back to Petersburg or where you can make the most time for your move in conjunction with Sherman." ALS (telegram sent), DNA, RG 107, Telegrams Collected (Bound); telegram sent, *ibid.*; copies, *ibid.*, RG 108, Letters Sent; DLC-USG, V, 46, 76, 108. *O.R.*, I, xlvi, part 3, 795. At 10:30 P.M., Sheridan telegraphed to USG. "I have telegraphed for the dispatches from Sherman that

you refer to—" Telegram received (at 11:45 P.M.), DNA, RG 107, Telegrams
Collected (Bound); *ibid.*, RG 108, Telegrams Received; copies, DLC-USG, V,
54; (2) DLC-Philip H. Sheridan. *O.R.*, I, xlvi, part 3, 795.

On the same day, Sheridan telegraphed to USG. "Is the reported assassination
of President Lincoln & Secy Seward which reached here last night true" Telegrams received (3), DNA, RG 107, Telegrams Collected (Unbound); (at 11:40
A.M.) *ibid.*, RG 108, Telegrams Received; copy, DLC-USG, V, 54. *O.R.*, I,
xlvi, part 3, 794. At 7:00 P.M., Brig. Gen. John A. Rawlins telegraphed to Sheridan. "The reported assassination of President Lincoln is true. He died yesterday
morning at 7:22. His murderer is supposed to be J. Wilkes Booth, who is still at
large. Mr. Seward is still living but in a very critical condition." Telegrams sent
(2), DNA, RG 107, Telegrams Collected (Bound); copies, *ibid.*, RG 108, Letters Sent; DLC-USG, V, 46, 76, 108. *O.R.*, I, xlvi, part 3, 794.

To Julia Dent Grant

Washington Apl. 16th *1865*

DEAR JULIA,

I got back here about 1 p. m. yesterday and was called immediately into the presence of our new President, who had already
been qualified, and the Cabinet. I telegraphed you from Baltimore
and told Beckwith to do the same thing from here.[1] You no doubt
received the dispatches. All seems very quiet here. There is but
little doubt but that the plot contemplated the distruction of more
than the President and Sec. of State. I think now however it has
expended itself and there is but little to fear. For the present I shall
occupy a room in the office which is well guarded and will be occupied by Bowers and probably two or three others.[2] I shall only go
to the Hotel twice a day for my meals and will stay indoors of eve-
nings. The change which has come upon the country so suddenly
will make it necessary for me to remain in the City for several days
yet. Gen. Halleck will go to Richmond to command there and Ord
to Charleston. Other changes which will have to be made, and the
apparent feeling that I should remain here until everything gets
into working order under the new régime will probably detain me
here until next Saturday.[3] If I can get home sooner I will do so. I
hope you will be in your house in Phila when I do go home. The

inconvenience of getting from the Phila depot to Burlington is about equal to the balance of the trip.

Love and kisses for you and the children.

ULYS.

ALS, DLC-USG.

1. On April 15, 1865, Samuel H. Beckwith telegraphed to Julia Dent Grant. "I am requested by the Lieutenant General to inform you of his safe arrival— Please inform Mrs. Dent   The President died this morning—See There are still hopes of Secretary Sewards recovery" ALS (telegram sent), DNA, RG 107, Telegrams Collected (Unbound). *O.R.*, I, xlvi, part 3, 757. On the same day, Mrs. Grant telegraphed to an unknown addressee. "Lt. Gen. Grant left here for Washington at 6 o'clock this morning." *Galena Gazette*, April 15, 1865.

2. On April 21, Bvt. Col. Theodore S. Bowers wrote to Maj. Gen. Christopher C. Augur. "The Lieutenant General desires that a guard consisting of two Sentinels during the day and five Sentinels at night be furnished his Head Quarters corner of F and 17th Streets, from the troops stationed at the War, Department Barracks, and that the Officer of the guard from which the Sentinels are taken, be instructed to report to Lieutenant Colonel Bowers Assistant Adjutant General at these Head Quarters for orders regarding the posting of the Sentinels, It is requested that the above mentioned arrangement may be carried into effect this evening, returning the guard now here which is furnished from Fry Barracks" Copies, DLC-USG, V, 46, 76, 108; DNA, RG 108, Letters Sent. *O.R.*, I, xlvi, part 3, 885.

3. April 22.

To Edwin M. Stanton

[Head] Qrs Armies U. S.

Washington, D. C., April 17th 1865

Respectfully refered to the Sec. of War. My own views are that it will be better to have Mosby's and White's[1] men in Maryland as paroled prisoners of War than at large as Guerrillas. I would exact howeve[r] that all should be required to register their names and residence with the nearest Provost Marshal to the place where they intend to live. I would also suggest the form of parole adopted with Gen. Lee's Army an exact copy of which will be found in the New York Herald of to-day. I would require each man to sign his own parole instead of allowing officers to sign for their men.

U. S. GRANT

Lt. Gn

AES, DNA, RG 107, Telegrams Collected (Unbound). *O.R.*, I, xlvi, part 3, 818. Written on a telegram of April 17, 1865, from Col. John L. Thompson, 1st N. H. Cav., Darnestown, Md., to Lt. Col. Joseph H. Taylor, adjt. for Maj. Gen. Christopher C. Augur. "Two hundred 200 white's & Moseby's men have sent word that they wish to be paroled at Edwards Ferry. They have been directed to come tomorrow. Shall I ~~meet~~ not send to your Hd qrs for blank paroles or can the Officers parole the men?" Telegram received (at 1:00 P.M.), DNA, RG 107, Telegrams Collected (Unbound); *ibid.*, RG 108, Letters Received. Printed as sent at 1:00 P.M. in *O.R.*, I, xlvi, part 3, 817.

1. Probably Lt. Col. Elijah V. White, 35th Va. Battalion.

To Maj. Gen. Edward R. S. Canby

Washington Apl. 17th 1865 [*1:30* P.M.]
MAJ. GEN. CANBY, MOBILE ALA. VIA CAIRO & NEW YORK.

I feel certain that you now have Mobile.[1] If so you have a large force that will no longer be required where it is. Commence operations immediately with all the force you can spare against Galveston Texas. Unless the forces in Louisiana and Texas surrender as Lee's Army has done, and Johnston's probably, a large force will start from Southwest Arkansas about the 1st of June to invade the state of Texas and wind up the war in that quarter. Your movement against Galveston will be co-operative.

U. S. GRANT
Lt. Gn.

ALS (telegram sent), DNA, RG 107, Telegrams Collected (Bound); telegram sent, *ibid.*; copies, *ibid.*, RG 108, Letters Sent; DLC-USG, V, 46, 76, 108. Variant text in *O.R.*, I, xlix, part 2, 382–83. On April 25, 1865, 5:00 P.M., Maj. Gen. Edward R. S. Canby, New Orleans, telegraphed to USG. "Your dispatch of the 17th has just been received. I came over from Mobile for the purpose of making the preparations directed in your order and in anticipation of it. I want light draft Sea going Steamers for service on the Gulf coast. The Quartermaster General does not appreciate the importance of these steamers and I beg that he may be directed to fill the requisitions heretofore made and which I renew today. In the last sixty days they would have repaid their cost tenfold. I return to Mobile tonight." LS (telegram sent), DNA, RG 107, Telegrams Collected (Unbound); telegram received, *ibid.*; (on May 1, 1:00 P.M.) *ibid.*, Telegrams Collected (Bound); *ibid.*, RG 108, Telegrams Received. *O.R.*, I, xlix, part 2, 467.

On April 26, noon, Bvt. Brig. Gen. Cyrus B. Comstock, Washington, D. C., telegraphed to USG, Raleigh, N. C. "A. J. Smiths Corps moved from Blakely for Montgomery on April 14. If Selma should be in rebel possession he would move on that place. Steele's command was to move via Alabama river for Selma on the 17th. Granger's corps to hold Mobile & mouth of Tombigby, the rebels having several gun boats up that river. Maury with probably 4000 to 6000 men went to Demotpolis. Gen Canby proposed to move from Selma against Demopolis. Our information was that Wilson only met Roddy's division at Selma the other two divisions of Forrests command being in Mississippi & not coming to time at that place. A. J. Smith should be at Selma or Montgomery before this. Gen. Canby will probably learn from Wilson of Shermans instructions & armistice before the despatch of the Secretary of War to Gen Canby in reference to them reaches him. Gen. Canby thinks Kirby Smith is trying to raise money enough to pay off his soldiers so that they will disband quietly instead of becoming guerillas. The river is very high, the whole country from Vicksburg to Cairo being under water & a crossing of any force almost impossible. When I left Mobile—the 15th, the news of Lee's surrender had not arrived. Do you wish any of us to join you?" ALS (telegram sent), DNA, RG 107, Telegrams Collected (Bound); telegram sent, *ibid.*; telegram received, *ibid.*, Telegrams Collected (Unbound). *O.R.*, I, xlix, part 2, 480.

On April 30, Canby telegraphed to USG. "General Smith occupied Montgomery on the twenty fifth inst & Genl Steele Selma on the twenty seventh,   The following dispatch has just been recd from Gen Wilson." Telegram received (on May 8, 1:20 A.M.), DNA, RG 108, Telegrams Received; copy, DLC-USG, V, 54. *O.R.*, I, xlix, part 2, 530. The appended telegrams are *ibid.*, pp. 347, 383.

On May 1, Canby telegraphed to USG. "At the request of Lieutenant General Taylor I had a personal conference with him, in the neighborhood of this city, on the twenty ninth (29th) ultimo designing to offer him the same terms as were given the Army of Northern Virginia. At the moment of starting, I received from General Wilson a copy of General Sherman's order to suspend hostilities, and consented to the application of this arrangement to that part of this Division east of the Mississippi. Yesterday, [t]he thirtieth (30th), I received from the Secretary [o]f War information that the armistice had been disapproved by the President, and immediately sent notice to General Taylor that hostilities would be resumed at the expiration of the 48 hours required by General Sherman's agreement. Wilson, Steele and Smith had previously received and acted upon General Sherman's order. Fortunately this action will involve no delay in operations, as the supplies for Smith's and Wilson's commands, will hardly reach them before the expiration of this period. I will be able to gather transportation enough for the movement upon Galveston by the fifteenth (15th) instant. The bulk of the expedition will sail from this place. I have proposed to Genl Taylor the surrender of his Army, upon the conditions given by you to General Lee, and expect his answer on the third (3d) instant." Telegram sent, DNA, RG 107, Telegrams Collected (Unbound); telegram received (on May 8, 3:00 A.M.), *ibid.*, Telegrams Collected (Bound); *ibid.*, RG 108, Telegrams Received. *O.R.*, I, xlix, part 2, 558–59.

On May 2, 10:00 P.M., Canby telegraphed to USG. "Lt Gen. Taylor surrenders on the terms proposed to him. I will meet him at Citronelle on the fourth (4th) instant, and will arrange that the troops and property within the limits of Gen. Thomas' command be surrendered to officers designated by him." Telegram sent, DNA, RG 107, Telegrams Collected (Unbound); telegram received (on May 8, 11:30 P.M.), *ibid.*, Telegrams Collected (Bound); *ibid.*, RG 108, Telegrams Received. *O.R.*, I, xlix, part 2, 573.

On May 6, 9:00 A.M., Maj. Gen. Napoleon J. T. Dana telegraphed to USG. "I have just received the following dispatch from Maj Gen. Canby through the Rebel Lines. 'Hd Qrs Army & Division of West Miss   Citronella Ala May 4th 1865   Lieut Gen Taylor has this day surrendered with the forces under his command on substantially the same terms as those accepted by Genl Lee. You will select & hold in readiness troops to garrison Jackson Brookhaven & Gallatin Infantry at the two (2) former & Cavalry at the latter point for the purpose of keeping constant communication between all three (3) points. The special duty of these troops will be to protect public and private property aginst Jay-Hawkers and other Evil-doers. The comdg officers will be instructed to maintain the strictest discipline & see that the people are treated with discretion & respect~~fully~~" Telegram received (on May 11, 3:10 P.M.), DNA, RG 107, Telegrams Collected (Bound); (on May 11, 3:15 P.M.) *ibid.*, RG 108, Telegrams Received; copy, DLC-USG, V, 54. The enclosure, printed as sent by Maj. Gen. Peter J. Osterhaus, chief of staff for Canby, is in *O.R.*, I, xlviii, part 2, 311.

On May 7, Canby telegraphed to USG. "The terms of the surrender of Dick Taylors forces includes all men and material within the limits of his command— His troops will at once be collected at points from which they can most conveniently be paroled and sent to their homes—The depots of supplies which appear to be very large will be guarded by his troops until the guards designated by me can relieve them—A number of river transports, impressed for the purpose of transporting the troops and supplies when the city was evacuated, will be sent down the river—Four blockade-runners the property of the Quarter Masters Dep. are included in the surrender to the army and will be very useful for coast service —The chiefs of the Property Dep. of Dick Taylors Army have been ordered by him to report to the Chiefs of my own staff to account for and turn over the property in their charge   The civil officers appear to be disposed to account for and turn over in good faith the property which they hold and I expect in a few days to get accurate accounts of all cotton belonging to the rebel Govt. within the states of Ala. and Miss. I shall keep the main body of the troops well together and make such detachments only as may be necessary to guard important points and the depots of supplies that will be turned over. I will open the telegraph line to Corinth and have requested Gen Thomas to open it from that place to Eastport The Mobile & Ohio and Mobile & Montgomery railroads can be put in running order in a short time and I will put them so far as they are within the limits of my command under the control of the Prest and Directors as agents of the military authorities until their legal status may be determined—Both will be needed for military purposes and in this arrangement will be quite as much under our control as if worked by ourselves   I will take immediate measures to garrison Apalachicola and Saint Marks to prevent their being used for any improper purposes   The Navy—fifteen officers and about 400 men with two 2 gunboats and two 2 Tugs— were surrendered at the same time to Admiral Thatcher" Telegram received (on May 15, 1:30 P.M.), DNA, RG 107, Telegrams Collected (Bound); *ibid.*, RG 108, Telegrams Received; copy, DLC-USG, V, 54. *O.R.*, I, xlix, part 2, 658–59.

Also on May 7, Maj. Gen. Cadwallader C. Washburn, Memphis, telegraphed to USG. "I have received the following telegram from Maj Gen Canby via Senatobia   ~~H~~ HeadQrs. Military, Division West Mississippi Citronle, May 4th, 65   MAJ, GEN C C WASHBURE Memphis—Lt Gen Taylor has this day surrendered to me with the forces under his Command on substantially the same terms as those accepted by Genl Lee   I have sent this information to Gen Thomas and requested that troops be sent from Memphis to Garrison Grenada as soon as gen Taylor notifies that the present garrison is relieved   Signed E R S CANBY Maj Genl   I am repairing the telegrh line and hope to be in direct communication in three (3) or four days with mobile. iIn the mean time I hold the telegh office at Senatobia & any despatches you may wish to send I can send them from there if the line is not disturbed"   Telegram received (on May 8, 11:50 P.M.), DNA, RG 107, Telegrams Collected (Bound); *ibid.*, RG 108, Telegrams Received; copies, *ibid.*, RG 393, District of West Tenn., Dept. of the Tenn., 16th Army Corps, Telegrams Sent; DLC-USG, V, 54. *O.R.*, I, xlviii, part 2, 340.

1. On April 9, Comstock telegraphed to USG. "Yesterday afternoon during a bombardment of Spanish Fort, A J Smiths skirmishers were pushed forward and about six p m gained a lodgement on the left of the enemys main line—They were reenforced during the night and at midnight the whole work was in our possession—The number of prisoners is about 600—The balance of the garrison it is supposed have escaped by boats—about 30 pieces of artillery captured"   Telegram received (on April 17, 1:00 P.M.), DNA, RG 107, Telegrams Collected (Bound); *ibid.*, RG 108, Telegrams Received; copy, DLC-USG, V, 54. *O.R.*, I, xlix, part 2, 294. Also on April 9, Canby telegraphed to USG and Maj. Gen. Henry W. Halleck. "I have the honor to report the capture this day of the rebel fortifications at Blakely with 2400 prisoners and twenty guns"   Telegrams received (2—on April 18, 1:30 P.M.), DNA, RG 107, Telegrams Collected (Bound). *O.R.*, I, xlix, part 2, 293. On April 10, Canby telegraphed to USG and Halleck. "Thirty one pieces of artillery were found in the Blakely works and thirty seven at Spanish fort—The prisoners at Blakely will reach 3000 Genls Diddell, Cockrell & Thomas included. At Spanish Fort 583 prisoners making a total of about 4000 including those captured by Steele on his way from Pensacola   One Gunboat surrendered but subsequently escaped—Our losses are severe in Garrards (C C) Andrews & Haskins Divisions"   Telegrams received (2—on April 20, 1:30 P.M.), DNA, RG 107, Telegrams Collected (Bound); copy, DLC-USG, V, 54. *O.R.*, I, xlix, part 2, 311. On the same day, Comstock telegraphed to USG. "The works around Blakely were carried by assault by Garrards aAndrews, Heckins divisions at six (6) P. M yesterday   about twenty five hundred (2500) prisoners were captured including Generals Sidell Cockrell & BThomas   Rebel officers state there are thirty eight (38) pieces of artillery in the works   Our loss is considerable"   Telegram received (on April 18, 1:30 P.M.), DNA, RG 107, Telegrams Collected (Bound); *ibid.*, RG 108, Telegrams Received; copy, DLC-USG, V, 54. *O.R.*, I, xlix, part 2, 311. On April 12, Canby, "Blakely Miss," telegraphed to Halleck, sending a copy to USG. "A boat expedition of 600 men was sent up last night to surprise and capture Batteries Tracy and Huger but found them abandoned by the enemy—Granger with 10000 men was thrown across the bay and now occupies Mobile which was evacuated last night, the enemy moving up the river— The bay and Blakely river is now open and one of our transports has just come up to this point—The depot at Starks wharf will be moved up at once. A. J Smith with 14000 move tomorrow for Selma & Montgomery by land—Steele with 10000 in a day or two by water—Grierson with 4000 Cavalry will operate on the east of the Alabama and Lucas with 2000 west of the Tombigbee. The results of our operations thus far has been greater than I have reported.   they will net on the East side 4.400 prisoners, 103 pieces of Artillery and ten flags—The reports of

what was captured in Mobile have not yet been recd   The Gunboats are not yet up but will probably work through tomorrow" Telegrams received (2—on April 20, 8:30 P.M.), DNA, RG 107, Telegrams Collected (Bound); *ibid.*, RG 108, Telegrams Received; copy, DLC-USG, V, 54. *O.R.*, I, xlix, part 2, 334. On April 14, 5:00 P.M., Canby telegraphed to USG. "We find in Mobile and its defences on the west side of the bay over 150 guns and a very large amount of Ammunition and Supplies of all kinds, and about 1000 prisoners   Inventories are now being taken and a detailed report will be forwarded as soon as they are completed—The quantity of Cotton will probably reach 30.000 Bales & there is a large amount of provisions and forage" Telegrams received (2—on April 22, 7:00 P.M.), DNA, RG 107, Telegrams Collected (Bound). *O.R.*, I, xlix, part 2, 356–57. On April 15, Canby, Mobile, wrote to USG. "In accordance with your instructions I have relieved General Comstock, who will return to you at once. He will be able to explain to you many things about which I have not written, and which cannot very well be explained in writing. I am not able yet to give you the exact results of our late operations, as the detailed reports have not yet been received; and it will take some time to get complete inventories of captured property. The artillery will exceed three hundred pieces of all classes, a very large proportion new guns, and in excellent condition. The number of prisoners, including the wounded, will reach five thousand, and from 8 to 1200 deserters remained in the city when it was abandoned. The captured cotton will be sent to New York to be consigned to the Quartermaster, and to be disposed of as the Secretary of War may direct.—I am under many obligations to General Comstock for his active and efficient assistance, and will make suitable acknowledgment in my official report." ALS, DNA, RG 108, Letters Received. *O.R.*, I, xlix, part 2, 362. On April 16, Maj. Thomas T. Eckert telegraphed to USG. "The above is from the Cipher Operator at Cincinnati. . . . Cairo says Clara Dean just arrived bringing news of Capture mobile" Telegram received, DNA, RG 108, Telegrams Received; copy, DLC-USG, V, 54.

To Maj. Gen. Edward O. C. Ord

Apl. 17th *1865* [5:00 P.M.]

MAJ. GEN. ORD, RICHMOND, VA

Ford, Manager of the theatre where the President was assassinated is now in Richmond. Have him arrested and sent under guard to Washington. Do not let it be noise[d] about that he is to be arrested until the work is done lest he escapes.

U. S. GRANT
Lt. Gn

ALS (facsimile telegram sent), Anderson Galleries Sale, Dec. 5–6, 1934, p. 73; telegram sent, DNA, RG 107, Telegrams Collected (Bound); telegram received, *ibid.*, Telegrams Collected (Unbound); (at 6:30 P.M.) Ord Papers, CU-B. *O.R.*, I, xlvi, part 3, 815. On April 17, 1865, 9:40 P.M. (sent at 10:00 P.M.), Maj.

Gen. Edward O. C. Ord telegraphed to USG. "Mr Ford ~~is reported to have~~ left town this A M 6 o clock for Baltimore ~~this~~ ~~E O C Ord~~ Genl Patrick has telegraphed to Baltimore that he be met at the boat and arrested" ALS (telegram sent), Ord Papers, CU-B; telegram received (on April 18, 1:15 A.M.), DNA, RG 107, Telegrams Collected (Bound); *ibid.*, RG 108, Telegrams Received. *O.R.*, I, xlvi, part 3, 815.

To Maj. Gen. John Pope

(Cipher)   Washington Apl. 17th/65 [*7:30* P.M.]
MAJ. GN. POPE, ST. LOUIS, MO.

I think now it will be well for you to send a proposition to Kirby Smith to surrender on the terms given Gn. Lee. Gen. Johnston has commenced a correspondence with Sherman on the subject, and Smith will see that with the vast Armies at our controll the state of Texas can and will be overrun and desolated if the war continues. On the theory that Mobile has fallen I have ordered Canby to arrange for operations against Galveston in co-operation with your movements which I informed him would start about the 1st of June. Go on with your preparations without intermission whilst you are negociating with Smith. I have directed 2.500 teams to be sent to Little Rock. Troops will also be sent in time.

U. S. GRANT
Lt. Gn

ALS (telegram sent), DNA, RG 107, Telegrams Collected (Bound); telegram sent, *ibid.*; telegram received (on April 18, 1865, 7:30 P.M.), *ibid.*, Telegrams Collected (Unbound); *ibid.*, RG 393, Dept. of the Mo., Telegrams Received. *O.R.*, I, xlviii, part 2, 110. On April 20, Maj. Gen. John Pope wrote to USG. "I have the honor to transmit enclosed a copy of my letter to Gen. E. Kirby. Smith offering the terms accorded by you to Gen. R. E. Lee. Also a copy of my letter of instructions to Col. Sprague. Col Sprague left yesterday for mouth of Red river." Copies (2), DNA, RG 393, Military Div. of the Mo., Letters Sent. *O.R.*, I, xlviii, part 1, 186. The enclosures are *ibid.*, pp. 186–88. On May 1, noon, Pope telegraphed to USG. "Quartermaster here has received orders from Qr. Mr. Genl. to buy no more horses, so Reynolds' Cavalry will remain without horses. Only about one third the necessary number has been sent. I have not yet heard from Officer I sent to Kirby Smith offering him same terms you gave to Lee. I have little doubt they will be accepted as soon as authentic information reaches Red river of surrender of all forces East of Chattahoochee [*Mississippi*] I incline strongly to belief that no campaign west of the Mississippi will be necessary, and therefore suggest that preparations for it be not hurried—Rivers are high and streams in Arkansas impassable. I would think it well to wait a couple of weeks to see what Smith may do. The high water is likely to keep up for six weeks so we can get what supplies we want up to Ft Smith for a considerable time yet. It seems useless to subject the Govt. to the great expense of getting ready for this campaign. It is certain that Kirby Smith won't surrender when the streams and swamps in Ark. are in such condition that we can not commence a land movement for some time." Telegram received (at 7:00 P.M.), DNA, RG 107, Telegrams Collected (Bound); *ibid.*, RG 108, Telegrams Received; copies, *ibid.*, RG 393, Military Div. of the Mo., Telegrams Sent; DLC-USG, V, 54. Printed (with variant text for the last two sentences) as received at 1:00 P.M. in *O.R.*, I, xlviii, part 2, 283. At 9:20 P.M., USG telegraphed to Pope. "You may suspend preparations for campaigning West of the Miss. for the present. If Kirby Smith attempts to hold out a force will be sent to overrun the whole country west of the Miss." ALS (telegram sent), DNA, RG 107, Telegrams Collected (Bound); telegram sent, *ibid.*; telegram received (marked as sent at 9:00 P.M., received on May 2), *ibid.*, RG 94, War Records Office, Army of the Potomac. *O.R.*, I, xlviii, part 2, 283.

To Maj. Gen. George H. Thomas

(Cipher)   *Washington, D. C.*, Apl. 17th *1864*5 [2:00 P.M.]
MAJ. GEN. THOMAS, NASHVILLE TENN.

The freedom of Va. from occupation by an armed enemy renders the occupation of East Tennessee in large force longer unnecessary. You may commence the withdrawel of the 4th Corps to Nashville immediately. It is desirable to hold all the territory we now have in sufficient force to protect it against roving bands that may yet infest the country but all force not necessary for that collect near Nashville as rapidly as possible, the 4th Corps in tact.

U. S. GRANT
Lt. Gen.

ALS (telegram sent), DNA, RG 107, Telegrams Collected (Bound); telegram sent, *ibid.*; copy, *ibid.*, RG 393, Dept. of the Cumberland, Telegrams Received. Printed as received at 8:00 P.M. in *O.R.*, I, xlix, part 2, 375. On April 17, 1865, 8:00 P.M., Maj. Gen. George H. Thomas telegraphed to USG. "Your telegram of two (2) p m to day received. Will immediately make arrangements to withdraw the Fourth (4th) Corps from East Tennessee to the vicinity of Nashville.—" Telegram received (at 11:35 P.M.), DNA, RG 107, Telegrams Collected (Bound); *ibid.*, RG 108, Telegrams Received; copies, *ibid.*, RG 393, Dept. of the Cumberland, Telegrams Sent; DLC-USG, V, 54. *O.R.*, I, xlix, part 2, 375.

To Charles W. Ford

———

Washington, Apl. 17th *1865*

Dear Ford,

Your letter enclosing $1450 00 was duly rec'd. At the time I was out attending to public duties which resulted as you know highly favorable to our cause. Since that the overwhelming disaster to the country in the assassination of the President drove from my mind for a time the fact that I owed you an acknowledgement.

I have every reason to hope that in our new pPresident we will find a man disposed and capable of conducting the government in its old channel. If so we may look for a speedy peace and return of a large part of our Army to their homes and families. For myself I would enjoy a little respite from my cares and responsibilities more than you can concieve. But I have health, strength and endurance and as long as they are retained I am willing to devote all for the public good.

My kindest regards to all old friends.

Yours &c.

U. S. Grant

ALS, USG 3.

To Maj. Gen. George G. Meade

———

(Cipher)   Washington Apl. 18th 1865 [*10:30* A.M.]

Maj. Gen. Meade, Burkesville Va.

The Cavalry was withdrawn from the front simply to be able to supply them with forage. If Sheridan is not called upon within a few days to go into North Carolina with the Cavalry the whole of it will be ordered to report to you.

U. S. Grant

Lt. Gn.

ALS (telegram sent), DNA, RG 107, Telegrams Collected (Bound); telegram sent, *ibid.*; telegram received, *ibid.*, Telegrams Collected (Unbound); *ibid.*, RG 94, War Records Office, Army of the Potomac. *O.R.*, I, xlvi, part 3, 822. On April 17, 1865, 10:00 P.M., Maj. Gen. George G. Meade telegraphed to USG.

"Major General Gibbon reports his arrival to day at Prospect Station, having completed the duty assigned him at Appomattox C H Brevet Major Genl Griffin Comd'g Fifth corps reached this point to day with his command. The Second, Sixth, and Fifth corps are now encamped in ~~vici~~ the vicinity of Burksville, Gen Parke reports all quiet along the line of the RailRoad—Maj Gen Wilcox, at Wilsons Station hearing of marauders on the Nottoway River, sent a detachment in that direction, who succeeded in capturing a camp with several wagons loaded with plunder, The party consisted of negroes, mostly belonging to this Army, Some were killed, and the rest made prisoners, I have also heard of parties of marauders operating to the south of this place, supposed to be stragglers from this, and the Confederate Army, To pursue and punish these offenders, will require on my part some cavalry force, I understand the cavalry corps has been moved to City Point, I would respectfully ask a cavalry force be assigned to this Army, and if practicable, the Division, which, until the recent operations was attached to it," Telegram received (on April 18, 1:00 A.M.), DNA, RG 107, Telegrams Collected (Bound); *ibid.*, Telegrams Collected (Unbound); *ibid.*, RG 108, Telegrams Received; copies (marked as sent at 9:45 P.M.), *ibid.*, RG 393, Army of the Potomac, Letters Sent; DLC-USG, V, 54; Meade Papers, PHi. *O.R.*, I, xlvi, part 3, 810–11.

On April 17, Bvt. Col. Theodore S. Bowers issued Special Orders No. 77. "Major General George G Meade, commanding Army of the Potomac, will while his army remains within the Dept of Va, report to Maj Gen H. W. Halleck, commanding that Department." Copies, DLC-USG, V, 57, 63, 65. *O.R.*, I, xlvi, part 3, 810.

On April 18, 10:00 A.M., Meade telegraphed to USG. "Your attention is called to the necessity of a permanent commander being assigned to the 5th corps.—My views upon this point have been made known to you—Should you be disposed to reassign Maj. Genl Warren I shall make no objection thereto." ALS (telegram sent), DNA, RG 94, War Records Office, Miscellaneous War Records; telegram received (at 1:30 P.M.), *ibid.*; *ibid.*, RG 107, Telegrams Collected (Bound); *ibid.*, RG 108, Telegrams Received. *O.R.*, I, xlvi, part 3, 822. On the same day, Bowers telegraphed to Meade. "Your dispatch calling attention to the necessity of a permanent commander for the 5th Corps is received. You will please continue it in the temporary command of Gen. Griffin for the present. Orders will be sent to General Warren in a few days." ALS (telegram sent), DNA, RG 107, Telegrams Collected (Bound); telegram sent, *ibid.*; telegrams received (2), *ibid.*, Telegrams Collected (Unbound). Printed as received at 7:20 P.M. in *O.R.*, I, xlvi, part 3, 823. See letter to Maj. Gen. Gouverneur K. Warren, May 6, 1865.

To Maj. Gen. Edward O. C. Ord

Washington Apl. 18th *18645*. [*11:00* P.M.]

[MA]J. GN ORD, RICHMOND VA.

Paroled prisoners belonging to N. C. S. C. Georgia Florida Alabama and in fact all the southern states must get to their homes through the Country. Those at [F]t Monroe must be turned back. Orders were given that their paroles should be a pass to go through our lines where it was necessary to get to their homes but we did not undertake to pay their passage nor to permit them to travel a roundabout way, through the loyal states for their convenience. All issues of forage and subsistence to them must also be discontinued.

U. S. Grant
Lt. Gn.

ALS (telegram sent), DNA, RG 107, Telegrams Collected (Bound); telegram sent, *ibid*.; telegram received, *ibid*., Telegrams Collected (Unbound); Ord Papers, CU-B. *O.R.*, I, xlvi, part 3, 826. On April 18, 1865, 10:00 p.m., USG telegraphed to Maj. Gen. Edward O. C. Ord. "Direct Gen. Patrick to give no more passes to paroled prisoners to come to Washington or the loyal states. They must get to their homes in their own way. ~~With the present feeling in the~~" ALS (telegram sent), DNA, RG 107, Telegrams Collected (Bound); telegram sent, *ibid*.; telegram received, *ibid*., Telegrams Collected (Unbound); Ord Papers, CU-B. *O.R.*, I, xlvi, part 3, 826. On April 19, Ord telegraphed to USG. "Your dispatch is received on the subject of sending paroled prisoners home. My impression is that the printed order furnished them by Gen Gibbon, promises them transportation home free where their routes home are in our lines. Large numbers are arriving here destitute. I shall refuse them forage and subsistence—but little of the former has been issued. It is too late to turn any—leaving yesterday, back from Fort Monroe—None will be allowed to leave today." Telegram received (at 10:15 a.m.), DNA, RG 107, Telegrams Collected (Bound); *ibid*., RG 108, Telegrams Received; copy, DLC-USG, V, 54. *O.R.*, I, xlvi, part 3, 835–36. See telegram to Maj. Gen. Edward O. C. Ord, April 19, 1865.

On April 14, 11:00 a.m., Ord telegraphed to President Abraham Lincoln. "Mr R M T. Hunter has just arrived under the invitation signed by Genl Weitzel He and Judge J A Campbell wish a permit to visit you at Washington. I think their communications important—" Telegram received (at 9:30 p.m.), DNA, RG 108, Telegrams Received; copy, DLC-USG, V, 54. *O.R.*, I, xlvi, part 3, 748. On April 16, Secretary of War Edwin M. Stanton endorsed this telegram. "Referred to the Lieutenant General with instructions that the President does not desire to see Messrs Hunter & Campbell or either of them at Washington and if their communication is an application for Executive Clemency to themselves it can be transmitted through the regular military channels for such consideration as he may be disposed to grant" AES, DNA, RG 108, Telegrams Received. At 4:00 p.m., Bvt. Col. Theodore S. Bowers telegraphed to Ord. "Your telegram to the President of 11 A. M. has been referred to the Lieutenant General with instructions that 'the President does not desire to see Messrs. Hunter and Campbell, or either of them, at Washington, and if there communication is an application for executive clemency to themselves it can be transmitted through the regular military channels for such consideration as he may be disposed to grant.' You will not therefore permit either of these parties to come to Washington, but will at once order Hunter to leave Richmond. You are reminded in this connection of the impropriety of addressing the President direct, and requested to address your communications to the Lieutenant General or Secret[ary] of War." ALS (telegram sent), *ibid.*, RG 107, Telegrams Collected (Bound); telegram sent, *ibid.*; telegrams received (2—one at 10:30 P.M.), *ibid.*, Telegrams Collected (Unbound); Ord Papers, CU-B. *O.R.*, I, xlvi, part 3, 796–97.

At 9:30 P.M., Bowers telegraphed to Ord. "Please send forward to this place immediately one of the best Regiments of Colored Troops you have, to attend the funeral ceremonies of President Lincoln on Wednesday. One that has seen service should be selected" ALS (telegram sent), DNA, RG 107, Telegrams Collected (Bound); telegram sent, *ibid.*; telegram received, *ibid.*, Telegrams Collected (Unbound). *O.R.*, I, xlvi, part 3, 797. On April 18, Brig. Gen. John A. Rawlins telegraphed to Ord. "Has the colored Regiment ordered at 9:30 on the 16th inst. yet started for Washington, and if so when did it start. Please answer." Telegrams sent (2), DNA, RG 107, Telegrams Collected (Bound); telegram received, *ibid.*, Telegrams Collected (Unbound); *ibid.*, RG 94, War Records Office, Miscellaneous War Records. *O.R.*, I, xlvi, part 3, 825. On the same day, Ord twice telegraphed to Rawlins. "The Regt left Petersburg at 5 a m yesterday for City Point where transportation was waiting for it I will procure a report from the latter point & forward at once" Telegram received (at 8:30 P.M.), DNA, RG 107, Telegrams Collected (Bound); *ibid.*, RG 108, Telegrams Received; copy, DLC-USG, V, 54. *O.R.*, I, xlvi, part 3, 826. "The Colored Regt left City Pt at daylight this morning" Telegram received (at 9:00 P.M.), DNA, RG 107, Telegrams Collected (Bound); *ibid.*, Telegrams Collected (Unbound). *O.R.*, I, xlvi, part 3, 826.

On April 17, Ord twice telegraphed to USG. "Yesterday Gen Gibbon telegraphed me that he then starts from Farmville with his Command having returned from Lynchburg where he paroled five thousand 5000 of Gen Lees army. When Gen Gibbon returns I want to see you. Shall I come to Washn or wait your arrival here The subject is of much importance" "There are a large number men 2 or 3000 prisoners in Libby many of them were here convalscent & in Hospital when the rebels Evacuated. they remained. Shall I parole them & send them home on same terms as Gen Lees army? I telegraphed the Secy of War on the fourteenth 14 when you were in Phila that I was trying to make the miltary Govt acceptable by Kindness where the interests of the Govt allowed it asking if my policy was not approved to be corrected." Telegrams received (at 7:00 P.M.), DNA, RG 107, Telegrams Collected (Bound); *ibid.*, RG 108, Telegrams Received; copies, DLC-USG, V, 54. *O.R.*, I, xlvi, part 3, 814. At 8:10 P.M., USG telegraphed to Ord. "Hold all prisoners of War you have until the disposition to be made of them is decided upon. Do not leave Richmond to come to Washington at present." ALS (telegram sent), DNA, RG 107, Telegrams Collected (Bound); telegram sent, *ibid.*; telegram received, *ibid.*, Telegrams Collected (Unbound). *O.R.*, I, xlvi, part 3, 814.

On April 18, 10:30 A.M., USG telegraphed to Ord. "Send two regiments of Infantry to Point Lookout without delay. One regiment at least should get off to day. It does not matter whether you [se]nd Black or White troops." ALS (telegram sent), DNA, RG 107, Telegrams Collected (Bound); telegram sent, *ibid.*; telegrams received (2), *ibid.*, Telegrams Collected (Unbound); *ibid.*, RG 94, War Records Office, Miscellaneous War Records. *O.R.*, I, xlvi, part 3, 825.

To Maj. Gen. Philip H. Sheridan

(Cipher)   Washington Apl. 18th 1865 [10:00 A.M.]
MAJ. GN. SHERIDAN, CITY POINT VA.

Some Cavalry should be left at Nottoway and Burkesville if it can possibly be fed. As soon as you think this can be done return Crook's Div. to Meade. The moment it is determined you will not have to go South with the Cavalry I will either order you to your old command or some new one.

U. S. GRANT
Lt. Gn.

ALS (telegram sent), DNA, RG 107, Telegrams Collected (Bound); telegram sent, *ibid.*; telegram received, *ibid.*, Telegrams Collected (Unbound). *O.R.*, I, xlvi, part 3, 825. On April 18, 1865, 7:00 P.M., Maj. Gen. Philip H. Sheridan, "Near Petersburg," telegraphed to USG. "The three divisions of Cavalry arrived here today and are comfortably encamped. At present I regard it as impossible to supply Cavalry at Nottoway or Burkeville on the Rail Road and I do not know how long this condition of things will exist. As soon as Genl Crooks division can be supplied then I will send it to Genl Meade. It should be allowed to remain here for a short time to recuperate the horses—they have been on short allowance of grain for some time and without any long forage and the animals are weak." Telegram sent, DNA, RG 107, Telegrams Collected (Unbound); telegram received (at 9:00 P.M.), *ibid.*, Telegrams Collected (Bound); *ibid.*, RG 108, Telegrams Received. *O.R.*, I, xlvi, part 3, 825.

On April 17, Brig. Gen. Rufus Ingalls, City Point, telegraphed to Brig. Gen. John A. Rawlins. "The Cavalry will start in to Petersburg where the forage can be sent by the Appomattox River—The Rail-Road between Sutherland and Nottoway is in bad condition—If some of the troops and trains of the Army of the Potomac could be brought nearer to this place they could be much better supplied and relieve the Road—I met Genl. McCallum at Fortress Monroe this morning—We agreed as to what should be done in Rail Road matters—I recommend that the Lieut. General approve of his suggestions—He will report tomorrow probably—I go to Richmond tomorrow to inspect my Department—My report of the Quartermasters Dept. property taken in Genl. Lee's surrender has been rendered to Genl. Meigs" ALS (telegram sent), DNA, RG 107, Telegrams Collected (Unbound); telegram received (at 11:00 P.M.), *ibid.*, Telegrams Collected (Bound); *ibid.*, RG 108, Telegrams Received. *O.R.*, I, xlvi, part 3, 809. At 11:30 A.M., Sheridan, City Point, telegraphed to Rawlins. "The cavalry is moving this morning to the vicinity of Petersburg where it can be quickly fitted up—Forage and supplies are now being sent to that point by water for us" Telegram received (at 12:30 P.M.), DNA, RG 107, Telegrams Collected (Bound); (2) *ibid.*, Telegrams Collected (Unbound); *ibid.*, RG 108, Telegrams Received; copies, DLC-USG, V, 54; (2) DLC-Philip H. Sheridan. *O.R.*, I, xlvi, part 3, 811.

On April 18, Sheridan, Petersburg, telegraphed to Rawlins. "The Cavalry is now going into camp near this place. My Hdqrs will be at this point." Tele-

gram sent, DNA, RG 107, Telegrams Collected (Unbound); telegram received
(at 8:30 P.M.), *ibid.*, Telegrams Collected (Bound); *ibid.*, RG 108, Telegrams
Received. *O.R.*, I, xlvi, part 3, 825.

To Maj. Gen. Winfield S. Hancock

(Cipher)   *Washington, D. C.*, Apl. 19th *1864*5 [*12:10* P.M.]
[MA]J. GN. HANCOCK, WINCHESTER VA
    You may receive all rebel Officers and soldiers who surrender
to you on exactly the same terms that were given t[o] Gen. Lee
except have it distinctly understood that all who claim homes in
states that never passed ~~ordnan~~ ordinances of secession have
[for]feited them and can only return on compliance with the Amnesty proclamation   Maryland Ky Delaware and Missouri are
such states. They may return to West Va. on their paroles.
                                        U. S. GRANT
                                        Lt. Gn.

ALS (telegram sent), DNA, RG 107, Telegrams Collected (Bound); telegram
sent, *ibid.*; copies, *ibid.*, RG 108, Letters Sent; DLC-USG, V, 46, 76, 108. *O.R.*,
I, xlvi, part 3, 838–39.
    On April 19, 1865, Maj. Gen. Winfield S. Hancock telegraphed to Maj.
Gen. Henry W. Halleck that Col. John S. Mosby had requested a ten-day truce.
Ibid., p. 839. At 5:30 P.M., USG telegraphed to Hancock. "If Mosby does not
avail himself of [t]he present truce end it and hunt him and his men down.
Guerrillas, after beating the Armies of the enemy, will not be entitled to quarter."
ALS (telegram sent), DNA, RG 107, Telegrams Collected (Bound); telegram
sent, *ibid.*; copies, *ibid.*, RG 108, Letters Sent; DLC-USG, V, 46, 76, (2) 108.
O.R., I, xlvi, part 3, 839. On the same day, Hancock telegraphed to USG. "I
have your dispatch concerning Mosby I have already informed him that there
would be no more truce with him after 12 M tomorrow and if he then Surrenders
there would only be a truce at the point of Surrender Sufficiently long to have
him sign the paroles" Telegram received (on April 20, 11:15 A.M.), DNA,
RG 107, Telegrams Collected (Bound); *ibid.*, RG 108, Telegrams Received;
copies, *ibid.*, RG 393, Middle Dept. and 8th Army Corps, Telegrams Sent; DLC-
USG, V, 54. *O.R.*, I, xlvi, part 3, 839.
    At 8:30 P.M., USG telegraphed to Hancock. "Send one Division of Infantry
and all the Cavalry you can spare to Washington at once. Send at least one
regiment of Cavalry even if hard to spare and a Brigade if disposable." ALS
(telegram sent), DNA, RG 107, Telegrams Collected (Bound); telegram sent,
ibid.; telegram received, *ibid.*, Middle Military Div., Telegrams Received. *O.R.*,
I, xlvi, part 3, 840. On the same day, Hancock telegraphed to USG. "I will send
at once a Div of Infantry, about six thousand (6000) strong, and a Brigade of

Cavalry as you direct," Copy, DNA, RG 393, Middle Dept. and 8th Army Corps, Telegrams Sent.

On April 20, Hancock twice telegraphed to Brig. Gen. John A. Rawlins. "At remount Camp near Harpers Ferry there are six thousand three hundred (6300) men of the dismounted Cav of Gen Sheridans & of the commands of this Valley & five batteries of horse artillery, Should any more men be required in the neighborhood of Washington I would suggest that the remount Camp be transfered to Geisboro or some such point. This dismounted Cav is generally well armed" "The Confederate officers & soldiers coming in here daily for parole amount to ~~the~~ about one hundred. A great many others have been paroled by my advanced Cav at Strasburg Woodstock & New Market in the valley embracing the small Commands in that section of Country also a great many of Mosbys men, guerillas, stragglers, & men on leave are coming in at other posts. In the Kanawha Valley the command of Lt Col Henshaw [*Hounshell*] which is being surrendered amounts to about four or five hundred men. Several other detachments have applied at Lewisburg to surrender on the same terms. They are understood to be of Gen Echols Command who himself has left. Col Mosby in person was met at Millwood today at 12 M when the truce with him ended. He stated & I have no doubt it is true from the corroboration of paroled officers & citizens that his command has disbanded with the exception of a few officers & soldiers. When Mosby found that no further truce or terms would be offered to him he was very much agitated. The Confederate officers & soldiers who have surrendered & the citizens are hostile to him. My impression is that ~~any~~ every thing in this country shows a state of pacification The worst band of guerillas in Loudon Co—Mobleys—have all been killed or surrendered. If Mosby is in Loudon Valley I will hunt him out" Telegrams received (on April 21, 8:05 A.M. and 8:15 A.M.), *ibid.*, RG 107, Telegrams Collected (Bound); *ibid.*, RG 108, Telegrams Received; copies, DLC-USG, V, 54. *O.R.*, I, xlvi, part 3, 868.

To Maj. Gen. Edward O. C. Ord

Washington, D. C. Apr. 19 *1865* [*5:30* P.M.]

MAJ GEN ORD RICHMOND

Your despatch recd. we cannot undertake to bear all the hardships brought on [in]dividuals by their treason and rebellion It was no part of the agreement that we should furnish homes subsistence or transportation to Lee's army After the surrender I ordered that the paroles of men should be a pass to go through our lines to reach their homes and that where transported on roads or vessels run by Govt. fare should not be collected I did not by any means intend that this should be an excuse for all who chose to come within our lines and stay there a public charge or that men going to N. C. or Ga should be furnished a pleasant passage through the North and Coastwise to their homes. Those living beyond our lines or in the seceded states before they can come north must qualify themselves as citizens by claiming and conforming to the Presidents amesty proclamation   Gen Halleck will start to Richmond tomorrow and he will take up and settle all presen[t] difficulties

U S GRANT
Lt Gen

Telegram sent, DNA, RG 107, Telegrams Collected (Bound); telegram received, *ibid.*, Telegrams Collected (Unbound); Ord Papers, CU-B. *O.R.*, I, xlvi, part 3, 836. On April 19, 1865, Maj. Gen. Edward O. C. Ord had telegraphed to USG. "Your order prohibiting passes via Northern routes to paroled prisoners, will leave a large number of destitute Officers and men here. The Railroad and Canal routes are all destroyed. There are no horses or mules or carriages left in this vicinity. Many of the paroled prisoners have their homes in Maryland Northern Kentucky and Tennessee: others have no home. Such for instance as came from Hampton, the coast of North Carolina, and where freedman's farms have been established on their former homes. These peoples money is worthless and they have no food—nor can they buy it or obtain labor here. They are coming here by thousands—Many of them have wi~~f~~ves and children here. It would be absurd to expect them with the bridges through the Country burnt, to foot it away or home. It is important to get them away from here. If I am not authorized either to feed them or send them away by the most expeditious routes I cannot be responsible for the consequences." Telegram received (at 4:00 P.M.), DNA, RG 107, Telegrams Collected (Bound); *ibid.*, RG 108, Telegrams Received; copy, DLC-USG, V, 54. *O.R.*, I, xlvi, part 3, 836.

To Maj. Gen. Christopher C. Augur

———

Washington, D. C., Apl. 20th 18645

MAJ. GEN. C. C. AUGUR,
COMD.G DEPT. OF WASHINGTON,
GENERAL,

In view of the large number of paroled Prisoners coming to Washington, and other late occurrences, it will be necessary to use the greatest vigilance to prevent disturbances in the City and District of Columbia. Increase the guards about public buildings and on the streets. Place pickets on all the roads leading out of the City where you have none now and strengthen those you already have.

The large additional force ordered here will enable you to do this, and as this increase of force will commence arriving to-morrow all the force you now have can be put on duty at once if necessary.

Give such orders to all guards in the City, and on the roads leading from it, as will best secure safety and prevent the escape of perpetrators if mischief is done.

By the agreement with Gen. Lee all paroled prisoners were to return to their homes. After the agreement it occured to Lee that many of his men lived within our lines. He asked me how they were to get there. I answered by giving an order that their paroles should be their pass for going through our lines where it was necessary for them to pass them to comply with their part of the agreement, and that when they traveled on govt. roads or vessels they would be transported free. It was never contemplated that they should come nNorth to reach homes in the Southern states nor that Govt. would undertake to furnish any of them transportation on private roads or vessels. All who come within your Dept. in violation of this interpretation of the agreement between Lee & myself may be turned back or taken up and imprisoned for violation of their parole, unless they qualify themselves as Citizens of the United States by obtaining the Presidents Amnesty.

> Very respectfully
> your obt. svt.
> U. S. GRANT
> Lt. Gn.

ALS, DNA, RG 393, Dept. of Washington, Letters Received. *O.R.*, I, xlvi, part 3, 868–69.

To Maj. Gen. George G. Meade

(Cipher)   Washington Apl. 20th 1865 [*8:50* P.M.]
MAJ. GEN. MEADE, HD QRS. A. P.

You may say to Mr. Dunn that the policy to be pursued towards rail-road companies South of the James River has not yet been decided upon and cannot be until it is known that the Govt.

can controll them. When the authority of the general Government
is acknowledged the policy will go as far towards free trade between the states and rights of loyal citizens to controll their property, rail-roads and all, as may be consistent with what remains of
the rebellion. The roads will never be allowed to resume operations
under disloyal Officers nor in the interest of disloyal stockholders.
It behooves all who wish to resume business under the old flag to
renew their allegiance to it under the Presidents Amnesty proclamation without delay.

U. S. GRANT, Lt. Gn

ALS (telegram sent), DNA, RG 107, Telegrams Collected (Bound); telegram
sent, *ibid.*; copies, *ibid.*, RG 108, Letters Sent; DLC-USG, V, 46, 76, 108; Meade
Papers, PHi. Printed as sent at 9:30 P.M. in *O.R.*, I, xlvi, part 3, 849. On April
20, 1865, 2:45 P.M., Maj. Gen. George G. Meade telegraphed to USG. "I transmit a despatch just handed me by Mr. Dunn—The Danville road is in working
order as far as the Staunton river. Mr. Dunn says there are no confederate troops
or authorities at Danville—that it was understood there that Johnston & Breckenridge had met Genl Sherman at Hillsboro, and that terms had been agreed
upon by which Johnstons army was to be disbanded & sent to their homes.—No
answer pending your instructions have been given to Mr. Dunn, who will await
here your decision.—" ALS (telegram sent), DNA, RG 94, War Records Office,
Army of the Potomac; telegram received (marked as sent at 3:00 P.M., received
at 5:00 P.M.), *ibid.*, RG 107, Telegrams Collected (Bound); *ibid.*, Telegrams
Collected (Unbound); *ibid.*, RG 108, Telegrams Received. Printed as sent at
3:00 P.M. in *O.R.*, I, xlvi, part 3, 848. The enclosure, from Lewis E. Harvie,
Danville, president, Richmond and Danville Railroad, to William S. Dunn, engineer of repairs, is *ibid.*, pp. 848–49. See *ibid.*, p. 877.
    On April 19, 8:45 P.M., Meade telegraphed to USG. "Maj. Wallach con-
federate army, reached here this P. M having left Danville yesterday. He reports
just previous to his departure a train arrived from ~~Danville~~ Greensboro having
some confederate officers in it who stated that Johnston was at Greensboro, and
that he had sent a flag of truce to Sherman who was in the vicinity—and that it
was understood the object of the flag was a proposition to surrender.—Maj.
Wallach is a brother of the Mayor of Washington & has come in to give his
parole.—" ALS (telegram sent), DNA, RG 94, War Records Office, Dept. of the
Cumberland; telegram received, *ibid.*; (marked as sent at 10:00 P.M., received
at 11:00 P.M.) *ibid.*, RG 107, Telegrams Collected (Bound); *ibid.*, Telegrams
Collected (Unbound); *ibid.*, RG 108, Telegrams Received. *O.R.*, I, xlvi, part
3, 832.
    At 9:00 P.M., USG telegraphed to Meade. "Send the 9th A. C. to Wash-
ington as rapidly as their places can be filled by such other troops from your
command as you may designate to take their place. Let the shipment of such as
can be spared before their places are filled be commenced at once." ALS (telegram sent), DNA, RG 107, Telegrams Collected (Bound); telegrams sent (2),
ibid.; copy, Meade Papers, PHi. *O.R.*, I, xlvi, part 3, 832. At 11:30 P.M., Meade
telegraphed to USG. "The order in cipher is received and will be executed at

once—" Telegram received (on April 20, 1:05 A.M.), DNA, RG 107, Telegrams Collected (Bound); *ibid.*, RG 108, Telegrams Received; copy, DLC-USG, V, 54. *O.R.*, I, xlvi, part 3, 833.

On April 20, 8:00 A.M., Meade telegraphed to USG. "Shall the 9th corps take with them their Artillery and supply trains?" Telegram received (at 11:30 P.M.), DNA, RG 107, Telegrams Collected (Bound); *ibid.*, RG 108, Telegrams Received; copies, DLC-USG, V, 54; (2) Meade Papers, PHi. *O.R.*, I, xlvi, part 3, 848. At 12:30 P.M., USG telegraphed to Meade. "The 9th Corps will bring everything with them." ALS (telegram sent), DNA, RG 107, Telegrams Collected (Bound); telegram sent, *ibid.*; copies, *ibid.*, RG 108, Letters Sent; DLC-USG, V, 46, 76, 108; Meade Papers, PHi. *O.R.*, I, xlvi, part 3, 848.

Also on April 20, Brig. Gen. Rufus Ingalls telegraphed to Brig. Gen. John A. Rawlins. "Sheridan left his wagons at Harpers Ferry He requires at least one hundred at Petersburg Can I take them from the ninth (9) Corps? I am told that Corps is under marching orders—What disposition shall be made of its means of transportation? I would suggest that artillery wagon trains &c Could be sent by land without much loss of time, if the Lt Genl should wish—" Telegram received (at 2:00 P.M.), DNA, RG 107, Telegrams Collected (Bound); *ibid.*, RG 108, Telegrams Received; copy, DLC-USG, V, 54. *O.R.*, I, xlvi, part 3, 849. At 4:45 P.M., USG telegraphed to Ingalls. "You may keep from the 9th Corps what wagons you deem necessary for Sheridan's Cavalry. If it is necessary for the 9th Corps to have any more I will direct some from Harper's Ferry to be brought up." ALS (telegram sent), DNA, RG 107, Telegrams Collected (Bound); telegram sent, *ibid.*; copies, *ibid.*, RG 108, Letters Sent; DLC-USG, V, 46, 76, 108. *O.R.*, I, xlvi, part 3, 850.

To Maj. Gen. Edward O. C. Ord

(Cipher)   Apl. 20th *1865* [*2:55* P.M.]
MAJ. GN. ORD, RICHMOND, VA,

The 3000 prisoners at Ft. Monroe bound for New Orleans Mobile &c. cannot be furnished transportation by Government. It was no part of the arrangement that they should receive transportation or be allowed to pass through our lines except when to reach their homes it was necessary to do so. The men living South of Richmond must get home through the country and if they come within our lines must do so either as prisoners of War who surrender their parole or as persons desirous of quiting the rebel cause and taking advantage of the Presidents Amnesty.

U. S. GRANT
Lt. Gn.

ALS (telegram sent), DNA, RG 107, Telegrams Collected (Bound); telegram sent (at 4:45 P.M.), *ibid.*; telegram received, *ibid.*, Telegrams Collected (Unbound). *O.R.*, I, xlvi, part 3, 865. On April 20, 1865, Maj. Gen. Edward O. C. Ord telegraphed to USG. "Respectfully forwarded to Lt. Genl. Grant for his orders in the case. . . . 'Ft. Monroe Va Apl 20. BR. GENL. M. R. PATRICK. P. M Genl Richmond. There are about three thousand 3.000 rebel paroled prisoners here awaiting transportation to New Orleans, Mobile. &c. The QrMr says he will send five 5 steamers with them. Should a guard be sent on these steamers? If so, I cannot procure guards at this point for more than two of the steamers. Please inform me whether I shall send guards on these steamers & so where I shall procure them. (sig) A GILCHRIST Capt & P m" Telegram received (at 1:40 P.M.), DNA, RG 107, Telegrams Collected (Bound); *ibid.*, Telegrams Collected (Unbound); *ibid.*, RG 108, Telegrams Received; copy, DLC-USG, V, 54. *O.R.*, I, xlvi, part 3, 864–65.

On May 3, Ord twice telegraphed to USG. "Genl Halleck authorized the sending away on transports some hundreds of destitute and starving Paroled prisoners who had found their way to Old Point and the Quarter master 'James' has a Vessel ready to sail with them to Savannah on Saturday next—he now reports that he is ordered ~~to~~ not to furnish transportation to any paroled prisoners —As your Order from Appomattox Court House of April 10th specially authorized free transporation to be furnished such paroled prisoners on Government transports I think there is some mistake on the part of the Quarter master Genl, and even if no such Order has issued these people Cant get home except by turning high way robers on the road and I presume it is not the desire of the Government to turn them loose on these terms" ALS (telegram sent), Ord Papers, CU-B; telegram received (at 1:00 P.M.), DNA, RG 107, Telegrams Collected (Bound); (at 12:35 P.M.) *ibid.*, RG 108, Telegrams Received. *O.R.*, I, xlvi, part 3, 1076–77. "I find I am mistaken in supposing your order from appomatox april tenth (10) allows any transportation home to Rebel prisoners going south. I shall try and dispose of the four hundred (400) at Old Point in another way" Telegram received (at 5:00 P.M.), DNA, RG 107, Telegrams Collected (Bound); *ibid.*, RG 108, Telegrams Received; copy, DLC-USG, V, 54. *O.R.*, I, xlvi, part 3, 1077.

To Maj. Gen. Edward O. C. Ord

(Cipher)   *Washington, D. C.*, Apl. 20th *18645* [*8:30* P.M.]
MAJ. GEN. ORD, RICHMOND VA,

[C]ol. Lamb, Lieuts. Lewis & Hawes can take the oath of allegiance and Amnesty oath and renew their allegiance, citizenship and rights to hold property by conforming to the Presidents Amnesty proclamation. This rule applies to all who are not excluded by the proclamation. Those who are excluded must make special application, to be refered to the President, before they can be allowed the privilege.

Gen. Jackson[1] can not be promoted just now but as you do not give up your Department command it will make no difference in his ~~present~~ position.

U. S. Grant

Lt. Gn.

ALS (telegram sent), DNA, RG 107, Telegrams Collected (Bound); telegram sent, *ibid.*; telegram received, *ibid.*, Telegrams Collected (Unbound); (on April 21, 1865) Ord Papers, CU-B. *O.R.*, I, xlvi, part 3, 865–66. On April 20, Maj. Gen. Edward O. C. Ord telegraphed to USG. "Colonel Lamb, Lieuts Lewis & Hawes C S A prisoners of war wounded and at Hampton Hospital desire to take the oath of allegiance   Surg McClellan reports that he believes they are actuated by a full conviction of their errors and true desire to return to the Union. Shall I let them do it. Others and paroled officers wish to take the oath of allegiance & go north on business   Shall I let them do so   Bt Br Gen Jackson is now commanding Division (late Birneys). Jackson will lose his place of Lieut Colonel as Inspr of the Dept by my going out   Can he not be made a full ~~Br Gen~~ Brig of Vols for gallant services in the field at Petersburg pursuing & Capture of Lees army so that he may continue in Command of the Division & get pay. He is only a Capt of regulars" Telegram received (at 5:15 P.M.), DNA, RG 107, Telegrams Collected (Bound); *ibid.*, RG 108, Telegrams Received; copy, DLC-USG, V, 54. *O.R.*, I, xlvi, part 3, 865.

1. Richard H. Jackson, born in Ireland in 1830, enlisted as a private in the U.S. Army in 1851, rising to 2nd lt. before the Civil War. Confirmed as bvt. brig. gen. on March 10, 1865, he was so assigned on April 10. *Ibid.*, p. 687; *ibid.*, I, xlvi, part 1, 1228–29.

To Maj. Gen. William T. Sherman

(Cipher)   *Washington, D. C.*, Apl. 20th *18645* [*11:00* A.M.] Maj. Gen. Sherman, Raleigh N. C. Telegraph to Ft. Monroe & from Morehead City N. C.

If Johnston surrenders his Army or is beaten so as to require no longer the force you have in the state of North Carolina march Slocum's and Howard's Armies to City Point by easy marches. Leave Schofield to occupy the state and give him all or as much as you think needed of the Cavalry. You need not march across with your troops unless you think it necessary.

U. S. Grant

Lt. Gn.

ALS (telegram sent), DNA, RG 107, Telegrams Collected (Bound); telegram sent, *ibid.*; telegram received, *ibid.*, Telegrams Collected (Unbound). *O.R.*, I, xlvii, part 3, 257.

On April 15, 1865, 9:30 A.M., Maj. Gen. William T. Sherman, Raleigh, N. C., telegraphed to USG and Secretary of War Edwin M. Stanton. "I send copies of a correspondence begun with Johnston which I think will be followed by terms of capitulation. I will accept the same terms as Genl Grant gave Lee and be careful not to complicate any points of civil policy. If any cavalry have started towards me caution them that they may be prepared to find all work done. It is now raining in torrents and I shall await Johnstons reply here and will propose to meet him at Chappel Hill. I have invited Governor Vance to return to Raleigh with the civil Officers of his staff. Have seen Ex-Governor Graham Mr Badger, Moore, Holden & others all of whom agree that the war is ~~ours~~ over and that the states of the South must resume their allegiance subject to the Constitution & laws of Congress and that the military power of the South must submit to the National arms. This great fact once admitted all the details are easy arranged" Telegram received (on April 17, 10:10 A.M.), DNA, RG 107, Telegrams Collected (Bound); *ibid.*, Telegrams Collected (Unbound); *ibid.*, RG 108, Telegrams Received; copy, DLC-USG, V, 54. *O.R.*, I, xlvii, part 3, 221. The enclosures are *ibid.*, pp. 206–7. On April 17, USG transmitted a copy of this telegram to Maj. Gen. Philip H. Sheridan. Telegrams sent (2), DNA, RG 107, Telegrams Collected (Bound).

On April 16, Bvt. Brig. Gen. Langdon C. Easton, Morehead City, N. C., telegraphed to USG. "The following is a copy of a telegram just received from Gen Sherman. I send it to you as he has directed me to keep you advised of his movements by every opportunity 'Raleigh N C April 16th 1865 GENL EASTON The capture of Selma is also announced in rebel papers I expect every hour an answer from Genl Johnston but shall start tomorrow toward Ashboro unless he makes clear and satisfactory terms (signed) W T SHERMAN M Genl' " LS (telegram sent), *ibid.*, Telegrams Collected (Unbound); telegram received (on April 18, 10:40 A.M.), *ibid.*, Telegrams Collected (Bound); *ibid.*, RG 108, Telegrams Received. Printed (with additional instructions from Sherman to Easton) as received on April 18, 10:45 A.M., in *O.R.*, I, xlvii, part 3, 229. At 10:00 P.M., Lt. Col. Roswell M. Sawyer wrote (and telegraphed) to USG. "In the absence of Gen Webster, Chief of Staff, I have the honor to forward, by Capt Anderson of the General's Staff, the following copy of a telegram just received from the Major General Comdg in the Field—'Raleigh Apl 16th 1865 To GEN WEBSTER I have appointed to meet Gen Johnston near Hillsboro tomorrow at noon. I have no doubt we shall arrange terms the same made with Lee's Army. Keep this to yourself for the present, but notify Genl Grant by any steamer leaving Morehead City. I will notify you of the result tomorrow Evening W. T. SHERMAN—Maj. Genl' " ALS, DNA, RG 107, Telegrams Collected (Bound). Printed as received on April 18, 10:45 A.M., in *O.R.*, I, xlvii, part 3, 228.

On April 17, USG telegraphed to Sherman. "The following dispatch from Gen. Wilson is forwarded for your information, also one to Maj. Eckert from Operator at Cincinnati . . . 'Hd. Qrs. Cavalry Corps M. D. Selma Ala April 4th 10. a. m., 1865 LT. GEN. GRANT ~~City~~ My Corps took this place by Assault late on evening of the second (2d). We have captured twenty (20) field guns, two thousand prisoners, besides over two thousand in hospital, and large quantity of military stores of all kinds. The Arsenals & foundrys with their Machinery are in my possession intact. I shall burn them today with every thing else useful to the enemy. I have already destroyed the iron works North of here, eight or ten in all, and very extensive. Forrest, Dick Taylor, Adams, Armstrong and Roddy succeeded in getting out in the darkness and confusion following the assault, by wading the swamp East of the City. The place is strongly fortified with two continuous lines, of parapet & redoubts, the outer one with a continuous stockade on the glacis, extending from the river above to river below City. They were defended by four 4 brigades of Cavalry and all the first & second class militia of this section, from six 6 to nine 9 thousand men The conduct of my troops, particularly that of Longs Division which made the attack, was magnificent. Gen. Long was wounded slightly in the head; Col. Dobbs Fourth (4th) Ohio killed Colonels Miller, McCormack and Biggs wounded. As it is my desire and intention to hold the place as long as possible I shall not relinquish my hold upon it except to secure other advantag[e.] If I can keep Forrest West of the Cawhaba until I have constructed bridge over the Alabama I will move against him, or Montgomery, as circumstances may determine. Operations Westward, rather than toward Montgomery will in my estimation assist Gen. Canby most. (signed) J. H. WILSON Bvt. Maj. Genl.' 'Cincinnati Apl. 16th 10 P M 1865 MAJ. ECKERT Cairo says Clara Dean just arrived bringing news of capture Mobile STEVENS" Telegrams sent (2), DNA, RG 107, Telegrams Collected (Bound); telegrams received (2), *ibid.*, Telegrams Collected (Unbound). The first enclosure is printed as addressed to Maj. Gen. George H. Thomas in *O.R.*, I, xlix, part 2, 217.

At 9:00 P.M., Sawyer wrote (and telegraphed) to USG. "The following telegram is just received from General Sherman, and forwarded to you by his direction. 'Raleigh April 17th—65—7 P. M. GEN. WEBSTER I have returned from a point twenty seven miles up the Railroad, where I had a long interview with Gen Johnston with a full and frank interchange of opinions—He evidently seeks to make terms for Jeff Davis and his Cabinet—He wanted to consult again with Mr Breckenridge at Greensboro, and I have agreed to meet him at noon tomorrow at the same place—We lose nothing in time as by agreement both armies stand still—and the roads are drying up—So that if I am forced to pursue I will be able to make better speed—There is great danger that the confederate armies will dissolve and fill the whole land with robbers and assassins—and I think this one of the difficulties that Johnston labors under—The assassination of Mr Lincoln shows one of the elements in the rebel army which will be almost as difficult to deal with as the main armies—Communicate substance of this to Genl Grant—and also that if Sheridan is marching down this way, to feel for me before striking the enemy—I dont want Johnston's Army to break up in fragments W. T. SHERMAN Major Genl Comdg'" ALS, DNA, RG 108, Letters Received; telegram received (on April 19, 2:30 P.M.), *ibid.*, Telegrams Received; *ibid.*, RG 107, Telegrams Collected (Bound); *ibid.*, Telegrams Collected (Unbound). *O.R.*, I, xlvii, part 3, 237. On April 19, 2:00 P.M., Maj. William G. Dickson, Fort Monroe, transmitted this telegram to USG. ALS (telegram sent), DNA, RG 107, Telegrams Collected (Unbound); telegram received (at 2:30 P.M.), *ibid.*, Telegrams Collected (Bound); *ibid.*, RG 108, Telegrams Received.

On April 18, Sherman wrote to USG and Maj. Gen. Henry W. Halleck. "I enclose herewith a copy of an agreemt made this day between Gen Joseph. E. Johnston and myself which if approved by the President of the United States will produce Peace from the Potomac and the Rio Grand. Mr Breckenridge was present at our conference in his capacity as Major General, and satisfied me of the ability of General Johnston to carry out to the full extent the terms of this agreemt, and if you will get the President to simply Endorse the copy, and commission me to carry out the terms I will follow them to the conclusion. You will observe that it is an absolute submission of the Enemy to the lawful authority of the United States, and disperses his Armies absolutely, and the point to which I attach most importance is that the dispersion and disbandmt of these Armies is done in such a manner as to prevent their breaking up into Guerilla Bands. On the other hand we can retain just as much of an army as we please. I agreed to the mode and manner of the surrender of arms set forth, as it gives the States the means of repressing Guerillas which we could not expect them to do if we stript them of all arms. Both Generals Johnston & Breckenridge admitted that slavery was dead and I could not insist on embracing it in such a paper, because it can be made with the states in detail. I know that all the men of substance south sincerely want Peace and I do not believe they will resort to war again during this Century. I have no doubt that they will in the future be perfectly subordinate to the Laws of the United States. The momt my action in this matter is approved, I can spare five Corps, and will ask for orders to leave Gen Schofield here with the 10th Corps and to march myself with the 14, 15, 17 20 and 23rd Corps, via Burksville, and Gordonsville to Frederick or Hagerstown there to be paid and mustered out. The question of Finance is now the chief one and every soldier & officer not needed should be got home at work. I would like to be able to begin the march north by May 1. I urge on the part of the President speedy action as it is important to get ~~both~~ the Confederate Armies to their homes as well as our own." ALS, *ibid.*, RG 94, Record & Pension Office, 520059. *O.R.*, I, xlvii, part 3, 243. The enclosures are *ibid.*, pp. 243–45. On April 20, 11:50 A.M., Maj. Henry Hitchcock, Fort Monroe, telegraphed to USG. "I have the honor to report my arrival at this place with important dispatches for yourself and General Halleck from Major General Sherman dated Raleigh, 18th inst., containing the conditions of an agreement made that day between General Sherman and the rebel General Johnston at a conference between them held near Durham's Station 28 miles N. W. of Raleigh, and forwarded immediately by General Sherman for your consideration. I leave here for Washington in half an hour on the 'Keyport,' dispatch boat. All was well at Raleigh, and the ~~Very respectfully~~ armies were to maintain the *status quo* for the present. Our cavalry head quarters were at Durham's Station: the bulk of the rebel army had crossed Haw River." ALS (telegram sent), DNA, RG 107, Telegrams Collected (Unbound); telegram received (marked as sent at noon, received at 2:30 P.M.), *ibid.*, Telegrams Collected (Bound); *ibid.*, RG 108, Telegrams Received. *O.R.*, I, xlvii, part 3, 257.

On April 19, USG telegraphed to Sherman. "The following dispatches are forwarded for your information" Telegrams sent (2), DNA, RG 107, Telegrams Collected (Bound); telegram received, *ibid.* USG transmitted a telegram of April 9 from Maj. Gen. Edward R. S. Canby to USG reporting the fall of Fort Blakely, Ala. (see telegram to Maj. Gen. Edward R. S. Canby, April 17, 1865, note 1) and a telegram of April 18 from Thomas to Halleck transmitting a report from Maj. Gen. George Stoneman (see *O.R.*, I, xlix, part 1, 323–25).

To Maj. Gen. Lewis Wallace

(Cipher)   Washington, Apl. 20th 1865 [*12:30* P.M.]
MAJ. GEN. WALLACE, BALTIMORE MD.

It was no part of the agreement that we were to transport or feed paroled prisoners. By the terms of the surrender they were allowed to return to their homes and I ordered that their paroles should be a pass to go through our lines where it was necessary to do so to reach their homes, and that when they traveled on roads or boats run exclusively by Government no fare would be collected. I did not calculate that men from N. C. S. C. & Ga. would expect to go home by way of New York. We furnish no transportation over private roads and those prisoners who have not homes in Maryland need not be allowed to remain but may be arrested if they attempt to do so.

U. S. GRANT
Lt. Gn.

ALS (telegram sent), DNA, RG 107, Telegrams Collected (Bound); telegram sent, *ibid.*; telegram received, *ibid.* O.R., I, xlvi, part 3, 873.

On April 15, 1865, Maj. Gen. Lewis Wallace, Baltimore, telegraphed to USG. "I have just returned & if agreeable would like to report to you in person." Telegram received (at 6:20 P.M.), DNA, RG 107, Telegrams Collected (Bound); copy, DLC-USG, V, 54.

On April 22, Wallace wrote to USG. "I have information that secret meetings have been held in this city, and in other parts of the Middle Department, relative to the rebel officer's and soldiers, who have returned to their homes under the terms of Lee's surrender. With a view to the preventtion of great trouble, I respectfully present the following point for your consideration and instructions. Under the laws of Maryland, a citizen who has left the state, and joined the rebel army, has lost his residence, and cannot, therefore, claim a home in its limits, That such is the law, and that, it has been so judicially decided, I beg leave to refer you to the accompanying opinion's of Honorables John C. King, Hugh L. Bond, and R. N. Martin, presiding Judge's of the highest respectability. After carefully studying the terms of surrender accepted by Genl Lee, I can see nothing which under the law, as stated by the Judges above named, precludes the state authorities from prohibitory action against returning rebel officers and soldiers. Following out that idea, it has occurred to me that I can have the trouble solved in this way. Suppose I suggest to His Excellency Gov Bradford the issuance, by him, of a proclamation declarative of the law of the state, upon the subject, and on that ground, prohibiting the return of rebel soldiers and officer's to Maryland, under penalty of prosecution for treason against the state. Such a mode, as you will perceive, cannot be construed as a molestation of the paroled men by the

U. S. authorities. Before making the suggestion however, I consider your advice
and instruction essential. The business, I assure you, is of the utmost importance." LS, DNA, RG 107, Letters Received from Bureaus; *ibid.*, RG 393,
Middle Dept. and 8th Army Corps, Letters Sent (Press). On May 2, Wallace
telegraphed to USG. "Have you seen my letter to you of the twenty second April?
If not, please look at it, and see one of the ~~troubles~~ peculiar troubles of my Department." ALS (undated telegram sent), *ibid.*, RG 107, Telegrams Collected
(Unbound); *ibid.*, RG 393, Middle Dept. and 8th Army Corps, Letters Sent
(Press); telegram received (at noon), *ibid.*, RG 108, Telegrams Received.

To Julia Dent Grant

Apl. 20th *1865*

DEAR JULIA,

I had made up my mind to go home last night, but the Sec. of
War wanted me to hold on here yet for a day or two. About the
time, or before, I would have started I received a dispatch from Ft.
Monroe stating that a messenger with very important despatches
from Gen. Sherman was on his way up.[1] I would have been compelled to await these. The bearer of dispatches has not yet arrived.

I will go home as soon as I can but this time will not be able
to remain long. It looks as if I was never to have any rest. I can
scarsely get to my meals without being followed up by dispatches
that require instant attention. I hope this condition of things will
change soon however.

I have had but one letter from you since you got home. Expect
one to-day and hope to hear that you are preparing to move to Phila.

I secured the position of P. M. of Richmond Va for Dr. Sharp
and telegraphed to Ford to send out word to him and tell him to
come on.[2] I also wrote to Nelly telling her of the appointment and
for her to send the Dr. if he did not before receive my dispatch. I received an answer from Ford however after he had sent the dispatch
out to the Dr. and learn that he left, or was to leave, yesterday for
Washington to go on and take charge of the office. Until it is regularly opened for the benefit of the community the Drs. position will
be that of Special Agt. of the P. O. Dept. with a salary of $1.500.

It will not be long I hope before the office can be opened when the place will be worth about $4,000.

Love and kisses for you and the children.

ULYS.

ALS, DLC-USG.

1. See telegram to Maj. Gen. William T. Sherman, April 20, 1865.
2. On April 18, 1865, 1:10 P.M., USG telegraphed to Charles W. Ford, U.S. Express Co., St. Louis. "Please send word to Dr. Alex. Sharp at Mr. Dent's to come to Washington immediately if he is willing to take the P. O. in Richmond." ALS (telegram sent), DNA, RG 107, Telegrams Collected (Bound); telegram sent, *ibid.*; copies, *ibid.*, RG 108, Letters Sent; DLC-USG, V, 46, 76, 108.

To Edwin M. Stanton

Washington D. C, Apl. 21st *1865*

HON. E. M. STANTON,
SEC. OF WAR,
SIR:

I have rec'd, and just completed reading the dispatches brought by Special Messenger from Gen. Sherman. They are of such importance that I think immediate action should be taken on them, and that it should be done by the President, in council with his whole Cabinet.

I would respectfully suggest whether the President should not be notified, and all his Cabinet, and the meeting take place to-night?

Very respectfully
your obt. svt.
U. S. GRANT
Lt. Gn.

ALS, DLC-Edwin M. Stanton. *O.R.*, I, xlvii, part 3, 263. On April 21, 1865, Secretary of War Edwin M. Stanton wrote to USG. "The memorandum or basis agreed upon between Genl Sherman and Gen Johnston having been submitted to the President, they are disapproved. You will give notice of the disapproval to Gen Sherman and direct him to resume hostilities at the earliest moment. The instructions given to you by the late President Abraham Lincoln on the 3d of

March by my telegraph of that date, addressed to you, express substantially the views of President Andrew Johnson, and will be observed by Genl Sherman. A copy is herewith appended. The President desires that you proceed immediately to the Hd Qrs of Gen Sherman and direct operations against the enemy" LS, DNA, RG 108, Letters Received. *O.R.*, I, xlvii, part 3, 263. The enclosure is *ibid.*

At 10:30 P.M., USG telegraphed to Maj. Gen. Edward O. C. Ord. "The memorandum of basis of arrangement made betweens Genls. Sherman and Johnston is disapproved by the President and Gen. Sherman is ordered to resume hostilities" Telegram received (on April 22), Ord Papers, CU-B.

To Maj. Gen. William T. Sherman

Washington, D. C., Apl. 21st *18645.*

MAJ. GEN. W. T. SHERMAN,
COMD.G MIL. DIV. OF THE MISS.
GENERAL,

The basis of agreement entered into between yourself and Gen. J. E. Johnston for the disbandment of the Southern Army and the extension of the authority of the general government over all the territory belonging to it, sent for the approval of the President, is received.

I read it carefully myself before submitting it to the President and secretary of War and felt satisfied that it could not possibly be approved. My reasons for these views I will give you at another time in a more extended letter.

Your agreement touches upon questions of such vital importance that as soon as read I addressed a note to the Sec. of War notifying him of their receipt and the importance of immediate action by the President, and suggested in view of their importance that the entire Cabinet be called together that all might give an expression of their opinions upon the matter. The result was a disapproval by the President of the basis laid down, a disapproval of the negociations altogether, except for the surrender of the Army commanded by Johnston, and directions to me to notify you of this decission. I cannot do so better than by sending you the enclosed copy of a dispatch penned by the late President, though signed by the Sec. of War, in answer to me on sending a letter received from

Gen. Lee proposing to meet me for the purpose of submitting the question of peace to a convention of Officers.

Please notify gGeneral Johnston immediately on receipt of this of the termination of the truce and resume hostilities against his Army at the earlyest moment you can, acting in in good faith.

The rebels know well the terms upon which they can have peace and just where negocations can commence, namely: when they lay down their Arms and submit to the laws of the United States. Mr. Lincoln gave them full assurances of what he would do I believe in his conference with commissioners met in Hampton Roads.

> Very respectfully
> your obt. svt.
> U. S. GRANT
> Lt. Gn.

ALS, NNP. *O.R.*, I, xlvii, part 3, 263–64. On April 25, 1865, Maj. Gen. William T. Sherman wrote to USG. "I had the ~~pleasure~~ honor to recieve your letter of April 21, with enclosures yesterday and was well pleased that you came along, as you must have observed that I had the Military control so as to adapt it to any phase the case might assume. It is but just that I should record the fact that I made my terms with General Johnston under the influence of the liberal terms you extended to the Army of Genl Lee at Appomatox C H on the 9th and the seeming policy ~~policy~~ of our Governmt as evinced by the call of the Virginia Legislature and Governor back to Richmond under yours and Presidents Lincolns very eyes. It now appears that this last act was done without consultation with you, or any Knowledge of Mr Lincoln, but rather in opposition to a previous policy well considered. I have not the least desire to interfere in the Civil Policy of our Governmt, but would shun it as something not to my liking, but occasions do arise when a prompt seizure of results is forced on Military Commanders not in immediate communication with the proper Authority. It is probable that the terms signed by Genl Johnston & myself ~~wa~~sere not clear enough on the point, well understood between us, that our negotiations did not apply to any parties outside the officers and men of the Confederate Armies, which would have been easily remedied. No surrender of an army not actually at the mercy of an antagonist, was ever made without 'terms,' and these always define the military status of the surrendered. Thus you stipulated that the officers and men of Lee's Army should not be molested at their homes so long as they obeyed the Laws at the place of their residence. I do not wish to discuss the points involved in our recognition of the State Governmts in actual existence, but merely state my Conclusions to await the solution of the future. Such ~~recognition~~ action on our part in no manner recognizes for a moment the So Called Confederate Government or makes us liable for its debts or acts. The Laws and acts done by the several States ~~in~~ during the Period of Rebellion, are void because done without the oath prescribed by the Constitution of the U S which is a 'condition precedent' We have a Right to use any sort of machinery to produce military results, and it is the commonest thing for Military Commanders to use the Civil Govermt in actual existence as a means to an end. I do believe we could and can use the present State Governmts lawfully, constitutionally and as the very best possible means to produce the object desired, viz entire and complete submission to the Lawful authority of the U S. As to punishmt for past crimes, that is for the Judiciary and can in no manner of way be disturbed by our acts, and so far as I can I will use my influence that Rebels shall suffer all the personal punishmt prescribed by Law, as also the Civil liabilities arising from their past acts. What we now want is the mere forms of Law by which common men may regain the positions of industry so long disturbed by the War. I now apprehend that the Rebel Armies will disperse; and instead of dealing with six or seven states, we will have to deal with numberless bands of desperados headed by such men as Mosby, Forrest, Red Jackson, & others who know not, and care not for danger or its consequences." ALS, PPRF. *O.R.*, I, xlvii, part 3, 302–3.

On April 22, Sherman had telegraphed to USG. "Wilson held Macon on the 30th [*20*] with Howell Cobb, G. W Smith and others as prisoners but they claimed the benefit of my armistice and he has telegraphed to me through the rebel lines for orders. I have answered him that he may draw out of Macon and hold his command for further orders unless he has reason to believe the rebels are changing the status to our prejudice—A Brigade of rebels offered to surrender to me yesterday but I prefer to make one grand final which I believe to be perfectly practicable—There will be no trouble in adjusting matters in N C. Ga and Ala., and I think South Carolina ought to be satisfied with Charleston and Columbia in ruins. All we wait is an answer from you and the President—Weather fine and roads good The troops ready for fight or home" Telegram received (on April 23, 10:30 A.M.), DNA, RG 107, Telegrams Collected (Bound); (2) *ibid.*, Telegrams Collected (Unbound). *O.R.*, I, xlvii, part 3, 277–78. Since this telegram arrived after USG's departure to meet Sherman, it may never have received his attention.

To Maj. Gen. Lewis Wallace

(Cipher)   Washington Apl. 21st 1865 [*9:30* A.M.]
MAJ. GEN. WALLACE BALTIMORE MD

Mrs. Cary is a resident of Baltimore and has had her home there throughout the War. She went to Richmond on a pass regularly obtained and now returns in the same way. She is of course restored to her former status and should be treated as if she had remained in Baltimore all the time. Mrs. Pegram left Baltimore and went South without permission. She should give satisfactory evidence of intention to remain quiet and peaceable to be allowed to stay. Her berievement should be counted in her favor however.

U. S. GRANT
Lt. Gn.

ALS (telegram sent), DNA, RG 107, Telegrams Collected (Bound); telegram sent, *ibid.*; telegram received, *ibid.* On April 21, 1865, Maj. Gen. Lewis Wallace telegraphed to USG. "Your telegram about Mrs Casey and Mrs Pegram received. Please see mine sent you in the early part of the evening asking instructions. I will add that these people have made themselves especially odious to loyal citizens of Baltimore." Telegram received, *ibid.*; *ibid.*, RG 108, Telegrams Received; copy, DLC-USG, V, 54. On April 22, Wallace wrote to USG. "Your telegram touching Mrs. Carey and Mrs. Pegram was recd. The truth is these ladies, if absolutely liberated, would not be safe in the city just at this time of public exasperation. I have been at great loss to know exactly the proper thing to do with them, under the circumstances. Desiring to conform to your wishes on the subject, I have paroled them, obligating them to report daily to Lt. Col. Woolley, Pro Marshal. My idea is that, as long as they are under this semblance of arrest, nothing more serious will happen them, provided they behave with common discretion. I would be obliged if you would inform me whether this action meets your approbation." ALS, DNA, RG 393, Middle Dept. and 8th Army Corps, Letters Sent (Press). In 1861, Henrietta (Hetty) Cary of Baltimore, after displaying a C.S.A. flag to U.S. troops marching past her house, went South. Hetty and her cousin, Constance Cary (later Mrs. Burton Harrison), became prominent in Richmond society. On Jan. 19, 1865, Hetty married C.S.A. Brig. Gen. John Pegram, who died in battle on Feb. 6. Her mother, Mrs. Wilson M. Cary of Baltimore, attended the wedding. Mrs. Burton Harrison, *Recollections Grave and Gay* (New York, 1911), pp. 58, 201–5. On Dec. 19, 1864, 10:45 [A.M.], Brig. Gen. John A. Rawlins telegraphed to Maj. Gen. Edward O. C. Ord. "Mrs Cary & two Other Ladies with passes from the President Secy of War & Gen Grant to pass through our lines into the Confederate Lines Are now on Steamer en route for Aikens Landing, you will please send a Couple of Ambulances to meet them at the Landing & get them through our lines at the earliest possible moment" Telegram received, DNA, RG 393, Dept. of Va. and N. C., Telegrams Received.

On Feb. 26, 1865, USG telegraphed to Lt. Col. John E. Mulford. "Please inform Col. Ould that Mrs. Cary and her daughter Mrs. Pegram will be permitted to pass through our lines to their home in Baltimore. Application has been made to me for such a pass." ALS (telegram sent), Kohns Collection, NN; copies, DLC-USG, V, 46, 74, 108; DNA, RG 108, Letters Sent. On Feb. 27, 3:45 A.M., Mulford telegraphed to USG. "Your dispatch received Will communicate to Mr Ould at once" ALS (telegram sent), *ibid.*, RG 107, Telegrams Collected (Unbound); telegram received (at 3:45 A.M.), *ibid.*, RG 108, Letters Received. *O.R.*, II, viii, 313. On Feb. 28, Bvt. Maj. Gen. John G. Barnard twice telegraphed to Lt. Col. Theodore S. Bowers. "Gen. Morris writes me that he will certainly arrest Mrs. Pegram if she returns to Baltimore Therefore please retain those passes for Mrs. Cary & Mrs. Pegram. ~~until~~" "It would be well to forward to Richmond a pass for Mrs. Cary *alone*. Telegraph me if there is any special boat coming up in a day or two." ALS (telegrams sent), DNA, RG 107, Telegrams Collected (Unbound). On the same day, Bowers telegraphed to Barnard. "Your letter of yesterday and telegrams of this evening received Your request will be complied with, General Ingalls will go up on a special boat on thursday to return probably on monday" Telegram received, *ibid.*, Telegrams Collected (Bound); copies, *ibid.*, RG 108, Letters Sent; DLC-USG, V, 46, 74, 108.

On April 16, 10:00 P.M., Rawlins telegraphed to Bvt. Brig. Gen. William W. Morris, Baltimore. "Mrs. Casey and Mrs. Pegram are on their way from Richmond to Baltimore. On their arrival in Baltimore require of them the oath of allegiance to the United States as a condition to their remaining there." Telegrams sent (2), DNA, RG 107, Telegrams Collected (Bound); telegram received, *ibid.*

On April 20, Wallace telegraphed to USG. "Mrs Carey and Mrs Pegram Refuse to take the oath of allegiance. I have arrested them & placed them in Confinement under guard. They are under Guard at Barrs Hotel where they will Remain until I can Recieve your instructions. Shall I Return them to Richmond Consulting the state of feeling in this City, at that at at this time, that I think that is the best that can be done with them" ALS (telegram sent), *ibid.*, Telegrams Collected (Unbound); *ibid.*, RG 393, Middle Dept. and 8th Army Corps, Telegrams Sent (Press); telegram received (at 10:25 P.M.), *ibid.*, RG 107, Telegrams Collected (Bound); *ibid.*, RG 108, Telegrams Received. At 11:30 P.M., USG telegraphed to Wallace. "I understand you are about sending Mrs. Cary & daughter South? Before doing so see the pass they have from me and report here the reason for sending them off and get my approval before doing so." ALS (telegram sent), *ibid.*, RG 107, Telegrams Collected (Bound); telegram sent, *ibid.*; telegram received, *ibid.*; *ibid.*, RG 109, Union Provost Marshals' File of Papers Relating to Two or More Civilians.

To Julia Dent Grant

Apl. 21st *1865*

DEAR JULIA,

It is now nearly 11 O'Clock at night and I have received directions from the Sec. of War, and President, to start at once for Raleigh North Carolina. I start in an hour. Gen. Meigs, Maj. Leet, Capt. Dunn, (Dunn is Capt. and Asst. Adj. Gn.) and Major Hudson go with me. I will write to you from Morehead City or New Berne.—I do hope you will have moved to Phila by the time I return. I can run up to Philadelphia easily; but to get to Burlington I have to give notice of my going to secure a train to take me the last end of the way.

I find my duties, anxieties, and the necessity for having all my wits about me, increasing instead of diminishing. I have a Herculean task to perform and shall endeavor to do it, not to please any one, but for the interests of our great country that is now begining to loom far above all other countries, modern or ancient. What a spectacle it will be to see a country able to put down a rebellion able to put half a Million of soldiers in the field, at one time, and maintain them! That will be done and is almost done already. That ₙNation, united, will have a strength which will enable it to dictate to all others, ₜₒ *conform to justice and right*. Power I think can go no further. The moment conscience leaves, physical strength will avail nothing, in the long run.

I only sat down to write you that I was suddenly required to leave on important duty, and not feeling willing to say what that duty is, you must await my return to know more.

Love and kisses for you and the children.

U. S. Grant

ALS, DLC-USG.

To Silas A. Hudson

———

Washington D. C, Apl. 21st *1865*

Dear Cousin,

I have just rec'd your letter of the 17th   Your views about our new President are just mine. It is impossible that an ordinary man should have risen to the position which M̶r̶ Pres. Johnson has and have sustained himself throughout. His start was in the South where he had an aristocracy to contend against without one advantage except native ability to sustain him. I am satisfied the country has nothing to fear from his administration. It is unpatriotic at this time for professed lovers of their country to express doubts of the capacity and integrity of our Chief Magistrate. All should give him a hearty support and recollect that whatever his policy it can not suit all and from his stand point he is better able to see the wants and true interests of the country than any other man. As to myself I believe I can truly say that I am without ambition. From the first I have tried to do what I thought my clear duty in putting down the rebellion. I never aimed or thought of my present rank in the Army until it was thrust upon me. The fears or clamors of the public can not change my course one ioto from what my own judgement tells me is right. Of course I like to have the approval of the public for it is their interest I am serving and what they approve can be more effectually done.

I am happy to state to you that Peter[1] has proven himself a capital Staff Officer. He has won the respect, and friendship for life, of all my Staff, most of whom are officers of the regular Army, by his quiet devotion to his duties, personal bravery and sound good sense. It is a great pity he did not go into the Cavalry at the begining of the War. It is the conviction of those who know him that he would now be one of our most sucsessful and dashing Cavalry Generals had he done so.

I will always be pleased to hear from you though I may not always find time to answer your letters.

> Yours Truly
> U. S. GRANT

ALS, State Historical Society of Colorado, Denver, Colo.

1. Bvt. Maj. Peter T. Hudson.

To Maj. Gen. Henry W. Halleck

Fort Monroe, Apl. 22, 1865, 4. p. m

GEN H. W. HALLECK, RICHMOND,

The truce entered into by Gen Sherman will be [e]nded as soon as I can reach Raleigh. Move Sheridan with his Cavalry toward Greenborough as soon as possible. I think it will be well to send one Corps of Infantry, also Cavalry. The infantry need not go farther than Danville, unless they secure Orders

> U. S. GRANT, Maj Gen

Telegram received, DNA, RG 107, Telegrams Collected (Unbound); copies (marked as sent at 3:30 P.M.), *ibid.*, RG 94, Letters Received, 223J 1865; *ibid.*, RG 108, Letters Sent; DLC-USG, V, 46, 76, 108. Printed with variant texts taken from USG's letterbooks and recipient's copy, both marked as received at

5:30 P.M., in *O.R.*, I, xlvi, part 3, 888; *ibid.*, I, xlvii, part 3, 276–77. The version in USG's letterbooks made clear his intention to have Maj. Gen. Philip H. Sheridan command both cav. and inf. On April 22, 1865, 7:00 P.M., Maj. Gen. Henry W. Halleck telegraphed to USG. "Orders have been sent to Genls Meade & Sheridan in complianc with your telegram of this date." ALS (telegram sent), DNA, RG 107, Telegrams Collected (Unbound); telegrams received (2), *ibid.*; *ibid.*, RG 108, Telegrams Received. *O.R.*, I, xlvi, part 3, 889; *ibid.*, I, xlvii, part 3, 277.

At 3:40 P.M., USG, Fort Monroe, telegraphed to Secretary of War Edwin M. Stanton. "As soon as dispatches can be got off for Halleck and Sheridan, I will start from here for Morehead City." ALS (telegram sent at 4:00 P.M.), DNA, RG 107, Telegrams Collected (Unbound); copies, *ibid.*, RG 108, Letters Sent; DLC-USG, V, 46, 76, 108. Printed as received at 5:00 P.M. in *O.R.*, I, xlvi, part 3, 888; *ibid.*, I, xlvii, part 3, 276.

At 9:30 A.M., Sheridan had telegraphed to USG. "If you desire me to make the march to join Gen Sherman, I will be ready to start on the 25th or 26th of this month" Telegram received (at 9:30 A.M.), DNA, RG 107, Telegrams Collected (Bound); *ibid.*, RG 108, Telegrams Received; copies, DLC-USG, V, 54; (2) DLC-Philip H. Sheridan. *O.R.*, I, xlvi, part 3, 894. Bvt. Col. Theodore S. Bowers endorsed the telegram received. "Will Major Eckert please have the foregoing despatch sent to Genl Grant at Fort Monroe, and instruct the operator at that place to see that it is delivered to the General on his arrival at old Point. General Grant left here last night on the steamer Keyport." ES, DNA, RG 108, Telegrams Received. *O.R.*, I, xlvi, part 3, 895.

At 3:10 P.M., Maj. Gen. Edward O. C. Ord telegraphed to USG. "I propose sending Sumners Regt 1st New York Mounted Rifles—A Regt of Infantry And Battery of Artillery to Fredericksburg—provided a sufficient force has not already been sent thereabouts from Washington—Shall I do so—" ALS (telegram sent), DNA, RG 94, War Records Office, Dept. of Va. and N. C.; telegram received (at 4:00 P.M.), *ibid.*, RG 107, Telegrams Collected (Bound). On the same day, Bowers telegraphed to Ord. "Your dispatch in relation to sending troops to Fredericksburg is received. Please consult Gen. Halleck on this subject, and be governed by his views and directions" ALS (telegram sent), *ibid.*; telegram received, *ibid.*, Telegrams Collected (Unbound); Ord Papers, CU-B.

To Edwin M. Stanton

HEADQUARTERS, MILITARY DIVISION OF THE MISSISSIPPI,
IN THE FIELD, Raleigh, Apl. 24th 1865 [*9:00* A.M.]
HON. E. M. STANTON,
SEC. OF WAR,
SIR:

I reached here this morning and delivered to Gen. Sherman the reply to his negociations with Johnston. He was not surprise but rather expected this rejection. Word was immediately sent to Johnston terminating the truce and information that civil matters could not be entertained in any convention between Army commanders.

Gen. Sherman has been guided in his negociations with Johnston entirely by what he thought was prescedents authorized by the President. He had before him the terms given by me to Lee's Army and the call of the rebel legislature of Va. authorized by Weitzel, as he supposed with the sanction of the President and myself. At the time of the agreement Sherman did not know of the withdrawal of authority for the meeting of that legislature. The moment he learned through the papers that authority for the meeting of the Va. legislature had been withdrawn he communicated the fact to Johnston as having bearing on the negociation had.

U. S. GRANT

Lt. Gen

ALS (telegram sent), Abraham Lincoln Book Shop, Chicago, Ill.; telegrams received (2), DNA, RG 107, Telegrams Collected (Unbound). *O.R.*, I, xlvii, part 3, 293. On April 25, 1865, 10:50 a.m., Secretary of War Edwin M. Stanton telegraphed to USG. "Your despatch received. The arrangement between Sherman & Johnston meets with universal disapprobation. No one of any class or shade of opinion approves it. I have not known as much surprise and discontent at any-thing that has happened during the war. No military news of importance has transpired since your departure   Hancock is here. Booth is still at large   Let me hear from you as frequently as possible. The hope of the country is that you may repair the misfortune occasioned by Sherman's negotiations." Telegram sent, DNA, RG 107, Telegrams Collected (Bound); telegram received (on April 27), *ibid.*, Telegrams Collected (Unbound); (on April 27, 9:30 a.m.) *ibid.*, RG 108, Telegrams Received. *O.R.*, I, xlvii, part 3, 301–2.

On April 23, 6:00 p.m., USG, Beaufort, N. C., had telegraphed to Stanton. "Have just ~~here~~ reached here and will start for Raleigh as soon as a train can be obtained. No news here from Sherman. I shall not telegraph to him that I am on the way." ALS (telegram sent), DNA, RG 107, Telegrams Collected (Unbound); copies, *ibid.*, RG 108, Letters Sent; DLC-USG, V, 46, 76, 108. *O.R.*, I, xlvii, part 3, 286.

On April 24, Brig. Gen. Innis N. Palmer, New Berne, N. C., telegraphed to USG. "Can you not stop over night with me on your return   If you Cannot stop please let me Know when you will pass through as I would like to see you" Telegram received, DNA, RG 107, Telegrams Collected (Unbound). On April 25, USG, Raleigh, telegraphed to Palmer. "Pleask ask the Naval Commander at New Berne and the Qr. Mr. to know if I can not have a vessel from there to-morrow evening to run to Ft. Monroe. I will go down in the 10 a. m. train in the morning and would like to start out two or three hours after my arrival." ALS (telegram sent), *ibid. O.R.*, I, xlvii, part 3, 309. On the same day, Palmer telegraphed to

USG. "The Steamer 'Edward Everett' will be ready for you to-morrow at any hour you may designate. Will you and Such ~~Staff~~ of your Staff as may be with you dine with me to-morrow   Colonel Whitford who commands the only rebel organization in this vicinity, has just come to my outer pickets to ask an interview with me. It is my opinion that he wishes to obtain the best terms he can for his command. I shall see him in an hour or two. What terms can I offer him? His command has been for three years in the vicinity of Kinston, but it has of course been much broken up of late." ALS (telegram sent), DNA, RG 107, Telegrams Collected (Unbound). *O.R.*, I, xlvii, part 3, 309. What appears to be USG's response to Palmer, declining the dinner invitation, was offered for sale by Kingston Galleries, 1963.

To Julia Dent Grant

In the Field Raleigh Apl. 25th *1865*

DEAR JULIA,

We arrived here yesterday and as I expected to return to-day did not intend to write until I returned. Now however matters have taken such a turn that I suppose Sherman will finish up matters by to-morrow night and I shall wait to see the result.

Raleigh is a very beautiful place. The grounds are large and filled with the most beautiful spreading oaks I ever saw. Nothing has been destroyed and the people are anxious to see peace restored so that further devastation need not take place in the country. The suffering that must exist in the South the next year, even with the war ending now, will be beyond conception. People who talk now of further retalliation and punishment, except of the political leaders, either do not conceive of the suffering endured already or they are heartless and unfeeling and wish to stay at home, out of danger, whilst the punishment is being inflicted.

Love and Kisses for you and the children,

ULYS,

ALS, PPRF.

To Edwin M. Stanton

Raleigh N. C. April 26, 1865—10 p m

FOR SEC OF WAR

Jeff Davis, with his cabinet, passed into South Carolina, with the intention, no doubt of getting out of the country, either by way of Cuba or across the Mississippi. Gen Sherman sent this information by way of Wilmington yesterday to Com. Dahlgreen and Gen Gilmore for them to be on the watch

I think it will be advisable to give the same information to naval commanders on the mississippi river and all post commanders

U S GRANT
Lieut Gen

Telegrams received (2), DNA, RG 107, Telegrams Collected (Unbound); copies, *ibid.*, RG 108, Letters Sent; DLC-USG, V, 46, 76, 108. Printed as received on April 28, 1865, 9:30 A.M., in *O.R.*, I, xlvii, part 3, 311; *O.R.* (Navy), I, xxvii, 163.

To Maj. Gen. Henry W. Halleck

Raleigh N C
10 p m April 26th 1865

MAJ GEN H W HALLECK
RICHMOND

Johnston surrendered the forces in his command, embracing all from here to the Chattahoochie, to Gen Sherman on the basis agreed upon between Lee and myself for the Army of Northern Virginia—

Please order Sheridan back to Petersburg at once—If you think proper a sufficient force may go on to Danville to take possession of all munitions of war that may be stored there

U S GRANT
Lt Genl

Telegram received (on April 28, 1865, 3:00 P.M.), DNA, RG 107, Telegrams Collected (Bound); (5) *ibid.*, Telegrams Collected (Unbound); copies, *ibid.*,

RG 108, Letters Sent; DLC-USG, V, 46, 76, 108. Printed as received on April 28, 9:30 A.M., in *O.R.*, I, xlvi, part 3, 954; *ibid.*, I, xlvii, part 3, 312. All versions of this telegram except those received in Washington have a final sentence instructing that a copy be sent to the secretary of war.

On April 26, 7:30 P.M., USG telegraphed to Secretary of War Edwin M. Stanton. "Sherman and Johnston had another interview to-day, and Johnston has surrendered on same terms as Lee accepted. I think the great bulk of the army will start for Washington overland in a few days. I will be guided by circumstances in the absence of any instructions from you. I think we will hold on here for some time." Printed as received on April 28, 10:00 A.M., *ibid.*, p. 311.

On April 26, 3:00 P.M., Maj. Gen. William T. Sherman, "Twenty Eight Miles from Raleigh," telegraphed to USG. "Genl Johnston was detained by an accident to his rail-road. We have now agreed substantially to the terms of Lees army for his at Greensboro and will sign the terms before parting. Better await my coming this evening" Telegram received (at 5:30 P.M.), DNA, RG 108, Telegrams Received; copy, DLC-USG, V, 54. *O.R.*, I, xlvii, part 3, 312. On the same day, Sherman, Durham, N. C., telegraphed to USG. "The convention is signed all right will be down in a couple of hours—" Telegram received, DNA, RG 108, Telegrams Received; copy, DLC-USG, V, 54. *O.R.*, I, xlvii, part 3, 312. The military convention specifying the terms of surrender had the signatures of Sherman and Gen. Joseph E. Johnston, and USG's endorsement "Approved." AES, DLC-William T. Sherman. *O.R.*, I, xlvii, part 3, 313.

Also on April 26, Brig. Gen. Rufus Ingalls telegraphed to Bvt. Col. Theodore S. Bowers. "The 6th Corps will be within fourteen miles of Danville to night—It has supplies to May 4th. The Engineer Brigade and Rail Road construction Corps will be at the Staunton River rebuilding the bridges tomorrow—The road from Manchester to Danville will be in running order in a few days—The Armies have about eight days forage on hand & there is an abundance in Depot here and at Burksville. The last of the 9th Corps will have embarked to night everything except Wagons" ALS (telegram sent), DNA, RG 107, Telegrams Collected (Unbound); telegram received (at 8:00 P.M.), *ibid.*, Telegrams Collected (Bound); *ibid.*, RG 108, Telegrams Received. *O.R.*, I, xlvi, part 3, 956.

To Maj. Gen. Henry W. Halleck

[( )Cipher)   *Washington, D. C.*, Apl. 29th *18645* [*11:30* A.M.] MAJ. GEN. HALLECK, ~~WASHINGTON~~,

Four Corps of the Army in N. C. will march to aAlexandria passing near Richmond leaving Raleigh probably [o]n the 1st of May. You may order the Army of the Potomac and all the Cavalry except such as you think necessary to retain in Va. over land to the same place starting as soon as they can be got off. Let them leave all ammunition and stores of every kind except provisions and forage behind or to be sent by water. ~~I hope the troops will come through in good order and without committing any acts of plunder or violence~~.

U. S. GRANT

Lt. Gn.

ALS (telegram sent), DNA, RG 107, Telegrams Collected (Bound); telegram sent, *ibid.*; telegram received, *ibid.*, Telegrams Collected (Unbound). *O.R.*, I, xlvi, part 3, 1005. On April 29, 1865, noon, USG again telegraphed to Maj. Gen. Henry W. Halleck. "Gen. Sheridan need not accompany his Cavalry across the Country but may return here by water with his Staff so soon as he sees his Cavalry started. All his Hd Qrs. escort, wagons & ambulances had better cross the Country. Foraging off the Country and all destruction of property I hope will be avoided." ALS (telegram sent), DNA, RG 107, Telegrams Collected (Bound); telegram sent, *ibid.*; telegram received, *ibid.*, Telegrams Collected (Unbound). *O.R.*, I, xlvi, part 3, 1005.

On April 30, 2:00 P.M., USG telegraphed to Halleck. "If Gen. Sheridan can be sent here immediately please send him and place Gen. Crooke in command of all the Cavalry." ALS (telegram sent), DNA, RG 107, Telegrams Collected (Bound); telegram sent, *ibid.*; telegrams received (2), *ibid.*, Telegrams Collected (Unbound). *O.R.*, I, xlvi, part 3, 1016. At 4:00 P.M., Halleck telegraphed to USG. "Orders have been sent to Genl Meade to move to Alexandria, & the same will be given to Genl Sheridan as soon as he reaches Petersburg. On further consultation with Genl Ord I am more fully convinced of the policy of withdrawal of the twenty fifth corps from Virginia Their conduct recently has been even worse than I supposed yesterday." ALS (telegram sent), DNA, RG 107, Telegrams Collected (Unbound); telegram received, *ibid.*; (at 6:00 P.M.) *ibid.*, Telegrams Collected (Bound); *ibid.*, RG 108, Telegrams Received. *O.R.*, I, xlvi, part 3, 1016. See telegram to Maj. Gen. Henry W. Halleck, April 30, 1865.

To Julia Dent Grant

———

Washington Apl. 29th *1865*

DEAR JULIA,

I have just returned after a pleasant trip to Raleigh N. C. where Gn. Sherman sucseeded in bringing Johnston to terms which are perfectly satisfactory to me and I hope will be well received by the country. I have not yet been able to look over the papers to see what has transpired in my absence. As your letters have been forwarded to Raleigh I do not know whether you have moved yet or are talking of doing so.[1] I certainly shall be able to go home within a few days but before doing so some orders looking to the reduction of the Army, and expenses of the Nation generally, must be attended to.

Love and Kisses for you and the children.

Ulys.

ALS, DLC-USG.

1. On April 29, 1865, George H. Stuart, Philadelphia, wrote to Julia Dent Grant. "It gives me great pleasure to inform you that after unlooked for delays, the dwelling presented to your honored husband on the 2nd January last, is now ready for your occupancy, The Committee will be most happy to have you take possession of the house No 2009 Chestnut St on Monday next May 1st, or on such other day as may be most convenient, We shall be pleased to have you communicate to Mr Knight the bearer of this note at what time you propose leaving for our City," ALS, USG 3.

To Maj. Gen. Napoleon J. T. Dana

___

(Cipher)   Washington, Apl 30th 1865 [*1:00* P.M.]
Maj. Gen. Dana, Vicksburg Miss.

Station troops at Rodney or that vicinity at once, with Cavalry to patroll the river, and prevent all rebels from crossing ~~the river~~. It is probable Davis and his Cabinet will try to cross. If they do it will be between the mouth of Big Black and Natchez. Call upon the Navy for co operation and make every preparation to intercept him if he should. Notify commander at Baton Rouge to the same effect and communicate here your action.

U. S. Grant
Lt. Gn.

ALS (telegram sent), DNA, RG 107, Telegrams Collected (Bound); telegram sent, *ibid.*; copies, *ibid.*, RG 108, Letters Sent; DLC-USG, V, 46, 76, 108. *O.R.*, I, xlviii, part 2, 248; (misdated May 1, 1865, and with variant text) *ibid.*, I, xlix, part 2, 557. On May 4, Maj. Gen. Napoleon J. T. Dana telegraphed to USG. "I have the honor to acknowlidge the receipt of your telegram of the first inst and in reply to State that the dispositions ordered therein had already been made by me and in addition Cavalry had been stationed at Fort Adams & Tunica" Telegram received (on May 8, 11:45 P.M.), DNA, RG 107, Telegrams Collected (Bound); *ibid.*, RG 108, Telegrams Received; copy, DLC-USG, V, 54. *O.R.*, I, xlviii, part 2, 309.

On April 29, 9:00 A.M., Bvt. Brig. Gen. Benjamin J. Sweet, Chicago, telegraphed to Secretary of War Edwin M. Stanton. "W. E. Wood formerly of Clyde

Wayne Co. New York refers to Jas Watson of same place resident last six years at Houston Texas reports that he crossed the Miss. river at Bruinsburg near Rodney fifty or sixty miles below Vicksburg on the 24th Feby last   That this point is a general crossing place for rebels & contraband articles, with knowledge and aid of gunboats number nine & Rattler patrolling river   thinks Jeff Davis can & will cross there unless intercepted   desires his name not to be used— Intelligent and seems truthful—" Telegram received (at 1:30 P.M.), DNA, RG 108, Telegrams Received; copy, DLC-USG, V, 54.

To Maj. Gen. Henry W. Halleck

(Cipher)   Washington Apl. 30th 1865 [*11:30* A.M.]
MAJ. GEN. HALLECK, ~~WASHINGTON~~ RICHMOND VA.

You may retain the 6th Corps for the present. Put the 25th in a Camp of instruction either at Bermuda Hundred or at City Point until some disposition is made of them for defense on the seacoast. Establish the best labor system you can to employ the idle and prevent their becoming a burthen upon the Govt.

U. S. GRANT
Lt. Gen.

ALS (telegram sent), DNA, RG 107, Telegrams Collected (Bound); telegram sent, *ibid.*; telegrams received (2), *ibid.*, Telegrams Collected (Unbound). Printed as received at 3:30 P.M. in *O.R.*, I, xlvi, part 3, 1016. On April 29, 1865, Maj. Gen. Henry W. Halleck had telegraphed to USG. "General Ord represents that want of discipline and good officers in the twenty fifth (25) corps renders it a very improper force for the preservation of order in this Dept. A number of cases of atrocious rape by these men have already occurred. Their influence on the colored population is also reported to be bad. I therefore hope you will remove them to garrison forts or for service on the southern coast, and substitute a corps from the Army of the Potomac (say, Wrights) temporarily. It seems very necessary to prevent the rush of the negro population into Richmond and to organize to a labor system in the interior immediately with the planting season, which will be over in two (2) or three (3) weeks. aUnless this is provided for there will be a famine in this state. fFor this purpose I shall occupy Fredericksburg Orange or Charlottesville Lynchburg and a few other points. To perform this duty properly requires officers and men of more intelligence and character than we have in the 25th Corps. I think that in a very short time the 24th Corps can do all the duty required. Affairs here are settling down quietly, more than five thousand people have offered to take the amnesty oath. aAmong these are many of Lees paroled officers. Four (4) offices have been opened for that purpose and all are densely crowded,   The rebel feeling in Virginia is utterly dead and with proper management can never be revived. As evidence of this the recusant clergymen have offered to pray for the President of the United States and to-

morrow all the Churches in Richmond will be reopened" Telegram received
(at 12:00 P.M.), DNA, RG 107, Telegrams Collected (Bound); *ibid.*, Telegrams Collected (Unbound); *ibid.*, RG 108, Telegrams Received; copy, DLC-
USG, V, 54. *O.R.*, I, xlvi, part 3, 1005–6.

On April 29, Maj. Gen. Edward O. C. Ord wrote to USG. "The Enclosed
was left me for you—I now send it—My impression is that as soon as excitement
will permit it The Officers of Genl Lees Army here had better get away—They
are here a tax on the Community (indirectly, in some instances) and scattered
would be less apt to breed discontent than together" ALS, DNA, RG 108,
Letters Received. *O.R.*, I, xlvi, part 3, 1013. Ord enclosed a letter of April 25
from Gen. Robert E. Lee to USG. "I have awaited your arrival in Richmond to
propose that the men and officers of the army of N. Va., captured or surrendered
on the 2d and 6th of April, or since that time, may be granted the same terms as
given to those surrendered by me on the 9th. I see no benefit that will result by
retaining them in prison; but on the contrary, think good may be accomplished
by returning them to their homes. Indeed, if all now held as prisoners of war
were liberated in the same manner, I think it would be advantageous. Should
there, however, be objections to this course, I would ask that exceptions be made
in favor of the invalid officers and men, and that they be allowed to return to
their homes on parole. I call your attention particularly to Genl. Ewell, the
members of the Reserves, Local Defence Troops, Naval Battalion &c. The Local
Troops were not performing military duty, and the Naval Battalion fell in the
line of march of the army for subsistence and protection. Understanding that
you may not reach Richmond for some days, I take the liberty to forward this
application for your consideration." Copy, ViHi. *O.R.*, I, xlvi, part 3, 1013.

On May 1, Halleck telegraphed to USG. "Would it not be well to retain here
all Regular troops of Meades & Shermans Commands & to fill them up with
recruits preparatory to mustering out the Volunteers? Many of the latter express
a strong desire to get home in time to put in their Crops—I understood from the
Secy of War that when Sherman left North Carolina that state fell within my
Command. Is it so understood still—" Telegram received (at 11:00 A.M.),
DNA, RG 107, Telegrams Collected (Bound); *ibid.*, RG 108, Telegrams Received; copy, DLC-USG, V, 54. *O.R.*, I, xlvi, part 3, 1055.

At 11:50 P.M., USG telegraphed to Halleck. "Please order Gens. Foster &
~~Kautz~~ Harris 24th Corps and Kautz 25th Corps to Washington to be here by
Thursday next. ~~They are wanted for a Military Commission.~~" ALS (telegram
sent), DNA, RG 107, Telegrams Collected (Bound); telegram sent, *ibid.*; telegram received (marked as sent at 11:40 P.M.), *ibid.*, Telegrams Collected
(Unbound). *O.R.*, I, xlvi, part 3, 1055. On May 2, Halleck endorsed a copy of
this telegram to Ord. AES, Ord Papers, CU-B. The officers requested served on
the commission trying the Lincoln conspirators.

On May 3, Halleck telegraphed to USG. "Genl Sheridan's command will
reach Petersburg to day. It will require some days to refit. Genl Sheridan has
been ordered to report to you in Washington." ALS (telegram sent), DNA, RG
107, Telegrams Collected (Unbound); telegram received, *ibid.*, Telegrams Collected (Bound); (at 1:00 P.M.) *ibid.*, RG 108, Telegrams Received. *O.R.*, I,
xlvi, part 3, 1073. On the same day, Maj. Gen. Philip H. Sheridan telegraphed
to USG. "A telegram from Maj: Genl Halleck directs me to turn over the Cavalry
to Maj: Genl. Crook and report to you in person at Washington. If there is no
urgent necessity for my reporting to you at once, I would like to remain here

for three or four (3 or 4) days to get in all the reports of the last Campaign, and to make out my own." Telegram sent, DNA, RG 107, Telegrams Collected (Unbound); telegram received, *ibid.*; (at 1:00 P.M.) *ibid.*, Telegrams Collected (Bound); *ibid.*, RG 108, Telegrams Received. *O.R.*, I, xlvi, part 3, 1076. On May 4, Brig. Gen. John A. Rawlins telegraphed to USG, Philadelphia. "Gen. Sheridan desires to remain three or four days at Petersburg for the purpose of getting up his reports. Can he do so." Telegrams sent (2), DNA, RG 107, Telegrams Collected (Bound); copies, *ibid.*, RG 108, Letters Sent; DLC-USG, V, 46, 76, 108. *O.R.*, I, xlvi, part 3, 1082. On May 5, USG telegraphed to Rawlins. "Genl Sheridan can remain in Petersburg as long as necessary to get up his reports." Telegram received (at 11:30 A.M.), DNA, RG 107, Telegrams Collected (Bound); *ibid.*, RG 108, Telegrams Received; copy, DLC-USG, V, 54. See *O.R.*, I, xlvi, part 3, 1087.

On May 4, 12:30 P.M., Rawlins telegraphed to Sheridan. "Maj Gen Wright ʜ will be directed to furnish you a ̶C̶o̶p̶y̶ ̶o̶f̶ his official report." Telegram sent, DNA, RG 107, Telegrams Collected (Bound); telegram received, *ibid.*, Telegrams Collected (Unbound). *O.R.*, I, xlvi, part 3, 1087. See *ibid.*, p. 1102. On May 8, USG endorsed a message of April 14 from Sheridan concerning the report of Maj. Gen. Horatio G. Wright. "Respy. referred to Maj Gen Meade, comdg. A of P. and attention invited to enclosed copy of despatch, of date 6th. inst. to Maj Gen Wright, comdg. 6th Army Corps; also, to copy of despatch to Maj Gen Sheridan of date April 6th. 1865. This Corps was not, by any order, at any time detached from your command, but under my instructions to M G. Sheridan, in answer to information, I had just recieved from him, he was authorized to assume the command of this Corps when it joined him, and it is considered a matter of simple justice that its action while under his command be reported to him. In your official report you will report the whole of the operations of that Corps on the 6th of April 1865 & Gen Wright will be required to make to you a report of the whole days operations, including the battle of Sailors Creek" Copies, DLC-USG, V, 58; DLC-Philip H. Sheridan. See *O.R.*, I, xlvi, part 3, 733.

To Maj. Gen. Joseph J. Reynolds

(Cipher)   Washington Apl. 30th/65 [*11:30* A.M.]
MAJ. GN. J. J. REYNOLDS, LITTLE ROCK, ARK.

You may release the prisoners you have on their taking the Amnesty oath and oath of allegiance exercising your discretion about those who should not have this privilege extended to them. Invite every one to lay down their arms on the same terms except you will only parole those who do not come within the Presidents Amnesty Proclamation.

U. S. GRANT
Lt. Gn

ALS (telegram sent), DNA, RG 107, Telegrams Collected (Bound); telegram sent, *ibid.*; copies, *ibid.*, RG 108, Letters Sent; DLC-USG, V, 46, 76, 108. *O.R.*, I, xlviii, part 2, 248; *ibid.*, II, viii, 521. On April 20, 1865, Maj. Gen. Joseph J. Reynolds telegraphed to Maj. Gen. Henry W. Halleck. "There are nearly 300 prisoners of war confined here, about two thirds of whom have heretofore applied to take the amnesty oath and of course would not be sent south when exchanged. The remainder have now applied to be released on parole believing the cause of the rebellion hopeless. What shall be done with them? A few desperate characters should be retained in prison." Telegram received (on April 25, 5:00 P.M.), DNA, RG 108, Telegrams Received; copy, DLC-USG, V, 54. *O.R.*, II, viii, 501.

To Maj. Gen. George H. Thomas

Washington Apl. 30th 1865 [*1:00* P.M.]

MAJ. GEN. THOMAS, NASHVILLE TENN.

Every effort should now be made to induce all armed bands of men in Tenn. Alabama and everywhere in reach of your command, to come in and surrender their Arms on the terms made by Lee & Johnston. Send out under Flag of Truce a summons to all bands you know of and report here the course you pursue. Make every effort to obtain intelligence of Davis Movements in the South and spare no pains in setting an expedition on foot to ketch him if he should be heard from.

U. S. GRANT
Lt. Gn.

ALS (telegram sent), USMA; telegram sent, DNA, RG 107, Telegrams Collected (Bound); copies, *ibid.*, RG 108, Letters Sent; *ibid.*, RG 393, Dept. of the Cumberland, Telegrams Received; DLC-USG, V, 46, 76, 108. *O.R.*, I, xlix, part 2, 522. On April 30, 1865, Maj. Gen. George H. Thomas telegraphed to USG. "Your cipher despatch of one (1) P M today just recd & will be attended to at once   I will despatch more fully tomorrow" Telegram received (at 7:30 P.M.), DNA, RG 107, Telegrams Collected (Bound); (at 7:20 P.M.) *ibid.*, RG 108, Telegrams Received; copies, *ibid.*, RG 393, Dept. of the Cumberland, Telegrams Sent; (misdated April 20) DLC-USG, V, 54. *O.R.*, I, xlix, part 2, 523. On May 1, Thomas telegraphed to USG. "In accordance with your instructions of one P M yesterday I have directed all my local commanders to send under flag of truce a summons to all armed band of men operating near their command, or who may be nearest them than to any other federal command, to come in and surrender on the same terms made by Lee and Johnston. əOn the twenty seventh (27) of April I directed to Gen's Stoneman, Wilson & Stedman to send out scouts & ascertain if possible the route Jeff Davis had taken & be prepared to pursue him on the first information of his whereabouts and use every exertion to capture him. I also gave the same instructions to Genls Granger Hatch and Washburne on the twenty eighth (28) & informed Maj Gen Canby & Admiral Lee that it was reported that Davis was endeavoring to escape across the Mississippi; that they might make arrangements for his capture Genl Stoneman has started his Cavy for South Carolina to scout down the east side of the Savannah River as far as possible as towards Augusta & had given Col Palmer instructions to forward a copy of the orders he recd to Genl Wilson for his guidance. These instructions were also forwarded to Maj Gen Wilson by Col Woodward ~~by~~ via Chattanooga. I ~~will~~ think it will be impossible for Davis to escape across the Country between this and Macon Montgomery or Vicksburg" Telegram received (at 7:10 P.M.), DNA, RG 107, Telegrams Collected (Bound); (at 7:20 P.M.) *ibid.*, RG 108, Telegrams Received; copies, *ibid.*, RG 393, Dept. of the Cumberland, Telegrams Sent; DLC-USG, V, 54. Printed as sent at 4:00 P.M. in *O.R.*, I, xlix, part 2, 549.

On April 29, 8:00 P.M., USG telegraphed to Thomas. "I have ordered Maj. Gn. J. E. Smith to Memphis to releive Maj. Gn. Washburn in command of West Tenn. He will report to you by letter." ALS (telegram sent), DNA, RG 107, Telegrams Collected (Bound); telegram sent, *ibid.*; copies, *ibid.*, RG 108, Letters Sent; DLC-USG, V, 46, 76, 108. *O.R.*, I, xlix, part 2, 514. As received by Thomas, however, "General Jeff. C. Davis" appeared in place of "Maj. Gn. J. E. Smith." Copy, DNA, RG 393, Dept. of the Cumberland, Telegrams Received. On April 30, Thomas telegraphed to USG. "Brig Gen B S Roberts is on his way to Memphis in compliance with Genl Orders from the War Dept Genl Davis being ordered to relieve Gen Washburn Gen Roberts will not be needed there He wishes to be ordered to report to Gen Pope [*if*] Gen Pope should be sent with a force to Texas The troops of the fourth Corps have arrived & are Encamped near this City The transportation will arrive by the End of this week" Telegram received (at 7:00 P.M.), *ibid.*, RG 107, Telegrams Collected (Bound); copies, *ibid.*, RG 393, Dept. of the Cumberland, Telegrams Sent; DLC-USG, V, 54. *O.R.*, I, xlix, part 2, 523–24.

On the same day, Thomas telegraphed to USG. "I forward the following just recd from Maj Gen Stedman for your information 'Near Dalton Ga April thirtieth (30) 1865 I have just met Col Merritt returning from Calhoun where he met Gen Woffard Confed. States Army who gave Col Woodall entrusted with your dispatch to Gen Wilson, an Escort & Rail Road transportation from Atlanta to macon where Gen Wilson now is The Confed forces under Cobb & Smith are surrendered to Gen Wilson who holds Macon with Cobb & Smith as prisoners Gen Woffard is willing to surrender himself & staff & all the force he can but is apprehensive if he surrenders most of his force will scatter to the hills Signed JAMES B STEEDMAN Maj Gen' Col Woodall was bearer of orders from me to Gen Wilson to insist on the Surrender of Macon with the Confed Genls Cobb & Smith. Their troops & all public stores in Macon at the time when Gen Shermans order to withdraw from before Macon reached him before insisting on the Surrender of Gen Woffard I thought it best to inform you of his apprehensions that most of his force will scatter to the hills & become bushwhackers in which Event it might become necessary to throw a federal force into that region to preserve quiet I have sufficient force for that purpose if it be deemed to be better ~~than~~ to request him to surrender than to permit him to preserve the peace of the Section—His force is an insignificant one & he assures me through Gen Judah that he is there for the sole purpose of preserving order until the State of Georgia can take the proper steps to return to her allegiance" Telegram received (at 7:30 P.M.), DNA, RG 107, Telegrams Collected (Bound); *ibid.*, RG 108, Telegrams Received; copies, *ibid.*, RG 393, Dept. of the Cumberland, Telegrams Sent; DLC-USG, V, 54. Printed as sent at 6:00 P.M. in *O.R.*, I, xlix, part 2, 523, 527. At 10:30 P.M., USG telegraphed to Thomas. "I think it advisable to get the surrender of Gen. Wofford and his men. Any that continue acts of hostilitiesy [h]ereafter will be regarded as outlaws and so treated. You can exercise your own judgement about sending more force to the front to protect that country but do not send any portion of the 4th Corps." ALS (telegram sent), DNA, RG 107, Telegrams Collected (Bound); telegram sent, *ibid.*; copies, *ibid.*, RG 108, Letters Sent; (misdated May 1) *ibid.*, RG 393, Dept. of the Cumberland, Telegrams Received; DLC-USG, V, 46, 76, 108. *O.R.*, I, xlix, part 2, 523.

On May 1, 10:00 P.M., USG telegraphed to Thomas. "Relieve Gn. Meredith from command at Paducah and direct him to report by letter to the A. G. for orders. Name his successor yourself. It is not necessary that a general officer should take his place." ALS (telegram sent), DNA, RG 107, Telegrams Collected (Bound); telegram sent, *ibid.*; copies, *ibid.*, RG 108, Letters Sent; (misdated May 2) *ibid.*, RG 393, Dept. of the Cumberland, Telegrams Received; DLC-USG, V, 46, 76, 108. *O.R.*, I, xlix, part 2, 549. On May 2, Thomas telegraphed to USG. "I have detained Col C. H. Carleton eighty ninth (89) O V, I & Capt fourth (4) U S Infty to relieve Brig Gen Meredith in command of Paducah" Telegram received (at 5:00 P.M.), DNA, RG 107, Telegrams Collected (Bound); *ibid.*, RG 108, Telegrams Received; copies, *ibid.*, RG 393, Dept. of the Cumberland, Telegrams Sent; DLC-USG, V, 54. *O.R.*, I, xlix, part 2, 564.

On May 3, Thomas twice telegraphed to USG, the second time at 4:00 P.M. "I forward the following despatch just recd from Maj Gen Stoneman for your information   as I have several days since directed Gen Stoneman to use every means in his power to capture Davis & as he has Col Palmer after him I have much hope of his success" "Are paroled prisoners of war surrendered by Lee now to be permitted to come to their former homes in Tenn? Many have come here with orders granting them that privilege made from your HdQrs. in the field in Virginia. Have I authority to release on parole prisoners of war in prison & hospitals in this Dept upon their taking the oath of allegiance? These prisoners were all captured in battle. Among them are Brig. Gen. Quarles of Tenn & Brig. Gen. Sears of La. both severely wounded." Telegrams received (at 5:00 P.M. and 8:00 P.M.), DNA, RG 107, Telegrams Collected (Bound); (at 4:50 P.M. and 7:50 P.M.) *ibid.*, RG 108, Telegrams Received; copies, *ibid.*, RG 393, Dept. of the Cumberland, Telegrams Sent; DLC-USG, V, 54. *O.R.*, I, xlix, part 2, 581. The enclosure in the first telegram is *ibid.*, p. 570.

Calendar

1865, FEB. 21. To Secretary of War Edwin M. Stanton transmitting information copied from Richmond newspapers.—*O.R.*, I, xlvii, part 2, 511. Similar telegrams of Feb. 27, March 3, 4, 7, 9, 10, 16 (addressed to Asst. Secretary of War Charles A. Dana), 20, 23, 24, and 29 (the last sent by Lt. Col. Theodore S. Bowers) are *ibid.*, I, xlvi, part 2, 824, 901, 914; *ibid.*, I, xlvi, part 3, 3, 51–52; *ibid.*, I, xlvii, part 2, 595–96, 659–60, 712–13, 753, 968; *ibid.*, I, xlvii, part 3, 3; *ibid.*, I, xlix, part 2, 120–21.

1865, FEB. 21, 1:50 P.M. Brig. Gen. Israel Vogdes, Norfolk, to USG. "A very intelligent man from Richmond, formerly a clerk, came in to-day. He represents the woods full of deserters and negroes, and says the evacuation [of] Richmond will disintegrate Lee's army. He is well posted in reference to railroad supplies, &c., around Richmond. His name is Charles Caulin. Do you desire to see him"—ALS (telegram sent), DNA, RG 94, War Records Office, Army of the Potomac; telegram received, *ibid.* *O.R.*, I, xlvi, part 2, 618. On the same day, Lt. Col. Theodore S. Bowers telegraphed to Vogdes. "Gen Grant directs me to acknowledge the receipt of your telegram, and to request you to send up Mr. Calnlin as you suggested." —Telegram received, DNA, RG 107, Telegrams Collected (Unbound). On Feb. 23 and 26, Vogdes sent information from deserters to USG.—*O.R.*, I, xlvi, part 2, 665, 710.

1865, FEB. 21. John Bigelow, chargé d'affaires, Paris, to USG. "The writer of the enclosed note, the distinguished Aeronaut Godard has requested me to take charge of it and to transmit it to you. I only consented to comply with his request upon being satisfied from his personal explanations that he has made some improvements in the art to which he has devoted all his mature life which promise to be susceptible of useful application to military operations. Mr Godard proposes to send me a detailed exposition of the new system of which he gives a glimpse in this note. I will see that it reaches you by the first opportunity after it comes to hand."—Copy, DNA, RG 84, France, Miscellaneous Letters Sent. On Feb. 20, Eugène Godard, "Aéronaute de l'Empereur," wrote to USG offering his services as a balloonist.—ALS (in French), USG 3. On March 3, Lt. Col. Adam Badeau wrote to Godard declining the offer.—ADf (in French), *ibid.*

1865, FEB. 22. To Secretary of War Edwin M. Stanton. "The following items are taken from todays Richmond papers. Our readers will Cheerfully forego their desire to be apprised of the pending military movements in the Carolinas when they are informed that our reticense is in Compliance with wishes which have been Communicated to all the newspapers. A report Comes from southwestern Va that Gillian with forty five hundred yankees is advancing into upper East Tennessee Their advance being now north of Greenville It is believed to be their intention to try & occupy the whole of the state at the time of the Coming Election Gilmores brigade of Kentucky Cavalry had an engagement last saturday at Balls Bridge in Lee Co Va.

twenty five miles north of Cumberland Gap resulting in a splendid victory to our arms. Our loss was not over 60 Killed & wounded. Rumors Can no more be stopped from Circulation Than sparks from going upwards There may be some truth in every rumor but it is hardly probable than a tithe of what one hears has really any foundation in fact: They start nobody Knows where or how but every one helps them on with more or less of amplification until like the snow ball what was once easily handled and even Cast from one to another it has by Continual accretions grown to such gigantic proportion as to tax the strength of the whole Community to stand up under it. By one man Beauregard is reported to have gone crazy—mind very much the worse for wear body dragged down by great exertion by another he has asked to be relieved By a third sherman is between Beauregard & Charlotte & by another the devil is to pay generally and the Confederacy is gone up. Put not your faith in rumor and do not permit yourselves to be very much frightened—The negro soldier bill—Yesterday during the consideration in secret session by the confederate senate of the bill to raise two hundred thousand negro soldiers a motion was made for its indefinite postponement & which was agreed to by a majority of one—This is equivalent to laying the bill upon the table but it can be called up at any time and we have reason to Know that it will be again taken up within the next few days & it will be passed—The measure is delayed not because of a want of strength on the part of its advocates but for a specific purpose"—Telegram received (as transmitted to Maj. Gen. John G. Parke and corps commanders), DNA, RG 94, War Records Office, Army of the Potomac; copies, *ibid.*, RG 393, 9th Army Corps, 1st Div., 3rd Brigade, Telegrams Received; *ibid.*, 2nd Div., Telegrams Received; Meade Papers, PHi; William C. Banning, Silver Spring, Md. Incomplete in *O.R.*, I, xlvi, part 2, 628–29; (incomplete) *ibid.*, I, xlvii, part 2, 526.

1865, FEB. 22.   To Cyrenius B. Denio, Washington. "Military Authorities Will please pass the Hon. C. B. Denio and I. H. Brown, from Washington D. C. to City Point Va."—Telegram sent, DNA, RG 107, Telegrams Collected (Unbound). Denio served three non-consecutive terms in the Ill. House of Representatives (1849–57) while living in Galena, and was later employed at Mare Island, Calif. Letters in DLC-Robert T. Lincoln; Lincoln, *Works*, VII, 401; *O.R.*, I, l, part 2, 115. An article appearing in the *Chicago Journal*, describing Denio as "an old personal acquaintance" of USG and reporting Denio's comments after spending three days at USG's hd. qrs., was reprinted in the *Galena Gazette*, March 6, 1865.

1865, FEB. 23.   To Secretary of War Edwin M. Stanton. "Col Fred. Winthrop 5th NewYork Vols Brevetted Brig Genl, and in command of a brigade, has not as yet been confirmed it is to be hoped he will be confirmed as he is a valuable Officer who cannot easily be replaced"—Copy, DNA, RG 94, ACP, S208 CB 1865. On March 1, Bvt. Lt. Col. Samuel F. Chalfin, AGO, wrote to USG. "I have the honor to acknowledge the receipt of your communication of the 23d ultimo, relative to the confirmation of Col. Fred. Winthrop, 5th New York Vols. as Brevet Brigadier General U. S. Vols. and to inform you in response that this officer was confirmed on the 20th ultimo. His commission will be forwarded to him as soon as signed."—Copy, *ibid.*, Letters Sent, Commissions and Returns. *O.R.*, I, xlvi, part 2, 770.

1865, FEB. 23. USG endorsement. "Respy. returned to the Hon W. D. McIndoe, M. C. 6th District Wisconsin, and his attention invited to endorsement hereon, and accompanying report of Insp Genl Schriver"—Copy, DLC-USG, V, 58. Written on a letter of U.S. Representative Walter D. McIndoe of Wis. concerning the treatment of enlisted men of the 38th Wis. by the officers.—*Ibid.*

1865, FEB. 24. To President Abraham Lincoln. "The sentence in the case of George Maynard forty sixth (46th) New York Vols has been suspended and the papers in the case were forwarded to you this morning.—" —Telegram received (at 4:45 P.M.), DNA, RG 107, Telegrams Collected (Bound); copies, *ibid.*, RG 108, Letters Sent; DLC-USG, V, 46, 74, 108. On Feb. 23, 11:25 A.M., Lincoln had telegraphed to USG. "Suspend execution of death sentence of George A. Maynard, Co. A 46th New-York Veteran Volunteers until further orders and forward record for examination."— Telegram sent, DNA, RG 107, Telegrams Collected (Bound); telegram received, *ibid.*, RG 393, Army of the Potomac, Miscellaneous Letters Received. Lincoln, *Works*, VIII, 313. See *ibid.*, p. 405. USG forwarded this telegram to Maj. Gen. John G. Parke.

1865, FEB. 24. To Secretary of War Edwin M. Stanton transmitting information copied from Richmond newspapers.—*O.R.*, I, xlvi, part 2, 668–69.

1865, FEB. 24. Asst. Secretary of War Charles A. Dana to USG. "I am directed by the Secretary of War to transmit for your consideration the inclosed extract from a recent letter submitted to the War Department by the Honorable Thomas Ewing, father-in-law of Major General Sherman, and father of Brigadier Generals Hugh and Thomas Ewing."—LS, DNA, RG 108, Letters Received. *O.R.*, I, xlvi, part 2, 669. Dana enclosed an extract from a letter of Feb. 22 from Thomas Ewing to Secretary of War Edwin M. Stanton. "Suppose Lee should determine to abandon Richmond, where will he go?—Will he not march his whole force upon Washington, leaving only enough for pickets and to amuse Grant and disguise his own movements. Is Washington so well guarded that it will resist the first onslaught? He could not hold it, but he might hope something from temporary possession of the capitol and insignia of sovereignty, and, at any rate, if he fell, to fall with eclat—and, indeed, he might hope to rouse the dormant energies of Northern sympathizers by so bold a stroke if successful even for a day. It is a contingency to be guarded against—indeed I do not know what else remains to him that will not involve disgraceful defeat and surrender.—"—Copy, DNA, RG 108, Letters Received. *O.R.,* I, xlvi, part 2, 669. Ewing's original letter is in DNA, RG 107, Letters Received.

1865, FEB. 25. Maj. Gen. Henry W. Halleck endorsement. "Respectfully referred to Lt Genl Grant for his information"—AES, DNA, RG 108, Letters Received. Written on a letter of Feb. 23 from Bvt. Maj. Gen. Montgomery C. Meigs to Secretary of War Edwin M. Stanton discussing the excessive number of horses sent to the Shenandoah Valley.—Copy, *ibid.* *O.R.,* I, xlvi, part 2, 656.

1865, FEB. 25. Moses Taylor, New York City, to USG. "The Citizens of New-York have confided to us the grateful duty of transmitting the proceedings of a Meeting held on the 22nd instant, in which they offer their cordial congratulations to the Country, on the recent successes of the Union Arms. In the performance of this duty, we beg to assure you of our hearty concurrence in the sentiments of the Resolutions and our admiration of the skill and gallantry evinced by the forces engaged in upholding the Flag of the Nation."—LS, USG 3. Copies of the resolution are *ibid.*

1865, FEB. 26. USG endorsement. "Respectfully forwarded to the Secretary of War, recommended and approved"—ES, DNA, RG 94, ACP, F134 CB 1865. Written on a letter of Feb. 25 from Brig. Gen. Robert S. Foster to President Abraham Lincoln recommending the appointment of Col. Harrison S. Fairchild, 89th N. Y., as brig. gen.—LS, *ibid.*

1865, FEB. 26, 10:15 A.M. To Maj. Gen. John G. Parke. "A party has just left here on the Cars for the front will you please send a spring wagon to the Station at which the cars stop for your head Qrs to report to Capt Robinet of my staff"—Telegram received (at 10:15 A.M.), DNA, RG 393, Army of the Potomac, Miscellaneous Letters Received.

1865, FEB. 26. Maj. Gen. Andrew A. Humphreys to USG. "There is a matter seriously affecting myself and other officers who hold commissions in the Regular Army and in the Volunteer Service, respecting which I wish to present my impressions, although the subject is one of such delicacy that I question even now whether silence may not be better than discussion. I refer to the recent promotions to the rank of Genl. Officer by Bvt. in the Regular Army, by which I find so low an estimate placed upon services in the field and so high a one upon the subordinate administrative duties, Chiefly not in the field. I have served three years continuously in the field without relaxation, and thought I had at least done something as a soldier and as a General of division. I did not suppose that at the end of the war I should find myself thrown back into my old place in the Engineers with simply my old rank, without even that Bvt. rank which I should have gained in any war of the same duration serving with my regular commission;

much less did I suppose that at the same time that I retired from the rank of a Genl. Officer in the service of the U S. to the rank of my old commission, I should find officers whom I had left in the Administrative Corps of the Army of the same rank as, or of less rank than, myself, and who have not served in the field, bearing the rank of Genl. Officers in the Regular Army, conferred on them by Bvt. for Bureau or exclusively administrative duties. Yet, it is plain from what is now occurring, that such must be the conclusion. I confess that the view which has been opened to me by a sight of the list of Bvts. in the Regular Army has been humiliating in the extreme, for I must believe that the duties I have been performing have been deliberately adjudged by the highest authorities to be inferior to those of Administration in subordinate branches of the Government, unless indeed, through some cause, no representation concerning the field services of myself and others have reached the Government. I beg that I may not be misunderstood. I raise no objection whatever to conferring such promotions as those I have noticed, but to the omission to confer others, an omission keenly felt by other officers as well as by myself. The brevets that have been given should follow not precede the promotion of those in the field. It is no answer to my statement to say that when the time arrives for officers of the Regular Army to return to their Corps and regts. the discrepancies in their positions will be rectified. To assert that the wrong will be rectified is no justification of its commission. If one of the two classes of officers must wait for reward it certainly should not be the class that fights the battles."—ALS, PHi. *O.R.*, I, xlvi, part 2, 707–8. A heavily cancelled draft of this letter, dated Jan. 28, is in the Humphreys Papers, PHi.

1865, FEB. 27, 12:30 P.M. To Secretary of War Edwin M. Stanton. "Since there has been Brevet's given to Asst, Adj't Quartermaster &C, in Washington ought not Col, Hardie to have it also? I telegraph this because I thought possibly it not being recommended by any one you may not have thought about it,"—Telegram, copies, DLC-USG, V, 46, 74, 108; DNA, RG 108, Letters Sent. James A. Hardie was appointed bvt. brig. gen. as of March 3.

1865, FEB. 27. J. S. Taggart, Norfolk, to USG. "If you should have an occasion to cross James river above Richmond with an Army, you will find a good Ford 75½ miles above Richmond by the Canal, and 3½ miles below scotts ferry. I am personally acquainted with this ford, and the water at ordeniry tide is not over two feet deep. I take the liberty to give you this information thinking perhaps it might be of service to you"—ALS, DNA, RG 108, Letters Received.

1865, FEB. 28. To Maj. Gen. John M. Schofield. "Please order the three (3) Companies of the first (1st) Connecticut Artillery that accompanied Genl Terry on the Fort Fisher expedition to rejoin their Reg't here without delay."—Telegram received (press), DNA, RG 107, Telegrams Collected

(Bound); copies, *ibid.*, RG 108, Letters Sent; *ibid.*, RG 393, Dept. of N. C., Telegrams Received; DLC-USG, V, 46, 74, 108.

1865, MARCH 1, 4:00 P.M. To Maj. Gen. John A. Dix. "I respectfully decline Genl Sanfords offer to furnish a Regiment for ~~G~~garrisoning Charlston We want no (3) three months men nor again do we want any ~~tor~~ troops except for such service as they may be called on to perform—"— Telegram received (at 5:00 P.M.), DNA, RG 107, Telegrams Collected (Bound); *ibid.*, RG 393, Dept. of the East, Letters Received; copies, *ibid.*, RG 108, Letters Sent; DLC-USG, V, 46, 74, 108. The same message also appears in USG's letterbooks as an endorsement by Lt. Col. Theodore S. Bowers to Secretary of War Edwin M. Stanton on a letter of Charles W. Sandford.—Copy, *ibid.*, V, 58.

1865, MARCH 1. To Lt. Col. John E. Mulford. "Please enquire of Col, Ould for Lieut, John-De-Witt Whiting 3d Ohio Vols, Captured with Straits Command, and if he can be speedily released, try and have it done"—Copies, DLC-USG, V, 46, 74, 108; DNA, RG 108, Letters Sent.

1865, MARCH 1. Lt. Col. Theodore S. Bowers to Maj. Gen. Edward O. C. Ord. "There are no spencer arms in depot here. The Ordnance officer has telegraphed to Washn to see whether they can be obtained. We can furnish you any number of Sharps carbines at once & they are regarded as a very efficient arm for sharp shooters."—Telegram received, Ord Papers, CU-B; copies, DLC-USG, V, 46, 74, 108; DNA, RG 108, Letters Sent.

1865, MARCH 1, 10:25 A.M. Lt. Col. John E. Mulford to Lt. Col. Frederick T. Dent. "Our prisoners will not be down tody, nor will they come until the water subsides I am unwilling to permit our men in their present condition to march 12 miles over such roads as we now have"—ALS (telegram sent), DNA, RG 107, Telegrams Collected (Unbound). *O.R.*, II, viii, 320.

1865, MARCH 2. USG endorsement. "Respectfully forwarded to the Secretary of War."—ES, DNA, RG 94, ACP, O24 CB 1865. Written on a letter of March 2 from Maj. Gen. Edward O. C. Ord to Brig. Gen. John A. Rawlins. "I beg to make the following nominations for promotion: Brig. Gen'l. John W. Turner U. S. Vol's. to be Maj. Gen'l. by Brevet for gallant and meritorious services—Campaign of 1864; on several ocasions before the enemy—to date from Octr. 1st 1864. Lieut. Col. Theodore Read U. S. Vols. A. A. G'l. Dep't of Va. to be Brig. Genl. by Brevet—a full recognition for gallantry before the enemy—to date from the capture of Fort Harrison, Sept. 29th 1864. Col. John E. Mulford, to be Brig. Gen'l. by Brevet for special services and highly meritorious conduct—to date from July 4th 1864. Major P. Ord, A. A. Gen'l. Vol's.—to be Lieut. Colonel by Brevet for gallant conduct in the campaign of 1864—to date from the capture of Fort

Harrison Sept. 29th 1864. Cap't. H. G. Brown A. D. C. U. S. Vols to be Major by Brevet for gallant and meritorious services in the Campaign of 1864 to date from the capture of Fort Harrison Sep't. 29th 1864. Major S. S. Seward, to be Lieut Colonel by Brevet for gallant and meritorious services in the campaign of 1864, to date from the attack on Petersburg July 30th 1864. 2nd Lieut. Tho's. G. Welles, 1st Conn. Cavalry—to be Captain by Brevet, in the Volunteers for gallant and meritorious services in the campaign of 1864—to date from the capture of Fort Harrison Sep't. 29th 1864. Capt. D. D. Wheeler, A. A. G'l. Vols.—to be Major by Brevet for gallant and meritorious services, in the campaign of 1864—to date from the capture of Fort Harrison Sept. 29th 1864. Capt.   Graves A. D. C. to Gen'l. Weitzell—to be Major by Brevet for gallant conduct during the campaign of the Summer of 1864, to date from capture of Fort Harrison Sept. 29th 1864. Lieut Col. Ed. W. Smith, Asst. Adj't. Gen'l. 25th A. C. to be Brevet Colonel for meritorious services in in the campaigns of 1863 and 1864 to date from Jan. 1st 1865. Lt. Col R. H. Jackson, Asst. Inspector General 25th Army Corps, to be Brevet Brigadier General for gallant and meritorious services in the campaign of 1864. This Officer was recommended for his Brevet by Gen. D. B. Birney, who made his case a special one for his services in the operations in September last, to date from Jany 1st 1865. Bv't. Major P. S. Michie, U. S. Engineers, to be Brevet Brig. Gen'l. for meritorious services in 1864 to date from 1st Jany 1865. Col. A. T. Voris 67th Ohio to be Brevet Brig. General for gallant and meritorious services in campaign of 1864, This Officer was also recommended by Maj. Gen. D. B. Birney, to date from 1st Jany. 1865. Capt. W. L. James A. Q. M. to be Bv't. Major for meritorious and faithfull services to date from 1st January 1865. Capt. C. E. Walbridge A. Q. M. to be Brevet Major for meritorious and faithfull services—to date from the 1st Jany. 1865. Capt. P. A. Davis, Ass't. Adj't. General to be Brevet Major, for gallant and meritorious services in campaign of 1864—to date from 1st January 1865. Capt. E. E. Lord, 3d N. Y. Vols. Commissary of Musters 24th Army Corps, to be Brevet Major for gallant and meritorious services in the campaign 1864, to date from 1st January 1865. Capt   Curry Com. Sub. to be Brevet Major and Lieut. Colonel, for long, faithfull and arduous services. Lieut. Col. M. P. Small, Com. Sub. 24th Army Corps, to be Colonel by Brevet for distinguished and meritorious services in the campaign of 1863 and 1864, to date from Jany. 1st. 1865."—LS, *ibid.*

1865, MARCH 2. USG pass. "Pass Mr. C. C. Leigh through all the Armies of the United States."—AES (facsimile), Long Island Historical Society, Brooklyn, N. Y. Written on a War Dept. pass of Feb. 27 for C. C. Leigh, National Freedmen's Relief Association, to travel to Norfolk, Charleston, and Savannah.—DS (facsimile), *ibid.* On Feb. 27, President Abraham Lincoln endorsed this pass. "I heartily commend Mr. Leigh's object, and bid him God speed in it."—AES (facsimile), *ibid.* Lincoln, *Works,* VIII, 321. On March 2, USG telegraphed to Brig. Gen. John W.

Turner, chief of staff for Maj. Gen. Edward O. C. Ord. "Mr Frederick Thompkins of London & Mr Leigh of New York City will visit the Army of the James about Eight Oclock tomorrow morning to specially visit the colored troops Please have horses at the landing for them and some staff officer to show them round. They are commended to your special courtesy." —Telegram received, DNA, RG 393, Dept. of Va. and N. C., 1st Military District, Telegrams Received. On April 26, Frederick Tomkins, Freed Men's Aid Society, London, wrote to USG concerning recent British publications.—ALS (incomplete), USG 3.

1865, MARCH 5. Brig. Gen. George H. Gordon, Norfolk, to USG. "I have three deserters from the 9th Va between the Appamatox & James— They left last Sunday A m—At that time cotton and tobacco was being removed from Petersburg to Richmond A new line of entrenchments being thrown up, running from Drury's Bluff in a direction two miles in rear of Petersburg"—ALS (telegram sent), DNA, RG 107, Telegrams Collected (Unbound); telegram received, *ibid.*; (at 6:15 P.M.) *ibid.*, RG 108, Letters Received. *O.R.*, I, xlvi, part 2, 847.

1865, MARCH 6. USG endorsement. "Respectfully forwarded to the Adjutant General of the Army, with the recommendation, that if their are any Assistant Adjutant Generals unassigned, or off duty, they be ordered to report to Maj. Gen. E. O. C. Ord, Comd'g. Army of the James, to relieve the Regimental Adjutants now acting, who are much needed with their proper commands."—ES, DNA, RG 94, Letters Received, 272A 1865. Written to accompany memoranda of officers absent from the Army of the James.—*Ibid.*

1865, MARCH 6. USG endorsements. "Respy. forwarded to the A G. of the Army, with the request that these officers be relieved from present duty and ordered to join their respective regiments without delay. There is a special necessity that Colored regiments have their full compliment of officers. Otherwise their efficiency is seriously is seriously impaired. I have therefore to recommend that no officer be detailed from Colored Troops, unless there is an absolute necessity for so doing" "Respy. forwarded to the A G. of the Army with the request the the within named officers be ordered to their respective Regiments at once, or mustered out of the service, that their place may be filled. It is essential to efficiency that Colored regiments have a full compliment of officers present for duty"—Copies, DLC-USG, V, 58. On March 7, Lt. Col. Theodore S. Bowers wrote to Maj. Gen. Edward O. C. Ord. "The list of Officers, absent from the Colored Troops of your Command, furnished by you, has been received and carefully considered. All Officers detached out of the Department of Virginia, have been ordered, to be relieved and returned to their respective Regiments. Those absent without leave, and those who have never joined their Regiment, are recommended to be dismissed the service, that their places may be filled.

The War Department has also been requested to make no further details of Officers from Colored Troops for fancy duty and to send to you Officers of the Commissary, Quarter Masters and Adjutant Generals Departments in sufficient number to relieve all Company Officers acting in these Departments. The enclosed extracts from the list referred to, are submitted for your action, with the recommendation that the Officers named therein be relieved from present duty and returned to their regiments, if it is possible to do so."—LS, DNA, RG 393, Dept. of Va. and N. C., 1st Military District, Two or More Name File. On March 17, Bvt. Brig. Gen. Edward D. Townsend wrote to USG. "In reply to your endorsements of the 6th inst., requesting that certain officers of colored troops be ordered at once to their regiments or mustered out of the service, I am directed to inform you that the following officers, being among those named in the communications forwarded, have been ordered to their regiments, viz; Col. C. J. Campbell, 23d U. S. Colored Troops, Capt. S. G. Gilbert 38th U. S. Colored Troops, Surg. A T. Augusta 7th U. S. Colored Troops, 1st Lieut. J. R Moore 23d U. S. Colored Troops, 1st Lieut. L. D. Dobbs, 19th U. S. Colored Troops, The following officers having been reported absent without leave, have been cited to appear before a Military Commission in this city, and should they fail to appear and render a satisfactory account of themselves, will be dismissed the service, viz; Captain Isaac C. Tytle, 115th U S. Colored Troops. Asst. Surg. Martin Phillips. 22d U S. Colored Troops. 2d Lieut. W. P. Brooks, 29th Conn. Vols. (Colored.) The following officers have been discharged the service for the causes stated, viz; Lieut. Col. W. E. W. Ross, 31st U. S. Colored Troops, honorably discharged the service on account of wounds by Special Order No. 119 of March 11th, 1865, from this office. 1st Lieut. Washington A. Huntly, 9 U. S. Colored Troops, and 2d Lieut. Samuel S. Simmons, 36th U. S. Colored Troops, dismissed the service by Special Orders, No. 75, of February 15th 1865 from this office. The name of 1st Lieut. Elisha Wood, 116th U. S. Colored Troops, does not appear upon the rolls of his regiment on file in this office. He was appointed by Brigadier General L. Thomas Adjutant General U. S. Army, September 6th 1864 and has not accepted. The same is true of 1st Lieut. John Morgan of the same regiment. Their appointments should be considered as vacated by their failure to accept. There is no record whatever in this office of S. B. Swisher, said to be Assistant Surgeon, 116th Regiment U. S. Colored Troops—there being no evidence of appointment a vacancy exists, unless recently filled by Major General Ord. 2d Lieut. William M. Titcombe, 38th Regiment U. S. Colored Troops, is reported on the Returns of his regiment as William A. Titcombe, 'sick at Point of Rocks Virginia.' Not having joined his regiment and not having been mustered into service, his appointment should be revoked by Major General Ord, and some one appointed in his place. Col. B. F. Tracy, 127th U. S. Colored Troops is retained as Commander of the Draft Rendezvous at Elmira N. Y. by direction of the Secretary of War. This letter has been delayed to announce the breaking up of the recruiting rendezvous in the rebel States. All officers on duty at said rendezvous, and on recruiting service in Maryland (principally officers of Colored Troops) have been ordered to join their regiments."— LS, *ibid.*, RG 108, Letters Received. Portions were written in tabular form.

1865, MARCH 6. To Col. George W. Bradley. "Pass Mrs. M. H. Slaughter to the 'Flag of Truce' steamer near Varina Va. by first steamer."—ADS, ViU. Mary Harker Slaughter (Mrs. John F. Slaughter) of Lynchburg, Va., was returning from taking her six-year-old son to a Philadelphia physician. —Lincoln, *Works*, VIII, 302–3; Rosalie Slaughter Morton, *A Woman Surgeon* (New York, 1937), p. 6.

1865, MARCH 7. USG endorsement. "Respy. forwarded to the Secretary of War, with the recommendation that Par. 19. of S. O. 278. AGO. series 1864, revoking the leave of absence granted Capt Hry. R. Mizner 18th U. S. Inf, to enable him to accept the Colonelcy of the 14th Reg. Michigan Volunteers, and orders him to report in person to his regiment, for duty under his rank as an officer of the regular army be revoked or recalled, and that he be restored to the command of the 14th Michigan, if the Colonelcy has not been filled. I made this recommendation without questioning the propriety of the order now recommended to be revoked. I approved the application for it, but Capt Mizner is an officer of fair ability, and from the spirit he manifest in his communication I believe the punishment suffered in his loss of rank thus long is sufficient, and that his restoration to rank will not prove inconsitant with the good of the service"—Copy, DLC-USG, V, 58. Written on a letter of Capt. Henry R. Mizner, 18th Inf., concerning his service as col., 14th Mich.—*Ibid.* See letter to John Robertson, Oct. 12, 1864.

1865, MARCH 7. To Maj. Gen. Henry W. Halleck. "Gen. Vogdes will be ordered to the Dept. of the South at once."—ALS (telegram sent), Kohns Collection, NN; copies, DLC-USG, V, 46, 74, 108; DNA, RG 94, Letters Received, 266A 1865; *ibid.*, RG 108, Letters Sent. Printed as sent at 6:00 P.M., received at 6:40 P.M., in *O.R.*, I, xlvi, part 2, 865. At 3:40 P.M., Halleck had telegraphed to USG. "Genl Scamman is seriously ill, & Genl Gillmore asks for Genl Vogdes to take his place. Can the latter be spared from Norfolk? The Dept of the South is deficient in good district commanders."—ALS (telegram sent), DNA, RG 107, Telegrams Collected (Bound); telegram received, *ibid.*; (at 5:30 P.M.) *ibid.*, RG 108, Letters Received. Printed as sent at 5:40 P.M. in *O.R.*, I, xlvi, part 2, 864. On the same day, USG telegraphed to Brig. Gen. Israel Vogdes, Portsmouth, Va. "Gen. Gilmore having made special application for your services orders will be sent to you by to-morrows Mail to report accordingly."—ALS (telegram sent), Kohns Collection, NN; copies, DLC-USG, V, 46, 74, 108; DNA, RG 108, Letters Sent. On March 8, Vogdes telegraphed to USG. "Will you order my Adjutant General, Capt. S. L. McHenry, to go with me. I will make a formal application for him. He was appointed through me, and always served with me."—ALS (telegram sent), *ibid.*, RG 107, Telegrams Collected (Unbound); telegram received, *ibid.* See *O.R.*, I, xlvi, part 2, 888; *ibid.*, I, xlvi, part 3, 54.

1865, MARCH 7.   Gov. Francis H. Peirpoint of Va., Alexandria, to USG. "There is great expectation that the Union Army will soon Ocupy Richmond; May I ask you to protect the Capitol ~~of~~ building of the state, and any records that may be left therein; Also the Governors Mansion which ~~also~~ belongs to the state. The Capitol building, is claimed to be a Monument of the architectural skill of Mr Jefferson. In the rotunda is the finest statue of Washington extant. The records if left will be of great value to the state and Federal government. I expect to ocupy the Governors Mansion and will gladly extend to you the hospitalities of the place when I get there"— ALS, DNA, RG 108, Letters Received. *O.R.*, I, xlvi, part 2, 885.

1865, MARCH 8, 6:30 P.M.   To Bvt. Brig. Gen. William Hoffman. "Please have Gen Trimble sent here for exchange."—Telegram received (at 8:00 P.M.), DNA, RG 107, Telegrams Collected (Bound); *ibid.*, RG 108, Letters Received; copies, *ibid.*, Letters Sent; DLC-USG, V, 46, 74, 108. *O.R.*, II, viii, 366. See *ibid.*, p. 375.

1865, MARCH 8.   To Lt. Col. John E. Mulford. "Please inform Col, Ould that I understand Mrs, Gen, Gracie with her three children, are anxious to go North to her friends and that if she will be permitted to go, we will receive her,"—Copies, DLC-USG, V, 46, 74, 108; DNA, RG 108, Letters Sent.

1865, MARCH 8.   Bvt. Maj. Gen. John G. Barnard, Washington, D. C., to USG. "I intended to have gone down with Gen. Ingalls but I have been far from well. I shall go down in a day or two."—ALS (telegram sent), DNA, RG 107, Telegrams Collected (Unbound).

1865, MARCH 9.   USG endorsement. "Respectfully forwarded to the Sec. of War as the application of Jas. C. Morrison for the appointment of his son to West Point."—AES, DNA, RG 94, Cadet Applications. Written on a letter of Feb. 21 from James C. Morrison, Cincinnati, to USG. "Great men do not always forget their small beginings, in this hope I desire to address you a few lines. You doubtless remember the fall of Ft Donelson, I desire to recall to your memory one who took a prominent part in that memorable struggle, I mean, my own boy, Capt. (then Lieut) Wm M. Raymond, Co D, 52 Inda Vol. Infantry. He was wounded in the Charge on that place, after his recovery, was promoted for his gallantry to the Captaincy of his Company, as such served at Corinth, Vicksburg &c was with Genl. Shermans Mississipi raid, then with Genl. A. J. Smith in his pursuit of Price through Arkansas and Missouri, finally was mortally wounded in the last Battle of Nashville and died Jan, 13th from his wounds. Now, my dear General, my youngest Son, Master Charles C, Morrison, (who is just 16 years of age) is very desirous of entering the Army, I think him too young, but am willing if he can get into the West Point Military Academy, that he should go into the regular Army. With an earnest desire on his part to do so, he has gone to Work after School hours and earned Money to pay his expenses to Washington, procured recommendations from his Teachers in the Woodward High School, from Rufus King Esq. President of our School Board, from the Hon. Judge Leavitt, from Generals Hooker, Wietzel, and Hays, all of whom examined him besides a general testimonial from all of our best business men. He is very studious, moral and industrious, stands third in his Class in School. He now asks me to get from you a request to the President to give him an appointment. Does he not deserve it? I am sure you would never have cause to regret it. Will you aid him in any way you can? If there was any vacancy in our Congressional district, he could get the place, but there will be none for 3 years, He therefore must look to the President. Hoping you will look favorably upon it and give it your *early attention* thereby laying me under great obligation . . ."—ALS, *ibid*. Charles C. Morrison, USMA 1871, was appointed in 1867.

1865, MARCH 9. USG endorsement. "This is respectfully referedd as the application of S. P. Brady for the appointment of his son to West Point. S. P. Brady is a man of standing in Detroit. ~~and~~ He is the son of Gen. Brady who served for so many years in our Army, and with great distinction in the War of /12 to /15 with Great Britten. He is the only male descendent of that old soldier and I would ask for his son, the Grandson of Gen. Brady, this appointment if it can be granted."—AES, DNA, RG 94, Cadet Applications. Written on a letter of Feb. 22 from Samuel P. Brady, Detroit, to USG. "One of my Sons, Samuel Brady, is exceedingly anxious to enter the army, tho' he is only desirous of doing so after quallifying himself with a West-Point education—I am without political influance—never had any—and never expect to have, and am not even on respectable personal terms with our Senator, Z Chandler. My hopes therefore for success rest entirely on the personal influance of a fiew friends—Among them I venture to ask the favour of a fiew lines from you to the President direct—If you feel that you can do me this kindness I doubt not it will have greater weight than all the recommendations it will be in my Sons power to obtain—No man knows better than yourself the Military history & character of my Father, and I cannot but feel that the Grandson of a soldier who entered the field of western warfare under the vetran Wayne in 1792, and (save a brief interval) served his country faithfully from that period until 1851, has not some little claim to an appointment 'at Large' Watching with interest and gratification your success and advancement, and hoping you will excuse me for asking even this much of your valuable time—. . ."—ALS, *ibid*.

1865, MARCH 9. To Maj. Gen. Edward O. C. Ord. "I have no objection to Gen. Kautz being absent for ten 10 days"—Telegram received (at 11:30 A.M.), Ord Papers, CU-B.

1865, MARCH 9. Maj. Gen. Edward O. C. Ord to Brig. Gen. John A. Rawlins. "Refugee from Richmond lately released from castle Thunder and deserted from Camp Lee left Richmond last night. Says that sunday monday or tuesday detachments of troops were moving through the City. Report was that Sheridans Cavalry had cut the Aqueduct at Dovers Mills and destroyed twelve or fifteen loaded boats. Some of the troops among them Wickhams Dismounted Cavalry went toward Dovers Mills some went toward to Hanover Junction. Detachments of troops are being picked up and sent to various points. Heard one party of Sheridans Cavalry was going to Louisa C H there was also a report three days ago in Richmond that Genls Sherman and Schofield had formed a junction. These reports were principally street rumors except the movement of Cavy westward"—Telegram received (at 2:40 P.M.), DNA, RG 108, Letters Received. *O.R.*, I, xlvi, part 2, 905. On the same day, USG forwarded a copy of this telegram to Secretary of War Edwin M. Stanton.—Telegram received (at 8:00 P.M.), DNA, RG 108, Letters Received.

1865, MARCH 9. Lt. Col. Theodore S. Bowers to Brig. Gen. George H. Gordon. "The necessities of the Hospitals at City Point are such as to render it necessary to procure supplies of Vegetables, fresh Oysters &c, for their use from the most available points, You will therefore permit such Officers, or Agent as Col. Morgan (M. R.) Chief Commissary may authorize and direct to purchase for the Commissary Department for the use of Hospitals exclusively and such products as Norfolk may afford This provission is designated purely for the benifit of Hospitals, and is not intended to effect any regulations which you have made of the subject of trade, further than herein expressed"—Copies, DLC-USG, V, 46, 74, 108; DNA, RG 108, Letters Sent. *O.R.*, I, xlvi, part 2, 908.

1865, MARCH 9. Lt. Col. Theodore S. Bowers to Brig. Gen. George H. Gordon. "From representations made to these Headquarters, the Lieutenant General is satisfied that Davis Hurd and E. S. Crittenden, now under charges for violation of orders regulating the purchase of supplies at Norfolk, should be discharged from custody. The Commissary Department made arrangements with one Mr. McGaffey to purchase supplies of vegetables, fish, &c., for the use of the Hospitals at City Point, and a permit was granted by Brig Gen M. R. Patrick, Provost Marshal General Armies operating against Richmond, to purchase these supplies wherever they could be obtained. Under this arrangement supplies have been purchased at Norfolk and brought here for six months past. No attempt was made during this time to enforce General Order No. 4 and its existence was not even known to General Patrick or the Commissary Department. Gen. Grant does not desire to shield from punishment parties who violate orders on trade or other subjects, but for the reasons named he directs that parties herein named be released from arrest. If in your judgment they are unfit persons to remain within your lines, you are at liberty to send them out"—LS, DNA, RG 109, Union Provost Marshals' File of Papers Relating to Two or More Citizens.

1865, MARCH 9.   Col. George D. Ruggles, adjt. for Maj. Gen. George G. Meade, to Lt. Col. Theodore S. Bowers. "Has General Grant received authority from the President to assign officers according to their brevet rank, without referring each case to him?"—ALS (telegram sent), DNA, RG 94, War Records Office, Army of the Potomac. *O.R.*, I, xlvi, part 2, 904. On the same day, Bowers telegraphed to Ruggles. "The Secy of War has authorized Genl Grant to assign officers under their Breveat rank where is desirable to avoid delay"—Telegram received (at 2:50 P.M.), DNA, RG 94, War Records Office, Miscellaneous War Records; copies, *ibid.*, RG 108, Letters Sent; DLC-USG, V, 46, 74, 108; Meade Papers, PHi. *O.R.*, I, xlvi, part 2, 904. See letter to Edwin M. Stanton, Feb. 26, 1865.

1865, MARCH 10.   To Maj. George K. Leet. "Please purchase & send by mail messenger a pair of thick soled number ten 10 children's walking shoes for Jesse."—Telegram received (at 11:00 P.M.), DNA, RG 107, Telegrams Collected (Bound).

1865, MARCH 10.   Maj. Gen. Edward O. C. Ord to USG. "Musketry and some shots from artillery are reported to have been heard from my lines for nearly an hour between eight and nine A M yesterday in the direction of Manchester. Today a deserter reports that parties from Richmond last night state this firing to have been upon the returned prisoners of war who refused to obey the order sending them at once to duty without furloughs and that it occured at Manchester . . . P. S. I think this might be published" "Col Mulford who is on good terms with the prisoners he takes back tells me that proper inducements are not held out to these men at the prison Camps to return to our lines and give them selves up after reaching the rebel army. Your least Order of 4th March with statement 'that they can go South have time to see their families and make arrangements for them to get North and send for them after reaching our lines should be sent to the prison Camps"—Telegrams received (at 4:00 P.M.), DNA, RG 108, Letters Received. *O.R.*, I, xlvi, part 2, 916–17.

1865, MARCH 10.   Maj. Gen. Edward O. C. Ord to Brig. Gen. John A. Rawlins. "~~Deserters and~~ refugees leaving Richmond last night state that gold ~~and~~ machinery ~~which~~ and tobacco which was Sent up toward Lynchburg is being returned—and that tobacco in quantitey is now sent up the R. Road toward Fredericksburg with a view of exchanging for Bacon—large quantity of tobacco stored in Richmond"—ADf, Ord Papers, CU-B.

1865, MARCH 11.   Act. Rear Admiral S. Phillips Lee, Mound City, Ill., to USG. "I request that I may be kept advised, by copies of the orders on the subject being sent me, of the limits of the different commands, and of the names of the commanding Generals of the Military Divisions and Departments in the West. I transmit herewith a set of my General Orders issued since assuming command of this Squadron, some of which indicate the necessity for the information I have requested."—ALS, DNA, RG 108, Letters Received. *O.R.*, I, xlix, part 1, 891; *O.R.* (Navy), I, xxvii, 92.

1865, MARCH 11.   Lt. Col. Theodore S. Bowers endorsement. "Respectfully referred to Maj. Gen. George G. Meade. Com'd'g Army of the Potomac."—AES, DNA, RG 109, Union Provost Marshals' File of Papers Relating to Individual Civilians. Written on a letter of March 8 from W. M. Jones, "Handcocks Station," to USG. "I have respectfully to represent to you that, I am an Old man, in my Seventy second year, and have been allowed to remain within your lines as a loyal citizen of the U. S. and have been kindly allowed to recve my rations from the Goverment by your ordir (I presume,)   But learning that Others on whose premaces the U. S. troops have been qurarterd has gotten cirtificats of the amount of damage done, I respectfully ask of you, to a commision or some one to ascertain the damage done to my plantation Building crops stock finceing &c as done by the different troops quarterered at and around my farm. I have further to say that I am inexperianced of such matters and Kindly ask of you your assistance, that I may be at some time remunerated, or my heirs."—ALS, *ibid.*

1865, MARCH 12.   To Secretary of War Edwin M. Stanton. "Gen, Meade says he can spare Gen, Schriver very well for a month, but should not like to spare him much longer"—Copies, DLC-USG, V, 46, 74, 108; DNA, RG 108, Letters Sent. *O.R.*, I, xlvi, part 2, 936. On the same day, Bvt. Brig. Gen. Edward D. Townsend had telegraphed to USG. "The Secretary of War Wishes to Know if General Schriver Inspector General Can be spared from his present duties to make a special Inspection under a resolution of Congress."—Telegram received, DNA, RG 108, Letters Received; copy, *ibid.*, RG 94, Letters Sent. *O.R.*, I, xlvi, part 2, 936. On the same day, USG telegraphed to Maj. Gen. George G. Meade. "The Secretary of War wishes to know if General Schriver Inspector General can be spared from his present duties to make a special inspection under a resolution of Congress"—Telegram received (at 11:35 A.M.), DNA, RG 94, War Records Office, Army of the Potomac; copies (2), Meade Papers, PHi. At 4:30 P.M., Meade telegraphed to USG. "Genl. Schriver can be spared for a month—I should not like him to be absent longer than that.—"—ALS (telegram sent), DNA, RG 94, War Records Office, Army of the Potomac; telegram received, *ibid.*, RG 108, Letters Received. See *O.R.*, I, xlvi, part 2, 948.

1865, MARCH 12.   USG endorsement. "Approved and respectfully forwarded to the Secretary of War. An early decision in these cases is requested, in order that the vacancies in their regiments (should they be appointed) may be filled."—ES, DNA, RG 94, ACP, I7 CB 1865. Written on a letter of March 11 from Brig. Gen. Rufus Ingalls to Bvt. Maj. Gen. Montgomery C. Meigs recommending that thirty-eight lts. serving as act. q. m. be appointed capt. and q. m.—LS, *ibid.*

1865, MARCH 12.   USG endorsement. "Approved and respectfully forwarded to the Secretary of War. A similar recommendation with approval has before been forwarded."—ES, DNA, RG 94, ACP, I6 CB 1865. Written on a letter of March 11 from Brig. Gen. Rufus Ingalls to Brig. Gen. John A. Rawlins recommending that Capt. William T. Howell and Capt. Edward J. Strang, both serving as depot q. m., be appointed bvt. lt. col. —LS, *ibid.*

1865, MARCH 12.   USG endorsement. "Approved and respectfully forwarded to the Secretary of War."—ES, DNA, RG 94, ACP, I5 CB 1865. Written on a letter of March 11 from Brig. Gen. Rufus Ingalls to Bvt. Maj. Gen. Montgomery C. Meigs recommending fourteen q. m. officers for promotion.—LS, *ibid.*

1865, MARCH 12.   Brig. Gen. George H. Gordon, Norfolk, to USG. "I have the honor to report that an expedition I sent to Murfrees Depot under Col. Lewis of the third N. Y. Cavalry reports today that he destroyed fifty bales of Cotton—burned the Depot—Warehouse and other buildings and was in waiting for another train en route with Cotton to the same place— Deserters have reported of late that large amounts of Cotton were coming into Murfrees Depot for the United states Gov't. to be shipped from Edenton—I send this direct as I understand Gen. Ord is in Washington."—ALS (telegram sent), DNA, RG 107, Telegrams Collected (Unbound); telegram received, *ibid.*, RG 108, Letters Received. *O.R.*, I, xlvi, part 2, 939.

1865, MARCH 13.   To Maj. Gen. Gouverneur K. Warren. "Please have Colonel [Major] Wagstaff, Ninety-first New York Volunteers, come down here this evening, bringing his personal baggage with him." "Has Major Wagstaff, Ninety-first New York Volunteers, received orders to report at these headquarters? If he has not, please order him to report in time to take the morning train."—*O.R.*, I, xlvi, part 2, 949. At 11:30 P.M., Warren telegraphed to USG. "Your dispatch of this p. m. was sent to Major Wagstaff as soon as received. I will send an order at once for him to report as you direct."—*Ibid.*, p. 950.

1865, MARCH 13.   Maj. Gen. Edward O. C. Ord to Brig. Gen. John A. Rawlins. "Deserters in this P. m say that Pickets Division is at Manchester & that firing, Artillery, was heard in the direction of Beaver Dam this morning Early,   No change reported on my front except possibly Coxs

Brigade has been relieved by some other troops,"—Telegram received, DNA, RG 108, Letters Received. *O.R.*, I, xlvi, part 2, 952.

1865, MARCH 13.   John Irving, U.S. Christian Commission, to USG. "Will you have the kindness to forward to me the letter from Col. Ould in response to our effort to reach agreement for the aid of our prisoners?"— ALS, DNA, RG 94, U.S. Christian Commission, Letters Sent (Press).

1865, MARCH 14.   USG endorsement. "Approved and respectfully forwarded to the Secretary of War."—ES, DNA, RG 94, ACP, G71 CB 1865. Written on a letter of the same day from Maj. Gen. John Gibbon to Lt. Col. Theodore S. Bowers requesting the appointment of officers to serve on the staff of the 24th Army Corps.—ALS, *ibid.*

1865, MARCH 14.   To Asst. Secretary of War Charles A. Dana. "I have the honor to inform you that the communication of Surgeon Hand, protesting against the order of General Shermans requiring the removal of Hospitals from Morehead City, forwarded to the Secretary of War by the Surgeon General and by him referred to me for my action, has been referred to Maj, Gen, J, M, Schofield, Commanding Department of North Carolina, with directions to examine into the matter, and to take such action as will best subserve the interest of the service,"—Copies, DLC-USG, V, 46, 74, 108; DNA, RG 108, Letters Sent.

1865, MARCH 14, noon.   To Maj. Gen. Henry W. Halleck. "I would like to have Gen. Benham ordered to take the place vacated by the capture of Gen. Kelly. He can be spared from here and he knows that country."—ALS (telegram sent), Hal Douthit, Sandusky, Ohio; copies, DLC-USG, V, 46, 74, 108; DNA, RG 108, Letters Sent. *O.R.*, I, xlvi, part 2, 961. See *ibid.*, p. 966.

1865, MARCH 14, 4:00 P.M.   To Maj. Gen. Henry W. Halleck. "A portion of the 45 U. S. Colored Troops ias in Washington, the balance here. Now that new troops are all being ordered there I think the regiment had better be together in the field. Please so order."—ALS (telegram sent), OClWHi; copies, DLC-USG, V, 46, 74, 108; DNA, RG 108, Letters Sent. *O.R.*, I, xlvi, part 2, 962. On March 15, noon, Halleck telegraphed to USG. "The balance of the U. S. Col Regt was sent to the front before the receipt of your telegram."—ALS (telegram sent), DNA, RG 107, Telegrams Collected (Bound); telegram received, *ibid.*; *ibid.*, RG 108, Letters Received. *O.R.*, I, xlvi, part 2, 986.

1865, MARCH 14.   To Col. Joseph Roberts, Fort Monroe. "Messrs Brown [&] Potter left New York this morning on Steamship Colorado for Fortress Monroe. Please instruct the Pro Marshal to give them a pass when they arrive to City Point"—Telegram received (press), DNA, RG 107, Telegrams Collected (Bound). On the same day, Maj. Gen. John A. Dix, New York City, had telegraphed to USG. "Mr James Brown senior partner of the house of Brown Bros and his son-in-law Mr Potter left this morning in the new Steamship 'Colorado' for for Ft monroe they would be much gratified to have your permission to go to City Point"—Telegram received, *ibid.*, RG 108, Letters Received.

1865, MARCH 14.   Lt. Col. Theodore S. Bowers endorsement. "Respectfully referred to Maj. Gen. Geo. H. Thomas Comd'g. Department of the Cumberland for report."—ES, DNA, RG 108, Letters Received. *O.R.*, II, viii, 369. Written on a letter of March 9 from C.S.A. Agent of Exchange Robert Ould to Lt. Col. John E. Mulford concerning the imprisonment of Charles W. Meeks.—LS, DNA, RG 108, Letters Received. *O.R.*, II, viii, 369. See *ibid.*, pp. 369–70.

1865, MARCH 15.   To Secretary of War Edwin M. Stanton. "The Richmond papers of today are received, but they Contain no news of interest— The following paragraph from the Examiner is all that is worth telegraphing—'This is once more almost a blank—Grant has been moving some troops from his left and Sending them again across the James River. This movement is Connected with other operations of which the War department is fully informed and which it has taken ample measures to meet. North and South Carolina—We are still without official despatches from the army under Genl. Johnston, but the progress of Sherman is evidently embarrassed by difficulties he did not expect and those Raleigh newspapers which but lately had no doubt that he would occupy Raleigh without opposition and then go where ever he pleased have Changed their minds—Everything that is Known from that quarter is encouraging there are other military movements on foot to which it would be premature to allude—' "—Telegram received (press), DNA, RG 107, Telegrams Collected (Bound). Incomplete in *O.R.*, I, xlvi, part 2, 986; (incomplete) *ibid.*, I, xlvii, part 2, 844.

1865, MARCH 15.   President Abraham Lincoln to USG. "Please allow the bearer, Robert E. Coxe, to pass through our lines to go South and return" —Lincoln, *Works*, VIII, 354. See *ibid.*, pp. 199–200.

1865, MARCH 15.   Col. Wardwell G. Robinson, Harrison's Landing, Va., to Lt. Col. Theodore S. Bowers. "The fires mentioned by you were not seen from this post. At sundown last evening I dispatched a scouting party toward the Chickahominy, who proceeded within four miles of the river, and who returned this morning about daylight. They saw no fires or indications of any."—*O.R.*, I, xlvi, part 2, 992. On the same day, Brig. Gen. Joseph B. Carr, Wilson's Wharf, Va., wrote to Bowers. "The fires were observed here last night. Supposed to be the woods on fire at some distance beyond the Chickahominy. A cavalry patrol just in report all quiet on this side of the river."—*Ibid.*, p. 993.

1865, MARCH 16. Lt. Col. Theodore S. Bowers pass. "Miss Smith will be afforded all facilities that Army Commanders afford to other State Agents. Free transportation will be given her on all Goverment steamers and Military Railroads. Guards and pickets will pass her accordingly."— Adelaide W. Smith, *Reminiscences of an Army Nurse during the Civil War* (New York, 1911), pp. 146–47.

1865, MARCH 17. Lt. Col. Theodore S. Bowers endorsement. "Respectfully referred to Maj. Gen. Geo. H. Thomas, Comd'g. Dep't. of the Cumberland for report in this case."—ES, DNA, RG 108, Letters Received. *O.R.*, II, viii, 371. Written on a letter of March 9 from C.S.A. Agent of Exchange Robert Ould to Lt. Col. John E. Mulford. "I have learned that Messrs. Ramsey, Sperry and Fox, citizens of Tennessee, are kept chained together and made to parade the streets of Knoxville. I will thank you to make inquiry into this matter, and if it is found to be true, that you will have them relieved from such ignominious punishment."—LS, DNA, RG 108, Letters Received. *O.R.*, II, viii, 370–71. Subsequent endorsements included a denial of the allegation.—*Ibid.*, pp. 371–72.

1865, MARCH 18, 9:00 P.M. To Secretary of War Edwin M. Stanton. "I would recommend the dis-continuance of the 19th Corp's organization and order Gen, Emory to report to Gen, Hancock for assignment,"—Telegram, copies, DLC-USG, V, 46, 75, 108; DNA, RG 108, Letters Sent. *O.R.*, I, xlvi, part 3, 27. See *ibid.*, pp. 16, 52.

1865, MARCH 18. To Asst. Secretary of War Charles A. Dana. "The Richmond papers of today are received—The Confederate Congress adjourned sine die at 3 oclock today. The President of the James river Canal calls on the farmers of Virginia to aid in repairing the canal—The Augusta papers say that A H Stevens has been in Georgia for ten days or more, that he has not yet been heard from and that they hope this silence will not continue—Vigorous efforts are making at Richmond for the organization of Colored troops—The following paragraphs ar[e] taken from the 'Richmond Whig' 'Mobile March 4th This city is strongly menaced. Genl Maury has issued a circular advising the people to prepare for the expected attack—He urges the non-combattants to leave. The Exchange Commissioner yesterday evening received information of the arrival in the bay of a large number of prisoners from Ship Island and New Orleans. They are expected up today. Maj Correll will effect such arrangements as will embrace all prisoners captured in this Department—' 'Mobile Mar. 5th 176 Navy & Army exchanged prisoners arrived in the city last night'. 'Mobile Mar 9th A Transport containing 2000 troops [e]ntered the bay yesterday through Grants Pass' 'Mobile Mar. 11th Fourteen Vessels more were

added to the fleet today, making twenty one in sight of the city,   Great
activity prevails with the enemy in the lower Bay. There is every indication
of any early attack—The enemy have fired a few shots at both shores'
'From Georgia!! Action of the Legislature on the Military question! Macon
March 4th. The House of Delegates has adopted a resolution requisting
Congress to repeal the conscript law and accept men from the States under
officers of their own choice. Yeas 61. Nays 46—' 'Sheridans Raid! Damage to the Canal etc: The Lynchburg papers of Monday and Tuesday bring
us some details of the raid through the upper country which in view of the
fact that Sheridan has communicated with Genl Grant from Columbia we
concieve to be puerile to withhold and therefore lay them before our
readers. The Virginian says that the yankee division sent in that direction
followed the Orange and Alexandria Rail Road as far as Buffalo river burning the Rail Road bridge at that point. Every bridge between Charlottesville
and Buffalo—(a distance of more than forty miles) has been destroyed and
much of the track torn up—though the extent of the damage done has not
been ascertained—The nearest approach they made to Lynchburg was New
Glasgow—17 miles distant, where a small party of them ~~raiders~~ burnt the
RailRoad Depot. On Wednesday a party estimated at from two to three
thousand appeared at Bent Creek supposed to be making for the South side
of James River. The fine bridge over the river being burnt on their approach
they contented themselves with loud curses upon our reserves who were
stationed on the other side of the river—They burned the boat of the James
River Canal Company at Bent Creek—They had captured four of our scouts
that were left in the hands of an equal number of their troops, who being
cut off from the main force by the burning of Tye River bridge gave themselves up to their prisoners and were brought to this city. The raiders burned
every mill they could find along James River, destroyed all the tobacco and
tobacco houses and carried away all the horses and negroes they could lay
hands upon—They shot about three hundred of their broken down horses
on the plantation of Mr W. B. Cabell below New Market and of course
took off all the horses belonging to that Gentleman they could find. It is said
that about three hundred yanekees crossed the river opposite Columbia on
Friday but recrossed to the north side immediately   The "Republican" of
Tuesday says that 'The raiders commenced at Bent Creek the work of destruction to the Canal which is reported to be very badly damaged from
about twenty five miles below here to Columbia and possibly further down
towards Richmond—Every lock on the Canal is said to have been destroyed;
in several places the banks have been blown away—The acqueduct at Columbia is said to be badly damaged—The destruction of private property
along the route of the raiders is represented to be immense—The people
were stripped of horses negroes and meat and bread & many were left
without a morsel of food.'—The situation in North Carolina! Our Danville
& North Carolina excha[nge] received yesterday threw some light upon the
situation of affairs in North Carolina—We venture to copy some of their
statements to relieve the solicitude of our own deeply interested people with-

out, we believe, conveying more information to the enemy than their most intelligent leaders have already inferred from previous developments or may now be in possession of—The Danville "Rigister" of Tuesday says that 'Our forces have probably withdrawn from Kinston and may be preparing to evacuate Goldsboro'. Goldsboro was all right yesterday afternoon! The Raleigh "Standard" of the same date (14th) says that 'Fayetteville was occupied several days since by the enemy in force—It is reported that the Cotton factories were burnt but we have ~~had~~ heard nothing as to the Arsenal or as to the treatment of the people of that place—Kinston is now in possession of the Enemy and Goldsboro seriously threatened—Our troops have contested the ground at various points with their accustomed courage & endurance. We believe the forces of the Enemy will be met at some point South of Raleigh. The Goldsboro "State Journal" of Sunday contains the following significant paragraph—The Editor of this paper is about to leave, his readers know why—In the course of a short time he hopes to meet them again. He feels he has been somewhat odious to the Enemy and he does not regret his course—They cant hurt him—He lives in hopes of being as he was—The newspaper press in the Confederacy! The Danville Register of Wednesday remarks that the recent movements of Sherman and Sheridan have greatly decreased the number of newspapers published in the country. In Virginia we have daily papers issued from four points—Richmond, Lynchburg, Danville and Petersburg, and one weekly at Clarksville. The number has been largely curtailed in North Carolina, Wilmington Fayetteville, Goldsboro, Newberne &c are in the hands of the enemy. The Yankees now publish a paper at Wilmington, Some think that Raleigh too may go, then Greensboro & Charlotte & Some smaller places will be alone left. In South Carolina it is even worse. The Mercury was removed from Charleston Some time before the occupation of the city by the enemy, and the Courier which remained was taken in charge by the Yankees, notwithstanding it opposed nullification in '32, and is now issued as a Yankee newspaper All the papers in Columbia have been discontinued. The South Carolinian is now published at Charlotte N. C.' "—Telegram received (at 3:30 P.M.), DNA, RG 107, Telegrams Collected (Bound).

1865, MARCH 18, 6:00 P.M. To Asst. Secretary of War Charles A. Dana. "I understand Gen, Ord is trying to buy some Tobacco that is now at Yorktown to issue to his Colored troops who are selling their Rubber blankets to Rebels to procure the article not having pay or credit to get it,"—Telegram, copies (marked as sent at 1:00 P.M.), DLC-USG, V, 46, (marked as sent at 6:00 P.M.) 75, 108; DNA, RG 108, Letters Sent. *O.R.*, I, xlvi, part 3, 28. At 1:30 P.M., Dana had telegraphed to USG. "I am informed that Gen Ord is making arrangments to buy a quantity of tobacco now on the Rappahannock from which he proposes to issue to his troops. Has this project your sanction?"—Telegram received, DNA, RG 107, Telegrams Collected (Bound); *ibid.*, RG 108, Letters Received. *O.R.*, I, xlvi, part 3, 28.

1865, MARCH 18, 2:30 P.M.   To Bvt. Maj. Gen. Montgomery C. Meigs.
"I approve Gn. Canby's recommendation of Winslow as volunteer Q. M."—
ALS (telegram sent), Kohns Collection, NN; telegram received (at 3:30
P.M.), DNA, RG 94, ACP, Q48 CB 1865; *ibid.*, RG 107, Telegrams Col-
lected (Bound). See *O.R.*, I, xlviii, part 1, 1092–93.

1865, MARCH 18.   To Brig. Gen. Alexander B. Dyer, chief of ordnance.
"There must be a large amount of Ordnance & Ordnance stores in the Departments of N. C. & the South which cannot be of use in Either of these
Departments & much of which might answer to fill requisitions from other
parts of the country   It probably will be advisable to send seige stores from
Charleston to Mobile bay without waiting requisitions"—Telegram received
(at 1:45 P.M.), DNA, RG 107, Telegrams Collected (Bound); *ibid.*, RG
156, Letters Received; copies, *ibid.*, RG 108, Letters Sent; DLC-USG, V,
46, 74, 108. *O.R.*, I, xlvii, part 2, 885; *ibid.*, I, xlix, part 2, 20. On the same
day, Dyer telegraphed to USG. "Telegram received   senior ordnance officer
Department of the south directed to Consult with his Commanding General
& send in Charge of an officer as Complete a seige train as Can be spared
from that Department to Mobile bay   Qr Mr notified"—Telegram received,
DNA, RG 108, Letters Received; copy, *ibid.*, RG 156, Letters Sent. *O.R.*,
I, xlix, part 2, 20.

1865, MARCH 18.   Maj. Gen. Edward O. C. Ord to Brig. Gen. John A.
Rawlins. "Deserters from Philips Legion Dubose brigade say that the brigade had orders about noon yesterday to be in readiness to move at any
moment. Between one & two oclock Brigade moved about half a mile to the
left—where the column about faced & returned to the old place & stacked
arms—As for down the line as he went he did not pass other troops the
whole line having moved to the left—The movement was caused by a
demonstration of our troops across white Oak swamp—Up to 8 oclock when
they left the brigade was still in readiness thought every thing was quiet
Deserter from Bryants brig. says brig. moved to the left & returned   thinks
it was caused by our review but heard rumors of our moving across white
Oak swamp—[— —] reports when he left the troops were in readiness
although every thing was quiet   our review could be seen and it seems the
enemy massed or prepared to mass on our review front"—ALS (telegram
sent), Ord Papers, CU-B. At 7:15 P.M. and 8:40 P.M., Ord telegraphed
to Rawlins. "The following despatch is received from Col West Com'd
Cav. Div. The disposition Ordered by the General Commanding has been
complied with   all is quiet—But few of the enemy have been seen   we
had a very tedious time crossing the Swamp   I have felt compelled to hold
fast to Charles City Cross Roads   Spear is there with his command covering communication, without him there we should be entirely cut off as the
enemy in parties dismounted are annoying him considerably   He reports
having lost thirteen (13) men   Nothing of Genl. Sheridan—We have a
party on the North bank of the Chickahominy at Bottoms Bridge—Signed

R M WEST Col Comdg." "A deserter reports that on the occasion of our review yesterday the enemy anticipated an attack and formed in line of battle, Afterward they sent two Brigades toward Mechanicsville to resist ~~an attack~~ Sheridans Cavalry I think the deserter mistaken and the Brigades were sent out because of the movement of my Cavalry."—LS and ALS (telegrams sent), DNA, RG 108, Letters Received; telegrams received, *ibid. O.R.,* I, xlvi, part 3, 32.

1865, MARCH 19. USG endorsement. "Approved, and respectfully forwarded to the Secretary of War. The recommendations of Gen's Ames and Terry are entitled to consideration"—ES, DNA, RG 94, ACP, A99 CB 1865. Written on a letter of March 12 from Bvt. Maj. Gen. Adelbert Ames to Secretary of War Edwin M. Stanton recommending Capt. Albert G. Lawrence for promotion to maj.—ALS, *ibid.* On Oct. 30, USG endorsed this letter. "Respectfully returned to the Adjt. Generals Office, for file."—ES, *ibid.* On Dec. 10, 1867, USG endorsed a letter of Lawrence requesting a diplomatic appointment, already endorsed by Bvt. Maj. Gen. Alfred H. Terry. "I have unbounded faith in all statements made by Gn. Terry but have no personal knowledge of the facts in Gn. Lawrence case." —AES, *ibid.*, RG 59, Applications and Recommendations, Lincoln and Johnson.

1865, MARCH 19. USG endorsement written on a letter of Lt. Col. Michael R. Morgan concerning appointments.—Kenneth W. Rendell, Inc., Catalogue 78, [*1972*], p. 21.

1865, MARCH 19, noon. To Maj. Gen. Henry W. Halleck. "Gen, Washburn as I understands makes his reports to Gen, Thomas, but for all purposes of keeping open navigation on the Miss, river, will obey instructions from Gen, Canby, For all local policy within the State of Tennessee he will be guided by instructions and orders from Gen, Thomas,"—Telegram, copies, DLC-USG, V, 46, 75, 108; DNA, RG 108, Letters Sent. Printed as received at 6:00 P.M. in *O.R.,* I, xlviii, part 1, 1214. See *ibid.*, pp. 1180, 1215.

1865, MARCH 19. To commanding officer, Norfolk. "You will permit G Crowleys vessel to proceed from Norfolk to White House there to report to Maj Genl Sheriden—"—Telegram received, DNA, RG 107, Telegrams Collected (Unbound); *ibid.*, RG 393, Dept. of Va. and N. C., 1st Military District, Telegrams Received.

1865, MARCH 20, 2:00 P.M. To Maj. Gen. Winfield S. Hancock. "Order Col Kellogg C. S., Col Newhall a. a. g. & surgeon Ghiselin to city Point to report to Maj Gen Sheridan. Those officers should start so as to take tomorrow's boat from Baltimore or Washington"—Telegram received (at 7:00 P.M.), DNA, RG 107, Telegrams Collected (Bound); *ibid.*, RG 393,

Middle Military Div., Letters Received; copies, *ibid.*, RG 108, Letters Sent; DLC-USG, V, 46, 75, 108. *O.R.*, I, xlvi, part 3, 58. On March 21, Hancock telegraphed to USG. "Your dispatch in cipher of the 20th was rec'd at 12 M today—It will be complied with at once"—Telegram sent, DNA, RG 108, Letters Received; telegram received, *ibid.*; *ibid.*, RG 107, Telegrams Collected (Unbound); (press) *ibid.*, Telegrams Collected (Bound). *O.R.*, I, xlvi, part 3, 68.

1865, MARCH 20. C.S.A. Agent of Exchange Robert Ould to USG. "Lt. Daniel Davis, a Confederate Officer, is held in close confinement, and at hard labor with convicts at Fort Warren. Some time ago a Federal Officer was selected in retaliation, and put in close confinement for Lt. Davis. When, however, the recent agreement was made about this class of prisoners, I immediately delivered the Federal Officer to your Authorities. Notwithstanding my prompt action, however, Lt. Davis is still retained in the manner I have mentioned. Capt. Gordon, and Major Armesy, of our service, were captured at the same time with Lt. Davis, and were held, like him, in close confinement. They, however, have been released and sent to us. Why Lt. Davis is retained, I cannot conceive. I have brought this case several times to the attention of your Authorities, but no action has been taken. I will thank you to cause him to be released and sent to us." "The following named Confederate Soldiers are now in close confinement in the Penitentiary, at Nashville. They are all privates, and belong to the commands indicated. Some, if not most of them, are dressed in convict clothes: H. L. Bell 10th Tenn. Cav. John O. Scarbrough 8th Ky. John S. Holder 4th Tenn. Z. F. Bailey, 8th Ky. Richard King, 8th Ky. J. Phillips, Lyon's Command H. F. Phillips Lyon's Command R. B. Vaughan 11th Tenn. Cav. Wm Andrews 1st Ky. Cav. Private Reaves 9th Tenn. T. K. Miller Forrest's Command Jesse Broadway Forrest's Command I will thank you to cause an order to be issued for their release and delivery."—Copies, DNA, RG 109, Ould Letterbook; Ould Letterbook, Archives Div., Virginia State Library, Richmond, Va. *O.R.*, II, viii, 413–14. The second letter was copied in tabular form.

On March 30, Bvt. Brig. Gen. William Hoffman endorsed the first letter. "Respectfully returned to Lieut General U S. Grant. Comd'g U. S. Army. Lieut Daniel Davis of the rebel army is at Fort Warren. under sentence to fifteen (15) years confinement at hard labor. Genl order 397. W. D.—A. G. O. Dec 16th 1863. He will be forwarded for exchange."—Copy, DNA, RG 249, Letters Sent.

1865, MARCH 20. Maj. Gen. Edward O. C. Ord to USG. "Gen Gibbon wants four (4) days leave to Settle Estate of his mother-in-law—Can he be spared"—Telegram received, DNA, RG 108, Letters Received. On the same day, Ord telegraphed to Brig. Gen. John A. Rawlins. "The following just recd from Gen Gibbon Your telegram is recd It would suit my business better to go at once but I would rather not go at all than run the risk of being absent should a movement take place. Please say to Gen Grant that under the circumstances I prefer to wait"—Telegram received, *ibid.*

1865, MARCH 20.   Amos Shinkle, Covington, Ky., to USG. "I trust you will excuse me for again troubling you, in a former letter I wrote you in regard to prisoners of the transports Champion's No 3 and 5, who were captured up Red river with Admiral Porters fleet, in Genl Banks expedition April 26. 1864., they are near Tyler Texas at Camp Fort as I understand, Since recieving your letter, Some of our exchanged Soldiers have returned home from that camp (where our men are confined) and inform us that the crew's of the Champions are held and are only to be exchanged for men held by our Govt. as Blockade runners, they claiming as the Champions were up the red river and attempting to run the blockade that they will only be exchanged for that kind of prisoners, these things I have not the Slightest doubt are correct, If any thing can be done for them I hope you will do it,"—ALS, University of Kentucky, Lexington, Ky.

1865, MARCH 21.   USG endorsement. "Respy referred Brig Gen W Hoffman, Com Gen Prisoners, who will please forward the parties within named for exchange, if they are held as within represented"—Copy, DLC-USG, V, 58. Written on a letter of March 7 from C.S.A. Agent of Exchange Robert Ould to Lt. Col. John E. Mulford enclosing a list of prisoners at Fort McHenry, Baltimore, and alleging their mistreatment.—*O.R.*, II, viii, 364. On April 20, Bvt. Brig. Gen. William Hoffman endorsed this letter. "Respectfully returned to Lieut Genl U S Grant. Comd'g. U S. Army. with reports received from the Comd'g. Officer of Ft. McHenry which show that there are no prisoners of War at that Fort. in irons or close confinement."—Copy, DNA, RG 249, Letters Sent.

1865, MARCH 21, 11:00 A.M.   Asst. Secretary of War Charles A. Dana to USG. "A person in confidential communication with Thompson & Tucker the rebel agents in Canada, whence he has just arrived reports that information had been received by them from Richmond to the 11th inst. It had been determined to unite the armies of Lee & Johnston, but at what point was ~~yet~~ still undecided. It was expected, but not yet absolutely resolved that Lee's [a]rmy would ~~evacuate~~ leave Richmond for the purpose."—ALS (telegram sent), DNA, RG 107, Telegrams Collected (Bound); telegram received, *ibid.*, RG 108, Letters Received. *O.R.*, I, xlvi, part 3, 62.

1865, MARCH 22.   USG endorsement. "Respectfully forwarded to the Secretary of War"—ES, DNA, RG 94, Letters Received, M146 1865. Written on the report of a board examining "Baxters Knapsack supporters." —DS, *ibid.* Other documents concerning the device, and a drawing of it, are *ibid.* On June 15, De Witt C. Baxter wrote to USG. "In the Spring of

1863 while the Army of the Potomac lay at Falmouth Va.—at my own expense—I equipped my regiment (the 72d Penna. Vols.) and each first Sergeant of the various regiments belonging to the 2d Divn 2d A. C. with my patent 'KnapSack Supporter' for the purpose of having the same thoroughly and practically tested. Of those issued then, many are still in use; to which I have never heard one word of objection but on the contrary have received the most flattering testimonials from Officers of every grade, and from none more satisfactory than the unanimous praise given it by the enlisted men who have so thoroughly tested it. Maj. Genl. Meade's recommendation for the issue of 25.000 came so late and the number so large that it became impracticable. I now respectfully ask that *one* regiment be equipped with my KnapSack Supporters for the purpose of experiment with a view of develloping whatever merit it may be found to possess, for the benefit of our Armies in future Military opperations; and would suggest the 3d Regt. 1st U. S. V. V. Col. Morgan (Wm H) comdg. to test and report"—ALS, *ibid.*, RG 108, Letters Received. On June 22, Bvt. Col. Theodore S. Bowers endorsed this letter. "Respectfully referred to Major General W. S. Hancock, Commanding Middle Mil'ty Division, who will please designate and cause to be equipped one regiment of his command with Baxters patent knapsack supporters for the purpose of testing their merits."—ES, *ibid.*

1865, MARCH 22. USG endorsement. "Respy. returned. This officer has not been, and is not now serving in the armies operating against Richmond. I learn unofficially that he was recently arrested at Baltimore by Col. Kellogg, Chief Commissary of the Mid Mil. Division. Further than this I can furnish no information in reference to him"—Copy, DLC-USG, V, 58. Probably written on a letter of March 17 from Bvt. Brig. Gen. Edward D. Townsend to USG. "The Secretary of War directs that Captain A. G. Randall, Commissary of Subsistence of Volunteers, be arrested and sent to Winchester, Virginia, for trial on charges preferred against him"—Copy, DNA, RG 94, Letters Sent.

1865, MARCH 22. To Maj. Gen. Henry W. Halleck. "I have no objection to the assignment of Gen Guy V Henry as proposed in your dispatch of this date"—Telegram received (on March 23, 1:20 P.M.), DNA, RG 94, Letters Received, 432H 1865. On March 22, 2:40 P.M., Halleck had telegraphed to USG. "Bvt Brig Genl Guy V. Henry, now on sick leave from Dept of Va. asks to be assigned for duty in the north-west, on recommendation of his physician. Genl Dodge asks for additional Genl officers. Is there any objection to this application of Genl Henry?"—ALS (telegram sent), *ibid.*, RG 107, Telegrams Collected (Bound); telegram received, *ibid.*; *ibid.*, Telegrams Collected (Unbound); (at 9:15 P.M.) *ibid.*, RG 108, Letters Received. On March 21, Bvt. Brig. Gen. Guy V. Henry, Washington, D. C., had written to USG. "I have the honor to request, that I may be ordered on duty in the North West. I make this request on account of my health that climate being recommended, for one with my disease."—ALS, *ibid.,* RG 94, Letters Received, 432H 1865. On May 25, Governor John Evans, Denver City, and others, addressed a petition to USG. "We, the undersigned Officers and Citizens of Colorado Territory, having learned that Brevet General Guy V Henry has asked to be relieved from duty in this District, on account of the great expense of living here,—he drawing only the pay of a Lieut of Artillery, as the Regiment of which he is Col. comes under the late order of the War Department, and is mustered out of service —would respectfully ~~request~~ pray that his request be not granted. but that his rank and pay be made such as to enable him to meet the great expensess of the Country—We, make this request because of the strict discipline and order he has established among the troops under his command, and because of the superior ability he has manifested in Controlling the ~~troops~~ affairs of this District—"—Copy, *ibid.,* ACP, H1118 CB 1864.

1865, MARCH 22. Brig. Gen. John A. Rawlins to Maj. Gen. Winfield S. Hancock. "under special orders number forty eight (48) you will under no circumstances permit familiesy supplies to go into virginia beyond the lines you actually hold. It will no doubt work hardships in many meritorious cases but we cannot control the use. They will be put to where ~~they will~~ beyond our reach. nor can those whom we would help   Hence the necessity of the strict enforcement of said order. The order does not apply to west virginia." —Telegrams received (2—on March 23, 1:20 P.M.), DNA, RG 107, Telegrams Collected (Bound); *ibid.,* RG 393, Middle Military Div., Letters Received; copy, *ibid.,* RG 107, Letters Received from Bureaus. *O.R.,* I, xlvi, part 3, 81. On March 21, Hancock had telegraphed to Rawlins. "I Would respectfully request to Know whether under the provisions of Special Order Number forty eight (48) I am at liberty to permit family Supplies to pass the lines I actually hold under any Circumstances   for example I do not hold Loudon County but have In my Command two Companies of Cavalry Composed of men from that County whose families live in Loudon & have been in the habit of getting Supplies across the Potomac—The same is the situation in part of West Virginia—"—Telegrams received (2), DNA, RG 107, Telegrams Collected (Unbound). *O.R.,* I, xlvi, part 3, 69.

1865, MARCH 22. Brig. Gen. Marsena R. Patrick to Lt. Col. Theodore S. Bowers. "I have the honor to enclose the orders relieving me and certain members of my staff from duty with the 'Army of Potomac.' As Captains Beckwith, Potter, and Scoville, and Lieut. Winfield, constitute my working staff as Provost Marshal General of Armies operating against Richmond, I respectfully request that they may be assigned to duty with me by an order from your office. The other officers, Surgeon Loughran and Captain Eddy, have rejoined their regiments. I would further suggest, that the jurisdiction of this office over all trade at City Point, whether afloat or ashore, be recognized in orders before the grounds are occupied on permits from the Army of the Potomac."—LS, DNA, RG 108, Letters Received.

1865, MARCH 22, 4:20 P.M. Bvt. Brig. Gen. Theodore Read, chief of staff for Maj. Gen. Edward O. C. Ord, to Brig. Gen. John A. Rawlins. "General Gordon sends the following information, received through a deserter from the 24th, Va. Cav., who reports, that the position which he occupied at Weldon afforded him a good opportunity to observe the amount of supplies passing through that place, the sources from whence it came, and its final destination:—All of the forage for Gen. Lee's army passes through Weldon. It is brought there on the Sea-Board, Raleigh and Gaston, and Weldon and Wilmington Rail Roads. Forage very scarce. All sugar and coffee lately issued to Genl. Lee's army has been carried through Weldon, and most of it came via Murfrie's Depot. Four hundred bales of cotton stored in Weldon, when informant left. Cotton seized by Conf'd't. Gov't. is turned over to Com. of Sub's't., who appoints agents to carry it into our lines and dispose of it. These agents are obliged to give security to amount of twenty thousand dollars, and are then allowed to take that amount of cotton out of Confederacy and exchange it for coffee, sugar and bacon. From six to twelve thousand pounds of bacon usually passed through Weldon daily, and most of it came from blockade runners, who gave it in exchange for cotton. Cotton trade dull, since late restrictions on all trade.— Cannot be disposed of, and is no longer sent to Murfree's Depot. Weldon is defended by one company with five pieces of Art'l'y, stationed north side of Roanoke River near R. R. Bridge.—Bridge is good, and very substantial. —Is used for carriages and foot passengers.—Is only bridge over river there. There are three companies of cavalry between Suffolk and Weldon,—called 12th N. C. Battalion,—commanded by Capt. Holliday.—Two companies at Borgan's Depot, and one with Hd Qrs at Murfrees pickets the Chowan and Blackwater. When Genl. Sherman was last heard from, he was at Fayetteville"—LS (telegram sent), DNA, RG 108, Letters Received; telegram received (at 4:20 P.M.), *ibid.* *O.R.*, I, xlvi, part 3, 77–78.

1865, MARCH 22. Chief John Ross and others, Washington, D. C., to USG. "The undersigned, Delegates of the Cherokee Nation duly appointed by authority of the National Council to look after the interests of our people in the City of Washington, being informed that an effort is being made to get the Indian Territory attached to the Department of Misso and Kansas, respectfully request the change asked for be not made. We are all entirely satisfied to remain under the command of Maj. Genl Reynolds in the Department of Arkansas. When heretofore attached to Kansas our cattle & corn have been stolen and our country ravaged under the auspices of the authorities sent to protect us—and we greatly fear that if we are again connected with that Department our people will be still further impoverished by the same kind of misrule. We further request that Major Genl

James G Blunt be not again placed in command in our Country."—DS, DNA, RG 108, Letters Received. *O.R.*, I, xlviii, part 1, 1237–38.

1865, MARCH 23. USG endorsement. "Respectfully forwarded to the Secretary of War. I see no advantages to the service, commensurate with the cost, that could be derived from the use of this shell."—ES, DNA, RG 94, Letters Received, 320A 1865. Written on the proceedings of a board, headed by Bvt. Brig. Gen. Henry L. Abbot, which examined "Mr R. L. Flemings incendiary shell."—DS, *ibid.*

1865, MARCH 23. USG endorsement. "Respy referred to Gen A B Eaton, Comy Gen. U S A. for his endorsement My long command in the west enables me to say that the duties of the subsistence Department, have been most efficiently performed by Col Hains, and I cheerfully endorse the recommendation for his promotion by Brevet. I am personally acquaintd with most of the signers of the within recommendation & know them not only to be original union men, but the most substantial and respectable citizens of St Louis."—Copy, DLC-USG, V, 58. Written on a letter of Feb. 27 from John O'Fallon and others, St. Louis, recommending Col. Thomas J. Haines for appointment as brig. gen.—*Ibid.*; *ibid.*, V, 49.

In Sept., 1863, John How, Giles F. Filley, Hugh Campbell, George Partridge, Brig. Gen. Robert Allen, and Brig. Gen. Albert G. Edwards had petitioned President Abraham Lincoln for the promotion of Haines.—DS, DNA, RG 94, ACP, 2605 (1872). On Oct. 26, USG endorsed this petition. "Respectfully forwarded to Hd Qrs. of the Army, Washington D. C. I know three of the signers of the within petition to be among the most prominant and respectable Union Citizens of St. Louis. I also know that Col Haines has filled his very responsible position to the entire satisfaction of the troops whom he has served and I believe with an eye single to the best interests of the Govt. If such promotions can consistently be made I would recommend the promotion of Col. Haines and also Lt. Col. Kilburn, Chief Com.y at Cincinnati to the rank of Brig. Gn."—AES, *ibid.* See *PUSG*, 9, 330*n.*

1865, MARCH 24. Secretary of State William H. Seward to USG. "The Honorable William Pickering, Governor of Washington Territory, informs me the Department that he is about to visit the Army and requests a letter of introduction, which is chearfully accorded to him."—ALS, Seward Papers, NRU.

1865, MARCH 24. Maj. Gen. John Gibbon to USG. "I received information today that a staff officer of C. M. Wilcox was at High Point N. C. which is 15 miles S. W. of Greensboro about the 9th of this month. Although this is not positive information of the presence of Wilcox's Div. there it may be confirmatory of other information which you may have, and I think it proper to report it."—Telegram received, DNA, RG 107, Telegrams Collected (Unbound). *O.R.*, I, xlvi, part 3, 102.

1865, MARCH 26. Bvt. Maj. Gen. Alexander S. Webb to USG. "I have telegraphed Mrs Webb that I will be down this eve' "—Telegram received (at 12:21 P.M.), CtY.

1865, MARCH 27. USG endorsement. "Respy forwarded to the Sec of War. I would recommend that Maj Gen Cadwalader be directed to inquire into each of the within cases, with authority to release and return to their regiments all men who appear to have been sufficiently punished, and whose conduct while in prison induces the belief that they will make faithful soldiers hereafter"—Copy, DLC-USG, V, 58. Written on a statement of March 22 of James Smith and others, Fort Delaware, asking to be restored to duty with the Army of the Potomac.—*Ibid.*; *ibid.*, V, 49.

1865, MARCH 27. USG endorsement. "Respy forwarded. I approve the suggestions of Major Stewart, and recommend, if deemed practicable, that orders be issued to carry them into effect"—Copy, DLC-USG, V, 58. Written on a letter of March 14 of Maj. Isaac S. Stewart, paymaster, suggesting measures to prevent the desertion of recruits.—*Ibid.*; *ibid.*, V, 49.

1865, MARCH 27. Brig. Gen. John A. Rawlins to Maj. Gen. Winfield S. Hancock. "Please order all medical officers belonging to Regiments of Cavalry now with Gen Sheridan to proceed to this place at once"—Telegram received, DNA, RG 107, Telegrams Collected (Unbound); (press) *ibid.*, Telegrams Collected (Bound); copies, *ibid.*, RG 108, Letters Sent; DLC-USG, V, 46, 75, 108. *O.R.*, I, xlvi, part 3, 215. On the same day, Hancock telegraphed to Rawlins. "There are six medical Officers at the remount camp all but one belonging to Regts now with Sheridan There are sixty one hundred men there mostly belonging to Sheridans Command I send three of them in the morning and will send the rest as soon as I can find Surgeons to relieve them"—Telegrams received (2—one on March 28, 9:45 A.M.), DNA, RG 107, Telegrams Collected (Unbound); (on March 28, 10:15 A.M.) *ibid.*, RG 108, Letters Received. *O.R.*, I, xlvi, part 3, 215–16.

1865, MARCH 27. Maj. Gen. Edward O. C. Ord to Brig. Gen. John A. Rawlins. "General Ludlow thinks that if the telegraph were instead of crossing Back river on Jamestown island at the upper end were to run down the island and cross over Back river at the lower end following the beach to the mouth of College creek (where there is a small post), & thence to Ft Magruder, it would be under better control than it now is—Can this alteration be made—"—LS (telegram sent), DNA, RG 107, Telegrams Collected (Unbound); telegram received, *ibid.*, RG 108, Letters Received. *O.R.*, I, xlvi, part 3, 209.

1865, MARCH 28. To Bvt. Brig. Gen. James A. Hardie. "I prefer that the gentlemen of the British Army whom you name would not come."— Telegram received (at 4:35 P.M.), DNA, RG 107, Telegrams Collected (Bound); (press) *ibid.* On the same day, Hardie had telegraphed to USG.

"Capt. Glynn, Capt. Northey and T Darnley Crosbie, of the British Army desire to visit the HeadQuarters Army Potomac—Is there any objection to their so doing?"—LS (telegram sent), *ibid.*; telegram received (at 3:55 P.M.), *ibid.*, RG 108, Letters Received.

1865, MARCH 28. To Bvt. Brig. Gen. William Hoffman. "Please forward Maj. N. Fitzhugh of Hampton's staff by first opportunity for exchange. He is at Ft Delaware."—ALS (telegram sent), Kohns Collection, NN; telegram received (misdated March 29), DNA, RG 107, Telegrams Collected (Bound); (at 9:45 A.M.) *ibid.*, RG 249, Letters Received. On Jan. 5, Lt. Col. Frederick T. Dent wrote a letter probably intended for C.S.A. Brig. Gen. William N. R. Beall. "Major Norman Fitz Hugh a brother-in law of my wife is a prisoner of war at Fort Delaware. at her suggestion I would respectfully request your influence to have him paroled and taken as one of your assistants his health is impaired and will be more so by confinement. could this be effected it will be a favour to her which will be fully appreciated—Mrs D is now living in Burlington New Jersey"—ALS, Confederate Museum, Richmond, Va. Dent mentioned the matter again in a letter of Jan. 8 to Beall.—ALS, *ibid.* On March 26, Dent wrote to his wife. "I did receive Norman's letter—and have been finding the officers who started the report have written to one of them who is now with Sherman —I have also handed his letter around among those who had heard the report as it was given here—and I think a great change of opinion has taken place in regard to the ~~feelings that~~ case and the feeling toward Norman has undergone a great change—"—ALS, John D. Burt, Redwood City, Calif.

1865, MARCH 29. USG endorsement. "Respectfully returned to the Secretary of War, with the recommendation that the monthly rate of commutation for officers servants be fixed at the cost prices of clothing issued to soldiers, as summed in General Orders at the time the commutation is made."—ES, DNA, RG 94, Letters Received, 345A 1865. Written on a letter of March 22 from Maj. Gen. Henry W. Halleck to USG. "I am directed by the Secty of War to forward the enclosed paper in regard to commutation price of Soldier's clothing, for your opinion & recommendation."—ALS, *ibid.*

1865, MARCH 29. To Maj. Gen. Horatio G. Wright. "Can you tell me where the Heavy artillery firing heard this morning was at?—"—Telegram received (at 8:35 A.M.), William C. Banning, Silver Spring, Md.

[*1865, March 29*]. Maj. Gen. Edward O. C. Ord to USG. "The firing on my front is simply picket firing. The men are firing away a great deal of ammunition unnecessarily. I have sent to have it stopped."—Copy (with penciled date), Ord Papers, CU-B.

1865, MARCH 30. Bvt. Brig. Gen. Edward D. Townsend, AGO, to USG. "In compliance with your request, I have the honor to transmit, herewith, a list of the major and Brigadier General's in the Regular Army, and of the Volunteer force, showing how and when said officers, are now employed." —Copy, DNA, RG 94, Commissions and Returns, Letters Sent.

1865, MARCH 30. Capt. Peter C. Hains, New Orleans, to Brig. Gen. John A. Rawlins. "You may recollect that in November 1863 Genl. Grant recommended me to the Governor of New Jersey for the position of Colonel of a Volunteer Regt—I received a letter from the Governor enclosing one from the Adjt. Genl. War. Dept—copies of which I send you, I do this to ask you if there is no hope of my being allowed to accept the position, after that answer—I have been trying hard to get into the field, & thought I had about succeeded when I got this—Genl. Hurlbut Comdg. the Dept, is anxious that I be allowed to accept the position, I am not in the field with Genl. Canby, I am in New Orleans & have been for about a year—If you deem proper I would like you to speak to the Genl—Comdg. about it. It was his recommendation that got me the appointment, perhaps he can devise some means by which I can be allowed to accept it—Please let me hear from you in regard to the matter . . ."—ALS (misdated 1864), DNA, RG 108, Letters Received. The enclosures are *ibid.* Hains remained in New Orleans. On June 8, Hains asked for leave to accept the position of col., 10th N. J., and, on June 16, USG endorsed this letter. "Respy. forwarded to the Sec of War with recommendation that the leave within asked be granted. Capt Haines is a most excellent officer and was by me recommended for the Colonelcy of a N. J. regiment more than a year since"—Copy, DLC-USG, V, 58.

1865, MARCH 31. Lt. Col. Ely S. Parker to Lt. Col. Theodore S. Bowers. "Major Wiley will call on you for an escort to guard cattle for Sheridan. You will order the escort from Sheridans remounted men"—Copies, DLC-USG, V, 46, 75, 108; DNA, RG 108, Letters Sent. *O.R.*, I, xlvi, part 3, 343. On the same day, Bowers wrote to Col. James Q. Anderson, 17th Pa. Cav., Remount Station, City Point. "You will immediately furnish mounted men under such necessary officers as you can spare to drive and guard a lot of beef cattle from the general cattle herd at City Point to Maj. Gen. Sheridan's command, in the vicinity of Dinwiddie Court House. The men will proceed as soon as they can be got in readiness to the Cattle Herd, from which they well start under the orders of Maj. Wiley, Depot Commissary, promptly at daylight tomorrow morning. You will report your execution of this order."—Copies, DLC-USG, V, 46, 75, 108; DNA, RG 108, Letters Sent.

1865, MARCH 31. Capt. Paul A. Oliver to Lt. Col. Theodore S. Bowers. "Our people came from Richmond yesterday, and brought the following information:—On Tuesday [*March 28*], General Lee and President Davis were together, the latter accompanying General Lee to the cars when he left. Our Richmond friends say that it is understood in official circles, that the forces of Lee and Johnston are to be joined. As a part of the preparations, either to leave wholly, or to take a new line in the rear of Petersburg, we have information that two pontoon bridges have been laid across the Appomattox; one just above Petersburg, and the other several miles above—their location is not more definitely fixed. Our friends say, that up to day before yesterday, only two brigades of Pickett's Division had passed to the Southside; namely, Hunton's and Terry's; and that Corse and Stewart were left on the north side. About one hundred pontoon boats were sent out on the Danville Road on Monday and Tuesday. Our Richmond friends say that the Post Office Department and the State Department are being moved from Richmond; and that the families of Mr. Davis, Secretary Mallory, Post Master General Regan, and that of Commissary General Northrop, have gone South; the information being repeated, that Mr. Davis' furniture had been sold, partly at auction and partly at private sale. We are told that the tunnel under Fort Harrison is progressing. From the large number of naval vessels in the James, the Richmond authorities seem to fear an attempt at passing the river by our navy and at or near 'the graveyard' (a place near the exchange ground) where there is only a passage sufficient for one ironclad, for four nights past, three wooden gunboats and one of the ironclads—the 'Fredericksburg'—have been sent down with instructions, that, if our fleet makes any demonstration, they are to be scuttled and sunk across the channel. When Fitz Hugh Lee's cavalry passed through Richmond on Monday, he took Paine's and Wickham's brigades with him, leaving Gary still on the enemy's extreme left. Paine's and Wickham's brigades were said to be in good condition. It is also understood that troops have been sent to the High Bridge over the Appomattox. The repairs on the Va. Central R. R. are being pushed forward, and it is said that the road will be run to Beaverdam Station on Sunday—a distance of forty miles. The Tredegar Iron Works are to be completely closed to-morrow. Some of the men have already been sent to Texas. Owing to the provisions which have been brought in, there is an increase in the amount of rations on hand. Hitherto the enemy have been able to provide for only one day ahead, and now our friends say that they have five or six days ahead. It is a matter of conversation among well informed people in Richmond, that a great battle will be risked, and if successful, Richmond will be held; if not, it will be evacuated. A report reached Richmond night before last, that Joe. Johnston evacuated Raleigh on the 28th instant."—ALS, DLC-Robert T. Lincoln. On April 1, Oliver wrote to Bowers. "Beyond the transfer of two Brigades of Picketts Division, from the North of the James, to South of the Appomattox, there is no change to notice in the enemys line in front of Bermuda Hundred & North of the James.—Mahones Division is still in front of Bermuda Hundred, between the Appomattox & the James.—Fields Division, & Kershaws Division, from Williamsburg Road to near Fort Harrison.—Next to this, Bartons Va Brigade & the Local Defence troops, extending to the river.— Garrys Cavalry Brigade is still in its old position, cossing the York River R Road, its left reaching to the New Bridge Road.—Deserters & prisoners received report nothing new.—I have telegraphed Genl Sharpe, & keep him advised of what is going on.—"—ALS, *ibid.*

1865, APRIL 6. Maj. Gen. Winfield S. Hancock, Winchester, Va., to USG. "Genl Terbert has Just returned from His reconnoisance he found nothing in the valley excepting a few hunded cavalry under Rosser at staunton he is satisfied from the reports from all the people that a movement of Picketts division was anticipated & quite a number of ~~the~~ his men are on furlough near here—some deserters from his division also report that it was the talk among the men that they were coming to the valley—"—Telegram received, DNA, RG 107, Telegrams Collected (Unbound); *ibid.*, RG 108, Letters Received. Printed as received at 9:10 P.M. in *O.R.*, I, xlvi, part 3, 616–17.

1865, APRIL 6. Commander Edward T. Nichols, U.S.S. *Mendota*, Hampton Roads, to Bvt. Col. Theodore S. Bowers. "Have just returned from Point Lookout—Was informed by naval officer Comdg that deserters from Longstreet Came in to the gunboats in York River yesterday and reported that he was between Pamunkey & Mattapony Rivers Cut off and without Supplies—you Can best judge of the reliability of this Story—"—Telegram received (at 5:20 P.M.), DNA, RG 108, Letters Received. *O.R.*, I, xlvi, part 3, 616. See *O.R.* (Navy), I, xii, 105.

1865, APRIL 6. Bvt. Brig. Gen. George H. Sharpe, Burkeville, Va., to Brig. Gen. John A. Rawlins. "Some refugees have Come in to our lines who left Danville Monday [*April 3*] night they say that Davis & Cabinet arrived Sunday at 2 P M & Mr Davis was taken to a Mr Sutherlands up the River where he remained up to Monday P M & is yet there as far as they know on sunday P M a despatch arrived from Beauregard at Greensboro saying that Stoneman had Captured High Point on the N C RR orders were then given not to transfer freight onto the Piedmont RR & Informant Knows that nothing went from Danville to Greensboro on Monday up to the time he left late in the Eve 3 frame buildings each 300 feet long at Danville filled with supplies troops on Stauntion River at Roanoke station withdrawn to Danville except one Company The Country between here & Danville filled with straglers mostly from N. C going home mostly unarmed heard that Johnston was ordered to join forces with Lee had ~~news~~ no news from Lynchburg Heard that Sherman was close up to Johnston but dont know where. No ~~words~~ works of Consequence at Danville a good deal of Militia there"—Telegram received, DLC-Robert T. Lincoln.

1865, APRIL 7. Maj. Gen. Godfrey Weitzel, Richmond, to USG. "The following has been found here"—Telegram received, DNA, RG 107, Telegrams Collected (Unbound). Weitzel appended a copy of a letter of March 9 from Gen. Robert E. Lee to Secretary of War John C. Breckinridge printed in *O.R.*, I, xlvi, part 2, 1295–96.

1865, APRIL 8.   Maj. Gen. George H. Thomas to USG. "I Send the following telegram just received from Gen Hatch for the information of the secy of war   I believe there is probability of its truth through the source from whence Gen Hatch derived it can[*not*] be strictly releid upon   'Eastport Miss Apl 6th 65   MAJ GEN THOMAS   A Scout just in reports as follows—Rebel telegram to Rienzi states Federal Cavalry at Selma whipped fForrest & burned the town   cavalry supposed wilsons   That forest had fallen back to Columbus   signed EDWARD HATCH Br Gen."—Telegram received, DNA, RG 107, Telegrams Collected (Unbound); *ibid.*, RG 108, Letters Received. Printed as addressed to Maj. Gen. Henry W. Halleck, received at 3:00 P.M., in *O.R.*, I, xlix, part 2, 269.

1865, APRIL 8.   Maj. Gen. Godfrey Weitzel, Richmond, to USG. "Bt. Brig Gen Collis Comdg troops at City Pt refuses to be relieved by my troops   will you please give the necessary orders"—Telegram received, DNA, RG 107, Telegrams Collected (Unbound); copy, *ibid.*, RG 393, 25th Army Corps, Telegrams Sent. *O.R.*, I, xlvi, part 3, 658. On the same day, Bvt. Brig. Gen. Charles H. T. Collis telegraphed to Bvt. Col. Theodore S. Bowers. "There are about four hundred remounted cavalry here—Would it not be well to send them forward with the recruits who are accumulating here"—ALS (telegram sent), DNA, RG 107, Telegrams Collected (Unbound). On the same day, Bowers telegraphed to Collis. "Send forward immediately, as far by railroad as possible, all troops of your command. They will come on until they meet the rebel prisoners and then take charge of them and conduct them to City Point. Use all possible diligence in the execution of this order."—*O.R.*, I, xlvi, part 3, 660. At noon, Collis telegraphed to Bowers. "My command of four Regiments about fifteen hundred men have started to meet the Prisoners   I could not obtain Railroad transportation—The Eleventh and fourteenth Infantry will go by Railroad this ~~evening~~—afternoon—My brigade will be some miles beyond Petersburg to night—"—ALS (telegram sent), DNA, RG 107, Telegrams Collected (Unbound); telegram received, *ibid.*, RG 108, Letters Received.

1865, APRIL 8.   Lt. Col. Ely S. Parker, Farmville, Va., to Lt. E. H. Rich. "There being no guard at this place to receive & Escort or guard prisoners you will proceed with your guard and prisoners to Burkesville Junction and deliver your prisoners to the Provost Guard at that place. Upon the Execution of this order you will rejoin your Corps without delay—"—ALS, Scheide Library, Princeton, N. J.

1865, APRIL 8.   Lt. Col. Ely S. Parker note. "Chief Commissary Army of the Potomac will furnish two sheep to Head Qrs of Lieut Gen Grant—"—ANS, Scheide Library, Princeton, N. J.

1865, APRIL 9.   To Bvt. Brig. Gen. William Hoffman. "I approve Newport News as a place for holding prisoners of War. It being in the Dept.

of Va. Gen. Ord will furnish guards."—ALS (telegram sent from Clifton, 9:30 A.M.), DNA, RG 107, Telegrams Collected (Unbound); Scheide Library, Princeton, N. J.; telegram received, DNA, RG 249, Letters Received. On April 8, Hoffman, City Point, had telegraphed to USG. "I am directed by the Secretary of War to consult you in reference to establishing a depot for prisoners of war near Fort Monroe. Newport News seems to be the most eligible place, and if you approve I will establish it there. Ten thousand to twenty thousand prisoners will require a guard of two regiments. To whom shall I apply for them?"—LS (telegram sent), *ibid.*, RG 107, Telegrams Collected (Unbound); telegram received, *ibid.*, RG 108, Letters Received. *O.R.*, II, viii, 477.

1865, APRIL 9. To Bvt. Col. Theodore S. Bowers. "Come out following the 5th Corps train. Direct Gn. Parke to push all prisoners of War to the rear as rapidly as possible."—ALS, DNA, RG 107, Telegrams Collected (Bound); Scheide Library, Princeton, N. J. *O.R.*, I, xlvi, part 3, 669.

1865, APRIL 9. Maj. Gen. George L. Hartsuff to "Asst Adjt Genl Genl Grants Hd Qrs In the field." "In what way can I assist you? Am able perhaps to contribute much assistance & am very desirous of doing so if I only knew what was most needed."—ALS (telegram sent), DNA, RG 107, Telegrams Collected (Unbound); copy, *ibid.*, RG 393, Dept. of Va. and N. C., Forces at Petersburg, Telegrams Sent. *O.R.*, I, xlvi, part 3, 680.

1865, APRIL 9. Lt. Col. Ely S. Parker to Maj. Gen. Philip H. Sheridan. "The Lt. Gen is informed that the trains you captured near here are without Guards and that every thing has been or is being carried away from them —He directs that you have them put in charge of your proper Staff Officers & have them guarded—"—ALS, Scheide Library, Princeton, N. J. *O.R.*, I, xlvi, part 3, 676.

1865, APRIL 11. To Mrs. E. C. Atchison. "Your son is safe & has behaved well in all the Battles."—Telegram received, DNA, RG 107, Telegrams Collected (Bound); (2) *ibid.*, Telegrams Collected (Unbound).

1865, APRIL 11. Maj. Gen. John Pope to USG. "The following dispatch from New Orleans just received   It has been confirmed by ~~teleg~~ intelligence from another source. Gen Reynolds cavalry is nearly all dismounted, Genl Canby having taken all the horses from arkansas. Whilst Reynolds might defend the posts he occupies, he has not force sufficient to oppose Kirby Smiths advance nor is there any force anywhere in this command for this purpose. It is not known what effect Lees surrender may have upon this movement but your immediate attention is invited to this dispatch   The montgomery papers say, 'A gentleman just from Richmond and a member of congress informs us that Gen Lee has ordered Kirby Smith to move with his whole army into Missouri. Our spies report that Kirby Smith is preparing to make this movement at the earliest possible moment' . . . 'St Louis Mo 11th Apl. The following despatch is just recd. To MAJ GEN POPE Comdg officer at Fort Riley & Comdg officer at Fort Scott both report standwaite at forks of white water & walnut which is one hundred (100) miles west of Fort Scott & fifty (50) miles south of Kansas line, with from six hundred to fifteen hundred men indians & whites—They have committed some depredations & claim to be the advance of a force moving north from Red river, I have sent all the force I have, four hundred mounted men from fort Scott out to attack & check them   signed G. M DODGE Maj Gen' "—Telegram received, DNA, RG 108, Letters Received. See *O.R.*, I, xlviii, part 2, 70.

1865, APRIL 11.   John U. McAlvin, city clerk, Lowell, Mass., to USG. "I have the honor to transmit herewith a copy of a 'Resolution of thanks for the recent victories of our armies,' this day passed by the City Council of the City of Lowell."—ALS, USG 3. The resolutions are *ibid.*

1865, APRIL 12.   President Abraham Lincoln to USG introducing John W. Forney, "principal editor of the Chronicle." Lincoln wrote that Forney "has some purpose to go to Richmond, on newspaper business. You could not oblige a truer man."—*The Collector*, LXXXIV, 816 (1971), p. 9.

1865, APRIL 12.   Bvt. Brig. Gen. William W. Morris, Baltimore, to USG. "In view of the peculiar state of affairs in this Dept and particularly the city of Balto and the disposition of the people who still insist upon being disloyal, I propose to issue an order that all rebel officers and soldiers who were paroled by Lee's surrender, who came to this Dept to remain until exchanged, Must report to the nearest Pro Mar and have their names registered and require them to abandon the rebel uniform while here—Unless some such order is issued the streets will be filled with rebel uniforms and women parading with them and the result will be trouble—Will such an order conflict with the terms of their parole or be approved by you."—ALS (telegram sent), DNA, RG 107, Telegrams Collected (Unbound); *ibid.*, RG 393, Middle Dept. and 8th Army Corps, Telegrams Sent (Press); telegram received, *ibid.*, RG 107, Telegrams Collected (Unbound); *ibid.*, RG 108, Letters Received. *O.R.*, I, xlvi, part 3, 727.

1865, APRIL 12.   Special Orders No. 75, Armies of the U.S. "Brevet Major Gen. J. G. Barnard, Chief Engineer Armies in the Field, will make full and complete surveys and Maps of the fortifications and defences of Richmond and Petersburg—On the completion of which he will report to the Lieut General commanding at Washington"—Copies, DLC-USG, V, 57, 63, 65. *O.R.*, I, xlvi, part 3, 719.

1865, APRIL [*13*].   Mary Lincoln to USG. "Mr Lincoln is indisposed with quite a severe headache, yet would be very much pleased to see you at the house, this evening about 8 o'clock & *I* want you to drive around with us to see the illumination"—ALS, Berkshire Museum, Pittsfield, Mass.

1865, APRIL 14.   USG endorsement. "I would recommend that Capt. Wright be breveted a Major of Volunteers"—Paul C. Richards, Catalogue 132 [1980], no. 88. Apparently written on a letter of Brig. Gen. Charles Cruft.

1865, APRIL 14.   President Abraham Lincoln to USG. "Please call at 11. A. M. to day insted of 9. as agreed last evening."—ALS (facsimile), MG 237, Pennsylvania State Archives, Harrisburg, Pa. Lincoln, *Works*, VIII, 411.

1865, APRIL 14.   Maj. Gen. Ambrose E. Burnside, New York City, to USG. "I have just asked the Secretary by telegraph not to muster me out by General Orders. If the order is issued I hope my name will be taken off, that I may be allowed to resign.   my resignation goes forward today. Please answer."—Telegram received (at noon), DNA, RG 108, Telegrams Received; copy, DLC-USG, V, 54. Burnside resigned as of April 15.

1865, APRIL 14.   Col. Benjamin L. E. Bonneville, Benton Barracks, Mo., to USG. "Could you be displeased, if I address you as of old? I know your good sense will rather be gratified at this proof of continued confidence in one whose great pride is, to have been your former commander. Allow me, my dear General, to congratulate you, upon the great work you have accomplished: believe me, when I say to you, your countrymen ever proud of your [works], will wreathe it with laurels, and claim it as the proudest ornament of their homestead—"—ALS (addressed to "Grant"), USG 3.

1865, APRIL 14.   Capt. Joseph B. Collins, 4th Inf., City Point, to Bvt. Col. Theodore S. Bowers. "The fourth U S. Infy arrived at this camp at 4 30 P M this day"—Telegram received (at 8:45 P.M.), DNA, RG 108, Telegrams Received; copy, DLC-USG, V, 54. *O.R.*, I, xlvi, part 3, 745.

1865, APRIL 14.   Hanson A. Risley, supervising special agent, U.S. Treasury Dept., to USG. "I have the honor to transmit by the hand of Col Loomis the application of D. Ferguson to take a cargo of goods specefied in the application or memorandum attached, to, Richmond Va; and having been informed that supplies of the character are needed there, I respectfully suggest that if so & you will cause orders to be given for the transportation of Mr Ferguson's and two other (or either) cargoes of provisions & merchandise, (not munitions of war) that clearance & permit will be given from this Department"—ALS, DNA, RG 366, 7th Special Agency. On April 17, Bvt. Col. Theodore S. Bowers endorsed this letter. "Permission is hereby granted for three Cargoes of goods, cleared by the Treasury Department, to be taken to Richmond, Virginia, for Sale there."—AES, *ibid.*

1865, APRIL 15. To U.S. Representative Elihu B. Washburne, City Point. "I will not go to Richmond for ten days or more. I can not leave here at present"—Telegram sent, DNA, RG 107, Telegrams Collected (Bound); telegram received, *ibid.* *O.R.*, I, xlvi, part 3, 758. On the same day, Washburne, Richmond, had telegraphed to USG. "When will you be here! If here by Monday I will remain   if not I will leave City Pt tomorrow morning & reach Washn Monday morning. Have you any news from Johnson."— Telegram received (at 8:15 P.M.), DNA, RG 108, Telegrams Received; copy, DLC-USG, V, 54.

1865, APRIL 17. Bvt. Col. Theodore S. Bowers to Absalom H. Markland, special agent of the Post Office Dept. "Lieutenant-General Grant directs that no mail matter be sent to Richmond addressed to citizens of that place until further orders. He further directs that you unseal and examine all letters in the mails addressed to citizens of Richmond and forward to these headquarters all such as contain contraband information."—*O.R.*, I, xlvi, part 3, 810.

1865, APRIL 17. Isaac F. Quinby, Rochester, N. Y., to USG. "While the whole people are plunged in the deepest grief at the death of our wise and most excellent President there is mingled with it a feeling of thankfullness that you, for whom the same blow was intended, so providentially escaped. If our hopes of the recovery of Secretary Seward are also realized the Nation will soon arouse itself from its almost stupor of grief, and forebodings of other calamities to follow in the train of this will give place to confidence in the ability of those at the head of our affairs to bring about the peace and National prosperity which seemed so well assured before this sad event. The people hope not less from you in the future than you have accomplished for them in the past, and I speak therefore not in the name of personal friendship alone, but in that of the Nation, when I ask you to take all wise precautions to guard against the assassins who may be watching their opportunity to strike at your life. With the most earnest wishes that your life may be long spared to your family and to the Nation . . ."—ALS, USG 3.

1865, APRIL 18. USG endorsement. "I have no objection to all Steamers now in the Red River at and above Alexandria, La., being run to New Orleans, La., laden with Cotton, the boats to be exempt from seizure if the property of Citizens loyal to the United States or who became so under the Presidents Amnesty ~~Proclamation~~ the Cotton to be sold to Government in accordance with Acts of Congress governing trade with the States in rebellion"—Copies, DLC-USG, V, 58; DNA, RG 108, Miscellaneous Papers, Papers of Theodore S. Bowers. "~~Letter~~ Endorsement on letter of Jas Harrison to Hon Hugh McCulloch Stating that in a recent trip to Red River he saw a number of Steamers, 12 or 15 in number & ownend by individuals who would be glad to save them by running within the lines of the U. S.

forces or to sell them to Union Men who could be permitted to run them within the lines under a gaurantee that they would not be seized or confiscated. If not saved in this way they will probably be destroyed by burning. Proposes to return & buy said Steamers & run them within the Union lines loaded with Cotton or other products at his own risk & requests permit to buy & bring them out without seizure or Confiscation, upon payment of duties required by revenue laws. Boats & cargoes to be reported to Collector at N Orleans soon as practicable after coming within our lines"—Copy, *ibid.*

1865, APRIL 18.   Maria Pearson, Stockwell, England, to USG. "I beg to say my husband George Pearson who joined your army in 1862 in the 1st Battalion 13th Infantry Co. G. has not answered my letters since June last causing me the greatest anxiety & having three little boys to bring up has urged me to take the liberty of addressing you hoping Sir you kindly condescend to reply to this"—ALS, DNA, RG 108, Letters Received. An endorsement reported that Private George Pearson deserted on Aug. 16, 1864.

1865, APRIL 19, 9:45 P.M.   To Col. Joseph Roberts, Fort Monroe. "Have Wm W. Wharton, a keeper of a litte store or Sutler store at Ft. Monroe arrested, and all his papers collected carefully and send the whole under guard to ~~Richmond~~ Col. Baker Washington. Send the man in irons."—ALS (telegram sent), DNA, RG 107, Telegrams Collected (Bound); telegram sent, *ibid.*; copies, *ibid.*, RG 108, Letters Sent; DLC-USG, V, 46, 76, 108. On the same day, Maj. J. S. Stevenson, Fort Monroe, telegraphed to USG. "Wm D. Wharton sutler at this place, left here for Baltimore on the evening of the ~~eighteenth~~ seventeenth five o'clock—I have arrested his employees and am examening his papers"—ALS (telegram sent), DNA, RG 107, Telegrams Collected (Unbound); telegram received (on April 20, 1:20 A.M.), *ibid.*, Telegrams Collected (Bound); *ibid.*, RG 108, Telegrams Received. On April 20, 9:30 A.M., USG telegraphed to the commanding officer, Baltimore. "W. D. Wharton, Sutler at Ft. Monroe left that place the evening of the 17th for Baltimore. If he can be found arrest him and send him [to] Col. Baker Washington."—ALS (telegram sent), *ibid.*, RG 107, Telegrams Collected (Bound); telegram sent, *ibid.*; telegram received, *ibid.*, RG 393, Middle Dept. and 8th Army Corps, Telegrams Sent (Press).

1865, APRIL 19.   USG pass. "Pass Mr L[ocke] to City Point and return" —ANS, WHi. Written on a letter of the same day from U.S. Senator Ira Harris of N. Y. to Bvt. Brig. Gen. James A. Hardie. "The bearer of this note, Mr Locke, has a brother at City Point, severely wounded—He desires to visit him and provide for his comfort—Mr Locke comes to me highly commended by some excellent citizens of New York and I solicit on his behalf the requisite facilities to enable him to reach his brother."—ALS, *ibid.* Dayton Locke received the pass.—Madison, Wis., *State Journal*, Aug. 17, 1885.

1865, APRIL 19. Maj. Gen. John Pope, St. Louis, to USG. "I transmit herewith, a letter written to the President some days since, but withheld until this time in consequence of the awful calamity which has befallen the Country. I do not deem it proper to withhold it longer, and I therefore submit it to your consideration, with the request that, if you approve it, you will forward it to its destination through the War Department. It is proper to state that the measures therein proposed, are substantially those adopted in Missouri, and which have led to such admirable results already, in the latter State. Already the whole of North Missouri has been turned over to the Civil Authorities of the State, troops and Provost Marshals having all been withdrawn except, from two or three Counties along the Missouri river. The Governor wrote me under date of the 14.th. inst., that the counties of Saint Louis, Jefferson, Franklin, Gasconade and Osage, are now in condition to be surrendered entirely, to the civil authorities, and I shall withdraw the Military, from all connection with Civil ~~officers~~ affairs in these Counties tomorrow. Every thing is working favorably to the same end in the Counties South of the Missouri, and I expect, in a few months, to leave Missouri entirely to the State authorities, and remove all the Military forces from the State. The fear of a raid by small bands from the Missouri forces under Sterling Price, renders the people of the Counties in question uneasy, and a little unwilling still, to dispense with the Military and rely upon their own resources. If the ~~tumult~~ summer passes off—as I hope it will—without such raids, the whole of the difficulties in Missouri, as far as the General Government is concerned, are ended. I believe that the same policy, substantially pursued in Arkansas, will assure the same results, as soon as the enemy is driven from the Red river; Even now, the policy could be safely applied in that portion of the State North of the Arkansas river. I only wish the approval of the Government to what I propose; so that I can make the needful arrangements in time to *begin* the policy with the disappearance of Kirby Smith's Army from the Red river, which I trust, will be early in the summer. Meantime I need not assure you that any other plan or policy in these matters adopted by the Government, I will execute with all zeal and all the energy I can command. I would be glad if you will submit this letter to the Secretary of War with the letter to the President, [if you should approve the views contained in the latter,] as it contains information which may perhaps, be useful in determining action upon the policy I suggest for Arkansas Civil affairs."—LS (brackets in original), DNA, RG 107, Letters Received. *O.R.*, I, xlviii, part 2, 132–33. See *ibid.*, pp. 125–32. On April 23, Bvt. Col. Theodore S. Bowers endorsed this letter. "Respectfully submitted to the Secretary of War."—AES, DNA, RG 107, Letters Received. *O.R.*, I, xlviii, part 2, 133.

1865, APRIL 20. USG endorsement. "Respectfully refered to the Sec. of the Treasury, Approved. I see no objection to the exportation of animals of any kind that are too valuable to be purchased for the use of the government but on the contrary it seems to me that these exports should be encouraged as a help to the finances of the country."—AES, DNA, RG 56, Div. of Captured and Abandoned Property, Letters Received, 494. Written on a statement of the same day of William D. W. Barnard. "Application is hereby respectfully made for permission to ship from the port of New York to Havana Cuba One Hundred pair of Horses to cost not less than Six Hundred Dollars a pair"—ADS, *ibid.*

1865, APRIL 20. To Bvt. Brig. Gen. Edward D. Townsend. "My attention has been called to the resignation of J. B. Atherton (Major) 22nd Iowa Vols, accepted by me in Special Orders No, 154 of June 8th 1863, and to facts which subsequently appeared in the case which are now on file in the Adjt, Genls Office, I would now like to have the order accepting Maj, Atherton's resignation revoked on the ground of it having been obtained on false statements and have him dishonorably discharged the Service from same date, for falsehood cowardice, and mis-conduct in the presence of the Enemy"—Copies, DLC-USG, V, 46, 76, 108; DNA, RG 108, Letters Sent.

1865, APRIL 20. USG endorsement. "I recommend that the within named Officers be ordered to join their regiment with the exception of Lt. French who, under the circumstances, I think should remain on present duty"—ES, DNA, RG 94, Letters Received, 572H 1865. Written on a letter of March 5 from Capt. Robert H. Hall, 10th Inf., Buffalo, N. Y., to Brig. Gen. Lorenzo Thomas requesting the return of officers of the 10th Inf.—LS, *ibid.*

1865, [APRIL 20]. USG memorandum. "I recommend the following officers for Brevets: Captain H. C. Robinett, A. D. C. to be Major of Volunteers by brevet. Captain Amos Webster, Assistant Qr. Master to be mMajor of Volunteers by brevet 1st Lieut. D. E. Porter, 1st Artillery, to be Captain by brevet in the Regular Service,—To date from April 9. 1865, for meritorious Services in the campaign against the Rebel Army of Northern Virginia, Commencing in front of Petersburg, Va, March 29. 1865, and ending April 9th 1865."—DS (undated; date on docket), DNA, RG 94, ACP, S420 CB 1865.

1865, APRIL 20. To George Peters. "Your favor of the 14th inst. and the Horse Equipments announced in it, have arrived safely. Allow me to thank you for this mark of your approval of my efforts in the restoration of peace and law over the whole of our beautiful land, . . ."—ALS, IHi.

1865, APRIL 20. Special Orders No. 78, Armies of the U.S. "1. . Brig. Gen. Edward A. Wild, U. S Vols, having been relieved from duty in the Dept of Virginia, and ordered to report to these Headqrs by Major General E. O. C. Ord, will proceed to his home, and from there report by letter to the Adjutant General of the Army, Washington D. C. for orders. 2. . Brig. Gen. Hugh Ewing, U. S. Volunteers will report in person to Major

General C. C. Augur, commanding Dept of Washington for orders."—
Copies, DLC-USG, V, 57, 63, 65. *O.R.*, I, xlvi, part 3, 847.

1865, April 21. USG endorsement. "It is important that this road should
be available to the Government. If the company cannot repair it, the Government should make the necessary repairs, and charge the cost of the same
against the earnings of the Company, or deduct from any claim the road
may have against the Government. If this is not done the road should be
seized by the Military. I prefer the former plan and will so direct if it meets
the approbation of the Secretary of War."—Copy, DNA, RG 92, Letters
Received by Gen. McCallum. Written on a copy of a telegram of April 3
from Maj. Gen. Grenville M. Dodge to Bvt. Brig. Gen. Daniel C. McCallum reporting nine bridges on the Iron Mountain Railroad washed away by
a freshet.—Copy, *ibid. O.R.*, I, xlviii, part 2, 20–21. See *ibid.*, p. 250.

1865, April 21. USG endorsement. "I recommend the dismissal of Col.
Jones."—ES, DNA, RG 94, ACP, J35 CB 1864. Written on a letter of
April 11 from Maj. Gen. Winfield S. Hancock to Brig. Gen. Lorenzo
Thomas reporting that Col. Amos B. Jones had twice been absent without
leave.—LS, *ibid.* Jones was dismissed as of May 8.

1865, April 21. USG endorsement. "Bvt. Lieut. Col. OBeirne will be
required to join his regiment immediately on the completion of the case
now being tried by the Court Martial of which he is a member. It appears
from the letter of the commander of the Dept. of the East that his services
on the Court cannot at once be dispensed with."—ES (not in USG's hand),
DNA, RG 94, Letters Received, 185E 1865. Written on a letter of April
12 from Maj. Gen. John J. Peck, New York City, to Brig. Gen. Lorenzo
Thomas stating that Bvt. Lt. Col. Richard F. O'Beirne was needed for
court-martial duty.—LS, *ibid.*

1865, April 21. Brig. Gen. Richard Delafield, chief of engineers, to
Brig. Gen. John A. Rawlins. "I have the honor to recommend to the Lieut.
Genl that instructions may be given to the Generals of Departments, to confine the labor on temporary field works, to such as can be performed by the
troops; to avoid all further expenditure in the employment of hired opera-
tives, and purchase of material; and to collect, and preserve, all tools, and
property appertaining to the Engineer Service; to the end, that they be held
for sale, or transportation to depots hereafter to be designated, or, held
ready for immediate use when required; also, the same instructions in relation to siege materiél, and bridge trains—The Chief Engineer has caused
property, and funds, to be forwarded to the Engineer officers assigned to
duty under the Generals Commanding in the field, which Commanders, are
the judges of the necessity and expediency of constructing the works of offense, and defense, as occasion may require: Hence, the Chief Engineer
cannot, with propriety, interfere in suspending any of the works in progress,

and therefore suggests that the Lieut. General call the attention of the Commanders in such localities as he may see fit, to the subject now presented.—In every department, attention may probably be given at once, to the collection of tools, property, and instruments, and great saving of treasure effected by early attention to this subject—. It is also recommended that the Department Commanders require their Engineer officers to keep on hand a specified supply of tools &c. to meet any emergency forwarding the residue to depots.—"—LS, DNA, RG 108, Letters Received. *O.R.*, I, xlvi, part 3, 875–76.

1865, APRIL 21.   Maj. Gen. John Pope to USG. "I have the honor to transmit enclosed a letter from Maj. Gen. Reynolds and some notes on the routes from Arkansas river to Red river made by Capt. Wheeler Chief Engineer Dept. of Arkansas. The difficulties and obstacles in the way, in carrying out the campaign proposed by me in my letter of the 8th inst. will be apparent to you. That they can be overcome is I think reasonably certain and that the decisive and speedy results which will be secured by the successful execution of this plan are worth the labor and privation, seems also not unreasonable to believe. I regret very much that Gen. Reynolds Comd'g. Dept. of Arkansas does not view favorably any movement south from the direction of the Arkansas river, but I know very well that I can safely confide in his zealous and faithful cooperation in any movement determined on. The difficulties, as you will observe, are found in the fact, that a belt of country nearly two hundred miles in breadth between the Arkansas and Red river, entirely destitute of supplies of any kind for man or animal, interposes between us and the enemy. This devastated and desolate region must be traversed by an army carrying all supplies with it over difficult and neglected roads. On the most Westerly routes from Ft. Smith grass in sufficient quantity to subsist our animals can be had. It is probable that the utterly destitute character of the country, may require the movement of our heaviest columns to be made from Ft. Smith. We shall need above all two things which indeed are vital to success:—1st. Western troops accustomed to long marches and to half rations and habituated to forage for themselves upon the country. I know no such troops except those in in the army of Sherman or Schofield. With the troops which have been occupied in Eastern Virginia, I would not be willing to undertake such a campaign. 2d. We shall need the very best and strongist mules and wagons which can be had. I respectfully request that you instruct Gen. Allen to send no wagons and mules to Arkansas except the very best and in the best condition. We need also at least two and better still *three* good pontoon trains. There are none in this command. I send you an estimate of the transportation required to render such a campaign practicable. I do not consider it certain that we shall be able to move as early as June. 1st. Whilst we might be ready, it is more than likely in view of the high waters which already prevail and of the continued wet weather indicating still greater floods, that the streams in Arkansas will be over their banks and the enemy's lands impassible until a later day. I believe, General, that the plan of operations I propose is practicable with energy and perseverance. That it will be difficult I know; but it promises complete results and is I think worth the effort and toil.— Nevertheless, I am by no means so committed to it that I am not ready and willing to adopt any other which may seem to you easier, less liable to failure and sufficiently satisfactory. There is no doubt that if Canby's forces, or the larger part of it, goes to the coast of Texas and can occupy such points as will intercept the rebel retreat across the Rio Grande, an easier and perhaps sufficiently successful movement can be made up Red river with the forces under my command, which you design for the movement from Arkansas river. I do not doubt that we could drive the enemy into Texas by advancing up Red river, even if we did not bring him to an engagement, and that having thus reached Shreveport we could, with that point as a base, occupy Eastern Texas as I proposed. This operation would be attended, I think, with little difficulty, abundant supplies would be at hand on the Red river and with Canby's forces at proper points in Texas, the final surrender or dispersion of the Rebel army under Kirby Smith would be certain. More time would be consumed in such a campaign, but it would meet with fewer obstacles and subject the troops to much less hardship and privation. I think it my duty to make these statements and suggestions for your consideration. There will be abundant time to make the change of plan if you think it best. Every thing can continue to go to Arkansas and if you conclude to adopt the Red river route, the arrival of troops at Little Rock will only mislead the enemy. The Arkansas river is high and is likely to remain so for a couple of months or more so that but a very few days would be needed to ship every thing to mouth of Red river. I enclose a map marked in red pencil with the movements I propose to make from the Arkansas in the event that the original plan is adhered to. I do not wish to subject the troops you send me to the unusual hardships of this campaign, nor to run any risk (which you do not understand and approve) of obscuring the brilliant record of your administration, nor to fail to present for your consideration a plan of operations easier and safer to execute and which may commend itself more favorably to you, from the fact that it will accomplish a satisfactory, though perhaps less complete and speedy result and that it will spare the troops who have undergone so much the severe labor and hardship essential to the success of the movement from Arkansas river. I need not tell you that I am ready to execute either plan with zeal and energy."—Copy, DNA, RG 393, Military Div. of the Mo., Letters Sent. *O.R.*, I, xlviii, part 2, 150–51. Some of the enclosures are *ibid.*, pp. 94–97, 151–52.

1865, APRIL 21. Bvt. Maj. Gen. Robert O. Tyler to Brig. Gen. John A. Rawlins. "I have the honor to enclose a communication adressed to me by Genl Beall Agent to purchase supplies for Rebel Prisoners of War. At present the fund from the sale of the Cotton is too low to furnish any large supply & any future relief must come from the United States. I consider the business of the Agency practically over, as concerns its capacity for furnishing relief to the large number of prisoners in our hands. I think that the proceeds of the cotton recently sold are already nearly absorbed by past transactions & but little remains for Genl Beall to do except to wind up his business & close his accounts—which may still occupy him a few weeks." —LS, DNA, RG 94, Letters Received, 260T 1865.

1865, APRIL 21. Brig. Gen. Rufus Ingalls to Bvt. Col. Theodore S. Bowers. "Our mail and other boats are detained off Point Lookout each day from *ten* to *fifteen* hours—I reported the matter to Genl. Meigs some days ago—The inspection is delayed entirely too long by the Officers at Point Lookout or those of the Navy—Cannot the examination be more prompt. It might be made by a special guard in the Chesapeake or at Fortress Monroe Va"—ALS (telegram sent), DNA, RG 107, Telegrams Collected (Unbound); telegram received (at 12:15 P.M.), *ibid.*, RG 108, Telegrams Received. *O.R.*, I, xlvi, part 3, 876. "The 2d Brigade of the 1st Divn 9th Corps has Embarked   It is probable the 3d Brigade will be embarked before night and the first Brigade tomorrow. I am told that Gen Meade has ordered six Batteries and the wagon trains to accompany the corps. Ifs it the wish of the Lieut Genl that the wagons shall be sent now?"—Telegram received (at 7:30 P.M.), DNA, RG 107, Telegrams Collected (Bound). *O.R.*, I, xlvi, part 3, 876.

1865, APRIL 22. Bvt. Brig. Gen. Bernard G. Farrar, St. Louis, to USG. "I respectfully request permission to visit Washington to tender my resignation"—Telegram received (at 5:00 P.M.), DNA, RG 107, Telegrams Collected (Bound).

1865, APRIL 24. Maj. Gen. John Pope to USG. "I have the honor to request 1st That I be permitted to take Maj Genl Dodge with me as Corps Commander on the projected campaign into Texas to command one of the Corps sent me from other Departments—I need say little to you of Genl. Dodge—He is one of the best, most earnest energetic & capable officers in the service and has unusual experience in the description of Campaign it is proposed to undertake—I should esteem it a real misfortune not to be able to have him with me—I do not wish him relieved for the purpose from the command of this Dept—Every thing can be left in good working order in charge of a reliable and trusty officer during his absence—2nd I wish Lt Col Fred Myers, brevetted a Brig General & made Chief Quartermaster of this Military Division & Army—I have several times recommended him for this promotion which he eminently deserves for service in the Field in Virginia & for valuable services under my command in the West—I trust you will procure for him this well earned promotion and have him assigned to his Bvt rank so as to give him rank sufficient for Chief Quartermaster of that Division in which there are several Quartermasters who are his seniors —3rd I desire to take with me Col. T J. Haines Chief C. S. He has served

with eminent ability & zeal as chief C. S in the West since the War began
& he is very anxious for a time to see some service in the Field—His duties
~~here~~ can be readily performed during his absence under his own direction &
I think he has fairly earned this indulgence by long & faithful service in this
Cit[y]—He is the best man I know for Chief C. S of an Army in the field
who can be found in the West & he is very anxious to go into this Campaign
I earnestly request General that unless you deem it inconsistent with the
public interest, you will grant these applications."—ALS, DNA, RG 108,
Letters Received. *O.R.*, I, xlviii, part 2, 176.

1865, April 24. Maj. Gen. John Pope to USG. "The enclosed letter concerning Indian affairs on the Upper Missouri river is respectfully transmitted for your information The writer is well known to me as a reliable
man, who has passed many years among the Indians in that region & is well
acquainted with the subject whereon he writes"—ALS, DNA, RG 94, Letters Received, 1072G 1865. Pope enclosed a letter of [April] 17 from C. E.
Galpin, Fort Rice, Dakota Territory, to Brig. Gen. Alfred Sully. "Since
my last to you, which I think was sometime in January—evry thing has
gone on well as we could expect with the Red Skins—And they still seem
desiring of meeting you in large numbers at this point in the Spring with
the purpose of making peace, and which can be fully accomplished, and in
very many Conversations with the principal men, and the Best of them,
they seemingly have a pretty good plan of their own in regard to the Band
of Santees living on Missouri River and the Devils Lake Country; however
they will not attempt this plan untill they have a council with you, and get
your ideas on the matter, though from what they say about it I feel Assured
you will highly approve of their Course—I am here e[ntir]ely in the dark
as to your future plans—&C—&C And from A letter I recd from Our friend
Col Bartlett some few days ago, I rather infered from it that you would
not be likely retained in your position, and seemingly there would be a
botch made of the adjusting these Indians Difficulties, which crtainly will
be done if you should not finish the work your self from this fact only your
intercourse with them for the last two Years—has inspired them with an
almost unbounded Confidence which no other man can obtain within that
time, And should new men now be sent unless they work with you, to Complete the work, you have so successfully Commenced, It will require more
time and expense to prepare the minds of the Indians to receive strangers
views on such matters, than it otherwise would take, with men that they
new and had already done business with events only give Confidence with
the Indians hence two years is better than one, and three is still better than
two. And certainly I should think it a great blunder and mistake should
your plans and Sugistions to the department not be fully carried into
execution. I pray & hope, not only for the Indians sake but for the good that
will be derived from your policy, upon the part of the Govm't for this
reason, I feel fully convinced, that it must turn out, in a lasting peace and
general good to the Country, Please let me hear from you at your leisure

moments. Correct me, and rest assured of evrything being done in my power for the consummation of your plans, &c"—ALS, *ibid.*

1865, APRIL 24. Maj. Gen. John Pope endorsement. "Respectfully transmitted for the information of the Gen'l. in Chief An expedition against these Indians was halted at the suggestion of Maj. Genl. Halleck, to allow Col. Leavanworth to make peace with these Indians. Leavanworth assured Genl. Halleck as I understand that he could do so. I do not believe that any satisfactory peace can be made until the Indians have been punished and the property they have plundered from the trains of traders returned."— Copy, DNA, RG 393, Military Div. of the Mo., Register of Letters Received. Written on a letter of April 12 from Bvt. Brig. Gen. James H. Ford, Fort Riley, Kan., probably the letter printed in *O.R.,* I, xlviii, part 2, 84.

1865, APRIL 24. David Heaton, supervising special agent, U.S. Treasury Dept., New Berne, N. C., to USG. "As Supervising Special Agent of the Treasury Department, charged with the performance of responsible and important duties in North Carolina I deem it proper to address you, respectfully, on a subject of much importance to the National Treasury. I have allusion to the proper management and disposition of captured and abandoned property. By the specific acts of Congress on this subject, approved, respectively, on the 12th of March 1863 and the second of July 1864, also by the orders of the Secretary of War and the Navy as well as the directions and orders of the President I understand that all captured and abandoned Property (except such as are termed munitions of War) are to be turned over to the Agents of the Treasury Department to be sold by them to the best advantage and the proceeds paid into the United States Treasury. These views are affirmed by a decision of the Supreme Court of the United States pronounced by the Chief Justice in the December term of 1864, a copy of which I herewith enclose. Under the forgoing acts and orders and by general and special Instructions received from time to time from the Secretary of the Treasury I have been performing my duty as Treasury Agent in this State for near two years. Nothing has occured by which I was to understand that the views above expressed were to be regarded in a different light until made aware of an order at Wilmington I understand it to have been issued by you at City Point on or about the 15th day of February last. I have no official copy of that order but am told that by its terms *all* captured and abandoned Cotton, Rosin, Turpentine, Tobacco and other contraband property not only at Wilmington but at other places in this State are to be taken posession of by the Provost Marshall General with the view of being turned over to the Quarter Masters Department, shipped to New York and disposed of through Military channels. I may mistake the exact terms of the order but the substance of the same, I infer, is correctly given. It only remains for me to say that in case the said order is practically applied in this State the important business of the Treasury Department must be most seriously embarrised. In various instances

I have already found this to be the case and under the impression that there must be some misapprehension about this matter, I have felt it a duty to address you, frankly, on the subject. As the proper representatiоnve of the Treasury in this State I have been ready and am now prepared not only at Wilmington but other places, to receive Captured and abandoned property and to dispose of the same in accordance with law and instructions. If I could have the active support of the Military Department in carrying out the important duties manifestly allotted to my charge, I cannot but express to you the beleif that a great releif could be given to the National Treasury in this hour of need. Much has already been done in this direction, even with our limited area for operations, and much more certainly can be done if our Department is permitted to proceed with the plans and policy which have been marked out."—LS, DNA, RG 366, 6th Special Agency, Unarranged Records.

1865, APRIL 26, 3:50 P.M.   Bvt. Col. Adam Badeau, New Berne, N. C., to USG. "Have just arrived with messages from Ord and one from Gen. Lee. Shall I report to you at Raleigh, or wait at Newbern I can start for there tonight."—ALS (telegram sent), DNA, RG 107, Telegrams Collected (Unbound). On the same day, Maj. George K. Leet telegraphed to Badeau. "The General directs me to say that you can come here by regular train tonight"—ALS (telegram sent), *ibid.*

1865, APRIL 27.   Gen. Robert E. Lee to USG. "I transmit for your perusal a communication just received, and ask your interposition in behalf of the authors. Similar statements have been made to me by officers of rank, which I have not thought it necessary to trouble you with, believing that the obstacles mentioned would be removed as soon as possible. This is still my conviction, and I should consider it unnecessary to call your attention to the subject, had I not been informed of orders issued by the military commanders at Norfolk and Baltimore, requiring oaths of paroled soldiers before permitting them to proceed on their journey. Officers and men on parole are bound in honor to conform to the obligations they have assumed. This obligation can not be strengthened by any additional form or oath, nor is it customary to exact them."—Copy, ViHi. *O.R.*, II, viii, 517. Lee enclosed a letter of April 23 from Alexander W. Vick and nine others, Fort Monroe, to Lee. "The undersigned Tennesseans, from the A. N. Va, paroled at Appomattox C. H., in strict accordance with the spirit and terms of our paroles; were on the speediest and most direct route, now open to travel, to our homes, when we were stopped here, where we have now been detained for several days. We see from the Baltimore American of Yesterday that Genl. Wallace, Comding '*The Middle Department*,' has issued an order that no paroled prisoners shall pass through that Dept. This leaves us no means of reaching home, by any practicable, or speedy route. We are sure this was neither Genl. Grant's or your understanding of the Capitulation. We do not know how our situation can be Communicated to Genl

Grant, in whose good-faith and magnanimity we have the utmost confidence, except through you. We therefore most respectfully, and earnestly appeal to you, with whom we have so long served, and upon whom we have learned so confidently to rely, to aid us in this emergency, by procuring from Genl. G. a permit for us to return to Tennessee via Baltimore, Cincinatti, Louisville, and Nashville—We cannot procure money to change our clothing short of Baltimore, as none of us had relations, or any business connexions in this section of Va. We will promise [after] reaching Baltimore to keep off the streets, and out of the way of any kind of popular excitement, until we can procure citizens clothes, and then to press on to our homes as rapidly, and quietly, as possible, concealing, as far as practicable, our character of paroled prisoners from all except the military authorities, to whom it may be necessary for us to report. Regretting this necessity for troubling you, at this time, with our affairs, assuring you of our continued highest regard and esteem, with our sincerest wishes for your future wellfare and happiness, . . ."—LS, DNA, RG 108, Letters Received. On May 1, USG endorsed this letter. "Respectfully refered to the Sec. of War with recommendation that I be authorized to telegraph to Ft. Monroe to clear out all the paroled prisoners there, ~~to~~ to give them passes to go through the North to their homes. I have no idea that it will lead to any harm to permit this." —AES, *ibid.* At 8:45 P.M., USG telegraphed to the commanding officer, Fort Monroe. "You may give the following ~~officers~~ prisoners now at Ft. Monroe passes, by my order, to their homes, ~~by my~~ via Baltimore and through the North towit; Majs. Vick, Randolph & Saunders, Capt. Cage, enlisted men Moore Franklin, Cochran, Oldham & Holder. The same privilege may be extended to any other prisoners you may have who want to pass by the North but others are not to be received for the purpose of getting this permission."—ALS (telegram sent), *ibid.*, RG 107, Telegrams Collected (Bound); telegram sent (at 9:00 P.M.), *ibid.*; telegram received (press), *ibid.*

1865, APRIL 29, 4:10 P.M.   To Maj. Gen. George G. Meade. "Please ascertain the whereabouts of Lieut. Mathew A. Bailey 188 N. Y. Vols. and inform me by telegraph."—ALS (telegram sent), DNA, RG 107, Telegrams Collected (Bound); telegram sent, *ibid.*; telegram received, *ibid.*, Telegrams Collected (Unbound); *ibid.*, RG 94, War Records Office, Army of the Potomac. On April 30, 12:20 P.M., Meade telegraphed to USG. "Lieut Mathew A. Barley 188th New York Vols, is present with his command in the 5th corps near Ford's Station on the ~~Railroad between Sutherland's Station and this point.~~ South Side R. Rd."—Telegram sent, *ibid.*; telegram received (at 3:20 P.M.), *ibid.*, RG 107, Telegrams Collected (Bound); (2) *ibid.*, Telegrams Collected (Unbound).

1865, APRIL 29.   Maj. Gen. John Pope endorsement. "Respectfully referred to the Genl. in chief of the Army with the request that Genl. Dodge's application be complied with. If quiet can be kept in Mo. for a month or two all concern for the State can be safely dismissed and it is very important that these returning soldiers who will be Bushwhackers and outlaws be intercepted before they get into Missouri."—Copy, DNA, RG 393, Military Div. of the Mo., Register of Letters Received. *O.R.*, I, xlviii, part 2, 234. Written on a letter of April 28 from Maj. Gen. Grenville M. Dodge, St. Louis, to Pope recommending that cav. be sent to southern Mo.—*Ibid.*

1865, APRIL 29. Bvt. Col. Theodore S. Bowers to Maj. Gen. Cadwallader C. Washburn. "I am directed to inform you that the papers, in the case of Miss Allison, forwarded by you, have been referred to Major General Dana Commanding Department of Mississippi, with the following endorsement: 'Respectfully referred to Maj. Gen. N. J. T. Dana Comdg Dept. of Miss., who will cause the $940 in gold within referred to, to be returned to Miss Allison from whom it was taken By command of Lt Gen. Grant, T. S BOWERS, Asst Adjt Genl. Headqr's Armies of the U S., April 29 1865—'" —LS, DNA, RG 109, Union Provost Marshals' File of Papers Relating to Individual Civilians. Other papers indicate that Harriet C. Allison, an "aged single Lady," attempted to take gold through the lines at Memphis about Feb. 1 in violation of orders; investigation established that she had no intention of using it except for her own support.—*Ibid.*

1865, APRIL 29. Bvt. Maj. Gen. James H. Wilson, Macon, Ga., to USG or Maj. Gen. George H. Thomas. "Genl Sherman has directed me to open a supply line for this command by way of Dalton and Atlanta. It will require forty (40) days to repair road there. But few materials for that purpose to be had at this end of line. Please give the necessary instructions to have the work begun at Dalton & pressed forward as rapidly as possible to Atlanta —I am making arrangements to have everything done from this end that our means will permit, Gen Cobb has turned over all Confederate supplies under his control on S, W, R R and done all in his power to assist us in buying from the people but it will be difficult to obtain a sufficient quantity of forage to last till new crop is ready. We shall soon begin to need small stores & clothing. They might be sent from Savannah or Augusta or up the Altamaha & Ackagee to Buzzards Roost. Both State & Confederate authorities seem anxious to give me all the assistance in their power. The people are well disposed & anxious for peace, By an agreement with Gen Cobb I have paroled all of the prisoners captured in Ga. besides the remnant of those brought from Ala. & if Croxtons brigade were moved to Dalton it could protect the R R repairers in that quarter in case a guard shall become necessary. There is enough C. S. A. Cotton in store here to pay for opening the road"—Telegram received (misdated April 28—received on May 5, 12:45 A.M.), DNA, RG 107, Telegrams Collected (Bound); *ibid.*, RG 108, Telegrams Received; copies, *ibid.*, RG 393, Military Div. of the Miss., Cav. Corps, Telegrams Sent; DLC-USG, V, 54. *O.R.*, I, xlix, part 2, 515. On the same day, Wilson again telegraphed to USG and Thomas. "Since writing my ~~telegr~~ last telegram Gen Cro£xton has joined me with his com-

mand in fine condition, After burning Tuscaloosa capturing three (3) guns
and a number of prisoners he moved toward Columbus fought Wirt Adams
near Eutaw moved thence to Halls Mill on Black Warrior, crossed Coosa
near Talladega fought & dispersed Genl Hills force between there & Blue
Mt burned several factories & Iron W[o]rks & thence marched via Carroll-
ton, Newman & Zublin to this place. Gen ~~Crafton~~ Croxton deserves great
credit & should be brevetted."—Telegram received (on May 5, 12:50 A.M.),
DNA, RG 107, Telegrams Collected (Bound); (misdated April 27) *ibid.*,
RG 108, Telegrams Received; copies, *ibid.*, RG 94, ACP, W1336 CB
1865; *ibid.*, War Records Office, Retained Records; *ibid.*, RG 393, Military Div. of the Miss., Cav. Corps, Telegrams Sent; DLC-USG, V, 54.
O.R., I, xlix, part 2, 515.

1865, APRIL 30.   To Secretary of War Edwin M. Stanton. "I would
respectfully recommend the appointment by Brevet of Brig, Gen, Charles
Deven to the rank of Maj, Gen, of Volunters, He has proven himself one
of the most gallant and devoted Officers, keeping with his Command always,
when it was in the field even when he was in a condition rendering him
entirely unable to walk or ride on horseback, As Gen, Deven will probably
be quitting the service soon, I would ask early action"—Copies, DLC-USG,
V, 46, 76, 108; DNA, RG 108, Letters Sent. *O.R.*, I, xlvi, part 3, 1015.

1865, APRIL 30.   USG endorsement. "Respectfully refered to Maj. Gn.
Halleck Comdg Mil. Div. of ~~Miss~~. Va. H. Clay Hart was one of the most
virulent secessionests in St. Louis when the rebellion broke out and went
South. Recently I heard of him being in New York City where he went no
doubt without authority and for no good purpose towards the Govt. Bruce
refered to is from the same place and of the same class and I believe has
pretended to represent Ky. in the rebel Congress. I think both should be
arrested and held until Hart avails himself of the Amnesty and Bruce receives pardon."—AES (undated), DNA, RG 109, Union Provost Marshals'
File of Papers Relating to Two or More Civilians; copy, DLC-USG, V, 58.
Written on a letter of March 20 from H. Clay Hart, Richmond, Va., to
USG. "Presuming upon former acquaintance with you at St. Louis, I request a passport through your lines for the purpose of having an interview
at Washington with my Cousin Hon. Montgomery Blair on business of importance to myself. Should you comply with my request please direct to
care of E. M. Bruce at this place. Of Course I will come under obligations
to convey no improper intelligence on my return. . . . P. S. It may be proper
to add that I do not now, nor have I ever held an office under this Government."—ALS, DNA, RG 109, Union Provost Marshals' File of Papers
Relating to Two or More Civilians.

1865, APRIL 30, 8:30 P.M.   To Brig. Gen. Rufus Ingalls. "Send the
Ambulances and other transportation of the 9th Corps through to Alexandria by land with the first troops marching."—ALS (telegram sent),

DNA, RG 107, Telegrams Collected (Bound); telegram sent, *ibid.*; copies, *ibid.*, RG 108, Letters Sent; DLC-USG, V, 46, 76, 108.

1865, [APRIL?].   To Secretary of the Treasury Hugh McCulloch. "Mr. _____ was a friend to me when I was in sore need of friends. He is desirous of going South to buy cotton, and I shall be obliged if you will give him whatever facilities for doing so you give to any one."—William Conant Church, *Ulysses S. Grant and the Period of National Preservation and Reconstruction* (New York and London, 1897), p. 59. Church stated that this letter was in the files of the U.S. Treasury Dept., that he provided its substance, and that the person recommended had the letter lithographed and distributed widely to Treasury agents.

1865, [*April*?].   USG endorsement. "Approved and recommended"—AES, DNA, RG 94, Amnesty Papers, 2998. Written on a letter of March 20 from Charles Green, Savannah, Ga., to President Abraham Lincoln stating that Green was a British subject who had lived in Savannah for over thirty years, that in 1861 he had carried $100,000 to England to enable Ga. to buy arms abroad, and that he had been arrested and imprisoned for four months on his return but had not violated his parole afterward.—ALS, *ibid.* President Andrew Johnson pardoned Green on July 29.

1865, [APRIL?].   Mrs. J. N. Ashton to USG. "On the first day of April, my brother John N. Cocke & my two sons R. N. Ashton & John C. Ashton (the two first named privates in Co K. 9th Regt Va Inft. Pickett's & the last named private in the Norfolk Light Artillery Blues) were captured, & are now held as prisoners of war at Pt Lookout by the U. S. Military Authorities. Each of these prisoners are ready & willing, to take the oath of allegiance to the United States & have so registered their names. My brother is a man of family, to the maintenance & suppor[t] of which, his presence is altogether essential. As a loyal woman of the United States I feel that it is my privilege to petition for their release. Hoping that you will agree with me that a magnanimous & considerate course pursued towards the prisoners would be the most efficient means of winning back their affections & restorings that feeling which should ever exist between the Citizens & the Government to which they owe allegiance   Hoping that it may be your pleasure to release them . . ."—ALS, ViHi.

Index

All letters written by USG of which the text was available for use in this volume are indexed under the names of the recipients. The dates of these letters are included in the index as an indication of the existence of text. Abbreviations used in the index are explained on pp. xvi–xx. Individual regts. are indexed under the names of the states in which they originated.